AMAZON PUBLISHING

MW01092258

i

The Definitive Guide to TradeStation™'s EasyLanguage & OOEL Programming

Volume I: Programming Guide

https://www.easylanguageOOEL.com

AMAZON PUBLISHING

Amazon Publishing is a leading trade publisher of fiction, nonfiction, and children's books with a mission to empower outstanding storytellers and connect them with readers worldwide. Amazon publishes emerging, bestselling and critically acclaimed authors in digital, print, and audio formats. With Amazon's drive for innovation and passion for books, they merge technology and art to support our authors and help their stories change the world.

For a list of available titles, please visit our Website at www.moneymentor.com/books.html.

For a download of the code examples presented in this book go to www.easylanguageOOEL.com and register as a Free Member.

COPYRIGHTS

COPYRIGHTS, TRADESTATION

♫ Easier Said than Done

- from the song by The Essex, 1963 (Linton/Huff)

Whatever your hand finds to do, do it with all your might.

      ■ Ecclesiastes 9:10

The human mind, once stretched to include a single new idea, does not shrink back to its original proportions."

      ■ Oliver Wendell Holmes

Until one is committed, there is hesitancy.

      ■   W. H. Murray

We must never assume that which is incapable of proof.

      ■ G. H. Lewes

Be sure of it; give me the ocular proof.

      ■ Shakespeare

Wise people either have the knowledge or they know where to go for the knowledge.

      ■ Mike Caprio

TABLE OF CONTENTS

AMAZON PUBLISHING..iii

COPYRIGHTS..vii

COPYRIGHTS, TRADESTATION..ix

DISCLAIMER...xi

DEDICATION..xiii

TABLE OF CONTENTS...xvii

FOREWORD...xxvii

PREFACE..xxix

ACKNOWLEDGMENTS...xxxi

CHAPTER 1...1

Introduction to the Basics 1

Who Is This Book For?...2

About These Books 3

What is EasyLanguage?..5

TradeStation Tidbits..6

   += and -=..6

   Reset Chart Scaling Range 6

   Transparent...7

   Optimizing with Data2 7

   Data2 Intricacies...7

   Alignment of Cells in RadarScreen 7

What Does Object-Oriented Mean?...7

Conventions 9

   Abbreviations, Acronyms & File Extensions 10

Introduction to TradeStation Basics 11

EasyLanguage Dictionary 16

Reserved Words and Skip Words 19

The EasyLanguage Development Environment (TDE) 21

   EasyLanguage Editor...21

   Menu Bar..22

   Output Bar..22

   Line Numbering 23

   Toolbar 23

   ToolBox Tab...23

   Creating and Modifying Code 23

   AutoComplete 24

   Member Association..24

   Properties Editor tab 25

Dictionary Tab 25

Component Tray 26

Summary...26

CHAPTER 2 ....**27**

Brushing Up on EasyLanguage 27

Introduction 27

Comments 28

Data Types..29

Inputs, Variables, Constants and Arrays 29

Boolean 29

Integers...29

Floating Point 30

String..30

Inputs 30

Variables...31

Constants 33

More Reserved Words...34

Statements 34

Numeric Expressions 34

Boolean Algebra...35

Symbolic Logic...35

Truth Tables...35

Logical Expression Operators 36

Bitwise Binary Operator 37

Decisions (Conditions) 37

If…Then..37

If…Then…Else 37

If…Then…Else…Begin 38

Nested If…Then Statements 39

IFF 39

Printing 40

User Functions...41

Common Usage...42

Series Function..42

Multiple Output Functions 42

Wrapper Functions..43

Loops and More..43

InfiniteLoopDetect...44

Once 44

Begin…End...45

For 45
To and DownTo 47
While 48
Repeat...Until 49
More About Strings 50
String Input 50
Placing Text (Strings) on Your Chart 51
Numeric Format Strings 52
Date and Time Format Strings 55
Date and Time 56
Date References 56
Date and Time Old School 57
Date and Time as Integers 57
Double DateTime Format 58
Date and Time OOEL Style 59
Switch…Case 83
A Brief Interlude 84
TokenLists, Vectors and Arrays 86
A Brief Look at TokenLists 86
More on Vectors and Arrays 86
Arrays 87
Fixed Length Arrays 88
Dynamic Arrays 88
Array Usage 89
Array_Compare 90
Array_Copy 90
Array_GetMaxIndex 91
Array_GetType 91
Array_SetMaxIndex 92
Array_SetValRange 93
Array_Sort 93
Array_Sum 94
Summary 94
CHAPTER 3 .... **97**
EasyLanguage Intricacies 97
Introduction 97
Spaces 97
Alerts 97
RunCommand 101
RunCommandOnLastBar (Function) 102

At$ 103
Analysis Commentary 103
Chart Type Reserved Word Values 106
Using ASCII 3rd Party Data 107
    Symbol Customize--3rd Party Data 108
    Symbol Lookup 3rd Party Data 110
PlaySound 114
PlayMovieChain 115
RaiseRunTimeError 116
InfoBox 116
Hello_World!_Ex#02 117
Time and Sales 118
    About the Time and Sales Window 118
Currency Conversion 124
Utilization Monitor 125
Summary 125
CHAPTER 4 127
Easing Into Object-Oriented EasyLanguage 127
Introduction 127
A Further Walk Through the EasyLanguage Dictionary 129
OOEL Coding Template 130
Classes 134
    About Classes in EasyLanguage 134
    Class Categories 135
AnalysisTechnique Class 136
    More About Event Handlers 138
Class Declaration (Instantiation) 139
Methods 139
Libraries 140
Namespaces 143
About Objects in EasyLanguage 144
Inheritance 145
Events 145
    Event Handlers 146
Provider Classes 147
About the ToolBox 148
Summary 148
CHAPTER 5 151
Debugging, Exceptions & Error Handling 151
Introduction 151

Divide by Zero 151

InfiniteLoopDetect 151

Printing as a Debugging Tool 152

Analysis Commentary as a Debugging Tool 152

Debug 154

    ClearDebug or ClearPrintLog 154

Exceptions 154

    Exception Class 154

    SystemException Class 155

Try…Catch…Finally 156

Throw (Reserved Word) 157

Summary 158

CHAPTER 6 .... **159**

Methods 159

Introduction 159

Override (Reserved Word) 159

Overloaded Methods 159

    How We Show Overloaded Methods 160

Useful Methods 160

Summary 162

CHAPTER 7 .... **165**

Hello World! 165

Introduction 165

Hello_World! #01 Revisited 165

Hello_World! #02: Print Log on First Bar 166

Hello_World! #03: Print Log on Last Bar 167

Hello_World! #04: String.Format () & Vector 168

Hello_World! #05: StreamWriter & StreamReader 169

Hello_World! #06: Using StreamReader to Read from a File 171

Hello_World! #07: String.Split to Stuff a Vector 172

Hello_World! #07a: Text Object Centered on Chart 175

Hello_World! #08a: Creates and Fills a GlobalValue 177

Hello_World! #08b: Creates and Displays the GlobalValue 178

Summary 179

CHAPTER 8 .... **181**

Collections: Dictionary, Vector etc. 181

Introduction 181

    TokenList 181

    Vector Class (Collection) 181

    Collection Classes 182

Dictionary Class (Collection) 182

    Examples for Clarification 183

GlobalDictionary Class...187

    Dictionary vs GlobalDictionary 194

Queue Class 194

Stack Class...198

TokenList Class 202

Vector Class 203

AppStorage 204

Summary...211

CHAPTER 9 ....**213**

Drawing Objects 213

Introduction 213

Drawing Objects 213

About DrawingObject Classes...214

    Adding Drawing Objects to Your EasyLanguage Code...........................214

    Alerts with Drawing Objects 215

DrawingObject Class 215

Object Class..220

DrawingObject Methods..221

    Setting Alerts for Drawing Objects 222

AlertConfiguration Class 223

    AlertFrequency Enumeration 224

Notification Class 225

TextLabel Class 226

Text at a Specific Location on Your Chart 232

HorizontalLine Class 238

VerticalLine Class 241

TrendLine Class...246

Rectangle Class 251

Ellipse Class 259

Summary...262

CHAPTER 10 ....**263**

Host Classes...263

Introduction 263

ChartingHost Class (Component)..263

PlatformClientHost Class (Component) 269

PortfolioHost Class (Component)..270

RadarScreenHost Class (Component) 273

StrategyHost Class (Component) 277

Summary 281
CHAPTER 11 .... **283**
Forms 283
Introduction 283
Form Class 283
Using WinForms Classes 286
　Control Classes 287
More About Control Classes 288
　Button 288
　Chart 288
　CheckBox 289
　ComboBox 289
　DataGridView 290
　DateTimePicker 290
　FastSymbolLookupComboBox 290
　Label 291
　LinkLabel 291
　ListView 292
　NumericUpDown 292
　ProgressBar 293
　RadioButton 293
　RichTextBox 294
　Slider 294
　TableLayoutPanel 294
　TextBox 295
　WebBrowser 295
　WebView2 296
Container Classes 297
　Form 297
　Panel 297
　GroupBox 298
　TabPage 298
Adding a Form to your EZL Code 302
About the ToolBox 302
About the Resource Editor 303
　Adding a Form to an Analysis Technique 304
　Editing a Form 304
　Using Events with Form Controls 304
Component Classes 304
ContainerControl Class 305

GroupBox Class 305

Panel Class 306

TabControl Class 310

TabPage Class 311

Control Class 311

Button Class 314

ButtonBase Class 315

CheckBox Class 316

ComboBox Class 317

DataGridView (DGV) 318

RadioButton Class 325

TextBox Class 326

Adding a Form..327

Editing a Form 328

Summary..328

CHAPTER 12 ....**331**

Provider Classes 331

Introduction 331

Best Practices with Data Providers...331

Data Provider Events 331

Data Provider States..331

Data Provider Update Reasons 332

RealTime 332

DataProviders and Functions 332

Using Data Providers 332

Account Class 333

AccountsProvider Class 335

SymbolAttributesProvider Class 339

OrdersProvider Class 340

PositionsProvider Class...341

QuotesProviderClass 345

PriceSeriesProvider Class (PSP) 346

Summary..350

CHAPTER 13 ....**351**

Order Tickets & Data Providers..351

Introduction 351

Benefits of Order Tickets..351

OrderTickets and DataProviders...352

Placing Orders with EasyLanguage 352

How They Compare 352

Updating an Order..355

Logging..355

Factors of Design..356

Enabling Order Placement Objects 356

Order Class...357

Examples of Order Tickets...360

Summary..367

CHAPTER 14 ....**369**

Using Excel...369

Introduction..369

Examples...369

Summary..379

CHAPTER 15 ....**381**

Fundamental Data Fields 381

Introduction..381

FundamentalFields Class 381

Summary..453

CHAPTER 16 ....**455**

Conclusion..455

REFERENCE & CONTACTS...**457**

TABLE OF EXAMPLES..**459**

TABLE OF FIGURES **465**

TABLE OF TABLES **469**

INDEX..**473**

PRODUCTS..**495**

Sunny J. Harris Products...495

ACCOLADES 496

SunnyBands..497

DynamicMovingAvg (DMA) & DMA_Histogram 497

PHW (Potential Hourly Wage) & PHW_Lower...............498

Who's On Top 498

DaySessions...499

CurrentPrice...499

DayOpenHiLo 500

SunnyBars 500

Ultimate-F Compounding..501

Pennant Finder...501

World Time 501

Samuel K. Tennis Products..503

Data Report Pro 503

SPGC Report Pro 504

Data Report Pro and SPGC Report Pro Bundle 504

Real Time Profit Loss Viewer..505

Scroll the Chart 505

Scroll the Chart Docked 506

ABOUT THE AUTHORS **507**

FOREWORD

Technical analysis is both art and science. The ability of technical analysis tools to reveal tradable patterns in today's lightning-fast, interconnected financial markets is determined by the skill and experience of their users. Luckily, skills can be taught, and experience can be shared. In Sunny Harris and Sam Tennis, readers get the best possible combination of both.

Sunny, one of the earliest users of System Writer, and then its descendant TradeStation, has been through the self-taught school of hard-knocks and built not one but two successful trading careers. She learned and, even more importantly, she took notes and delights in conveying what she has learned to serious students of market behavior and trading. Sam speaks code as easily as he speaks English. He saw patterns in code and wrote EasyLanguage to help bridge the gap between coding and trading. Together, these two consummate professionals provide rare insight, not just into the workings of the software, but into a process for gaining the fluency and dexterity required to realize your own trading ideas and strategies.

I tried my hand at coding when Apple released the Apple II graphic interface in 1977, but quickly learned I had no aptitude, despite being trained at Cornell as an engineer. At that time, I was lucky enough to meet up with Jim Schmitt, a computer science professor at Loyola University with whom I soon partnered to develop CompuTrac software for the Apple II, which we released in 1979 and to launch the Technical Analysis Group (TAG) conferences and seminars which, over the course of twenty years, allowed thousands of talented technicians from around the U.S. and the world to share their ideas and learn from one another, including Sunny Harris and Sam Tennis. Sunny attended 11 TAG conferences over the years and Sam attended them all, speaking at many and travelling the world with them.

Technical analysts have always been a breed apart, intuitively recognizing the symphonic patterns inherent in market data and attempting to identify and isolate repetitive movements with sufficient specificity and predictability to trade them profitably. Most traders, even most technicians, rely upon patterns identified by others and use off-the-shelf tools with limited sets of parameters to perform their testing and analysis. Elite technicians (like you) want to see what others miss. You want an edge over traders using black box strategies and limited parameters. You want to ask "what if…"; and to test out sophisticated ideas and compound strategies against realistic data over various timeframes.

Sunny Harris and Sam Tennis wrote this book for you. Their decades of experience as well as their mutual drive to share their knowledge with others and their superb communication skills make this book the quintessential guide for sophisticated technicians who want to maximize the power of TradeStation.

I wish you a profitable journey.

Tim Slater
Founder, CEO, CompuTrac, Inc.
President, TAG/DowJones Seminars

PREFACE

Welcome to an experience! These books are more than coding manuals, they are more than trading manuals, they are more than an EZL manual: they are the complete reference and how-to-guide you wish you had years ago. Additionally, the **Programming Guide (Volume I)** includes Advanced EasyLanguage techniques that were not within the scope of my *TradeStation Made Easy!* book (TSME).

Because the complete manuscript is more than 1,300 pages, I have divided it into two volumes: **Volume I—The OOEL Programming Guide** and **Volume II--The OOEL Reference Guide**. This allows the reader to have both books open on the desk and refer easily to both instead of flipping back and forth in one heavy book. And against advice I have opted to publish them in color because of the abundance of charts herein.

My fifth trading book, *TradeStation Made Easy!*[2] covered learning TradeStation step-by-step rather than reading the vendor's A to Z documentation. I found it untenable to sit down and memorize the Users' Manual without having any idea what should be first, second and third. So, I wrote the book.

This book, *The Definitive Guide to TradeStation's EasyLanguage and OOEL Programming*, is based on the same concept: that Object-Oriented EasyLanguage (OOEL) is impossible to learn on your own unless you were born a computer programmer.

Unlike my previous tome[3], which took 12 years to write, and spurred on by the twice weekly 3 hours' programming lessons with Samuel K. Tennis, this book should be a straightforward one-year project. I shouldn't say easy, since it is never truly easy to learn a new programming language but making it easy is exactly what Sam and I are doing for you with this book.

As long as TradeStation (TS) doesn't release a new version while I'm writing this book, as they did many times during the years I was writing *TradeStation Made Easy!,* we should meet the deadline[4].

I should mention here that Samuel K. Tennis is the author of *Ask Mr. EasyLanguage* published by Traders Press. He is also the lead programmer who brought us EasyLanguage and System Writer, the predecessor of TradeStation. Sam has graciously donated his time and superior knowledge to coding the examples, teaching me OOEL and helping write and edit these books.

The Definitive Guide to TradeStation's EasyLanguage & OOEL Programming is intended for those who are familiar with what I call Vanilla EasyLanguage (VEZL or just EZL or Classic EasyLanguage or even Legacy EZL) and want to delve in further. Students of these books should be very familiar with classic EZL itself before attempting to learn this more advanced and at the same time more primitive coding language for traders.

Furthermore, these books are more than just OOEL. They are also books with Advanced EasyLanguage concepts that are not found elsewhere.

Having taught myself EasyLanguage (EZL)[5] many years ago as a trader looking for a way to test my ideas, I began by using the predecessor to TradeStation when it was but a DOS program for daily data, called System Writer, and later System Writer Plus (SWP) program of the year for a number of years by Omega Research, which grew into TradeStation Securities. I loved it! Finally, a way to test strategies other than using a spreadsheet or paper and pencil.

The only challenge is that I started writing this book not knowing much at all about OOEL other than it is daunting. I have avoided it too long and now I am determined to learn it. At the same time, I am learning to program OOEL, I am doing what I did with my first book[6]: keeping notes and turning them

---

[2] TradeStation Made Easy! (TSME), 746 pages, John Wiley & Sons, 2011

[3] This is actually my seventh book. My fourth book was Going Vegan! with Linda Blair; my sixth book was ghost-written and edited for Murray Ruggiero: Using EasyLanguage 9.x.

[4] It actually ended up taking two years to write these books.

[5] Along with some expert tutelage from Bill Cruz, co-founder of Omega Research

[6] My first book was *Trading 101—How to Trade Like a Pro* published in 1996 by John Wiley & Sons.

into a book for you and others like you.

How, you ask, am I going to proceed to learn something so difficult on my own? Memorize the TradeStation (TS) documentation and somehow make sense of it? No, I am going to take the easy path. Turning to the world's expert on EZL, who also is a master at OOEL, I have enlisted a friend of mine: Sam Tennis.

I have known Samuel K. Tennis for more than thirty years. To me he is just Sam. But to the world, he is "Mr. EasyLanguage." He is the expert on TradeStation and EasyLanguage. Of course—because he is the one who created them in the first place. Specifically, Sam wrote and led the group that programmed TradeStation's predecessors System Writer and System Writer Plus except for charting and the interpreter. Now that's an accomplishment!

Sam and I have been to so many of the same workshops, conferences, and tradeshows, including the famous TAG Seminars (Technical Analysis Group), over the years, both as students and speakers, that we knew each other in passing before we became friends. I have so much respect for Sam that I wanted no one else to help me write this book.

This is a very special book because, while I speak EasyLanguage (EZL) fluently, I will be learning OOEL from Sam at the same time I write this book and I record the steps it took to learn to program OOEL. I have never tackled the OOEL language because EZL was just that, easy, and OOEL was daunting with lots of very specific coding skills one must learn.

As a mathematician, I have programmed in many languages over the years, starting with Basic and Fortran at Lockheed Missiles and Space in Sunnyvale, CA in 1970. Also using COBOL and Assembler Language at Lockheed, I fell in love with programming. When you do what you love for a living, you never work a day in your life. It was and still is that way with me. I feel the same way about trading the financial markets. Having been a full-time trader for over 42 years I am taking on a new hobby: programming in OOEL.

Having the experience of learning these languages on my own, not in college, I believe I can teach you too. It really isn't all that hard, it just takes the right teacher and a lot of perseverance.

And! You are about to learn it alongside me. Sam and I meet for three hours on Tuesdays and Thursdays[7] over Zoom with him coding and teaching and me learning the basic concepts so I can teach them to you. We hope you enjoy and profit from our work.

The second book is the companion book to *The Definitive Guide to TradeStation's EasyLanguage and OOEL* which is **Volume I—Programming Guide**. **Volume II** is the **OOEL Reference Guide** to all the concepts in **Volume I** and to wonderful things we haven't covered but you will want to know. The Reference Guide is your best friend. It lists all the classes, all the Reserved Words, a complete unfolding of the **Dictionary** and a quick way to find where a TradeStation command is.

This book is the Appendix section of the first book, divided into a second volume to allow you to keep both on your desk and flip back and forth as you learn.

It is a separate volume also because 1,300 pages are just too many to publish in a single book.

I have a new website just for readers of this book: https://www.easylanguageOOEL.com where you are free to download the code that is explored herein. Any questions you may have can be submitted there.

Sunny and Sam

---

[7] That was in the beginning. For the last 6 months we have been meeting Tuesday through Friday evenings inclusive for 3-4 hours.

ACKNOWLEDGMENTS

Thank you to my previous editor Pamela van Giessen for originally telling me I could write, when I was sure I couldn't, and for encouraging me to write my previous five Wiley books. I really thought I had nothing to say.

Thanks to William R. (Bill) Cruz, co-founder of TradeStation, who helped me along the way, many years ago, with learning the intricacies of EasyLanguage when we were both just beginning.

And a huge debt of gratitude to Samuel K. Tennis[8] for patiently teaching me TradeStation's Object-Oriented EasyLanguage (OOEL)! Not only did we get a book out of the deal, but I also got an education that will last me a lifetime.

To Chris Davy[9] for being such a brilliant OOEL programmer and helping me along with the writing, proofing, and verifying that our **OrdersProvider** and **Positions Provider** code is viable and for contributing heavily to the chapters on Order Tickets & Data Providers.

And a special thanks to my assistant Diane Donges for working so hard so many hours helping me with all my many projects and especially this one.

To my wife I am eternally grateful for understanding and appreciating me as no one else ever has. I greatly admire you for being such an amazing physician and partner; thank you for believing in me; thank you for standing by my side through thick and through thin, through rich and through poor. It's not easy living with a trader.

---

[8] Samuel K. Tennis is the lead programmer we must thank for EasyLanguage in the first place. Sam wrote the design spec and lead the team who created it all.

[9] Christopher G. Davy is a trading system developer and the programmer who headed up the TradeStation EasyLanguage Forum and a consummate OOEL expert. His contact information is in Appendix VII.

CHAPTER 1

Introduction to the Basics

In This Chapter

- Who Is This Book For?
- About These Books
- What is EasyLanguage?
- TradeStation Tidbits
- What Does Object-Oriented Mean?
- Conventions
- Introduction to TradeStation Basics
- EasyLanguage Dictionary Intro
- Reserved Words & Skip Words
- EasyLanguage Development Environment (TDE)
- Summary

This book is one of a kind. It is more than a book; it is an experience. It is written by a mathematician/computer programmer who is a full-time trader, who taught herself EasyLanguage many years ago, and who doesn't know squat about Object-Oriented EasyLanguage (OOEL) coding. Yet! Lest you think I'm handing you a crock, hang on a second. By the time this book is half-way done I will be proficient at OOEL largely due to the expert tutelage of Samuel K. Tennis (Sam), and further instruction by Christopher G. Davy[10] (Chris). A huge thank you to them both!

TradeStation[F11] is considered the premiere trading software for individual traders and professional traders alike. Especially if you want to write programs for your trading. I have been an end-user of the software since 1987 when I started using System Writer (no charting just calculations). Clearly, since Sam Tennis was the designer and lead programmer of the software, he has been using it a lot longer than I have. System Writer Plus added charting, more language features and still used the Borland Pascal run-time compiler.

The draw, at the time, for me was real-time data and a language with which to program and test my ideas. The language was very easy to use, and my passion was in testing strategies to find something successful with which to trade. I was, and still am, a proponent of testing before trading.

Many people with whom I come in contact don't want to test their strategies. Either they don't program, or they believe they can make more money using discretionary "feelings." I have found over the years that those who don't test their systems don't want to know the answer.

It is said that hypothetical performance results … have no bearing on future results. But what else is there? You cannot trade future results. That data doesn't exist yet. Even though you can't take every factor into account when programming and testing, if you don't do it, you will surely be stepping into shark infested waters.

While EasyLanguage (EZL) was miles ahead of any competing products, it nevertheless benefitted from adding tools for programmers to use in handling the more intricate features of charting, programming, and testing in an easy to learn programming language.

In 2009, with the release of version 9.0, TradeStation Securities Group introduced an extension to its EasyLanguage programming language called Object-Oriented EasyLanguage (OOEL). While its early claim to fame was the ease of use of EasyLanguage, this new extension is clearly not easy. It is definitely a computer programming language.

As an aside, I recently had occasion to need a program that would compare two files looking for matches and unique entries. First, I thought about using C++ or Java to write a little program to do it

---

[10] Christopher (Chris) Davy, EasyLanguage systems developer, OOEL expert, worked for TS as master of the Forum. See more in the References at the end of the second book.

[11] www.TradeStation.com

for me. Then I realized that the program could be written just as well in OOEL by using CSV files. I could easily write (print) a file from within EZL, but I didn't know how to read one. The EZL programmer I turned to, Chris, took a look at the task and wrote it in OOEL post haste. That's how extensible OOEL is.

Upon reflection the simple truth is that programming a computer, no matter how friendly the programming language, is never easy. Becoming a good coder takes study, sometimes years of study. It is the intent of this book to walk the reader through that learning process in small and simple steps that will make the process comfortable. I have recently noticed the tendency of some of my competitors to use the paraphrase "EasyLanguage Isn't," and I herewith forgive them their lack of imagination.

Computer manuals aren't meant to be read cover to cover. The TS Users' Manual is no exception. *TradeStation Made Easy!*, however, was intended to be read from cover to cover with pauses along the way to try the examples. *Ask Mr. EasyLanguage* was also written to be read cover to cover. This book and its companion are also meant to be read from cover to cover. Hopefully it will be an informative and enjoyable experience for you. After reading this book, you will be more prepared to go back and use the TS manuals with ease and as reference.

In *Trading 101—How to Trade Like a Pro* I wanted to introduce to basic concepts of trading to the general public. In *Trading 102—Getting Down to Business* my hope was to introduce the concepts of system design and testing as well as treating your trading as a business. *TradeStation Made Easy!* was intended as a procedural guide to getting comfortable with programming TradeStation's EasyLanguage (EZL). This book, *The Definitive Guide to TradeStation's EasyLanguage & OOEL Programming* is for EZL "speakers" who want more. There is a dearth of documentation and explanation for OOEL. It basically doesn't exist. One can find a few things on the TS Forum, but there is, until now, no comprehensive book that starts at step A and goes to step Z. These books are to fill the gap.

Who Is This Book For?

I know, I should have said "For Whom is this Book?" My daughter Colby (now deceased) had a T-shirt that said: "I walk a fine line between having friends and correcting their grammar." I agree! I'm usually a stickler for correct grammar[12], and this is what one needs to do to be a good programmer. Keep your code pretty. What do I mean by pretty? To see the programming rules that make code pretty, go to my website (www.moneymentor.com) and click on Books & Articles → Articles → Articles by Others and read Chris Davy's "EasyLanguage Coding Best Practices." Obey all the syntax rules. More on that later when we get to Coding Templates. Programming is all about syntax. Getting the syntax correct, however, doesn't mean you will have coded a successful (money making) strategy, but it does mean that there are no coding syntax errors. It doesn't even mean that your code will do what you want it to do; it just means there are no syntax errors. Hopefully, this book will walk you through the correct coding practices and give you some ideas so that you too can program OOEL.

Not for novices, this book is for folks who already know EasyLanguage and want to get deeper into the machinations that standard EZL doesn't address. We assume that you can already open TS and crank up the TS Development Environment (TDE). We also assume that you are versed in programming with EasyLanguage. Things have been moved around from version 9.5 to version 10, but they are still there, somewhere. If you need help with the version change, give Sunny a call[13]. Or check out **Volume II—Appendix I: Where's the Command?**

What if you want precise control of EZL order entry tickets or want to base your next decision on the real-time equity (as opposed to your system's equity) in your account? Can't do that with vanilla EZL, so you either don't do it or you resort to OOEL.

On the TS Forum (where you go to get trading ideas and trading help) I found a comment as follows:

[12] My grandsons call me the GrammarNazi
[13] 1-760-908-3070 PTs

"I have been playing with some of the ToolBox objects and having some success modifying a few of the simpler examples, but it seems that a lot of the documentation of the new OOEL stuff is kind of 'self-referential.' Everything strange seems to be explained by something else strange. Would it be possible to get some straightforward explanations of what these things do, without referencing only the newer terminology?"

That really says it all. And that's what this book is for, to explain and give examples of coding with OOEL, assuming you know EZL, and make OOEL not so much a mystery.

There are key words used in OOEL that are not part of EZL classic (or vanilla or legacy). For instance, we are going to define and use these concepts:

- Array
- Class
- Collection
- Dictionary
- Form
- Library
- Member

- Method
- Namespace
- Null
- Object
- Region
- Using
- Vector

and many more strange words just like these. But, unlike the user's complaint in the quote above, we will be defining them in easy-to-understand, non-self-referential language.

About These Books

These books do not cover every aspect of OOEL. In fact, these books will lead to other books we will write, smaller specialty books covering single topics. The language is so complex that you will only learn it all by studying the Dictionary and trying to come up with examples, or by scouring the EasyLanguage Forum. After reading these books, however, you will have a solid understanding of object-oriented programming as it pertains to TS.

This begs the question, why do you want to learn OOEL?

Why on Earth would you want to learn this "looks so much more difficult" language when you can use classic EZL? I am glad that you asked. One reason is because you can do so much more. You can control the inner workings and intricacies of TS; you can create applications for yourself or to sell. You can get around the inherent limitations of EZL.

TS's EasyLanguage (EZL) is more than just software; it's a full-fledged programming language. And with the advent of the new Object-Oriented EasyLanguage beginning in TS version 9.0 it is more like Pascal, a lower-level language, than any easy language. Albeit the easiest to use of the complex trading tools, it is still so full of features that it can't help but be difficult in spots.

The chapters in **Volume I** are organized as below. **Volume II** contains all the Appendices, including Where Is the Command?, Dictionary Unfolded, Classes, Reserved Words, Error Codes, and ASCII Character Codes.

Chapter 1: Introduction, where we introduce the prerequisites and re-introduce you to information you might have forgotten. We also discover the meaning of Object-Oriented, Definitions and Setup, TS Basics, Reserved and Skip Words, and Introduction to your best friend and ally on this journey, the EasyLanguage Dictionary.

Chapter 2: Where we address **EasyLanguage** (EZL) **Brush-Up**, Rules & Regulations, More Reserved Words, EasyLanguage Dictionary Lightly Explored, Boolean Algebra, User Functions, Methods, Strings, Date and Time, Switch…Case, Alerts, Commentary, Arrays, Coding Templates, Your First Program and EasyLanguage Intermediate Essentials.

Chapter 3: EasyLanguage Intricacies. This is the essential memorizing part of this book. We will explore Easing into Object-Oriented EasyLanguage, Libraries, Namespaces, Classes, Objects,

Inheritance, Provider Classes, Resource Editor and the ToolBox.

Chapter 4: Easing into Object-Oriented Programming. We begin this chapter with a further walk through the Dictionary, but not the last. You'll get an OOEL coding template, learn what Libraries, Namespaces, Classes and Objects are. You will learn about inheritance and several different Classes, Properties, Methods, use of OOEL DateTime Objects and utilities as well as the beginnings of drawing objects and object manipulation.

Chapter 5: Debugging, Exceptions and Error Handling. No matter who is writing code there are always mistakes ("bugs[14]"), whether just typos or putting a comma when you meant to put a semicolon. When that happens, your code won't compile (verify). You might get an unintelligible error message or one that pinpoints the error and the line number. It happens. Worse yet are the logic error that Verify but do not yield the desired result. This chapter is meant to assist you in locating and diagnosing your errors, oversights, and omissions. For a full list of the error codes, see **Volume II—OME Reference Guide**.

Chapter 6: Methods. Methods are localized subroutines. That is it in short. You declare your Method in your code and refer to it like a local subroutine. You cannot reference it out of the study, strategy etc. in which you have it. This is called "scope." Here I explain how to use them and give you several Methods you will want to copy and paste into your code.

Chapter 7: Hello World! This is the program every new programmer learns first. We present 8 different, and each more progressive, looks at using EZL and then OOEL to create stimulating Hello World! examples. We will print to the Print Log and introduce **StreamReader** and **StreamWriter**. We are going from simplistic to OOEL in this chapter.

Chapter 8: Collections: **Dictionary, Vector** etc. I touched briefly on these subjects in Chapter 2, but here we go into more depth. We also used **TokenList** and **Vector** Classes in Chapter 7 in the Hello_World! examples, before having fully explained them. Please refer to Chapter 7 for the examples. How does the Dictionary differ from a **Dictionary** or **GlobalDictionary**? Here's where we explain them both. Further, we discuss **AppStorage** and the **Queue** and **Stack** Classes.

Chapter 9: Drawing Objects There are objects, and then there are objects. The word "object" can refer to a class of items or it can refer to a single object in your code or on your chart. We are going to examine both, starting with the Analysis Technique class. A myriad of classes and their properties is in **Volume II—Reference Guide**. The EZL **DrawingObject** classes allow you to create drawing objects on a chart from your Analysis Technique (AT) and to programmatically manage their appearance and position. The Trendline and TextLabel Objects parallel the functionality of the legacy EZL **TL_xxx** and **Text_xxx** reserved words. The **Ellipse, HorizontalLine, Rectangle**, and **VerticalLine** Objects are equivalent to the drawing tools you were able to manually insert in a chart.

Chapter 10: Host Classes. The EZL Host classes provide you with the ability to control several of the main TS apps from your EZL code. For example, the **ChartingHost** class contains Properties and Methods that allow you to monitor key and mouse clicks in your chart as well as providing control over the color and position of components in the chart. The **PlatformClientHost** allows access to the active account number in TS and lets you set an event to monitor changes in the account number made by other components. The **PortfolioHost** is the top-level portfolio object that is used to access portfolio state values when they are executed from a Portfolio Maestro (PM) Strategy Group. The **RadarScreenHost** allows access to click events within a RadarScreen window. The event returns additional information from the event hander using the **PlotClickEventArgs** and **CellClickEventArgs** classes. The **StrategyHost** Class allows you to access strategy automation, backtesting, connections, signals, and strategies on the current chart.

Chapter 11: Forms allow you to display a custom form window or dialog box as part of a TS Analysis

---

[14] The first recorded use of the term "bug", with regards to an error or malfunction in a machine, comes from none other than Thomas Edison. In an 1878 letter to an associate. The term was further popularized by Admiral Grace Hopper, creator of one of the first programming languages.

Technique (AT), Strategy, or TradingApp (TA). The ToolBox includes a collection of components that may be 🖱 Double-Clicked to insert them into the AT that is currently open in the EZL editor. Once in the editor, object-oriented code for the component is automatically generated (DGC). The object code is protected (not intended to be edited directly) but the values contained in the component generated code can be modified using the Properties editor.

Chapter 12: Data Providers. There are two main groups of data providers: market data and trading data. The data providers listed below must each be studied in-depth. They each have a specific set of information they make available to an application. Some are straight-forward and other quite complex with some unique and possibly un-anticipated behaviors and limitations.

Chapter 13: Order Tickets & Data Providers. It seems to be everyone's dream to have an automated system that does the chart monitoring and order placement by itself. Set it up once and leave. We all want an automated money-making machine. Everyone dreams of printing money. This chapter covers the machinations of creating order tickets to submit directly to the TS servers. With this facility you can create automated strategies if you want.

Chapter 14: Using Excel within EZL. Who would ever think that you could use Microsoft Excel from within OOEL? Built in. Well, you can, and thankfully this chapter shows you how. You can specify a Workbook and Worksheet name and output real-time data to it from TS. You can then manipulate, conduct analyses on it and display that information with Excel features that are not available in TS.

Chapter 15: Fundamental Data Fields. Even though I am a technical trader I sometimes like to look at the metrics of fundamental data. One can draw trendlines on fundamental data. While most fundamental data is delayed, not by minutes but by days or weeks or sometime even months, the general trend is of interest to me. The fields available are numerous, far beyond anything I can memorize. This chapter is one that should be browsed and then read so you can know what is available when you decide to explore fundamental fields.

Chapter 16: Conclusion

Appendices: These are in **Volume II—Reference Guide.** Here you are going to find more than you might imagine. I have worked at including all you could ever hope to know in the Appendices from Where Is the Command? to a comprehensive listing of classes and error messages, to a full listing of Reserved Words, and one that lists the ASCII character code.

Website Link for Supplemental Material:

https://www.EasyLanguageOOEL.com Sign up as a Free Member and establish a password and you will get access to the code downloads. They are all in one big ELD file but to access the individual components you will need their names.

What is EasyLanguage?

EasyLanguage (EZL) is TS's proprietary command language that lets you specify your trading ideas in "plain English" and test them before you trade. TradeStation's proprietary Object-Oriented EasyLanguage (OOEL) is not so English-like. It is a full-fledged programming language that uses more primitive constructs to allow you greater power within the framework of TradeStation (TS) and EasyLanguage (EZL).

> 📝 For the examples in this book, the ones that are just snippets of code will not be available on the www.EasyLanguageOOEL.com website. They are usually just a few lines and often are not complete routines and won't compile. Those you can type yourself. The rest are available for you to download just by becoming a free member.

EXAMPLE 1.01—Classic EZL Print to File

To print "Hello World!" to a file, using Classic EasyLanguage (EZL) looks like this:

```
Print (File ("C:\OME_Files\MyFile#1.TXT"),"Hello World!") ;
```

EXAMPLE 1.02—OOEL Print to File

Achieving the same goal with Object-Oriented EasyLanguage (OOEL) looks like this:

```
Using elSystem.IO ;
Vars  :  StreamWriter SW  (NULL) ;
SW  = StreamWriter.Create ("C:\OME_Files\MyFile#2.TXT", TRUE) ;
SW.WriteLine ("Hello World!") ;
SW.Close () ;
```

Now you've seen your first OOEL program! Type Example 1.01 and Example 1.02 in the TDE (TS Development Environment), then put them each on a chart and see what happens.

EasyLanguage (EZL) is used to create custom indicators and strategies for financial charts. Its functionality can be extended with the use of DLL's. But in these books, we are going to venture into the labyrinth that is object-oriented programming.

TS's EasyLanguage is more than just software; it's a full-fledged programming language. And with the advent of the new Object-Oriented EasyLanguage (OOEL) beginning in TS version 9.0 it is more like a lower-level language than any easy language. Albeit the easiest to use of the complex trading tools, it is still so full of features that it can't help but be difficult in spots.

All software comes with stumbling blocks. I have yet to open a software box, install and use the product with no problems along the way. Furthermore, TS's EasyLanguage is more than just software; it is a trading language.

TradeStation Tidbits

Sometimes there are often hard to find features in TS that are quite useful. I'm trying to put these in one place, in the beginning. These are handy utilities and I'm not going into depth here, but they are features you might need sometime.

Speaking of difficulties finding features, I've included an Appendix in the **Volume II—Reference Guide** called **Where is the Command?** That should help you find hidden commands.

+= and -=

In brief, += is a concatenation operator. In its simplest sense the statement `Count += 01;` is (computationally) the same as `Count = Count + 01;` It adds the item on the right of the equal sign to the item on the left. There is another usage such as `myTokenList += StrItem01;` or `myTokenList += "StrItem01, StrItem02, StrItem03;` or even `myEventHandlerChain += myEventHandler ;` At first look this appears very different, but it actually is not. The += operator is TYPE sensitive. The first `Count +=` example was adding (or appending) an Integer value. The first `myTokenList +=` example is appending a single value (StrItem01) to the **TokenList** and the second reference is adding a list of items (StrItem01, StrItem02, StrItem03) to a **TokenList** object. The `myEventHandlerChain +=` example is adding an Event Handler Method to a list of Event Handlers. You see? They appear very different but, according to type, they are exactly the same as `myObject = myObject + AnotherObject` where `AnotherObject` is of Type "Int", "Double", "String", **TokenList**, Event Handler, etc. OK, the Event Handler list takes a few more brain cells to grasp but it is adding one Event Handler to a collection of zero or more Event Handlers.

Reset Chart Scaling Range

Ever scroll around on a chart and lose the scaling, so it looks like all or some of your data seems to be gone? If at any point you changed the scaling by dragging the axis so you could better see details on your chart, then this can be a handy trick. After the chart has been re-scaled ⮎ Right-Click on the chart and click Reset Scaling Range. Clever, huh?

Transparent

Did you know that one of the color choices in TS is Transparent? Not a highly advertised feature. Wherever you name a color in your code, or you edit an indicator that has a color selection, one of the choices is the word **Transparent**. If you color something transparent it disappears! You can, in the same manner, make it partially transparent–"see through." Handy for moving drawing objects into the background, still there but not as "in your face". You can make the borders "less loud" than the contents, i.e., lighten up the outside border or the interior fill of a **Rectangle**. For more information see **Chapter 9** on Drawing Objects.

Optimizing with Data2

One "undocumented feature" we discovered is when optimizing it is necessary (if you wish to complete, or even effectively start, the optimization run) that Data1, Data2 and any other data series are set to load the same start and end dates (or end date and days, weeks, months, or years back). It can save you lots of time and frustration to know this fact in advance, instead of trying to figure it out when your Optimization freezes at "Waiting for data".

Data2 Intricacies

There are proper ways to reference Data2 and some that work but are not proper:

When aliasing for Data2 (or Data3, etc.) you may say Close [01] of Data2 but not Close of Data2 [01]. You can legally say (Close of Data2) [01]. You can also say things like (High [01] - Low [01]) of Data2 or (High - Low) [01] of Data2 which will give you the Range of Data2 one bar ago. You will get the same results with Average (Close, 10) of Data2, Average (Close of Data2, 10) and Average (Close of Data2, 10) of Data2. To inspect the results, use the following example.

EXAMPLE 1.03—Diagnosing Proper Use of Data2 [OME_Data2]

To determine whether there is any difference between the structures we present this example which shows the same results no matter which form you choose.

```
if  atCommentaryBar  then begin
  CommentaryCL ("Data1  ", vrt_MMDDYYYY (Date of Data1), ", ",
vrt_HHMM_pm (Time of Data1), ", ", vrt_Format (Close of Data1)) ;
  CommentaryCL ("Data2  ", vrt_MMDDYYYY (Date of Data2), ", ",
vrt_HHMM_pm (Time of Data2), ", ", vrt_Format (Close of Data2)) ;
  CommentaryCL ("C[1] of Data2  ", (Close [01]) of Data2) ;
  CommentaryCL ("2 Methods  ", (High [01] - Low [01]) of Data2, " or
", (High - Low) [01] of Data2) ;
end ;
```

Alignment of Cells in RadarScreen

There's a nifty trick you can do with RadarScreen. Did you know that you can set the alignment of the cells to Left, Right or Middle? Sam taught me this one. I never thought to look.

In a RadarScreen window with your indicator on it, 🖰 Right-Click on the indicator and go to Studies → Edit Indicator for All Symbols. Click on the Style selection, pick the Plot you want to modify and make your selection beside the word Align.

What Does Object-Oriented Mean?

Object-oriented programming is based on the concept of objects. In object-oriented programming data structures, or objects, are defined, each with its own properties or attributes. Object-oriented software

is designed by using objects that interact with one another. Think of objects as people, places and things for the time being.

Just the other day I noticed (since I'm thinking about objects now) that my Adobe Acrobat software has objects, too. Looking at the panel to the left, halfway down is a section headed OBJECTS. Likewise in Figure 1.01 is a window from Microsoft Word, showing the use of objects there. They are all over the place and I hadn't noticed.

A few years ago, just for fun, I took a class with my grandson that covered a programming language called Alice. Alice is a block-based programming environment that makes it easy to create animations, build interactive narratives, or program simple games. Essentially, Alice is a learning tool that introduces the novice to the concept of object-oriented programming.

While an object in OOEL might be a vertical line, or a trendline, or a rectangle, in Alice an object is a person, place or thing.

In the beginning lesson, I learned to make Alice glide across a frozen pond moving her legs back and forth to appear to be skating. Alice was the object I was manipulating. Likewise, in OOEL objects are things you can manipulate. (Remember this for later.)

One can create code to make Alice appear to move across the screen, but Alice doesn't actually move until you press the Play button.

I Googled "what is an object in OOP" and encountered the same problem the user (several pages above) was complaining about. The definition I found was circular:

Each object is an instance of a particular class or subclass with the class's own Methods or procedures and data variables.

Wow! Still, I don't know what they mean by that! What is a class? A subclass? We will know soon. TS is considered the premiere trading software for individual traders and professional traders alike. I have been an end-user of the software since 1986 or 1987 when I started using System Writer (no charting just calculations). Clearly, since Sam led the development department and designed the software, he has been using it a lot longer than I have. System Writer Plus added Charting and more language features but still used the Borland Pascal compiler of the original and has Pascal features.

The draw, at the time, for me was real-time data (vs End-of-Day only) a language with which to program and test my ideas. The language was very easy to use, and my passion was in testing strategies to find something successful with which to trade. I was, and still am, a proponent of testing before trading.

Many people with whom I come in contact don't want to test their strategies. Either they don't program, or they believe they can make more money using discretionary "feelings." I have found over the years that those who don't test their systems don't want to know the answer.

It is said that hypothetical performance results…have no bearing on future results. But what else is there? You cannot trade future results. That data doesn't exist yet. Even though you can't take every factor into account when programming and testing, if you don't do it, you will surely be stepping into shark infested waters.

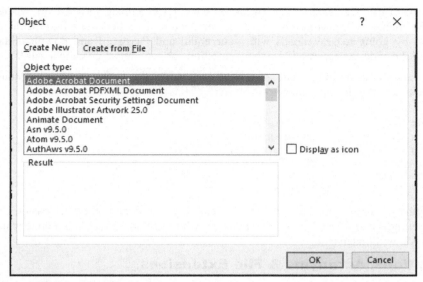

FIGURE 1.01—Objects in Microsoft Word

While EZL was miles ahead of any competing products by version 9.0, it nevertheless benefitted from adding tools for programmers to use in handling the more intricate features of charting, programming, and testing.

With version 9.0 TS Securities Group introduced an extension to its EZL programming language called Object-Oriented EasyLanguage (OOEL). While its claim to fame had been the ease of use of EZL, and the English-like command structure (verbose), this new language (OOEL) is a fully extensible programming language. In structure OOEL is reminiscent of the programming language Pascal (though Pascal had no Objects at the time) and has features of C++ that make it truly powerful.

In the next chapter we will discover the meaning of terms like object, class, and namespace and they will begin to make sense. It wasn't that long ago that we didn't know the meaning of gigabyte (much less terabyte) and it was just a matter of getting used to it; the same will be true of OOEL words by the end of Chapter 2.

Conventions

You have already encountered some of the conventions in this book. When I use the `Courier New` font, it designates coding examples. Here's how I will be representing code throughout the book:

```
Print (File ("C:\OME_Files\MyFile#1.TXT"),"Hello World!") ;
```

All programming code herein is designated by using the typeface Courier New.

All classes and namespaces are shown in the typeface **bold Arial Narrow** while EZL specific terms and EZL Reserved Words are in **Bold Times New Roman** type.

I've used a few symbols in the book and some typefaces to separate code from text. An arrow (→) means to pull-down the menu and choose the next command. You can read it as "go to".

A mouse symbol (🖰) means to use the mouse to pull-down or click to the command. Important notes are in blue boxes. Everything else is pretty much self-explanatory.

In the code presented herein I have eliminated blank lines from Sam's pretty code in many cases to conserve space. In your own code be liberal with blank lines between sections of your program to make for readability. Think of them as paragraphs with double spacing between them.

In cases where a line of code is too long to present on one line, it extends to the next line. It is not as "pretty" that way, but it must be.

For your ease-of-use we have a new website: www.EasyLanguageOOEL.com where you can download the coding examples in this book. All you need to do is become a free member. They are located there by going to Downloads with your email and Password and downloading the ELD containing all the code. As always, if you have questions or comments, give me a call.[15]

Sam likes to line things up in his code, so you will encounter this convention in the examples. He's pretty nit-picky about it. For instance, you will see:

```
Vars   :
  String DQ           (DoubleQuote),
  String NL           (NewLine),
  String myVectObj    (""),
  Bool   Debug        (FALSE),
  Double Dummy        (0.00),
  Int    Loop         (00) ;
```

so that everything is pretty, lined up. and easy-to-read. It makes debugging much easier. I've taken to doing it myself now and it helps. Now if you wonder why there are spaces in our code where they are not needed, you will understand.

Abbreviations, Acronyms & File Extensions

Herewith I am collecting a simple list of abbreviations I am using in these books for your ease of use.

AC   Analysis Commentary
AME   *Ask Mr. EasyLanguage* by Samuel K. Tennis
AP   AccountsProvider
AT   Analysis Technique (Indicator, PaintBar, ShowMe)
CL   Carriage Return / Line Feed or a NewLine character
CONST   Constant - a Declaration Statement
CRLF   Carriage Return / Line Feed, #OD #OA in Hex
CSV   File Extension - Comma Separated Values
DGC   Designer Generated Code
DGV   DataGridView - an Object
DICT   Dictionary - an Object
DLL   File Extension - Dynamic Link Library
DOP   File Extension – Data Order Parameter
DP   DataProvider
DQ   DoubleQuote
ELA   File Extension - EasyLanguage Archive (TS 4 and earlier)
ELD   File Extension - EasyLanguage Document File
ELP   File Extension - EasyLanguage Project File
ELS   File Extension - EasyLanguage Storage (TS 5)
ELX   File Extension - EasyLanguage Project XML definition file
eNum   Enumeration or Enumerated Value
EZL   EasyLanguage
F3   Verify. Press Function Key 3 or F3
FC   Fast Calc
GD   GlobalDictionary - elSystem.Collections.GlobalDictionary
GDict   GlobalDictionary
GV   Global Variables
HL   HorizontalLine - an Object
HTML   File Extension - HyperText Markup Language
IBOG   IntrabarOrderGeneration compiler directive (a variant of IOG)
IBP   IntraBarPersist variable declaration
INI   File Extension – Initialization File

---
[15] (760) 908-3070 PT.

IOG	IntrabarOrderGeneration compiler directive (a variant of IBOG)
JSON	File Extension - JavaScript Object Notation
LE	Long Entry
LIBB	Look Inside Bar Backtesting
LX	Long Exit
MBB	MaxBarsBack (Maximum number of bars study will reference)
NaN	Not a Number
NL	NewLine
OME	*The Definitive Guide to TradeStation's EasyLanguage & OOEL* [16]
OOEL	Object-Oriented EasyLanguage
OP	OrdersProvider
OT	OrderTicket
PSP	PriceSeriesProvider – an object
RE	Resource Editor (form graphical design tool)
RS	RadarScreen
SAP	SymbolAttributesProvider
SE	Short Entry
SJH	Sunny J. Harris
SKT	Samuel K. Tennis
SWP	System Writer Plus
SX	Short Exit
TA	TradingApp
TApp	TradingApp
TDE	TradeStation Development Environment
TMP	File Extension - Temporary File
TS	TradeStation
TSD	File Extension - TradeStation Desktop
TSME	TradeStation Made Easy! by Sunny J. Harris
TSW	File Extension - TradeStation Workspace
TXT	File Extension - Text File
VAR	Variables - a Declaration Statement
VL	VerticalLine – an Object
VRT	Vista-Research and Trading
WAV	File Extension - an Audio File
XLXS	File Extension - Microsoft Excel File
XML	File Extension - Extensible Markup Language

Introduction to TradeStation Basics

To effectively utilize the information herein you should have TS running and have brought up the TDE (TS Development Environment). Take a look at the following figures to get a picture of what I mean.

---

[16] These books were originally named "…Object-Oriented EasyLanguage Made Easy!"

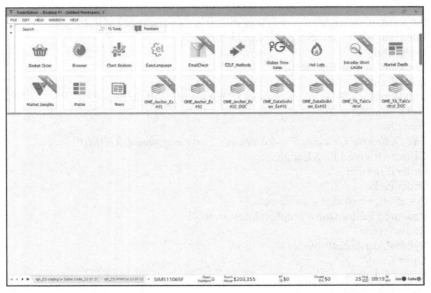

FIGURE 1.02—TS When You First Open It

> ✍ There is a reported bug (since 9.0 I believe) in TradeStation. If you click in a Chart or RadarScreen to "Edit EasyLanguage" and you do NOT have the TDE already open then the TDE will open that single document and forget all of the documents you previously had open. Very frustrating, I usually crash the TDE when this happens to preserve my list of open files.

On the screen you see in Figure 1.02, the EZL icon is in the first row of apps (applications) fourth one over from the left. It looks like a gear. Clicking on that icon takes you directly to the TDE (TradeStation Development Environment). It will generally open any code you previously had open. If none was open previously you will come to an open environment that looks like Figure 1.03.

> ✍ From within the platform you can also click File, New Application and EasyLanguage is (currently) the fourth item.
> It is fairly simple to create a shortcut to the Development Environment on your desktop.

You can also see several icons showing a stack of books. Those are TradingApps for this book. Notice that they all start with OME_ which signifies OOEL Made Easy!

I have three more apps that you probably won't have: EMailCheck, Intraday Short Locate or Market Insights on yours. The first one, EmailCheck, I had Chris do for me; the others I got from the TradeStation Forum. Sign-in to your account and ✍ click on Support → TS → EasyLanguage Support and search away. I found this app under a search for "intraday."

Next let's get to the place we program indicators, strategies, and apps. To do so you will need to click on Apps (mine is on the top in the ribbon) followed by selecting the EZL icon (the gear-like picture). You can also get there by ✍ File → New Application and selecting EasyLanguage. This will bring up the TradeStation Development Environment (TDE). This is where you will program all your code. It used to be called the EZL PowerEditor, but it's more than that now.

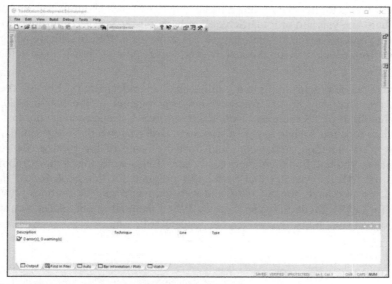

FIGURE 1.03—The TS Development Environment (TDE)

Here is where you do your programming. The blank slate; *tabula rasa*. In its current state there is nothing to write on. To bring up a blank study or a template document you need to see Figure 1.04.

Starting with the blank screen from Figure 1.03 we go to ⏷ File in the upper left corner and pull-down to → New and over to select the type of document you want to create. You can also click on the top left icon. The selections are:

- ActivityBar
- Function
- Indicator
- PaintBar

- ProbabilityMap
- ShowMe
- Strategy
- TradingApp

These choices are the same whether you are using EZL or OOEL; you start with a blank document and then decide what to type in to create your trading analysis. It's seamless. To explore what "words" you can use, you explore the Dictionary, which lives at the right-hand edge of my default configuration of TS. You will find all the familiar words like **Plot**, **Buy**, **Sell**, **If**, **Then** etc. under the selection **easylanguage.ell**.

The good and the bad of the Dictionary is that ALL the commands for both EZL and OOEL are there for you to sort through. If you are an expert EZL programmer, then it isn't distracting to have them all in one place because you will know what you are looking for. But if you are new to OOEL, most of the language will be foreign to you and it might be difficult to differentiate which is which. We will do a little EZL brush up in a few minutes, but it will not be the basic stuff covered in TSME. Keep reading; we'll get there.

Typically, we begin with an Indicator (Study), though not always. An indicator will plot lines or bars on your chart from which you develop trading plans. If you can program your indicator and have a schematic for how to use it in trading, then you can program the Strategy. Studies also include PaintBars, and ShowMes. In the main menu bar of a TS workspace, you will also find Strategies and Study Groups.

If you have an idea that you want programmed and don't feel you can quite get there by yourself, give me a call or shoot me an email.[17] We can program it for you. Between me, Sam and Chris, we can get just about anything done.

---

[17] sunny@moneymentor.com or 1-760-908-3070 PT.

Next, EZL/OOEL wants to give the routine a name, enter any notes about its use, and select whether to make it for Chart Analysis and/or RadarScreen[18] or both. Lastly, you can pull-down to the Template selection and bring up a pre-made template to give you some ideas. Before long we will give you some OOEL templates from which to begin. Soon, however, we are going to brush up on some plain vanilla EZL.

In order to keep my code organized, I put my initials and an underscore (_) before the name of any routine I program. That way all my routines show up together in the list, instead of dispersed throughout the hundreds of TS routines I have collected from various sources, not just my own. For instance, my colors function's name is `sjh_f_Colors`. Broken down that's my initials, underscore, f to let me know it's a function, underscore and then the name of the routine. Be sure to choose descriptive names so you will find them more easily later. Believe me, this is more important than you will believe at first. All the routines that Sam and I program for this book follow the convention `OME_routinename`. We have, for this book and website, named all the routines provided with the initials OME_ (for OOEL Made Easy) so that you'll find them all in one place. You will find these .ELD files on our website: https://www.EasyLanguageOOEL.com..

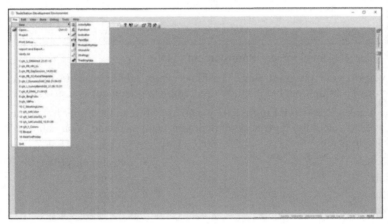

FIGURE 1.04—From the TDE: 🖰 File → New → Document Type

> 📝 The term ELD refers to a disk file of type EasyLanguage Document, which is a container of one or more Analysis Techniques. You use the Import/Export Wizard to import Analysis Techniques from an .ELD file. You use that same Import/Export wizard to export Analysis Techniques from the TDE to an .ELD file.

Develop a system early for naming and storing your ELD files for archival purposes.

Looking at Figure 1.05 below we are going to begin a new indicator by using the command sequence, from the TDE:

🖰 File → New → Indicator to bring up the New Indicator box (see Figure 1.04 above).

For our first indicator, we are going to do what all computer programming manuals do for the first example. We will code a little routine called `Hello_World!  #01`. Later we will program the same thing in OOEL.

When you get to the OOEL part, know that there is a template for you to model your code after in **Chapter 4—OOEL Coding Template.** Feel free to change it to suit your needs.

---

[18] If you don't know what RadarScreen is, you should read "TradeStation Made Easy!" before reading this book. RadarScreen is a spreadsheet configuration in which to display and compare indicators.

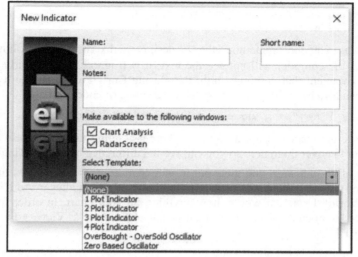

FIGURE 1.05—🖱 File → New → Indicator

Do not select a template; I will handhold you through the example. For this first example, give your indicator an appropriate name (like `OME_Hello_World!_Ex#01`). Also enter some descriptive text now in the Notes for future reference. TS only displays the Notes in a few places but where it does it helps. If you want to know how to create and update EZL templates, then send Sam an email[19] one day and ask him to run through the basics with you.

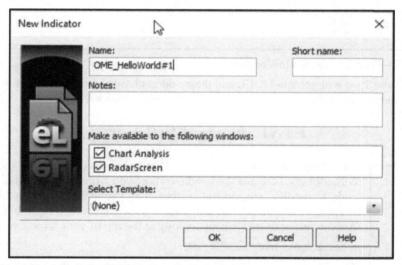

FIGURE 1.06—Creating Hello_World!_Ex#01 Indicator

Having selected and named as above, you are now ready to begin typing on that blank slate. But, what to type? Let's start out with a simple **Print** statement. Just type what I have in the example below, and we are on our way.

Why have I given you something so simple to start with? Because we are going to do the same thing with OOEL in **Chapter 7**. You've got to start somewhere.

EXAMPLE 1.04—Hello_World!_Ex#01 [Hello_World!_Ex#01]

```
// Hello_World!_Ex#01
```

[19] sktennis@vista-research.com or sktennis@EasyLanguageOOEL.com

```
// This is how to write a comment
{ or you could write a comment this way }
Print (" Hello World! #1 ") ;
```

Before I go on, in case you don't remember, the // designates that the text that follows is a comment, for this line. Thus, the compiler will not see the text; it will ignore it. The Curly Braces (French Braces) denote a comment that continues until the closing Curly/French Brace. It can extend over multiple lines. It can also be entirely contained within one line of code as in :

```
Print ("This line " + {"does not contain " + }"contains a comment.") ;
```

Now how do we see the results of our program? Where is it going to print? These are questions for newbies, but I want to cover them here so you can see the difference between EZL and OOEL.

To see the results of an indicator, you must put it on a chart so it will run. Open up a chart of your favorite symbol and put our indicator on the chart. Reminder: it's ⊕ Studies → Add Study → Indicator → OME_Hello_World!_Ex#01. It won't show anything on your chart. In order for you to see the output you will need to open the Print Log, which you do as follows: ⊕ View → EasyLanguage Print Log, or CTRL-SHIFT-E.

Here is the Print Log I got. What about you?

×	Hello World! #1
🗗	Hello World! #1
	Hello World! #1
▼	Hello World! #1
	Hello World! #1
	Hello World! #1

Print Log

FIGURE 1.07—Print Log for HelloWorld#01

In **Chapters 3** and **7** we will get into OOEL and there address how to make it print only once instead of once for each bar and explore other renditions of this indicator in OOEL.

EasyLanguage Dictionary

The Dictionary (as opposed to a Dictionary Object) lives in the upper right corner of my TDE aka the window where you type your EZL code and bring up code to modify, seen in the sidebar. The Dictionary does not live in the TS charting environment, it is only available where you will be coding, in the TDE. Another place to find it is by looking at the top of your screen, with the toolbar icons. It looks like this: 🖳.

The Dictionary is just like you would think, it's the repository of all the commands that are embedded into EZL, both EZL and OOEL. (I'm tempted to call them EasyLanguage and HardLanguage. Sam wanted to call it TradeSpeak but Bill overruled him.) Each item has a corresponding definition and links to other related items. The bad news is they ALL are in the Dictionary and there are no filters to reduce the clutter to just what you are looking for. That is not strictly true because there IS a search feature, but it does not do what I wish for.

The EZL Dictionary contains all the Reserved Words and functions and commands that can be used when creating EZL (or OOEL) documents in the TDE. That means that lots of stuff you won't use as a legacy EZL programmer is in there along with all the EZL commands for OOEL programmers. It makes browsing that much more difficult.

The EasyLanguage Dictionary is organized by category (**LibraryName.ell**), so it is easy to find the words needed to express your trading ideas. This Dictionary also provides notes, examples, and parameter values to help you quickly understand what each word means and how the word can be incorporated within your study. **Volume II—Reference Guide**: **Appendix V** contains a full listing of the Reserved Words and their meanings.

Just like learning any foreign language, learning to program both "vanilla" EasyLanguage (EZL) and learning Object-Oriented EasyLanguage (OOEL) is really a matter of memorizing nouns and verbs. Once you are familiar with the most commonly used nouns and verbs you will be able to write EZL/OOEL programs. Start by browsing the Appendices in **Volume II—Reference Guide**.

We will soon give you a list of the more commonly used words and commands. My suggestion for now is "explore the Dictionary." The more "nouns and verbs" you memorize and understand, the more programming you will be able to accomplish.

For the moment, start with finding where the Print statement lives. To find a command that we want for EZL, we look in the Dictionary under **easylanguage.ell**. Putting "print" into the search bar in the Dictionary brings us to the environment in Figure 1.08. The third item in the list is Print, which is not the same as Printer.

Investigating the **Print** command by clicking on **Print** in the list gives us the information in Figure 1.09.

Here you can see a brief summary of the Print command. What it does not do is tell me the details I am looking for. For that let's click on the hyperlinked Print word at the bottom of that figure. That brings up a wealth of information, including how to print to the Print Log, a File or the default Printer. Now we are talking. We will use this information later. For now, we just want to know how to find things in the Dictionary.

Print is pretty innocuous; we just want to get accustomed to using the Dictionary. Seeing our familiar Print command where it lives in the overall Dictionary helps us to feel more comfortable with the daunting task of learning the huge volume of commands in there. It should make you comfortable when we start memorizing and becoming familiar with OOEL commands.

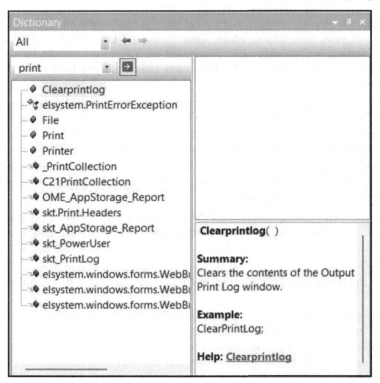

FIGURE 1.08—Finding the Print Command

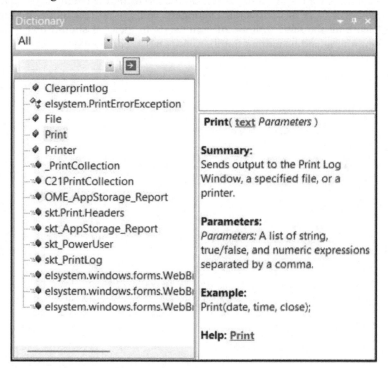

FIGURE 1.09—Elucidating the Print Command

Now let us get a little more familiar with the Dictionary. Clear the search so you again see the list of libraries (they end in .ell). Click on **easylanguage.ell** to open the library. Now we need to find print;

time for some brainiac work. Messaging? Nope. Output? Bingo! In short, that is how you search for and locate the term of interest.

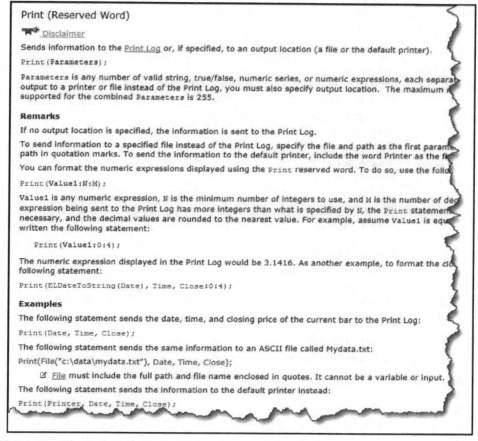

Print (Reserved Word)

🔫 Disclaimer

Sends information to the Print Log or, if specified, to an output location (a file or the default printer).

`Print(Parameters);`

Parameters is any number of valid string, true/false, numeric series, or numeric expressions, each separat... output to a printer or file instead of the Print Log, you must also specify output location. The maximum ... supported for the combined Parameters is 255.

Remarks

If no output location is specified, the information is sent to the Print Log.

To send information to a specified file instead of the Print Log, specify the file and path as the first param... path in quotation marks. To send the information to the default printer, include the word Printer as the f...

You can format the numeric expressions displayed using the Print reserved word. To do so, use the follo...

`Print(Value1:N:M);`

Value1 is any numeric expression, N is the minimum number of integers to use, and M is the number of dec... expression being sent to the Print Log has more integers than what is specified by N, the Print statemen... necessary, and the decimal values are rounded to the nearest value. For example, assume Value1 is equ... written the following statement:

`    Print(Value1:0:4);`

The numeric expression displayed in the Print Log would be 3.1416. As another example, to format the clo... following statement:

`Print(ELDateToString(Date), Time, Close:0:4);`

Examples

The following statement sends the date, time, and closing price of the current bar to the Print Log:

`Print(Date, Time, Close);`

The following statement sends the same information to an ASCII file called Mydata.txt:

`Print(File("c:\data\mydata.txt"), Date, Time, Close);`

☑ File must include the full path and file name enclosed in quotes. It cannot be a variable or input.

The following statement sends the information to the default printer instead:

`Print(Printer, Date, Time, Close);`

FIGURE 1.10—The Full Definition of Print

Now we can move on. Feel free to explore the Dictionary to your heart's content. And then some, do not be shy. Learn all you can. It will be time well spent. Then come back here and let's brush up a bit on EZL "vanilla" and some Reserved Words before we get into the hard stuff.

Reserved Words and Skip Words

There is a set of words that are reserved for use by TS and EZL. For instance, it wouldn't make sense for you to name a variable Buy when there is a command called Buy in the language itself. This would be a big conflict and the interpreter wouldn't understand what you meant. Words like these are called Reserved Words.

The first words we need to know in the Reserved Words list are self-explanatory.

- Open (O)
- High (H)
- Low (L)
- Close (C)
- Date (D)
- Time (T)

- UpTicks
- DownTicks
- Ticks
- Volume (V)
- OpenInt (OI)

You should not use these words in your code for other than their intended meaning. The short form of the word is in parentheses.

There are more. In fact, with the advent of OOEL there are lots more reserved words. See **Volume II—Reference Guide, Appendix V: Reserved Words** for the full list. In **Chapter 2** we will discover many more reserved words. For now, just remember the words above are not words you can use as variables or inputs in your programming.

Here are some more Reserved Words, which should be self-explanatory.

Symbol	Meaning
#	Character used to denote compiler directives
(	Open parenthesis, used in formulas
)	Close parenthesis, used in formulas
*	Multiplication sign
+	Addition sign
-	Subtraction sign
/	Division sign
//	Comment
=	Equals sign
<	Less Than sign
<=	Less Than or Equal sign
>	Greater Than sign
>=	Greater Than or Equal sign
<>	Not Equal sign
[ ]	BarsAgo reference; Array or Collection Index; Attribute statements
{ }	Comment of 1 or more lines

TABLE 1.01—More Reserved Words

There are also Skip Words that EZL ignores. These are:

- A
- An
- At
- Based
- By
- Does
- Is
- Of
- On
- Place
- Than
- The
- Was

These skip words are for your use in making your code easier to read. For instance, these two sentences are the same, but the second one is easier to read.

```
Buy 2 contracts next bar Market ;
Buy 2 contracts next bar at the Market ;
```

Writing the statements above reminds me of another EZL convention: you must end each sentence with a semicolon (;). That way EZL/OOEL knows you are finished with this sentence and ready to begin another. If you forget your semicolon the EZL compiler (**F3**) will tell you, but it won't always get the location correct. It gets confused sometimes. The other way to verify (compile) your code is to go to the top ribbon of the TDE and choose ⌐ Build → Verify. You can also get there through ⌐ File → Verify. The **F3** shortcut is preferable for me, but you are welcome to use the menu bars.

TS/EZL also has several OOEL KeyWords which are essential in your programming. These KeyWords came with a newer version of EZL and relate, largely, to OOEL Programming.

This list is alphabetical, not in order of importance.

- asType
- Catch
- Finally
- In
- isType
- Method
- New
- Once
- Out
- Override
- Throw
- Try
- Using

The EasyLanguage Development Environment (TDE)

Sam: The TDE has gone through so many 'revisions' over the years – originally the PowerEditor and now the 'Development Environment' – I think I still prefer the PowerEditor! Change for the purpose of change – the software user's worst nightmare. A lesson learned well by the WordPerfect team!

EasyLanguage Editor

The Editor into which you type your EZL sentences is much like a word processor, in that you type words and sentences and EZL will try to highlight your syntax errors and give you related messages. And just like Microsoft Word, it starts out blank: *tabula rasa*. Likewise, where MSWord tells you of grammatical errors and spelling mistakes, EZL will tell you something you may type next or when something in your code will not compile.

If you get an error number that you don't recognize, flip back to **Volume II—Reference Guide, Appendix VI: Error Codes** to get a better idea. The PowerEditor is now called the TDE or TS Development Environment since it is so much more than just an editor. You will be writing programs and compiling (verifying) them in the TDE. I use the **F3** key to compile my code. Of course, you are free to use the command sequence ⟨🖱 Build → Verify to verify as well.

In the olden days, before TS became a brokerage house, when you pressed **F3** and your code was correct, the compiler would respond with "Excellent!" No longer; legal restrictions don't allow that as it might make you think your code would be profitable. It now so it simply puts Verified or Not Verified in the bar at the bottom of the page.

You can even develop programs that have facility beyond TS. For instance, I asked Chris to use EZL to give me a program that could compare two files and output a file containing the differences. He did it with OOEL! Now I can load two CSV files into the program and get as output a file that is the difference between the two input files. It's great for keeping my email lists up to date. It has nothing to do with TS or plotting or strategies; it simply uses the reading and writing facilities of OOEL to parse the files and create a difference file. OOEL is just that powerful!

When you click on the Apps menu in the top bar of TS 10.0 or click View → TradingApp Launcher, it brings up all the applications available in TS. Here's what it looks like, see Figure 1.11.

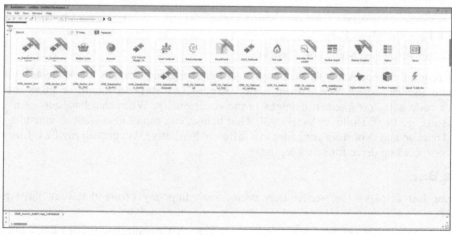

FIGURE 1.11—The Application Menu (Apps)

The applications standardly available are:

- Basket Order
- Browser
- Chart Analysis
- Hot Lists

- Market Depth
- Matrix
- News
- OptionStation Pro

- Portfolio Maestro
- Quick Trade Bar
- RadarScreen
- Research
- Scanner
- Time and Sales
- TradeManager

- TradeManager Analysis
- TradingApp Store
- TradingApp Store Updates
- Walk-Forward Optimizer

You will notice that in Figure 1.11 (my own Apps toolbar) there are more apps than the ones I just listed for you. If you were to look at Sam's toolbar you would see that it is full of TradingApps. Why? Because we have downloaded and installed apps from the TradingApp Store[20] and Sam has written many. You will probably want to as well. In fact, there are TradingApps in the code provided in this book. And by the time we are done with this book, you will be writing apps of your own which will live on your toolbar.

Menu Bar

The menu bar provides access to most of the editing and formatting commands used in the TDE. Clicking on a menu title displays a drop-down menu from which you can select the available commands.

Drop-down window menu categories on the menu bar include File, Edit, View, Build, Debug, Tools, Window, and Help. Clicking on a menu title displays a drop-down menu from which you can select commands.

The Standard toolbar includes commonly used icons to access the same menu command with a single click. To customize (add, remove, or reposition) the icons on the toolbar use the Tools → Customize menu sequence and drag those elements to the toolbar that you want to have access to. Drag away and drop (anywhere off the menu) those you do not want or drag to a different location (still on the menu) to change the order.

FIGURE 1.12—The Menu Bar

For more information, see Menu and Toolbar.

To Verify (compile) your Analysis Technique (AT) after making changes, click the 🖉 Verify icon on the main toolbar, select Verify from the ⊕ Right-Click shortcut menu, or press the F3 key. Sometimes code gets corrupted. It happens to me occasionally. When that happens, or if you have imported stuff, go to ⊕ Build → Verify All. That helps. You might also want to consider doing an automated backup and exporting your files to a different hard drive. I export all my EZL files regularly to my Drobo[21] backup drive for safe keeping.

Output Bar

The Output Bar displays the verification status, including any errors that may have prevented verification.

In Figure 1.13 I have introduced an error so you can see what a compilation error looks like. What is Error (#30286) I hear you ask.

I have an Appendix just for that. See **Volume II—Reference Guide** for a full listing of **Error Codes** and their meanings.

---

[20] Which has been discontinued since we began writing these books.

[21] Drobo is a brand of external storage devices.

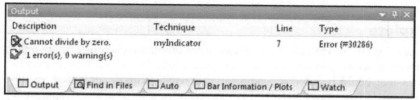

FIGURE 1.13—Output Bar

The Output Bar includes an Output tab and Find in Files tab as well as several other tabs. These are used to display verification messages (output) and to find specified text by searching through a set of files.

Line Numbering

I like to have my code lines numbered for ease of use in debugging. If you get an error message that says your error is on line 47, how do you know where that is? You turn on line numbering.

Line numbering is an EZL Code Editor feature that lets you add sequential numbers to each line of code in an Analysis Technique (AT).

Use the ⤴ Tools → Options main menu sequence to access the General tab and check or un-check Line Numbers to change the setting. If you forget that then you can always look in **Volume II— Reference Guide, Appendix I: Where Is the Command?**

Toolbar

The Standard toolbar displays icons for accessing common editing commands used in the TS Development Environment.

Click on an active (not grayed out) icon to execute a command. Use the ⤴ View → Toolbars menu sequence to show or hide the Standard toolbar and to Customize toolbar commands.

ToolBox Tab

The ToolBox includes a context-sensitive set of design components that let you add specific objects to your AT that can be modified using the Properties Editor to minimize writing code.

Creating and Modifying Code

The EZL Editor, aka TS Development Environment (TDE), is used to create and modify ATs including studies, strategies, and functions.

The EZL Editor is a word processor-like text editor for editing ATs including Studies, Strategies, TradingApps, and Functions that contain EZL statements that combine Reserved Words, Functions, and Methods.

Before you can use the editor, you'll need to either open an existing AT or create a new one.

Use the ⤴ File → Open menu sequence or click the second Open icon to access the window, specify a type (Indicator, Strategy, etc.), and select a document from those listed.

Use the ⤴ File → New menu sequence, or click the left most New icon, to create a new Analysis Technique of a specified type (Indicator, Strategy, etc.). Enter a Name for the document and other related information, like Notes, about its use.

The EZL Editor features include color coded elements to make your reading easier to read. By default, they are: Green comments, Blue reserved words, Purple functions, Olive pre-declared variables, DarkRed string text and Black user code. For instance:

EXAMPLE 1.05—Hello_World!_Ex#03

```
if (CurrentBar <= 01) then begin
  Print ("Hello World! #03") ;
  // prints on the first bar on the chart
```

```
end ;
```

AutoComplete

The EZL Code Editor in the TDE also provides an AutoComplete technology that monitors your typing and can prompt you with a pop-up window displaying a list of Reserved Words, Functions, Methods, and Properties that could be used to complete your entry. This helps speed up development by minimizing the need to memorize statement syntax and by reducing keyboard input and by referencing the Appendices or Dictionary.

You can change the Enable AutoComplete settings on the General tab of the Options dialog box (🖰 Tools → Option menu sequence).

As you begin typing at the beginning of a line, a list box appears showing the range of words that match your typing. Select any item in the list and press the Enter key (or click again) on the highlighted word to have it inserted into your code window. In addition, a word is highlighted when it is the only one that matches your current typed input and will be inserted when the Enter key is pressed (or when clicked again).

For example, with AutoComplete enabled, typing `GetR` will highlight the complete function name **GetRGBValues** and will insert it into your code when pressing the Enter key or 🖰 Double-Clicking a listed item. I'm a mouser, but Sam is a keyboardist. He says: if typing, then pressing Enter is faster than moving the mouse.

Often EZL "gurus" turn off AutoComplete because they think it slows down production. We are not doing any large projects here so Sam and I both keep it enabled.

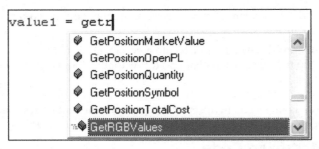

FIGURE 1.14—Using AutoComplete

Also, when typing a reserved word or function followed by a parenthesis, an AutoComplete tool tip appears providing additional information about the word such as possible parameters and a brief summary. For example, when typing the reserved word **NumToStr** in the editor you will see the following prompt popup as soon as the opening parentheses is typed:

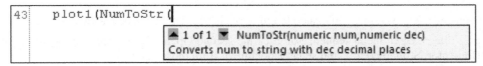

FIGURE 1.15—AutoComplete PopUp

The AutoComplete tool tip remains in view while you type any additional parameters for that word. Clicking the mouse again at any time removes the prompt.

Member Association

Another AutoComplete feature is triggered when you type a marker character, such as a period or parenthesis, and will display a popup list box showing the members (objects, properties, etc.) that are associated with your entry. Highlight any item in the list (using the mouse or arrow keys) and press the Enter key (or click again) on the highlighted word to have it inserted into your code window. In addition, a word is highlighted when it is the only one that matches your current typed input and will be inserted when the Enter key is pressed (or when clicked again).

For example, with AutoComplete enabled, as you type the period character after account (see below), a list of available properties for the Account Object will be displayed for you to select.

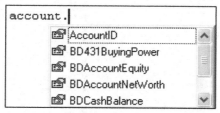

FIGURE 1.16—AutoComplete for Account

Properties Editor tab

The Properties Editor is used to modify the values of design components that have been included in your Analysis Technique. Values changed in the Properties Editor are automatically transferred into the protected Designer Generated Code (DGC) region of your document.

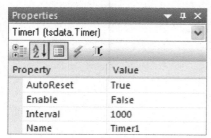

Click ▼ to select an available component from the drop-down list at the top of the Properties Editor to display and edit the properties, events, and inputs for the component.

Click the 🖩 Property icon to display or change property values for a component. Click on a specific Property Value to change it, then type/select a new value.

Click the ℃ Input icon to create an input for a value. The component code section is automatically updated with your change.

Click the 🖋 Event icon to display or change the event handler(s) for a component. Click on a specific event Value to change it, then type, double-click or select the name of the Event Handler.

Clicking the ⊞ Categorized icon displays items by category and clicking the ⒜ Alphabetical icon displays items in ascending order.

Dictionary Tab

The Dictionary lists libraries and their members in a tree-like structure. In the left panel is the Objects pane that allows you to view the contents of the various elements contained in a Namespace or selected from a Search. Multiple levels of detail for each element can be displayed by clicking + or − to unfold or fold the view.

The Members Pane is on the right side of the Dictionary and displays the members of the elements selected in the Objects pane. These can include EZL words, Functions, Properties, Methods, Events, and Enumerated Value (eNum) items. The icon preceding the name of the member identifies its type. See **Table 2.13 in Chapter 2** for a list of icons, aka the **Dictionary Exploration Aid**.

The Description pane is at the bottom right of the Dictionary and displays detailed information about the currently selected Element or Member. In brief, Elements are on the left and Members are in the top right. Related information may be available by clicking on the Help link (if shown) at the bottom of the description.

See **Volume II—Reference Guide, Appendix II: The Dictionary Unfolded**.

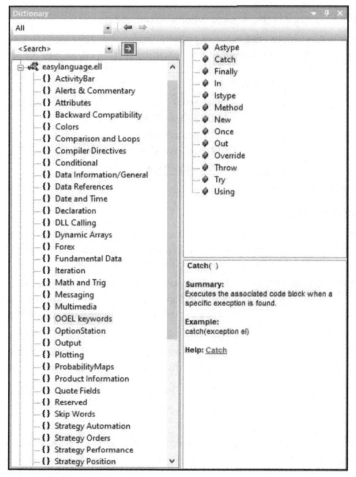

FIGURE 1.17—Introduction to the Dictionary

The pane that shows Class items grouped by Namespace; the upper right pane shows the members of a selected class, and the lower right pane shows a description of the selected member.

Component Tray

The Component Tray displays the components that are included in the currently selected Analysis Technique. Components are found in the ToolBox and includes design templates that can be dragged into a document.

Summary

We have looked briefly at the Dictionary the EZL Editor, the Output tab, the Properties Editor and the TDE. Sometimes the TDE is called the PowerEditor or the EZL Editor. There is more to come. I hope you have spent some time browsing through them, especially the Dictionary, by yourself. We have also looked at Reserved Words and Skip Words. We have briefly examined the Print statement and printed to the EZL Print Log.

In the next chapter we will get to the EZL brush up. We would suggest that you ask Sam for a pdf copy of *Ask Mr. EasyLanguage* or pick up a copy of *TradeStation Made Easy!* to facilitate your learning. Preferably both as all the basics are in those books.

CHAPTER 2
Brushing Up on EasyLanguage

In This Chapter

- Introduction
- Comments
- Data Types
- Inputs
- Variables
- Constants
- Boolean Algebra
- Decisions (Conditions)
- Printing
- User Functions
- Loops & More
- More About Strings
- Date & Time
- Date & Time Old School
- Switch … Case
- A Brief Interlude
- Token Lists, Vectors & Arrays
- Summary

Introduction

This chapter is not a substitute for reading *TradeStation Made Easy!* or *Ask Mr. EasyLanguage.* Chapter 2 will quickly get into some essentials of EZL but will not lead you by the hand as those books do. I will lead you by the hand when we get into OOEL in **Chapter 3**. For this chapter I will borrow liberally from Sam's book *Ask Mr. EasyLanguage.*[22]

We have lightly brushed on the Dictionary, Reserved Words and Skip Words above. Now we will take a longer look at some of the concepts from Intermediate EZL areas. You should already be familiar with these concepts, but some EZL programmers who are proficient with most things have not had a use for things like **Analysis Commentary** or **Switch…Case** statements. This is the chapter in which we will briefly delve into the concepts listed above. In this chapter I am not covering the easy parts of EZL. I am making the assumption that you already program EZL and know the material in *TradeStation Made Easy!* We will jump right past all that material and cover a few of the more advanced topics, with the idea in mind that you already have the training that allows you to understand without handholding. We are also including issues here that will be addressed with OOEL in the chapters that follow.

If this material exceeds your current knowledge, you should study the following:

- *TradeStation Made Easy!* (Sunny J. Harris)
- *Ask Mr. EasyLanguage* (Samuel K. Tennis)
- *Using EasyLanguage 9.*x (Murray Ruggiero Jr & Sunny J. Harris)
- *EasyLanguage Learning-by-Example Workbook* 2010 (William Brower)
- EasyLanguage Essentials (TS)
- *Easing Into EasyLanguage: Foundation Edition, Hi-Res Edition and Advanced Topics 2021* (George Pruitt)

I know I have mentioned these books before. Take it as I think they are very important.

In this chapter I will go faster than I did in TSME.[23] I'm assuming that you already speak EZL and just need a tune-up and perhaps the addition of a few concepts that might become necessary later in the book. Here we go.

---

[22] All references to the material in *"Ask Mr. EasyLanguage"* (AME) retain the copyright/trademark to Samuel K. Tennis of www.Vista-Research.com. All material gleaned from AME is noted with AME so you can distinguish it.

[23] *TradeStation Made Easy!* Sunny J. Harris 2011 Wiley

Comments

This is the easiest topic I've ever covered. Comments are simply in place to allow the program to ignore characters, words, sentences, and paragraphs that are designated as the software allows, often to annotate your code and make it easier to understand. Comments assist in making your code more readable and easier to refer back to at a later time. The EZL interpreter ignores them, but you shouldn't.

Different software products have constructed their interpreters and compilers to recognize comments by different methods. For instance, JavaScript uses the designators // to comment a single line and /* and */ to contain more than one line. Anything between the beginning and end designators is ignored by the interpreter. In the derivatives of C (C, C+, C++ and C#) the comments are the same as JavaScript: // for a single line and /* with */ for multiple lines. Further, in HTML comments are designated as: <!-- -->.

They are all different; IMHO[24] they should standardize.

TS (EZL) uses the designator // for single line comments and { } to bracket a partial line, one line or multiple lines.

For instance:

```
// this is a single line comment
{
this is a block, or multiline comment
here is the second line
}
If    TRUE   then ; // this is always executed
If    FALSE  then ; // this is never executed
```

Buyer beware: there is a bug (design feature) in EZL that causes some curly braces { } comments to fail, that is it stops automatically syntax coloring. It does not, however, affect the execution of code. The bug appears when you use curly braces (aka French Braces) inside of curly braces, like this:

```
// Your code before the comment
{
  Comment
  {
    Another comment
  }
}
```

In this case, EZL will quit syntax coloring the outer comment when it encounters the closing inner comment, and the rest will look just like regular code (black). It does not affect the execution of the code, however. At this point in time the solution is to use // comments throughout if you need to nest comments.

Sam and I use a little convention that makes the French Braces easier to spot in our code. So that they stand apart in code we designate them with following and preceding asterisks. It looks like this:

```
{ *
Vars  :
  elSystem.windows.forms.Form Container_Form(NULL),
  elSystem.windows.forms.Label Label5(NULL),
  elSystem.windows.forms.Label Label4(NULL),
  elSystem.windows.forms.Label Label3(NULL),
  elSystem.windows.forms.GroupBox GroupBox1(NULL)  ;
* }
```

Further, it is a good idea to follow good programming habits so that you can come back years later (I still have code dating back to 1991) and quickly read the code to see what it is intended to do, and so

---

[24] IMHO: In my humble opinion.

that others can read your code and understand it. From "EasyLanguage Coding Best Practices" by Chris Davy we read:

> Consistency is important. Develop a coding style and coding practices as well as overall design practices that you use in all your code. You will come to depend upon code in that structure and will already have some understanding of old code that you go back to months after last working on it.

If you would like to read his whole document (and I would suggest it), go to my website: https://www.moneymentor.com/articlesOthers.html.

In **Chapter 4** I will give you a coding template to help you get started. A large part of programming is documenting. It is very important that you comment your code well so you can come back to it later and recall what you meant to do. Good commenting (record keeping) starts at the point of creation and should include each and (almost) every time you touch the code. Like so many things it is, or becomes, a good habit. Commenting also helps with debugging your code, and it makes it so that another programmer can read it and make sense of your code.

Data Types

Inputs, Variables, Constants and Arrays

These data constructs can be declared of various types or flavors. These include Bool (Boolean or True/False), Int (Integer or whole numbers), Float (Floating Point), Double (Floating Point) and String (text or characters). Variables (but not Inputs, Constants or Arrays) may also be declared of an Object Class but we will cover that in great detail later in this volume. To cloud the water more a User Functions may have an Input of an Object Class.

Boolean

Data fields declared as type Bool have two possible values, either True or False. See the section Boolean Expressions to learn more about using these very important tools in your programming.

Integers

The **Int** reserved word is used in a variable declaration statement to explicitly set the data type of a variable to integer (no decimal portion; a whole number). If you do not declare a specific type, EZL will auto-detect and set the variable type when verifying. For example, if an un-typed variable is assigned a whole number value in a calculation, it will be recast as an integer automatically.

REMARKS

The **Int** keyword is an alias of the **elSystem.int32** Class and allows you to use the Methods associated with that class (such as .**ToString ()**) on variables declared with the **Int** data type.

EXAMPLE 2.01—Variable Declarations

In the main body of a document:

```
Vars  : int MyVar1 (120) ;
// in this case, the data type is optional, and the initial
// value is required
```

In a Method:

```
Vars  : int MyVar2 ;
// in this case, the data type is required, and no initial
// value is allowed
```

There is also a "Long Int" (Int-64) that greatly extends the potential size that may be represented.

Floating Point

Floating Point values are generally of type Double. The Float type is a legacy back to 32-bit processors and really retained for backward compatibility. The Double 64-bit type has a very large capacity (1.7E +308 (15 digits) to 1.7E +308) meaning lots of digits (15) to the left and/or right of the decimal place. The value 123456.789012345 should satisfy the needs of most any requirement in Technical Analysis.

String

There is another type of variable you can declare: string.

This reserved word can be used in two different ways. It can be used to explicitly declare the data type of an input or variable in a study or function, and it can be used to declare the expected data type of an input to a function. The function usage is illustrated below.

When used to declare the expected data type of an input to an EZL function, this reserved word indicates that the input is expected to be a string expression passed by value. It can be used, as in the examples shown below, to declare a string input that has historical values available (a series input), or a string input that does not have historical values available (a simple input).

REMARKS

String can be used for inputs that can be either **StringSimple** or **StringSeries**.

> ☑ The Simple and Series suffixes are only valid when declaring an Input to a User Function.

EXAMPLE 2.02—A Variety of String Formats [OME_Strings]

```
Input: MyMessage (String) ;
// declares the constant MyMessage as a text string value to
// be used in a User Function.
Input: NewMessage (String) ;
// declares the constant NewMessage as a text string value
// to be used in a function.
once begin
  Print (String.Format ("{0:X}" ,  1234      )) ; // 4D2
  Print (String.Format ("{0:X8}" , 1234      )) ; // 000004D2
  Print (String.Format ("{0:X}" ,  255       )) ; // FF
  Print (String.Format ("{0:X4}", 255        )) ; // 00FF
  Print (String.Format ("{0:X}" ,  82879     )) ; // 143BF
  Print (String.Format ("{0:X}" ,  123456789)) ; // 75BCD15
End ;
```

Inputs

The word **Input(s)** is a Reserved Word. The first and most commonly used Declaration Statement is the **Input** declaration statement. Many beginning programmers find the **Input** statement to be confusing. Users are often comfortable using a function, such as Average or Sum within MS Excel. The Average function in Excel requires that you supply a range of cells. The **Input** in EZL is essentially identical to this user-specified range value.

For instance, TS gives us the generic function Average. You must specify what you want to average and over what time period.

The syntax for the Input statement is the Reserved word **Input** or **Inputs** followed by a colon (:), the name of the Input followed by the default value in parentheses. The default value will also serve to define the type of this input, whether Numeric, Boolean or String. Additional inputs may be appended by using a comma as a list separator. The **Input** statement is terminated by a semicolon. For instance:

```
Inputs: Price (Close) ;
```

or

```
Inputs: Length (12), DoReport (False), Name ("Buy") ;
```

The Input statement for a Function is a special case. You cannot specify a default value inside the Function. Instead of a default value, you are required to use one of the type identifiers (Numeric, NumericSimple, NumericSeries, NumericRef, TrueFalse, TrueFalseSimple, TrueFalseSeries, TrueFalseRef, String, StringSimple, StringSeries. StringRef, ObjectSimple, or ObjectRef) Key Words. An example follows:

```
Inputs: Price (NumericSeries) , Length (NumericSimple ;
```

This explanation from *Ask Mr. EasyLanguage* page 40.

EXAMPLE 2.03—Input Declaration Statements

```
Inputs: double Price (Close), int Length (10);
```

declares the inputs `Price`, as a double-precision floating-point value (`Close`), and `Length`, as an integer value (10).

```
Inputs: int Length (10) [DisplayName = "LengthInBars", Tooltip =
"Enter the number of bars over which to calculate."];
```

declares an integer input, `Length`, with a default value of 10. The display name of this input is "LengthInBars", and the tooltip for this input is "`Enter the number of bars over which to calculate.`"

Variables

The word **Variable** is a Reserved Word. You may also use the words **Var**, **Vars**, and **Variables**, all meaning the same thing. I like to use **Vars** as my code lines up nicely with it. Whichever word you choose, the Reserved Word always is followed by a colon (;) and after the variables are declared, ends with a semicolon (;).

There are three main data types: String, Numeric, and True/False (or Boolean). Numeric types are further broken down into the following subsets:

Integers – 32 bit signed integer (whole numbers only).

Single floats – A real number represented as 4 bytes, floating point.

Double floats – A real number represented as 8 bytes, floating point. (This provides the highest precision when calculating large numbers and reduces the chance of rounding discrepancies.)

The range of these types is as follows:

Type	From	To
Integer	-2,147,483,648	2,147,483,647
Single Float	3.4E -38 (7 digits)	3.4E + 38 (7 digits)
Double Float	1.7E -308 (15 digits)	1.7E +308 (15 digits)

TABLE 2.01—Numeric Precision

There are three reserved words used to identify the three numeric subtypes: Int for integers, Float for single floats, and Double for double floats.

EXAMPLE 2.04—Declaring Variables

```
Vars  :
    String DQ        (DoubleQuote),
    String NL        (NewLine),
    Bool   Debug     (FALSE),
    Double Dummy     (0.00) ;
```

The reserved word Variable (or Var, Vars, Variables) is used to specify the name of a user-declared variable, or variables, separated by commas, its/their initial value, and optional data type. This must be done before a user-declared variable can be used in an assignment statement or formula. Multiple variables' names may be declared using a single Variable statement where the names are separated by commas.

Usage (Common)

Variable: Name (Value) ;

Where `Name` is the unique name of the user-declared variable, and `Value` is either a Numeric, True/False, String, or Null value used as the initial value of the variable. The common form of the variable declaration statement appears in the main body of an Analysis Technique and requires that an initial value be included in parentheses following the name.

The variable declaration syntax for the main body of an AT is slightly different than for a variable declaration in your **Method** (see below). In the main body declaration, an initial value is required after the variables name and any data type is optional.

Usage (Complete)

Variable: <IntraBarPersist> <DataType> VarName(InitialValue<,datan>)<, <IntraBarPersist> <DataType> VarName(InitialValue<,datan>)> ;

IntraBarPersist indicates that a variable's or array's value can be updated on every tick. By default, variable values are only updated at the close of each bar. By default, the value of these will be updated at the close of each bar. For example,

```
Variable: IntraBarPersist Count(0) ;
Count = Count + 01 ;
```

DataType is the optionally supplied data type (float, double, int, bool, string, or class) of the variable, typically used to conserve memory.

VarName is the user specified variable name. Variable names may include alphanumeric characters, underscores (_), periods (.), dollar signs ($), the "at" symbol (@), and the pound sign (#).

InitialValue is the initial value of the variable.

DataN is an optional parameter that identifies the data stream the variable is tied to and may be Data1 through Data50.

Usage (Method)

Variable: DataType Name ;

Where `Name` is the unique name of the user-declared variable, and `DataType` (required) defines the type of value (Float, Double, Int, Bool, String, or Class) that may be assigned to the variable.

The variable declaration rules in a local Method are slightly different than for a variable declaration in the main body of an Analysis Technique (see above). In a Method, the data type is required, and no initial value is allowed after the variables name.

REMARKS

A variable name can contain up to 20 alphanumeric characters plus the period (.), the underscore (_), the pound sign (#), the dollar sign ($) and possibly more. Feel free to explore. However, it's not really a good idea to use the period as it can get confused with the OOEL meaning of a period (dot).

A variable name cannot start with a number or a period (.) but it can start with an underscore (_).

The default value of a variable is declared by a value in parenthesis after the input name. The value can be **Numeric**, **Boolean** or **String**.

Multiple variables names may be declared using a single **Variable** statement where the names are separated by commas.

While variables and constants used to be limited to something like 30 characters, I haven't found the limit to their length now. We stopped checking at 50 characters, so clearly you can name them something ridiculously long. It does appear that Inputs are capped at 32 characters.

EXAMPLE 2.05—Variables

```
Variables: Count(10), Done (FALSE), Str ("George") ;
```

declares the variable `Count` and initializes the value to ten, `Done` is initialized to the Boolean value False and a String variable is declared and initialized to "George".

```
Var: MADiff(0), MyAverage(0);
```

declares the variables `MADiff` and `MyAverage` and initializes their values to zero.

Constants

Similarly, there is a reserved word called **Const** where you can declare one or more constants.

The reserved word **Const** (or **Consts**, **Constant**, **Constants**) is used to specify the name of a user-declared constant, its value, and optional data type. This must be done before a user-declared constant can be used in an assign statement or formula. Multiple constant names may be declared using a single **Const** statement where the names are separated by commas.

Usage (Common)

Const: Name(Value) ;

Where Name is the unique name of the user-declared constant, and Value is either a Numeric, or True/False value that sets the value of the constant.

Usage (Complete)

Const: <DataType> VarName(ConstantValue) <, <DataType> VarName(ConstantValue)> ;

Const is the constant declaration statement that may alternately be typed as Consts.

DataType is the optionally supplied data type (float, double, int, and bool) of the constant.

VarName is the user specified constant name that can be up to a ridiculous number of characters (used to be 20 characters) long and must begin with an alphabetic character or an underscore (_)(names are not case sensitive).

ConstantValue is the constant value.

REMARKS

A constant name can contain alphanumeric characters plus the period (.) and the underscore (_). The use of a period is not, however, recommended.

A constant name cannot start with a number or a period (.).

A constant name may not contain the "#" character but may contain the "@" or "$" symbols.

The value of a constant is declared by a number in parenthesis after the constant name.

Multiple constants' names may be declared using a single Const statement where the names are separated by commas.

The use of the reserved words Const, Consts, Constant, and Constants is identical.

EXAMPLE 2.06—Declaring Pi as a Constant

```
Const: Pi(3.14159265) ;
```

Declares the constant Pi and sets the value as specified where the type is set based on the value.

```
Consts: int MyValue(1025), float MyFactor(27.3618) ;
```

Declares the constant `MyValue` as an integer value of 1025 and `MyFactor` as a float value of 27.3618.

More Reserved Words

Statements

Those EZL reserved words that perform comparisons, carry out associated actions, and control other program operations are called **Statements**.

These include statements such as the `Plot`, `If...Then` structures, and variable declaration statements. Just like a sentence represents a complete thought in the English language, an EZL statement represents a complete instruction that results in some program action.

For example, the following statements are used to declare a variable and conditionally execute two additional statements that calculate and plot a 10-bar average of the Close:

EXAMPLE 2.07—Plotting a 10-bar Average of the Close [OME_3BarMAV]

```
Var  : MovAvg (0.00) ;
If  (CurrentBar > 10)  then begin
  MovAvg  = Average (Close, 10) ;
  Plot1 (MovAvg) ;
End ;
```

The following is a list of frequently used EZL statements.

Statement	Action
plot1-99	Plots a line, marker, or text on a chart or grid
if...then	Executes one or more statements when an if condition is True
else	Executes one or more statements following Else when the preceding condition is not True
begin	Specifies the beginning of a block of statements to be conditional executed
end	Specifies the end of a block of statements
for	Executes one or more statements within a loop using a counter variable
while	Executes one or more statements within a loop while a condition is True
variable	Declares one or more user defined variables to an initial value
input	Declares one or more input values of a specified type and with a default value
array	Declares one or more array variables to contain a specified number of cells with a default value
print	Sends output to the Print Log
commentary	Sends output to a Commentary window
once	Specifies that the EZL statement or Begin...End block that follows will only be executed once

TABLE 2.02—Frequently Used EZL Statements

Numeric Expressions

A numeric expression is a combination of values and/or operators that result in a number; their return type is numeric.

EXAMPLE 2.08—Numeric Expressions

```
8
8 + 4
Close
High - Low
```

☑ It is important to remember that arithmetic operations are order dependent (precedence of operators). The order of operations is a rule that tells the correct sequence of steps for evaluating a math expression. We can remember the order using PEMDAS: Parentheses,

Exponents, Multiplication and Division (from left to right), Addition and Subtraction (from left to right).

EXAMPLE 2.09—Using Parentheses for Clarification

```
8 + 5 * 4 - ( 6 + 10 / 2 ) = 8 + 20 - ( 6 + 5 ) = 28 - 11
```

Boolean Algebra

Symbolic Logic

If you use the Internet to search for information, you probably have used symbolic logic. You might not have realized it, however. If I wanted to find information about economic indicators and bonds on the Internet, I might say:

SEARCH FOR: economic AND indicators AND bonds

Probably the result of this search would yield thousands of matches. Many of the matches would not be what I am looking for. For instance, the search would probably yield "bail bonds" —hopefully not something I am looking for.

To tell the search engine not to give us bail bonds as a match we could perform this search:

SEARCH FOR: (economic AND indicators AND bonds) AND NOT bail

Using **AND** as the operator doesn't present much in the way of difficult logic. Two other concepts, OR and NOT raise the bar just a bit higher. These three operators are called Boolean operators, after George Boole. Boolean algebra is the algebra of logic.

Truth Tables

AND and OR

For a statement containing expressions separated by ANDs to be True, all the expressions must be True. For a statement containing expressions separated by ORs to be True, at least one of the expressions must be True.

If I say, "Sunny is 6-feet tall AND has red hair," the statement is True, because both expressions are True. If I say, "Sunny is 6-feet tall AND has green hair," the statement is False, because both expressions must be True, and I do not have green hair. If I say, "Sunny is 5-feet tall OR has red hair," the expression is again True, because one of the expressions is True: I have red hair. OR is a less stringent operator than AND.

A quick and easy way to evaluate conditional statements is by looking up the answer in a "truth table," as seen in Tables 2.03 and 2.04 below:

	Operator		Result
True	And	True	True
True	And	False	False
False	And	True	False
False	And	False	False

TABLE 2.03—AND Truth Table

	Operator		Result
True	Or	True	True
True	Or	False	True
False	Or	True	True

	Operator		Result
False	Or	False	False

TABLE 2.04—OR Truth Table

EXAMPLE 2.10—Using AND and OR

```
High = High of 1 Bar Ago    False
H > H[1] AND H[1] > H[2]     True
O[1] < C[1] OR O < C     True
```

In EZL a Boolean expression is an expression that uses the AND, OR, or NOT reserved words. You should always use parentheses to force the order of evaluation. Do not assume that there is an operator precedence of ANDs being evaluated before ORs.

For example:

'A and B or C and D' will not be evaluated the same as '(A and B) or (C and D)' when A and B are False and C and D are True.

Logical Expression Operators

When used in a logical expression, AND returns True when the Boolean values on either side of the AND are both True, as in the table below:

Expression 1	Expression 2	Exp 1 AND Exp 2
True	True	True
False	True	False
True	False	False
False	False	False

TABLE 2.05—Logical Expression AND Truth Table

An example of a statement using the AND operation would be:

```
If Plot1 Crosses Above Plot2 AND Plot2 > 5 Then...
```

AND is used here to determine if the direction of the cross of the values `Plot1` and `Plot2`, and that `Plot2` is greater than 5 are both True on the bar under consideration. If either is False, the condition returns False.

```
If  Value1 Crosses Above Value2
AND Value1 > Value1[1]   Then...
```

AND is used here to determine if the direction of the cross of the variables `Value1` and `Value2`, and that `Value1` is greater that `Value1` of one bar ago are both True on the bar under consideration. If either is False, the condition returns False.

NOT

If you want to negate a Boolean variable, a condition, or an expression, you use the operator NOT. If the expression is False, then NOT the expression is True; likewise, if the expression is True then NOT the expression is False. Be sure to use parentheses.

EXAMPLE 2.11—Boolean Expressions Demonstrating Using NOT

```
Condition1  =  TRUE ;
Condition2  = FALSE ;
Print (Not Condition1) ; // prints False
Print (Not Condition2) ; // prints True
```

EXAMPLE 2.12—Using NOT

```
If  Not (Close < Open)
  Then  Buy {"LE"}  next bar at close ;
```

```
If  Not (Close < Open)
   then Buy ("LE") next bar at close or higher ; // stop
```

Bitwise Binary Operator

When used with integer values, the AND keyword functions as a bitwise operator, following the rules of the table below:

Bit 1	Bit 2	Bit 1 And Bit 2
1	1	1
0	1	0
1	0	0
0	0	0

TABLE 2.06—Binary AND Truth Table

Respective bits from each integer will be compared. If both bits are 1, the resulting bit will be 1. Otherwise, the resulting bit will be 0.

So, the integer expression (2 AND 6) = 2 (x0010 AND x0110 = x0010).

Decisions (Conditions)

EZL provides several ways to construct loops and conditions. The simplest version of a block statement is the `begin...end` block. From there we progress into more and more complex blocks. First the Begin…End block.

If...Then...

If "something" happens, then we will do "consequence" is the focus of this chapter. More specifically, it is the "something" we will tackle here. The "something" is called a condition.

EXAMPLE 2.13—If…Then Statement

A typical statement you might see in an indicator would look like this[25]:

```
If  High < High[01] and High[01} > High[02]
   Then  Plot1[01] (High[01] + 05 points, "MktTop") ;
```

In **Chapter 1** we talked about the form of the statement itself, from a syntax perspective. In the first part of this chapter, we have been talking about conditions, from a symbolic logic perspective. Conditions always evaluate to True or False.

If...Then...Else

We can add to the complexity of the evaluation by adding an ELSE condition. IF "something" THEN "one consequence" ELSE "another consequence."

If it is raining outside, then we will take the umbrella, else we will leave it at home. The condition in this sentence is "it is raining outside." The consequence is what we do if the condition is True-the "somethingelse." By default, there is an implied second consequence in the sentence. The implied part is what happens if the condition is False. In this case, the implied consequence is we don't take the umbrella.

If we wanted to be very precise in our statement, with no assumptions as to what is implied, we would write:

IF (it is raining outside) THEN (we will take the umbrella) ELSE (we will not take the umbrella);

Statements like that are called **If…Then…Else** statements. In the above example the **Else** is redundant since it is not assumed to be the first consequence.

---

[25] From AME page 47

A NOT truth table is pretty simple. IF the statement is True, NOT the statement is False and if the statement is False then NOT the statement is True. In symbolic logic notation you will often see the tilde (~) symbol or the prime (') symbol used to denote NOT. For instance, you might see ~T=F, or you might see T=F'. Not that this (tilde and prime) is Mathematics, and not EasyLanguage.

EXAMPLE 2.14—Using NOT

```
If  Not (Close < Open)
  Then Buy {"LE.01"}  this bar at close
// stop if not (Close < Open)
  Else Buy ("LE.02") next bar at close or higher ; // or stop
```

I had correspondence with a TS user some time ago, but it still is a good illustration of Conditions. It went like this:

I would like to be able to enter on the same bar that confirms a signal. For example, conditions 1, 2, and 3 are met but I only want to enter on tomorrow's open if it is below today's close. Seems from reading the EZL Users Guide that it is not possible, but that can't be, can it??

From: sunny@moneymentor.com Sent: August 24, 1999 8:16 am
Mary, Try this. Let me know if it does what you want.

```
Condition1 = High[0] > High[1] ;
Condition2 = High[1] > High[2] ;
If  Condition1 AND Condition2 and Open Next Bar <  Close [00]
  Then Buy ("LE") tomorrow Close - (1 point) STOP ;
```

Sometimes programming is like the old saying: You've gotta kiss a lot of frogs before you find a Prince. As we are creating examples for this book sometimes, we must spend hours finding just one error. It can certainly be tedious at times.

One time I spent hours, many, trying to find out why my code wouldn't verify. I called the late Murray Ruggiero Jr and asked if he could take a look at it. He graciously agreed to. He then sent it to Sam. An hour later Murray called me back and said: "Sunny, are you blind?" Why, I asked. "Can't you tell a lowercase l from a 1?"

If...Then...Else...Begin

IF is used to introduce a condition that will be evaluated to determine execution of additional code.

REMARKS

If can only be used to begin an **If...Then** or **If...Then...Else** statement.

EXAMPLE 2.15—If...Then

```
If Condition1 Then
  {Your Code goes here} ;
```

If is used here to start the If...Then statement. Your code will be executed if `Condition1` returns a value of True. If `Condition1` is False, your code will not be executed.

EXAMPLE 2.16—Else Begin

```
If Condition1 AND Condition2 Then Begin
  {Your Code Line1}
  {Your Code Line2, etc.}
End
Else Begin
  {Your Code Line3}
  {Your Code Line4, etc.}
End ;
```

If is used here to start the If...Then...Else statement. The Line1 and Line2 code will be executed if Condition1 and Condition2 return a value of True. If Condition1 or Condition2 is False, the Line3 and

Line4 code will be executed.

Another example of **If…Then…Else** from Sam's book *Ask Mr. EasyLanguage* (AME) is found on page 50:

EXAMPLE 2.17—If…Then…Else

```
If High    > High[01]  then begin
   Value1  = Open [00] ;
   Value2  = Close[00] ;
end
else begin
   Value1  = Open [01] ;
   Value2  = Close[01] ;
end ;
```

Nested If…Then Statements

You can include ifs within ifs if you like. Here is what a nested **If…Then** statement looks like[26].

```
If  Close  > Close[01]  then begin
  If  Open  > Open[01]
     then   Buy  ("le.#1") 300 shares at Market
     else   Sell Short ("se.#1") 100 Shares at Market ;
End ;
```

If the first condition is False, no further action is taken. If, however, the first condition is True EZL obeys the Then Begin command and evaluates the second nested **If…Then** statement. If that statement is True EZL executes the Then part of that statement. If the second nested **If…Then** statement returns a False value TS moves on to the else portion of the nested statement and takes that action.

Here's another example from AME:

```
If  High > High[01] then begin
   If  High / High[01] > 1.02
      Then  Buy ("le.#1") 500 shares at Market
      Else  Buy ("le.#2") 100 Shares at Market ;
End ; // old syntax, will not verify, Next Bar required
```

IFF

The IFF Built-In Function is used to conditionally return one of two specified numeric values. I always read it "if this then that else the other." Like an Excel expression.

USAGE

Iff (Name = "George", 01, 00)

This function returns the TrueVal if Test is True and FalseVal if Test is False.

EXAMPLE 2.18—Using IFF to compare prices

```
Value1 = IFF (Close > Open, 01, -01) ;
```

There are more User Functions like this one for use with Boolean expressions and with Strings. They are IFFLogic and IFFString. Their use is obvious, as IFFLogic tests logical (Boolean) expressions and returns a Boolean (True/False) value. IFFString tests the first string expression and returns one of two possible Boolean values.

USAGE

IFFLogic(Test, TrueVal, FalseVal)

---

[26] AME page 51

IFFString(Test, TrueVal, FalseVal)

EXAMPLE 2.19—Using IFF_Logic and IFF_String User Functions

```
Value1 = IFFLogic (Close > Open, Close > Close[01], Open < Open[01])
;
Plot1 (IFFString (Close > Open, "True", "False") ;
```

Printing

Printing is great for outputting information for later reference. It's also a great debugging tool. (Refer to **Analysis Commentary** for another helpful debugging tool.) The **Print** command takes several forms. It can be short and sweet, or it can be complex. There are optional parameters in the Print function.

The simplest form of the Print command is as follows, no extra parameters.

USAGE

Print ("Easy Print") ;

Print statements in their easiest incarnation put their output to the Print Log. If yours is not showing on your desktop, just go to ⏷ View and pull down to EZL Print Log or use the shortcut CTRL-SHIFT-E.

To send the output to a file or your default printer you will need to specify that. To go directly to your default printer the form of the Print statement is:

```
Print (Printer, Date, Time, Close) ;
```

If it goes nowhere or to the wrong printer, you'll have to take that up with Windows in the system settings, to set the printer you want to be the default.

You can also print to a file using this format:

```
Print (File ("C:\OME_Files\myData.txt"), Date, Time, Close) ;
```

where you specify the disk drive, folder, file name of your choice with an optional extension (i.e., .txt).

> ☑ Print to File always deletes the previous content of the file on the first execution of the Print to File statement.

It makes sense, now that we are discussing output to a file, to give you a couple of ways to manipulate files. You can add to the file specified above by using the **FileAppend** structure. Example 2.20 shows you how that can be accomplished.

EXAMPLE 2.20—Adding to a File with FileAppend

```
FileAppend ("C:\OME_Files\myData.txt", "Hello " + GetSymbolName + "
World!  The date and time is " + NumToStr (Date, 00) + " " + NumToStr
(Time, 00) + " - Classic Append to File, requires a NewLine." +
NewLine) ;
```

But what if you want to get rid of a file from within EZL? Then you use the **FileDelete** command and be sure that the string you specify is a valid path (fully qualified file specification). The structure of the command is `FileDelete("str_Filename") ;`

> ☑ FileAppend does not delete the previous contents, if any. You may want to delete it in your Once block. Unlike the Print (File()) statement FileAppend will accept a variable as the File Specification. FileAppend does NOT include the Carriage Return + Line Feed characters so you want to append " + NewLine" after the line of data values. You can only print string values, or string representations of your Numeric values often using the NumToStr function.

EXAMPLE 2.21—Deleting a File with FileDelete

If you wanted to delete a file when an Analysis Technique was initially applied, you could use the following syntax:

```
If BarNumber = 1 Then FileDelete ("C:\OME_Files\myData.txt") ;
```

to delete the specified file.

Alternately you can use this syntax:

```
Once begin
    FileDelete ("C:\OME_Files\myDate.TXT") ;
end ; // Once, and only once
```

`Print (File ()) ;` automatically, and with no regard to your desire, deletes any existing file prior to writing the first line to the file.

You don't need to create the file (á la FileCreate or something). When you print to a file that doesn't exist EZL creates it for you as long as the folder exists. Further, when you have the file you want to use open in Notepad (or other editor) you will get an error message that tells you something like "Error Creating File" and it will toggle the Status of your Analysis Technique (AT) to OFF.

User Functions

An EZL User Function is a set of EZL statements that returns one or more values to the function caller, depending what type of function it is. A function only returns one value; a multiple-output function can return more (see below). Like Studies (Indicators, PaintBars, ShowMe and ActivityBar studies), functions have their own document type in EZL. That is, the code for a function resides in a different code document than the code for the indicator, PaintBar, ShowMe study, Strategy, or other Analysis Technique that calls the Function.

As an aggregate these Studies and Functions are called Analysis Techniques (AT).

A function call is an EZL expression that calls an EZL function. Such calls, by default, appear in purple in the code editor. Many of the built-in studies in the TS platform call EZL functions.

There is another type of Function called a Built-In Function. Built-In Functions are written in EZL so you can view the code, but they are Read-Only so if you want to make modifications you must copy and paste the code into a User Function with a different, though probably related, name of your creation. An example of this is "skt_AverageFC" where Sam "corrected" a perceived flaw in the Built-In Function.

For instance, the RSI Indicator calls the Built-In Function RSI.

A function's statements can be used to calculate a mathematical formula, test for a Boolean condition, format a string or perform any other EZL action. All EZL functions must return a value. You can also use a function like this:

`If myBooleanFunction then` ; where the function is called but the return value is not expressly used and while the function is called no consequence is implemented.

In the code for the function, then, an assignment statement must appear that assigns a value to the function. The data type of the returned value (integer, Boolean, string, double-precision floating-point, etc.) is set in the properties of the function. For example, a statement like the following might appear in the code for a function named `MyFunc` that always returns the value 1 to the caller:

```
MyFunc = 01 ;
```

That's a bit simplistic. How about this next one? I
have a set of functions in my EZL library for every
color name in their color picker window and then
some. If you want the functions for yourself, visit
www.moneymentor.com and go to Comments and
let me know. I'll be happy to send them to you for
free. Be sure to say in the comments what it is you
want.

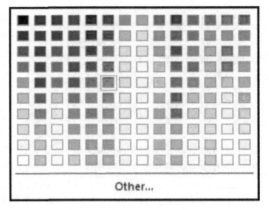

```
BlueViolet = 14822282 ;
```

This returns the numeric value for the color name,
which is also the name of the function. To learn
more about the RGB values, see **Volume II—
Reference Guide, Appendix III: Color Class.**

Common Usage

A function's return value can be assigned to a variable in the code that calls the function.

For example, in the following line of code, the function calculates the average closing price over 10
bars and assigns the returned value to a pre-declared variable:

```
Value1 = Average (Close, 10) ;
```

Series Function

A series function automatically stores its own previous values and executes on every bar (even if used
within a conditional statement). Most functions are simple functions, not series functions. Prices, such
as Open, High, Low and Close are built-in series functions as you can refer to previous values with
statements such as:

Close[01] // means close of one bar ago and

Close[10] // refers to the closing value 10 bars ago

Multiple Output Functions

Some functions need to return more than a single value and do this by using one or more output
parameters within the parameter list. Built-in multiple output functions typically preface the parameter
name with an "o" to indicate that it is an output parameter used to return a value. These are also known
as "input/output" parameters or 'passed by reference' parameters because they are declared within a
function as a 'ref' type input (i.e., **NumericRef, TrueFalseRef, StringRef** etc.) which allows it to
output a value, by reference, to a variable in the EZL code calling the function.

A multiple-output function will contain one or more Inputs passed by reference and, optionally, normal
Inputs as required by the function.

The values of the input parameters are passed into the multiple-output function, but not modified by
the function. The values of the input/output parameters are passed into the multiple-output function,
modified by it, and the modified values are then inherited by - or output to - the calling routine.
Technically, a pointer to the original variable in memory is passed in and the actual variable is
modified. Only the address of the variable is passed in.

The input/output parameters are often used for output purposes only, i.e., the incoming values are
ignored. The outputs are in addition to the function return. In multiple output functions, the function
return is generally used to return an error code, though sometimes the return may simply be a dummy
value.

For example, the following built-in function looks for the 2nd highest Close over the last 30 bars. The
first four parameters are inputs used to specify:

- what price to find

- over how many bars
- which occurrence (1st, 2nd, etc.)
- look for the highest or lowest.

The fifth and sixth parameters are outputs. The function uses one output parameter to assign the 2nd highest Close to `Value2` and a second output parameter to assign the number of bars ago it occurred to `Value3`. The function itself returns the status of the search (1 if successful or -1 if an error occurred) to `Value1`.

EXAMPLE 2.22—Using Multiple Output Functions

```
Vars  : oExtremeVal (0), oExtremeBar (0) ;
Value1 = NthExtremes (Close, 30, 02, 01,
                    oExtremeVal, oExtremeBar) ;
Value2 = oExtremeVal ;
Value3 = oExtremeBar ;
```

Wrapper Functions

When looking at the EZL code for a built-in function you may find the term "wrapper function." This refers to a single-return function that references a multiple-output function to obtain the return value. Calling a single-return wrapper function helps make your EZL code simpler by avoiding the need to set up output parameters or understand multiple output functions.

The built-in single-return wrapper functions that call the multiple output functions are specialized calling routines designed to offer simplified, alternate pathways to the functionality of the underlying multiple-output functions. In the wrapper functions, the input/output parameters are declared as local variables and generally initialized to zero. They are passed through to the multiple-output function without further modification. After the call, the wrapper function picks out the single output of interest and assigns it as the return of the wrapper function.

EXAMPLE 2.23—Using a Wrapper Function [OME_f_ADX]

For example, the ADX function returns the average directional movement index value that is one of several output parameters of the DirMovement function as follows.

```
Inputs:
    Length (numericsimple) ; // a constant >= 1
Vars  :
    oDMIPlus   (0.00),
    oDMIMinus  (0.00),
    oDMI       (0.00),
    oADX       (0.00),
    oADXR      (0.00),
    oVolty     (0.00) ;

Value1 = DirMovement (High, Low, Close, Length, oDMIPlus, oDMIMinus,
oDMI, oADX, oADXR, oVolty) ;

OME_f_ADX  = oADX ;
```

In the examples above you can see the variable names preceded by an "o". These values are accessible outside of the routine they are in.

Loops and More

EZL contains three types of iterative (loop) statements, the **For** loop, the **While** loop and the **Repeat…Until** loop. **To** and **DownTo** are only used in For loops, but the variation is shown here.

Some loops can count up and some can count down. They usually require a specific format which includes the word **Begin** at the end of the line which starts with **For**, followed by lines of code that do something inside the loop, followed by the word **End**; signifying the loop has ended. The **For** statement includes a starting level and an ending level and an instruction to count up or down. Counting up is specified by the word **To**. Counting down is specified by the word **DownTo**. The starting and ending values can be numbers, variables, or inputs. **For** loops repeat an instruction a fixed number of times.[27]

One of the pitfalls of running a loop is the possibility of executing it endlessly by misstating your loop values. To that end there is a Reserved Word that will detect the problem.

InfiniteLoopDetect

The InfiniteLoopDetect keyword (Reserved Word) directive allows you to enable or disable infinite loop detection in an EZL document. Infinite loop detection logic will always be enabled by default (i.e., if no attribute is present detection logic will be enabled). If the same attribute appears more than once in a document, an error message will appear during verify.

EXAMPLE 2.24—Turn Off Infinite Loop Detect

```
[InfiniteLoopDetect = FALSE]
// Turns off infinite loop detection
```

> ✑ Attributes are local to the document (function, indicator, strategy, etc.) in which they are used so it is possible to have a function with detection disabled but the calling Analysis Technique with the logic enabled. Also, attributes are evaluated at compile time only so their values cannot be changed at run-time.

Once

The Once statement or Once Begin…End block is a compiler directive to limit the contained code to executing only once. The nice thing about it is that you don't run that contained code on every bar of your chart. In **Chapter 7** we will further examine our Hello World! code (from **Chapter 1**) and discover just how valuable this construction is. Without it the TS engine would go through the statements from top to bottom.

The format of the block is:

```
Once ([optional Boolean expression])
   {follow by single statement or statement block}
[begin]
  Statement(s)
[end]
```

EXAMPLE 2.25—Simple Once Statement

The simplest form of the Once statement is as follows:

```
Once Condition1 =  TRUE ; // Once, and only once
```

EXAMPLE 2.26—Once Begin…End Block

```
once begin
  isOnAuto = GetAppInfo (aiStrategyAuto) = 01 ;
  // Intended for use within a strategy
  if Debug then Print ("Is on Auto = ", isOnAuto:5) ;
end ; // Once, and only once
```

EXAMPLE 2.27—Once Begin to Clear PrintLog

```
Once Begin
  ClearPrintLog ;
```

---

[27] Paragraph courtesy William (Bill) Brower in *EasyLanguage Learning by Example* 2010 page 29

```
End ; // Once, and only once
```

Clear the Print Log and print a header the first time the market position is long.

```
Once (MarketPosition > 00) Begin
  ClearPrintLog ;
  Print ("Log Header") ;
End ; // Once, and only once
```

Begin...End

The **Begin…End** construct allows you to insert code that will process multiple statements. The **Begin…End** allows you to group multiple statements together into compound statements. The block statement starts with the reserved word begin and is terminated with the reserved word **End** followed by a semicolon. The only exception to this rule is when the **End** precedes an **Else**.

Every complete statement must end in a semicolon. Most complex statements contain statements that make up portions of the complete statement without an intervening semicolon. An example would be `if True then xxx else yyy ;` or `if True then xxx else yyy` are sub statements of the complex statement. A complex (or compound) statement may include complete statements (with semicolon) inside a **Begin…End** block. The statement `if xxx then ; begin...end ;` is actually two statements - the **Begin…End** block is **not** part of the **If…Then** statement due to the statement terminator following the **Then**.

EXAMPLE 2.28—A Simple Begin…End Block

```
If Result = FALSE then begin
  Print ("The result is not True.") ;
end ;
```

EXAMPLE 2.29—Complex Begin…End Block

Begin is used here twice to include the execution of Line1 and Line2 only when `Condition1` is True and execute Line3 and Line4 only when `Condition1` is False.

```
If Condition1 Then Begin
  {Your Code Line1}
  {Your Code Line2, etc.}
End
Else Begin
  {Your Code Line3}
  {Your Code Line4, etc.}
End ;
```

For

The **For** loop is used where there is a predetermined number of iterations to be processed. Counting the inside bars within the ten most recent bars is an example of knowing the number of iterations in advance.

Template 1

```
For Counter = Start To Quit
begin...end ; // for loop
```

Template 2

```
For Counter = Start DownTo Quit
begin...end ; // for loop
```

The **For** command always appears with a **Begin…End** block and is sometimes referred to as a **For…Begin** command. The For command is always followed by a set of variables that define the starting and ending number of steps to execute the loop. This structure is fairly complex until you get accustomed to it, and then it will become second nature, so don't start worrying yet.

For is always followed by a variable name (`Value5` in Example 2.30). The command tells the computer to perform a set of actions a specified number of times. The variable counts the number of times as it steps through the loop. Each time it reaches the **End**; statement it increments (in Template 1) or decrements (in Template 2) the variable until it reaches the ending value specified in the command.

> ✍ After the For Loop the counter variable will hold a value one greater (or less in a DownTo loop) than the maximum parameter. The loop terminates when the counter exceeds the variable but then ends the loop, leaving the variable one greater (or less in a DownTo loop) than the stoppping value without executing the rest of the code in the loop. To confirm this for yourself, include a Print statement to print the values.

EXAMPLE 2.30—Using the For Loop

This next example shows how the For Loop is initiated. It will be executed for each value of `Value5` from `Length` to `Length + 10`.

```
For Value5 = Length To Length + 10
Begin
  {Your Code Goes Here}
End ; // for loop
```

EXAMPLE 2.31—A Simple Loop

Let's break down the process by following code:

```
Value2  = 00 ;
For Loop = 01 TO 03 begin
  Value2  = Value2 + 01 ;
end ; // for loop
```

The computer will do the actions in the **Begin…End** block with `Loop` set to 1. When it reaches the **End**; statement it will loop back up to the top and set `Loop` to 2 (it incremented Loop by 01) and do the actions in the **Begin…End** block again, this time with `Loop` set to 02. When it reaches the **End**; statement it will loop back up to the top and set `Loop` to 03 and do the actions in the **Begin…End** block again, this time with Value1 set to 4. And one more time. This time, when the computer reaches the **End** statement, it looks at Loop, sees that it is at 4 (greater than 3, the ending value specified in the **For** statement) and it falls through the end statement to the next line of code keeping the values most recently determined. `Value2` will have the ending value of 4.

The starting value for the variable does not have to be 1; you can start the loop at 4, or 7, or any integer you choose. In fact, you can start the loop at 0. You can even start with a negative value like -1 and end with a positive number. EZL assumes that you will always be incrementing (or decrementing) by 1 (though other languages allow one to use a negative incremental value).

For instance, if you wanted to investigate market action during the last month of the year you could increment from 330 through 365, counting and analyzing the days, one day at a time.

EXAMPLE 2.32—Using For to Average Closing Values

This example calculates an average of closing values from the current bar back 9 bars—that's ten samples. Before starting, however, it zeroes out any old data from `Value2`, to be safe. The computer will run through the loop until `Loop` reaches 9, accumulating the sum of the previous `Value2` and the Close of `Loop Bars Ago`. It will finish that evaluation and then stop the loop at the **End ;** statement. After completion of the loop, the computer evaluates `Value3 = Value2 /10`, which averages the accumulated sum collected in the **For** loop.

```
Value2  = 00 ;
For Loop = 00 TO 09 begin
  Value2 = Value2 + Close [Loop] ;
```

```
end ;
Value3  = Value2 / 10 ;
```

EXAMPLE 2.33—A Function Using a For Loop [OME_f_ForLoop]

A generalized example of the use of the **For** loop is found in the EZL built-in function Average. Let's take a look at that code for this function:

```
// OME_f_ForLoop
// Function to Calculate a Simple Moving Average
Inputs:
 Double Price     (NumericSeries),
 Int    Length    (NumericSimple) ;
Vars  :
 Int    Loop      (00),
 Double Sum       (0.00),
 Double RetVal    (0.00) ;

Sum  = 0.00 ;
For Loop  = 00 TO (Length - 01) begin
  Sum  = Sum + Price [Loop] ;
end ; // for loop
If  Length  > 00
  then  RetVal  = Sum / Length
  else  RetVal  = 0.00 ;
OME_f_ForLoop  = RetVal ;
```

> ☑ This is a function. Since I've named it with my OME convention, when you import the .eld from our website you will also need to observe the new function name. Another of my conventions is to name all Indicators sjh_I_xxx, functions sjh_f_xxx, and RadarScreen studies sjh_R_xxx etc.

EXAMPLE 2.34—For Loops [OME_ForLoop]

This example illustrates finding Inside Bars:

```
Inputs: MinVal(00), MaxVal (10),
        Inside (High[00] < High[01] and Low[00] > Low [01]) ;
Vars  : Loop (00),        Count (00),  Done(FALSE) ;
Count = 00 ;
//start off with zero inside bars
For Loop = MinVal to MaxVal begin
  Print (Loop:6:0, Inside[Loop] :6) ;
  if  Inside[Loop]
    then Count = Count + 01 ; // increment counter
end ;  //end for loop
if  (Count  > 00)
  then Print ("I found ", Count:1:0, " Inside Bars.")
  else Print ("No inside bars found within ",
          MaxVal:1:0, " bars.") ;
```

To and DownTo

These words are used as a part of a **For** statement where the execution values will be decreasing to a finishing value.

REMARKS

DownTo will always be placed between two arithmetic expressions.

EXAMPLE 2.35—DownTo

```
For Value5 = Length DownTo 00 Begin
  { your code here }
```

```
End ;
```

And the example from AME is:

```
For VarName = HiVal DownTo LoVal begin
  { body of loop goes here... }
End ;
```

An error is displayed whenever writing a **For** loop and the word **To** or **DownTo** is omitted. The correct syntax for a **For** loop is:

```
For Loop = 01 To 10 Begin
  {statements}
End ; // for loop

For Loop = 10 DownTo 01 Begin
  {statements}
End ; // for loop
```

EXAMPLE 2.36—Illustration of To Structure[28]

```
For VarName = StartVal To StopVal begin
  { body of loop goes here... }
end ; // for loop
```

While

This Reserved Word initiates a **While** loop statement.

REMARKS

A **While** loop statement defines a set of instructions that are executed until a True/False expression returns False. The number of iterations the **While** loop performs depends on the value returned by the True/False expression following the **While** Reserved Word.

> ✎ The True/False expression must eventually return False to break the loop. If the expression does not evaluate to False, the While loop will continue indefinitely and create an infinite loop.Often the While loop has two conditions, one is the expected outcome and the other is a method of terminating the loop when no True condition is found. For example Count < 10000 works if you are incrementing Count within the Begin...End portion of the While statement.

EXAMPLE 2.37—Structure of While

```
While Condition1 Begin
 {Your Code Here};
  Condition1 = SomeCondition ;
End ; // while loop
```

While is used here to initiate the code contained in the **Begin...End** section until `Condition1` returns a value of False. If `Condition1` is False, the **While** loop is not executed.

If the initial value of `Condition1` is False then the **While** Loop never executes. As contrast, the Condition of a **Repeat Until** Loop is checked at the bottom, so it is always executed at least once.

Template 3

```
WHILE (something is true)
BEGIN...END ; // while loop
```

EXAMPLE 2.38—While Loop with No Ending Value

In Example 2.33 we used the **For** statement to calculate an average, by specifying the beginning and

---

[28] AME page 52

ending values for the loop. In this example we will only specify the ending value using the **While** statement, and let the loop run as long as (while) the statement is True.

```
While Value1 <  10 begin
  Value1 = Value1 + 01 ;
  Value2 = Value2 + Close[Value1] ;
end ; // while loop
Value3  = Value2 / 10 ; // (or * 0.10)
```

For and **While** are similar statements; they are both used for looping. The difference is in the **For** loop you specify the start and end, and in the **While** loop you keep doing it until the condition is no longer True.

EXAMPLE 2.39—Using a While Loop to Put a Leading Zero on a String

If you have a string that is only 2 characters, and the rest of your strings are 5 characters long, to have a leading zero (so your report lines up) you can append the leading zeroes as follows:

```
Inputs: Int    Length    (10) ;
Vars  : String myStr     ("") ;

myStr  = NumToStr (Length, 00) ;
while StrLen (myStr) <  05 begin
  myStr  = "0" + myStr ;
end ; // while loop
```

The **While** loop is used when there is a variable, or indeterminate, number of iterations to be processed. If, for instance, I wanted to know the bar number of the most recent inside bar, then the number of iterations is indeterminate.

EXAMPLE 2.40—Using the While Loop[29] to Find Inside Bars [OME_WhileLoop]

```
Loop = MinVal ;
Done = FALSE ;
while  Loop <= MaxVal and Done = FALSE begin
  if Inside [Loop]
    then Done = TRUE
    else Loop = Loop + 01 ;
end ;  // end while loop
if Done
  then Print ("Most recent Inside Bar was ",
              Loop:1:0, " bars ago.")
  else Print ("No Inside Bar found within ",
              MaxVal:1:0, " bars.") ;
```

Repeat...Until

Evaluates one or more statements in a loop and exits the loop only when the until condition is True.

USAGE

Repeat <statement(s)> Until <condtion> ;

Template 4

```
Repeat
// any other statement(s) ;
  UntilCondition = SomeCondition ;
until UntilCondition ; // repeat until loop
```

---

[29] AME pages 52-53

REMARKS

There is no need to use the **Begin…End** keywords to group more than one program statement, as all statements between **Repeat** and **Until** are treated as a block.

The **Repeat** loop is like the **While** loop, however, with the repeat statement, the conditional test occurs at the bottom of the loop. This means that the program statement(s) which constitute the loop body will be executed at least once.

More About Strings

String expressions consist of any combination of string literals (ASCII characters within quotation marks), string variables, string constants, string inputs or string functions. Their return type results in a string.

EXAMPLE 2.41—Using Strings

```
"A" + "B"
"Symbol = " + GetSymbolName
"346"
"MSQ97A"
"Volume is increasing"
```

String Input

A string input allows you to assign a name to a string expression. Inputs provide tremendous flexibility in that once you assign a string expression to an input, you can then reference that input throughout your Analysis Technique to retrieve its corresponding expression. This is especially helpful when using lengthy string expressions in your formulas although string constants would be better used for lengthy text.

> ☑ Input values cannot use variables. Input values may be assigned to variables. Also, string inputs are case-sensitive.

EXAMPLE 2.42—Using String Expressions

The example below assigns the string expression "Yes" to the input `YesNo`. This allows you to use `YesNo` anywhere you would reference "Yes".

```
Input: YesNo ("Yes") ;
If YesNo = "Yes" then {your operation here} ;
```

Strings can also be date and time format strings and Custom Date and Time Format strings.

EXAMPLE 2.43—Manipulating Strings

Much like Excel EZL provides you with tools to manipulate and interpret values in a string. The table below shows you the tools available for use with strings.

Here are a few samples of using string manipulation found in various OME_xxx routines, where xxx stands for the descriptor for the routine.

```
Slow_TL = TextLabel.Create (Slow_DT, "  " + NumToStr (Slow_Len, 00))
;
Str  = NumToStr (Loop, 00) ;
adate = ELDateToString(date) ;
HoldDate  = ELDateToString (JulianToDate (IntPortion
(MyBaseDateTime))) ;
Ndx  = InStr (TmpStr, Delim) ;
Str  = LeftStr (TmpStr, Ndx - 01) ;
```

Name	Brief Description	Type
DoubleQuote	Will embed a double-quote (") character in a string.	Reserved Word

Name	Brief Description	Type
ELDateToString	Returns a 10-character date string in MM/DD/YYYY format from an EZL date	TS Function
InStr	Returns the location of String2 within String1.	Reserved Word
LeftStr	Returns the leftmost character(s) of a text string.	Reserved Word
LowerStr	Used to convert a string expression to lowercase letters.	Reserved Word
MidStr	Returns the middle portion of a text string.	Reserved Word
NewLine	Adds carriage return/linefeed in FileAppend and Commentary/file output strings.	Reserved Word
NumToStr	Converts the specified numeric expression to a string expression.	Reserved Word
RightStr	Returns the rightmost (ending) portion of a text string.	Reserved Word
Spaces	Specifies the number of blank spaces to add to a text or Commentary string.	Reserved Word
StrLen	The number of characters that make up a text string.	Reserved Word
StrToNum	Returns the numerical value of a text string, zero if the string not numeric.	Reserved Word
UpperStr	Used to convert a string expression to uppercase letters.	Reserved Word

TABLE 2.07—String Functions

Sam has a group of "make it easier" tricks he uses for expedience. One is DQ and another is NL. The DQ function simply is a call to the **DoubleQuote** Reserved Word mentioned in the table above. The code in the function is simply:

```
Vars  :
  String DQ  (""),
  String NL  ("") ;
Once begin
  DQ  = DoubleQuote ;
  NL  = NewLine ;
End ; // Once, and only once
```

Using this functionality is simpler than typing DoubleQuote each time you need it and reduces the text in the EZL code.

More succinctly, setting up the DoubleQuote and NewLine in a String Variable or Constant declaration uses less overhead since you don't need to call a function.

EXAMPLE 2.44—Assigning DoubleQuote to DQ and NewLine to NL

```
Vars  :
  String DQ (DoubleQuote),
  String NL (NewLine) ;
```

After that you only need to type DQ when you want a double quote or NL when you want a new line. Using this convention is especially useful when you already have double quotes in your string and need nested double quotes, then you simply type DQ. For instance:

```
myStr = "Buy (" + DQ + "LE" + DQ + " next bar at market ;" + NL ;
```

Placing Text (Strings) on Your Chart

Here's a real-world example. In my SunnyBands© code I use a single string which is composed by concatenating single strings into a longer string that gets printed on the chart (at the **LastBarOnChart**) location. Notice the use of a previously defined variable NL which translates to the EZL **NewLine**.

EXAMPLE 2.45—Concatenating Strings to Place on Chart

```
myStr  = j_CrossOver + " on top at " +  NumToStr (j_CrossTime, 0) + "
from " + NumToStr (j_CrossValue, 02) + NL + "MidAngle= "  + NumToStr
(j_MidAngle, 02) + NL + "Diff_Inner=" + NumToStr ((UpperInnerBand –
LowerInnerBand), 02) + NL + "Diff_Outer=" + NumToStr ((UpperOuterBand
– LowerOuterBand), 02) ;
```

The resultant plot is shown in Figure 2.01 below.

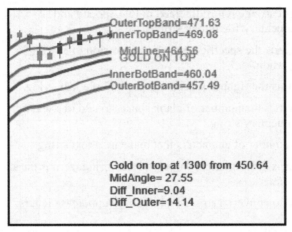

FIGURE 2.01—Strings on a Chart

Numeric Format Strings

You can create a standard or custom numeric format string, which consists of one or more numeric specifiers, to define how to format numeric data using Composite Formatting of strings.

Standard Numeric Format Strings

Standard numeric format strings are used to format common numeric types. A standard numeric format string takes the form Axx, where:

- A is a single alphabetic character called the format specifier. Any numeric format string that contains more than one alphabetic character, including white space, is interpreted as a custom numeric format string. For more information, refer to Custom Numeric Format Strings (see below).
- xx is an optional integer called the precision specifier. The precision specifier ranges from 0 to 99 and affects the number of digits in the result. Note that the precision specifier controls the number of digits in the string representation of a number. It does not round the number itself.

The following table describes the standard numeric format specifiers and displays sample output produced by each format specifier. Note that the string representations of numeric values typically vary by culture.

Specifier	Name	Description	Example
"C" or "c"	Currency	Result: A currency value. Supported by: All numeric types. Precision specifier: Number of decimal digits.	1234.5678 ("C") → $1,234.57 1234.5678 ("C4") → $1,234.5678
"D" or "d"	Decimal	Result: Integer digits with optional	1234 ("D") -> 1234

Specifier	Name	Description	Example
		negative sign. Supported by: Integral types only. Precision specifier: Minimum number of digits.	-1234 ("D6") → -001234
"E" or "e"	Exponential	Result: Exponential Notation. Supported by: All numeric types. Precision specifier: Number of decimal digits.	1052.0329112756 ("E") → 1.052033E+003 -1052.0329112756 ("e2") → -1.05e+003
"F" or "f"	Fixed-Point	Result: Integral and decimal digits with optional negative sign Supported by: All numeric types. Precision specifier: Number of decimal digits.	1234.567 ("F") → 1234.57 1234 ("F1") → 1234.0 -1234.56 ("F4") → - 1234.5600
"G" or "g"	General	Result: The more compact of either fixed-point or scientific notation. Supported by: All numeric types. Precision specifier: Number of significant digits.	-123.456 ("G") → - 123.456 -1.234567890e-25 ("G") → -1.23456789E-25
"N" or "n"	Number	Result: Integral and decimal digits, group separators, and a decimal separator with optional negative sign. Supported by: All numeric types. Precision specifier: Desired number of decimal places.	1234.567 ("N") → 1,234.57 1234 ("N1") → 1,234.0 -1234.56 ("N3") → - 1,234.560
"P" or "p"	Percent	Result: Number multiplied by 100 and displayed with a percent symbol. Supported by: All numeric types. Precision specifier: Desired number of decimal places.	1 ("P") → 100.00 % -0.39678 ("P1") → -39.7 %
"X" or "x"	Hexadecimal	Result: A hexadecimal[30] string. Supported by: Double, Int, and Int64 Precision specifier: Minimum number of digits in result.	255 ("X") → FF 255 ("x4") → 00ff 123456789 ("X4") → 75BCD15
Any other single character	Unknown	Throws a format exception at runtime.	Error

TABLE 2.08—Standard Numeric Format Strings

Custom Numeric Format Strings

The following table describes the custom numeric format specifiers and displays sample output produced by each format specifier. Note that the string representations of numeric values typically vary by culture.

Specifier	Name	Description	Examples
"0"	Zero placeholder	Replaces the zero with the corresponding digit if one is present; otherwise, zero appears in the result string.	1234.5678 ("00000") → 01235 0.45678 ("0.00") →

[30] Hexadecimal is base 16 represented by the characters 0123456789ABCDEF so FF is 256 in decimals.

Specifier	Name	Description	Examples
			0.46
"#"	Digit placeholder	Replaces the "#" symbol with the corresponding digit if one is present; otherwise, no digit appears in the result string. Note that no digit appears in the result string if the corresponding digit in the input string is a non-significant 0. For example, 0003 ("####") -> 3.	1234.5678 ("#####")→ 1235 0.45678 ("#.##")→ .46
"."	Decimal point	Determines the location of the decimal separator in the result string.	0.45678 ("0.00") → 0.46
","	Group separator and number scaling	Serves as both a group separator and a number scaling specifier. As a group separator, it inserts a localized group separator character between each group. As a number scaling specifier, it divides a number by 1000 for each comma specified.	Group separator specifier: 2147483647 ("##,#")→ 2,147,483,647 Scaling specifier: 2147483647 ("#,#,,")→ 2,147
"%"	Percentage placeholder	Multiplies a number by 100 and inserts a percentage symbol in the result string.	0.3697 ("%#0.00") → %36.97 0.3697 ("##.0 %") → 37.0 %
"‰"	Per mille placeholder	Multiplies a number by 1000 and inserts a per mille symbol in the result string.	0.03697 ("#0.00‰") → 36.97‰
"E0" "E+0" "E-0" "e0" "e+0" "e-0"	Exponential Notation	If followed by at least one 0 (zero), formats the result using exponential notation. The case of "E" or "e" indicates the case of the exponent symbol in the result string. The number of zeros following the "E" or "e" character determines the minimum number of digits in the exponent. A plus sign (+) indicates that a sign character always precedes the exponent. A minus sign (-) indicates that a sign character precedes only negative exponents.	987654 ("#0.0e0") → 98.8e4 1503.92311 ("0.0##e+00") → 1.504e+03 1.8901385E-16 ("0.0e+00") → 1.9e-16
"\"	Escape character	Causes the next character to be interpreted as a literal rather than as a custom format specifier.	987654 ("\###00\#") → #987654#
'string' "string"	Literal string delimiter	Indicates that the enclosed characters should be copied to the result string unchanged.	68 ("# ' degrees'") → 68 degrees 68 ("#' degrees'") → 68 degrees
;	Section Separator	Defines sections with separate format strings for positive, negative, and zero numbers.	12.345 ("#0.0#;(#0.0#);-\0-") → 12.35 0 ("#0.0#;(#0.0#);-\0-") → -0-

Specifier	Name	Description	Examples
			-12.345 ("#0.0#;(#0.0#);-\0-") → (12.35)
			12.345 ("#0.0#;(#0.0#)") → 12.35
			0 ("#0.0#;(#0.0#)") → 0.0
			-12.345 ("#0.0#;(#0.0#)") → (12.35)
Other	All other characters	The character is copied to the result string unchanged.	68 ("# °") → 68 °

TABLE 2.09—Custom Numeric Format Strings

For casual debugging I usually use the old-fashioned **Print** statement. When your needs become more precise, as in generating Printed Reports for instance, then the **string.format ()** has a lot of latitude. In brief, the format is this: within the parentheses you place a format string, it may be a string literal, input value, a constant or a string variable followed by a list of parameters to match the numbered items in your format string. For example:

```
CommentaryCL (String.Format ("{00}{01}{00} {02} {03}", DoubleQuote,
Symbol, Date, Time)) ;
```

The format items which are an integer value inside curly braces identifies which item from the list of parameters goes where. The parameters are zero-based. You can have more parameters than are used but you cannot have more items than you do parameters. You will notice I am using parameter zero (Double Quote) twice. The order of the parameters makes no difference if you place the correct integer where it needs to be. This statement would yield the exact same output.

```
CommentaryCL (String.Format ("{03}{02} {03} {01} {00}", Time, Date,
Symbol, DoubleQuote)) ;
```

Date and Time Format Strings

You can create a standard or custom date and time format string, which consists of one or more date specifiers, to define how to format date and time data using Composite Formatting of strings.

Standard Date and Time Format Strings

A standard date and time format string uses a single format specifier to define the text representation of a date and time value. Any date and time format string that contains more than one character, including white space, is interpreted as a custom date and time format string; for more information, refer to Custom Date and Time Format Strings below.

The following table describes the standard date and time format specifiers and displays a result string produced by each format specifier. Note that the string representations of date and time values typically vary by culture. See the Example section for EZL code samples.

Specifier	Description	Example
"d"	Short date pattern	2009-06-15T13:45:30 → 6/15/2009

TABLE 2.10—Short Date Pattern

Custom Date and Time Format Strings

A custom format string consists of one or more custom date and time format specifiers. Any string that is not a standard date and time format string (i.e., containing more than one character) is interpreted as a custom date and time format string.

The full table in **Chapter 4** describes the custom date and time format specifiers and displays a resultant string produced by each format specifier. Note that the string representations of date and time values typically vary by culture. See the website www.EasyLanguageOOEL.com for downloads of the .ELD files.

Date and Time

Classic EZL has two ways to refer to dates and times. The first is by legacy Integer methods such as `Value1 = Date` ; The second is through using the Double **DateTime** functionality.

The next example is a particularly useful function for converting TS formatted dates to common strings.

EXAMPLE 2.46—Converting EZL Dates to Strings

```
// Function OME_DateToString to convert TS Dates to
// Common Form Dates:
// EL date, ie, yr102 = yr2002:
Inputs: DateSelect (NumericSimple) ;
Vars  : YearPortion( "" ), StringMonth( "" ), StringDay( "" ) ;
YearPortion = NumToStr( 1900 + IntPortion( DateSelect * 0.0001), 0) ;
if DateSelect >= 1000000 then // ie, if a 2000 date
    StringMonth = MidStr (NumToStr (DateSelect, 0), 04, 02)
else // ie, if a 1900 date
    StringMonth = MidStr (NumToStr (DateSelect, 00), 03, 02) ;
StringDay = RightStr (NumToStr (DateSelect, 0), 2) ;
// return:
OME_DateToString = StringMonth + "/" + StringDay + "/" + YearPortion ;
```

This function accepts an EZL date (i.e., 1211119) and returns the date string 11/19/2021.

Date References

You can always do it the old-fashioned way, as Sam does in his "vrt_MMDDYYYY" and "vrt_HHMM_pm" User Functions[31] but there is an easier way. The OOEL **DateTime** Class has Methods to deal with these various number bases (12 months 24 hours, 7 weekdays, 60 minutes, etc.) for you. It is worth your time to learn to use them.

DateTime is a double precision decimal value that represents the combination of a Julian Date and time using the standard Windows Date format (i.e. day.time). The whole number portion of **DateTime** is the date portion (i.e., using the year 1900 as a base) and the decimal portion represents the time that transpired for the day (starting at midnight). For example, the return value for the **DateTime** property on the 12:00:00pm bar of 11/01/2002 will be 37561.50000. More about this later on.

One thing to keep in mind when dealing with either Date or Time values is that simple math will not product reliable results. Sure, adding two minutes to 10:30am will return 10:32am but add ten minutes to 11:55am will result in 11:65am which may not yield the results you are looking for. This is because Time values are a combination of base 60 and base 24 rather than the base ten you have learned to work with all your life. Similarly, an **ELDate** format is a combination of Year (base 10), Month (base 12) and Day of Month (base 28-31).

EXAMPLE 2.47—Another Date Format

---

[31] sktennis@vista-research.com

```
If Date = ELDate (12,01,1999) Then Value1 = High ;
```

EXAMPLE 2.48—Formatting Dates with Sam's Function

```
Print (vrt_MMDDYYYY (BarDateTime.ELDate) ;
```

Date and Time Old School

There are several main formats for dates and times in EZL.

Integer based Date and Time reserved words and the functions return the bar end date in legacy format as an integer and the bar end time as an integer, respectively, with a precision to the minute.

ComputerDate and **ComputerTime** reserved words—returns the computer date and time respectively as an integer value with time having a precision to the minute.

Double based DateTime reserved words, **ComputerDateTime**—returns the computer clock date and time as a double value, with precision to the second. This double format is referred to as a Julian time but also as **DateTime**, which can be confusing. The value is returned using the standard Windows Date format (Date.Time). The reference to it as a DateTime was established before the DateTime Class was instituted.

DateTime class (new style) an OOEL class in which the date and time are combined into a single value, with a precision to the second. The equivalent to the date and time of a bar is the reserved word **BarDateTime**, which is the **DateTime** of the end of a bar. **DateTime.Now()** returns the computer clock time.

Date and Time as Integers

Date and Time are Reserved Words that return an Integer (whole number, no decimal portion) value. These are legacy EZL, simple and easy to use, no real explanation required here. There are many User Functions, Built-In Functions and other Reserved Words that require parameters using the Date and Time words, including **TL_New** and **TEXT_New**, so understanding what they are and how they can and cannot be used is important.

Date

The reserved word Date returns an integer (a whole number, no decimal portion) containing the date of the active bar in TS's YYYMMDD format where YYY is (the year – 1900), MM is the month and DD is the day of the month. This format is a rather clever solution to the 'Y2K (year 2000) bug' that allows for backward compatibility to all pre-2k data, as least if stored in ASCII (American Standard Code for Information Interchange) format.

Associated with a date are many reserved words and functions, one is **DayOfWeek** which returns an integer representing the day of the week, where 0 is Sunday and 6 is Saturday. You use it by inserting `DayOfWeek (cDate)` in your code. `DayOfWeek (1011024)` returns a value of 3 because October 24, 2001 was a Wednesday. There is also **DayOfMonth** where `DayOfMonth (1011024)` returns a value of 24. Also provided are: **Month (Date)**, **Year (Date)**, **DayOfMonth (Date)**, **DateToJulian (Date)**, **CalcDate (Date, N)** and more. When you need it, open the Dictionary and search, or just peruse the appropriate section(s).

You can also convert a date to Julian format and back with **DateToJulian** and **JulianToDate**. This is useful when you want to do arithmetic with a date because you are dealing with base 28-31, base 12 and base 10 all stored in one number. For example, October 31 + 1 is October 32, not November 1. Convert your date to Julian, do your arithmetic and then convert the result back to TS Date format. Sam's vrt_AddDate User Function, as well as the built-in CalcDate function, do this for you.

For instance: `DateToJulian (991024)` returns a value of 36457 for the date October 24, 1999.

Time

The Reserved word **Time** returns an integer (a whole number, no decimal portion) containing the time in the 24-hour, or military, format of HHMM where HH is the hour and MM is the minute(s). The value returned is the closing time of the active bar.

Similar to the Date mentioned above you cannot do simple math on a time value, base 60 and base 24, remember? There is a built in CalcTime function as well as the skt_AddTime User Function.

Double DateTime Format

This format contains the date as the integer portion of the double and the time as the fractional portion of the double. On occasion this format is the only format returned from a reserved word, such as GetAppInfo (aiLeftDispDateTime), and therefore you do need to know how to convert it to a date and time or a DateTime object.

The following method shows the conversion from a Double **DateTime** to integer **Date** and **Time** and then to a **DateTime** object.

EXAMPLE 2.49—Converting Julian Time Date [OME_DateTime_Julian]

```
using elSystem ;
method DateTime DTFromJulian (double julian)
Vars  :
    int LegacyDate,
    int LegacyTime ;
begin
  LegacyDate = JulianToDate (IntPortion (julian)) ;
  LegacyTime = (HoursFromDateTime (julian) * 100 ) +
MinutesFromDateTime (julian) ;
  return DateTime.FromELDateAndTime (LegacyDate, LegacyTime) ;
end ; // "DTFromJulian" method
```

DateTime as a Double

Double is a format used by Microsoft to return a Julian date (base 1900) value in the Integer portion of the Double and a time value in the decimal, or fractional, portion of the double. The fractional portion is a percent of the 24-hour day because, in an example TS provided, a value of 0.50 corresponded to Noon (12:00pm), twelve hours or halfway through the 24-hour day.

DateTime is a double precision decimal value that represents the combination of a Julian Date and time using the standard Windows Date format (i.e.,. day.time) .The whole number portion of **DateTime** is the date portion (i.e., using the year 1900 as a base) and the decimal portion represents the time that transpired for the day (starting at midnight). For example, the return value for the **DateTime** property on the 12:00:00pm bar of 11/01/2002 will be 37561.50000.

Return a DateTime as Double

ComputerDateTime returns a Double **DateTime** value

LastCalcDateTime returns a Double **DateTime** value

Pass in a DateTime as Double

Here are examples of all the ways you can format **DateTime**:

```
DateTimeToString(DateTime) Print (DateTimeToStr (ComputerDateTime)) ;
DateToString (DateTime)  Print (DateToStr (ComputerDateTime)) ;
TimeToString (DateTime)  Print (TimeToStr (ComputerDateTime)) ;
DayFromDate (DateTime)
DayOfWeekFromDate (DateTime)
HoursFromDateTime (DateTime)
MinutesFromDateTime (DateTime)
MonthFromDateTime (DateTime)
SecondsFromDateTime (DateTime)
YearFromDateTime (DateTime)
```

Create a DateTime as Double

Here are the ways:

```
StringToDateTime ("12/31/2021 11:38:00 PM")
StringToDate ("12/31/2021") string expression of the date in
"MM/DD/YY" or "MM/DD/YYYY" format
StringToTime ("10:44:00 OM") string expression of the date in
"HH:MM:SS TT" format
EncodeDate(YY, MM, DD) Value1  = EncodeDate (2022, 12, 31) ;
EncodeTime (HH, MM, SS, mm) Value1  = EncodeTime (14, 59, 20, 14) ;
```

These Reserved Words use modifiers from "Date and Time Format Strings", "Custom Date and Time Format Strings". Peruse the documentation carefully because Case is very specific. My choices below are specific because I am looking specifically for leading zeroes for alignment purposes. Your desires may be different, so have fun experimenting.

```
FormatDate ("MM/dd/yyyy", myDateTime)
FormatTime ("HH:mm.ss", myDateTime)
```

Here is the code snippet I was using to test some of these Functions and Reserved Words. The code is in the Snippets file on www.EasyLanguageOOEL.com. Feel free to play around and change the formatting parameters.

```
Once begin
  Print ("LastCalcJDate=", LastCalcJDate:4:6, ", ComputerDateTime=",
ComputerDateTime:4:4) ;
// See Composite formatting
//Print (String.Format("{0:MM/dd/yy HH:mm:ss}", Date)) ;
// Date is an integer = Fails
//Print (String.Format("{0:MM/dd/yyyy HH:mm:ss}", ComputerDateTime)) ;
// ComputerDateTime is Double DateTime - Fails
  Print (String.Format("{0:MM/dd/yyyy HH:mm:ss}", BarDateTime)) ;
// BarDateTime is DateTime object - works
// Monday, June 15, 2009
// Verifies, but Fails with "Format specifier was invalid" in
// Event Log window.
// Reason is that ComputerDateTime is a Double DateTime, not
// an elSystem.DateTime Class Object.
//  Print (String.Format("{0:D}", ComputerDateTime)) ;
  Print (String.Format("{0:D}", BarDateTime)) ;
// works because BarDateTime is a DateTime Class Object
  Print (BarDateTime.Format ("%m/%d/%Y %H:%M:%S")) ;
  Print (BarDateTime.Format (":D")) ;
  Print (String.Format ("Entered on {00} at {01}.", vrt_MMDDYYYY
(Date), vrt_HHMM_pm (Time))) ;
  Print (DateToString (ComputerDateTime ())) ;
  Print (FormatDate ("MM/dd/yyyy", ComputerDateTime)) ;
  Print (FormatTime ("HH:mm.ss", ComputerDateTime)) ;

  Print (Name) ;
  Print (Name + "(" + NumToStr (10, 00) + ")") ;
end ;
```

Date and Time OOEL Style

As well as the **DateTime** Class there is a **TimeSpan** Class, which represents the duration of a period of time, or can represent a time-of-day.

The Double **DateTime** 'ComputerDateTime' is not a very useful format and can be easily replaced by the **Now** property of the **DateTime** Class. Therefore, this Reserved Word is infrequently used.

The **Date** and **Time** reserved words are legacy functionality that in most instances can be handled much more simply but may also be accessed by use of the **DateTime** Class. There are Methods to convert Date and Time to **DateTime** objects and vice-versa.

If you expect to use any object-oriented programming classes (such as DrawingObjects), learning to use the **DateTime** Class is necessary. Except for the legacy functions that require date and time as inputs, one can code almost exclusively using **DateTime** classes if preferred.

Calculations with Date and Time

We mentioned this before, but it cannot be said enough. One cannot just add some number of minutes to a Time value and expect it to be correct. Similarly, one cannot just add some number of days to a Date integer and expect it to be correct. For instance, September 30 + 1 = September 31. Not a valid date.

This can become very important when it comes to optimizing Date and Time values. The solution is to have the Time input(s) be in 'MinutesSinceMidnight' format and Date input(s) be in Julian format.

There are reserved words and functions designed to facilitate calculations with the Date and Time values. The bulk of these can be found by opening the **easylanguage.ell** library in the Dictionary and then opening the Date and Time Namespace, searching for Date in the TDE Dictionary and then selecting the {} Date and Time item. The CalcDate, CalcTime, MinutesToTime, TimeToMinutes and other functions are also useful for doing arithmetic with these values. See Figure 2.02 to see where to find the Dictionary output for these terms.

The **DateTime** Class comes with a host of Properties and Methods to assist with these conversions. With OOEL all these features come encapsulated in the Class itself!

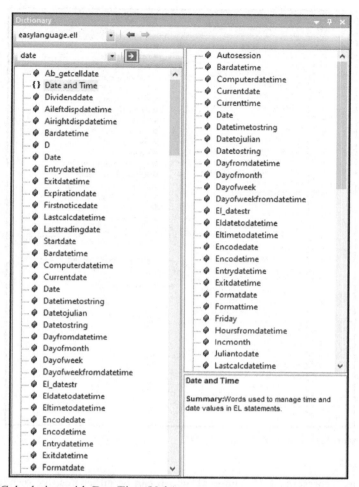

FIGURE 2.02—Calculating with DateTime Values

> ☑ SKT: Unlike OOEL Namespaces, the EZL Namespace does not need to be declared in a Using statement nor do you need to type a dot (.) operator before Date. These are some sort of hybrid, or intermediate, Namespaces that are inherently included in the AT by default. Confusing, I know, but they are doing some fancy footwork behind the curtain to make Classic EZL play nice with OOEL. I would have to say the engineer(s) who designed this (thank you Armando Martinez) did an amazing job! From what I can learn if I am 'Mr. EasyLanguage' then Armando is 'Mr. OOEL'.

DateTime Class

Almost everything that can be done with Double Date and Time can be done with the **DateTime** class, plus several additional things. In addition, there are several functions and classes in EZL that require the use of the **DateTime** class as parameters. The **DateTime** and **TimeSpan** classes usage is eased by including the following using statement at the start of your code:

```
using elSystem ;
```

From the TDE Dictionary the Methods of the **DateTime** Class are shown below. See Figure 2.03.

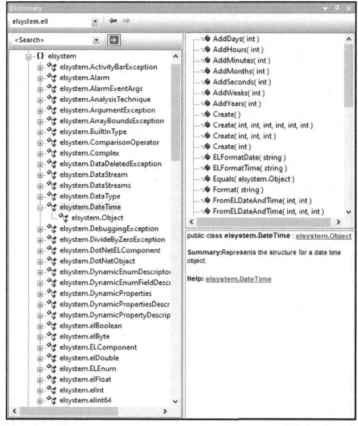

FIGURE 2.03—Methods of the DateTime Class

TimeSpan Class

The **TimeSpan** Class represents a time interval, which can be either positive or negative. This class along with the **DateTime** Class gives one the tools with which to do nearly anything one needs to do with dates and times within EZL.

You can add and subtract times using a DateTime value.

NAMESPACE: elSystem

The following calculates and displays a new time that is 3 hours, 20 minutes, and 12 seconds greater than the current time:

EXAMPLE 2.50—Using DateTime.Now with TimeSpan

```
using elSystem ;
Vars  : myDT NewTime (NULL) ;
NewTime  = myDT.Now + TimeSpan.Create (03, 20, 12) ;
Print ("Current Time: ", myDT.Now.tostring (),
        " New Time: ", NewTime.tostring ()) ;
```

Just to show that it can be done, in the example above I inserted spaces to align the dot operators.

EXAMPLE 2.51—Print Log TimeSpan Manipulations [OME_TimeSpan_Ex#01]

In this example we use the **TimeSpan** Class to calculate two **DateTime** values, one forward and one backward using addition and subtraction. Then we report it to the Print Log.

```
Using elSystem ;
```

```
 Inputs:
  Int     Fore_Days    (02),
  Int     Fore_Hours   (00),
  Int     Fore_Mins    (00),
  Int     Fore_Secs    (00),
  Int     Back_Days    (03),
  Int     Back_Hours   (00),
  Int     Back_Mins    (00),
  Int     Back_Secs    (00) ;

 Vars  :
  TimeSpan Fore_TS   (NULL),
  DateTime Fore_DT   (NULL),
  TimeSpan Back_TS   (NULL),
  DateTime Back_DT   (NULL) ;

 // ============================================================

 // Working Storage Section
 Consts:
  String App_Type    ("Study"),
  String App_Name    ("OME_I_TimeSpan_Ex#01"),
  String App_Note    ("OOEL Explore the DateTime and TimeSpan
 Classes"),
  String App_Vers    ("01.00.00") ;

 Vars  :
  String DQ          (DoubleQuote),
  String NL          (NewLine),
  Bool   Debug       (FALSE),
  Double Dummy       (0.00) ;

 // ============================================================

 method TimeSpan TimeSpan_Init (Int myDays, Int myHours, Int myMins,
 Int mySecs)
 Vars  :
  TimeSpan myTS ;
 begin
  Print ("TimeSpan_Init") ;
  myTS  = TimeSpan.Create (myDays, myHours, myMins, mySecs) ;
  Return myTS ;
 end ; // "TimeSpan_Init" method

 // ------------------------------------------------------------

 method void TimeSpan_Report (TimeSpan myTS)
 begin
  Print ("TimeSpan_Report (" + myTS.toString () + ")") ;
  Print ("myTS.Days = ", myTS.Days.toString ()) ;
  Print ("myTS.Hours = ", myTS.Hours.toString ()) ;
  Print ("myTS.MilliSeconds = ", myTS.MilliSeconds.toString ()) ;
  Print ("myTS.Minutes = ", myTS.Minutes.toString ()) ;
  Print ("myTS.Seconds = ", myTS.Seconds.toString ()) ;
  Print ("myTS.TotalDays = ", myTS.TotalDays.toString ()) ;
  Print ("myTS.TotalHours = ", myTS.TotalHours.toString ()) ;
  Print ("myTS.TotalMilliSeconds = ", myTS.TotalMilliSeconds.toString
 ()) ;
  Print ("myTS.TotalMinutes = ", myTS.TotalMinutes.toString ()) ;
  Print ("myTS.TotalSeconds = ", myTS.TotalSeconds.toString ()) ;
```

```
end ; // "TimeSpan_Report" method

// ============================================================

once begin
  Fore_TS   = TimeSpan_Init (Fore_Days * +01, Fore_Hours * +01,
Fore_Mins * +01, Fore_Secs * +01) ;
  Back_TS   = TimeSpan_Init (Back_Days * -01, Back_Hours * -01,
Back_Mins * -01, Back_Secs * -01) ;
  Fore_DT   = BarDateTime + Fore_TS ;
  Back_DT   = BarDateTime + Back_TS ;

  Print ("BarDateTime = ", BarDateTime.toString (), ", Fore = ",
Fore_DT.toString (), ", Back = ", Back_DT.toString ()) ;
  Print (NL, "Report the properties of the 'Fore_TS'.") ;
  TimeSpan_Report (Fore_TS) ;
  Print (NL, "Report the properties of the 'Back_TS'.") ;
  TimeSpan_Report (Back_TS) ;

  Print (NL, "Example using 'FromELDateAndTime' rather than 'Create'
method.") ;
  Fore_TS   = TimeSpan.FromELDateAndTime (Fore_Days * 2400, 00) ;
  TimeSpan_Report (Fore_TS) ;
end ; // Once, and only once
```

And below is the output from the Print Log.

```
Example using 'FromELDateAndTime' rather than 'Create' method.
TimeSpan_Report (2. 0. 0. 0.  0)
myTS.Days = 2
myTS.Hours = 0
myTS.MilliSeconds = 0
myTS.Minutes = 0
myTS.Seconds = 0
myTS.TotalDays = 2.0
myTS.TotalHours = 48.0
myTS.TotalMilliSeconds = 172800000.0
myTS.TotalMinutes = 2880.0
myTS.TotalSeconds = 172800.0
```

FIGURE 2.04—Print Log Output for TimeSpan Manipulations

See **Volume II—Reference Guide, Appendix III: Classes** for the Properties and Methods of this Class.

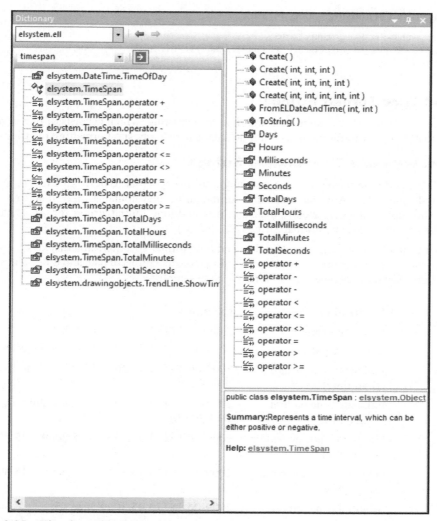

FIGURE 2.05—TimeSpan Class Members

The rest of the Date and Time section gets a bit messy, I fear. I wrote code to explore for myself how the various formatting schemes work and Sunny, bless her diligent heart, stuck it in the book. For the next few pages, we will be jumping around between the three methods of representing Date and Time values a bit.

Formatting DateTime

There are multiple approaches available to formatting a datetime as a string:

Quick and Easy – no flexibility:

```
MyDTText = MyDateTime.ToString () ;
```

DateTime.Format Method – very flexible:

[See the Format Codes in the **DateTime** class help topic for the various options available.]

```
// 03/08/20 11:34:16
MyDTText = MyDateTime.Format ("%m/%d/%y %H:%M:%S") ;
// Wed May 05, 2010
MyDTText = MyDatetime.Now.Format (Format ("%a %b %d, %Y")) ;
```

Using Composite Formatting – Very Flexible:

```
// See Composite formatting
MyDateText = String.Format("{0:MM/dd/yy HH:mm:ss"}, Date1) ;
// Monday, June 15, 2009
MyDateText = String.Format("0:D}, Date1) ;
```

Date and Time Format Strings

You can create a standard or custom date and time format string, which consists of one or more date specifiers, to define how to format date and time data using Composite Formatting of strings.

Standard Date and Time Format Strings

A standard date and time format string uses a single format specifier to define the text representation of a date and time value. Any date and time format string that contains more than one character, including white space, is interpreted as a custom date and time format string; for more information, refer to Custom Date and Time Format Strings (see below).

The following table describes the standard date and time format specifiers and displays a result string produced by each format specifier. Note that the string representations of date and time values typically vary by culture. See the Example section for EZL code samples.

Specifier	Description	Examples
"d"	Short date pattern.	2009-06-15T13:45:30 → 6/15/2009
"D"	Long date pattern.	2009-06-15T13:45:30 → Monday, June 15, 2009
"f"	Full date/time pattern (short time).	2009-06-15T13:45:30 → Monday, June 15, 2009 1:45 PM
"F"	Full date/time pattern (long time).	2009-06-15T13:45:30 → Monday, June 15, 2009 1:45:30 PM
"g"	General date/time pattern (short time).	2009-06-15T13:45:30 → 6/15/2009 1:45 PM
"G"	General date/time pattern (long time).	2009-06-15T13:45:30 → 6/15/2009 1:45:30 PM
"M", "m"	Month/day pattern.	2009-06-15T13:45:30 → June 15
"O", "o"	Round-trip date/time pattern.	DateTime values: 2009-06-15T13:45:30 (DateTimeKind.Local) → 2009-06-15T13:45:30.0000000-07:00 2009-06-15T13:45:30 (DateTimeKind.UTC) → 2009-06-15T13:45:30.0000000Z 2009-06-15T13:45:30 (DateTime Kind.Unspecified) → 2009-06-15T13:45:30.0000000 DateTimeOffset values: 2009-06-15T13:45:30-07:00 → 2009-06-15T13:45:30.0000000-07:00
"R", "r"	RFC1123 pattern.	2009-06-15T13:45:30 → Mon, 15 Jun 2009 20:45:30 GMT
"s"	Sortable date/time pattern.	2009-06-15T13:45:30 (DateTimeKind.Local) → 2009-06-15T13:45:30 2009-06-15T13:45:30 (DateTimeKind.Utc) → 2009-06-15T13:45:30

Specifier	Description	Examples
"t"	Short time pattern.	2009-06-15T13:45:30 → 1:45 PM
"T"	Long time pattern.	2009-06-15T13:45:30 → 1:45:30 PM
"u"	Universal sortable date/time pattern.	With a DateTime value: 2009-06-15T13:45:30 → 2009-06-15 13:45:30Z With a DateTimeOffset value: 2009-06-15T13:45:30 → 2009-06-15 20:45:30Z
"U"	Universal full date/time pattern.	2009-06-15T13:45:30 → Monday, June 15, 2009 8:45:30 PM
"Y", "y"	Year month pattern.	2009-06-15T13:45:30 → June, 2009
Any other single character	Unknown specifier.	Throws a run-time FormatException .

TABLE 2.11—Standard Date and Time Format Specifications

Custom Date and Time Format Strings

A custom format string consists of one or more custom date and time format specifiers. Any string that is not a standard date and time format string (i.e., containing more than one character) is interpreted as a custom date and time format string.

The following table describes the custom date and time format specifiers and displays a result string produced by each format specifier. Note that the string representations of date and time values typically vary by culture. See the Example section for EZL code samples.

Specifier	Description	Examples
"d"	The day of the month, from 1 through 31.	2009-06-01T13:45:30 → 1 2009-06-15T13:45:30 → 15
"dd"	The day of the month, from 01 through 31.	2009-06-01T13:45:30 → 01 2009-06-15T13:45:30 → 15
"ddd"	The abbreviated name of the day of the week.	2009-06-15T13:45:30 → Mon
"dddd"	The full name of the day of the week.	2009-06-15T13:45:30 → Monday
"g", "gg"	The period or era.	2009-06-15T13:45:30.6170000 → A.D.
"h"	The hour, using a 12-hour clock from 1 to 12.	2009-06-15T01:45:30 → 1 2009-06-15T13:45:30 → 1
"hh"	The hour, using a 12-hour clock from 01 to 12.	2009-06-15T01:45:30 → 01 2009-06-15T13:45:30 → 01
"H"	The hour, using a 24-hour clock from 0 to 23.	2009-06-15T01:45:30 → 1 2009-06-15T13:45:30 → 13
"HH"	The hour, using a 24-hour clock from 00 to 23.	2009-06-15T01:45:30 → 01 2009-06-15T13:45:30 → 13
"K"	Time zone information.	With DateTime values: 2009-06-15T13:45:30, Kind Unspecified → 2009-06-15T13:45:30, Kind UTC → Z 2009-06-15T13:45:30, Kind Local → -07:00 (depends on local computer

Specifier	Description	Examples
		settings)
		With DateTimeOffset values: 2009-06-15T01:45:30-07:00 → -07:00 2009-06-15T08:45:30+00:00 → +00:00
"m"	The minute, from 0 through 59.	2009-06-15T01:09:30 → 9 2009-06-15T13:29:30 → 29
"mm"	The minute, from 00 through 59.	2009-06-15T01:09:30 → 09 2009-06-15T01:45:30 → 45
"M"	The month, from 1 through 12.	2009-06-15T13:45:30 → 6
"MM"	The month, from 01 through 12.	2009-06-15T13:45:30 → 06
"MMM"	The abbreviated name of the month. .	2009-06-15T13:45:30 → Jun
"MMMM"	The full name of the month.	2009-06-15T13:45:30 → June
"s"	The second, from 0 through 59. .	2009-06-15T13:45:09 → 9
"ss"	The second, from 00 through 59.	2009-06-15T13:45:09 → 09
"t"	The first character of the AM/PM designator.	2009-06-15T13:45:30 → P
"tt"	The AM/PM designator.	2009-06-15T13:45:30 → PM
"y"	The year, from 0 to 99.	0001-01-01T00:00:00 → 1 0900-01-01T00:00:00 → 0 1900-01-01T00:00:00 → 0 2009-06-15T13:45:30 → 9 2019-06-15T13:45:30 → 19
"yy"	The year, from 00 to 99.	0001-01-01T00:00:00 → 01 0900-01-01T00:00:00 → 00 1900-01-01T00:00:00 → 00 2019-06-15T13:45:30 → 19
"yyy"	The year, with a minimum of three digits.	0001-01-01T00:00:00 → 001 0900-01-01T00:00:00 → 900 1900-01-01T00:00:00 → 1900 2009-06-15T13:45:30 → 2009
"yyyy"	The year as a four-digit number.	0001-01-01T00:00:00 → 0001 0900-01-01T00:00:00 → 0900 1900-01-01T00:00:00 → 1900 2009-06-15T13:45:30 → 2009
"yyyyy"	The year as a five-digit number.	0001-01-01T00:00:00 → 00001 2009-06-15T13:45:30 → 02009
"z"	Hours offset from UTC, with no leading zeros.	2009-06-15T13:45:30-07:00 → -7
"zz"	Hours offset from UTC, with a leading zero for a single-digit value.	2009-06-15T13:45:30-07:00 → -07
"zzz"	Hours and minutes offset from UTC.	2009-06-15T13:45:30-07:00 → -07:00
":"	The time separator.	2009-06-15T13:45:30 → :
"/"	The date separator.	2009-06-15T13:45:30 → / (2009/06/15)
"string"	Literal string delimiter.	2009-06-15T13:45:30 ("arr:" h:m t) →

Specifier	Description	Examples
'string'		arr: 1:45 P 2009-06-15T13:45:30 ('arr:' h:m t) → arr: 1:45 P
%	Defines the following character as a custom format specifier.	2009-06-15T13:45:30 (%h) → 1
The escape character.	2009-06-15T13:45:30 (h \h) → 1 h	
Any other character	The character is copied to the result string unchanged.	2009-06-15T01:45:30 (arr hh:mm t) → arr 01:45 A

TABLE 2.12—Custom Date and Time Format Specifiers

EXAMPLE 2.52—Custom Date and Time Formats [OME_DateTime_Ex#01]

```
Using elSystem ;

// Working Storage Section
Consts:
  String App_Type    ("Study"),
  String App_Name    ("OME_DateTime_Ex#01"),
  String App_Note    ("OOEL Made Easy; Demonstrate DateTime Formats"),
  String App_Vers    ("01.00.00") ;

Vars  :
  String DQ          (DoubleQuote),
  String NL          (NewLine),
  Bool   Debug       (FALSE),
  Double Dummy       (0.00) ;

once begin
// Date (Reserved Word) :
//    This reserved word returns a numeric expression
//    representing the EasyLanguage date of the close of the
//    bar being analyzed. The date is an EasyLanguage date,
//    so, it is a numeric expression of the form YYYMMDD,
//    where YYY is years since 1900, MM is the month, and DD
//    is the day of the month.
  Print ("Int : ") ;
  Print (" Date = ", Date:6:4,
     ", Time = ", Time:6:4,
    NL, " CurrentDate = ", CurrentDate:6:4,
     ", CurrentTime = ", CurrentTime:6:4) ;
  Print (String.Format ("Entered on {00} at {01}.",
              vrt_MMDDYYYY (Date), vrt_HHMM_pm (Time))) ;

// ComputerDateTime (Reserved Word) :
//    This reserved word returns a double-precision decimal
//    DateTime value for the current computer time.
  Print (NL + "Double : ") ;
  Print (" LastCalcJDate = ", LastCalcJDate:4:6,
       ", ComputerDateTime = ", ComputerDateTime:4:4) ;
  Print (" DateToString (ComputerDateTime ()) = ",
          DateToString (ComputerDateTime ())) ;
  Print (" FormatDate (" + DQ + "MM/dd/yyyy"
                    + DQ + ", ComputerDateTime) = ",
          FormatDate ("MM/dd/yyyy", ComputerDateTime)) ;
```

```
        Print (" FormatTime (" + DQ + "HH:mm.ss"
                            + DQ + ", ComputerDateTime) = ",
             FormatTime ("HH:mm.ss", ComputerDateTime)) ;

    // See Composite formatting
      Print (NL + "OOEL DateTime Class : ") ;
    // fails - Date is an Integer, not a DateTime Object
    //  Print (String.Format("{0:MM/dd/yy HH:mm:ss}", Date)) ;

    // fails - ComputerDateTime is Double, not DateTime Object
    //  Print (String.Format ("{0:MM/dd/yyyy HH:mm:ss}",
                        ComputerDateTime)) ;
      Print (" String.Format (" + DQ + "{0:MM/dd/yyyy HH:mm:ss}"
                        + DQ + ", BarDateTime) = ",
             String.Format ("{0:MM/dd/yyyy HH:mm:ss}",
                        BarDateTime)) ;

    // Fails with "Format specifier was invalid" displayed in
    //   the Event Log window.
    // Reason is that CumputerDateTime is a Doudle DateTime, not
    //   an elSystem.DateTime Class Object.
    // Print (String.Format("{0:D}", ComputerDateTime)) ;

    // works because BarDateTime is a DateTime Class Object
      Print (" String.Format (" + DQ + "{0:D}"
                            + DQ + ", BarDateTime) = ",
             String.Format ("{0:D}", BarDateTime)) ;

    // Notice the DateTime.Format Method uses different format
    //   codes than the String.Format Method
      Print (" BarDateTime.Format (" + DQ + "%m/%d/%Y %H:%M:%S"
                            + DQ + ") = ",
             BarDateTime.Format (" | %m/%d/%Y %H:%M:%S | ")) ;

    // does not appear to do anything?  Not even a blank line.
      Print (BarDateTime.Format ("? %D")) ;
      Print (" BarDateTime.Format (" + DQ + "? %D" + DQ + ") = ",
             BarDateTime.Format ("? %D")) ;

    // Print the Analysis Technique Name
      Print ("Analysis Technique Name = ", Name) ;
    // Print the Symbol Name
      Print ("Symbol Name = ", Symbol) ;
      Print (DQ + Name + DQ + " (" + Symbol + ")") ;
    end ; // Once, and only once
```

elSystem.DateTime Class

Object **DateTime** is a Class in the elSystem namespace. The **DateTime** Class has a Format method with its own set of 'format specifiers'. In the TDE Dictionary click to open the 'elSystem.ell library (.ell)', click to open the '{} elSystem' namespace and select 'elSystem.DateTime'. In the lower right pane click the link for "Help: elSystem.DateTime", see the "Format Codes (used with the Format Method)" section near the bottom. Within that help page you will discover an entirely different (in both definitions and syntax) set of formatting tools. The general format is "DateTimeObj.Format (parameter string)". ex: Print (BarDateTime.Format ("D")) ;

See "Date and Time Format Strings" in the TDE Help system. The sample code on that page is named "!ex_CompositeFormatting". General format is "String.Format (parameter string, parameter list)". ex: Print (String.Format ("{0:MM/dd/yyyy HH:mm:ss}", BarDateTime)) ; notice that the Case is very specific.

```
The very important difference between "String.Format ()" and
"myDateTime.Format ()".
  Print (String.Format("{0:D}", ComputerDateTime)) ;
// fails because it is a Double
  Print (String.Format("{0:D}", BarDateTime)) ;
//  Succeeds because it is an Object
```

Functions or Reserved Words that return a **DateTime** Object

> `EntryDateTime (Num)` returns a **DateTime** Object

> `ExitDateTime (Num)` returns a **DateTime** Object

Summarizing, you can do composite formatting with Integer Date and Time values but any formatting of that date or time value must be accomplished using a User Function (or Method) and the formatted string then passed to the Format Method. Ex: Print (String.Format ("Entered on {00} at {01}.", vrt_MMDDYYYY (EntryDate), vrt_HHMM_pm (EntryTime))) ;

You can do limited formatting using Double **DateTime** values but if you want more advanced features, such as ensuring a leading zero so columns align, then I believe you will have to first extract the Date and Time values then use User Functions to give you the formatting you desire. I have lots of examples of this, but they are not really within the purview of a book on OOEL.

Composite Formatting

The composite formatting feature takes a composite format string and list of objects as input. A composite format string consists of fixed text intermixed with indexed placeholders, called format items, that correspond to the objects in the list. The formatting operation yields a result string that consists of the original fixed text intermixed with the string representation of the objects in the list.

The composite formatting is supported by:

String.Format, which returns a formatted result string. See the **elString.Format Method**.

StreamWriter.WriteLine, which outputs a formatted line. See the **StreamWriter WriteLine** Method.

See Appendix III: Classes in Volume II—Reference Guide.

Composite Format String

A composite format string and object list are used as arguments of Methods that support the composite formatting feature. A composite format string consists of zero or more runs of fixed text intermixed with one or more format items. The fixed text is any string that you choose, and each format item corresponds to an object in the list. The composite formatting feature returns a new result string where each format item is replaced by the string representation of the corresponding object in the list.

EXAMPLE 2.53—String.Format in a Print statement

```
Vars  : string newString ("Fred") ;
Print (String.Format ("Name = {0}, Hours = {1:hh}", newString,
elSystem.DateTime.Now)) ;
```

The fixed text is "Name = " and, "Hours = ". The format items are "{0}", whose index is 0, which corresponds to the object `newstring`, and {1:hh}, whose index is 1, which corresponds to the object **elSystem.DateTime.Now**.

Format Item Syntax

Each format item takes the following form and consists of the following components:

{index[,alignment][:formatString]}

The matching braces ("{" and "}") are required.

Index Component

The mandatory index component, also called a parameter specifier, is a number starting from 0 that identifies a corresponding item in the list of objects. That is, the format item whose parameter specifier is 0 formats the first object in the list, the format item whose parameter specifier is 1 formats the second object in the list, and so on.

Multiple format items can refer to the same element in the list of objects by specifying the same parameter specifier.

Each format item can refer to any object in the list. For example, if there are three objects, you can format the second, first, and third object by specifying a composite format string like this: "{1} {0} {2}". An object that is not referenced by a format item is ignored.

Alignment Component

The optional alignment component is a signed integer indicating the preferred formatted field width. If the value of alignment is less than the length of the formatted string, alignment is ignored, and the length of the formatted string is used as the field width. The formatted data in the field is right-aligned if alignment is positive and left-aligned if alignment is negative. If padding is necessary, white space is used. The comma is required if alignment is specified.

```
Print (String.Format("{0:MM/dd/yy HH:mm:ss} {1,-8} TODAY: {2:MM/dd/yy}
V={3} YESTERDAY: {4:MM/dd/yy} V={5} ",DateTime.Now, Symbol,
PSP.Time[0], PSP.Volume[0], PSP.Time[1], PSP.Volume[1])) ;
```

The -8 left justifies the symbol (index 1), padding it to 8 characters in length with blanks.

> ✎ Alignment will give better results in the Print Log or text window when using a fixed width font, such as Courier,

Format String Component

The optional formatString component is a format string that is appropriate for the type of object being formatted. Specify a standard or custom numeric format string if the corresponding object is a numeric value, a standard or custom date and time format string if the corresponding object is a **DateTime** object, or an enumeration format string if the corresponding object is an enumeration value. If formatString is not specified, the general ("G") format specifier for a numeric, date and time, or enumeration type is used. The colon is required if formatString is specified.

Formatting Types

Different types of data values can use specialized format specifiers to determine how to format the data when converting it into a string. For more information, refer to the following:

- Numeric Format Strings (Standard and Custom)
- Date and Time Format Strings (Standard and Custom)
- TimeSpan Format Strings (Standard)

EXAMPLE 2.54—Composite Formatting [OME_StringManipulation]

```
Once begin
  Print ("LastCalcJDate=", LastCalcJDate:4:6, ", ComputerDateTime=",
ComputerDateTime:4:4) ;
// See Composite Formatting
  Print (String.Format("{0:MM/dd/yyyy HH:mm:ss}", BarDateTime)) ;

// Monday, June 15, 2009
// Fails with "Format specifier was invalid" in Event Log
// Reason is that CumputerDateTime is a Double DateTime,
// not an elSystem.DateTime Class Object.
//  Print (String.Format("{0:D}", ComputerDateTime)) ;
  Print (String.Format("{0:D}", BarDateTime)) ;
// works because BarDateTime is a DateTime Class Object

  Print (BarDateTime.Format ("%m/%d/%Y %H:%M:%S")) ;
```

```
   Print (BarDateTime.Format (":D")) ;
   Print (String.Format ("Entered on {00} at {01}.", vrt_MMDDYYYY
(Date), vrt_HHMM_pm (Time))) ;
   Print (DateToString (ComputerDateTime ())) ;
   Print (FormatDate ("MM/dd/yyyy", ComputerDateTime)) ;
   Print (FormatTime ("HH:mm.ss", ComputerDateTime)) ;

   Print (Name) ;
   Print (Name + "(" + NumToStr (10, 00) + ")") ;
end ;
```

EXAMPLE 2.55—Composite Formatting [OME_CompositeFormatting]

```
using elSystem ;
using elSystem.Srawing ;
using elSystem.Windows.Forms ;
using tsData.Common;
using tsData.MarketData ;
using tsData.Trading ;

Vars  :
   int Int32(12345678),
   int64 BigInt(1234567890),
   TimeSpan TS1(null),
   TimeSpan TS2(null),
   DateTime DT1(null) ;

Once begin
   ClearPrintLog();
   //-------------------------------------------------------
   //   Standard Numeric
   //-------------------------------------------------------
   print("STANDARD NUMERIC");
   print("{0:C}, 12345.6789", "=", String.Format("{0:C}", 12345.6789));

   print("{0:C4}, 12345.6789", "=", String.format("{0:C4}",
12345.6789));

   print("{0:D}, 123", "=", String.format("{0:D}", 123));

   print("{0:D4}, 123", "=", String.format("{0:D4}", 123));

   print("{0:X}, 123", "=", String.format("{0:X}", 123));

   print("{0:X4}, 1234", "=", String.format("{0:X4}", 1234));

   print("{0:X4}, 123456789", "=", String.format("{0:X4}", Int32));
   print("{0:X4}, 1234567890", "=", String.format("{0:X4}", BigInt));

   //-------------------------------------------------------
   //   Custom Numeric
   //-------------------------------------------------------
   Print (NewLine, "CUSTOM NUMERIC") ;
   Print ("'{0:###,###,##0}', 12345", "=", String.format
("{0:###,###,##0}", 12345)) ;

   Print ("'{0:0.00}', 0.45678 ", "=", String.format ("{0:0.00}",
0.45678 ));

   Print ("'{0:0.00}', 0.45678 ", "=", String.format ("{0:0.00}",
```

```
123.45678 ));

   Print ("'{0:0.00}'", 123.45678 ", "=", String.format ("{0:0.00}",
123.45678 ));

   Print ("'{0:###,##0.00}'", 12321.45678 ", "=", String.format
("{0:###,##0.00}", 12311.45678 ));

   Print("'{0:###%}'", .12", "=", String.format("{0:###%}", .12));

   Print ("'{0:##e+00}'", 987654", "=", String.format ("{0:##e+00}",
987654));


   //-------------------------------------------------------------
   //  Standard DateTime
   //-------------------------------------------------------------
   Print (NewLine, "STANDARD DATETIME");
   DT1 = DateTime.Create (2018, 09, 06, 11, 05, 23) ;
   Print ("DT:d", "=", String.Format ("{0:d}", DT1)) ;
   Print ("DT:D", "=", String.Format ("{0:D}", DT1)) ;
   Print ("DT:f", "=", String.Format ("{0:f}", DT1)) ;
   Print ("DT:F", "=", String.Format ("{0:F}", DT1)) ;
   Print ("DT:g", "=", String.Format ("{0:g}", DT1)) ;
   Print ("DT:G", "=", String.Format ("{0:G}", DT1)) ;
   Print ("DT:o", "=", String.Format ("{0:o}", DT1)) ;
   Print ("DT:O", "=", String.Format ("{0:O}", DT1)) ;
   Print ("DT:r", "=", String.Format ("{0:r}", DT1)) ;
   Print ("DT:R", "=", String.Format ("{0:R}", DT1)) ;
   Print ("DT:s", "=", String.Format ("{0:s}", DT1)) ;
   Print ("DT:t", "=", String.Format ("{0:t}", DT1)) ;
   Print ("DT:T", "=", String.Format ("{0:T}", DT1)) ;
   Print ("DT:u", "=", String.Format ("{0:u}", DT1)) ;
   Print ("DT:U", "=", String.Format ("{0:U}", DT1)) ;
   Print ("DT:y", "=", String.Format ("{0:y}", DT1)) ;
   Print ("DT:Y", "=", String.Format ("{0:Y}", DT1)) ;


   //-------------------------------------------------------------
   //  Custom DateTime
   //-------------------------------------------------------------
   Print (NewLine, "CUSTOM DATETIME") ;
   Print ("DT:M/d/y H:m:s", "=", String.Format("{0:M/d/y H:m:s}", DT1))
;
   Print ("DT:MM/dd/yy HH:mm:ss", "=", String.Format ("{0:MM/dd/yy
HH:mm:ss}", DT1)) ;
   Print ("DT:MM/dd/yyyy HH:mm:ss", "=", String.Format ("{0:MM/dd/yyyy
HH:mm:ss}", DT1)) ;
   Print ("DT:MM/dd HH:mm", "=", String.Format ("{0:MM/dd HH:mm}",
DT1)) ;
   Print ("DT:MMM dd, yyyy HH:mm:ss", "=", String.Format ("{0:MMM dd,
yyyy HH:mm:ss}", DT1)) ;


   //-------------------------------------------------------------
   //  Standard TimeSpan
   //-------------------------------------------------------------
   Print(NewLine, "STANDARD TIMESPAN");
   TS1 = TimeSpan.Create(14, 24, 12) ;
   TS2 = TimeSpan.Create (02, 14, 24, 12, 311) ;

   Print ("14:24:12:c" , "=", String.Format ("{0:c}", TS1));
   Print ("14:24:12:g" , "=", String.Format ("{0:g}", TS1));
```

```
   Print ("14:24:12:G" , "=", String.Format ("{0:G}", TS1));

   Print ("2 14:24:12,311:c" , "=", String.Format ("{0:c}", TS2));
   Print ("2 14:24:12,311:g" , "=", String.Format ("{0:g}", TS2));
   Print ("2 14:24:12,311:G" , "=", String.Format ("{0:G}", TS2));

   //-----------------------------------------------------
   //   Enumeration
   //-----------------------------------------------------
   Print(NewLine, "ENUMERATION");

   Print ("Enum", "=", String.Format ("{0}", elSystem.timezone.Local))
;
   Print ("Enum", "=", String.Format ("{0}",
tsData.Trading.OrderAction.Buy)) ;
   Print ("Enum", "=", String.Format ("{0}", FontStyle.Bold));

   //-----------------------------------------------------
   //   Alignment
   //-----------------------------------------------------
   {* Note: To get proper alignment in the EasyLanguage Print Log you
can change to a fixed width font, such as Courier, by Right-Clicking
in the Print Log window and selecting Preferences > Font and choosing
Courier.
   *}

   Print (NewLine, "ALIGNMENT");

   Print (String.format("{0,-20}   {1,-8}
{2,10}","Date","Symbol","Price"));

   Print (String.format("{0,-20:MM/dd/yy HH:mm:ss}   {1,-8}   {2,10:C2}
", DateTime.Now, Symbol, Close));

   // Date {0} and Symbol {1} are left justified (a negative
   // alignment number)
   // Price {2} is right justified (a positive alignment
   // number)

   //-----------------------------------------------------
   //   Mixed text example
   //-----------------------------------------------------
   Print(NewLine, "MIXED TEXT EXAMPLE");

   Print(String.format("At {0:g} the last price for {2} was {1:C2}",
DateTime.Now, Last, Symbol)) ;
      // Note that indexed items in string can be in a
      // different order than the items in the list

      Print (String.format ("Standard Date Format: {0:G} and Custom Date
Format: {0:MM/dd/yy} using the same index element",DateTime.Now)) ;
      // Shows two different date formats using
      // the same indexed item
End ;
```

The Print Log for this example is shown in Figure 2.06 just below. It is enlightening to see all the different possibilities.

```
DATETIME EXAMPLES
End of Feb: 02/29/2020
COMPOSITE FORMATTING: Today=08/18/22 Yesterday=08/17/22 1-month
```

```
ago=07/18/2022
DATETIME.FORMATTING:  Today=08/18/22 Yesterday=08/17/22 1-month
ago=07/18/2022
NOW = 08/18/22 17:16:02
NOW = 08/18/22 17:16:02
XMAS = 12/25/19 00:00:00
XMAS = 12/25/19 08:15:30
'12/25/19 10:30:00' => 12/25/2019 10:30:00
'12/25/30 10:30:00' => 12/25/2029 10:30:00 - NOTE 21st Century
'12/25/30 10:30:00' => 12/25/2030 10:30:00 - NOTE 20th Century

DATETIME PARSE WITH NON-US STRING EXAMPLES
'1/2/2020 using d/m/y ' ==> 01/02/2020 00:00:00 - EXPECTING
THIS TO BE Feb. 1, not Jan. 2
'13/12/2020 using d/m/y ' ==> 12/13/2020 00:00:00 - Handles
correctly
'11/12/2020 using d/m/y ' => 11/12/2020 00:00:00 - EXPECTING
Dec. 11 BUT GET Nov 12
'2020/1/2 using y/m/d ' => 01/02/2020 00:00:00 - Handles
correctly
'2020/11/13 using y/m/d ' => 11/13/2020 00:00:00-Handles
correctly
2020/13/11 using y/m/d CAUSES AN EXCEPTION

DATETIME PARSE WITH ERRONEOUS STRING EXAMPLES
'12/45/30 10:30:00' string date invalid

DATETIME DISPLAY EXAMPLES
BarDateTime = 08/11/22 15:10:00

DATETIME COMPARISON EXAMPLES
01/01/20 08:00:00 < 01/03/20 10:15:00
01/03/20 10:15:00 > 01/01/20 08:00:00
Converted Date and Time = 08/11/2022 15:10:00 - Note 0 seconds
Converted Date and Time = 08/11/2022 15:10:40
DOW: #=4 Thu Thursday
DOW: #=4 Thu Thursday

TIMESPAN EXAMPLES
01/03/2020 10:15:00 - 01/01/2020 08:00:00 = 2.09 Total Days
50.25 TotalHours  3015.00 TotalMinutes  180900.00 TotalSeconds
Timespan Duration: 2.02:15:00
08/18/22 17:16:02 time 0. 9.30. 0.  0
Total Days = 3.07
Total Hours = 73.75
Total Minutes = 4425.00

MORE DATETIME EXAMPLES
FirstBar Of New Day: 08/12/2022 00:00:00
FirstBar Of New Day: 08/14/2022 15:05:00
FirstBar Of New Day: 08/15/2022 00:00:00
FirstBar Of New Day: 08/16/2022 00:00:00
FirstBar Of New Day: 08/17/2022 00:00:00
```

```
FirstBar Of New Day: 08/18/2022 00:00:00
```

FIGURE 2.06—Output in the Print Log

DateTime Related Tasks

This section contains code that demonstrates the use of the **DateTime** and **TimeSpan** classes to accomplish common tasks.

EXAMPLE 2.56—DateTime Examples [OME_DateTime]

```
#Region - Usings -
//------------------------------------------------------------
// Namespace containing DateTime and TimeSpan classes
//------------------------------------------------------------
using elSystem;
#endRegion

#Region - Variables_Study -
//------------------------------------------------------------
// Variable declaration
//------------------------------------------------------------
variables:
    DateTime MyDT(null),
    DateTime MyDT1(null),
    DateTime MyDT2(null),
    DateTime MyToday(null),
    DateTime MyYesterday(null),
    DateTime MyMonthAgo(null),
    DateTime MyNow(null),
    DateTime MySpecificDate(null),
    DateTime MyBarDT(null),
    DateTime MyBeforeDT(null),
    DateTime MyAfterDT(null),
    DateTime MyEqualAfterDT(null),

    int DOW(0),

    TimeSpan MyTS(null);
#endRegion

#Region - TimeSpan and DateTime Methods -
//------------------------------------------------------------
// TimeSpan and DateTime Methods
//------------------------------------------------------------
method string FormatTimeSpan (TimeSpan ts)
begin
  if ts.Days <> 0 then
  begin
    return String.Format ("{0}.{1:00}:{2:00}:{3:00}",
      ts.Days, ts.hours, ts.minutes, ts.seconds) ;
  end
  else begin
    return String.Format("{0:00}:{1:00}:{2:00}",
      ts.hours, ts.minutes, ts.seconds);
  end ;
end ;

ethod string FormatTimeSpanHM(TimeSpan ts)
begin
  return String.Format ("{0:00}:{1:00}", ts.hours, ts.minutes) ;
```

```
end ;

method TimeSpan TimePartOfDateTime (DateTime dt)
begin
  return TimeSpan.Create (dt.Hour, dt.Minute, dt.Second) ;
end ;

method DateTime DatePartofDateTime (DateTime dt)
begin
  return DateTime.Create(dt.Year, dt.Month, dt.Day);
end;
#endRegion

#Region - Sample Code -
once
begin
  ClearPrintLog ;

//------------------------------------------------------------
//------------------------------------------------------------
// DATETIME CLASS
//------------------------------------------------------------
//------------------------------------------------------------
  Print("DATETIME EXAMPLES");

//------------------------------------------------------------
// Today - date part only
//------------------------------------------------------------
    MyToday = DateTime.Today;

//------------------------------------------------------------
// Yesterday - date part only
//------------------------------------------------------------
MyYesterday = DateTime.Today;
MyYesterday.AddDays(-1);

//------------------------------------------------------------
// A month ago - date part only
//------------------------------------------------------------
MyMonthAgo = DateTime.Today ;
MyMonthAgo.AddMonths (-1) ;

//------------------------------------------------------------
// Last day of a month - February
//------------------------------------------------------------
MyDT = DateTime.Create(2020, 2, 1) ;
MyDT.AddMonths(1) ;
MyDT.AddDays(-1) ;
Print(String.format ("End of Feb: {0:MM/dd/yyyy}", MyDT)) ;

//------------------------------------------------------------
// Two ways of formatting a DateTime to a string
//------------------------------------------------------------
Print (String.format ("COMPOSITE FORMATTING: Today={0:MM/dd/yy}
Yesterday={1:MM/dd/yy} 1-month ago={2:MM/dd/yyyy}", MyToday,
MyYesterday, MyMonthAgo)) ;
Print ("DATETIME.FORMATTING:  Today=", MyToday.Format ("%m/%d/%y"), "
Yesterday=", MyYesterday.Format ("%m/%d/%y"), " 1-month ago=",
MyMonthAgo.Format ("%m/%d/%Y")) ;

//------------------------------------------------------------
```

```
// Now
//------------------------------------------------------------
MyNow = DateTime.Now ;
Print (String.format ("NOW = {0:MM/dd/yy HH:mm:ss}", MyNow));

MyNow.SetToCurrentTime() ;
Print (String.format ("NOW = {0:MM/dd/yy HH:mm:ss}", MyNow));

//------------------------------------------------------------
// Declare a specific date
//------------------------------------------------------------
MySpecificDate = DateTime.Create(2019, 12, 25) ;
Print (String.format ("XMAS = {0:MM/dd/yy HH:mm:ss}", MySpecificDate))
;
MySpecificDate = DateTime.Create(2019, 12, 25, 8, 15, 30) ;
Print(String.format ("XMAS = {0:MM/dd/yy HH:mm:ss}", MySpecificDate))
;

//------------------------------------------------------------
// Convert string into a DateTime US Format for date (m/d/y)
//------------------------------------------------------------
MySpecificDate = DateTime.Parse ("12/25/19 10:30:00") ;
Print (String.format ("'12/25/19 10:30:00' => {0:MM/dd/yyyy
HH:mm:ss}", MySpecificDate)) ;

MySpecificDate = DateTime.Parse ("12/25/29 10:30:00");
Print (String.format ("'12/25/30 10:30:00' => {0:MM/dd/yyyy HH:mm:ss}
- NOTE 21st Century", MySpecificDate)) ;

MySpecificDate = DateTime.Parse ("12/25/30 10:30:00") ;
Print (String.format("'12/25/30 10:30:00' ==> {0:MM/dd/yyyy HH:mm:ss}
- NOTE 20th Century", MySpecificDate)) ;

//------------------------------------------------------------
// String conversion handling non-US format
//------------------------------------------------------------
Print(NewLine + "DATETIME PARSE WITH NON-US STRING EXAMPLES");
    MySpecificDate = DateTime.Parse ("1/2/2020 ");
    Print (String.format ("'1/2/2020 using d/m/y ' ==> {0:MM/dd/yyyy
HH:mm:ss} - EXPECTING THIS TO BE Feb. 1, not Jan. 2",
MySpecificDate));

MySpecificDate = DateTime.Parse("13/12/2020 ");
Print (String.format ("'13/12/2020 using d/m/y ' ==> {0:MM/dd/yyyy
HH:mm:ss} - Handles correctly", MySpecificDate));

MySpecificDate = DateTime.Parse("11/12/2020 ");
Print (String.format ("'11/12/2020 using d/m/y ' => {0:MM/dd/yyyy
HH:mm:ss} - EXPECTING Dec. 11 BUT GET Nov 12",
MySpecificDate));

MySpecificDate = DateTime.Parse("2020/1/2 ");
Print (String.format ("'2020/1/2 using y/m/d ' => {0:MM/dd/yyyy
HH:mm:ss} - Handles correctly", MySpecificDate));

MySpecificDate = DateTime.Parse("2020/11/13 ") ;
Print (String.format ("'2020/11/13 using y/m/d ' => {0:MM/dd/yyyy
HH:mm:ss}-Handles correctly", MySpecificDate));

Try
```

```
  MySpecificDate = DateTime.Parse ("2020/13/11 ") ;
  Print (String.format ("'2020/13/11 using y/m/d ' => {0:MM/dd/yyyy
HH:mm:ss} - Handles correctly", MySpecificDate)) ;
Catch (Exception ex)
  Print ("2020/13/11 using y/m/d CAUSES AN EXCEPTION") ;
end ;

//-----------------------------------------------------------
// String conversion handling erroneous string
//-----------------------------------------------------------
Print (NewLine + "DATETIME PARSE WITH ERRONEOUS STRING EXAMPLES") ;
if not DateTime.TryParse ("12/45/30 10:30:00", MySpecificDate)
then begin
  Print (String.Format ("{0} string date invalid", "'12/45/30
10:30:00'")) ;
end ;

//-----------------------------------------------------------
// Display BarDateTime
//-----------------------------------------------------------
Print (NewLine + "DATETIME DISPLAY EXAMPLES") ;
MyBarDT = BarDateTime ;
Print (String.Format ("BarDateTime = {0:MM/dd/yy HH:mm:ss}", MyBarDT))
;

//-----------------------------------------------------------
// Comparison
//-----------------------------------------------------------
Print (NewLine + "DATETIME COMPARISON EXAMPLES") ;
MyBeforeDT = DateTime.Parse ("1/1/2020 08:00:00") ;
MyAfterDT = DateTime.Parse ("1/3/2020 10:15:00") ;
MyEqualAfterDT = DateTime.Parse("1/3/2020 10:00:00") ;

if  MyBeforeDT < MyAfterDT  then  Print (String.Format ("{0:MM/dd/yy
HH:mm:ss} < {1:MM/dd/yy HH:mm:ss}",
MyBeforeDT, MyAfterDT)) ;
If  MyAfterDT > MyBeforeDT  then  print (String.Format("{0:MM/dd/yy
HH:mm:ss} > {1:MM/dd/yy HH:mm:ss}", MyAfterDT, MyBeforeDT)) ;
if  MyAfterDT = MyEqualAfterDT  then  Print (String.Format
("{0:MM/dd/yy HH:mm:ss} = {1:MM/dd/yy HH:mm:ss}",  MyAfterDT,
MyEqualAfterDT)) ;

//-----------------------------------------------------------
// Conversion from Date and Time
//-----------------------------------------------------------
MyDT = DateTime.FromELDateAndTime (Date, Time);
Print(String.format("Converted Date and Time = {0:MM/dd/yyyy HH:mm:ss}
- Note 0 seconds", MyDT)) ;

MyDT = DateTime.FromELDateAndTime (Date, Time, 40);
Print (String.format ("Converted Date and Time = {0:MM/dd/yyyy
HH:mm:ss}", MyDT)) ;

//-----------------------------------------------------------
// DayOfWeek - A bit clumsy
//-----------------------------------------------------------
DOW = StrToNum(MyNow.Format("%w")) astype int ;
Print (String.Format ("DOW: #={0} {1:ddd} {1:dddd}", DOW, MyNow));

DOW = DayOfWeek (MyNow.ELDate) ;
Print (string.format ("DOW: #={0} {1:ddd} {1:dddd}", DOW, MyNow)) ;
```

```
//------------------------------------------------------------
//------------------------------------------------------------
// TIMESPAN CLASS
//------------------------------------------------------------
//------------------------------------------------------------
Print (NewLine + "TIMESPAN EXAMPLES");
MyTS = MyAfterDT - MyBeforeDT;
Print (string.format ("{0:MM/dd/yyyy HH:mm:ss} - {1:MM/dd/yyyy
HH:mm:ss} = {2:F2} " + "Total Days {3:F2} TotalHours {4:F2}
TotalMinutes {5:F2} TotalSeconds", MyAfterDT, MyBeforeDT,
MyTS.TotalDays, MyTS.TotalHours, MyTS.TotalMinutes,
MyTS.TotalSeconds)) ;

//------------------------------------------------------------
// Format TIMESPAN using method
//------------------------------------------------------------
Print (string.format ("Timespan Duration: {0}", FormatTimeSpan
(MyTS))) ;

//------------------------------------------------------------
// TimeOfDay Check with TimeSpans
//------------------------------------------------------------
MyDT = DateTime.Parse ("09:30") ;
MyTS = MyDT.TimeOfDay ;

If DateTime.Now.TimeOfDay  > MyTS
then begin
  print (String.Format ("{0:MM/dd/yy HH:mm:ss} time {01}",
DateTime.Now, MyTS)) ;
end
else begin
  print (String.Format ("{0:MM/dd/yy HH:mm:ss} time before or equal to
{1}",  DateTime.Now, MyTS)) ;
end ;

//------------------------------------------------------------
// Compute the difference between two DateTimes
//------------------------------------------------------------
MyDT1 = DateTime.Parse("12/30/2019 09:30:00") ;
MyDT2 = DateTime.Parse("1/2/2020 11:15:00") ;
MyTS = MyDT2 - MyDT1 ;

Print(String.Format("Total Days = {0:F2}", MyTS.TotalDays)) ;
Print(String.Format("Total Hours = {0:F2}", MyTS.TotalHours)) ;
Print(String.Format("Total Minutes = {0:F2}", MyTS.TotalMinutes)) ;

Print (NewLine + "MORE DATETIME EXAMPLES") ;

End ;

//------------------------------------------------------------
// Check for new Date
//------------------------------------------------------------
if  BarDateTime.Day <> BarDateTime[1].Day
and BarStatus(Datanum + 1) = 02
then begin
    Print (String.Format ("FirstBar Of New Day: {0:MM/dd/yyyy
HH:mm:ss}", BarDateTime)) ;
End ;
```

```
//----------------------------------------------------------
// END OF CODE
//----------------------------------------------------------
#endRegion
```

And now here's the output from the **Print Log**:

```
Last Day of Feb: 02/29/2020
COMPOSITE FORMATTING: Today=02/19/20 Yesterday=02/18/20 1-month
ago=01/19/2020
DATETIME.FORMATTING:  Today=02/19/20 Yesterday=02/18/20 1-month
ago=01/19/2020
NOW = 02/19/20 10:47:41
NOW = 02/19/20 10:47:41
XMAS = 12/25/19 00:00:00
XMAS = 12/25/19 08:15:30
'12/25/19 10:30:00' => 12/25/2019 10:30:00
'12/25/30 10:30:00' => 12/25/2029 10:30:00 - NOTE 21st Century
'12/25/30 10:30:00' => 12/25/1930 10:30:00 - NOTE 20th Century
```

FIGURE 2.07—Output to the Print Log for DateTime Example

```
'1/2/2020 using d/m/y ' ==> 01/02/2020 00:00:00 - EXPECTING THIS TO BE
Feb. 1, not Jan. 2
'13/12/2020 using d/m/y ' => 12/13/2020 00:00:00 - Handles correctly
'11/12/2020 using d/m/y ' => 11/12/2020 00:00:00 - EXPECTING Dec. 11
BUT GET Nov 12
'2020/1/2 using y/m/d ' => 01/02/2020 00:00:00 - Handles correctly
'2020/11/13 using y/m/d ' => 11/13/2020 00:00:00 - Handles correctly
2020/13/11 using y/m/d CAUSES AN EXCEPTION
```

FIGURE 2.08—Output to the Print Log for DateTime Parse Example

```
'12/45/30 10:30:00' string date invalid
```

FIGURE 2.09—DateTime Parse with Erroneous String

```
BarDateTime = 02/11/20 08:40:00
1/01/20 08:00:00 < 01/03/20 10:15:00
01/03/20 10:15:00 > 01/01/20 08:00:00
Converted Date and Time = 02/11/2020 08:40:00 - Note 0 seconds
Converted Date and Time = 02/11/2020 08:40:40
DOW: #=3 Wed Wednesday
DOW: #=3 Wed Wednesday
```

FIGURE 2.10—DateTime Display Examples

```
01/01/20 08:00:00 < 01/03/20 10:15:00
01/03/20 10:15:00 > 01/01/20 08:00:00
Converted Date and Time = 02/11/2020 08:40:00 - Note 0 seconds
Converted Date and Time = 02/11/2020 08:40:40
DOW: #=3 Wed Wednesday
DOW: #=3 Wed Wednesday
```

FIGURE 2.11—DateTime Comparison Examples

```
01/03/2020 10:15:00 - 01/01/2020 08:00:00 = 2.09 Total Days  50.25
TotalHours  3015.00 TotalMinutes  180900.00 TotalSeconds
Timespan Duration: 2.02:15:00
02/19/20 10:47:41 time is after 0. 9.30. 0. 0
Total Days = 3.07
Total Hours = 73.75
```

```
Total Minutes = 4425.00
```

FIGURE 2.12—TimeSpan Examples

```
FirstBar Of New Day: 02/12/2020 08:35:00
FirstBar Of New Day: 02/13/2020 08:35:00
FirstBar Of New Day: 02/14/2020 08:35:00
FirstBar Of New Day: 02/18/2020 08:35:00
FirstBar Of New Day: 02/19/2020 08:35:00
```

FIGURE 2.13—More DateTime Examples

Switch...Case

There are times when you want to do A if X happens and B if Y happens and C if Z happens. Rather than write a string of **If** statements (and the possibilities for your choices could be many) EZL has a convenient statement block to allow you to line them up and knock them down with far fewer statements and less computer resources.

Let us assume that you want to align your text depending on something you have predetermined. You have a default case (it is always good practice to include a default, so you don't end up with a value out of bounds) of "centered" which is what you want most of the time and depending on your conditions you want it either right- or left-justified. For this you can use the **Switch...Case** block as follows:

EXAMPLE 2.57—Using Switch...Case to Designate Horizontal Styles

```
begin
   switch myStyle begin
     case 00 : hStyle  = HorizontalStyle.Right ;
     case 01 : hStyle  = HorizontalStyle.Left ;
     case 02 : hStyle  = HorizontalStyle.Center ;
     default : hStyle  = HorizontalStyle.Center ;
   end ;  // switch/case statement
end ;
```

☑ Though the Switch statement does require a Begin...End block a Case statement within the Switch does not require a Begin...End block though you can use them if it makes it easier to read and understand.

EXAMPLE 2.58—Switch...Case with Begin...End

```
Switch (value1)
Begin
  Case 02: value2 = 00 ;
  Default: value2 = 01 ;
end;  // switch/case statement
```

With a **Switch...Case** block control passes to the statements whose case-expression matches the value of the switch (expression). The **Switch** statement can include any number of **Case** instances, but no two **Case** constants within the same **Switch** statement can have the same constant value.

☑ Once the statements associated with a matching case are evaluated, control passes to the end of the switch statement. This is an implied break and is different than a similar structure found in some other languages that require an explicit break.

REMARKS

A single case statement can carry multiple values, as the following example shows:

```
Case 1, 2, 3, 4, 5, 6, 20: Value1 = Lowest (Close, 03) ;
```

Ranges like this are also valid:

```
     Case 1 to 6, 20: Value2 = Highest (High, 05) ;
```

In both examples above, if case-expression equals any number between 1 and 6 or equal to 20, a function is called and assigned to a value.

In addition, logical operators may be used with case statements including: >, <, >=, <=, <> and =.

```
     Case > Average (Close, 50): Value1 = Close ;
```

You can also use the EZL skip word "is" for better clarity as in the following:

```
     Case is < Average (High, 75) : Value1 = High ;
```

EXAMPLE 2.59—Using Switch and Case

```
Switch (Value1) Begin
   Case 1 to 5:
     Value2 = Value2 + 1 ;
   Case 10, 20, 30 :
     Value3 = Highest (High,10) ;
   Case is > 40:
     Value3 = Value3 + 1 ;
   Default:
     Value5 = Value5 + 1 ;
End ; // switch/case statement
```

The above **Switch** statement increments `Value2` when the **Switch** expression (`Value1`) is a value from 1 to 5; assigns `Value3` to the highest high of 10 bars ago when the **Switch** expression is either 10, 20 or 30; increments `Value4` for all switch expression values above 40; and increments `Value5` for any other values of the **Switch** expression.

A Brief Interlude

Before stepping into the next section, I need to tell you a bit about Classes, Methods, and the other strange words we will get into as we proceed to OOEL structures. I need to give you some OOEL concepts before we get to the next section.

I hate to jump ahead a chapter but, I need to for just a second. You will spend lots of time as you learn OOEL exploring the Dictionary. You need some guidance in the beginning. In the table below are little graphics characters you are about to encounter which have their own special significance.

Look at the following table and you will have had your second exposure to OOEL. These are the possible symbols and their meanings. I know it won't mean a lot to you yet, but when you explore the Dictionary, it will help to know the symbols. This table appears again in Chapter 4.

Symbol	Meaning
◇	Class
▱	Enumeration
⚡	Event
⚒	Library
◆	Method or Function
{}	Namespace or Category
≚	Operator
▣	Property
◈	Reserved Word

TABLE 2.13—Dictionary Exploration Aid

Do it now. Bring up the TDE and then find the little icon that is third from the right and looks like 🗗

. This takes you to the Dictionary. (I said third because under the narrow pulldown icon with a ▼ lies Add or Remove Buttons. Do not forget to check that tiny, lower down-arrow because if your window is sized small then the buttons may be off screen, but the command should appear in that pull down!

FIGURE 2.14—Finding the Dictionary on the Toolbar

Having found and clicked on the Dictionary icon (do this, at least, several times because muscle memory is built through successful repetition), you are presented with a list, shown in Figure 2.15 The first view is of the available Libraries in the TDE. Clicking on the ⊞ symbol in front of any of the choices will allow you to explore what lives beneath that library. For now, I just want you to know that it is there. The selection you will want to explore for now is the **easylanguage.ell** library, where you will find all the EZL terms with which you are already familiar. Take a moment to search for several of the terms we have introduced previously in this chapter, or anything that catches your eye. Remember – repetition!

Figure 2.15 shows the first view of the Dictionary with 10 Libraries exposed. To explore further, just click on a ⊞ sign.

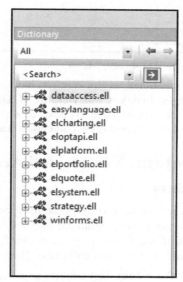

FIGURE 2.15—On First Clicking on the Dictionary Icon

The EZL commands you are already familiar with are shown under the second listing on Figure 2.16, **easylanguage.ell**. In Figure 2.16 I've opened up the menu (unfolded) so you can see what is accessible there.

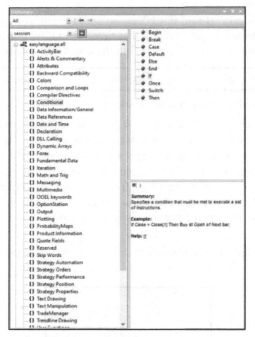

FIGURE 2.16—The EasyLanguage.ell (Library) Menu

In this figure I have clicked on **{} Conditional**, as I'm sure you have seen these terms before. Notice in the right panel that you can see **Begin**, **Break**, **Case**, **Default**, **If**, **Once**, **Switch** and **Then**. I'll leave it to you to click on the symbol beside each of those terms to see what lies beneath. Remember to look the symbols chart in Tables 2.13 or 4.04, **Dictionary Exploration Aid** to see what the symbols signify.

TokenLists, Vectors and Arrays

A Brief Look at TokenLists

TokenLists are much like vectors in that they contain multiple entries (a collection that is not in **elSystem.Collections**), though these are comma delimited like a .CSV file. The list must contain one or more string values as a collection of items. Any text or item added, updated, or inserted that contains commas will have separate items added to the item collection. Duplicate values may be added.

That's almost all I'm going to say about **TokenList** Objects until we get into **Chapter 8** and discuss **Vector** and **Array** Classes more in-depth.

More on Vectors and Arrays

Vectors (OOEL) and **Arrays** (Classic/Legacy EZL) are structures that allow for multiple values inside a single reference. For instance, this is one way to visualize a vector: (0, 1, 1, 2, 3, 5, 8, 13). There are eight components in the vector, all Fibonacci numbers. This can also be visualized as a one-dimensional spreadsheet.

323.55	420	375.6	779.4	123.4

FIGURE 2.17—Visualizing a Vector

Another mental image would be a row of mailboxes on a postal route in a Rural Route, or even a bank of mailboxes (two dimensional) in an apartment lobby.

To refer to cells in the vector we address them much like in a spreadsheet, only not quite. While a spreadsheet has A B C at the top to refer to the columns and 1 2 3 down the side to reference the rows, elements in an EZL vector are referred to as Vector(0), Vector(1), Vector(3) etc. It can be a bit confusing as vectors and arrays both start their numbering from zero (0). Generally, we do not put anything in the 0 element, but you must nevertheless know it is there.

In essence a vector is a one-dimensional array. The power of vectors is seen when you realize that the contents don't have to be characters, strings, or numerals. You can also include objects in a vector!

Arrays, on the other hand, can be multi-dimensional. In the figure below we have a visualization of an array that is four cells by four cells.

3100.50	3065.25	3222.75	2511.25
3104.50	3076.25	3245.50	2389.50
3126.75	3086.25	3254.00	2458.00
3124.50	3076.25	3248.50	2424.25

FIGURE 2.18—Visualizing a Two-Dimensional Array

We will look at Vectors and **Vector** Class in Chapter 8.

Arrays

The words **Array** and **Arrays** are used synonymously to declare variables that can contain multiple data elements.

REMARKS

The declaration of an array creates a name that refers to a grouped set of data elements within an Analysis Technique (AT); these arrays can be numeric values, True/False comparisons, or strings. Arrays allow you to group and reference data elements with an index number. This is where Loops become powerful. Like variables you can organize and annotate your code with functional names that describe the nature of the calculation or purpose of the data.

Arrays in EZL start at data element zero, however, all built-in functions that operate on arrays ignore the zero element, so it is advised not to use the zero element.

An array may be described as a table of variables. That is, an array can hold many values just as a single variable holds a single value. You are already comfortable using arrays when you refer to Open, High, Low and Close since they are arrays. It's not that different. For instance, High of 01 bar ago is referring to the next to last element in the High array. Using an array has the advantage of allowing manipulation of the values in all or part of the array at once. That is, all the values can be averaged or sorted as a group. This would be a much more difficult task with individual variables. Additionally, an array is convenient for storing and retrieving values that occur on intermittent or non-consecutive bars. As an example, consider Inside Bars, Key Reversals or Pivot Points.

The elements in an array may be organized in a single dimension or multiple dimensions. Once again, in spreadsheet terms, a 1-dimensional array has 1 column; a 2-dimensional array has multiple columns and rows; a 3-dimensional array has two 2-dimensional spreadsheets one on top of the other. (Width, Height and Depth or Volume, Weight, and Distance). The human mind has trouble comprehending more than a three-dimensional Array but with sketches and diagrams you can model it out.

The **Array** reserved word has two forms: **Arrays** and **Array**, each is functionally equivalent, and each must be followed by a colon (:) then a list of array names separated by commas (,) .

> ✎ Array names like variables are unique to the AT they are declared in; you can use the same name over again in any other AT, but you cannot use the same name within the same AT, for example, declaring an array with the same name as a variable. Also, remember to avoid naming arrays with the same name as an EZL reserved word.

USAGE (COMMON)

Array: ArrayName (Value) ;

Where `ArrayName` is the unique name of the user-declared array, and `Value` is either a Numeric, True/False or String value used as the initial value of the array.

USAGE (COMPLETE)

> ☑ The angled brackets (less than and greater than) used in the declarations below denote that the parameter is optional. The angled brackets themselves are never typed into EZL code in this context.

Array: <IntraBarPersist> <DataType> ArrayName (InitialValue<,datan>) <, <IntraBarPersist> <DataType> ArrayName (InitialValue<,DataN>)> ;

Array is the array declaration statement that may alternately be typed as Arrays.

IntraBarPersist indicates that this array's values can be updated on every tick. By default, array values are only updated at the close of each bar. If you ever need IntraBarPersist (IBP) on an array, consider using a Vector instead.

DataType is the optionally supplied data type (float, double, int, bool, string) of the array, typically used to conserve memory.

ArrayName is the user specified array name that can be up to a ridiculous number of characters long (in the past limited to 20) and must begin with an alphabetic character (names are not case sensitive)

InitialValue is the initial value of the array elements which may determine the DataType of the Array.

DataN is an optional parameter that identifies the data stream the array is tied to and may be data1 through data50.

Fixed Length Arrays

The declaration of a fixed length array must specify the maximum element reference number and given an initial default value for each element; arrays are generally initialized to 0 but can be initial set to any useful value.

EXAMPLE 2.60—Single-Dimension Array Declaration

```
Array: WeeklyHighs[52](0.00), WeeklyLow[52](0.00) ;
```

(Declares a single dimension 53 element array of integers, 0 to 52, and initializes each element to 0)

EXAMPLE 2.61—Multi-Dimensional Array Declaration

```
Arrays: VolumeHighs[05,20](00), VolumeLow[05,20](00) ;
```

(Declares a two-dimensional array, 6 elements by 21 elements, or 126 elements, and initializes each element to 0)

An **Input** or a **Constant** can be used to declare the size of a Fixed-Length Array:

```
Consts:
  Int    MaxRows (100),
  Int    MaxCols (05) ;
Arrays:
  Double myArray [MaxRows, MaxCols] (Close) ;
```

Declares a 101 x 6 Data Structure (Array) initialized to the first bar's Close.

> ☑ Remember to avoid using data element zero if you are going to use any of the built-in array functions.

Dynamic Arrays

The declaration of a dynamic array is the same as that of a fixed array except that the maximum element reference number is left blank. At this time, only single dimension dynamic arrays are supported.

EXAMPLE 2.62—Dynamic Array

For example, to declare a dynamic array of integers named `MyDynamicIntArray` you would type the following into your EZL Analysis Technique:

```
Array: int MyDynamicIntArray[](00) ;
```

And to set the third element to 1 you would have to first increase the size of the array and then assign the value as follows:

```
Array_SetMaxIndex(MyDynamicIntArray, 10) ;
MyDynamicIntArray[2] = 01 ;
// note that [2] is the third element since arrays
// are zero-based
```

Other than having to resize the dynamic array prior to use dynamic arrays will behave exactly as existing Arrays do (though slower). Note that while you can use a dynamic array in place of an existing array the reverse is not true. The new dynamic array functions will not accept static arrays as inputs which is due to the fact the dynamic and static arrays are treated differently internally.

Array Usage

Arrays are often used with loops to store values based on successive calculations that use a counter as an index number. Because EZL allocates space for each index number, avoid declaring an array larger than necessary.

EXAMPLE 2.63—Single-Dimension Array Declaration

```
Array: WeeklyHighs[52](0), WeeklyLow[52](0)
```

(declares a single dimension 53 element array, 0 to 52, and initializes each element to 0).

EXAMPLE 2.64—Assigning Values to a Single-Dimension Array in a Loop

```
Vars  : Loop (00) ;
Arrays: PrevCloses [05] (00) ;
For  Loop = 01 to 05 begin
  PrevCloses [Loop]  = Close [Loop] ;
End ; // for loop
```

EXAMPLE 2.65—Retrieving Values from a Single-Dimension Array in a Loop

```
Vars  : Loop (00), SumCloses (0.00) ;
Arrays: PrevCloses[05](00) ;
SumCloses  = 00 ;
For  Loop = 01 to 05  begin
  SumCloses  = SumCloses + PrevCloses[Loop] ;
End ; // for loop
```

EXAMPLE 2.66—Multidimensional Array Declaration

```
Array: VolumeHighs[05,20](00), VolumeLows[05,20](00) ;
```

(Declares a two-dimensional array, 6 elements by 21 elements, or 126 elements, and initializes each element to 00)

> ☑ Remember to avoid using data element zero if you are going to use any of the built-in array functions.

Array names like variables are unique to the study they are declared in; you can use the same name over again in any other study, but you cannot use the same name within the same study, for example, declaring an array with the same name as a variable. Also, remember to avoid naming arrays with the same name as an EZL reserved word.

A number of reserved words are available for use with dynamic arrays, including; **Array_Compare**, **Array_Copy**, **Array_GetMaxIndex**, **Array_GetType**, **Array_SetMaxIndex**, **Array_SetValRange**, **Array_Sort**, and **Array_Sum**.

These are defined in the next sections.

Array_Compare

This reserved function compares a range of elements between the first and second dynamic array and returns an integer value identifying any differences.

USAGE

```
Array_Compare(SrcArrayName, SrcElement, DestArrayName, DestElement,
NumElements);
```

RETURN

A value of 0 will be returned if all respective elements in the range of `NumElements` for both arrays are equal. If they are not, the following values will be returned:

+1 A value in the range of `SrcArrayName` is greater than its counterpart in `DestArrayName`.

-1 A value in the range of `SrcArrayName` is less than its counterpart in `DestArrayName`.

+2 An error has occurred in the comparison (incompatible array types, Out of Bounds range error, etc.).

PARAMETERS

Name	Description
SrcArrayName	Name that identifies the first dynamic array to compare and is the name given in the array declaration.
SrcElement	An integer representing the starting element to begin comparing in the first array.
DestArrayName	Name that identifies the second dynamic array to compare with and is the name given in the array declaration.
DestElement	An integer representing the starting element to begin comparing in the second array.
NumElements	An integer representing the number of elements to compare.

TABLE 2.14—Array Compare Parameters

EXAMPLE 2.67—Comparing Elements of an Array

Compares a range of 6 array elements starting with element 4 of the first dynamic array to element 5 of a second dynamic array.

```
Array_Compare (FirstArray, 04, SecondArray, 05, 06) ;
```

Array_Copy

This reserved function copies `NumElements` elements from the dynamic array identified by `SrcArrayName` starting with the element at `SrcElement` and copies them to the array identified by `DestArrayName` starting with the element at `DestElement`. The `SrcArrayName` and `DestArrayName` can be the same value and in the case of an overlap this function will ensure that the original source elements are copied before being overwritten.

USAGE

Array_Copy (SrcArrayName, SrcElement, DestArrayname, DestElement, NumElements) ;

RETURN

A value of 0 will be returned if the copy is successful, otherwise one of the following values will be returned:

-1 Unknown error

-2 Invalid ScrArrayName or DestArrayName

-3 Invalid SrcElement or DestElement

-4 Destination array is different type than source array

-5 Invalid or out of range NumElements

PARAMETERS

Name	Description
SrcArrayName	Name that identifies the dynamic array to copy from and is the name given in the array declaration
SrcElement	An integer representing the starting element to begin copying from in the source array.
DestArrayName	Name that identifies the dynamic array to copy to and is the name given in the array declaration
DestElement	An integer representing the starting element to begin copying to in the destination array.
NumElements	An integer representing the number of elements to copy.

TABLE 2.15—Array_Copy Parameters

This next one copies a range of 12 array elements from element 5 of the first dynamic array to element 8 of a second dynamic array:

```
Array_Copy (FirstArray, 05, SecondArray, 08, 12) ;
```

Array_GetMaxIndex

Returns the index of the last element of a dynamic array. Note that the actual number of elements that an array can hold is the MaxIndex+1.

USAGE

Array_GetMaxIndex (ArrayName) ;

RETURN

An integer value greater than or equal to 0 will be returned if the function is successful. This value is equivalent to the MaxIndex value used when declaring a static array.

PARAMETERS

Name	Description
ArrayName	Identifies the dynamic array for which you want to get the size and is the name given in the array declaration.

TABLE 2.16—Array_GetMaxIndex Parameters

EXAMPLE 2.68—Getting the Size of an Array

Value2 will contain the maximum index value of 8 for the specified dynamic array.

```
Array: MyDynArray[](0) ;
Condition1 = Array_SetMaxIndex (MyDynArray, 8) ;
//… other easylanguage statements
Value2 = Array_GetMaxIndex (MyDynArray) ;
```

Array_GetType

Identifies the data type of the elements in the dynamic array identified by ArrayName

USAGE

Array_GetType (ArrayName) ;

RETURN

A value of -1 will be returned if `ArrayName` is invalid, otherwise the function will return one of the following values:

    1 - Unknown

    2 - Boolean

    3 - String

    4 - Integer

    6 - Float

    7 - Double

PARAMETERS

Name	Description
ArrayName	Identifies the dynamic array to inspect and is the name given in the array declaration.

TABLE 2.17—Array_GetType Parameters

`Value2` with a type of 4 (integer) for the specified dynamic array:

```
Arrays: int MyDynArray [] (00) ;
Condition1 = Array_SetMaxIndex (MyDynArray, 08) ;
//… other EasyLanguage statements
Value2 = Array_GetType (MyDynArray) ;
```

Array_SetMaxIndex

Resizes a dynamic array. A dynamic array can be made larger or smaller and if made larger each new element will be initialized to the value used when the dynamic array was first created.

USAGE

Array_SetMaxIndex (ArrayName, MaxIndex) ;

PARAMETERS

Name	Description
ArrayName	Identifies the dynamic array to resize and is the name given in the array declaration.
MaxIndex	An integer representing the index of the last element and is equivalent to the MaxIndex value used when declaring a static array. This value can be greater than or equal to 0.

TABLE 2.18—Array_SetMaxIndex Parameters

REMARKS

Returns a Boolean value indicating success or failure.

EXAMPLE 2.69—Changing the Size of a Dynamic Array

Changes the size of a newly created dynamic array to a maximum index value of 7.

```
Arrays: MyDynArray[] (00) ;
//..other easylanguage statements
Condition1 = Array_SetMaxIndex (MyDynArray, 07) ;
```

Array_SetValRange

This reserved function places the value `Val` into each element of the dynamic array identified by `ArrayName` starting with element `BegElementNum` and ending with element `EndElementNum`.

USAGE

Array_SetValRange (ArrayName, BegElementNum, EndElementNum, Val) ;

RETURN

A value of 0 will be returned if the function is successful in setting the values, otherwise one of the following values will be returned:

- -1 - Unknown error
- -2 - Invalid ArrayName
- -3 - BegElementNum or EndElementNumB is out of range
- -4 - Val is wrong type

PARAMETERS

Name	Description
ArrayName	Identifies the source dynamic array to compare and is the name given in the array declaration.
BegElementNum	An integer representing the first element in the range of values to be set to the value Val.
EndElementNum	An integer representing the last element in the range of values to be set to the value Val.
Val	Identifies the value to be set and can be a Boolean, string, integer, float or double.

TABLE 2.19—Array_SetValName Parameters

Sets elements 5 through 12 of the specified array to a string value of "OK".

```
Value1 = Array_SetValRange (MyDynArray, 05, 12, "OK") ;
```

Array_Sort

This reserved function sorts a range of elements in a dynamic array in either ascending or descending order.

USAGE

Array_Sort (ArrayName, BegElementNum, EndElementNum, SortOrder) ;

RETURN

An integer value of 0 will be returned if the function is successful in setting the value else one of the following values will be returned:

- -1 - Unknown error
- -2 - Invalid `ArrayName`
- -3 - `BegElementNum` or `EndElementNum` is out of range
- -4 - `SortOrder` is invalid

PARAMETERS

Name	Description
ArrayName	Identifies the source dynamic array containing elements to be sorted and is

Name	Description
	the name given in the array declaration
BegElementNum	An integer representing the first element in the range of sorted values.
EndElementNum	An integer representing the last element in the range of sorted values.
SortOrder	A True/False value that specifies if the sort is Ascending (True) or Descending (False).

TABLE 2.20—Array_Sort Parameters

Performs an ascending sort on the specified dynamic array from elements 1 through 5.

```
Value1 = Array_Sort0 (MyDynArray, 01, 05, True) ;
```

Array_Sum

This reserved function that sums a range of elements in the specified dynamic array.

USAGE

Array_Sum (ArrayName, BegElementNum, EndElementNum) ;

RETURN

Returns the numeric sum of the values in the specified range If the array contains string or Boolean (True/False) elements, a 0 is returned.

Returns the numeric sum of the values in the specified range. If the array contains string elements, a 0 is returned. If the array contains Boolean (True/False) elements, the number of True elements is returned.

PARAMETERS

Name	Description
ArrayName	Identifies the source dynamic array containing elements to be summed and is the name given in the array declaration.
BegElementNum	An integer representing the first element in the range of values to be summed.
EndElementNum	An integer representing the last element in the range of values to be summed.

TABLE 2.21—Array_Sum Parameters

EXAMPLE 2.70—Adding the Values in a Dynamic Array

Value1 will contain the sum of values contained in the specified dynamic array from elements 4 through 10.

```
Value1 = Array_Sum (MyDynArray, 04, 10) ;
```

Summary

It has been a heady chapter, but well worth it. Lots of logic has been required.

We have introduced concepts perhaps better covered in an elementary or intermediate book about EZL. But before we get into the really difficult stuff, I wanted to refresh a few concepts for you. These topics included variables, constants, strings, Boolean algebra, user functions, loops, strings, and switch…case. And more.

We have covered a broad range of topics from the **TokenList** and Vector Classes to Arrays and Array manipulation tools. We have also discussed Fixed Length (Static) Arrays and Dynamic Arrays. Why discuss Arrays here when this is supposed to be an OOEL book? Because it is not covered elsewhere.

The next chapter covers EZL Intricacies and Advanced EZL topics.

CHAPTER 3
EasyLanguage Intricacies

In This Chapter

- Introduction
- Spaces
- Alerts
- Run Command
- At$
- Analysis Commentary
- Chart Type Reserved Word Values
- Using ASCII 3rd Party Data
- PlaySound

- PlayMovieChain
- RaiseRunTimeError
- InfoBox
- Hello_World! #2
- Time and Sales
- Currency Conversion
- Utilization Monitor
- Summary

Introduction

H ere we have a conglomeration of some more esoteric features not covered elsewhere. They range from useful tools to shortcuts.

This chapter is a refresher of some of the important EZL features with which you should already be familiar before you even dream of venturing into OOEL programming. You should have a firm grasp of these basic Classic EZL terms and their proper usage before delving too deeply into OOEL because everything is based on these building blocks.

Spaces

Spaces adds the specified number of blank spaces into the line of text output by using this format:

```
Print (Spaces (Cnt)) ;
```

Cnt is the numeric expression indicating the number of spaces to be inserted.

EXAMPLE 3.01—Adding Spaces to Your Strings

```
Print ("Close" + Spaces (05) + NumToStr (Close, 03)) ;
```

The above example results in five blank spaces between the string "Close" and the closing price.

Alerts

Alerts can be very handy when using an indicator that could use an alarm-type popup box to alert you to some condition. For example, I have alerts on my SunnyBands© indicator to tell me when price crosses over or under the bands, and when it crosses the midline.

I'll show you what I mean. By ⊕ Double-Clicking on the indicator, TS brings up a popup that has several choices: General, Inputs, Alerts, Style, Color, Scaling and Advanced. Select the Alerts choice. Now you have the following to choose from, Figure 3.01. If you check the ☒ Enable Alert choice you get more choices. Do you want the alert to sound once, once per bar, or continuously? I usually choose continuously so it's really annoying and gets my attention. Then I can turn it off when I have reacted to the alert.

I also like the **Use the global messaging** preferences. See Figure 3.01. Check the radio button and then click the ⬚Configure... button. This will take you to Notification Preferences where you can choose your sound, whether you want a visual notification and whether you want to send an email or text to yourself, or even to another person. Think about alerting your clients. The only trick to this one is you must know your SMTP (Simple Message Transfer Protocol) address to make it work. In Chapter 9 we are going to address setting Alerts for Drawing Objects in OOEL.

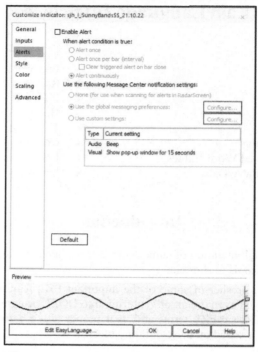

FIGURE 3.01—The Alerts Box

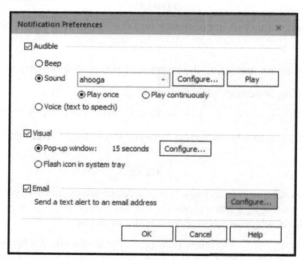

FIGURE 3.02—The Configuration Box for Notification Preferences

Here below are the statements you may use when creating and using the Alerts.

Name	Brief Description
#BEGINALERT	Instructions between #BEGINALERT and #END are only executed if the alert is enabled for the Analysis Technique.
#BEGINCMTRYORALERT	Instructions between #BEGINCMTRYORALERT and #END when either the Alert or Commentary conditions

Name	Brief Description
	exist.
#END	Used to terminate an alert or Commentary block statement.
Alert	When True, triggers an alert for an indicator or study. The alert description is optional.
AlertEnabled	Returns True if the Enable Alert check box is selected. Note that at the time of this writing AlertEnabled is broken; it behaves exactly as CheckAlert.
Cancel	Used in conjunction with Alert to cancel a previously triggered alert.
CheckAlert	Returns True for the last bar when Enable Alert check box is selected.
OneAlert	Alert only once per bar.
Pager_DefaultName	Returns the string containing of the default Message Recipient as specified in the Messaging tab under the File → Desktop Options menu.
Pager_Send	Sends a text message to a specified pager recipient (if pager module enabled).
PlaySound	Plays the specified sound file (.wav file).
RunCommand	Allows you to run a Command Line instruction or Macro from within an EZL Study.
RunCommandOnLastBar	Allows you to run a Command Line instruction or Macro from within an EZL Study.
elSystem.Environment.Start	Allows you to run an external program.
TL_GetAlert	Gets the alert status of a specified trendline.
TL_SetAlert	Sets the alert status for a specified trendline.

TABLE 3.01—Useful Statements When Issuing Alerts

EXAMPLE 3.02—Alerts in SunnyBands© Indicator

```
#BeginAlert
If  CheckAlert  then begin
// Alert criteria
  if  Price1 crosses over UpperInnerBand
  then  Alert ("Cross OVER UPPER INNER SunnyBand", "Symbol")
  else
    if  Price2 crosses under LowerInnerBand
    then Alert ("Cross UNDER LOWER INNER SunnyBand") ;
end ;
#end
```

Here's what my SunnyBands indicator looks like on a chart: When price penetrates the bands, the Alert pops up.

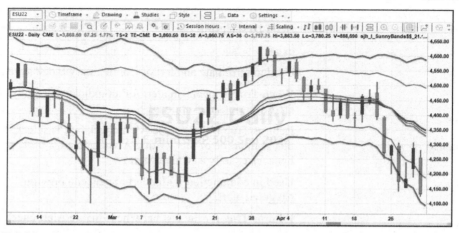

FIGURE 3.03—SunnyBands

EXAMPLE 3.03—Alerts from Sam's AME

An example from Sam's *Ask Mr. EasyLanguage* page 108:

```
If CheckAlert then Alert = FastMA crosses above SlowMA ;
```

Then he states that he prefers the following method:

```
If CheckAlert then begin
  If  FastMA crosses above SlowMA  then  Alert = TRUE ;
End ;
```

> Actually, this is very old technology (you could not even pass in a string of text) and I (Sam) have moved on to much rather more sophisticated Alert handling. You can probably find an example somewhere in the OME files, or I can write an article for my Vista-Research FaceBook page (https://www.facebook.com/VistaResearch/).

Sometimes you don't want the alert to sound on every single tick. I trade a 5-minute chart and it can get really annoying to have the alert constantly sounding. Fixing this is as simple as a setting in the Alerts box.

🖰 Right-Click on the indicator and bring up the Customize Indicator control box. Next click on the Alerts choice (third one down) and select Enable Alert and the Radio Button that says Alert once per bar (interval) and check the box that says Clear triggered alert on bar close. Now it will only sound the alert when the bar closes.

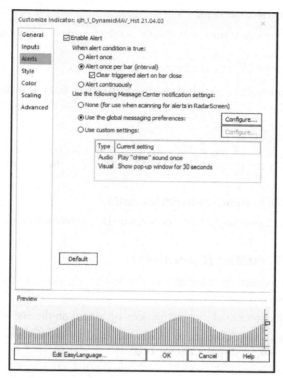

FIGURE 3.04—Alert on Bar Close

RunCommand

RunCommand allows you to run a Command Line instruction or Macro from within any EZL study.

EZL does not check the validity of the string that is specified for the keyword. If the command is not valid, a message will be displayed in the Events Log.

This command is intended for advanced users who understand how create EZL code for use in charting applications that utilize macros.

USAGE

RunCommand (CommandOrMacro) ;

PARAMETERS

Name	Type	Description
CommandOrMacro	String	Sets a string value that is either a command line MACRO, or an actual command line instruction sequence.

TABLE 3.02—RunCommand

See Command Line Reference in **Volume II—Reference Guide** for a list of supported command line strings.

REMARKS

You cannot historically back-test the results of orders placed into the market with RunCommand.

> ☑ If the Update value intra-bar check box is enabled in a study or strategy that calls the reserved word 'RunCommand', it could execute the Command Line instructions or Macro on every tick causing unintended processing issues.

EXAMPLE 3.04—Using RunCommand

Run the 'CustBuyMarket' macro if time is 10:00am and the Close price is greater than the Open price.

```
If  Time = 1000 AND Close > Open  Then
   Value1 = RunCommand (".CustBuyMarket MSFT, 500") ;
```

Run the three command line instructions if Condition1 is TRUE. Each instruction set can contain one or more command sets.

```
If  Condition1  Then Begin
   Value1=RunCommand(".NWS") ;
   Value1=RunCommand (".BuyLimit MSFT, 500 ;; .NewChart;; MSFT") ;
   Value1=RunCommand (".BuyLimit DELL, 500 ;; .NewChart;; DELL") ;
End ;
```

RunCommand is called from **RunCommandOnLastBar**.

To view all the appropriate Command Lines, see Volume II—Reference Guide, Appendix V: Reserved Words.

RunCommandOnLastBar (Function)

The **RunCommandOnLastBar** function allows you to run a Command Line instruction or Macro from within any EZL study.

This function only runs the command line instructions or Macro on the last bar of data.

EZL does not check the validity of the string that is specified for the keyword. If the command is not valid, a message will be displayed in the Events Log.

USAGE

RunCommandOnLastBar(CommandOrMacro);

RETURNS (INTEGER)

The value **1** when it runs on the last bar of data, otherwise it returns **0**.

PARAMETERS

Name	Type	Description
CommandOrMacro	String	Sets a string value that is either a command line MACRO, or an actual command line instruction sequence.

TABLE 3.03—RunComandOnLastBar Parameters

REMARKS

You cannot historically back-test the results of orders place into the market with **RunCommandOnLastBar**.

If the Update value intra-bar check box is enabled in an Indicator that calls the reserved word **RunCommand**, it could execute the command line instructions or MACRO on every tick, this is probably not what you are intending.

EXAMPLE 3.05—Using RunCommandOnLastBar

Run the 'CustBuyMarket' MACRO if time is 10:00am and the Close price is greater than the Open price.

```
If Time = 1000 AND Close > Open Then
   Value1 = RunCommandOnLastBar (".CustBuyMarket MSFT, 500") ;
```

Run the function three times if Condition1 is True. Each instruction set can contain one or more command sets.

```
If  Condition1  Then Begin
```

```
    Value1=RunCommandOnLastBar (".NWS") ;
    Value1=RunCommandOnLastBar(".BuyLimit MSFT, 500 ;; .NewChart;;
MSFT");
    Value1=RunCommandOnLastBar(".BuyLimit DELL, 500 ;; .NewChart;;
DELL");
    End ;
```

At$

At$** is used in trading strategies to anchor exit prices to the bar where the entry order was placed. **At$ must be used in conjunction with an entry order that has an assigned label such as `from Entry ("EntryNameGoesHere")`.

The **At$** must be executed on every bar of data. To be specific, you must not place the exit order within an **If** block such as `if MarketPosition = +01`.

EXAMPLE 3.06—Using At$ in a Strategy to Isolate the Signal Bar

The following order buys when the 10-bar moving average crosses over the 20-bar moving average, placing a stop loss order 1 point under the Low of the bar where the cross over occurred by appending **At$** to the Sell statement.

```
If Average (Close,10) Crosses Over Average(Close,20)
  Then  Buy ("MA Cross Over") next bar at market ;
Sell ("1x.Stop") next bar from entry ("MA Cross Over") At$ Low - 01
point stop ;
```

EXAMPLE 3.07—Using At$ from AME[32]

```
Sell ("1x.At$") all Contracts
  from Entry ("le.Main#A")
  at$ Lowest ( Low, 03) stop ;
```

It is important to remember that the **At$** exit must be executed on the Order Generation bar so it cannot be with other exits which I normally surround with an `if MarketPosition > 0` statement (for long exits).

Analysis Commentary

This is different than the non-executable comments described above. Analysis Commentary is where you write comments for different bars on a chart, triggered by turning Commentary on and then clicking your mouse on that bar. One can get rather complex in Commentary by adding links and colors with HTML. I'll show you that in a minute. While you should tell your code to look for a **CommentaryBar** with **atCommentaryBar**, you must also create your Commentary Line with Commentary with no Carriage Return / Line Feed pair or **CommentaryCL** which can include the **NewLine** construct. You can set up the string in advance in a variable, or you can do it on the fly, as in the example below.

A popup window will appear if you have Commentary permitted in your code and if you have clicked on a bar using the Analysis Commentary cursor and provided that that bar has Commentary for it.

EXAMPLE 3.08—Using Analysis Commentary

```
doCmtry  = atCommentaryBar ;        // set the switch
if  doCmtry  then  CmtryStr  = "" ; // clear contents
if  doCmtry  then  CmtryStr += "whateverstringyouwish" ;
```

In the area where you display all the Commentary you use:

---

[32] AME = "*Ask Mr. EasyLanguage*" page 167 by Samuel K. Tennis

```
If CmtryStr  > "" then CommentaryCL (CmtryStr) ;
```

☑ If you want to have multiple statements or lines of Commentary in the output you would want to place a NewLine character after each string as in CmtryStr += "Something interesting happened on this bar." + NewLine.

Commentary allows you to click on specific bars that you want to examine and see what your variables are on those bars only, no need to scroll through hundreds or thousands of print lines to find those specific bars.

The next example is code from my SunnyBands© indicator (see Figure 3.08) showing you how I display all the relevant values from within the indicator. Here you can see how to add meaningful descriptive text about several output values to make the popup window insightful. This code displays the values of the SunnyBands, the values of the DMA (DynamicMovingAverage), and the Angle of the DMA MidLine.

EXAMPLE 3.09—A Real-World Example of Analysis Commentary

```
CommentaryCL ("UIB=", o_UpperInnerBand, ", LIB=", o_LowerInnerBand, ",
UOB=", o_UpperOuterBand, ", LOB=", o_LowerOuterBand, ", MidLine=",
o_MidLine, ", MidAngle=", o_MidAngle, ", DMA Gold=", o_DMAValueGold,
", DMA_Purple=", o_DMAValuePurple) ;
```

You can see the results of this effort in Figure 3.08, after I finish explaining the process.

When you quit clicking on bars and do something else to change the cursor then the Commentary is deactivated. When you close the Commentary window Analysis Commentary is also disabled.

Here's a fun aside that you can achieve with Analysis Commentary: you can imbed HTML code to the Commentary you write to display all kinds of things in the Commentary box that pops up when you click on a bar on the chart. Included in the example below is a function (Sam starts them with "@" to make them easily distinguishable and because that's how it was done in System Writer) called "vrt_MMDDYYYY. You can get this function from Sam by shooting him an email at sktennis@vista-research.com. In the meantime, you can write little functions for calculating the date format from an EZL date and likewise with the EZL time. I am not going to teach you HTML in this book, so if you don't already speak it, Google how to specify links and bold text.

EXAMPLE 3.10—Testing HTML eMail Sending [OME_HTML_Email]

```
Inputs:
  j_Address ("sktennis@vista-research.com"),
  j_Subject ("Test Subject"),
  j_Prompt  ("Click Here to Send EMail"),
  ShowCmtry ( TRUE) ;
Vars:
  string NL (NewLine) ;
#beginCmtry
if CheckCommentary and ShowCmtry then begin
  CommentaryCL ("Study : '<strong>","TestMailto",
  "</strong>' ",@vrt_MMDDYYYY (Date),
  " ", @vrt_HHMM_pm (Time),
  HTML_HRef_MailTo (j_Address,  j_Subject,
  NL + j_Prompt)) ;
end ; // expert Commentary enabled for this bar
#end
```

☑ This will only function if you have an Email client installed in Windows applications.

Insert this indicator on a chart. Then go the top of your chart, on the right, and click on the tiny, little button that is grayed out with a chevron (>>) and a pulldown to expose Analysis Commentary. This turns it on, changing your cursor to look like an arrow with a cartoon bubble. In Figure 3.06 you can see the result of the code, the Commentary cursor in the lower right, and the pop-up Commentary box in the center.

FIGURE 3.05—Analysis Commentary for the Code in Figure 3.08

This little routine does the email part of HTML.

Sam has more HTML functions if you are interested. Just email him at sktennis@vista-research.com; they are available for the asking. This next one (see Example 3.11 for the code and Figure 3.07 for the outcome) shows how to link to a website from a Commentary bar.

EXAMPLE 3.11—HTML Code to Link to a Website [OME_HTML2Website]

```
Inputs:
 String j_Address ("https://www.MoneyMentor.com"),
 String j_Prompt  ("Click Here to Link"),
 Bool   ShowCmtry ( TRUE)
   ;
VARS:
 string NL (NewLine) ;
#beginCmtry
if  CheckCommentary and ShowCmtry
then begin
  CommentaryCL ("Study : '<strong> TestLink, </strong>",
  @vrt_MMDDYYYY (Date), " ", @vrt_HHMM_pm (Time),
  HTML_HRef_Link (j_Address, "" , j_Prompt)) ;
end ; // expert Commentary enabled for this bar
#end ;// end of Commentary
```

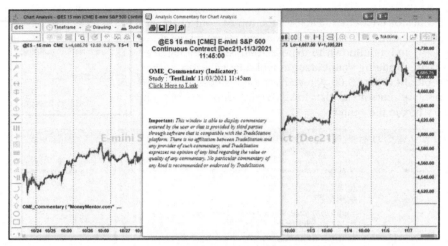

FIGURE 3.06—HTML Link to Website [OME_HTML2Website]

In my SunnyBands Indicator I have both a HTML link and color coding to match the indicator values. It makes for easy reading and quick analysis. The output to the Commentary window follows, in Figure 3.07.

FIGURE 3.07—SunnyBands Commentary Window

Now that's what I call beautiful! Notice in the Figure above that I have color coded the values to match the colors of the bands on the chart. Further, the price quotes (Open, Close etc.) are color coded to reveal the direction of the market. If the last tick was down, the prices are red; if the last tick was up, the prices are green.

Chart Type Reserved Word Values

The following table provides examples of the values that would be returned by the EZL Reserved Words associated with symbol settings for a chart.

The following table gives examples of the available values:

Chart Type	Box Size	Rev Size	Bar Type	Bar Interval	Interval Type
10 tick	0	0	0	10	0
100 shares	0	0	0	100	0
10 minute	0	0	1	10	0
Point & Figure 2x3	2	3	5	1	0
Point & Figure 2x4	2	4	5	10	1
Point & Figure 3x5 Daily	3	5	5	0	2
Kagi 2 Fixed Price 1 minute	0	2	8	1	1
Kagi 5%	0	5	8	0	2
Kase 3	3	0	9	5	1
Line Break 3	0	3	10	30	1
Momentum 2	2	0	11	0	2
Range	2	0	12	1	1
Renko 2.5	2.5	0	13	1	0

TABLE 3.04—Chart Type Reserved Word Values

Using ASCII 3rd Party Data

In addition to using data obtained from the TS Data Network, you can plot 3rd party data in a Chart Analysis or RadarScreen window from previously created ASCII or MetaStock (9.x or greater) data files stored on your computer or local area network. For example, this allows you to use proprietary data that may have been generated through another application (such as Excel) or that was obtained for exotic markets not currently supported by the TS Data Network.

There are two types of supported 3rd party data files:

ASCII data—A delimited text file that supports a variety of user customization options including the ability to specify different kinds of delimiters and the number and order of data fields. Each line of data represents a tick or a bar interval and contains a date/time stamp along with user definable price data.

MetaStock data (daily only)—A specific format that is not user definable and can be used to plot daily, weekly, monthly, and point & figure bars. MetaStock data must be version 9.x or greater.

> ☑ The first time you plot from a 3rd party data file, you may be asked to verify the date format, symbol description, and sessions. These settings are saved in the Symbol Attributes file so that the next time you type or select the 3rd party symbol the information will be automatically retrieved.

Symbol attribute (attributes.ini) **file**—A text file that stores default, symbol-specific, and root-specific symbol attributes for 3rd party data files that reside within the same directory as the symbol attributes file. When you import the data in your file to TS it will create the attribute.ini file for you. It is worth opening the file sometime to take a look at the information stored there. You can just open it with Notepad or Notepad++.

> ☑ When you first plot from a 3rd party data file, you may be asked to verify the field order if it hasn't already been specified in a header row. This field order information is then stored in a separate Data Order Parameter (.dop) file so that is can be automatically retrieved the next time you select the 3rd party symbol.

Data Order Parameter (.dop) **file**—A delimited text file containing a single header line that defines the field order of a specific data file or all data files (AllData.dop) that reside in the same directory. A SymRoot.DOP (ex: IBM.dop) in the folder will override the AllData.dop file.

☑ If your 3rd party data is associated with an exchange that isn't supported by the TS data network, you can create and maintain this information in your own exchange file.

Symbol Customize--3rd Party Data

The format for a 3rd Party symbol is:

+PREFIX:Symbol_Data

The plus (+) sign indicates that the symbol represents 3rd party data.

PREFIX is the text name you associated with the data source location (file directory) on the **Add/Edit Data Source** dialog box from the **Symbol Lookup -- 3rd Party** tab. See Figure 3.08 below.

A colon (:) always follows the PREFIX.

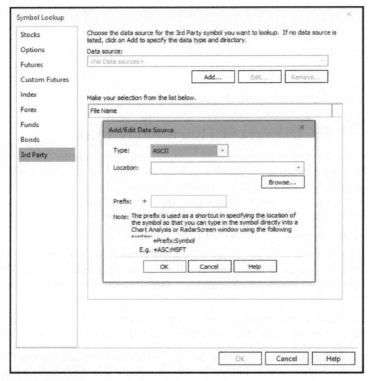

FIGURE 3.08—Third Party Data Menus

Symbol Data is either the root name of the 3rd party data file (the portion of the file name before the period and any extension) or the full 3rd party data file name (including the period and extension).

EXAMPLE 3.12—Two Examples of Custom Data Symbols

```
+ASC:Ticks2001
+MY:CIndex.txt
```

Symbol data from an external ASCII file can be read by TS if the text information in the file is properly formatted. This topic provides information about customizing the data fields and optional header in a 3rd party ASCII data file.

- Each ASCII file may only contain data for a single symbol.
- Each line of data in the file must be followed by a carriage return.
- Each field in a line must be delimited by a comma, tab, or space. No other delimiters are permitted.
- An optional header line may be included in the file to define the order of the fields on each

line within the file.
- The header must be the first line of the file.

The following table lists acceptable field names:

Field Name	Short Name	Purpose
Date		Date of the bar or tick
Time		Closing time of the bar or tick
Open	O	Opening price of the bar
High	H	High price of the bar
Low	L	Low price of the bar
Close	C	Closing price of the bar or tick
Volume	V	Volume of the bar
OpenInt	OI	Open Int of the bar
Other		Reserved as placeholder to skip a column

TABLE 3.05—Acceptable Field Names for 3rd Party Data

An example of a header line and matching data would be:

```
"Date","Time",O,H,L, "Close", "Volume", "OpenInt"
12/12/2003,1340,53,55,48,49.200000,0
```

The Date must be entered using one of the following formats:

Proper Date Formats			
mm/dd/yy	mm-dd-yy	mm.dd.yy	mmddyy
mm/dd/yyyy	mm-dd-yyyy	mm.dd.yyyy	mmddyyyy
yy/mm/dd	yy-mm-dd	yy.mm.dd	yymmdd
yyyy/mm/dd	yyyy-mm-dd	yyyy.mm.dd	yyyymmdd
dd/mm/yy	dd-mm-yy	dd.mm.yy	ddmmyy
dd/mm/yyyy	dd-mm-yyyy	dd.mm.yyyy	ddmmyyyy

TABLE 3.06—Acceptable Date Formats

When using a two-digit year, the years less than 30 are assumed to be 21st century and the years 30-99 are assumed to be 20th century. Since this will "break" in 2030 (only 7 years hence) TS will have to do something clever to fix this assumption.

All times need to be in exchange time, in 24-hour format and can be entered using one of the following formats:

Proper Time Formats	
hhmmss	hh:mm:ss
hhmm	hh:mm

TABLE 3.07—Acceptable Time Formats

Examples of time formats would be:

  11:15:04 AM can be entered as 111504 or 11:15:04

  2:20:36 PM would be entered as 142036 or 14:20:36

  3:30 PM would be entered as 1530 or 15:30

The file cannot contain any characters besides letters, numbers, the permitted delimiters (in my experience only comma works), the permitted date and time separators, and carriage returns.

The file name limit is a maximum of 18 characters including prefix and extension such as `ABC:1234567890.CSV`.

The symbol name should not be included in the data file itself. However, if it is, one can have it ignored using the 'Other' field in a header file. The symbol name, however, should be a part of the file name since this is what will be assumed as the symbol in the platform. For instance, in `MSFT.txt`, `MSFT` will be assumed to be the symbol name.

The two mandatory fields are Date and Close. Other fields that may be added to the file are optional.

The fields Open, High, and Low must all be included if any one of them is included (e.g., you couldn't just have Date, Open, High, and Close).

While either Volume or Open Interest can be 0, any line that has 0 for Open, High, Low or Close will be ignored.

A data file must contain at least 1 line of data to be valid. This line is in addition to the header if there is a header (since the header is optional).

All dates and times must be in forward chronological order (oldest date/time to newest date/time).

In the case of daily data, no duplicate dates are allowed. In the case of intraday data, no duplicate date/time pairs are allowed. In the case of tick data, there are no such restrictions. Chronological order is required. Acceptable file intervals are:

1 tick	Any file that is detected to be a tick file should be presumed to be a 1 tick file
1 minute	Any file that is detected to be an intraday file should be presumed to be a 1-minute file
Second	
Daily	
Weekly	
Monthly	

Symbol Lookup 3rd Party Data

Now that you have your datafile set up, you will want to locate the datafile in TS, format it and put it on your chart. It's not intuitive. Or at least it wasn't for me. Go to **Data** on the menu bar and select **Add Symbol**. Then click the **Prompt for Editing** checkbox so TS doesn't get ahead of you. Next to where it says **Symbol:** is a button that says **Lookup**. ⌐ Click that button. (I have run across clients who say, "mash the button.") Just click it.

FIGURE 3.09—Add Symbol Dialog Box

In Figure 3.10 you'll see what comes next: the **Symbol Lookup** dialog box. (Yes, this is redundant with Figure 3.08). Click on 3rd Party and it will show you a dropdown that says **<No Data sources>**. This is where you click **Add** and specify the location of your data. The selections are ASCII or

MetaStock. For this exercise we are going to choose **ASCII**. Under the Location: dropdown (mine is empty at this point) ᗢ click on the **Browse...** button. See Figure 3.11—Add/Edit Data Source.

FIGURE 3.10—Symbol Lookup

For use in a later chart, I have a CSV file named GAS3.txt on my C:\ drive. It is named the same as the symbol I will use when I import the data. I wanted to see a comparison of gasoline prices at the pump (historically) on the same chart as oil futures prices. I am going to Browse to my C:\ drive; it doesn't let me specify the datafile just yet. I am specifying the symbol to be GAS3. TS automatically names it with the +Prefix.

Now it gives me a selection of file names that are in acceptable formats and from that I select GAS3.txt and click **OK**. Next you will select the format for the dates you have in your file and click **Next.** After that you will need to give your custom symbol a Description, Category, Exchange, Sessions etc. This can be trial and error. Often mostly error. But keep trying.

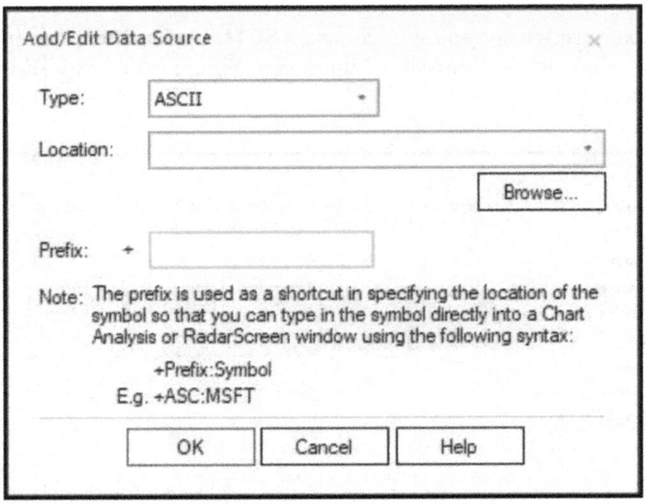

FIGURE 3.11—Add/Edit Data Source

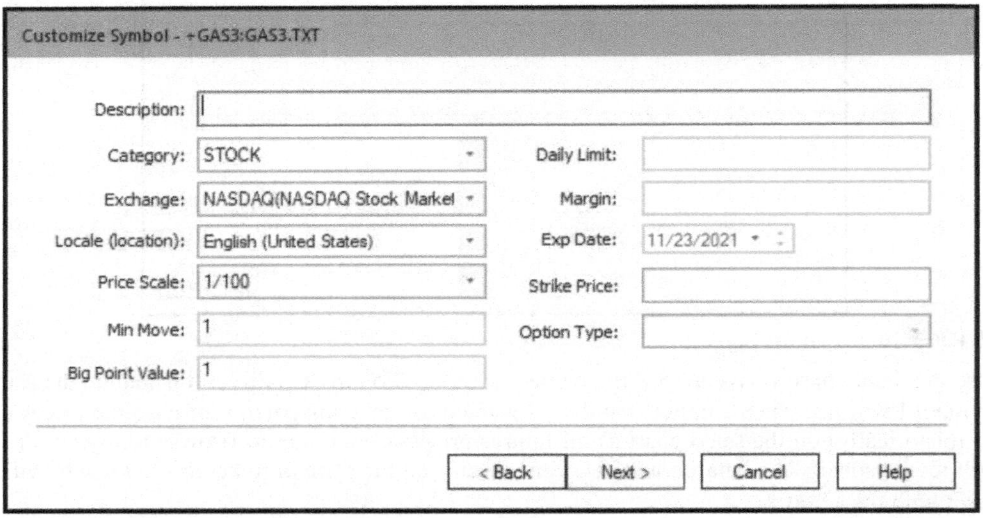

FIGURE 3.12—Customize Your Symbol

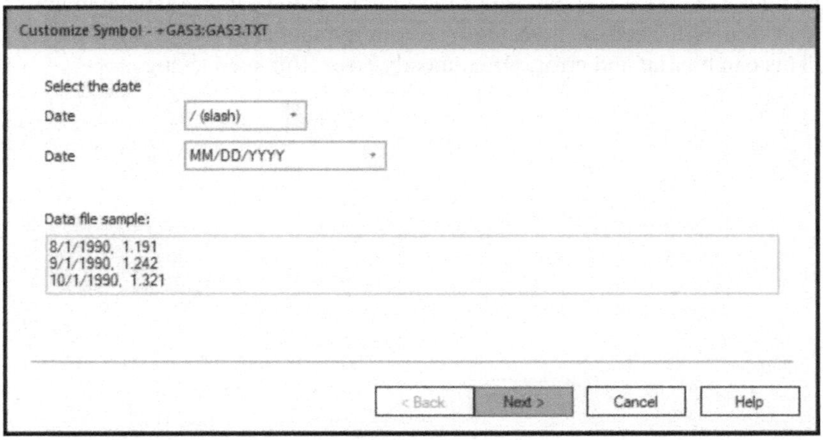

FIGURE 3.13—Tell TS What Format Your Dates Are In

After all this, when you try to put your data on a chart you might get an error message like the one in Figure 3.14.

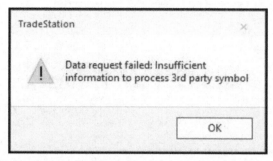

FIGURE 3.14—Error Message: Data Source Is Not Properly Formatted

I kept getting this error message again and again until I realized that in the header Date and Close must have double quotes around them and that you cannot use tabs in the file.

It is imperative that your .txt file look like, similar to, the data in Figure 3.15 below. Any variations will result in an error message. I also found out the hard way that I had a date and price duplicate in the file, and it won't work with that either.

```
"Date","Close"
8/1/1990,1.191
9/1/1990,1,242
10/1/1990,1.321
11/1/1990,1.334
12/1/1990,1.341
1/1/1991,1.250
2/1/1991,1.139
3/1/1991,1.025
4/1/1991,1.052
5/1/1991,1.113
6/1/1991,1.138
7/1/1991,1.104
8/1/1991,1.099
```

FIGURE 3.15—Proper Formatting of Your Datafile

It also turns out that the last line of your file must contain a **return/enter** so that TS knows when your file is finished, much like an EOF (end-of-file) marker.

After all that, here is the resultant chart, in Figure 3.16, so you can see what the final product looks like.

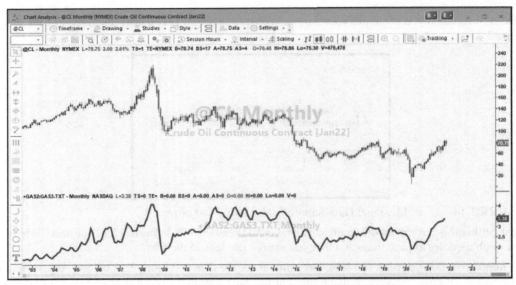

FIGURE 3.16—Gasoline Prices at the Pump vs Crude Light (through 2021)

Curious, isn't it, that from 2009 to 2014 when crude oil was pretty much flat that prices at the pump were nearly as high as they had been in mid-2008. (Note: I wrote this, and did the chart, before the war in Ukraine and spiking gas prices.)

PlaySound

This reserved word finds and plays the specified sound file (.wav file). The reserved word returns a value of True if it was able to find and play the sound file, and it returns a value of False if it is not able to find or play it.

USAGE

PlaySound (myWavFile) ;

`myWavFile` is any text string expression that represents the full path and file name of the sound file to be played. Only .wav files can be played.

REMARKS

The specified file must be a *.wav audio file.

> ✏ It is recommended that you use this reserved word only on the last bar of the chart, otherwise, you may find that the .wav file is played more often than you intended. For example, if your intention is to play a .wav file whenever a certain bar pattern occurs, and this pattern occurs 50 times in the price chart, the trading strategy, Analysis Technique, or function will play the .wav file 50 times when it is applied to the price chart. Also, the .wav file is only played once per bar, even if the event occurs more than once intrabar (unless the Update value intra-bar option is enabled, in which case, the .wav file will play with each new tick while the event is True).

EXAMPLE 3.13—Using PlaySound

```
Condition1  = PlaySound ("C:\Sounds\ThatsABuy.wav") ;
```

This statement plays the sound file `Thatsabuy.wav` that resides in directory `c:\sounds`.

EXAMPLE 3.14—PlaySound on Key Reversal

The following statements play the sound file `Thatsabuy.wav` when there is a key reversal pattern on the last bar of the chart:

```
If  LastBarOnChart and Low < Low[1] and Close > High[1]
  then  Condition1 = PlaySound("c:\sounds\Thatsabuy.wav") ;
```

EXAMPLE 3.15—Sunny's BingTicks© Indicator

I use the **PlaySound** feature everyday while I'm trading. I have a little indicator called BingTicks that plays a sound with every tick of the market. I chose a "bing" sound for upticks, a "bonk" sound for downticks and a "click" for sideways. If you would like to download the Sounds folder, just go to MoneyMentor.com → Resources → Downloads. It's free.

Here's the code:

```
If  Time <> Time[01]  then begin
  If  Close > Close[01]
  then  Condition1 = PlaySound ("C:\Sounds\C7x400.wav")
  else
    If Close = Close[1]
    then  Condition1 = PlaySound ("C:\Sounds\Click.wav")
    else  Condition1 = PlaySound ("C:\Sounds\C5x050.wav") ;
end ;
```

I have yet another indicator (Strategy) called `sjh_S_PositionsAsSpeech` that uses **PlaySound** to play my recorded voice announcing the position I'm in ("long", "short", "flat") followed by the number of contracts I have on ("One", "Two", …). And in the automated SunnyBands© strategy I'm working on I again use **PlaySound** to say "BuyBuyBuy" or "SellSellSell" in Sam's voice. That way I don't lose focus on my trading screen and start looking at something else, like the book I'm writing.

> ☑ Your assignment, student, is to replicate this behavior using a Variable and a Switch…Case Statement. Submit your solution to www.moneymentor.com.

PlayMovieChain

This reserved word plays a V clip and returns a True/False expression representing the success of the operation. If the reserved word was able to play the video clip, it returns a value of True, if it was not, it returns a value of False.

USAGE

Print (PlayMovieChain (Movie_ID)) ;

`Movie_ID` is a numeric expression representing the ID number of the video clip.

REMARKS

The reference number should be a whole positive number.

NOTES

Once you have created a video clip using the reserved word **MakeNewMovieRef** and added .avi files to the video clip, you are ready to play it. We recommend you use the reserved word **PlayMovieChain** only on the last bar of the chart or on bars where the Commentary is obtained (using the **atCommentaryBar** or **LastBarOnChart** reserved words). Otherwise, you may find that the video clip is played more often than you need it to.

If your intention is to play the video clip when a certain bar pattern occurs, and this pattern occurs 50 times the price chart, the trading strategy, Analysis Technique, or function will play the video clip 50 times when applied to the price chart.

EXAMPLE 3.16—Play a Video Clip at Commentary Bar

The following statements create and play a video clip on the bar where Commentary is obtained:

```
Vars  : ID (-1) ;
If BarNumber = 01 Then Begin
  ID = MakeNewMovieRef;
```

```
    Print (AddToMovieChain (ID, "C:\MyMovie.avi")) ;
    Print (AddToMovieChain (ID, "C:\MyOtherMovie.avi")) ;
End;
If  LastBaronChart  Then
    Print (PlayMovieChain (ID)) ;
```

Notice that the video clip is created, and the video files are added to it only once by using an **If…Then** statement to check for the first bar of the chart. If we don't use this **If…Then** statement (or a **Once** block), the indicator will create as many video clips as there are bars in the chart.

RaiseRunTimeError

This causes a user specified run-time error message to be generated. The message will display in the Event Log when an error is raised from the Chart Analysis window and will display upon rolling the mouse pointer over the 'E' error indication in a RadarScreen cell.

USAGE

RaiseRunTimeError (strReason)

`strReason` is a string expression that contains the text of the user specified error message.

EXAMPLE 3.17—RaiseRunTimeError

`RaiseRunTimeError("My Own Error Message")` will generate an error and will display the specified message. Compare this to **Analysis Commentary**, where you must click on a specific bar on your chart to see the message.

An example from my own code is

```
    RaiseRunTimeError ("A problem occurred with this " + App_Type + ",
    please contact Sunny J. Harris.") ;
```

You will get this message if you don't have the right `j_Key` password in the indicators you licensed from me.

InfoBox

The **InfoBox** function is used to display a popup window that shows a message specified by the calling Analysis Technique or strategy. The form (box) is closed by clicking the OK button. The location of the **InfoBox** popup will be relative to the upper left corner (X pixels over and Y pixels down) of the platform window containing the Analysis Technique that calls the function.

The **InfoBox** does not pause EZL execution to await an answer, it is information only.

USAGE

InfoBox (Message, Caption, Pos_XPixels, Pox_YPixels)

RETURNS (number) Always returns a 1.

PARAMETERS

Name	Type	Description
Message	String	Specifies the info message to display to the user.
Caption	String	Specifies the caption to display at the top of the info box popup window.
Pos_XPixels	Integer	Specifies the X location to plot the info box popup relative to the upper left corner of the calling window (pixels to the right).
Pos_YPixels	Integer	Specifies the Y location to plot the info box popup relative to the upper left corner of the calling window (pixels down).

TABLE 3.08—InfoBox Parameters

REMARKS

EZL code continues to run even when this form is visible. This function can be called, and will create an info box, on historical bars, but calling it on every bar in history will cause the code to run more slowly than it would otherwise. Because it takes longer to run, the **Abort** button may appear on the chart. See notes within the **InfoBox** function code for additional details.

Suggested uses would be to display some information about an invalid Input value (ex: "Length must be greater than zero." on the first bar of data or using **LastBarOnChart**.

> ☑ No attempt should be made to make the InfoBox form modal[33], as this will interrupt EZL processing. Also, the caller should not attempt to delay continuation of the code pending user response to the dialog box.

EXAMPLE 3.18—Engaging the InfoBox

Displays a warning message to the user based on a condition in the calling Analysis Technique.

```
Value1 = InfoBox ("Invalid operation","My Warning", 50, 50) ;
```

EXAMPLE 3.19—InfoBox with Two Moving Averages

In this example I've used two simple moving averages on the chart for reference and am displaying an **InfoBox** when the averages either cross under or cross over each other. It's a nice way to let yourself, or your user, know when the crossover has happened.

```
Value1  = Average (Close, 10) ;
Value2  = Average (Close ,20) ;
Plot1 (Value1, "FastAvg") ;
Plot2 (Value2, "SlowAvg") ;
if  LastBarOnChart  then begin
   if  Value1 crosses over Value2
      then  Value3 = InfoBox ("Crossing Over", "MAV Crossing", 30, 30) ;
   if  Value1 crosses under Value2
      then  Value3 = InfoBox ("Crossing Under", "MAV Crossing", 50, 50)
;
end ; // last bar on chart
```

The popup box appears at the pixels you have specified, and looks like this:

FIGURE 3.17—InfoBox PopUp

Clearly, I could have made it much more complex with concatenation of strings that were more descriptive, but you get the picture.

Hello_World!_Ex#02

Remember the first program we wrote? In Chapter 1?

Let's bring it up front again so we can examine it and progress further with it. Here is what the code

---

[33] Modal dialog boxes require the user to respond before continuing the program. Modeless dialog boxes stay on the screen and are available for use at any time but permit other user activities.

looked like:

```
Print   ("Hello_World!_Ex#01") ;
```

You have now given the instruction to print the words "Hello_World!_Ex#01" in the EZL **Print Log**. When you put the indicator on your chart it will produce the string of text over and over. Why does it print over and again and not once? Because the code is executed on each and every bar of data and you (OK, we) did nothing to limit the output. Stick with me, there is a method to my madness!

Let's make a modification to take care of this. If we want, we can specify that it only be printed on the last bar of the chart, like this:

EXAMPLE 3.20—Print Only on Last Bar

```
if  LastBarOnChart  then begin
  Print ("Hello_World!_Ex#02") ;
end ;  // prints on the last bar on the chart
```

Of course, because the last bar is continually being renewed with a new last bar, this configuration prints "Hello_World!_Ex#02" many times in the EZL **Print Log**.

Here is another modification to the above: how about printing only on the first bar of the chart?

EXAMPLE 3.21—Printing Only on the First Bar of the Chart [OME_Hello_World! Ex#02]

```
if  (CurrentBar <= 01)  then begin
  Print ("Hello_World!_Ex#02") ;
  // prints on the first bar on the chart
end ;
```

And lo and behold it does indeed print "Hello_World!_#02" just once in the **Print Log**. This is very simple code, and it works fine, but if you have a more complex application and have selected **Auto Detect MaxBarsBack** it might execute multiple times.

As an aside, if you don't have the **Print Log** on your Desktop, you can bring it up in either of two ways:

CTRL-SHIFT-E

or

View → EasyLanguage Print Log

We will be getting into many more configurations of Hello World! in the next chapter. Hold on tight.

Understanding the **Print** statement fully and using it constantly is essential to debugging your code. In some cases, like when 'update tick-by-tick' is enabled, it may be necessary to print to file then examine the file contents afterwards. This is an extremely time consuming and detail-oriented task and I recommend that you develop code, as long as you possibly can, with update tick-by-tick or **IntrabarOrderGeneration** OFF.

Time and Sales

About the Time and Sales Window

In the Time and Sales window you can monitor Level I trades, as well as changes in the Best Bid[34] and Best Ask prices. Level 1 trades are the actual trades taking place for a specific security. The Time and Sales window supports data for stocks, stock options, indexes, index options, forex, futures, futures options, and funds. You can display either real-time or historical data.

> ☑ Level 2 data builds on Level 1 data by also displaying market depth. Market depth means

---

[34] The term "best bid" refers to the highest quoted [rice available that somebody is willing to purchase a particular security, and so reflects the best price that somebody could sell at the market.

the market's ability to trade large orders without impacting the price of a symbol. Level 2 data requires a subscription to the datafeed and an extra fee. Users with Level 2 data will see the national best bid and offer (NBBO) and also see the next best 30 bid/ask prices, as well as the size for each price level, all in real-time.

If you choose real-time data, you can display a certain number of ticks, a certain time-period (in minutes), or all ticks recorded for the day. If you choose historical data, which is useful for examining the history of a security, you can display tick data recorded for a specific day or for a specific day and time-period (up to 5 days back). The Time and Sales window can also help you gauge the support and resistance of certain price points in addition to the volume behind each trade. For these reasons, this window is often used in conjunction with the Market Depth window.

☑ To create a Time and Sales window, click the Time and Sales ⓒ$ icon on the Apps tab. A new Time and Sales window is displayed.

Layout

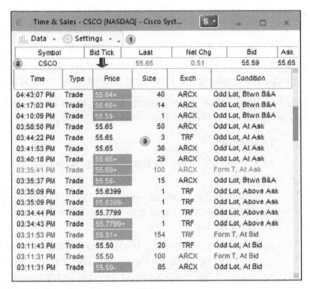

FIGURE 3.18—Time and Sales Window for CSCO

☑A maximum number of 10,000 items may be displayed from the first requested date and/or start time.

① **Toolbar**—Provides drop-down menus that control the features and settings of the window.

② **Quote Bar**—Displays only the best Bid and best Ask data for a symbol.

This information is also known as Level 1 data. The default layout includes the following information for each symbol: Bid, Last, Net Chg, Open, High, Low, and Close. You can choose which columns to display in the Quote Bar and the order in which they are displayed. For more information, see Customizing Time and Sales Columns in the EZL Help files.

☑ Use the View → Quote Bar menu sequence to toggle the display of the Quote Bar. A check mark appears next to the Quote Bar menu item to indicate that it has been selected for display.

③ **Detail Pane**—The Detail pane shows time stamped quotes for each type of market event.

This provides detailed information in a column format: Time, Type, Price, Size, Exchange, and Condition. The most current market activity is shown in the top row. A new row is displayed for each trade, or when the price or volume of the best Bid or best Ask changes. Each event is displayed as a different color for easier viewing, as shown in the picture above.

> 📝 For Forex quotes, a referred value in the Condition column indicates that the price is provided for reference only. Referred quotes are ignored by TS and cannot be used by TS to trigger activation rules, strategies, stops, limits, or any other price based trade.

Referred Quote

A reference price available for Forex markets that appears in the Time and Sales window. A referred quote price is ignored by TS and cannot be used by TS to trigger activation rules, strategies, stops, limits, or any other price-based trade.

Time and Sales Condition/Subtype Reference

The reference table below (Table 3.09) contains possible subtypes that may appear along with the following market items in the Conditions column of the Time and Sales window.

- Above Ask
- At Ask
- At Bid
- Below Bid
- Btwn B&A (Between Bid and Ask)

By default, subtypes are highlighted in black with white text, unless otherwise noted. You may change the color of individual subtype items using the Time and Sales Customize Window dialog box.

> 📝 Note that the following table contains definitions for the most common trade subtypes sent by the exchanges and is not an all inclusive list of possible subtypes.

Subtype	Definition
Acquisition	A transaction made on the exchange as a result of an exchange acquisition.
Average Price	A trade where the price reported is based upon an average of the prices for the transactions in a specific security during all or any portion of the trading day.
Basket Index	A trade involving paired basket orders, the execution of which is based on the closing value of the index. These trades are reported after the close when the index closing value is determined.
Bilat Block Trade	A bilateral, off-book trade of a standard Eurex product.
Block Trade	A privately negotiated futures, options or combination transaction that is permitted to be executed apart from the public auction market.
Bunched Sold	A Bunched Sold Trade is a Bunched Trade that was reported late (later than 90 seconds after the occurrence of the first trade aggregated in the Bunched Trade report). Nasdaq will process a Bunched Sold Trade as a Sold Trade, that is, Out of Sequence Trade, when updating the security's last sale information.
Bunched Trade	A trade representing an aggregate of two or more Regular trades in a security occurring at the same price, either simultaneously or within the same 60-second period, with no individual trade exceeding 10,000 shares. Nasdaq will process a Bunched Trade as a Regular last sale when updating the security's last sale information.
Burst Basket	A trade wherein the equity specialists, acting in the aggregate as a market maker, purchase or sell the component stocks required for execution of a specific basket trade.
Canceled	A trade that is voided by the buyer or seller. Highlighted in black with

Subtype	Definition
	red, strike-through text.
Cash	A transaction that calls for the delivery of securities and payment on the same day the trade took place.
CCX/EFP Trade	Chicago Climate Exchange/Exchange for Physical Trade.
Close Price	A transaction executed by the listing market to establish the official Consolidated Close Price as indicated by the listing market.
Cross Trade	A trade transaction resulting from a market center's crossing session.
Crossed	The transaction that constituted the trade-through was executed at a time when a protected bid was priced higher than a protected offer in the National Market System (NMS) stock.
Custom Basket Cross	One of the following: A trade of two paired split (where the customer requires only a portion of the standardized basket) orders in which the market maker or member organization facilitates both sides of the remaining portion of the baskets; or A combination of a split basket and an entire basket where the market maker facilitates the remaining shares of the split basket only.
Derivatively Priced	A transaction that constituted the trade-through was the execution of an order at a price that was not based, directly or indirectly, on the quoted price of the security at the time of execution, and for which the material terms were not reasonably determinable at the time the commitment to execute the order was made (REG NMS 611b7).
Distribution	Sale of a large block of stock in such a manner that the price is not adversely affected.
DNTP	Delta-Neutral Trading Products - Combinations of related futures and option contracts with a position delta close to zero. With a DNTP, either both the futures and the option legs have the same underlying, or the futures product is the underlying of the option.
EFP Basis	Exchange for Physical Basis.
EFP Block Trade	Exchange for Physical Block Trade.
EFP/EFS Contra	Exchange for Physical/Exchange for Swap Contra Block Trade.
EFR Trade	Exchange for Risk Trade - A position in an Over-the-Counter (OTC) swap or other OTC derivative in the same or related instrument for a position in the corresponding futures contract.
EFS Basis	Exchange For Swap Basis.
EFS Block Trade	Exchange For Swap Block Trade.
EOO Trade	Exchange of Options for Options Trade - A position in an OTC option (or other OTC contract with similar characteristics) in the same or related instrument for an option position.
Exchange for Physical	A position in the underlying physical instrument for a corresponding futures position.
Filtered from Chart	A bad tick that is filtered out automatically from displaying in any TS window aside from the Time and Sales window. Highlighted in black with yellow, strike-through text.
Form T	A trade executed after the normal trade reporting day has ended. This

Subtype	Definition
	type of trade is not applicable for UTP[35] exchange participants.
Intermarket Sweep	Intermarket sweep order means a limit order for a stock that meets the following requirements: When routed to a trading center, the limit order is identified as an intermarket sweep order; and Simultaneously with the routing of the limit order identified as an intermarket sweep order, one or more additional limit orders, as necessary, are routed to execute against the full displayed size of any protected bid, in the case of a limit order to sell, or the full displayed size of any protected offer, in the case of a limit order to buy, for the stock with a price that is superior to the limit price of the limit order identified as an intermarket sweep order. These additional routed orders also must be marked as intermarket sweep orders.
Intraday Trade Detail	The Intraday Trade report indicates the trade was included as part of a transaction that involves a group or "bunch" of orders executed at the same time and price and previously reported by the market center as a single cumulative trade report.
Next Day	A transaction that calls for delivery of securities between one and four days after the trade date. The time period is agreed upon by the buyer and the seller; the time period is not noted with the transaction.
Odd Lot	An order amount for a security that is less than the normal unit of trading for that particular asset. Odd lots are considered to be anything less than the standard units of trade.
Open Price	The transaction or group of transactions reported as a result of a single-priced opening event by the market center.
Opening Delay	Postponement of the opening of trading in a security for a participant.
Opening/Reopening Trade Detail	An opening/reopening trade detail report indicates the trade was included as part of an opening or reopening transaction previously reported by a market center on an aggregated basis.
Out of Sequence	A transaction that printed late; may include the following types of transactions: Cash (only) Market, Average Price Trade, Next Day (only) Market, and Sold. Cash (only) Market - A security settling in cash all day on a participant or consolidated basis, such as a Common, Preferred, or Right that is nearing expiration. This type of settlement is similar to a Cash Trade, except that Cash (only) Market trades qualify to update a security's trading range (high, low, last) during the day. Participants can elect to report different settlements in the same security during the day based on their own settlement requirements. For example, one participant can report trades as Cash (only) Market trades while another participant can report trades as regular or next day settlement. For Network B bonds, Cash (only) Market can be used to report transactions in a regular way market. Average Price Trade - A trade where the price reported is based upon an average of the prices for transactions in a security during all or any

---

[35] Under the Securities and Exchange Act of 1934, a U.S. exchange can offer "unlisted trading privileges" for securities listed on other U.S. exchanges. This practice promotes competition among the U.S. markets and exchanges, increasing opportunities for investors to obtain the best execution of their orders.

Subtype	Definition
	portion of the trading day. Next Day (only) Market - The same as a Cash (only) Market trade but the settlement is on the next day. Sold - Indicates that a trade was reported out of sequence and at a different time than the actual transaction time.
Price Variation Trade	Indicates a regular market session trade transaction that carries a price that is significantly away from the prevailing consolidated or primary market value at the time of the transaction.
Prior Reference Price	An executed trade that relates to an obligation to trade at an earlier point in the trading day or to a prior referenced price. A Prior Reference Price Trade may be the result of an order that was lost or misplaced or a SelectNet order that was not executed on a timely basis.
Referred Quote	A forex price that is provided for reference only. Referred quotes[36] are ignored by TS and cannot be used by TS to trigger activation rules, strategies, stops, limits, or any other price-based trade.
Rule 127	A trade that is always outside of the present quotation and meets one or both of the following conditions: Volume of 10,000 shares or more; and/or Dollar value of $200,000 or more.
Rule 155	Offered by a specialist, the sale of a block at one "clean-up" price or at the different price limits on his book. If the block is sold at a "clean-up" price, the specialist should execute all executable buy orders on his book at the same price.
Seller	A special transaction that gives the seller the right to deliver stock at any time within a specified period, ranging from 2 to 60 calendar days. A stock offered as a Seller's trade may command a lesser price than if offered as a Regular trade.
Sold Last	Used when a trade prints in sequence but is reported late.
Split Trade	An execution in two markets when the specialist or market maker in the market first receiving the order agrees to execute a portion of it at whatever price is realized in another market to which the balance of the order is forwarded for execution.
Stock Option Trade	Identifies cash equity transactions which are related to options transactions and therefore potentially subject to cancellation if market conditions of the options leg(s) prevent the execution of the stock-option order at the price agreed upon.
Stopped	In accordance with Amex Rule 109, a "stopped stock" transaction may occur under several circumstances, including when an Amex specialist executes market-at-the-close orders in a stock, where the specialist is holding simultaneously both buy and sell market-at-the-close orders. The specialist is required, under section (d) of the rule, to report the "pair off" transaction as "stopped stock." In addition, a "stopped stock" transaction may occur when a broker, trying to get a better price for the customer's market order than the currently available price, asks the specialist to "stop the stock." The specialist guarantees the broker the

[36] A reference price available for Forex markets that appears in the Time and Sales window. A referred quote price is ignored by TS and cannot be used by TS to trigger activation rules, strategies, stops, limits, or any other price-based trade.

Subtype	Definition
	current "stopped" price but does not immediately execute the order. The order is used by the specialist to improve the quote in order to obtain a better price. If the next trade is at the "stopped" price, the order is "elected" and executed by the specialist at the stopped price rather than at an improved price. The execution at the stopped price is designated as "Stopped Stock." Depending on the timing of the trade report message, one of three sale condition modifiers may be used to identify a stopped stock transaction: 1 = Stopped Stock – Regular Trade. 2 = Stopped Stock – Sold Last. 3 = Stopped Stock – Sold Out of Sequence.

TABLE 3.09—Time and Sales Condition/Subtype Reference

Currency Conversion

When strategy backtesting a symbol that is based in a different currency than your TS account it may be useful to apply a currency conversion factor when calculating profit and loss. In TS, you have the option of having profit and loss values converted based on either the symbol or the TS account.

TS no longer allows real-time trading of Forex on its standard platform. To trade currencies. One needs to open a forex TS account through https://www.TS-international.com/global/forex-trading/. TS still collects the data live, but you'll need special access to trade a forex account.

> ☑ Since this writing TradeStation has come out with a Crypto Trading TradingApp.

Like other Compiler Directives (Attributes) either there may only be one or only the last one will have any effect on the execution of the AT. In other words, when the code is verified, it determines the state of the attribute, and that state is used throughout. If you had one statement [BaseCurrency = Symbol] at the top of the code, and later you attempt to switch using [BaseCurrency = Account] the entire calculation will use the final state of the Attribute, which is Account.

That said, one can always analyze a strategy using the same familiar tools and do historical testing with standard TS.

Strategy Properties for All

By default, a new strategy uses the currency of the symbol. If the symbol currency is different from that of your TS account, click ⏏ Studies → Edit Strategies → Properties for All → General → Base Currency.

From the tab, change the Base Currency setting to either Account or Symbol. Values on the Strategy Properties window (commissions, trade size value, etc.) will display based on the selected currency conversion factor. In addition, built-in stops, studies, and strategies will be impacted by this setting.

EXAMPLE 3.22—Trading with Foreign Currencies (Forex)

If you're using a Forex symbol such as USDJPY that trades in Yen and you have Currency Based On set to Account (where your account is based in U.S. dollars), the profit and loss values in your strategy, including built-in stops, will use a currency conversion factor that converts Yen ¥ values to dollars. On the other hand, if you're using the USDJPY forex symbol and have Currency Based On set to Symbol, all strategy profit and loss calculations and built-in stops will not use currency conversion since none is needed for Yen to Yen.

```
if BarsSinceExit (01) = 00 and MarketPosition (01) <> 00  then begin
   Print ("Trade Closed : MP(1)=", MarketPosition (01), ", Entry=",
```

```
EntryPrice (01), ", Exit (01)=", ExitPrice (01)) ;
   switch MarketPosition (01) begin
     case +01 :
       if  ExitPrice (01)  > EntryPrice (01)
         then  Print ("Adjusted Profit/Loss is ", ExitPrice (01) -
EntryPrice (01) + ProfitCF) ;
         else  Print ("Adjusted Profit/Loss is ", ExitPrice (01) -
EntryPrice (01) + LossCF) ;
     case -01 :
       if  EntryPrice (01)  > ExitPrice (01)
         then  Print ("Adjusted Profit/Loss is ", ExitPrice (01) -
EntryPrice (01) + ProfitCF) ;
         else  Print ("Adjusted Profit/Loss is ", ExitPrice (01) -
EntryPrice (01) + LossCF) ;
   end ; // switch/case statement
end ; // we just closed a position
```

Strategy Backtesting

During strategy backtesting, profit and loss calculations can be made on any bar where a strategy trade is exited or partially exited. The essence of the profit and loss calculation is the difference between entry and exit price (exit - entry for long and entry - exit for short) for the shares or contracts traded, including commissions and slippage. In addition, when the symbol currency is different than the account currency, a currency conversion factor is applied that uses either the bid or ask price depending on whether the position was exited at a loss or profit, respectively. The Currency section on the Studies → Edit Strategies → Properties for All dialog box is used to change this setting (see above).

EasyLanguage Reserved Words

The **ProfitCF** and **LossCF** EZL reserved words are available (for Forex) to assist you in obtaining the currency conversion factor for any bar when writing custom rules for trade size or profit and loss calculations. As with bar properties such as **Date**, **Open**, **Volume**, etc., the **ProfitCF** and **LossCF** reserved words are bar properties that provide values both historically and real-time. When used without the optional BarsBack parameter the word returns the value for the current bar, and with the BarsBack parameter (enclosed in square brackets) it returns the value for that number of bars ago.

Utilization Monitor

Ever wonder how much of your computer's resources your indicator or strategy is using? I know I have some intense calculating going on in some of my studies, but I never knew just how much until a student asked me how to measure it.

To see the resources being consumer go to: Settings → EasyLanguage Utilization Monitor There you will find statistics on Calculations, Average Execution Time, Maximum Execution Time and more. It will show you what needs to be streamlined for faster execution.

Summary

In this chapter we have covered some more esoteric features of TS and EZL not covered elsewhere. They ranged from useful tools to shortcuts to foreign currency.

This chapter was a refresher of some of the important EZL features you should already be familiar with before you even dream of venturing into OOEL programming. You should have a firm grasp of these basic Classic EZL terms and their proper usage before delving too deeply into OOEL because everything is based on these building blocks.

Some things in this chapter you may never use, but you can imagine scenarios where they might be useful. For instance, I have never used **PlayMovieChain**, but I can imagine using it as Expert Commentary on my SunnyBands Automated 5-minute S&P strategy to alert users to certain market conditions or to the reasons behind the signal they just got.

I do use **PlaySound** every day in my BingTicks© indicator which plays a sound with every tick of the market: bing for up, bong for down, and click for sideways.

RaiseRunTimeError and Analysis Commentary are invaluable. My SunnyBands indicator has Commentary for each bar to tell you the values of each band, the values of the DMA Gold and Purple, the MidLine and MidAngle and several more.

I also use **InfoBox** to give me more information about my indicators and Alerts to tell me quickly when price is crossing over or under my SunnyBands or over or under my MovAvg_3Lines.

Hello_World!_Ex#02 was our next venture into EZL programming and will lead soon to more sophisticated OOEL versions of Hello World!

Not a feature limited to OOEL, we examined Currency Conversion and the Utilization Monitor. These are topics not covered elsewhere and I thought they should be included to make this a complete guide to TS, EZL, and OOEL.

CHAPTER 4
Easing Into Object-Oriented EasyLanguage

In This Chapter

- Introduction
- A Further Walk Through the EZL Dictionary
- OOEL Coding Template
- Classes
- AnalysisTechnique Class
- Class Declaration (Instantiation)
- Methods

- Libraries
- Namespaces
- About Objects in EZL
- Inheritance
- Events
- Provider Classes
- About the ToolBox
- Summary

Introduction

Here we go. This is what you bought the books for. Finally, I will explain namespaces, properties, regions, objects, classes, and dot operators. And maybe more. Your assignment is to go through this chapter quickly the first time and then come back and re-read it for content.

You will not understand everything in this chapter the first time through. I'm bringing in many terms that are going to be explained later. Nevertheless, you need to see what you can comprehend now and later we will go into it in more depth.

Herein we define the otherwise unintelligible words that constitute the nomenclature of OOEL: **Namespace**, **Object**, **Method**, **Class**, **Using**, **Void**, **Region** and more.

This chapter is the foundation for the remainder of this book. It may be a labor of love to read this chapter and understand it. You may need to re-read the chapter several times for the contents to sink in. That's alright, just do it. In fact, read through it once over without pausing for what you don't yet understand. Just give it a good brush-over. Then tomorrow, come back and read it again more slowly. And, the third time, study it. You will begin to understand the concepts just by reading through a few times.

It is important to know that object-oriented code is unlike classic EZL in that while the classic version executes your code from top to bottom, object-oriented code does not. Object-oriented code contains, or may contain, Methods which are like subroutines embedded in the code. Methods are similar to, but very different than, User Functions. I put a demarcation, something like `//=== Main Code ==` after the declaration section and before my **Once** block. Actually, I put two and place a list of my Method headers between them, as a reminder to respect this rule. Your Methods declarations must precede the first line of executable code.

For example, here's a template for this idea:

```
Inputs: …
Vars  : …
// ==============Methods Declared ================
{*
Method Void App_Init ()
 *}
// =========== Method Declarations ==============
Method void App_Init ()
Begin
End ; // "App_Init" method
// ========= Main (Executable) Code Block ========
Once begin
  App_Init () ;
```

```
end ; // Once, and only once
//  Your code after this…
```

The Method reserved word allows you to create a named subroutine within an AT that consists of a sequence of zero or more statements that perform an action, a set of input parameters to customize those actions, and possibly a return value.

REMARKS

Methods are local to the AT and local variables declared within a Method are active only within the scope of that Method. The EZL statements within a Method are only executed when the Method is called. Unlike top-down programming, a Method can be called from anywhere within the AT, Methods do not need to be declared before (higher in the code block) than where you call them. Unlike EZL functions, the Method is only available in the AT you are in. You cannot call it from outside the AT.

More on Methods later in this chapter.

SYNTAX SAMPLE

```
method double myMethod (int Param1)
vars  : double myVar ;
begin
// EasyLanguage statements
  return myVar ;
end ; // "myMethod" method
```

The data type of the Method always appears between the Method reserved word and the name you give to the method. A return statement in the method is used to return a value that is the same data type as the method. If a method does not include a return statement, the word Void is used as the Data Type. If the data type of the Method is **Void** then the Method has no return value and the Return statement is optional.

Methods can accept optional input parameters within the parenthesis following the method name. The parentheses are required, even if empty. The data type of the inputs must be specified in front of each input parameter name.

Local variables that are only used within a method are declared after the method declaration statement and before the **Begin…End** statement containing the body of the Method.

> ☑ The variable declaration rules in a local method are slightly different than for a variable declaration in the main body of an AT. In a Method, the Variable data type is required and no initial value is allowed after the variable's name.

EXAMPLE 4.01—Method to Plot Real-Time Equity

The following Method reads and displays account information from the `AccountsProvider1` object that was created using the **AccountsProvider** component. When `ShowInformation(0)` is called, the first plot displays the AccountID of the first Account in the provider collection (`acctIndex` is 0) and the second plot displays the Real Time Net Worth value for the same account. Since this Method does not return a value its return type is void. Void means that the content of the item is empty or void or does not exist. Void functions are stand-alone statements. Void can refer to a data type or object that does not have a return a value or type. It may or may not perform a function, other than storing a value for other processes to use.

When void is used as a function return type, it indicates that the function does not return a value.

```
Method void ShowInformation (int acctIndex)
begin
  if  (AccountsProvider1.Count  > 00)
  then begin
    Plot1 (AccountsProvider1.Account [acctIndex].AccountID, "Account
ID") ;
    Plot2 (AccountsProvider1.Account [acctIndex].RTAccountNetWorth,
```

```
"RT Net Worth") ;
  End ;  // plotting
end ;  // count greater than zero
```

A Further Walk Through the EasyLanguage Dictionary

Exploring the Dictionary is your new pastime. To truly understand OOEL you will need to spend sleepless nights clicking and reading, clicking, and reading. **Appendix II** of the **Reference Guide** is called **The Dictionary Unfolded**. By this I mean that you will want to uncheck the AutoHide option and keep the Dictionary open in the TDE. Then click on all the little **+** signs and see what's under them. In **Volume II—Reference Guide, Appendix II** I have clicked on the **+** signs and listed much of it for you. When you first read it, your job will be to just note the things that are available. You won't be able to memorize them all but say the name out loud so your brain will know they are there. Later, when you want to achieve a programming goal, you will have an ah-ha moment and know that the answer was somewhere, and you can go looking for it. If you don't even know it is there, it is much more difficult to find it.

This little interlude does not replace your study of the Appendix where everything is unfolded for you. Here I just want to give you an overview.

The first view of the Dictionary is shown in Figure 4.01. Here we see the first level of the Dictionary with only the Libraries showing. Each has a little **+** sign in front of it, meaning that there is more beneath it.

When you are looking at one **Class** or **Object** it is a wise idea to click on any **+** beneath the top level one as **Properties**, **Methods**, **Events** and **Operators** (jointly referred to as the **Members** of the Class) are inherited so not all the options you require will necessarily be visible at the top level.

Also take note of the **Namespace** under which the **Class** or **Object** falls. You will need this information when typing the **Using** statement(s).

> ✍ Actually, in general terms, it remains a class until it becomes instantiated as an Object of type ClassName. An exception are Enumerations (Enums).

The Search feature can be useful, but it can sometimes be difficult to find that same item once you cancel the Search—this is part of why I mentioned the Namespace in the paragraph above.

> ✍ It would be helpful if the TS Documentation Team were to add a Namespace field in the Description Pane (the section in the lower right). See;
> https://help.tradestation.com/10_00/eng/tsdevhelp/tsdev/about_dictionary.htm for a better idea what I am referring to.

FIGURE 4.01—Preview Level of the Dictionary

OOEL Coding Template

To make your code readable by others who might want to learn from it, or even to help you debug it or read and understand it months or years later, you should choose a template to which you adhere and stick with it. Example 4.02 shows a combination of the templates Sam and I use for the OOEL code in these books. You can create one that works for you.

EXAMPLE 4.02—OOEL Coding Template [OME_CodingTemplate]

```
{*
Type  : Study
Name  : Study_Name (OME_CodingTemplate)
Notes : Description (Example of a coding template for use with OOEL)
Create: Jun 24, 2021  01.00.00
   This has both Sunny's and Sam's templates sort of
     co-mingled. The reader can pick and choose which style
     and portions fit their requirements.
     Once you have the template the way you like it click
     "File" and "Save as Template"
Usage : Note on how to use your study, any data requirements, etc.
Note  : After you get it all set up click on "File", "Save as
Template"

EasyLanguage translation provided
  for Sunny J. Harris
   of MoneyMentor.com
  and Ask Mr. EasyLanguage
   by Samuel K. Tennis
   of Vista-Research (c) 2021-2023

Any unauthorized use of this material may constitute
  a violation of U.S. and International Copyright Laws.
*}
```

```
//----------------------------------------------------------
#region - Documentation -
//----------------------------------------------------------


{===============================================================
  Copyright 2021-2022 Sunny J Harris. ALL RIGHTS RESERVED.
  Written by:
      name      Sunny J. Harris and Samuel K. Tennis
      addr      123 Easy St, Simpleville, IL 60606
      phone     1-760-908-3070


  This code is for educational purposes only.
  Trading is speculative and risky. You might lose everything.
  No warranties of any kind are made with respect to this code, or its
  use.
  Distribution to another person or use on more than one computer can
  result in prosecution to the full extent allowable by law.
 ===============================================================}


  {*


  IDENTIFICATION
  ==============
  Name:             Name of Routine
  Note     :        Note describing the project
  Type:             Indicator
  TS Version:       10.0 Update 62
  Created:          Date of Creation
  Updated:          Date of Editing


  ----------------------------------------------------------------
  DOCUMENTATION
  =============
  This indicator does .....
  Type:  Function [Indicator]  ShowMe   Strategy   PaintBar
  ----------------------------------------------------------------
  INPUTS & EXPLANATIONS
  =====================
   j_input01( 1234 )      // first input value
   j_input02( 7654 )      // second input value
   ...
  ----------------------------------------------------------------
  FUNCTIONS CALLED
  ================
  xxx


  HISTORY
  =======
  Date        By    Version         Task
  ---------   ---   --------        -------------------------------
  08/27/21    SJH   21.08.27        * Created
  08/29/21    SJH   21.08.29        * Modified to do xxx
  ----------------------------------------------------------------
  TO DO LIST
  ==========
  Date        Version         Task
  ---------   --------        -------------------------------------
  20210920    21.09.20        Add this to the To Do List
  ----------------------------------------------------------------
  *}
```

```
#endRegion
[LegacyColorValue =  TRUE] ;
// means you can only use 16 standard colors, not RGB values

#Region - Usings
using elSystem ;
using elSystem.Collections ;
using elSystem.Drawing ;
using elSystem.IO ;
using elSystem.Net ;
using elSystem.xml ;
using elSystem.Windows.Forms ;
using Platform ;
using tsData.Common ;
#endRegion

#region - Data Declarations

// Working Storage Section
Inputs:
 Bool    ShowCmtry    (FALSE),
 Bool    WalkForward ( TRUE) ;

Consts:
 String App_Type     ("Study"),
 String App_Name     ("Study_Name"),  // "OME_CodingTemplate"
 String App_Note     ("Description"),
// "Example of a coding template for use with OOEL")
 String App_Vers     ("01.00.00 (21.09.20)") ;

Vars  :
 String DQ           (DoubleQuote),
 String NL           (NewLine),
 String CmtryStr     (""),
 String AlertStr     (""),
 Bool   doCmtry      (FALSE),
 Bool   doAlert      (FALSE),
 Bool   KeepGoing    ( TRUE),
 Bool   Debug        (FALSE),
 Double Dummy        (0.00) ;
#endRegion

// =======================================================
//    METHODS
// =======================================================
{*
 * List of Methods
 *}
#Region - Method Initialized

method void AnalysisTechnique_Initialized (elSystem.Object sender,
elSystem.InitializedEventArgs args)
begin
  Print (App_Name, ".AnalysisTechnique_Initialized      ") ;
end ; // "AnalysisTechnique_Initialized" method

// -------------------------------------------------------

method void AnalysisTechnique_UnInitialized (elSystem.Object sender,
elSystem.UnInitializedEventArgs args)
```

```
begin
  Print (App_Name, ".AnalysisTechnique_UnInitialized      ") ;
end ; // "AnalysisTechnique_UnInitialized" method

// ----------------------------------------------------

method void AnalysisTechnique_WorkspaceSaving (elSystem.Object sender,
elSystem.WorkspaceSavingEventArgs args)
begin
  Print (App_Name, ".AnalysisTechnique_WorkspaceSaving     ") ;
end ; // "AnalysisTechnique_WorkspaceSaving" method

// ----------------------------------------------------

method void App_Init ()
begin
  Print ("App_Init") ;
end ; // "App_Init" method

// ----------------------------------------------------

method void EachBarProcessing ()
begin
  Print ("EachBarProcessing") ;
  Plot1 (myPrice, "myPrice", Default, Default, Default) ;
  if  doAlert  then begin
    AlertStr += "myAlert" + NL ;
    if  AlertStr  > ""  then  Alert (AlertStr, Symbol) ;
  end ;
end ; // "EachBarProcessing" method

// ----------------------------------------------------

method void LastBarProcessing ()
begin
  Print ("LastBarProcessing") ;
end ; // "LastBarProcessing" method

#endRegion

// ========================================================
// Main Code Body
// ========================================================

// Your Main Executable Code Goes Here

once begin
  App_Init () ;
  KeepGoing  =  TRUE ;
end ; // Once, and only once

doCmtry  = AtCommentaryBar ;
if  doCmtry  then  CmtryStr = "" ;
doAlert  = CheckAlert or doCmtry ;
if  doAlert  then  AlertStr = "" ;

if  KeepGoing  then begin
  if  (Date [00]  > Date [01])  then begin
  end ; // first bar of new day
```

```
    EachBarProcessing () ;
end ; // keep going / walk forward
if  atCommentaryBar
and WalkForward
and KeepGoing  then  KeepGoing  = FALSE ;

if  LastBarOnChart  then begin
  LastBarProcessing () ;
end ; // only on the last bar of data

//-------------------------------------------------------
//    END OF CODE
//-------------------------------------------------------

#beginCmtry
if  CheckCommentary and ShowCmtry  then begin
  CommentaryCL (skt_Commentary_Header (App_Type, App_Name, App_Note,
App_Vers),
               skt_Commentary_Notes  (CmtryStr),
               skt_Commentary_Alert  (AlertStr)) ;

end ; // expert Commentary enabled for this bar
#end

{*
Custom Programming Services provided by:

             Samuel K. Tennis
             Vista-Research
                PO Box 343562
       Florida City, Florida 33034
       cell  :  1(850) 582-7342
       fax   :  1(510) 743-8274
       eMail :sktennis@vista-research.com
       eMail :sktennis@EasyLanguageOOEL.com
         http://www.vista-research.com
         http://www.facebook.com/vistaresearch
       AIM   : SKTennis
       GMail : SKTennis
       Yahoo : SamuelKTennis
       Skype : SamuelKTennis
  *}
```

The TDE includes one or more templates for Indicator, PaintBar, ShowMe, Strategy and more. Unfortunately, no template is provided for User Functions so that is where your personalized copy-and-paste version is a god send. So you can type in a blank code window your default template for this type of AT then 'Save As' a template, giving it your own name. Let me know if this topic is on interest, perhaps we shall provide a booklet describing this process in greater detail.

Classes

About Classes in EasyLanguage

An OOEL Class defines the structure for an object that can contain members such as Properties, Methods, Events and Operators. Much like a blueprint, a class describes the actions (behavior) an object can perform and the information (data) it can access.

The **elSystem.Object** Class is the ultimate parent (as far as I know) of all classes in OOEL.

Objects—Instances of a Class that allow users to access the Members defined by the class from which it is created. Multiple instances of the same class may be declared and used in an AT.

Properties—Members of a class that allow your code to read and/or write stored values. Each instance of a specific class (object) shares the same property definitions but can have different property values specific to that object.

Methods—Members of a class that perform specific actions (much like a function) within a class such as data retrieval and calculations. Methods often accept parameters (input values). They can return data of a specified type or can be void (not return a value). Methods always require parentheses, even if they are empty. Example: `myObject.toString () ;`

With methods, unlike functions, you may choose to ignore the value returned by a method and doing so inadvertently can lead to obscure errors!

Constructors—Special methods (New and/or Create) that are invoked (executed) each time a new instance of a class (object) is created. Use constructors to initialize the state of your new object.

Events—Members of a class which trigger the execution of an event handler. For instance, the Alarm Class defines an object that triggers an event when a specified time is reached.

Dot Operator—The period symbol (.) to the right of an object name is used to refer to a child element of an object (such as a property, method, or event). For instance, in the expression PositionProvider1.Count, the dot operator indicates that the term Count is referring to an element of the object named PositionProvider1 that returns the number of available positions.

Class Categories

Although each class has a unique set of members (Properties, Methods, Events and Operators), it is useful to think of them belonging to broad categories so that you'll have a better idea of what similar classes are designed to do. For example, all the Control classes used in Forms have some common properties and methods.

Components—Classes that are designed to be added to an AT from the TS Development Environment (TDE) ToolBox and will automatically generate protected (read only) code that contains objects whose properties and events can be managed using the Properties Editor. A number of components, such as Data Providers and **OrderTickets**, are found in the tsData Namespace sections of the Dictionary.

> ☑ SKT: Anything available as a Component, which can be added to the Component Tray using the ToolBox or added to a Form usin103..g the ToolBox and the Resource Editor, and thereby generates Designer Generated Code (DGC), can also be created using pure code. I do not, virtually ever, use the Component Tray. I just cannot see an advantage to it. Sunny finally showed me where it actually visually resides. I write the code myself. You may start out with the Component Tray then later, if you decide. graduate to writing the code where you have greater control and less chance of a catastrophic error and losing the ability to verify your code. One bit of advice: copy the DGC periodically and paste it in a comment block at the bottom of your code. You can paste it in anywhere but at the bottom is most convenient for me, why scroll through it to get to code you are actively editing.

Collections—Classes that allow you to create objects which may contain a collection (zero or more) of values that can be modified, stored and retrieved using common programming models including dictionaries, stacks, queues, and vectors. Think of a data structure, a sidewalk {one dimension}, a wall {two dimensions}, a room {three dimensions} or a house {more than three dimensions} built using information.

Collections are listed in **Appendix III of Volume II—Reference Guide** alphabetically, along with classes.

One concept we did not touch upon as thoroughly as we might have is the Events associated with some Collection Classes and the amount of control they may provide. **GlobalDictionary** objects communicating between ATs in real time are a prime example.

Enumerations—Enumerated Lists of named values that consist of a set of named constants called enumerators that typically allow you to evaluate a state or action associated with a property of a class.

Although you CAN use the integer value of an enumerated value it is Best Practice, and always the recommended way, to employ the Enum value instead. Examples will appear in the source files, which you may download at www.EasyLanguageOOEL.com.

Exceptions—Classes that are typically used to identify errors and will be used to throw an exception (error message) if the condition is True. The Exception base class provides a common set of methods and properties that may be accessed for these exceptions. See **Try…Catch** for more on this topic.

Support Classes—Classes that are designed to be used by higher level classes (such as Component Classes) and generally reside in the same Namespace as the classes that reference them.

System Classes—Classes that provide a general framework for other classes and typically reside under the **elSystem.ell** library.

> ✍ Unlike 'some other' object-oriented programming languages, EZL does not provide one the ability to create one's own classes. The classes that already exist are the only ones to which you have access.
>
> The one caveat to this, that I believe I have discovered and proven, is the AnalysisTechnique class itself: your local methods alter the structure of this Object.

AnalysisTechnique Class

This is the base class for an AT object. All EZL Analysis Techniques (AT) (ActivityBar, Indicator, PaintBar, ProbabilityMap, ShowMe, Strategy, TradingApp, User Function etc.) are automatically created as an instance of the **AnalysisTechnique** Class which allows you to access information about the AT from other objects using the listed properties. No "Using Namespace" required. The **AnalysisTechnique** Class has properties available including 'Symbol' (actually a Quote Field I believe) and 'Name'. The Class also has AppStorage. You can also create your own Event Handler methods that respond to the Initialized, UnInitialized and WorkspaceSaving events.

The **AnalysisTechnique** Class may be referenced, if it makes you more comfortable, by using the term 'Self'. For example:

```
Once
   self.Initialized      += App_Initialized ;
   self.UnInitialized    += App_UnInitialized ;
   self.WorkspaceSaving  += App_WorkspaceSaving ;
end ; // Once, and only once
```

To use the **Initialized**, **UnInitialized** and **WorkspaceSaving** events for an Analysis Technique when using the Resource Editor you need to do the following:

After creating an EZL Analysis Technique document, open the Properties window.

Select the **AnalysisTechnique** Object from the combo box at the top of the Properties window.

Click ⚡ to go to the Events tab.

Double-click on the **Initialized**, **WorkspaceSaving**, and/or **UnInitialized** Event to create an Event Handler method in your Analysis Technique document.

> ✍ Doing this will create Designer Generated Code (DGC) meaning you cannot just copy the text and paste it somewhere else and expect it to run. Export the .eld file instead.

NAMESPACE: elSystem

PROPERTIES

	Name	Type	Description
📑	AppStorage	object	A **Dictionary** of name-value pairs that will be persistent when an Analysis Technique is closed-reopened, re-verified, or has its inputs modified. AppStorage is an instance of the **Dictionary** class. Any object can be placed in AppStorage. However, only native data type values (int, bool, string, float, double, byte) and "serializable" objects that contain native data type elements (see below for a list of "serializable" Objects) should be expected to retain all of their values "permanently" (that is, beyond the time during which the Analysis Technique is running). Thus, for example, an integer value can be stored in AppStorage and retrieved from AppStorage even after the computer has been restarted. But an instance of the Position class cannot be so stored and retrieved since the Position class is not "serializable." If instances of the following classes contain only the native data types, then the instances (objects) are serializable: 1) Dictionary 2) Vector 3) Stack 4) Queue If desired, EZL code can be written to put values into AppStorage when the WorkspaceSaving event fires (see below for details on the WorkspaceSaving event). Values can be placed in AppStorage at any time, but it is sometimes convenient to store values when the workspace is saved (that is, when the WorkspaceSaving event fires).
📑	DataNum	int	The number of the data stream (zero-based) to use for the Analysis Technique.
📑	DataStreams	object	Used to access additional information about the data streams used by the Analysis Technique. See DataStreams for more info.
📑	DrawingObjects	object	Used to add, delete, and access drawing objects in a chart. See DrawObjects for more info.
📑	Name	string	The name of the Analysis Technique.

TABLE 4.01—AnalysisTechnique Properties

METHODS

	Name	Description
⦿	GetDataNum ()	Gets the number of the data stream used by the Analysis Technique.
⦿	GetParent ()	The AnalysisTechnique object that called this Analysis Technique.

TABLE 4.02—AnalysisTechnique Methods

EVENTS

	Name	Description
⚡	Initialized	Event handler that is called when the Analysis Technique first runs. See **InitializedEventArgs** for the properties returned by the handler's args parameter.
⚡	UnInitialized	Event handler that is called as the Analysis Technique is shutting down and prior to finishing calculation. See **UnInitializedEventArgs** for the properties returned by the handler's args parameter.
⚡	WorkSpaceSaving	Event handler that is called when a workspace containing the Analysis Technique is to be saved. See **WorkSpaceSavingEventArgs** for the properties returned by the handler's args parameter.

TABLE 4.03—AnalysisTechnique Events

INHERITANCE HIERARCHY

elSystem.Object
  elSystem.AnalysisTechnique

More About Event Handlers

The Initialized event can be used to call an Event Handler method that contains code that is called only once prior to calculations commencing in the AT. The Initialized Event Handler might be used to perform one time initialization of variables or perform any other operation that needs to occur at the time the AT first runs and not thereafter.

Likewise, the UnInitialized event can be used to call an Event Handler method that contains code that is called prior to the calculation of the AT finishing. The UnInitialized Event Handler might be used to execute any cleanup code required to be run before the AT shuts down. This could happen when the AT is removed from an analysis window or when a window, workspace, or desktop is closed. The UnInitialized Event is also called prior to recalculation. However, in the case of an exception error there are times that the UnInitialized Event Handler may not get called.

> ☑ An UnInitialized Event may be fired after the contents of the AT have been saved to its workspace, so this event should not be used to store values (such as AppStorage) associated with the Analysis Technique.

The WorkSpaceSaving Event occurs when the workspace containing the AT is about to be saved. This event fires before the AnalysisTechnique UnInitialized Event occurs, so creating a method to handle this event is a good place to store values associated with an AT, such as AppStorage values, that need to be updated before the AT is closed.

> ☑ More about AppStorage in Chapter 8 and in **Volume II—Reference Guide, Appendix III.**

Class Declaration (Instantiation)

Before a Class can be used as an Object in EZL, it needs to be instantiated which consists of declaring a new object variable of the class type and creating a new instance of the class as an object.

To make the code more readable you can add a **Using** statement(s) to avoid retyping Namespace prefixes when referencing Classes and their Members.

EXAMPLE 4.03—Employing Using Statements

```
// EasyLanguage Class Declaration:
// define namespaces your code & declared classes might use

// used to reference system base classes:
using elSystem;

// used to reference TS trading classes:
using tsData.Trading;

// object declaration
Vars :
// define an object variable of type AccountsProvider
AccountsProvider myAcctProvider (null) ;
// Instantiate an object of the class specified
myAcctProvider = new AccountsProvider ;
```

Methods

A Method implements an action that you can ask an object to perform; not the most sensible name, but it is what the software industry uses. In OOEL, objects can have methods, but TS also uses the term Method for a block of code in the EZL "file" that can be invoked from one or more than one place in the program (presumably because they can't call it a "function" as that term already means something else).

More about methods is explained in **Chapter 6** where we give you samples and useful snippets of code.

They are identical, actually–your AT is an Object, it has Properties (such as 'Name' and AppStorage) and it has Events (Initialized, UnInitialized, WorkSpaceSaving,) plus any methods you create that are local to this AT. It seems that AT is the only Class in OOEL that you can modify.

The Method reserved word allows you to create a named "subroutine" within an AT that consists of a sequence of statements to perform an action, a set of (optional) input parameters to customize those actions, and possibly a return value. In this chapter we will only cover methods cursorily and devote a whole chapter to discovering Methods in depth.

Methods are not restricted to OOEL. Any job you need to carry out in your main code body, especially if it is repetitive, might be a candidate for a Method. For example, if you use one set of code if you are long and another if you are short, and only the plus and minus signs change. Some numeric process, a string manipulation, shifting an array–if you could do it in a User Function then you can do it in a Method. OK, I (Sam) do not think you can pass an Array to a method as an Input. Variables in Methods have no BarsBack history. All those points can be resolved with clever coding. I very frequently reduce ten lines of code in my main code body to "doPlots ()" or "EachBarProcessing ()" – single line calls that move minutia out of my way and allow me to view more of the main code body on the screen at one time!

REMARKS

Methods are local to the AT and local variables declared within a Method and are active only within the scope of that Method. The EZL statements within a Method are only executed when the Method is called. A Method can be called from anywhere within the AT in which it resides. You can think of a Method as a local subroutine that resides in the body of your code.

One benefit of Methods to an EZL programmer is that they allow an action to be applied at several different points in the program, without having to duplicate the code to carry out that action. A secondary benefit is that they allow a block of statements to be parceled up and given a descriptive name, allowing the code that applies the Method to be short; understanding, and finding errors in, a block of code is easier if it can all be seen on the screen without scrolling, than if you must scroll up and down to see the code.

Libraries

When you click on the Dictionary icon from the menu bar at the top of the screen (from within the TDE) it will bring up a list of the Libraries in EZL. If you are like me, you may want the Dictionary to stay open all the time while you are learning and exploring available choices. To do this select the Dictionary Tab that typically resides vertically at the right side of the TDE. Then click on the ▼ to bring up the Window Position selector. Uncheck Auto Hide and check Docking instead.

First, however you need to know what a Library is because each of the items in the pull-down menu is a library. If you look it up in Google, here is what you see:

> In computer science, a library is a collection of non-volatile resources used by computer programs, often for software development. These may include configuration data, documentation, help data, message templates, pre-written code and subroutines, classes, values or type specifications.

Okay! Now we really understand, right? Wrong! Wait 'til I define Namespace in just a bit. I'm afraid these concepts only get clearer with use.

All the EZL-type commands live in a library called **easylanguage.ell**. And all the charting commands live in a library called **elcharting.ell**. This will make a little bit more sense when we open the libraries in Figure 4.03 and look at what lies inside them. (Hint: lots of classes.)

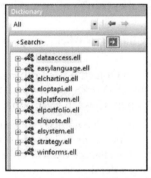

FIGURE 4.02—The Libraries in the First Level of the Dictionary

Name	Description	Related
easylanguage	Contains references to legacy EasyLanguage reserved words and functions.	
elsystem	Contains base classes that are used by tsdata classes and other elsystem classes.	
elsystem.collections	Contains base classes that are used to create different types of collection objects.	
elsystem.elcomponentmodel	Contains base classes that are used to describe the editing behavior of components.	
elsystem.windows.forms	Contains classes that are used to create forms controls and containers.	
elsystem.io	Contains base classes that are used to handle input/output system exceptions.	
elsystem.excel	Contains base classes that are used to access data from Excel spreadsheet files.	
elsystem.xml	Contains base classes that are used to manage data in XML files.	
strategy	Contains classes that are used to manage strategies and strategy automation.	
tsdata.common	Contains classes that are used by other tsdata namespaces.	
tsdata.marketdata	Contains classes that are used to access market data such as price quotes, market levels, and fundamental values.	
tsdata.trading	Contains classes that are used to manage trades, positions, and account information.	

FIGURE 4.03—Namespaces and Their Descriptions

Conveniently, TS gives us the quick reference to namespaces in Figure 4.06. Once again, they are using circular logic in telling me "… that contain classes that are used to…" what then is a class? Back to the oracle, for Google's definition of class:

> In object-oriented programming, a class is an extensible program-code-template for creating objects, providing initial values for state (member variables) and implementations of behavior (member functions or Methods).

Once again, it isn't elucidating. To understand what a class is in OOEL we must first know what an object is. Turns out that you can think of an object as a person, place or thing. A **Trendline** is a thing: an object. A **Form** is an object. A **Vector** is an object.

Other programming languages have objects, too. Recall that I mentioned in the beginning of this book that my Adobe Acrobat program has objects. The objects are defined by the application, but the concept is the same. The objects in Acrobat are things like Flip Horizontal, Flip Vertical, Crop and Rotate.

A class is a group of one or more objects that have similar attributes. With humans, all who have black hair is a class of humans; all who are taller than 6' tall is a class of humans (to which I belong).

Namespaces are used much like folders and files in your computer's directory. They are employed for grouping symbols, identifiers and functions similar in nature together. We could consider a state, like California, to be a namespace and cities under that and streets and then house numbers. Population might be a Method within both State and City with Input parameters (filters) such as Sex, AgeRange, Ethnicity, EmploymentStatus, etc. There also may be enumerated lists defining the accepted values (ex: Gender may be Male, Female, Other) for the filter inputs. This gives us the unique representations we need to identify what namespace you live in. I remind myself that it is a space where names live.

Names in classes cannot have more than one meaning. Sunny Harris and Sunny Harris would not be unique and so we can't have two Sunny Harris' in one class. Likewise, we have a namespace on our computer called directories with folders and files under that.

There are ten libraries listed above in Figure 4.02. We can guess at some of the functions that lie under the top-level container names, but to really get an idea of what is going on under the namespace we need to take a closer look. **easylanguage.ell** seems pretty self-explanatory, but what is under something like **eloptapi.ell**? Let's find out.

> ☑ SKT: It is important to differentiate the Library (.ell) from the actual Namespace ({}). Unlike what the TS help frequently states, the Library name is NOT a parent for the actual Namespace. As an example "Using elQuote.Quote ;" will not verify, the correct Namespace is "Quote". So, in the paragraph before "elOptApi.ell" is the Library name and "tsOpt" is the Namespace name."
>
> Because it came straight from the TS Help engine it took me a long time to spot this error.

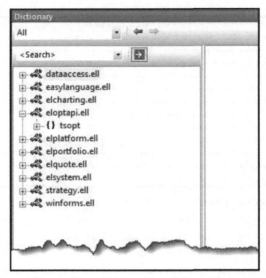

FIGURE 4.04—Second Level Shows Namespace tsOpt under eloptapi.ell

The next level, when you click on **eloptapi.ell**, gives us more information, but it is not overly revealing. The library **eloptapi.ell** contains the namespace **tsopt**. At least I've figured out what it means, though; el is for EasyLanguage, opt is for Optimization and api is for Application Programming Interface.

An API lets two applications talk to each other. An API is a set of programming tools, potentially including documentation, that is used to create a widget of some sort—the widget is not the API. It is an end-product. When you use Facebook or send an instant message, you are using an API. When you use an application on your mobile phone, the application connects to the Internet and sends data to a server. The server then retrieves that data, interprets it, performs the necessary actions, and sends it back to your phone. The application then interprets that data and presents you with the information you wanted in a readable way.

What then is under the newly revealed **{ } tsopt** (which probably stands for TS Optimization)? Click on the **+** sign to the left of **{ } tsopt** to reveal the Classes contained within the Namespace. See Figure 4.05. The list is very long, and not all are included in this figure, but you get the idea. If you want to see a full listing of these items, go to **Volume II—Reference Guide, Appendix II: Dictionary Unfolded**. You might also want to download a copy of *EasyLanguage Optimization API* on the TS Forum. It is not what this book is—it is not easy. But you can quickly get an idea of what OOEL code looks like with a great deal of explanation of its use.

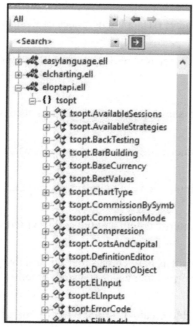

FIGURE 4.05—Cascading Menu Under tsopt

Notice that each subsequent Class has **tsOpt** preceding the description and then a period (.). This gives us more information about the subspace. All these things have to do with optimization.

Clicking again on the **+** sign opens one more layer. You may want to click more than once, so we can see what lives under the main headings. Now, however, when I click on **tsopt.AvailableSessions** information appears in the box to the right of the panel revealing the properties of that Class. They are:

- Create () (method)
- GetSessionName (int) (method)
- Count (property)
- Session (property)

Only more time with the Dictionary will reveal greater meanings; either that or turn now to **Volume II—Reference Guide, Appendix II: The Dictionary Unfolded** and read through it briefly one (or more) time(s).

Everything you need to know lives in the Dictionary. When I watch Sam program on Tuesdays and Thursdays, I see him exploring the Dictionary for the correct syntax for what it is he's looking up. No need to memorize formats, just the function of the commands. Just like when I need the Print command for a program in EZL, I go to my book *TradeStation Made Easy!* to find the full definition of the command, as I don't have it memorized. More on the Dictionary later.

Just as an example, when I am creating the Event Handler(s) for a button click I find the click event then copy the parameters I need to paste into the Event Handler parameter list.

Namespaces

Namespaces (also called a name scope) represent a logical grouping of classes that relate to one another. The EZL class library includes the following main namespaces that appear when expanding the xxx.ell folders in the Dictionary:

tsdata

Contains the Common, MarketData and Trading Namespaces

tsdata.common

Contains classes that are used by other tsData Namespaces as well as elsewhere.

tsdata.marketdata

Contains classes that are used to access market data such as price quotes, market levels, and fundamental values.

tsdata.trading

Contains classes that are used to manage trades, positions, and account information.

charting

Contains classes that are used to interface with a chart analysis window.

platform

Contains classes that are used to interface with the main platform and settings.

quote

Contains classes that are used to interface with a quote (grid) window.

elSystem

Contains several Namespaces as well as base classes that are used by tsdata classes and other elSystem classes as well as classes that perform some general system function or report error conditions.

elSystem.collections

Contains base classes that are used to create different types of collection objects.

elSystem.drawing

Contains classes that are used to describe the color and font characteristics of form controls and drawing objects.

elSystem.DrawingObjects

Contains classes that are used to create and manipulate drawing tools (trendlines, text, rectangles, etc.) in a chart window.

elSystem.io

Contains base classes that are used to handle input/output system exceptions.

elSystem.Office.Excel

Contains base classes that are used to access data from Excel spreadsheet files.

elSystem.xml

Contains base classes that are used to manage data in XML files.

strategy

Contains classes that are used to manage strategies and strategy automation.

elSystem.Windows.Forms

Contains classes that are used to create forms controls and containers.

About Objects in EasyLanguage

An object in EZL is a declared instance of a class, which has been instantiated, that contain all members (such as Properties, Methods, enumerated lists and Events) of the class. An object is created through instantiation which involves declaring an object variable and then using a constructor statement like **New** Reserved Word or the **Create ()** Method to create the object instance into that object variable. See **Class Declaration** for a generic class declaration and an initialization example.

Once an object has been created (instantiated), you can access the object properties (values) that are specific to that object instance, and you can use the object methods to perform actions that have been defined as behaviors of the object.

Properties are attributes that allow your EZL code to read and/or write stored values. Each instance of a class (object) shares the same property definitions but can have different property values specific to that object.

An example might be 'Symbol' which may be the symbol on the chart or a symbol you set the Property to.

```
myObject.Symbol  = "IBM" ;
```

Methods are actions that can be performed by an object and often act using values from properties. Methods can accept parameters (input values). They can return data of a specified type or can be void (not return a value). Another way of thinking about Methods is that they are local functions.

Events are object actions that trigger a call to a Method called an Event Handler that can handle the action. For example, a timer object can call an 'Elapsed' event handler when the time value has counted down to zero.

Inheritance

In object-oriented programming, inheritance is the mechanism of basing an object or class upon another object or class, retaining similar implementation. An inherited class is called a subclass of its parent class. Trendline is a subclass of DrawingObjects (the 'Parent'), for instance.

Inheritance is one of the most important aspects of object-oriented programming. The key to understanding Inheritance is that it provides code re-usability. In place of writing the same code, again and again, we can simply inherit the members of one class into the other.

In short, classes and objects can have properties in common and belong to higher classes or objects. SubClasses/SubObjects get their members from the parent class/object.

Here we should refer back to the table presented in Table 2.13, where we could see all the symbols used in the Dictionary. I'll display it again for your convenience.

Symbol	Meaning
	Class
	Enumeration
	Event
	Library
	Method or Function
	Namespace or Category
	Operator
	Property
	Reserved Word

TABLE 4.04—Dictionary Exploration Aid

I bring this to the fore for you so that you can browse through the Dictionary and know what is what. Let's find a class, for instance. The graphic symbol in the left column resembles a genealogy chart with descendants. There is a yellow, larger, box with a red and a green, smaller, box coming off it. When you see this icon, you will know that you have found a class.

Classes are listed in **Volume II—Reference Guide: Appendix III**.

Events

According to Wikipedia:

An event can be defined as "a significant change in state. For example, when a consumer purchases a car, the car's state changes from "for sale" to "sold". A car dealer's system architecture may treat this state change as an event whose occurrence can be made known to other applications within the architecture. From a formal perspective, what is produced, published, propagated, detected, or consumed is a (typically asynchronous) message called the event notification, and not the event itself, which is the state change that triggered the message emission. Events do not travel, they just occur. However, the term event is often used metonymically to denote the notification message itself, which may lead to some confusion. This is due to Event-Driven architectures often being designed atop message-driven architectures, where such communication pattern requires one of the inputs to be text-only, the message, to differentiate how each communication should be handled.

Events are essentially actions—"something happens" then the program "responds." For instance, there are Events for the following: Click event, StateChanged, Updated, ElementSelected, AlarmEvent, Initialized, TimerElapsed and more. You will find events listed under their respective class in **Volume II—Reference Guide**: **Appendix III**.

Event Handlers

Perhaps the easiest way to explain Event Handlers is like this: Consider the **Button** Class. You create a button on your Form. The button is useless until you give it some meaning. Without an Event Handler, it will just sit there. To get it to do something you need to define how the button will react when it is clicked. Once you click the Button a Click Event is fired. You need to set up the Event Handler to respond to that Click Event.

The basic shell of an Event Handler can look like this:

```
Method void replaceMe (elSystem.Object Sender, … args)
Begin
  Print ("replaceMe") ;
End ; // "replaceMe" method
// I fill in the "replaceMe" after I properly
// name my event handler
```

Now go to the Dictionary and search for the Click event, (you will need to 'dumpster dive' until you get to **elSystem.Windows.Forms.Control** to find the Click event). See Figure 4.06.

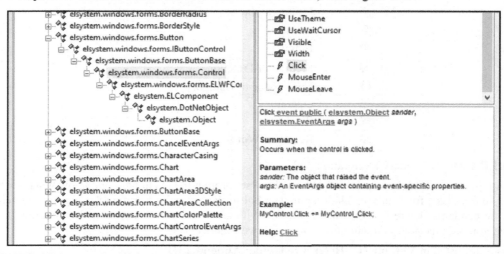

FIGURE 4.06—Button.Click Event from the Dictionary

Highlight and copy this Method to the clipboard; and then paste within the empty parentheses the Parameters the Event Handler expects, starting with **elSystem.Object** and ending with args. It is just easier and safer than typing it all, although the Sender part is always the same and could be part of the template. Now remove the "event public" from the code and you are set to go. When the Button is clicked it will fire the Event which you can now properly handle.

One more thing. You also might want to add `if Debug then` before the **Print** statement, though I usually add it later when the noise in the **Print Log** becomes too great.

Provider Classes

The use of **DataProviders** and **OrderTickets** will be addressed in Chapters 12 and 13. This is only a cursory look at the concept and the requisite classes before we go on.

In OOEL, provider classes represent a group of component classes whose names end with the word Provider and are used to access data from one or more classes referenced in the Provider, including changes to the data in real-time. The provider classes inherit characteristics from the **tsdata.common.DataProvider** class that allows you to connect an event handler method in your EZL code to a provider **Updated** event or **StateChanged** event. An **Updated** event fires when the provider is loaded for the first time and, thereafter, when the data contained in the provider is updated real-time. The **StateChanged** event reports a change in the loaded or unloaded state of the provider. Providers also inherit from the **elSystem.elComponent** class that allows you to double-click and drop a provider component from the toolbox into your AT and to edit the values for the component using the Properties Editor.

Probably the most satisfying Provider Class to just play around with is the **SymbolAttributesProvider**, just so much meat to go with the potatoes.

PROVIDERS

Name	Description
AccountsProvider	Gets account balance and other information from specified TS accounts.
FundamentalQuotesProvider	Gets information from specified fundamental fields for a symbol.
MarketDepthProvider	Gets market depth bid and ask levels regarding specified ECN books for a symbol.
NewsProvider	Gets news items for specified symbols and date ranges.
OrdersProvider	Gets updated order status information based on user specified filters.
PositionsProvider	Gets information about positions from specified TS accounts.
PriceSeriesProvider	Gets a historical price series for a specified symbol and interval, including real-time updates.
QuotesProvider	Gets information from specified quote fields for a symbol.
RSSProvider	Gets RSS news items from a specified RSS feed and web address.
SymbolAttributesProvider	Gets information and attributes for a specified symbol.
TimeAndSalesProvider	Gets information about Level I trades as well as changes in the best bid and best ask prices.

TABLE 4.05—List of Provider Classes

About the ToolBox

The ToolBox includes a collection of components that may be placed into the AT that is currently  open in the EZL editor simply by ⌐ Double-Clicking the desired component. Once in the editor, object-oriented code for the component is automatically generated as Designer Generated Code (DGC). The object code is protected (not intended to be edited directly) but can be viewed by clicking the ⌐ View menu and selecting Designer Generated Code (DGC). The values contained in the component generated code can be modified using the Properties Editor.

☑ To copy the text from the Designer Generated Code window press Ctrl-A (Select All) then Ctrl-C (Copy). You can now press Ctrl-V (Paste) to insert the text into a comment block in the main AT.

Using the ToolBox

ToolBox components are grouped into sections that may be expanded/collapsed using the +/- buttons next to each section tab title.

To find the ToolBox you may follow this pathway:

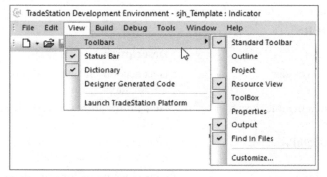

Or ⌐ Right-Click on the ToolBox tab in your TDE window.

To add a component to your code you may create a variable declaration for the object or click a component to select it and then ⌐ Double-Click it into the EZL editor. See **EasyLanguage Components** for details.

To add a new section tab to the ToolBox, click ▼ on the ToolBox title bar (or ⌐ Right-Click in a blank area of the ToolBox and select Add Tab). You can also ⌐ Right-Click on a tab to remove or rename a tab.

To add or remove components to a tabbed section of the ToolBox, ⌐ Right-Click on the tab and select Choose Items. From the Choose ToolBox Items dialog box, place a check mark next to items to be included and uncheck items to be removed. Click OK when done.

Summary

In this chapter I have covered a wide range of material aiming to prepare you to code OOEL and Sam has given you a lot of examples.

I have led you through the Dictionary and the vocabulary you need to understand Libraries, Namespaces, Classes, Instantiation, Objects, Inheritance, Events and Provider Classes. We have also defined Methods and explored the use of Date and Time manipulation.

Using the ToolBox is very useful when creating Forms using the Resource Editor. It certainly makes it easier. It is especially useful to new OOEL programmers.

Once you study the DGC for a while you will get the hang of coding without the ToolBox.

Sam uses the ToolBox and Resource Editor during the Sandbox[37] portion of his development process. He also copies the DGC and pastes it into a comment section at the bottom of his source code. When prototyping is complete, he creates a new AT (not Save As…) and pastes in the code. He then cuts and pastes the DGC where appropriate in the code he is working on. No more DGC.

---

[37] Sandbox: an isolated testing environment that enables users to run programs or open files without affecting the application.

CHAPTER 5
Debugging, Exceptions & Error Handling

In This Chapter

- Introduction
- Divide by Zero
- Infinite Loop Detection
- Printing as a Debugging Tool
- Analysis Commentary as a Debugging Tool

- Debug
- Exceptions
- Try…Catch…Finally
- Throw
- Summary

Introduction

No matter who is writing code there are always mistakes ("bugs[38]"), whether just typos or putting a comma when you meant to put a semicolon. When that happens, your code won't Verify. You might get an unintelligible error message or one that pinpoints the error and the line number. It happens. This chapter is meant to assist you in locating and diagnosing your errors).

We will explore several possibilities for you to consider. Hope it helps.

Divide by Zero

It is always illegal to divide a number by a value of zero. This results in a divide by zero error. The answer is infinity. But infinity is an undefined term to a computer. Within reason one should always test for a non-zero divisor prior to performing a division operation. Wherever possible replace division with multiplication. For example, replace `/ 2` with `* 0.50`.

To catch yourself so as not to cause this error, you should always check the numbers in your code before attempting a division. For instance, first check the denominator for not equal to zero. This can be accomplished as follows:

EXAMPLE 5.01—Checking for Divide by Zero

```
If Divisor <> 0 then Value1 = Numerator / Divisor ;
```

Another way to accomplish the same thing is to avoid the division and multiply instead.

EXAMPLE 5.02—Multiplying Instead of Dividing

If you, for instance you want to divide by 2 just multiply by 0.5 (the reciprocal of 2) instead.

```
Value1 = Numerator * 0.50 ;
```

InfiniteLoopDetect

You don't ever want to get caught in an infinite loop and have to CTRL-ALT-DEL to kill the application. It can just spoil your day.

The **InfiniteLoopDetect** keyword directive allows you to enable or disable infinite detection in an AT. Infinite loop detection logic will always be enabled by default (i.e., if no attribute is present detection logic will be enabled). If the same attribute appears more than once in a document, an error

---

[38] The first recorded use of the term "bug", with regards to an error or malfunction in a machine, comes from none other than Thomas Edison, in an 1878 letter to an associate. The popularity of the term is credited to Admiral Grace Hopper, computer programming pioneer.

message will appear during Verify.

EXAMPLE 5.03—Infinite Loop Detection

```
[InfiniteLoopDetect = FALSE]
// Turns off infinite loop detection
```

Attributes are local to the document (function, indicator, strategy, etc.) in which they are used so it is possible to have a function with detection disabled but the calling Analysis Technique with the logic enabled. Also, attributes are evaluated at compile time only so their values cannot be changed at run-time.

Printing as a Debugging Tool

Printing is probably the first resort for most EZL programmers, especially new ones. It is very easy to throw Print statements around the suspect code and inspect the Print Log. No complexity, no fuss, no muss.

When I was recently making improvements to my CPC© Index indicator, I was getting zeros when I expected values. So, I put **Print** statements above and below where I thought the values should have been calculated. Example 5.04 shows you one of my **Print** statements.

EXAMPLE 5.04—Using a Print Statement to Locate Errors

```
Print ("AvgWin= ", AvgWin, ", AvgLoss= ", AvgLoss, ", AvgTrade= ",
AvgTrade) ;
```

The extra space following the equal sign is to separate the values and their descriptions and make the output prettier and easier to read. Turns out the printout was also displaying zero values. What now? In this case I found out by scouring the code that I hadn't assigned them values, so of course they were all zero. Easy to fix.

Sometimes you want to print with every bar of data. In that case having the date and time of the bar is helpful.

EXAMPLE 5.05—Printing DateTime, Open, High, Low and Close

```
Print (BarDateTime.toString (), ", ", Open:2:4, , ", ", High:2:4, , ",
", Low:2:4, , ", ", Close:2:4) ;
// add variables to the 'chain'
```

There are times where you wish to limit the print to only a specific time period. There are ways to do that as well.

EXAMPLE 5.06—Printing Data Between Selected Dates

```
If  Date  > 1210501 and Date <  1211001  then Print …
If  Date  = 1210501 and Time  > 1000 and time <  1400  then Print …
```

Analysis Commentary as a Debugging Tool

Sometimes you want to click on a specific bar on your chart and examine the data and output at that bar. You might want to do this at several bars in sequence to debug your code and completely understand what's going on in it.

To invoke the Analysis Commentary (AC) you need to do three things:

Check if Commentary is turned on by having a statement in your code that uses the **CheckCommentary** reserved word in an if statement. (This is not mandatory; it is just good form.) This reserved word returns True if the user clicks on a chart with the AC pointer on the specified bar. False is returned if the pointer has not been inserted, or if the pointer was inserted on a different bar. In other words, as your EZL code is evaluated from the first bar following the **MaxBarsBack** buffer up to the final bar of data on one bar, if you clicked the AC Cursor on a bar (which is what lead to the recalculation, in this example) then on one, and only one, bar the **atCommentaryBar** will be True.

Include one or more **Commentary** and/or **CommentaryCL** statements in your code that consists of concatenated strings that you want to appear in the Commentary window. The CL means Carriage Return/Line Feed.

Click on the Commentary pointer in your charting, which usually lies on the top right of the Chart Analysis window and looks like this: ⬒. I know, it's difficult to see and almost looks grayed out, but it's there. If you don't see it, invoke the Classic Charting Tools toolbar in the Customize dialog box by clicking the last little q to the right of Settings on the menu bar to get to ☝ Customize → Toolbars ☑ Charting Tools Classic and then click Apply.

If you only wanted code to be evaluated for the bar where the user had inserted the Analysis Commentary Tool, you could use the syntax in Example 5.07 below.

> ✍ Concatenated (also catenated) Strings can be a string representative of numeric, Boolean or string value; same rules apply as with Print statements.

For instance, the following example shows you a short piece of minimalist code that gets you started.

EXAMPLE 5.07—The Minimum Code for Invoking Commentary

```
If  atCommentaryBar  Then Begin
  {Your Code Here}
  CommentaryCL (BarDateTime.toString (), ", ", Open:2:4, , ", ",
High:2:4, , ", ", Low:2:4, , ", ", Close:2:4) ;
// add variables to the 'chain'
End ;  // Check Commentary
```

In the following example I have used HTML because it makes the Commentary window so pretty. Remember that we use Sam's convention for **NewLine** instead of typing it out each time, so you need to have a String declared in your **Vars:** or **Consts:** statement that says `String NL (NewLine);` so that you can say NL instead of **NewLine**.

EXAMPLE 5.08—Minimum Code for Using Analysis Commentary

```
Vars  : String NL (NewLine) ;
if CheckCommentary then begin
  CommentaryCL ("Study : '<strong>", "SunnyBands" ,"</strong>' ",
// Close
  "<FONT size='" + NumToStr (03,00)
              + "' Face='"  + "Courier New"
              + "' Color='" + jColor + "'>"  +
              "Close= " + "</FONT>" , Close, NL,
// Open
  "<FONT size='" + NumToStr (03,00)
              + "' Face='"  + "Courier New"
              + "' Color='" + jColor + "'>"  +
              "Open=  " + "</FONT>" , Open, NL,
// High
  "<FONT size='" + NumToStr (03,00)
              + "' Face='"  + "Courier New"
              + "' Color='" + jColor + "'>"  +
              "High=  " + "</FONT>" , High, NL,
// Low
  "<FONT size='" + NumToStr (03,00)
              + "' Face='"  + "Courier New"
              + "' Color='" + jColor + "'>"  +
              "Low=   " + "</FONT>" , Low, NL) ;
```

The above example is code from my SunnyBands© indicator. You can see how nicely the values line up using the Courier New font and how I can change the colors based on whether the close was up or down using HTML.

```
sjh_I_SunnyBands$$_21.10.22
Study : 'SunnyBands' 04/05/202
https://www.moneymentor.com
Close=  15148.25
Open=   15155.50
High=   15162.75
Low=    15144.50
```

FIGURE 5.01—Using HTML in Commentary

Debug

Here's an example of how to engage Debug:

EXAMPLE 5.09—Using Debug [OME_Debug]

```
// Global Variable Declarations
Vars  : // Global Variable Declarations
Bool   Debug (FALSE) ;
// control over Global debugging output

// Local debug control
Method void MyMethod ()
Vars  :
 Bool   Debug ;
Begin
  Debug  =  TRUE ; // local debug variable
  If  Debug
    then  Print ("some information goes here…") ;
End ; // "myMethod" method
```

You can later comment out the local variable declaration and the Debug = TRUE statement to return to global debug setting.

ClearDebug or ClearPrintLog

These reserved words both clear the contents of the Print Log window. Usually this is put in a **Once** statement at the top of your code.

Exceptions

An exception is an event which occurs during the execution of a program that disrupts the normal flow of the program's instructions. When an error occurs EZL allows you to intercept normal handling of the error and designate special processing instructions to deal with it.

Exception Class

The Exception Class defines the base class for exception objects used to handle system error conditions when executing EZL code.

NAMESPACE: elSystem

PROPERTIES

	Name	Description
🖾	Category	Gets the category of the exception.

	Name	Description
📭	Data	Gets a collection of key/value pairs that provide additional user-defined exceptions about the error condition.
📭	HelpLink	Gets or sets a link to the help file associated with this exception.
📭	InnerException	Gets the exception instance that caused the current exception.
📭	Message	Gets a message that describes the current exception.
📭	Source	Gets or sets the name of the application or the object that causes the error.
📭	StackTrace	Gets the call sequence string of the code up to the point of the exception.
📭	TargetSite	Gets the name of the Method that throws the current exception.

TABLE 5.01—Exception Class Properties

METHODS

	Name	Description
🔷	Create ()	Initializes a new instance of the class.
🔷	Create (Message, ex)	Initializes a new instance of the class with the specified error Message and a reference to the inner ex (Exception object) that is the cause of this exception.
🔷	GetBaseException ()	Gets the exception that is the root cause for one or more exceptions.
🔷	ToString ()	Returns a string representation of the current exception.
🔷	UnInitialize ()	Deallocates memory and performs any necessary cleanup.

TABLE 5.02—Exception Class Methods

INHERITANCE HIERARCHY

elSystem.Object
  elSystem.SystemException
  elSystem.Exception

SystemException Class

This defines the base class for system exception objects used to handle system error conditions.

NAMESPACE: elSystem

PROPERTIES

	Name	Description
📭	Category	Gets the category of the exception.
📭	Data	Gets a collection of key/value pairs that provides additional user-defined exceptions about the error condition.
📭	HelpLink	Gets or sets a link to the help file associated with this exception.
📭	InnerException	Gets the exception instance that caused the current exception.
📭	Message	Gets a message that describes the current exception.
📭	Source	Gets or sets the name of the application or the object that causes the

	Name	Description
		error.
🖼	StackTrace	Gets the call sequence string of the code up to the point of the exception.
🖼	TargetSite	Gets the name of the Method that throws the current exception.

TABLE 5.03—SystemException Class Properties

METHODS

	Name	Description
◈	Create (Message, ex)	Initializes a new instance of the class with the specified error Message and a reference to the inner ex (Exception object) that is the cause of this exception.
◈	GetBaseException ()	Gets the exception that is the root cause for one or more exceptions.
◈	ToString ()	Returns a string representation of the current exception.

TABLE 5.04—SystemException Class Methods

INHERITANCE HIERARCHY

elSystem.Object
  elSystem.SystemException

Try...Catch...Finally

Many things you will want to do with OOEL will require you to first see if some condition will cause an exception in your code.

There are some operations that are inherently liable to cause an error (examples could be reading from a file, writing to a file, referencing fields within a **Vector**) and there is a way to code around this.

The **Try**, **Catch** and **Finally** reserved words work together to make up a code structure that is used to test for exceptions and handle them when they occur. Generally, a **Try...Catch...Finally** statement consists of a **Try** block is followed by one or more **Catch** clauses to handle exceptions and, optionally, a **Finally** block to clean up resources before exiting the statement. The guarded code in the **Try** block is executed until an exception is thrown or until all the **Try** block code is successfully executed. If an exception is thrown, the **Catch** block is examined for a statement that handles the exception. If no **Catch** statement is found, the system generates an error message and program execution may possibly halt. If a **Finally** block is present, it will be the last set of code executed in the statement regardless of whether any exceptions have been thrown.

REMARKS

Try...Catch...Finally blocks are used to handle anticipated exceptions in your code so that you may deal with the exception and/or display a specific error message to the user.

Try is used to test for an occurrence of an anomalous situation (exception) during the program execution.

Catch is used to execute additional code in response to specified exception cases.

Finally is used to execute code after any **Try...Catch** blocks complete. It is useful for cleaning up any resources allocated in the **Try** block as well as running any code that must execute even if there is an exception. Control is always passed to the **Finally** block regardless of how the **Try** block exits.

The following describes the order of processing in a **Try...Catch...Finally** block.

Control reaches the **Try** statement by normal sequential execution. The guarded section within the

Try block is executed.

If no exception is thrown during execution of the guarded section, the **Catch** clauses that follow the **Try** block are not executed. Execution continues at the statement after the last **Catch** clause following the associated **Try** block.

If an exception is thrown during execution of the guarded section or in any code the guarded section calls (either directly or indirectly), the **Catch** handlers are examined in order of their appearance following the **Try** block.

If a matching **Catch** handler is found, the **Catch** handler is executed and the program resumes execution following the last handler (that is, after the **End** statement of the **Try…Catch** Block). Control can only enter a **Catch** handler through a thrown exception.

If a matching **Catch** handler is not found, program execution resumes after the last handler.

If a **Finally** block is present, the code within the block is executed just before the **Try…Catch** block is exited. This is used to guarantee that a block of statements executes regardless of how the preceding **Try** block is exited.

EXAMPLE 5.10—Using Try…Catch…Throw to Trap an Error [OME_TryCatchThrow]

In this example, an xmldocument file object is created when the Analysis Technique is initialized, and an attempt is made to load the file specified in the **Try** block. If the file is not found, a FileNotFoundException is thrown and is caught by the matching catch clause that includes a **Throw** statement to generate a user defined message that appears in the Event Summary message section of the TS Events Log.

> 🖉 You can also use Catch (exception) to handle any exception which can be useful when troubleshooting.

```
var: elSystem.xml.xmlDocument doc (null) ;
method void AnalysisTechnique_Initialized (elSystem.Object sender,
elSystem.InitializedEventArgs args)
begin
  doc = new elSystem.xml.xmlDocument;
  try
    doc.Load ("C:\testing123.xml") ;
    catch (elSystem.IO.FileNotFoundException ex)
      throw ex.create ("User-defined: File is not in the specified
directory") ;
  end ;  // try / catch statement
end ; // method
```

EXAMPLE 5.11—Pseudo_Code Try…Catch…Finally

The following pseudo-code shows the structure of a **Try…Catch…Finally** block with a **Finally** clause:

```
Try
// statements to be tested for an exception
  Catch (elSystem.Exception ex)
  // statements that handle a general exception
  Finally
  // statements that always executes after any try
  // or catch statements are executed
end ;
```

Throw (Reserved Word)

The **Throw** Reserved Word is used to generate a specific program exception message. This message is displayed in the TS Event Log and typically consists of a diagnostic message.

REMARKS

Throw is used to create an instance of an exception that will be displayed in the Event Log.

EXAMPLE 5.12—Throw a User-Defined Message

```
throw ex.create ("User-defined error message") ;
```

EXAMPLE 5.13—Trap Errors Using Try…Catch [OME_TryCatch]

This example is from the Using Excel chapter, which is later in this book, but it's important here for the **Try…Catch…Throw** part of this chapter.

```
Once begin
  try
    rowReaderWeekly  = StreamReader.Create (FileNameW) ;
   catch (FileNotFoundException ex)
     throw Exception.Create ("Specified file not found." ) ;
  end ; // what is this the end of, anyway?

  if  rowReaderWeekly.EndOfStream  then
    throw Exception.create ("User specified file empty.") ;
      getFileDateTime () ; // some undefined method, I presume
  // read first file lines text, get date & time
    While barDateTime  > fileDateTime begin
  // skip through file to a line after current bar
      getFileDateTime () ;
  // exits if barDateTime <= fileDateTime
    end ; // while loop
  end ; // try catch with no finally
end // Once, and only once
```

Summary

In this chapter we have addressed some of the EZL (classic) concepts that you will need in the OOEL environment. They are not strictly OOEL, but you will use them heavily when we get to more elaborate OOEL programming.

We have looked into debugging, and using printing as a debugging tool, using analysis Commentary as a debugging tool, exceptions and error handling. We also covered using Try…Catch…Finally and throw to capture errors. Further we investigated conquering divides by zero and infinite loop detection.

Now, finally, we will next get into using Methods, in the next chapter.

CHAPTER 6
Methods

In This Chapter

- Introduction
- Override
- Overloaded Methods
- Useful Methods
- Summary

Introduction

Here it is six-months after I began writing this book, not knowing much about OOEL[39] and I know what **Methods** are. They are localized subroutines. That is it in short. You declare your Method in your code and refer to it like a local subroutine. You cannot reference it out of the AT you have it in. In other words, the Scope of a Method is local to the AT which contains it. This should be no surprise, the only exception to this rule is a User Function. **GlobalDictionaries** skirt around this issue.

A **Method** consists of the keyword Method, a return type, the method name, and a set of parentheses. Inputs to the Method may be included inside the parenthesis. The parentheses are required both when declaring and when calling a Method. A return type of **Void** may be used if no value is to be returned. Unlike a User Function which is external to the code of the AT (Analysis Technique) a Method has full access to any Inputs, Constants and Variables declared higher in the code stream. Any variables declared within a Method are local in scope to that Method. The variables are recreated on each call to the Method and have no history (BarsBack).

Override (Reserved Word)

Use **Override** to modify a Method, a property, an indexer, or an event. An override Method provides a new implementation of a member inherited from a base class. The Method overridden by an override declaration is known as the overridden base Method. The overridden base Method must have the same signature as the override Method.

It seems that Override is of no actual interest to an OOEL programmer as we are unable to create our own classes, but OOEL does contain Override Methods, behind the scenes.

REMARKS

You cannot override a non-virtual or static Method. The overridden base Method must be virtual, abstract, or override.

An override declaration cannot change the accessibility of the virtual Method. Both the override Method and the virtual Method must have the same access level modifier.

EXAMPLE 6.01—Declaration with Override

```
Method override void Initialize ()..
```

Overloaded Methods

Several classes in EZL use Methods that are "overloaded" meaning that the Method can accept multiple parameter types. When a call is made to an overloaded Method, EZL automatically

---

[39] But lots about legacy EasyLanguage.

determines how the call will be processed based on the parameter's data type.

For example, the **StreamWriter** Class has a **Method** named **Write (parameter)** which writes data to a file. The parameter can be of type Boolean, string, double, float, int, int64, or object. In any of these cases, **Write** will handle the parameter appropriately and send data to the file.

There is at least one example of an overloaded Method among the ATs supplied with the source code from the books: https://www.EasyLanguageOOEL.com.

How We Show Overloaded Methods

In classes with overloaded Methods, the Method name is listed multiple times, as shown below. These all represent the same Method. The documentation shows that the Method works with any of the parameter types indicated.

	Name	Description
◈	Write (Bool)	Writes the text representation of a Boolean value to the file.
◈	Write (String)	Writes a string to the file.
◈	Write (Double)	Writes the text representation of a 4-byte floating-point value to the file.
◈	Write (Float)	Writes the text representation of an 8-byte floating-point value to the file.
◈	Write (Int)	Writes the text representation of a 4-byte signed integer to the file.
◈	Write (Int64)	Writes the text representation of an 8-byte signed integer to the file.
◈	Write (elSystem.Object)	Writes the text representation of an object to the file by calling ToString on that object.

TABLE 6.01—Overload Method

Useful Methods

This section includes some Methods that can be very useful in your own code. They are included here all together in one place for your convenience. Just copy what you want and paste it into your code. Or download the whole thing from www.EasyLanguageOOEL.com by becoming a free member and cut and paste what you want.

When you use the **#Region** command you make it very convenient for yourself in a hidden way. Not only can you read the code more easily, but you can also open the Outline view in your TDE and find each **#Region** statement under their respective **Begin** blocks because each one will have **#Region** in it and if you click on it in the Outline view it will take you right to that section of code.

EXAMPLE 6.02—Helper Methods [OME_HelperMethods]

```
// == HELPER METHODS =======================================
// ---------------------------------------------------------

#Region - - - Method Header
method String Method_Header (String AppName, String MethodName, String
MethodArgs)
Vars   :
 String RetVal ;
begin
   RetVal  = String.Format ("({00}.) {01} ({02})", AppName, MethodName,
MethodArgs) ;
```

```
    Return RetVal ;
end ; // "Method_Header" method
#endRegion

// --------------------------------------------------------

#Region - - - Int NumToText
method String NumToText (Int Value)
// receives a method argument and return a string of it
Vars  :
 Int    Val,
 String RetVal ;
begin
  Val  = Value ;
  RetVal  = NumToStr (Val, 00) ;
  Return RetVal ;
end ; // "NumToText" method
#endRegion

// --------------------------------------------------------

#Region - - - NumToText of Double Value
method String NumToText (Double Value, Int Decimals)
// receives a method argument and return a string of it
Vars  :
 Double Val,
 String RetVal ;
begin
  Val  = Value ;
  RetVal  = NumToStr (Val, Decimals) ;
  Return RetVal ;
end ; // "NumToText" method override
#endRegion

// --------------------------------------------------------

#Region - - - Price to Text
method String PriceToText (Double Value)
// receives a method argument and return a string of it
Vars  :
 Double Val,
 String RetVal ;
begin
  Val  = Value ;
  RetVal  = vrt_Format (Val) ;
  Return RetVal ;
end ; // "PriceToText" method
#endRegion

// --------------------------------------------------------

#Region - - - BooltoText
method String BoolToText (Bool Value)
// receives a method argument and return a string of it
Vars  :
 Bool   Val,
 String RetVal ;
begin
  Val  = Value ;
  if  Val  then  RetVal  = " TRUE"
```

```
              else  RetVal  = "FALSE" ;
//  RetVal  = skt_Bool_Str (Val) ;
  Return RetVal ;
end ; // "BoolToText" method
#endRegion

// -----------------------------------------------------------

#Region - - - IFFtoText
method String IFFToText (Bool Value, String ifTRUE, String ifFALSE)
// receives a method argument and return a string of it
Vars  :
 Bool   Val,
 String RetVal ;
begin
  Val  = Value ;
  if  Val  then  RetVal  = ifTRUE
          else  RetVal  = ifFALSE ;
//  RetVal  = skt_IFF_Str (Val, ifTRUE, ifFALSE) ;
  Return RetVal ;
end ; // "IFFToText" method
#endRegion

// -----------------------------------------------------------

// this little method illustrates using an input as a
// working variable and a return value
#Region - - - AddDelimiter
method String AddDelimiter (String StrIn, String Delim)
begin
  if  StrIn > ""  then  StrIn  = StrIn + Delim ;
  Return StrIn ;
end ; // "AddDelimiter" method
#endRegion
// ===========================================================
```

Summary

In this chapter we have covered several examples of using **Methods**. We have given you sample code for many useful Methods from which you can copy and paste the parts you find valuable.

An **Input** to a Method may be declared with the **Out** reserved word which makes it similar to the **Ref** Inputs to a User Function.

A Method declared as type **Void** may contain one or more return statements, but no return value is allowed.

To the best of my knowledge an **Array** may not be passed to a Method as an Input, nor may a Method return an **Array** though a Method may access Arrays created Globally and manipulate them internally.

EXAMPLE 6.03—Using Methods

```
Method void store_Swing (Int Swing_Dir)
Begin
  Switch Swing_Dir begin
    Case +01 : hi_Array [00] = Swing_Info ;
    Case -01 : lo_Array [00] = Swing_Info ;
  End ; // switch/case statement
End ; // method
```

Using Methods you can get your Main Code Body down to a very streamlined state, for example:

```
Once begin
  App_Init () ;
End ;
BarByBarProcessing () ;
doPlots () ;
if  LastBarOnChart  then  doReports () ;
```

where `BarByBarProcessing`, `doReports` and `doPlots` are **Methods** previously declared.

Now on to Hello World!

CHAPTER 7

Hello World!

In This Chapter

- Introduction
- Hello_World!_Ex#01   Revisited
- Hello_World!_Ex#02   Print Log on First Bar
- Hello_World!_Ex#03   Print Log on Last Bar
- Hello_World!_Ex#04   String.Format and Intro to Vector Class
- Hello_World!_Ex#05   StreamWriter and StreamReader
- Hello_World!_Ex#06   StreamReader to Read from a File
- Hello_World!_Ex#07   Stream.Split to Stuff a Vector
- Hello_World!_Ex#07a   Text Object Centered on Chart
- Hello_World!_Ex#08a   Creates and Fills a GlobalValue
- Hello_World!_Ex#08b   Creates and Displays the GlobalValue (used with #08a)
- Summary

Introduction

It seems like I could have found a way to get back to the Hello_World! programs before now. I just couldn't find a way to work it in during all the setup and definitions-type stuff you had to learn. So, here we get back to it. Now we will explore several ways to program the Hello_World! indicators. As said previously, this is the section that every computer user's manual starts with. We are going from simplistic to OOEL in this chapter.

Since we are printing to the **Print Log** you find it easier to read the output if you clear it after each test, or you will get thoroughly confused about its contents.

It has been a long time (chapter-wise) since I first introduced and so I am going to bring it forward here and go through the exercise again. Then I will add more examples to get into the OOEL use of enhancing the same basic idea. Bear with me as I repeat myself.

Hello_World! #01 Revisited

Hello_World! #01prints to the **Print Log** with every bar of the chart. If the Print Log is not showing at the bottom of your workspace, you can do CTRL-SHIFT-E to view it, or you can go up to 🖱 View → EasyLanguage Print Log. Then you can see what we are printing.

```
Print ("Hello_World! #1") ;
```

You can quickly see that this is neither efficient nor what we really want as it prints lots and lots of Hello Worlds as it prints on every bar of the chart. The beginning of the Print Log looks like this. It goes on for every bar ad infinitum. This demonstrates several important concepts. First, it is often good practice to include the date and time of the bar in the output. Second it is often important to limit the output by some mechanism.

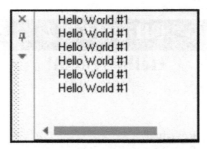

FIGURE 7.01—The results of the Hello_World!_Ex#01 Print statement

Hello_World! #02: Print Log on First Bar

To test the 'print only once per bar' I strongly advise setting (🖰 Customize → General tab) **MaxBarsBack** to its Default of 50. In other words, turn OFF Auto-Detect.

We can limit the printing to a single bar by adding code to test for the first bar on the chart.

EXAMPLE 7.01—Using CurrentBar <= 01 to Print a Single Line

```
if  (CurrentBar <= 01)  then begin
  Print ("Hello_World!_Ex#02") ;
end ;  // test for Current Bar
```

This **Begin…End** block allows printing only on the first bar of the chart. Again, it prints to the Print Log. The Print Log for this one has only one line, which by our coding is the first bar on the chart.

We could change the **Print** statement by putting in code to print the **BarNumber** to verify that it is indeed the first bar. Or we could print the date and time to convince yourself that it is the first bar. I'll leave that to you. As they used to say in my math books "the exercise is left to the reader."

There is another way to achieve the same results. We can use a **Once Begin…End** block and again print on the first bar of the chart. It looks like this:

EXAMPLE 7.02—Once and Only Once

```
once begin
  Print ("Hello_World! #02") ;
end ; // Once, and only once
```

The **Once** Block allows the code to execute only on the first bar of the chart and be ignored after that.

This is not exactly what we want either unless you are doing something for which you want data only on the first bar of the chart. Or printing Headers to an output file. Or deleting a file before writing to it. In any case, we have discovered two ways to do something on at the beginning of the data.

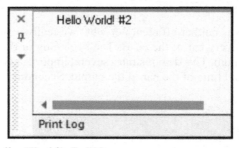

FIGURE 7.02—Printing Hello_World!_Ex#02

Hello_World! #03: Print Log on Last Bar

Next let's only print to the last bar on the chart. The following code should do just that.

EXAMPLE 7.03—Code for Printing on the Last Bar

```
if  LastBarOnChart  then begin
   Print ("Hello_World! #03") ;
end ; // test for last bar of data
```

That's better. Now only when the chart is at the last bar on the chart should the program print into the Print Log.

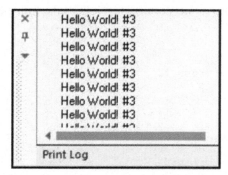

FIGURE 7.03—The Print Log for my first effort of Hello_World!_Ex#03

But that's not what is happening. It's a little befuddling because this code prints `Hello World! #3` repeatedly in the **Print Log**. Sam reminded me that since my chart is of the @ES and it trades 23 hours a day that I probably had **Update-Intrabar** checked. Sure enough, when I went to ⏱ Studies → Edit Studies → Customize here's what I found.

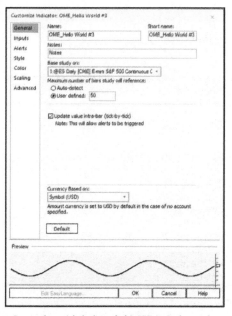

FIGURE 7.04—Update Value Intra-bar (tick-by-tick) Was Selected

I unchecked the box, Cleared the Print Log and did CTRL-R to refresh the chart, and lo and behold it prints `Hello_World!_#03` only one time!

Hello_World! #04: String.Format () & Vector

Hello_World! #04 demonstrates the **String.Format** Method and how to create and stuff values into a **Vector**. The **Print** statement demonstrates that the count is zero-based, showing that you need to subtract 1 from count to access the location of the last element. The elements of a **Vector** are referenced using square brackets [ ] similar to "close of one bar ago" and must always be type-cast.

For example, `myString = myVect[01] asType String ;`

EXAMPLE 7.04—Using the String.Format Method and a Vector [OME_Hello_World!_Ex#04]

This example Prints "Sam and Sunny" and creates a Vector with eight names in it. It then displays the names and the count of the items in the Vector. Then it finds the fifth element and prints the contents of that element.

```
Using elSystem ;
Using elSystem.IO ;
Using elSystem.Collections ;

Vars  :
Vector           myVect    (NULL) ;

// Working Storage Section
Inputs:
 Bool   ShowCmtry    (FALSE) ;

Consts:
 String App_Type     ("Study"),
 String App_Name     ("OME_Hello_World!_Ex#04"),
 String App_Note     ("Hello from Sunny and Sam to the WHOLE World"),
 String App_Vers     ("01.03.00") ;

Vars  :
 String DQ           (DoubleQuote),
 String NL           (NewLine),
 Double Dummy        (0.00) ;

// ========================================================
// Main Code Body (Executable code follows)
// ========================================================

once begin
  Print (App_Name) ;
  Print (String.Format ("{00}{01}{00} and {00}{02}{00}", DQ, "Sam",
"Sunny")) ;
  myVect  = Vector.Create () ;
  myVect.Push_Back ("Sunny") ;
  myVect.Push_Back ("Sam") ;
  myVect.Push_Back ("Pat") ;
  myVect.Push_Back ("George") ;
  myVect.Push_Back ("Pumpkin") ;
  myVect.Push_Back ("Diane") ;
  myVect.Push_Back ("Eric") ;
  myVect.Push_Back ("Sally") ;
  Print ("Count = ", myvect.Count:2:0, ", the collection goes from
zero to ", myvect.Count - 01:2:0) ;
  Print ("Item #5  = ", DQ, myVect [05] asType String, DQ) ;
end ; // Once, and only once
```

For this example, nothing shows on the chart, so there's nothing to display for you. But the output to the Print Log follows:

```
OME_Hello_World!_Ex#04
"Sam" and "Sunny"
Count = 8, the collection goes from zero to  7
Item #5  = "Diane"
```

FIGURE 7.05—Hello_World!_Ex#04 Output in the Print Log

Hello_World! #05: StreamWriter & StreamReader

In addition to reading from a file with **StreamReader** we can write to a file with **StreamWriter**. In this next example we are creating a file called MyTextFile.txt on the C:\ drive in the \OME_Files\ directory. Then we write one line, flush the buffer, and close the file. Then in Hello_World!_Ex#05b we open the file with **StreamReader**, read the text line and print it to the Print Log.

EXAMPLE 7.05—Using StreamWriter to Create a File Within a Method
[OME_Hello_World!_Ex#05a]

This example and the next use **StreamWriter** while Hello_World!_Ex#05b uses **StreamReader** also.

```
Inputs:
  String File_Path    ("C:\OME_Files\"),
  String File_Name    ("MyTextFile"),
  String File_Ext     (".TXT"),
  Bool   Append       (FALSE) ;
Vars :
  String File_Spec    ("") ;

Using elSystem ;
Using elSystem.IO ;
Using elSystem.Collections ;

Vars  :
Vector         myVect  (NULL) ;

// Working Storage Section Inputs:
  Bool   ShowCmtry   (FALSE) ;

Consts:
  String App_Type   ("Study"),
  String App_Name   ("OME_Hello_World!_Ex#05a"),
  String App_Note   ("Hello from Sunny and Sam to the WHOLE World"),
  String App_Vers   ("01.04.00") ;

Vars  :
  String DQ         (DoubleQuote),
  String NL         (NewLine),
  Double Dummy      (0.00) ;

method void Create_TXT_File ()
Vars  :
  Int    Loop,
  String myStr,
  StreamWriter   mySW ;

begin
  File_Spec  = File_Path + File_Name + File_Ext ;
  mySW = StreamWriter.Create (File_Spec, Append) ;
```

```
  for Loop  = 00 to myVect.Count - 01 begin
// extract one element from the vector
   myStr   = myVect [Loop] asType String ;
// output the name to a line in a text file
// contained in File_Spec
// terminate the line of output with a CR/LF
// (carriage return / line feed)
   mySW.WriteLine (myStr) ;
 end ; // for loop

 mySW.Flush () ; // Flush the file
 mySW.Close () ; // Close the file
end ; // "Create_TXT_File" method

// ========================================================
// Main Code Body (Executable code follows)
// ========================================================

once begin
 Print (App_Name) ;

 Print (String.Format ("{00}{01}{00} and {00}{02}{00}", DQ, "Sam",
"Sunny")) ;
 myVect  = Vector.Create () ;
 myVect.Push_Back ("Sunny") ;
 myVect.Push_Back ("Sam") ;
 myVect.Push_Back ("Pat") ;
 myVect.Push_Back ("George") ;
 myVect.Push_Back ("Pumpkin") ;
 myVect.Push_Back ("Diane") ;
 myVect.Push_Back ("Eric") ;
 myVect.Push_Back ("Sally") ;
 Print ("Count = ", myvect.Count:2:0, ", the collection goes from
zero to ", myvect.Count - 01:2:0) ;

 Create_TXT_File () ;
end ; // Once, and only once
```

And here is the output that goes to the Print Log:

```
OME_Hello_World!_#05a
"Sam" and "Sunny"
Count = 8, the collection goes from zero to  7
```

FIGURE 7.06—Print Log Output from Hello_World!_Ex#05a

EXAMPLE 7.06—Using StreamReader and StreamWriter [OME_Hello_World!_Ex#05b]

Here we have another example of using **StreamWriter** but this time we are adding complexity with **StreamReader**. Again, we are using a file called C:\OME_Files\Scrap.txt and are writing a single line of text to the file.

```
#Region elSystem_IO
Using elSystem.IO ;
Vars  :
 StreamReader SR (NULL),
 StreamWriter SW (NULL) ;
Vars  :
 String myTxt    ("") ;
if LastBarOnChart  then begin
```

```
SW  = StreamWriter.Create ("C:\OME_Files\Scrap.TXT") ;
SW.WriteLine ("Hello_World!_#05b") ;
SW.Flush () ;
SW.Close () ;
SR  = StreamReader.Create ("C:\OME_Files\Scrap.TXT") ;
myTxt  = SR.ReadLine () ;
SR.Close () ;
Print (myTxt) ;
end ;
#endRegion
```

Put this indicator on your chart and you will find a .txt file on your C:\ drive named Scrap.txt in the C:\OME_Files\ directory. Open it up and you will see one line that reads: Hello_World!_Ex#05b. See Figure 7.07. At the same time, the indicator printed Hello_World!_Ex#05b to your EZL Print Log.

FIGURE 7.07—Contents of Scrap.txt File

Hello_World! #06: Using StreamReader to Read from a File

Here's an example of reading the contents of the file C:\OME_Files\MyTextFile.txt to get the names (which we wrote to the file in Example 7.05—Hello_World!_#05a) and then pushing them into a **Vector**. We then increment the **While** Loop value and read another line and push it into the Vector. While reading the names from the file we print the location in the **Vector** and the name that was found. You can see these results in Figure 7.08.

EXAMPLE 7.07—Hello_World!_#06 Using StreamReader [OME_Hello_World!_Ex#06]

```
Inputs:
  String File_Path    ("C:\OME_Files\"),
  String File_Name    ("MyTextFile"),
  String File_Ext     (".TXT"),
  Bool   Append       (FALSE) ;
Vars  :
  String File_Spec    ("") ;

Using elSystem ;
Using elSystem.IO ;
Using elSystem.Collections ;

Vars  :
  StreamReader    mySR    (NULL),
  StreamWriter    mySW    (NULL),
  Vector          myVect  (NULL) ;

// Working Storage Section

Consts:
  String App_Type    ("Study"),
  String App_Name    ("OME_Hello_World!_Ex#06"),
  String App_Note    ("Hello from Sunny and Sam to the WHOLE World"),
  String App_Vers    ("01.05.00") ;
```

```
Vars  :
 String DQ              (DoubleQuote),
 String NL              (NewLine),
 String myStr           (""),
 Int    Loop            (00),
 Double Dummy           (0.00) ;


// ===========================================================
// Main Code Body (Executable code follows)
// ===========================================================

once begin
  Print (App_Name) ;

  myVect  = Vector.Create () ;

  File_Spec  = File_Path + File_Name + File_Ext ;
  mySR  = StreamReader.Create (File_Spec) ;
  while not mySR.EndOfStream begin
    myStr  = mySR.ReadLine () ;
    myVect.push_back (myStr) ;
    Print ("#", Loop:2:0, ", ", DQ, myStr, DQ) ;
    Loop += 01 ;
  end ; // while loop

// close the file so it does not get damaged or lost
  mySR.Close () ;
end ; // Once, and only once
```

As a reminder, the file which we created in Example 7.05—Hello_World!_#05a looks like this:

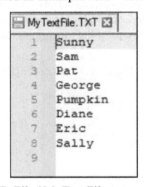

FIGURE 7.08—Contents of C:\OME_Files\MyTextFile.txt

Hello_World! #07: String.Split to Stuff a Vector

This next example returns a vector of elements that were delimited by the Separator string (",").

It reads the text file created in Hello_World!_#05a (one name per line) and then writes the names to a CSV file as a single line of comma separated values. Then it reads the CSV file into a String Variable and uses the **String.Split** Method treating the Variable as a **TokenList** and separating the values into a **Vector**.

EXAMPLE 7.08—Hello_World!_#07 [OME_Hello_World!_Ex#07]

This example reads the names, writes them to a CSV file, reads the CSV file into a variable, separates the values into a vector and prints out the contents of the vector to the Print Log.

```
Inputs:
```

```
   String File_Path      ("C:\OME_Files\"),
   String File_Name      ("MyTextFile"),
   String TXT_File_Ext   (".TXT"),
   String CSV_File_Ext   (".CSV"),
   Bool   Append         (FALSE) ;

Using elSystem ;
Using elSystem.IO ;
Using elSystem.Collections ;

Vars  :
 Vector          TXT_Vect  (NULL),
 Vector          CSV_Vect  (NULL) ;

// Working Storage Section

Consts:
 String App_Type   ("Study"),
 String App_Name   ("OME_Hello_World!_#07"),
 String App_Note   ("Hello from Sunny and Sam to the WHOLE World"),
 String App_Vers   ("01.05.00") ;

Vars  :
 String DQ         (DoubleQuote),
 String NL         (NewLine),
 String myStr      (""),
 Int    Loop       (00),
 Double Dummy      (0.00) ;

// ==========================================================

method void Read_TXT_File ()
Vars  :
 String File_Spec,
 String myStr,
StreamReader mySR;
begin
  Print ("Read_TXT_File - Read the names and stuff them in the
Vector.") ;
  File_Spec  = File_Path + File_Name + TXT_File_Ext ;
  if  TXT_Vect  = NULL  then  TXT_Vect  = Vector.Create () ;  //
initialize the vector
  mySR  = StreamReader.Create (File_Spec) ;
  while not mySR.EndOfStream begin
    myStr  = mySR.ReadLine () ;
    TXT_Vect.Push_Back (myStr) ;
  end ; // while loop
  mySR.Close () ;
end ; // "Read_TXT_File" method

// ----------------------------------------------------------

method void Read_CSV_File ()
Vars  :
 String File_Spec,
 String myStr,
 StreamReader mySR ;
begin
  Print ("Read_CSV_File - Read the CSV file (TokenList) and stuff them
in the Vector.") ;
```

```
   File_Spec   = File_Path + File_Name + CSV_File_Ext ;
   mySR  = StreamReader.Create (File_Spec) ;
   myStr   = mySR.ReadLine () ;
   mySR.Close () ;

   if  CSV_Vect  = NULL  then  CSV_Vect  = Vector.Create () ;  //
initialize the vector
   CSV_Vect  = mystr.Split (",") ; // break StrIn into fields

   for Loop   = 00 to CSV_Vect.Count - 01 begin
      Print ("#", Loop:2:0, " Hello ", CSV_Vect [Loop] asType string,
"!") ;
   end ; // for loop
end ; // "Read_CSV_File" method

// ------------------------------------------------------------

method void Create_CSV_File ()
Vars  :
 String File_Spec,
StreamWriter mySW ;
begin
   File_Spec  = File_Path + File_Name + CSV_File_Ext ;
//  mySR  = StreamReader.Create (File_Spec) ;
   mySW  = StreamWriter.Create (File_Spec, Append) ;
   for Loop   = 00 to TXT_Vect.Count - 01 begin
// we need to separate the fields with a comma
      if Loop   > 00
         then  myStr   = "," + TXT_Vect [Loop] asType String
         else  myStr   =       TXT_Vect [Loop] asType String ;

// output the list of names to a text file contained
// in File_Spec
      mySW.Write (myStr) ;
   end ; // for loop
   mySW.Close () ;
end ; // "Create_CSV_File" method

// ============================================================
// Main Code Body (Executable code follows)
// ============================================================

once begin
   Print (App_Name) ;

   TXT_Vect   = Vector.Create () ;
   CSV_Vect   = Vector.Create () ;
   Read_TXT_File () ;
   Create_CSV_File () ;
   Read_CSV_File () ;
end ; // Once, and only once
```

And now, in Figure 7.09, is the resultant output to the Print Log.

```
OME_Hello_World!_#07
Read_TXT_File - Read the names and stuff them in the Vector.
Read_CSV_File - Read the CSV file (TokenList) and stuff them in the Vector.
# 0 Hello Sunny!
# 1 Hello Sam!
# 2 Hello Pat!
# 3 Hello George!
# 4 Hello Pumpkin!
# 5 Hello Bobbit!
# 6 Hello Eric!
# 7 Hello Sally!
```

FIGURE 7.09—Print Log Output from Hello_World! #7

Hello_World! #07a: Text Object Centered on Chart

EXAMPLE 7.09—Hello_World! #07a [OME_Hello_World!_Ex#07a]

In this example we **Push_Back** names into a **Vector** and write them to a file with **StreamWriter**. Then we use the function **OME_Floating_Text** to place the text on the chart at the center.

```
Inputs:
  String File_Path    ("C:\OME_Files\"),
  String File_Name    ("MyTextFile"),
  String File_Ext     (".CSV"),
  Bool   Append       (FALSE) ;
Vars  :
  String File_Spec    ("") ;

Using elSystem ;
Using elSystem.IO ;
Using elSystem.Collections ;

Vars  :
  StreamWriter   mySW     (NULL),
  Vector         myVect   (NULL) ;

// Working Storage Section
Consts:
  String App_Type    ("Study"),
  String App_Name    ("OME_Hello_World!_Ex#07a"),
  String App_Note    ("Hello from Sunny and Sam to the WHOLE World"),
  String App_Vers    ("01.04.00") ;

Vars  :
  String NL          (NewLine),
  String myStr       (""),
  Bool   Debug       (FALSE),
  Int    Loop        (00) ;

// =======================================================
// Main Code Body (Executable code follows)
// =======================================================

once begin
  myVect  = Vector.Create () ;
  myVect.Push_Back ("Sunny") ;
  myVect.Push_Back ("Sam") ;
  myVect.Push_Back ("Pat") ;
```

```
    myVect.Push_Back ("George") ;
    myVect.Push_Back ("Pumpkin") ;
    myVect.Push_Back ("Diane") ;
    myVect.Push_Back ("Eric") ;
    myVect.Push_Back ("Sally") ;

    File_Spec  = File_Path + File_Name + File_Ext ;
    mySW  = StreamWriter.Create (File_Spec, Append) ;

    for Loop  = 00 to myVect.Count - 01 begin
      if Loop  > 00
        then  myStr  = "," + myVect [Loop] asType String
        else  myStr  =        myVect [Loop] asType String ;
      mySW.Write (myStr) ;
    end ; // for loop

// terminate the line of output with a CR/LF (carriage
// return / line feed)

    mySW.WriteLine () ;
// mySW.Write (NewLine) accomplishes the same thing
// close the file so it does not get damaged or lost
    mySW.Close () ;
end ; // Once, and only once

Once (LastBarOnChart) begin
  if OME_Floating_text (App_Name + NL + App_Note, "Black", "Arial",
10, 50, 50, FALSE)  then ;
end ; // Once, and only once
```

And in Figures 7.10 and 7.11 we have the output to the chart and from the Print Log.

FIGURE 7.10—Chart for Hello_World!_#7a

```
Read_TXT_File - Read the names and stuff them in the Vector.
Read_CSV_File - Read the CSV file (TokenList) and stuff them in the Vector.
# 0 Hello Sunny!
# 1 Hello Sam!
# 2 Hello Pat!
# 3 Hello George!
# 4 Hello Pumpkin!
# 5 Hello Bobbit!
# 6 Hello Eric!
# 7 Hello Sally!
```

FIGURE 7.11—Print Log for Example 7.09—Hello_World!_#07a

Hello_World! #08a: Creates and Fills a GlobalValue

In this example we create a **GlobalValue** and concatenate two inputs, assign the result to the **GlobalValue**, and print the **GlobalValue** to the Print Log.

EXAMPLE 7.10—Hello_World!_Ex#08a

```
#Region Declarations
Inputs:
  String myChannel        ("Hello_World!_Ex#08"),
  String Message#1        ("Hello World! from "),
  String Message#2        ("Workspace Name"),
  String GV_Name          ("Hello World!") ;

Using elSystem ;

Vars  :
  GlobalValue  myGV       (NULL) ;

// Working Storage Section
Consts:
  String App_Type         ("Study"),
  String App_Name         ("OME_Hello_World!_Ex#08a"),
  String App_Note         ("Demonstrate the GlobalValue Class"),
  String App_Vers         ("01.01.00") ;

Vars  :
  String DQ               (DoubleQuote),
  String NL               (NewLine),
  Double Dummy            (0.00) ;

#endRegion
// ========================================================
// Methods section
// ========================================================

method void GV_Updated (elSystem.Object sender,
elSystem.GlobalValueUpdatedEventArgs args)
begin
  Print (skt_Method_Header (App_Name, "GV_Updated", "")) ;
end ; // "GV_Updated" method

// ========================================================
// Main Code Body (Executable code follows)
// ========================================================
```

```
once begin
  Print (App_name, ", ", DQ, myChannel, DQ, ", ", DQ, GV_Name, DQ, ",
", Message#1, ", ", DQ, Message#2) ;
  myGV                = GlobalValue.Create () ;
  myGV.Channel        = myChannel ;
  myGV.Name           = GV_Name ;
  myGV.StringValue    = Message#1 + Message#2 ;
  myGV.Updated       += GV_Updated ;
  myGV.Load           =   TRUE ;
end ; // Once, and only once

if  LastBarOnChart  then begin
  Print (App_Name, " : myGV = ", DQ, myGV.StringValue, DQ) ;
end ;
```

This was an exercise to demonstrate the use of objects of the **GlobalValue** Class. And here is the result, from the **Print Log**.

```
OME_Hello_World!_Ex#08a, "Hello_World!_Ex#08a", "Hello World!", Hello World! from , "Workspace Name
(OME_Hello_World!_Ex#08a) GV_Updated ()
OME_Hello_World!_Ex#08a : myGV = "Hello World! from Workspace Name"
```

FIGURE 7.12—Print Log Output from Hello_World!_Ex#08a

Hello_World! #08b: Creates and Displays the GlobalValue

This example creates a **GlobalValue** and prints its contents to the Print Log demonstrating that the **GlobalValue** is accessible in an independent AT. Hence the word Global. As an extension of this example, we leave it to the reader to determine whether this can be used on a separate chart as well. See GlobalValue Class in **Volume II—Reference Guide, Appendix III: Classes**.

EXAMPLE 7.11—Hello_World!_Ex #08b

```
#Region Declarations
Inputs:
 String myChannel       ("Hello_World!_Ex#08"),
 String GV_Name         ("Hello World!") ;

Using elSystem ;

Vars  :
 GlobalValue  myGV       (NULL) ;

// Working Storage Section
Consts:
 String App_Type       ("Study"),
 String App_Name       ("OME_Hello_World!_Ex#08b"),
 String App_Note       ("Demonstrate the GlobalValue Class"),
 String App_Vers       ("01.01.00") ;

Vars  :
 String DQ             (DoubleQuote),
 String NL             (NewLine),
 Double Dummy          (0.00) ;

#endRegion

// =========================================================
// Methods section
// =========================================================
```

```
method void GV_Updated (elSystem.Object sender,
elSystem.GlobalValueUpdatedEventArgs args)
begin
  Print (skt_Method_Header (App_Name, "GV_Updated", "")) ;
end ; // "GV_Updated" method

// ==========================================================
// Main Code Body (Executable code follows)
// ==========================================================

once begin
  Print (App_name, ", ", DQ, myChannel, DQ, ", ", DQ, GV_Name, DQ) ;
  myGV               = GlobalValue.Create () ;
  myGV.Channel       = myChannel ;
  myGV.Name          = GV_Name ;
  myGV.Updated      += GV_Updated ;
  myGV.Load          =  TRUE ;
end ; // Once, and only once

if  LastBarOnChart  then begin
  Print (App_Name, " : myGV = ", DQ, myGV.StringValue, DQ) ;
end ;
```

And the output from Hello_World!_#08b:

```
OME_Hello_World!_Ex#08b, "Hello_World!_Ex#08", "Hello World!"
OME_Hello_World!_Ex#08b : myGV = "Hello World! from Workspace Name"
```

FIGURE 7.13—Output from Hello_World!_#08b

Summary

And you thought Hello_World! would be simple! We have discovered several, and each different, methods of outputting to the **Print Log** and to external files. We have used simple **Print** statements, limited the printing to the first bar on the chart or the last bar on the chart. We have used string formatting and vectors and **GlobalValues** to exhibit a wide range of possibilities. We have also used Methods of the **String Class: String.Format ()** and **String.Split ()**.

CHAPTER 8

Collections: Dictionary, Vector etc.

In This Chapter

- Introduction
- Dictionary Class (Collection)
- GlobalDictionary Class
- Queue Class
- Stack Class

- TokenList Class
- Vector Class
- AppStorage
- Summary

Introduction

I touched briefly on these subjects in Chapter 2, but here we go into more depth. We also used **TokenList** and **Vector** Objects in Chapter 7 in the Hello_World! examples, before having fully explained them. Please refer to Chapter 7 for the examples.

How does the Dictionary differ from a **Dictionary** or **GlobalDictionary**? I know it can get confusing. The Dictionary is a development and programming tool accessed from the menu toolbar at the top of your TDE screen by clicking on the [⊠] icon. You can look EVERYTHING up there. If that's confusing, refer to **Volume II—Reference Guide, Appendix II: The Dictionary Unfolded.**

TokenList

TokenList is a collection of String expressions separated by commas. You address them by index number, starting with index number zero (0), much as one would a **Vector** or an **Array**. Think of a **TokenList** as a one row CSV (Comma Separated Values) file. **TokenList** Objects may contain alphanumeric values but not objects. Examples of using **TokenList** and **Vector** Classes were presented in the previous chapter, but here we get into the precise definition and usage. Any text or item added, updated, or inserted that contains commas will have separate items added to the item collection. Duplicate values may be added.

EXAMPLE 8.01—Working with TokenList Objects

```
MyTokenList.Add ("Symbol1");
// adds the first string value as item 0
MyTokenList.Add ("Symbol2");
// adds the second string value as item 1
MyTokenList.Insert (01,"Symbol3");
// inserts a new string value at item 1
MyList   = MyTokenList.Value ;
// MyList contains the comma-delimited string values
"Symbol1,Symbol3,Symbol2"
RemoveAt (00) ; // deletes the first item in the list
MyString  = Item[0] ;
// MyString will contain the string value for the
// first item which is now "Symbol3"
```

It can get confusing because **TokenList** is from the **tsData.Common** Namespace, not **elSystem.Collections**, but it does indeed contain a collection of zero or more strings. As most all **Classes** we will encounter, it has a **Count** property that returns the number of items in the **Collection**. Accessing the Collection uses a zero-based Index so that valid elements are from 00 to Count – 01.

Vector Class (Collection)

A **Vector** is a data structure containing zero or more elements. Like all objects, when you declare an **Object** it is given the initial value of **NULL**. A **Vector** is declared as in:

```
Vars: Vector myVect (NULL) ;
```

and must be instantiated using the new reserved word or the **Create ()** Method of the object. The elements of a Vector are referenced using square brackets very similar to an array, but you must always typecast (asType Double, etc.) the values referenced from a **Vector**. As usual the **Vector** has a Count property, and it must be greater than zero before you attempt to access any items. A check for a value greater than zero should be made prior to an attempt. Also, as usual, the items are referenced using a zero-based index so `myVect.Count - 01` is the last item available.

I am not covering Arrays in this chapter as we went over them in depth in Chapter 2. However, to properly make use of the extensive features of **TokenList** and **Vector** Objects we need to examine some **Collection** Classes, specifically the **Dictionary** and **GlobalDictionary** Classes. We will also cover **Queue** and **Stack** lightly.

Collection Classes

Collection Classes in EZL refer to classes that organize information into different types of data structures. These are all to be found in the **elSystem.collections** Namespace. I bring this up here because you will need them for **Vectors**, **Dictionaries**, **Queues** and **Stacks**. The Collections most frequently used are Vector, **GlobalDictionary**, and **Dictionary**. Other Collections of value, but not covered extensively here are **Queue** and **Stack**. We mention **TokenList** here because, even though it is not actually of the **Collections** Namespace it is very highly correlated.

The elements of the collection classes are:

- **Dictionary** Class
- **GlobalDictionary** Class
- **Queue** Class
- **Stack** Class
- **Vector** Class

These classes are generally Serialized data structures that contain 0 or more items. Every Collection has a Count property which can be used to query for the number of elements it has. Each of the different collections in the Namespace has unique features. The most frequently used Classes are **Vector**, **Dictionary** and **GlobalDictionary** but there are also **Queue** and **Stack** Classes available.

A major difference between **Vector** and the **Queue** and **Stack** Classes is that the **Queue** and **Stack** are read-only while the **Vector** class is read/write. That means that you can only read the next element (i.e., the last or first element governed by the fact that a **Queue** is FIFO[40] and a **Stack** is LIFO.)

The properties and Methods for these Collections are covered in **Volume II: Reference Guide** listed alphabetically.

Dictionary Class (Collection)

A **Dictionary** defines the structure of an object that represents a collection of key/value pairs that let you save values for use by a single EZL Analysis Technique or strategy. See **GlobalDictionary** Class below for a similar collection that allows values to be shared between Analysis Techniques in the same or different windows.

Elements are added to the **Dictionary** using the **Add (sKey, oValue)** Method where `sKey` is string containing the unique key name and `oValue` is the value to be stored.

An element (key and value pair) is removed from the **Dictionary** using the **Remove (sKey)** Method. The **Contains (sKey)** Method is used to determine if an element key exists in the **Dictionary**.

Dictionaries can contain all kinds of elements, even objects that are not serializable[41] while since

---

[40] FIFO: First In First Out; LIFO: Last In First Out

[41] "Serializable" means the process of making a representation as a string of values (say a comma separated list of values) that is added to the GlobalDictionary, and then the receiving Dictionary deserializes this data (parses the CSV to obtain all

trendlines <u>are</u> serializable the whole topic of Serializable is undocumented and one must search the Forums diligently using the Advanced Search feature to really learn more about it. Basically, an object must be able to be broken down into **String** values to be serialized—a **TrendLine** consists of, for example, two **DTPoint** objects (date, time, price) and some properties such as thickness, color, extend left and right—all that information can be converted and stored as strings.

To create a **TrendLine** one must specify the beginning date/time price pair (to create a **DTPoint**) and the ending date/time price pair. This information is serializable whereas the **TrendLine** itself may not be. I believe the action is invisible and done 'behind the curtain.'

NAMESPACE: elSystem.Collections

PROPERTIES

	Name	Type	Description
🖾	Count	int	Gets the number of elements contained in the **Dictionary**.
🖾	Items	string	Gets or sets the value of the element with the specified key.
🖾	Keys	vector	Gets the vector collection of sorted keys from the **Dictionary**.
🖾	Values	vector	Gets the vector collection of sorted values from the **Dictionary**.

TABLE 8.01—Dictionary Class Properties

METHODS

	Name	Description
🔹	Add (key,value)	Adds an element with the provided key and value to the Dictionary.
🔹	Clear ()	Removes all elements from the Dictionary.
🔹	Contains (key)	True if the dictionary contains an element with the specified key.
🔹	Create ()	Initializes a new instance of the Dictionary Class.
🔹	Remove (key)	Removes the element with the specified key from the Dictionary.

TABLE 8.02—Dictionary Class Methods

INHERITANCE HIERARCHY

elSystem.Object
　elSystem.Collections.Dictionary

That was a handful, right? So now on to the Examples!

Examples for Clarification

These two examples should help clarify the above definitions. The first example creates a **Dictionary** to hold swing highs and swing lows. These are then plotted on a chart and the first 11 (0 through 10) are printed in the **Print Log**.

EXAMPLE 8.02—Using Two Dictionaries to Store Swing Highs & Swing Lows
[OME_Swings_in_Dict_Ex#01]

The two **Dictionaries** are called, respectively, `hi_Dict` and `lo_Dict`. The code counts the number of

---

the values needed to create the trendline in the receiving application. Objects other than collections added to a GlobalDictionary cannot be retrieved as the same type of object on the receiving Dictionary event handler. The GlobalDictionary only supports certain types of objects when passed between applications. If the objective is to pass the information about a trendline from one chart to another, the object must be serializable in the sending side and the deserialized values passed back into an object. Note that the result is two different objects. Updating one does not result in the other being updated unless the information is serialized and deserialized.

Swings in each **Dictionary** and plots the swings on a chart. It then prints the results of the first 11 (0 through 10), just so you can "see" that they are in the Dictionary.

There are a few of Sam's (skt_) special functions used herein. You may get access to them by emailing him at sktennis@vista-research.com or by registering as a Free member and downloading them from https://www.EasyLanguageOOEL.com.

```
Inputs:
 Int     Strength      (02) ;

Vars   :
 Int     Length        (Strength + 01),
 Int     swHiBar       (-01),
 Int     swLoBar       (-01),
 String  Str           (""),
 Double  ATR_Val       (00) ;

#Region - - - Dictionary_Declarations
Using elSystem ;
Using elSystem.Collections ;
Vars  :
 Dictionary hi_Dict (NULL),
 Dictionary lo_Dict (NULL) ;
#endRegion // Dictionary_Declarations

// Working Storage Section
Inputs:
 Bool    ShowCmtry     (FALSE),
 Bool    WalkForward   ( TRUE) ;

Consts:
 String App_Type       ("Study"),
 String App_Name       ("OME_Swings_in_Dict_Ex#01"),
 String App_Note       ("Demonstrate storing Swing Highs and Lows in a
Dictionary"),
 String App_Vers       ("01.00.00") ;

Vars  :
 String DQ             (DoubleQuote),
 String NL             (NewLine),
 String CmtryStr       (""),
 String AlertStr       (""),
 Bool   doCmtry        (FALSE),
 Bool   doAlert        (FALSE),
 Bool   KeepGoing      ( TRUE),
 Bool   Debug          (FALSE),
 Int    lOOP           (00),
 Double Dummy          (0.00) ;

// ===========================================================

method Dictionary Dictionary_Create ()
// If you uncomment the local DEBUG variable you can print // ONLY
this specific method
Vars  :
// Bool Debug,
 Dictionary myDict ;
begin
  if  Debug  then  Print ("Dictionary_Create") ;
  myDict  = Dictionary.Create () ;
  Return myDict ;
```

```
    end ; // "Dictionary_Create" method

    // ----------------------------------------------------------

    method void Build_Key (out String myKey, Int myDate, Int myTime)
    // demonstration of using OUT to return a value
    begin
     myKey = NumToStr (myDate, 00) + ":" + NumToStr (myTime, 00);
    end ; // "Build_Key" method

    // ----------------------------------------------------------

    method Dictionary Dictionary_AddItem (Dictionary myDict, Int myDate,
    Int myTime, Double Price)
    Vars  :
     String myKey,
     Double myVal ;
    begin
      if  Debug  then  Print ("Dictionary_AddItem ") ;
      myKey  = NumToStr (myDate, 00) + "_" + NumToStr (myTime, 00) ;
      myVal  = Price ;

    // Item has already been added. Key in dictionary
    //  myDict.Add (myKey, myVal) ;
      if  myDict.Contains (myKey)
        then  myDict.Items [myKey]  = Price asType Double
        else  myDict.Add (myKey, myVal) ;
      Return myDict ;
    end  ; // "Dictionary_AddItem" method

    // ==========================================================

    once begin
      hi_Dict  = Dictionary_Create () ;
      lo_Dict  = Dictionary_Create () ;
      Length      = Strength + 01 ;
      KeepGoing  =  TRUE ;
    end ; // Once, and only once

    doCmtry  = AtCommentaryBar ;
    if  doCmtry  then  CmtryStr  = "" ;
    doAlert  = CheckAlert or doCmtry ;
    if  doAlert
     or doCmtry  then  AlertStr  = "" ;

    if  KeepGoing  then begin
      if  (Date [00]  > Date [01])  then begin
      end ; // first bar of new day

      ATR_Val  = skt_AverageFC (TrueRange, 14) ;
      swHiBar  = SwingHighBar (01, High, Strength, Length) ;
      swLoBar  = SwingLowBar  (01,  Low, Strength, Length) ;

      if  swHiBar  > -01  then begin
        Dictionary_AddItem (hi_Dict, Date [swHiBar], Time [swHiBar], High
    [swHiBar]) ;

      Plot1 [swhiBar] (High [swHiBar] + ATR_Val * 0.50, "swHi", Default,
    Default, Default) ;
      if  doAlert  then  AlertStr += "Swing High Detected" + NL ;
```

```
  if  Debug  then  Print ("swHI : BarsAgo=" + NumToStr (swHiBar, 00) +
", Date=" + vrt_MMDDYYYY (Date [swHiBar]) + ", Time=" + vrt_HHMM_pm
(Time [swHiBar]) + ", Price=" + vrt_Format (High [swHiBar]) + ",
BarNo=" + NumToStr (BarNumber [swHiBar], 00)) ;
  end ; // Swing High Detected (swHiBar > -01)


  if  swLoBar  > -01  then begin
    Dictionary_AddItem (lo_Dict, Date [swLoBar], Time [swLoBar],  Low
[swLoBar]) ;

    Plot2 [swLoBar] ( Low [swLoBar] - ATR_Val * 0.50, "swLo", Default,
Default, Default) ;
    if doAlert  then  AlertStr += "Swing Low Detected" + NL ;
    if  Debug  then  Print ("swLO : BarsAgo=" + NumToStr (swLoBar, 00)
+ ", Date=" + vrt_MMDDYYYY (Date [swLoBar]) + ", Time=" + vrt_HHMM_pm
(Time [swLoBar]) + ", Price=" + vrt_Format ( Low [swLoBar]) + ",
BarNo=" + NumToStr (BarNumber [swLoBar], 00)) ;
  end ; // Swing High Detected (swLoBar > -01)


  if  AlertStr  > ""  then  Alert (AlertStr, Symbol) ;


  if  LastBarOnChart  then begin
    Print ("My Swing High Dictionary has ", hi_Dict.Count:2:0, "
elements and the Swing Low Dictionary has ", lo_Dict.Count:2:0, "
elements.") ;
    for Loop  = 00 to 10 begin
      if  hi_Dict.Count  > Loop and lo_Dict.Count  > Loop  then begin
        Str  = NumToStr (Loop, 00) ;
        if  Str.Length < 02  then  Str  = "0" + Str ;
        Print (String.Format ("#{00}  hi = {01} : {02}, lo =  {03} :
{04}", Str, hi_Dict.Keys [Loop], hi_Dict.Values [Loop], lo_Dict.Keys
[Loop], vrt_Format (lo_Dict.Values [Loop] asType Double))) ;
      end ; // avoid an error if insufficient elements
    end ; // for loop
  end ; // last bar on chart
end ; // keep going / walk forward
if  atCommentaryBar and WalkForward and KeepGoing
  then  KeepGoing  = FALSE ;

#BeginCmtry

if  CheckCommentary and ShowCmtry  then begin
  CommentaryCL (skt_Commentary_Header (App_Type, App_Name, App_Note,
App_Vers),
                skt_Commentary_Notes  (CmtryStr),
                skt_Commentary_Alert  (AlertStr)) ;

end ; // expert Commentary enabled for this bar
#end
```

Here's what they look like on a chart:

FIGURE 8.01—Swing Highs and Swing Lows from the Dictionary

And here is the output from the Print Log:

```
#00  hi = 1000110_1400 : 1457.50, lo =  1000105_1400 :  1361.50
#01  hi = 1000114_1400 : 1461.50, lo =  1000112_1400 :  1415.25
#02  hi = 1000120_1400 : 1461.50, lo =  1000131_1400 :  1333.50
#03  hi = 1000127_1400 : 1405.00, lo =  1000215_1400 :  1357.50
#04  hi = 1000209_1400 : 1431.25, lo =  1000228_1400 :  1304.00
#05  hi = 1000303_1400 : 1391.00, lo =  1000307_1400 :  1309.50
#06  hi = 1000310_1400 : 1392.75, lo =  1000315_1400 :  1333.00
#07  hi = 1000324_1400 : 1532.75, lo =  1000321_1400 :  1421.75
#08  hi = 1000404_1400 : 1503.25, lo =  1000330_1400 :  1452.00
#09  hi = 1000410_1400 : 1502.50, lo =  1000404_1400 :  1389.50
#10  hi = 1000419_1400 : 1418.50, lo =  1000417_1400 :  1302.75
```

FIGURE 8.02—Results from the Print Log

GlobalDictionary Class

The **GlobalDictionary** Class allows you to set up a collection of key/value pairs that can be shared between EZL Analysis Techniques and strategies. The **GlobalDictionary** class includes many of the same properties and methods as the **Dictionary** class.

There are two ways the **GlobalDictionary** can be configured. In one form, the **GlobalDictionary** class is used to share values within the same window type. In the other, the **GlobalDictionary** is configured to share with additional window types.

EXAMPLE 8.03—Creating an Instance of GlobalDictionary

To create an instance of **GlobalDictionary** to share values within same window type:

```
myGlobal = GlobalDictionary.create (FALSE, "GDictName") ;
```

EXAMPLE 8.04—Creating an Instance of a Shared GlobalDictionary

To create an instance of GlobalDictionary to share values beyond the same window type or between two charts when multi-core charting[42] is enabled.

```
myGlobal = GlobalDictionary.create (TRUE, "GDictName");
```

Elements are added to the **GlobalDictionary** using the **Add(sKey, oValue)** method where sKey is a string containing the element name and oValue is the value to be stored.

---

[42] When you select ⏷ File → Preferences → Performance the Custom radio button will show you the MultiCore settings

Elements (key and value) are removed from the **GlobalDictionary** using the **Remove ()** Method.

EXAMPLE 8.05—Using GlobalDictionary with Pivots [OME_Swings_in_Dict_Ex#02]

In this example we are storing the highs and lows using two dictionaries to place high swings in the first Dictionary and low swings in the second and print the results to the **Print Log**. The pivots are drawn on the chart, see Figure 8.03 below.

```
Inputs:
 Int     Strength      (02) ;

Vars  :
 Int     Length        (Strength + 01),
 Int     swHiBar       (-01),
 Int     swLoBar       (-01),
 String Str            (""),
 Double ATR_Val        (00) ;

// ----------------------------------------------------
#Region - - - Dictionary_Declarations
Using elSystem ;
Using elSystem.Collections ;

Vars  :
 Dictionary hi_Dict (NULL),
 Dictionary lo_Dict (NULL) ;
#endRegion // Dictionary_Declarations
// ----------------------------------------------------
#Region - - - myGlobalDictionary

Inputs:
 String gDict_Name     ("Pivots"),
 Bool   isShared       ( TRUE) ;

Vars  :
 String myKey          (""),
 String gDict_Spec     (""),
 Vector myVect         (NULL),
GlobalDictionary gDict  (NULL) ;

#endRegion // myGlobalDictionary
// ----------------------------------------------------

// Working Storage Section
Inputs:
 Bool   ShowCmtry   (FALSE),
 Bool   WalkForward (FALSE) ;

Consts:
 String App_Type      ("Study"),
 String App_Name      ("OME_Swings_in_Dict_Ex#02"),
 String App_Note      ("Demonstrate storing Swing Highs and Lows in a
GlobalDictionary"),
 String App_Vers      ("01.02.03") ;

Vars  :
 String DQ            (DoubleQuote),
 String NL            (NewLine),
 String CmtryStr      (""),
 String PowerStr      (""),
 String AlertStr      (""),
```

```
      Bool    doCmtry      (FALSE),
      Bool    doAlert      (FALSE),
      Bool    KeepGoing    ( TRUE),
      Bool    Debug        (FALSE),
      Int     Loop         (00),
      Double  Dummy        (0.00) ;

   // ===========================================================
   {*
    * List of methods
   method Dictionary Dictionary_Create ()
   method GlobalDictionary gDict_Create (Bool Shared, String gDict_Name)
   method void gDict_Cleared     (elSystem.Object sender,
   elSystem.Collections.ItemProcessedEventArgs args)
   method void gDict_ItemAdded (elSystem.Object sender,
   elSystem.Collections.ItemProcessedEventArgs args)
   method void gDict_ItemChanged (elSystem.Object sender,
   elSystem.Collections.ItemProcessedEventArgs args)
   method void gDict_ItemDeleted (elSystem.Object sender,
   elSystem.Collections.ItemProcessedEventArgs args)
   method String gDict_BuildKey (String Key, Int myDate, Int myTime)
   method Dictionary Dictionary_AddItem (Dictionary myDict, String myKey,
   Double Price)
   method GlobalDictionary GDict_StuffIt (GlobalDictionary gDict, String
   Key, Double Value)
   method void GDict_MergeDicts () // String Key, Double Value)
   method void App_Init ()
    *}
   // ===========================================================

   method Dictionary Dictionary_Create ()
   // If you uncomment the local DEBUG variable you can print ONLY this
   specific method
   Vars  :
   // Bool Debug,
    Dictionary myDict ;
   begin
   //  Debug  =  TRUE ;
      if  Debug  then  Print ("Dictionary_Create") ;
      myDict  = Dictionary.Create () ;
      Return myDict ;
   end ; // "Dictionary_Create" method

   // -----------------------------------------------------------

   method GlobalDictionary gDict_Create (Bool Shared, String gDict_Name)
   // If you uncomment the local DEBUG variable you can
   // print ONLY this specific method
   Vars  :
   // Bool Debug,
    GlobalDictionary myDict ;
   begin
   //  Debug  =  TRUE ;
      if  Debug  then  Print ("gDict_Create (", Shared:5, ", ",
   gDict_Name, ")") ;
      myDict  = GlobalDictionary.Create (Shared, gDict_Name) ;
   //  myDict  = GlobalDictionary.Create (gDict_Name) ;
      myDict.Cleared      += gDict_Cleared ;
      myDict.ItemAdded    += gDict_ItemAdded ;
      myDict.ItemChanged += gDict_ItemChanged ;
```

```
   myDict.ItemDeleted += gDict_ItemDeleted ;
   Return myDict ;
end ; // "gDict_Create" method

// -----------------------------------------------------------

method void gDict_Cleared (elSystem.Object sender,
elSystem.Collections.ItemProcessedEventArgs args)
begin
  if  Debug  then  Print ("gDict_Cleared") ;
end ; // "gDict_Cleared" method

// -----------------------------------------------------------

method void gDict_ItemAdded (elSystem.Object sender,
elSystem.Collections.ItemProcessedEventArgs args)
begin
  if  Debug  then  Print ("gDict_ItemAdded") ;
end ; // "gDict_ItemAdded" method

// -----------------------------------------------------------

method void gDict_ItemChanged (elSystem.Object sender,
elSystem.Collections.ItemProcessedEventArgs args)
begin
  if  Debug  then  Print ("gDict_ItemChanged") ;
end ; // "gDict_ItemChanged" method

// -----------------------------------------------------------

method void gDict_ItemDeleted (elSystem.Object sender,
elSystem.Collections.ItemProcessedEventArgs args)
begin
  if  Debug  then  Print ("gDict_ItemDeleted") ;
end ; // "gDict_ItemDeleted" method

// -----------------------------------------------------------

method String gDict_BuildKey (String Key, Int myDate, Int myTime)
// demonstration of using the OUT keyword to return a value\
Vars  :
// Bool Debug,
 String myKey ;
begin
  myKey  = Key + "_" + NumToStr (myDate, 00) + "_" + NumToStr (myTime,
00) ;
  Return myKey ;
end ; // "gDict_BuildKey" method

// -----------------------------------------------------------

method Dictionary Dictionary_AddItem (Dictionary myDict, String myKey,
Double Price)
Vars  :
 Double myVal ;
begin
  if  Debug  then  Print ("Dictionary_AddItem ") ;
  myVal  = Price ;
// Item has already been added.  Key in dictionary
//  myDict.Add (myKey, myVal) ;
  if  myDict.Contains (myKey)
```

```
    then  myDict.Items [myKey]  = Price asType Double
    else  myDict.Add (myKey, myVal) ;
  Return myDict ;
end  ; // "Dictionary_AddItem" method

// --------------------------------------------------------

method GlobalDictionary GDict_StuffIt (GlobalDictionary gDict, String
Key, Double Value)
begin
  if  Debug  then  Print ("GDict_StuffIt") ;
  if  gDict.Contains (Key)
    then  gDict.Items [Key]  = Value asType Double
    else  gDict.Add (Key, Value asType Double) ;
  Return gDict ;
end ; // "GDict_StuffIt" method

// --------------------------------------------------------

method void GDict_MergeDicts () // String Key, Double Value)
Vars  :
 Int     Loop,
 Vector Keys,
 Vector Vals ;
begin
  if  Debug  then  Print ("GDict_MergeDicts") ;
  Keys  = hi_Dict.Keys ;
  Vals  = hi_Dict.Values ;
  for Loop  = 00 to hi_Dict.Count - 01 begin
    gDict = GDict_StuffIt (gDict, Keys [Loop] asType String, Vals
[Loop] asType Double) ;
  end ; // for loop

  Keys  = lo_Dict.Keys ;
  Vals  = lo_Dict.Values ;
  for Loop  = 00 to lo_Dict.Count - 01 begin
    gDict = GDict_StuffIt (gDict, Keys [Loop] asType String, Vals
[Loop] asType Double) ;
  end ; // for loop
end ; // "GDict_MergeDicts" method

// --------------------------------------------------------

method void App_Init ()
Begin
  if  Debug  then  Print ("App_Init") ;
  gDict_Spec  = gDict_Name ;
  hi_Dict  = Dictionary_Create () ;
  lo_Dict  = Dictionary_Create () ;
  gDict  = gDict_Create (isShared, gDict_Spec) ;
  Length  = Strength + 01 ;
end ; // "App_Init ()" method

// ========================================================

once begin
  App_Init () ;
  PowerStr  = "" ; // special case with PowerStr
  if  skt_PowerUser (CustomerID)  then begin
    PowerStr += "Top " + vrt_MMDDYYYY (DateTime.Now.ELDate) + " " +
```

```
    vrt_HHMM_pm (DateTime.Now.ELTime) + NL ;
      end ;
      KeepGoing = TRUE ; // WalkForward/KeepGoing
    end ; // Once, and only once

    if (CurrentBar <= 01) then begin
    end ; // first bar of data

    doCmtry = AtCommentaryBar ;
    if doCmtry then CmtryStr = "" ;
    //if doCmtry then PowerStr = "" ;
    doAlert = CheckAlert or doCmtry ;
    if doAlert
     or doCmtry then AlertStr = "" ;

    if KeepGoing then begin // WalkForward/KeepGoing
      if (Date [00] > Date [01]) then begin
      end ; // first bar of new day

      if (BarStatus (01) = 02) then begin
        ATR_Val = skt_AverageFC (TrueRange, 14) ;
        swHiBar = SwingHighBar (01, High, Strength, Length) ;
        swLoBar = SwingLowBar (01, Low, Strength, Length) ;

        if swHiBar > -01 then begin
          myKey = gDict_BuildKey (skt_DataCompress_Str (Bartype,
    BarInterval) + "_HI", Date [swHiBar], Time [swHiBar]) ;
          Dictionary_AddItem (hi_Dict, myKey, High [swHiBar]) ;

          Plot1 [swhiBar] (High [swHiBar] + ATR_Val * 0.50, "swHi",
    Default, Default, Default) ;
          if doAlert then AlertStr += "Swing High Detected" + NL ;
          if Debug then Print ("swHI : BarsAgo=" + NumToStr (swHiBar,
    00) + ", Date=" + vrt_MMDDYYYY (Date [swHiBar]) + ", Time=" +
    vrt_HHMM_pm (Time [swHiBar]) + ", Price=" + vrt_Format (High
    [swHiBar]) + ", BarNo=" + NumToStr (BarNumber [swHiBar], 00)) ;
          end ; // Swing High Detected (swHiBar > -01)

        if swLoBar > -01 then begin
          myKey = gDict_BuildKey (skt_DataCompress_Str (Bartype,
    BarInterval) + "_LO", Date [swLoBar], Time [swLoBar]) ;
          Dictionary_AddItem (lo_Dict, myKey, Low [swLoBar]) ;

          Plot2 [swLoBar] ( Low [swLoBar] - ATR_Val * 0.50, "swLo",
    Default, Default, Default) ;
          if doAlert then AlertStr += "Swing Low Detected" + NL ;
          if Debug then Print ("swLO : BarsAgo=" + NumToStr (swLoBar,
    00) + ", Date=" + vrt_MMDDYYYY (Date [swLoBar]) + ", Time=" +
    vrt_HHMM_pm (Time [swLoBar]) + ", Price=" + vrt_Format ( Low
    [swLoBar]) + ", BarNo=" + NumToStr (BarNumber [swLoBar], 00)) ;
          end ; // Swing High Detected (swLoBar > -01)

        if AlertStr > "" then Alert (AlertStr, Symbol) ;
      end ; // BarStatus

    // if LastBarOnChart then begin
      Once (LastBarOnChart and BarStatus (01) = 02) begin
        if skt_PowerUser (CustomerID) then begin
          PowerStr += " LastBar Top " + vrt_MMDDYYYY
    (DateTime.Now.ELDate) + " " + vrt_HHMM_pm (DateTime.Now.ELTime) + NL ;
          end ;
```

```
        Print ("My Swing High Dictionary has ", hi_Dict.Count:2:0, "
  elements and the Swing Low Dictionary has ", lo_Dict.Count:2:0, "
  elements.") ;
        gDict_MergeDicts () ;
        Print ("After the merger, GDict has ", gDict.Count:2:0, "
  entries.") ;

        Print ("First 10 elements: ") ;
        for Loop  = 00 to 10 begin
          if  hi_Dict.Count  > Loop and lo_Dict.Count  > Loop  then begin
            Str  = NumToStr (Loop, 00) ;
            if  Str.Length <  02  then  Str  = "0" + Str ;
            Print (String.Format ("#{00}  hi = {01} : {02}, lo =  {03} :
  {04}", Str, hi_Dict.Keys [Loop], vrt_Format (hi_Dict.Values [Loop]
  asType Double), lo_Dict.Keys [Loop], vrt_Format (lo_Dict.Values [Loop]
  asType Double))) ;
            end ; // avoid an error if insufficient elements
          end ; // for loop

        Print ("First 100 elements: ") ;
        for Loop  = 00 to MinList (gDict.Count - 01, 100) begin
          if  gDict.Count  > Loop  then begin
            Str  = NumToStr (Loop, 00) ;
  // if  Str.Length <  03  then  Str  = "0" + Str ;
            while  Str.Length <  03  begin  Str  = "0" + Str ;  end ; //
  while loop
            Print (String.Format ("#{00}  {01} : {02}", Str, gDict.Keys
  [Loop], vrt_Format (gDict.Values [Loop] asType Double))) ;
            end ; // avoid an error if insufficient elements
          end ; // for loop
        if  skt_PowerUser (CustomerID)  then begin
          PowerStr += "  LastBar Bottom " + vrt_MMDDYYYY
  (DateTime.Now.ELDate) + " " + vrt_HHMM_pm (DateTime.Now.ELTime) + NL ;
          Print (PowerStr) ;
          end ;
      end ; // last bar on chart

  end ; // WalkForward/KeepGoing
  if  atCommentaryBar and WalkForward and KeepGoing
    then  KeepGoing  = FALSE ;

  #beginCmtry
  if  CheckCommentary and ShowCmtry  then begin
    CommentaryCL (skt_Commentary_Header (App_Type, App_Name, App_Note,
  App_Vers),
                  skt_Commentary_Notes  (CmtryStr),
                  skt_Commentary_Alert  (AlertStr),
                  skt_Commentary_Power  (PowerStr)) ;

  end ; // expert Commentary enabled for this bar
  #end
```

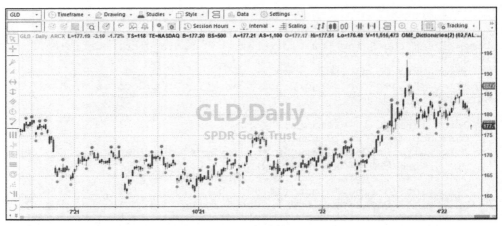

FIGURE 8.03—Swings from the Dictionaries on a Chart

```
#02 hi = 1000120_1300 : 1.01, lo = 1000131_1300 : 0.73
#03 hi = 1000203_1300 : 0.86, lo = 1000208_1300 : 0.79
#04 hi = 1000218_1300 : 1.42, lo = 1000225_1300 : 1.22
#05 hi = 1000224_1300 : 1.39, lo = 1000303_1300 : 1.20
#06 hi = 1000313_1300 : 3.13, lo = 1000321_1300 : 1.81
#07 hi = 1000323_1300 : 2.14, lo = 1000330_1300 : 1.47
#08 hi = 1000331_1300 : 1.83, lo = 1000404_1300 : 1.19
#09 hi = 1000410_1300 : 2.3, lo = 1000417_1300 : 1.31
#10 hi = 1000418_1300 : 1.87, lo = 1000424_1300 : 1.51
My Swing High Dictionary has 733 elements and the Swing Low Dictionary has 748 elements.
```

FIGURE 8.04—Output from the Print Log

Dictionary vs GlobalDictionary

This can be a difficult concept to grasp. Basically, we examined the difference between a **Dictionary** and a **GlobalDictionary**. We saw how we can input and retrieve items from each.

What the examples demonstrate is capturing Pivot (swing) points for highs and lows and storing them in two local Dictionaries. We then merge the two sets in sequential order and store the result in a **GlobalDictionary** which is shared.

A **GlobalDictionary** may be shared between EZL Analysis Techniques and even across Chart Analysis and RadarScreen windows. It may even be shared across Workspaces. There is a topic on the TS Forum demonstrating how to share a **GlobalDictionary** with an external Python application. A **Dictionary** is local and may not be inherently shared, but a **Dictionary** may be created locally and passed through a Collection such as a **GlobalDictionary** and be used by the recipient.

Queue Class

The **Queue** Class defines the structure of an object that represents a collection of elements accessed on a first-in, first-out (FIFO) basis.

Elements are added to the end of the **Queue** using the **enQueue**(object) Method where elements can reference different object types.

Elements are removed from the beginning of the **Queue** using the **Dequeue** Method. The **Peek**() Method reads the first element without removing it.

EXAMPLE 8.06—Strategy Using Queue [OME_Queue_Ex#01]

In this example we take the closed-out trade and store the entry and exit information and store them in a queue, using push. On the last bar we remove them from the queue and print them in the Print Log.

```
    Using elSystem ;
    Using elSystem.Collections ;

    Vars  :
     Vector myVect          (NULL),
     Queue  myQueue         (NULL) ;

    // Classic EasyLanguage Declarations

    Inputs:
     String Mode_Note       ("-1=Short; 0=All Entries; +1=Long"),
     Int    en_Mode         (00) ;

    Inputs:
     String Time_Note       ("Allow entries within limits."),
     Int    Beg_Time#1      (0900),
     Int    End_Time#1      (1500),
     Int    Beg_Time#2      (-01),
     Int    End_Time#2      (-01),
     String EoD_Note        ("Exit and stop trading."),
     Int    EoD_Exit_Time (1545) ;
    Vars  :
     Bool   Time_OK         (FALSE) ;

    Inputs:
     String Date_Note       ("Allow entries within date range."),
     Int    Beg_Date        (0990101),  // Jan 01, 1999
     Int    End_Date        (1991231) ; // Dec 31, 2099
    Vars  :
     Bool   Date_OK         (FALSE) ;

    // Working Storage Section
    Inputs:
     Bool   ShowCmtry       ( TRUE),
     Bool   WalkForward ( TRUE) ;

    Consts:
     String App_Type        ("Strategy"),
     String App_Name        ("OME_Queue_Ex#01"),
     String App_Note        ("Demonstrate storing trades in a Queue
    Collection"),
     String App_Vers        ("01.00.00") ;

    Vars  :
     String DQ              (DoubleQuote),
     String NL              (NewLine),
     String CmtryStr        (""),
     String OrderStr        (""),
     String myStr           (""),
     Bool   doCmtry         (FALSE),
    // String AlertStr       (""),
    // Bool   doAlert        (FALSE),
     Bool   KeepGoing       ( TRUE),
     Bool   Debug           (FALSE),
     Double Dummy           (0.00) ;

    // Main Code Body

    once begin
      myQueue  = Queue.Create () ;
```

```
    KeepGoing  =  TRUE ;
end ; // Once, and only once...

if  (CurrentBar <= 01)  then begin
end ; // first bar of data

doCmtry  = AtCommentaryBar ;
if  doCmtry  then  CmtryStr  = "" ;
if  doCmtry  then  OrderStr  = "" ;
//doAlert  = CheckAlert ;
//if  doAlert
// or doCmtry  then  AlertStr  = "" ;

if  KeepGoing  then begin
  if  (Date [00]  > Date [01])  then begin
    Date_OK  = vrt_Date_OK (Date, Beg_Date, End_Date) ;
  end   ; // first bar of new day

  Time_OK  = (BarType > 01 and BarType <> 14)
        or (BarType = 01 and BarInterval  = 1440)
        or  skt_Time_OK (Beg_Time#1, End_Time#1, Beg_Time#2,
End_Time#2, Time_OK) ;

  if  MarketPosition (01) <> 00
  and BarsSinceExit  (01)  = 00
  then begin
    myVect  = Vector.Create () ;
    myVect.Push_Back (MarketPosition (01) asType Int) ;
    myVect.Push_Back (EntryDate      (01) asType Int) ;
    myVect.Push_Back (EntryTime      (01) asType Int) ;
    myVect.Push_Back (EntryPrice     (01) asType Double) ;
    myVect.Push_Back (MaxContracts   (01) asType Int) ;
    myVect.Push_Back (ExitDate       (01) asType Int) ;
    myVect.Push_Back (ExitTime       (01) asType Int) ;
    myVect.Push_Back (ExitPrice      (01) asType Double) ; //
    myVect.Push_Back ((BarsSinceEntry (01) - BarsSinceExit (01) + 01)
asType Int) ; // duration of the trade in bars
    myQueue.Enqueue (myVect) ;
// add an element to the Queue
  end ; //  we just closed a trade

// Entry Signals
  if  Date_OK and Time_OK and en_mode  > -01
  then begin
  end ; // Long Entry Signals

  if  Date_OK and Time_OK and en_mode <  +01
  then begin
  end ; // Short Entry Signals

// Exit Signals
  if  (MarketPosition = +01)  then begin
    if  (BarsSinceEntry <= 01)  then begin
    end ; // first bar of trade

    if   EoD_Exit_Time  > -01
    and  Time [00] >= EoD_Exit_Time
    and  Time [01] <= EoD_Exit_Time
    then begin
      Sell        ("lx.EoD") next bar at market ;
```

```
        if  doCmtry  then  OrderStr += "Sell         (" + DQ + "lx.EoD" +
DQ + ") next bar at market ;" + NL ;
      end ; // End of Day Exit
    end ; // currently long

  if  (MarketPosition  = -01)  then begin
    if  (BarsSinceEntry <= 01)  then begin
    end ; // first bar of trade

    if   EoD_Exit_Time  > -01
    and   Time [00] >= EoD_Exit_Time
    and   Time [01] <= EoD_Exit_Time
    then begin
      BuyToCover ("sx.EoD") next bar at market ;
      if  doCmtry  then  OrderStr += "BuyToCover (" + DQ + "sx.EoD" +
DQ + ") next bar at market ;" + NL ;
      end ; // End of Day Exit
    end ; // currently short

  Once  (skt_LastBarOnChart)  begin
    Print ("Demonstrate the Queue Collection.  ", myQueue.Peek
().GetType ().toString (), ", ", myQueue.Peek ().toString ()) ;
    myStr  = "" ;
    while myQueue.Count  > 00 begin
      myVect  = myQueue.Dequeue () asType Vector ;
// must type cast the return value
      myStr  = String.Format ("{00} Entry: {01} {02} {03} {04} Units;
Exit:  {05} {06} {07} duration {08} bars",
        skt_iff_Str  (myVect [00] asType Int  > 00, "Long", "Short"),
        vrt_MMDDYYYY (myVect [01] asType Int),
        vrt_HHMM_pm  (myVect [02] asType Int),
        vrt_Format   (myVect [03] asType Double),
        myVect [04] asType Int,
        vrt_MMDDYYYY (myVect [05] asType Int),
        vrt_HHMM_pm  (myVect [06] asType Int),
        vrt_Format   (myVect [07] asType Double),
        myVect [08] asType Int) ;
        Print (myStr) ;
      end ; // while loop
    Print ("Notice that the last item printed is the first trade in
the sequence") ;
    end ; // Once, and only once, on the last bar

end ; // keep going / walk forward
if  atCommentaryBar and WalkForward and KeepGoing
  then  KeepGoing  = FALSE ;

#beginCmtry
if  CheckCommentary and ShowCmtry  then begin
  CommentaryCL (skt_Commentary_Header (App_Type, App_Name, App_Note,
App_Vers),
    skt_Commentary_Notes  (CmtryStr),
    skt_Commentary_Order  (OrderStr)) ;
  myStr  = "" ;
  while myQueue.Count  > 00 begin
    myVect  = myQueue.Dequeue () asType Vector ;
// must type cast the return value
    myStr  = String.Format ("{00} Entry: {01} {02} {03} {04} Units;
Exit:  {05} {06} {07} duration {08} bars",
      skt_iff_Str  (myVect [00] asType Int  > 00, "Long", "Short"),
```

```
      vrt_MMDDYYYY (myVect [01] asType Int),
      vrt_HHMM_pm  (myVect [02] asType Int),
      vrt_Format   (myVect [03] asType Double),
      myVect [04] asType Int,
      vrt_MMDDYYYY (myVect [05] asType Int),
      vrt_HHMM_pm  (myVect [06] asType Int),
      vrt_Format   (myVect [07] asType Double),
      myVect [08] asType Int) ;
      CommentaryCL (myStr) ;
   end ; // while loop
 end ; // expert Commentary enabled for this bar
 #end
```

```
Short Entry: 07/16/2021 01:00pm 654.68 100 Units; Exit: 08/02/2021 01:00pm 700.00 duration 12 bars
Long Entry: 08/02/2021 01:00pm 700.00 100 Units; Exit: 08/23/2021 01:00pm 685.44 duration 16 bars
Short Entry: 08/23/2021 01:00pm 685.44 100 Units; Exit: 09/01/2021 01:00pm 734.08 duration 8 bars
Long Entry: 09/01/2021 01:00pm 734.08 100 Units; Exit: 11/18/2021 01:00pm 1106.55 duration 56 bars
Short Entry: 11/18/2021 01:00pm 1106.55 100 Units; Exit: 12/01/2021 01:00pm 1160.70 duration 9 bars
Long Entry: 12/01/2021 01:00pm 1160.70 100 Units; Exit: 12/08/2021 01:00pm 1052.71 duration 6 bars
Short Entry: 12/08/2021 01:00pm 1052.71 100 Units; Exit: 12/31/2021 01:00pm 1073.44 duration 17 bars
Long Entry: 12/31/2021 01:00pm 1073.44 100 Units; Exit: 01/19/2022 01:00pm 1041.71 duration 13 bars
Short Entry: 01/19/2022 01:00pm 1041.71 100 Units; Exit: 02/17/2022 01:00pm 913.26 duration 22 bars
Long Entry: 02/17/2022 01:00pm 913.26 100 Units; Exit: 02/22/2022 01:00pm 834.13 duration 3 bars
Short Entry: 02/22/2022 01:00pm 834.13 100 Units; Exit: 03/21/2022 01:00pm 914.98 duration 20 bars
Long Entry: 03/21/2022 01:00pm 914.98 100 Units; Exit: 04/18/2022 01:00pm 989.03 duration 20 bars
Short Entry: 04/18/2022 01:00pm 989.03 100 Units; Exit: 06/08/2022 01:00pm 720.26 duration 37 bars
Notice that the last item printed is the first trade in the sequence
```

FIGURE 8.05—Example 8.06 Output to Print Log

Stack Class

The **Stack** class allows you to create a collection of data elements accessed on a last-in, first-out (LIFO) basis.

NAMESPACE: elSystem.Collections

An element is added to the top of the stack collection using the **Push(oElement)** method where oElement is the data to be added.

EXAMPLE 8.07—Adding an Element to the Top of a Stack

```
myStackObj.Push (oElement);
//adds oElement at the top of the stack
```

Elements are read from the top of the stack using the **Peek ()** Method.

EXAMPLE 8.08—Plotting a String from a Stack

```
Plot1 (myStackObj.Peek ().tostring()) ;
//displays element at top of stack as a string
```

Elements are removed from the stack using the **Pop()** method.

EXAMPLE 8.09—Remove the Element at the Top of a Stack

```
myStackObj.pop ();
//removes element at top of stack
```

EXAMPLE 8.10—Use a Stack to Store Trade Information [OME_Stack_Ex#01]

And now for the ultimate example. From the brilliant mind of Sam Tennis, we have an extensive example that is in fact a Strategy. Add your Strategy to the chart along with this example and you will get output of the **Stack** results to the **Print Log**, see Figure 8.06.

```
  Using elSystem ;
  Using elSystem.Collections ;

  Vars  :
   Vector myVect          (NULL),
   Stack  myStack         (NULL) ;

// Classic EasyLanguage Declarations

  Inputs:
  String Mode_Note        ("-1=Short; 0=All Entries; +1=Long"),
   Int    en_Mode         (00) ;

  Inputs:
   String Time_Note       ("Allow entries within limits."),
   Int    Beg_Time#1      (0900),
   Int    End_Time#1      (1500),
   Int    Beg_Time#2      (-01),
   Int    End_Time#2      (-01),
   String EoD_Note        ("Exit and stop trading."),
   Int    EoD_Exit_Time (1545) ;
  Vars  :
   Bool   Time_OK         (FALSE) ;

  Inputs:
   String Date_Note      ("Allow entries within date range."),
   Int    Beg_Date       (0990101),  // Jan 01, 1999
   Int    End_Date       (1991231) ; // Dec 31, 2099
  Vars  :
   Bool   Date_OK         (FALSE) ;

// Working Storage Section
  Inputs:
   Bool   ShowCmtry      ( TRUE),
   Bool   WalkForward ( TRUE) ;

  Consts:
   String App_Type       ("Strategy"),
   String App_Name       ("OME_Stack_Ex#01"),
   String App_Note       ("Demonstrate storing trades in a Stack
Collection"),
   String App_Vers       ("01.00.00") ;

  Vars  :
   String DQ             (DoubleQuote),
   String NL             (NewLine),
   String CmtryStr       (""),
   String OrderStr       (""),
   String myStr          (""),
   Bool   doCmtry        (FALSE),
   Bool   KeepGoing      ( TRUE),
   Bool   Debug          (FALSE),
   Double Dummy          (0.00) ;

// Main Code Body

once begin
  myStack  = Stack.Create () ;
  KeepGoing  =   TRUE ;
end ; // Once, and only once...
```

```
if  (CurrentBar <= 01)  then begin
end ; // first bar of data

doCmtry  = AtCommentaryBar ;
if  doCmtry  then  CmtryStr  = "" ;
if  doCmtry  then  OrderStr  = "" ;

if  KeepGoing  then begin
  if  (Date [00]  > Date [01])  then begin
    Date_OK  = vrt_Date_OK (Date, Beg_Date, End_Date) ;
  end  ; // first bar of new day

  Time_OK  = (BarType > 01 and BarType <> 14)
         or (BarType = 01 and BarInterval  = 1440)
         or  skt_Time_OK (Beg_Time#1, End_Time#1, Beg_Time#2,
End_Time#2, Time_OK) ;

  if  MarketPosition (01) <> 00
  and BarsSinceExit  (01)  = 00
  then begin
    myVect  = Vector.Create () ;
    myVect.Push_Back (MarketPosition (01) asType Int) ;
    myVect.Push_Back (EntryDate        (01) asType Int) ;
    myVect.Push_Back (EntryTime        (01) asType Int) ;
    myVect.Push_Back (EntryPrice       (01) asType Double) ;
    myVect.Push_Back (MaxContracts     (01) asType Int) ;
    myVect.Push_Back (ExitDate         (01) asType Int) ;
    myVect.Push_Back (ExitTime         (01) asType Int) ;
    myVect.Push_Back (ExitPrice        (01) asType Double) ;

    myVect.Push_Back ((BarsSinceEntry (01) - BarsSinceExit (01) + 01)
asType Int) ; // duration of the trade in bars
    myStack.Push (myVect) ; // add an element to the Stack
  end ; //  we just closed a trade

// Entry Signals
  if  Date_OK and Time_OK and en_mode  > -01
  then begin
  end ; // Long Entry Signals

  if  Date_OK and Time_OK and en_mode <  +01
  then begin
  end ; // Short Entry Signals

// Exit Signals
  if  (MarketPosition  = +01)  then begin
    if  (BarsSinceEntry <= 01)  then begin
    end ; // first bar of trade

    if  EoD_Exit_Time  > -01
    and  Time [00] >= EoD_Exit_Time
    and  Time [01] <= EoD_Exit_Time
    then begin
      Sell        ("lx.EoD") next bar at market ;
      if  doCmtry  then  OrderStr += "Sell        (" + DQ + "lx.EoD" +
DQ + ") next bar at market ;" + NL ;
    end ; // End of Day Exit
  end ; // currently long
```

```
    if  (MarketPosition  = -01)  then begin
      if  (BarsSinceEntry <= 01)  then begin
      end ; // first bar of trade

      if   EoD_Exit_Time  > -01
      and  Time [00] >= EoD_Exit_Time
      and  Time [01] <= EoD_Exit_Time
      then begin
        BuyToCover ("sx.EoD") next bar at market ;
        if  doCmtry  then  OrderStr += "BuyToCover (" + DQ + "sx.EoD" +
  DQ + ") next bar at market ;" + NL ;
      end ; // End of Day Exit
    end ; // currently short

    Once  (skt_LastBarOnChart)  begin
      Print ("Demonstrate the Stack Collection.  ", myStack.Peek
  ().GetType ().toString (), ", ", myStack.Peek ().toString ()) ;
      myStr  = "" ;
      while myStack.Count  > 00 begin
        myVect  = myStack.Pop () asType Vector ;
  // must type cast the return value
        myStr  = String.Format ("{00} Entry: {01} {02} {03} {04} Units;
  Exit:  {05} {06} {07} duration {08} bars",
          skt_IFF_Str  (myVect [00] asType Int  > 00, "Long", "Short"),
          vrt_MMDDYYYY (myVect [01] asType Int),
          vrt_HHMM_pm  (myVect [02] asType Int),
          vrt_Format   (myVect [03] asType Double),
          myVect [04] asType Int,
          vrt_MMDDYYYY (myVect [05] asType Int),
          vrt_HHMM_pm  (myVect [06] asType Int),
          vrt_Format   (myVect [07] asType Double),
          myVect [08] asType Int) ;
        Print (myStr) ;
      end ; // while loop
      Print ("Notice that the last item printed is the final trade in
  the sequence") ;
    end ; // Once, and only once, on the last bar


  end ; // keep going / walk forward
  if  atCommentaryBar and WalkForward and KeepGoing
    then  KeepGoing  = FALSE ;


  #beginCmtry


  if  CheckCommentary and ShowCmtry  then begin
    CommentaryCL (skt_Commentary_Header (App_Type, App_Name, App_Note,
  App_Vers),
      skt_Commentary_Notes  (CmtryStr),
      skt_Commentary_Order  (OrderStr)) ;
      myStr  = "" ;
    while myStack.Count  > 00 begin
      myVect  = myStack.Pop () asType Vector ;
  // must type cast the return value
      myStr  = String.Format ("{00} Entry: {01} {02} {03} {04} Units;
  Exit:  {05} {06} {07} duration {08} bars",
        skt_IFF_Str  (myVect [00] asType Int  > 00, "Long", "Short"),
        vrt_MMDDYYYY (myVect [01] asType Int),
        vrt_HHMM_pm  (myVect [02] asType Int),
        vrt_Format   (myVect [03] asType Double),
        myVect [04] asType Int,
```

```
        vrt_MMDDYYYY (myVect [05] asType Int),
        vrt_HHMM_pm  (myVect [06] asType Int),
        vrt_Format   (myVect [07] asType Double),
         myVect [08] asType Int) ;
      CommentaryCL (myStr) ;
    end ; // while loop
  end ; // expert Commentary enabled for this bar
  #end
```

The output from this example, to the Print Log, follows in Figure 8.06.

```
Short Entry: 04/15/2011 01:00pm 5.13 100 Units; Exit: 04/25/2011 01:00pm 5.34 duration 6 bars
Long Entry: 03/30/2011 01:00pm 4.82 100 Units; Exit: 04/15/2011 01:00pm 5.13 duration 13 bars
Short Entry: 03/17/2011 01:00pm 4.65 100 Units; Exit: 03/30/2011 01:00pm 4.82 duration 10 bars
Long Entry: 02/02/2011 01:00pm 4.83 100 Units; Exit: 03/17/2011 01:00pm 4.65 duration 31 bars
Short Entry: 12/06/2010 01:00pm 6.27 100 Units; Exit: 02/02/2011 01:00pm 4.83 duration 41 bars
Long Entry: 10/22/2010 01:00pm 4.14 100 Units; Exit: 12/06/2010 01:00pm 6.27 duration 31 bars
Short Entry: 10/08/2010 01:00pm 4.09 100 Units; Exit: 10/22/2010 01:00pm 4.14 duration 11 bars
Long Entry: 09/29/2010 01:00pm 4.24 100 Units; Exit: 10/08/2010 01:00pm 4.09 duration 8 bars
Short Entry: 09/23/2010 01:00pm 3.98 100 Units; Exit: 09/29/2010 01:00pm 4.24 duration 5 bars
Long Entry: 09/15/2010 01:00pm 4.20 100 Units; Exit: 09/23/2010 01:00pm 3.98 duration 7 bars
Notice that the last item printed is the final trade in the sequence
```

FIGURE 8.06—Stack Example #01 Output to Print Log

TokenList Class

This is a base class for manipulating a comma-separated list of string values as a collection of items.

NAMESPACE: tsData.Common

Any text or item added, updated, or inserted that contains commas will have separate items added to the item collection. Duplicate values may be added.

This snippet example is not a fully defined routine so it will not be in the downloads. It is just to illustrate manipulating a **TokenList**.

```
MyTokenList.Add("Symbol1");
  // adds the first string value as item 0
MyTokenList.Add("Symbol2");
  // adds the second string value as item 1
MyTokenList.Insert(0,"Symbol3");
  // inserts a new string value at item 0
MyList = MyTokenList.Value;
  // MyList contains the comma-delimited string values
  // "Symbol3, Symbol1, Symbol2"
MyTokenList.RemoveAt(0);
  // deletes the first item in the list
MyString = MyTokenList.Item[00];
  // MyString will contain the string value for the first
  // item which is now "Symbol1"
  // Remember that we removed item 0
```

> It may be a good practice to force all text used with the TokenList to be either upper or lower case.

PROPERTIES

	Name	Type	Description
	Count	int	Gets the number of items contained in the list.
	IsReadOnly	bool	True indicates that the list is read-only.

	Name	Type	Description
🖼	Item[index]	string	Gets or sets the value of the string item with the specified index.
🖼	Value	string	Gets or sets the string containing the full list of comma-separated string items.

TABLE 8.03—Properties of the TokenList Class

METHODS

	Name	Description
🔩	Add (name)	Adds an item with the provided string value (name) to the list.
🔩	Clear ()	Removes all items from the list.
🔩	Clone ()	Creates a copy of the current instance.
🔩	Contains (name)	True if the list contains an item with the specified string value (name).
🔩	Create ()	Initializes a new instance of the class.
🔩	Create (values)	Initializes a new instance of the class using the specified comma-delimited list of values.
🔩	IndexOf (name)	Get the index of the list item with the specified string value (name).
🔩	Insert (index, name)	Inserts a string value (name) at the specified index position.
🔩	Remove (name)	Removes the first occurrence of a specified string value (name) from the list.
🔩	RemoveAt (index)	Removes a string value item from the list at a specified index position.
🔩	ToString (string)	Gets the full list of string values as a comma-delimited string.

TABLE 8.04—Methods of the TokenList Class

OPERATORS

	Name	Description
📇	operator +=	Adds a string value item to the list.
📇	operator -=	Removes the specified string value item from the list.

TABLE 8.05—Operators of the TokenList Class

INHERITANCE HIERARCHY

elSystem.Object
  tsData.Common.TokenList

Vector Class

As discussed briefly in Chapter 8, a **Vector** is like a string in that it contains a "list" of items. There is often more than one character in a string. There can be more than one element in a **Vector**. In fact, one can store Objects, in addition to numbers or strings, in a Vector. That's the beauty of it. One can even put another vector in a vector, referred to as a Vector of Vectors.

The **Vector** class allows you to create a collection of data elements referenced by an index (zero-based). Data elements may be inserted, read, and deleted from anywhere within the Collection.

An element is added to the vector collection several ways: using **Insert (iIndex, oElement)** to add the element in front of the `iIndex` element. where `oElement` is the data to be added or using **Push_Back (oElement)** to add the element to the end of the collection.

On our website (https://www.EasyLanguageOOEL.com) we have included OME_Vector_Ex#01 in the downloads. It is not included in this book but is an excellent example of reading from a file and putting fields into a vector. This example delves into **Vector, String.Split (), TokenList, StreamReader, Array** and Loop structires!

INHERITANCE HIERARCHY

elSystem.Object
elSystem.Collections.Vector

You may add an element to the Vector Collection in a couple of ways:

```
insert(iIndex, oElement)
//  to add the element in front of the iIndex element, where
//  oElement is the data to be added
```

or

```
push_back (oElement)
// to add the element to the end of the collection.
```

EXAMPLE 8.11—Adding and Element to a Vector using Push_Back

```
myVectorObj.insert(iIndex, oElement);
//adds oElement at position iIndex in the collection
myVectorObj.push_back(oElement);
//adds oElement as the last element of the collection
```

Elements are read from the vector using square brackets [`iIndex`] that specify the index of the element to read. Elements are written to the vector using square brackets [`iIndex`] to place `oElement` in an existing `iIndex` position.

EXAMPLE 8.12—Demonstrates Retrieving and Storing Values in a Vector

```
Plot1 (myVectorObj[iIndex].tostring ()) ;
// displays oElement at iIndex as a string
myVectorObj[iIndex] = myInput ;
//replaces oElement at element iIndex, overwriting content
```

Elements are removed from the vector using the **Erase (iIndex)** to remove the `iIndex` element of the collection or by using **Pop_Back ()** to remove the last element in the collection.

EXAMPLE 8.13—Demonstrates Two Ways of Removing an Item from a Vector

```
myObj  = myVectorObj.Erase (iIndex) ;
//removes element at iIndex
myObj  = myVectorObj.Pop_Pack () ;
//removes element at end of collection
```

AppStorage

AppStorage is a member of the **AnalysisTechnique** Class and is itself a **Dictionary**. It is an Object of the **Dictionary** Class, or more specifically **elSystem.collections.Dictionary**.

Every AT has an **AppStorage** except the user function which shares the **AppStorage** of its parent.

EXAMPLE 8.14—Analysis AppStorage Ex #01 [OME_AppStorage]

If the code in this example does not execute and show output in the **Print Log**, then most likely the Designer Generated Code (DGC) that was included in the original ELD file was not found. In this event, you will need to go to the bottom of the ELD and un-comment the DGC. You can either enable the three commented lines in the **Once** block or 🖰 Double-Click on the three Event Handlers in the Properties tab to create the DGC code.

```
{*
This example uses the AppStorage dictionary property to save the time
the workspace that contains this indicator was last saved. The
EasyLanguage Print Log will display a text message when one of the
associated update events has been triggered.
*}

method void AnalysisTechnique_Initialized (elSystem.Object sender,
elSystem.InitializedEventArgs args)
begin
  If (AppStorage.Contains("WorkspaceSavingTime") = False) then
    AppStorage.Add("WorkspaceSavingTime",
elSystem.Datetime.CurrentTime) ;

  Print("Initialized Event - Saved value is
",(AppStorage["WorkspaceSavingTime"] astype
elSystem.DateTime).ToString ()) ;
End ;

method void AnalysisTechnique_WorkspaceSaving (elSystem.Object sender,
elSystem.WorkspaceSavingEventArgs args)
begin
  AppStorage["WorkspaceSavingTime"] = elSystem.DateTime.CurrentTime ;

  Print("WorkspaceSaving Event - Updated value to
",(AppStorage["WorkspaceSavingTime"] astype
elSystem.DateTime).ToString ()) ;
End ;

method void AnalysisTechnique_UnInitialized( elSystem.Object sender,
elSystem.UnInitializedEventArgs args )
begin
  Print ("UnInitialized Event") ;
End ;

plot1 (Close, "C") ;
```

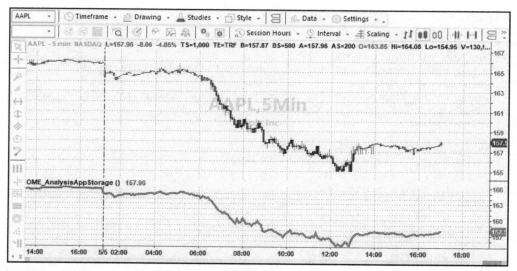

FIGURE 8.07—Analysis AppStorage

```
UnInitialized Event
Initialized Event - Saved value is 6:14:32 PM
UnInitialized Event
Initialized Event - Saved value is 6:14:32 PM
```

FIGURE 8.08—AppStorage Print Log

The following is the listing of the Designer Generated Code (DGC) just so you can see what it looks like. The DGC is available by accessing the **View** menu and you can copy the contents by the standard Windows method of CTRL-A and CTRL-C (select all and copy).

```
{ This method gets called by EasyLanguage one time at
  the beginning to create and initialize the components }

method override void InitializeComponent()
begin

  //--------------------------
  //analysistechnique
  //--------------------------

  //-------------------------------------------
  //                    Events
  //-------------------------------------------
  self.initialized += analysistechnique_initialized ;
  self.uninitialized += analysistechnique_uninitialized ;
  self.workspacesaving += analysistechnique_workspacesaving ;
end ;
```

☑ I have it on good authority that the InitializeComponent method should be called only from Designer Generated Code. Instead, if you are writing an AT that does not use DGC then use a Once block. Example 8.15 calls an App_Init method from its Once block.

EXAMPLE 8.15—Using AppStorage to Output the Contents of Various Collections [OME_AppStorage_Report]

```
Using tsData.Common ;
Using elSystem ;
Using elSystem.Collections ;

Inputs:
 Bool   DoPrint       ( TRUE),
 String Print_Note#0  ("The Report data is returned as a String to the
Print Log window if TRUE, "),
 String Print_Note#1  (" do you want it Printed (TRUE) or as
Commentary (FALSE)?"),
 String Print_Note#2  (" The ShowCmtry (Show Commentary) Input must be
<b>TRUE</b> to display as Commentary!"),
 String Indent        ("") ;

Vars :
 String myStr         ("") ;

// Working Storage Section
Inputs:
 Bool   ShowCmtry    (FALSE) ;

Consts:
 String App_Type     ("Study"),
 String App_Name     ("OME_AppStorage_Report"),
 String App_Note     ("Test the User Function of the same name"),
```

```
   String App_Vers      ("01.03.00") ;

Vars  :
  String DQ            (DoubleQuote),
  String NL            (NewLine),
  String CmtryStr      (""),
  String AlertStr      (""),
  Bool   doCmtry       (FALSE),
  Bool   doAlert       (FALSE),
  Bool   Debug         (FALSE),
  Double Dummy         (0.00) ;

method void Init_App ()
Vars  :
  Int            Loop,
  GlobalDictionary myGDict,
  Dictionary myDict,
  Dictionary BarDict,
  Vector     myVect,
  Stack      myStack,
  Queue      myQueue,
  TokenList  myTokenList ;
begin
  Print (App_Name, "(" + App_Type + ")." + "Init_App") ;

  if  AppStorage.Contains ("App_Name")
    then  AppStorage       ["App_Name"]  = App_Name
    else  AppStorage.Add  ("App_Name",    App_Name) ;

  if  AppStorage.Contains ("App_Note")
    then  AppStorage       ["App_Note"]  = App_Note
    else  AppStorage.Add  ("App_Note",    App_Note) ;

  myGDict   = GlobalDictionary.Create (FALSE, "myGDict") ;
  myDict    = Dictionary.Create () ;
  BarDict   = Dictionary.Create () ;
  myVect    = Vector.Create () ;
  myStack   = Stack.Create () ;
  myQueue   = Queue.Create () ;
  myTokenList  = TokenList.Create () ;

  if  BarDict.Contains ("01) Date")
    then  BarDict       ["01) Date"]    = vrt_MMDDYYYY (Date)
    else  BarDict.Add  ("01) Date",      vrt_MMDDYYYY (Date)) ;

  if  BarDict.Contains ("02) Time")
    then  BarDict       ["02) Time"]    = vrt_HHMM_pm (Time)
    else  BarDict.Add  ("02) Time",      vrt_HHMM_pm (Time)) ;

  if  BarDict.Contains ("03) Open")
    then  BarDict       ["03) Open"]    = vrt_Format (Open)
    else  BarDict.Add  ("03) Open",      vrt_Format (Open)) ;

  if  BarDict.Contains ("04) High")
    then  BarDict       ["04) High"]    = vrt_Format (High)
    else  BarDict.Add  ("04) High",      vrt_Format (High)) ;

  if  BarDict.Contains ("05) Low")
    then  BarDict       ["05) Low"]     = vrt_Format (Low)
    else  BarDict.Add  ("05) Low",       vrt_Format (Low)) ;
```

```
   if  BarDict.Contains ("06) Close")
     then   BarDict        ["06) Close"]    = vrt_Format (Close)
     else   BarDict.Add  ("06) Close",      vrt_Format (Close)) ;

   if  BarDict.Contains ("07) Volume")
     then   BarDict        ["07) Volume"]  = NumToStr (Volume, 00)
     else   BarDict.Add  ("07) Volume",     NumToStr (Volume, 00)) ;

   if  myDict.Contains ("BarDict")
     then   myDict         ["BarDict"]      = BarDict
     else   myDict.Add  ("BarDict",         BarDict) ;

   for Loop  = 10 DownTo 00 begin
     if  myGDict.Contains (NumToStr (CurrentBar + Loop, 00))
       then  myGDict      [NumToStr (CurrentBar + Loop, 00)] =  NumToStr
(CurrentBar + Loop, 00)
       else  myGDict.Add (NumToStr (CurrentBar + Loop, 00),    NumToStr
(CurrentBar + Loop, 00)) ;

     if  myDict.Contains (NumToStr (CurrentBar - Loop, 00))
       then  myDict       [NumToStr (CurrentBar - Loop, 00)] = NumToStr
(CurrentBar - Loop, 00)
       else  myDict.Add (NumToStr (CurrentBar - Loop, 00),    NumToStr
(CurrentBar - Loop, 00)) ;

     myVect.Push_Back (Loop) ;

     myStack.Push (High [Loop]) ;

     myQueue.enQueue (CurrentBar - Loop) ;

     myTokenList.Add (NumToStr (Loop, 00)) ;
   end ; // for loop

   if  AppStorage.Contains ("myDict")
     then   appStorage      ["myDict"]       = myDict
     else   appStorage.Add  ("myDict",        myDict) ;

   if  AppStorage.Contains ("myGDict")
     then   appStorage      ["myGDict"]       = myGDict
     else   appStorage.Add  ("myGDict",        myGDict) ;

   if  AppStorage.Contains ("myQueue")
     then   appStorage      ["myQueue"]       = myQueue
     else   appStorage.Add  ("myQueue",        myQueue) ;

   if  AppStorage.Contains ("myStack")
     then   appStorage      ["myStack"]       = myStack
     else   appStorage.Add  ("myStack",        myStack) ;

   if  AppStorage.Contains ("myTokenList")
     then   appStorage      ["myTokenList"] = myTokenList
     else   appStorage.Add  ("myTokenList",   myTokenList) ;

   if  AppStorage.Contains ("myVect")
     then   appStorage      ["myVect"]       = myVect
     else   appStorage.Add  ("myVect",        myVect) ;

end ; // "Init_App" method
```

```
once begin
  Print ("AnalysisTechnique.Name = ", DQ, AnalysisTechnique.Name, DQ)
;
  Init_App () ;
end ; // Once, and only once

if  (CurrentBar <= 01)  then begin
end ; // first bar of data

doCmtry  = AtCommentaryBar ;
if  doCmtry  then  CmtryStr  = "" ;
doAlert  = CheckAlert ;
if  doAlert
 or doCmtry  then  AlertStr  = "" ;

if  skt_LastBarOnChart
 or doCmtry
then begin
  Print ("Last bar, Calling OME_AppStorage_Report.") ;
  myStr  = OME_AppStorage_Report (DoPrint) ;
  if  doPrint  then  Print (myStr) ;
end ; // on the last bar

#beginCmtry

if  CheckCommentary and ShowCmtry  then begin
  CommentaryCL (skt_Commentary_Header (App_Type, App_Name, App_Note,
App_Vers),
                skt_Commentary_Notes  (CmtryStr),
                skt_Commentary_Alert  (AlertStr)) ;

  CommentaryCL ;
  if  doPrint  = FALSE
  then begin
    CommentaryCL (myStr) ;
  end
  else begin
    CommentaryCL (Print_Note#0 + NL + Print_Note#1 + NL +
Print_Note#2) ;
  end ;
end
else begin
  CommentaryCL (Print_Note#0 + NL + Print_Note#1 + NL + Print_Note#2)
;
end ; // expert Commentary enabled for this bar
#end
```

The output from the example looks like that shown in Figure 8.09 below.

```
AnalysisTechnique.Name = "OME_AppStorage_Report"
OME_AppStorage_Report(Study).Init_App
Last bar, Calling OME_AppStorage_Report.
AnalysisTechnique.Name = "OME_AppStorage_Report"

OME_AppStorage_Report (Function (String, Simple)).Once
StepThruAppStorage
    : #000, "App_Name", "OME_AppStorage_Report"
    : #001, "App_Note", "Test the User Function of the same name"
    : #002, "myDict", "elSystem.Collections.Dictionary"
      : Dict:      #000, "-1", "-1"
      : Dict:      #001, "-2", "-2"
```

```
: Dict:          #002, "-3", "-3"
: Dict:          #003, "-4", "-4"
: Dict:          #004, "-5", "-5"
: Dict:          #005, "-6", "-6"
: Dict:          #006, "-7", "-7"
: Dict:          #007, "-8", "-8"
: Dict:          #008, "-9", "-9"
: Dict:          #009, "0", "0"
: Dict:          #010, "1", "1"
: Dict:          #011, "BarDict", "elSystem.Collections.Dictionary"
   : Dict:      Dict:       #000, "01) Date", "07/14/2010"
   : Dict:      Dict:       #001, "02) Time", "01:00pm"
   : Dict:      Dict:       #002, "03) Open", " 3.59"
   : Dict:      Dict:       #003, "04) High", " 4.03"
   : Dict:      Dict:       #004, "05) Low", " 3.55"
   : Dict:      Dict:       #005, "06) Close", " 3.97"
   : Dict:      Dict:       #006, "07) Volume", "20980550"

: #003, "myGDict", "elSystem.Collections.GlobalDictionary"
: GlobalDict: #000, "1", "1"
: GlobalDict: #001, "10", "10"
: GlobalDict: #002, "11", "11"
: GlobalDict: #003, "2", "2"
: GlobalDict: #004, "3", "3"
: GlobalDict: #005, "4", "4"
: GlobalDict: #006, "5", "5"
: GlobalDict: #007, "6", "6"
: GlobalDict: #008, "7", "7"
: GlobalDict: #009, "8", "8"
: GlobalDict: #010, "9", "9"

: #004, "myQueue", "elSystem.Collections.Queue"
: Queue:      #000, "-9"
: Queue:      #001, "-8"
: Queue:      #002, "-7"
: Queue:      #003, "-6"
: Queue:      #004, "-5"
: Queue:      #005, "-4"
: Queue:      #006, "-3"
: Queue:      #007, "-2"
: Queue:      #008, "-1"
: Queue:      #009, "0"
: Queue:      #010, "1"

: #005, "myStack", "elSystem.Collections.Stack"
: Stack:      #000, "4.03"
: Stack:      #001, "3.73"
: Stack:      #002, "3.61"
: Stack:      #003, "3.58"
: Stack:      #004, "3.5"
: Stack:      #005, "3.33"
: Stack:      #006, "4.0"
: Stack:      #007, "4.62"
: Stack:      #008, "5.18"
: Stack:      #009, "6.08"
: Stack:      #010, "5.0"

: #006, "myTokenList", "10,9,8,7,6,5,4,3,2,1,0"
: TokenList:  #000, "10"
: TokenList:  #001, "9"
: TokenList:  #002, "8"
```

```
           : TokenList:     #003, "7"
           : TokenList:     #004, "6"
           : TokenList:     #005, "5"
           : TokenList:     #006, "4"
           : TokenList:     #007, "3"
           : TokenList:     #008, "2"
           : TokenList:     #009, "1"
           : TokenList:     #010, "0"

      : #007, "myVect", "elSystem.Collections.Vector"
           : Vector:        #000, "10"
           : Vector:        #001, "9"
           : Vector:        #002, "8"
           : Vector:        #003, "7"
           : Vector:        #004, "6"
           : Vector:        #005, "5"
           : Vector:        #006, "4"
           : Vector:        #007, "3"
           : Vector:        #008, "2"
           : Vector:        #009, "1"
           : Vector:        #010, "0"
```

FIGURE 8.09—Output from Example 8.15: [OME_AppStorage_Ex#02]

Summary

We have examined the **TokenList** and **Vector** Classes in this chapter. We also addressed **Collection Classes**, **Dictionary**, **GlobalDictionary**, **Queue**, **Stack**, **Vectors** and **AppStorage**.

Collections can be used to help you organize, manipulate, and share nearly any information imaginable; the sky is the limit, the pearl is your oyster. When you start combining **Vector** and **GlobalDictionary** a whole world of shared connectivity opens up to you. Want your Strategy and Study to talk to each other? Want your RadarScreen to display values from a Chart? The world really is your oyster, and that shell is half full!

A **GlobalDictionary** may be shared between EZL Analysis Techniques and even across Chart Analysis and RadarScreen windows. It may even be shared across Workspaces. A **Dictionary** is local and may not be inherently shared, but a Dictionary may be created locally and passed through a Collection such as a **GlobalDictionary** and used by the recipient.

These can be difficult concepts to grasp. Basically, we examined the difference between a **Dictionary** and a **GlobalDictionary**. We saw how we can input and retrieve items from each.

CHAPTER 9
Drawing Objects

In This Chapter

- Introduction
- Drawing Objects
- About DrawingObject Classes
- DrawingObject Class
- Object Class
- DrawingObject Methods
- AlertConfiguration Class
- Notification Class
- TextLabel Class
- Text at a Specific Location on Your Chart
- HorizontalLine Class
- VerticalLine Class
- TrendLine Class
- Rectangle Class
- Ellipse Class
- Summary

Introduction

There are objects, and then there are objects. The word "object" can refer to a class of items or it can refer to an object on your chart. We are going to examine both, starting with the **AnalysisTechnique** Class. A myriad of classes and their properties is in **Volume II—Reference Guide: Appendix III**.

The EZL Drawing Object Classes allow you to create drawing objects on a chart from your AT and to programmatically manage their appearance and position. The **TrendLine** and **TextLabel** Objects parallel the functionality of the legacy EZL TL_xxx and Text_xxx reserved words. The **Ellipse**, **HorizontalLine**, **Rectangle**, and **VerticalLine** Objects are equivalent to the drawing tools you can manually insert in a chart.

I could have addressed some of the following concepts in an earlier chapter, but I felt it expedient to introduce these topics in the chapter where they are being used.

Drawing Objects

There are drawing objects such as horizontal line, vertical line, trendline, **TextLabel**, text, arc, rectangle, arrows, ellipse and more. If you'll look under **Drawing** on the menu bar at the top of your chart you will see what I'm talking about. Drawing Tools from the Platform however are rather different from **DrawingObjects** though they can be found and manipulated using the **ChartingHost** Class.

DrawingObjects can be added to your charts with the use of OOEL Read the following section: **About Drawing Object Classes** to see how.

The base class from which all other classes are derived is called the **Object** Class. Every Method and Property in the **Object** Class is available in all objects in the system, although derived[43] classes can and do override some of the base Methods.

The base Class **Object** contains a very few Methods and operators that are common to all Objects. Each additional Class in the Inheritance Hierarchy brings its own set of zero or more Properties, Methods and / or Alerts to the mix. It pays to look at the parent Classes to find the Member(s) you need.

---

[43] A class whose members are inherited is called the base class, and the class that inherits those members is called the derived class.

About DrawingObject Classes

The OOEL **DrawingObject** classes allow you to create drawing objects on a chart from your Analysis Technique and to programmatically manage their appearance and position. The **TrendLine** and **TextLabel** Objects parallel the functionality of the legacy EZL **TL_xxx** and **Text_xxx** reserved words. The **Ellipse, HorizontalLine, Rectangle,** and **VerticalLine** Objects are equivalent to the drawing tools you are able to manually insert in a chart, except that these can be manipulated programmatically.

Adding Drawing Objects to Your EasyLanguage Code

To use OOEL drawing objects, you should have the following elements:

Declare a variable for each type of object to be used. The class type of each variable must be appropriate for the object it will reference. Remember to include the namespace identifier **elSystem.DrawingObjects** in front of the specific class type unless you have previously added a **Using** statement for the namespace. In this example, myHorizLine1 and myTrendLine1 are the names of the variables being created for each drawing object type.

```
using elSystem.DrawingObjects ;
using elSystem ;
Vars  : HorizontalLine myHorizLine1 (null),
// declare myHorizLine as a HorizontalLine type
TrendLine myTrendLine(null),
// declare myTrendLine as a TrendLine type
BNPoint BNPoint1(null), BNPoint BNPoint2(null);
// declare bar number points 1 & 2
```

Create an instance of each drawing object at the point locations specified.

```
myHorizLine = HorizontalLine.Create (last-.02);
// create a horizontal line at .02 below the last price
myPoint1 = BNPoint.Create (barnumber + MaxBarsBack-10, close[10]);
// create first trendline point 10 bars to the left of
// the current bar
myPoint2 = BNPoint.Create (BarNumber + MaxBarsBack, close) ;
// create second trendline point at current bar
myTrendLine = TrendLine.Create (myPoint1, myPoint2) ;
// create a trend line and assign it to myTrendLine
```

Note that you can also create the above trendline without needing to define **BNPoint** objects by directly specifying the **BNPoint** values when creating the trendline instance, as follows:

```
myTrendLine1 = TrendLine.Create (BNPoint.Create (BarNumber +
MaxBarsBack - 10, close[10]), BNPoint.Create (BarNumber, close)) ;
```

Add drawing objects (e.g., **TrendLine, HorizontalLine**) to the **DrawingObjects** Property of the AnalysisTechnique Object.

```
DrawingObjects.Add (myHorizLine) ;
DrawingObjects.Add (myTrendLine) ;
```

Associate an Event Handler with the objects (to call the DOClick Method when either drawing object is clicked).

```
myHorizLine1.Click += DOClick ;
myTrendLine1.Click += DOClick ;
```

Finally, write the Method(s) to be called when a drawing object click event happens.

```
method void DOClick (Object sender, ChartElementClickEventArgs args)
begin
// Your EasyLanguage code to handle a drawing object that
// has been clicked
End ;
```

Alerts with Drawing Objects

You can set alerts for **TrendLine, HorizontalLine,** and **VerticalLine** drawing objects so that they will notify you when specified alert criteria occur.

INHERITANCE HIERARCHY

elSystem.Object
  elSystem.DrawingObjects.DrawingObject
   elSystem.DrawingObjects.[ClassType]

DrawingObject Class

The **Object** Class is the base class from which all other classes are derived. Every Method in the **Object** Class is available in all objects in the system, although derived classes can and do override some of the base Methods.

NAMESPACE: elSystem.DrawingObjects

Objects can be drawn with the Drawing Tool in the classic way, or they can be done programmatically from within OOEL code. There is an immense amount of control of these objects from within OOEL. The **TrendLine** and **TextLabel** Objects parallel the functionality of the legacy EZL **TL_xxx** and **Text_xxx** reserved words. The **Ellipse, HorizontalLine, Rectangle,** and **VerticalLine** objects are equivalent to the drawing tools you were able to manually insert in a chart.

The available traits are listed below. The classes and explanations appear below that.

Ellipse—Draws an ellipse based on two points, the starting point at the upper left and the ending point at the lower right of a bounding rectangular area. The border line and fill pattern characteristics can be user specified.

HorizontalLine—Draws a horizontal line that intersects a specified price. The line color, style and thickness can be user-specified.

Rectangle—Draws a rectangle based on two BN (BarNumber), DT (DateTime) or XY points, the starting point at the upper left and the ending point at the lower right corner of the rectangle. The border line and fill pattern characteristics can be user specified.

TextLabel—Displays a text object at a specified point. The color, font style and horizontal/vertical centering can be user-specified.

TrendLine—Draws a trendline between two points, the starting point and the ending point. The line characteristics and left/right extension properties can be user-specified.

VerticalLine—Draws a vertical line that intersects a specified time interval. The line style and thickness can be user specified.

There are also Point Classes in addition to the Drawing Classes. These consist of **BNPoint, DTPoint** and **XYPoint**.

BNPoint—Used to define a drawing object point based on a bar number and a price value. Objects positioned with a **BNPoint** will move along with the bars they are anchored to.

DTPoint—Used to define a drawing object point based on a bar date/time stamp and a price value. Objects positioned with a **DTPoint** will move along with the bars they are anchored to.

XYPoint—Used to define a drawing object (**Ellipse, Rectangle,** or **TextLabel**) point based on a chart X and Y location (relative to the upper left corner of the chart window). Objects positioned with an **XYPoint** will not move as the bars are scrolled.

We will examine these in turn though not necessarily in the above order.

Let's start with a simple example. The following code makes use of **DTPoint** to locate text at the **BarDateTime** so we can have the values of the moving average appear to the right of the moving average itself. For this example, I asked Sam to just write me an easy, vanilla moving average. So that's what he named it.

As you will quickly notice when you import the code and put it on your chart, the code is missing something, because the values plotted to the right of the chart print over and again with each new bar. We will correct this in the following example.

Notice the lines where I set the **VStyle**. The first line uses a hard coded "2" whereas the second example uses the **eNum** (Enumerated Value) **VerticalStyle.Center**. It is right and proper to use the eNum whenever possible as this will automatically adjust to any changes to the OOEL definitions.

EXAMPLE 9.01—A Vanilla Moving Average [OME_MovAvg_Vanilla]

```
Inputs:
 Double Price        (Close),
 Int    Fast_Len     (09),
 Int    Slow_Len     (18) ;

Vars  :
 Double Fast_Val     (0.00),
 Double Slow_Val     (0.00) ;

// Working Storage Section

Consts:
 String App_Type     ("Study"),
 String App_Name     ("OME_MovAvg_Vanilla"),
 String App_Note     ("OOEL Made Easy"),
 String App_Vers     ("01.00.00") ;

Fast_Val  = Average (Price, Fast_Len) ;
Slow_Val  = Average (Price, Slow_Len) ;

Plot1 (Fast_Val, "Fast MAvg", Default, Default, Default) ;
Plot2 (Slow_Val, "Slow MAvg", Default, Default, Default) ;

Using elSystem.DrawingObjects ;

Vars  :
 DTPoint    Fast_DT  (NULL),
 DTPoint    Slow_DT  (NULL),
 TextLabel Fast_TL  (NULL),
 TextLabel Slow_TL  (NULL) ;

if  LastBarOnChart  then begin
  Fast_DT  = DTPoint.Create (BarDateTime, Fast_Val) ;
  Slow_DT  = DTPoint.Create (BarDateTime, Slow_Val) ;
  Fast_TL  = TextLabel.Create (Fast_DT, "  " + NumToStr (Fast_Len,
00)) ;
  Slow_TL  = TextLabel.Create (Slow_DT, "  " + NumToStr (Slow_Len,
00)) ;
// center the text on the value of the line.
  Fast_TL.VStyle  = 02 ; // VerticalStyle.center
  Slow_TL.VStyle  = VerticalStyle.center ;
  DrawingObjects.Add (Fast_TL) ;
  DrawingObjects.Add (Slow_TL) ;
end ;
```

FIGURE 9.01—A Vanilla Moving Average with Labels

We will get on with the classes and definitions in a bit, but let's look at some more things we can do with drawing objects in OOEL. In this next example we are going to specify the font to use as well as font size and color. And we are going to remove the expired text, so it doesn't write over itself. We are calling this one Strawberry since it's a little more flavorful than Vanilla.

EXAMPLE 9.02—Code for Moving Average Strawberry [OME_MovAvg_StrwBry]

```
Using elSystem.Drawing ;
Using elSystem.DrawingObjects ;

Inputs:
 Double Price        (Close),
 Int    Fast_Len     (09),
 Int    Slow_Len     (18),
 Int    Fast_Col     (DarkGreen),
 Int    Slow_Col     (Red) ;

Vars  :
 Double Fast_Val     (0.00),
 Double Slow_Val     (0.00) ;

// Working Storage Section

Consts:
 String App_Type     ("Study"),
 String App_Name     ("OME MovAvg Strawberry"),
 String App_Note     ("OOEL Made Easy"),
 String App_Vers     ("01.02.00") ;

Fast_Val = Average (Price, Fast_Len) ;
Slow_Val = Average (Price, Slow_Len) ;

Plot1 (Fast_Val, "Fast MAvg", Fast_Col, Default, Default) ;
Plot2 (Slow_Val, "Slow MAvg", Slow_Col, Default, Default) ;

Inputs:
 String Font_Name    ("Arial"),
 Int    Font_Size    (10),
 String Font_Color   ("Red") ;

Vars  :
 Font       myFont   (NULL),
 Color      myColor  (NULL) ;
```

```
Vars :
 DTPoint   Fast_DT  (NULL),
 DTPoint   Slow_DT  (NULL),
 TextLabel Fast_TL  (NULL),
 TextLabel Slow_TL  (NULL) ;

if  LastBarOnChart  then begin
// Remove previous DrawingObject from the Chart if it exists
  if  Fast_TL <> NULL  then DrawingObjects.Delete (Fast_TL) ;
  if Slow_TL <> NULL   then DrawingObjects.Delete (Slow_TL) ;

// Create the DateTime Point object
  Fast_DT  = DTPoint.Create (BarDateTime, Fast_Val) ;
  Slow_DT  = DTPoint.Create (BarDateTime, Slow_Val) ;
  Fast_TL  = TextLabel.Create (Fast_DT, " " + NumToStr (Fast_Len, 00))
;
  Slow_TL  = TextLabel.Create (Slow_DT, "         " + NumToStr
(Slow_Len, 00)) ;

// center the text on the value of the line.
  Fast_TL.VStyle  = 02 ;
// VerticalStyle.center
  Slow_TL.VStyle  = VerticalStyle.center ;

// Set the font size
  myFont  = Font.Create (Font_Name, Font_Size) ;
  Fast_TL.Font  = myFont ;
  Slow_TL.Font  = myFont ;

// Set the font color
  myColor  = Color.fromARGB (Fast_Col) ;
  Fast_TL.Color  = myColor ;

  myColor  = Color.fromARGB (Slow_Col) ;
  Slow_TL.Color  = myColor ;

  DrawingObjects.Add (Fast_TL) ;
  DrawingObjects.Add (Slow_TL) ;
end ;
```

The next figure shows how pretty it turns out (Figure 9.02).

FIGURE 9.02—Strawberry Moving Average Displays Lengths to the Right

☑ The Persist property allows the default behavior of drawing objects created in an indicator using the "Update value intra-bar" setting to be overridden. By default, the EZL run-time environment will not allow multiple instances of a drawing object to be created on an intra-bar basis. This behavior is intended to simplify the code required when creating drawing objects. If the Persist property is set to True, multiple instances can be created. This property is useful when creating drawing objects in events not related to bar updates. Note this is an advanced feature and in most cases, should be left with the default value False.

☑ SKT: I always assume "Update tick-by-tick" is disabled (just like I always assume MaxBarsBack has been set), so I sometimes forget the extra step of checking **BarStatus** for a closed bar prior to creating a DrawingObject!

PROPERTIES

	Name	Type	Description
	AutoShow	bool	Reserved for future enhancement.
	Color	object	Gets or sets the Color object representing the color of the drawing object (or border color in the case of Rectangle and Ellipse objects). See **Color** class.
	Count	int	Gets an integer representing the number of points in the drawing object collection.
	ID	int	The ID assigned to legacy TrendLines and TextLabels. For all non-legacy drawing objects the ID is -1.
	Lock	bool	True indicates that the user may not drag the drawing object on a chart; False allows dragging.
	OverrideTooltips	bool	True indicates that the drawing object overrides the displays of tooltips. (TS >= 10)
	Persist	bool	True if the drawing object instance should remain displayed between intra-bar updates. The default behavior is False which expects that your code will recreate the drawing object on each tick update.
	Points[Indx]	object	Gets or sets an element within the collection of points used to create the drawing object.
	ShowInPlotSubgraph	bool	True indicates that this drawing object will be displayed in a subgraph.
	Tag	object	Gets or sets an arbitrary value that allows you to store additional info with the drawing object.

TABLE 9.01—DrawingObject Properties

METHODS

	Name	Description
	ClearTooltips ()	Clears all the ToolTip rows associated with the DrawingObject.(TS >= 10)
	RemoveTooltipRow (index)	Removes a ToolTip row at the specified index. (TS >= 10)

	Name	Description
⚹	SetTooltipHeader (text)	Sets the text for the header of the DrawingObject ToolTip. Note that at least one row must exist for the ToolTip to display. (TS >= 10)
⚹	SetTooltipRow (index, column1, column2)	Sets the ToolTip row at the specified index. The text string column 1 appears in the left column and text string column 2 appears in the right column. (TS >= 10)

TABLE 9.02—DrawingObject Methods

EVENTS

	Name	Description
⚡	Click	Occurs when the DrawingObject is clicked. The Event Handler Method's args parameter should be of type DrawingObjectEventArgs.
⚡	Moved	Occurs while the DrawingObject has been moved and the mouse has been released. Also occurs if any of the DOPoints for the DrawingObject is changed. The Event Handler Method's args parameter should be of type DrawingObjectMovedEventArgs. (TS >= 10)
⚡	Moving	Occurs while the DrawingObject is being moved. The Event Handler Method's args parameter should be of type DrawingObjectMovedEventArgs. (TS >= 10)
⚡	SubGraphResize	Occurs when a subgraph is resized, including its first display. The Event Handler Method's args parameter should be of type SubGraphResizeEventArgs.

TABLE 9.03—DrawingObject Events

INHERITANCE HIERARCHY

elSystem.Object
  elSystem.DotNetObject
    elSystem.elComponent
      elSystem.DrawingObjects.DrawingObject

The **DrawingObject** Class is the Parent class to all the DrawingObject Classes we have been discussing here. All these Class Members are inherited by each **DrawingObject** Class of the DrawingOhjects Namespace. Pretty much, if it has "DrawingObject' in its inheritance then it is a DrawingObject and not a supporting Class (ex: the **DOPoint** Class or **StyleType** which is an enumerated list.)

Object Class

The Object Class is the ancestor of all classes. It is the base class from which all other classes are derived. Every Method in the Object Class is available in all objects in the system, although derived classes can, and often do, override some of the base Methods.

The Methods and Operators included here apply to all Object Classes.

NAMESPACE: elSystem

METHODS

	Name	Description
⧫	Clone ()	Creates a duplicate of the current Object.
⧫	Equals (obj)	True when the specified obj (object) is equal to the current object instance.
⧫	Equals (objA, objB)	True when the specified object instances (objA and objB) are considered equal.
⧫	GetType ()	Gets the type of the current Object instance.
⧫	ReferenceEquals (objA, objB)	True when the specified object instances (objA and objB) are the same instance.
⧫	ToString ()	Converts the value of this Object instance to a string.

TABLE 9.04—Object Class Methods

OPERATORS

	Name	Description
⧎	operator <>	True with two objects are not equal.
⧎	operator =	True with two objects are determined to be equal.

TABLE 9.05—Object Class Operators

INHERITANCE HIERARCHY

None

DrawingObject Methods

Drawing objects have Methods that can be applied to them and used to compare or duplicate (clone) objects. Further there are operators you can use with them to determine whether two objects are equal (=) or not equal (<>) and to clone an object. You can even set Alerts for Drawing Objects. See Tables 9.04 and 9.05 above for details.

DrawingObject Classes are as follows, which includes **Point** Classes:

- AddEventArgs
- AlertConfiguration
- AlertEventArgs
- AudibleConfiguration
- BNPoint
- Color
- DeleteEventArgs
- DOPoint
- DrawingObject
- DrawingObjectEventArgs
- DrawObjects
- DTPoint
- Ellipse
- Font
- HorizontalLine
- Notification
- PointType
- PopUpConfiguration
- PriceAlert
- Rectangle
- SoundConfiguration
- TextLabel
- TimeAlert
- TrendLine
- UpdateEventArgs
- VerticalLine
- VisualConfiguration

We will examine many, though not all, these **DrawingObject** Classes. I'll leave you to discover the ones I don't cover in **Volume II—Reference Guide**. They all have similar properties.

To use OOEL drawing objects, you should have the following elements:

Declare a variable for each type of object to be used. The class type of each variable must be appropriate for the object it will reference. Remember to include the namespace identifier **elSystem.DrawingObject** in front of the specific class type unless you have previously added a Using statement for the namespace. In this example, myHorizLine1and myTrendLine1 are the names of the variables being created for each drawing object type.

EXAMPLE 9.03—Preparation for Inserting Drawing Objects

```
using elSystem.DrawingObjects ;
using elSystem ;
// declare myHorizLine1 as a HorizontalLine type:
vars: HorizontalLine myHorizLine1(null),
// declare myTrendLine1 as a TrendLine type:
TrendLine myTrendLine1(null),
// declare bar number points 1 & 2:
BNPoint BNPoint1 (null), BNPoint BNPoint2 (null) ;
```

EXAMPLE 9.04—Placing Drawing Objects on Your Chart

```
// create a horizontal line at .02 below the last price:
HorizontalLine.Create (Close - 0.02) ;
// create first trendline point 10 bars to the left of the current
bar:
myPoint1 = BNPoint.Create (BarNumber - 10, close[10]);
// create second trendline point at current bar:
myPoint2 = BNPoint.Create (barnumber, close) ;
// create a trendline and assign it to myTrendLine:
myTrendLine1 = TrendLine.Create (myPoint1, myPoint2) ;
```

☑ You can also create the above trendline without needing to define BNPoint objects by directly specifying the BNPoint values when creating the trendline instance.

EXAMPLE 9.05—Defining a TrendLine with BNPoint

```
myTrendLine1 = TrendLine.Create (BNPoint.Create (Barnumber-10,
close[10]), BNPoint.Create (barnumber, close)) ;
```

You must add drawing objects (e.g., **TrendLine, HorizontalLine**) to a the **DrawingObjects** property of the Analysis Technique if you want them to appear on a chart.

Here's how you do it:

```
DrawingObjects.Add (myHorizLine1) ;
DrawingObjects.Add (myTrendLine1) ;
```

You will need to associate an Event Handler with the objects (to call the **DOClick** Method when either drawing object is clicked).

```
myHorizLine1.Click += DOClick ;
myTrendLine1.Click += DOClick ;
```

Setting Alerts for Drawing Objects

You can set alerts for **TrendLine, HorizontalLine**, and **VerticalLine** drawing objects so that they will notify you when specified alert criteria occur.

The **Alert** Property of the **TrendLine, HorizontalLine**, and **VerticalLine** drawing objects refers to properties of the **AlertConfiguration** class and related classes that allow you to set an alert for a drawing object and to create custom notification preferences for the alert if you don't want to use the global notification preferences of the TS platform.

The following code enables alerts for a **TrendLine** drawing object, `myTL`, using the global notification settings from the TS platform.

```
myTL.Alert.Enable = True;
myTL.Alert.GlobalNotification = True;
```

By default, alerts will be fired continuously if the alert criterion is True. To fire the alert only once per bar, use the following:

```
myTL.Alert.Frequency = AlertFrequency.OncePerBar ;
```

The **Alert** property of **Trendline** and **HorizontalLine** drawing objects also references a **PriceCondition** Property that lets you set the type of price breakout for alerts. The **VerticalLine** refers to a similar property to set a time breakout alerts. The following changes the price condition for `myTL`.

```
myTL.Alert.PriceCondition = PriceCondition.Breakoutintra_interbar ;
```

You can also set up your own notification criteria for this specific alert instance and enable just those options. In the following, a synthesized voice will announce the alert and the TS alert icon will flash at the lower right of your windows screen. You'll also need to disable global notification to allow your custom alert notification criteria to be sent.

```
myTL.Alert.Notification.AudibleEnable = True ;
myTL.Alert.Notification.AudibleConfiguration.Options =
AudibleOptions.Voice ;
myTL.Alert.Notification.VisualEnable = True ;
myTL.Alert.Notification.VisualConfiguration.Options =
VisualOptions.flashicon ;
myTL.Alert.GlobalNotification = False ;
```

The next bit of sample code associates an Event Handler Method with the **Fired** event of the Alert property. Whenever the alert condition is met, the alert event will fire, and the Method will be called. You can then use your own code to determine how to handle the **Alert**. If you did nothing else, the Method would exit without sending any alert notifications. However, setting the **args.Trigger** flag to True allows notifications to be sent after exiting the Method.

```
myTL.Alert.Fired += GotAlert;
method void GotAlert (elSystem.object sender,
elSystem.DrawingObjects.AlertEventArgs args )
begin
// put your own code here to handle an alert that has fired
args.Trigger = True ;
// continue processing using your alert notification
// settings
End ;
```

AlertConfiguration Class

This is a base class containing common **Properties**, **Methods**, and **Events** used to enable and configure the alert criteria of a drawing object. **AlertConfiguration** members are inherited by the **PriceAlert** and **TimeAlert** Classes that make up the **Alert** property of **HorizontalLine**, **TrendLine**, or **VerticalLine** drawing objects.

See **Using Alerts** for more information.

NAMESPACE: elSystem.DrawingObjects

PROPERTIES

Name	Type	Description
Enable	bool	True to enable alert notifications for a drawing object.
Frequency	enum	Gets or sets how frequently alerts will be triggered. See AlertFrequency for a list of possible values.
GlobalNotification	bool	True to use the global messaging preferences from the TS platform as your notification criteria.
Notification	object	Provides access to properties of the Notification Class that are used to enable and configure the Audible, Email, and Visual notification criteria for the alert.

TABLE 9.06—Alert Configuration Properties

EVENTS

	Name	Description
⚡	Checked	Occurs every time the alert criteria is evaluated. The handler's args parameter is of type AlertEventArgs. Set the args.Triggered property to True to continue with an alert notification message.
⚡	Fired	Occurs before the alert is fired. The handler's args parameter is of type AlertEventArgs. Set the args.Triggered property to True to continue with an alert notification message.

TABLE 9.07—Alert Configuration Events

INHERITANCE HIERARCHY

elSystem.Object
 elSystem.EventArgs
  elSystem.DrawingObjects.AlertConfiguration

AlertFrequency Enumeration

These values describe how often an alert notification will be triggered. Enumerated Values are listed in **Volume II—Reference Guide** in **Appendix IV**.

NAMESPACE: elSystem.DrawingObjects

ENUMERATED VALUES

	Name	Value
▦	Continuously	2
▦	Once	0
▦	OncePerBar	1

TABLE 9.08—AlertFrequency Enumeration

EXAMPLE 9.06—Method Shows How to Output Alert Configuration Settings

This is only a partial listing of the 500 lines of code available to make use of several alert types. I'm not going to print it all here, but you can download it at https://www.EasyLanguageOOEL.com by becoming a free member.

```
method String AlertConfiguration_Report (AlertConfiguration myAC)
Vars :
 String RetVal ;
begin
```

```
  if  Debug  then  Print (Method_Header (App_Name,
"AlertConfiguration_Report", "")) ;

  RetVal  = "(Enable=" + BoolToText (myAC.Enable) + ", Frequency=" +
myAC.Frequency.toString () + ", GlobalNotification=" + BoolToText
(myAC.GlobalNotification) + ", Notification=" + Notification_Report
(myAC.Notification) + ")" ;
  Return RetVal ;
end ; // "AlertConfiguration_Report" method
```

Notification Class

Used by the **AlertConfiguration** Class to determine the types of notifications that will be generated when an Alert is triggered. Both audible and/or visual alerts may be set.

The xxx**Enable** properties determine whether a particular type of notification is active. **AudibleConfiguration** includes properties to specify additional information about audio notifications and **VisualConfiguration** includes properties to specify information about visual notifications.

NAMESPACE: elSystem.DrawingObjects

PROPERTIES

	Name	Type	Description
🖳	AudibleConfiguration	object	Gets or sets properties of the AudibleConfiguration object used to set the type of audible notifications.
🖳	AudibleEnable	bool	True to enable audible notifications.
🖳	EmailEnable	bool	True to enable email notifications.
🖳	VisualConfiguration	object	Gets or sets properties of the VisualConfiguration object used to set the type of visual notifications.
🖳	VisualEnable	bool	True to enable visual notifications.

TABLE 9.09—Notification Class Properties

METHODS

	Name	Description
⬥	Create ()	Initializes a new instance of the Notification Class.

TABLE 9.10—Notification Class Methods

INHERITANCE HIERARCHY

elSystem.Object
  elSystem.DrawingObjects.Notification

EXAMPLE 9.07—Method Illustrating Configuring a Notification

```
method HorizontalLine HorizontalLine_SetAlert (HorizontalLine myHL,
Bool EnableAlert, Double Price)
begin
  if  Debug  then  Print (Method_Header (App_Name,
"HorizontalLine_SetAlert", "")) ;
  myHL.Alert.Enable  = EnableAlert ;
  myHL.Alert.GlobalNotification  = doGlobalNotifi ;
  Return myHL ;
end ; // "HorizontalLine_SetAlert" method
```

TextLabel Class

Similar to the classic **Text_New** set of drawing tools, the **TextLabel** Class fills the same niche but much more robustly. Using a **TextLabel** object you have control over a variety of properties and access to a number of Methods. The members of the top level **TextLabel** Class are listed in the tables to follow.

PROPERTIES

	Name	Type	Description
	Font	object	Gets or sets the font object used to set font parameters. See **Font Class** for more details.
	HStyle	enum	Gets or sets the horizontal position of the text relative to the anchor point. See **HorizontalStyle** enumerated list.
	PointValue	object	Gets or sets the DrawingObject point, initially set in the Create method. The DOPoint object allows changes to the Price (but NOT the PointType).
	TextString	string	Gets or sets the text string to be displayed. TextString will overwrite any text in TextLabel.Create(DTPoint, "some text");
	VStyle	enum	Gets or sets the vertical position of the text relative to the anchor point. See **VerticalStyle** enumerated list.

TABLE 9.11—TextLabel Properties

METHODS

	Name	Description
	Create ()	Initializes a new instance of the class.
	Create (DTPoint, string)	Initializes a new instance of the TextLabel Class. The first parameter is a DTPoint object representing the location of the text; the second parameter is the string to be displayed.
	Create (DTPoint, string, int)	Initializes a new instance of the TextLabel Class. Parameters include a DTPoint point value representing the position of the text, the text string to be displayed, and an integer representing the datanum on which to display the text.
	Create (BNPoint, string)	Initializes a new instance of the TextLabel Class. Parameters include a BNPoint object representing the location of the text and the string to be displayed.
	Create (BNPoint, string, int)	Initializes a new instance of the class using the BNPoint object, text string, and the data number.
	Create (XYPoint, string)	Initializes a new instance of the TextLabel Class using the XYPoint object, and text string.
	Create (XYPoint, string, int)	Initializes a new instance of the TextLabel Class using the XYPoint object, text string, and the data number.
	SetPointValue (value)	Sets a new position for the text label as a DTPoint, BNPoint, or XYPoint value.

TABLE 9.12—TextLabel Methods

INHERITANCE HIERARCHY

elSystem.Object

```
  elSystem.DotNetObject
   elSystem.elComponent
     elSystem.DrawingObjects.DrawingObject
       elSystem.DrawingObjects.TextLabel
```

It is easy to place text on your chart by using the Drawing Tool → Text sequence in the menu bar at the top of your chart. But what if you want it at a specific location? Let's not jump into the code we've already examined in the previous chapter, but rather start with a simpler example.

In this example we are going to place a **TextLabel** Object of "My Text" on the upper left corner of a chart. There is a lot to this one, as there are several **Methods** in the code to locate the **TextLabel**, but it is a fitting example of a single, simple **TextLabel**. This is also a very good example of using methods.

EXAMPLE 9.08—Using XYPoint to Anchor Text [OME_TextLabel_Ex#01]

```
    Inputs:
    Bool    Show_Text ( TRUE),
    // Enable or Disable the TextLabel
    String Message    ("My Text"),
    // text you want displayed
    String myColor     ("Red"),
    Int     XLoc      (20),
    // pixels from the left edge
    Int     YLoc      (20),
    // pixels from the top edge
    Int     Data_Num  (01) ;
    // Define which data series to address

    Vars  :
    IntraBarPersist
    Int     DNum      (Data_Num),
    // Variable analog for the Data_Num Input
    IntraBarPersist
    Int     sgUL_X    (00),   // Upper  Left XLoc
    IntraBarPersist
    Int     sgUL_Y    (00),   // Upper  Left YLoc
    IntraBarPersist
    Int     sgLR_X    (00),   // Lower Right XLoc
    IntraBarPersist
    Int     sgLR_Y    (00),   // Lower Right YLoc
    IntraBarPersist
    Int     sgXLoc    (XLoc), // XLoc initial value, TextLabel_Update will
    adjust it
    IntraBarPersist
    Int     sgYLoc    (YLoc) ;
    // YLoc initial value, TextLabel_Update will adjust it

    #Region - - - OOEL Declarations

    Using elSystem ;
    Using ElSystem.Drawing ;
    Using ElSystem.DrawingObjects ;

    // Declarations for Objects
    Vars  :
    TextLabel  TheTL  (NULL) ;

    #endRegion // OOEL Declarations

    // Working Storage Section
    Consts:
```

```
  String App_Type      ("Study (OOEL)"),
  String App_Name      ("OME_TextLabel_#01"),
  String App_Note      ("Draw a TextLabel in corner of the chart"),
  String App_Vers      ("01.02.00") ;

Vars  :
  String DQ            (DoubleQuote),
  String NL            (NewLine),
  Bool   Debug         (FALSE) ;

// ============================================================
// My Methods ================================================

method void App_Init ()
// The user passes in the Data Number (Data1 = 01)
// and decrement it
begin
Print (skt_Method_Header (App_Name, "App_Init", "Data#" + NumToStr
(Data_Num, 00))) ;

// DataNum is zero based so Data1 = 0; Data2 = 1, etc.
   DNum  = Data_Num ;
   if  DNum  <  00  then  DNum  = 00 ;
// default to zero (Data1)
   if  DNum   > 00  then  DNum -= 01 ;
// Decrement if one or above

end ; // "App_Init" method

// ------------------------------------------------------------
method TextLabel TextLabel_Init (Int XLoc, Int YLoc, String Message,
String myColor, Int DNum)

Vars  :
 String myStr,
 XYPoint      myXY,
 DTPoint      myDT,
 TextLabel    myTL ;
begin
   if  Debug  then begin
     myStr  = "X=" + NumToText (XLoc) + ",Y=" + NumToText (YLoc) + DQ +
Message + DQ + "," + myColor + ", DNum=" + NumToText (DNum) ;

     Print (skt_Method_Header (App_Name, "TextLabel_Init", myStr)) ;
   end ;

   myTL  = TextLabel.Create (XYPoint.Create (XLoc, YLoc), Message,
DNum) ;
   if  myTL  = NULL  then begin
    Print ("Error : TextLabel_Init, TheTL = NULL. Abort!") ;
     Return myTL ;
   end ;
// error report - it never hurts to report an error
// and avoid a crash
   myTL.Color    = Color.FromName (myColor) ;
   myTL.Persist  = TRUE ;
   myTL.SubgraphResize += TextLabel_SubgraphResize ;
   DrawingObjects.Add (myTL) ;

   Return myTL ;
end ; // "TextLabel_Init" method
```

```
   // --------------------------------------------------------

method void TextLabel_SubgraphResize (elSystem.Object sender,
elSystem.DrawingObjects.SubgraphResizeEventArgs args)
// called on initialization and when resized
begin
   if  Debug  then  Print (App_Name, "TextLabel_SubgraphResize", ) ;
   sgUL_X  = args.UpperLeft.X ;
   sgUL_Y  = args.UpperLeft.Y ;
   sgLR_X  = args.LowerRight.X ;
   sgLR_Y  = args.LowerRight.Y ;

   if  Debug  then  Print ("UL_X=", sgUL_X:2:0, ", Y=", sgUL_Y:2:0, ",
LR_X=", sgLR_X:2:0, ", Y=", sgLR_Y:2:0, ", SG :  X=", sgXLoc:2:0, ",
Y=", sgYLoc:2:0) ;

   TextLabel_SetLocation () ;
end ; // "TextLabel_SubgraphResize" method

   // --------------------------------------------------------

method void TextLabel_SetLocation ()
begin
   sgXLoc  = sgUL_X + XLoc ;
// compute the horizontal offset within the SubGraph
   sgYLoc  = sgUL_Y + YLoc ;
// compute the vertical offset within the SubGraph
   TheTL.SetPointValue (XYPoint.Create (sgXLoc, sgYLoc)) ;
end ; // "TextLabel_SetLocation" method

   // --------------------------------------------------------

method TextLabel TextLabel_Update (TextLabel oldTL, Int XLoc, Int
YLoc, String Message, String myColor, Int DNum)

Vars  :
 String myStr ,
  TextLabel   myTL ;
begin
   if  Debug  then begin
     myStr = "X=" + NumToText (XLoc) + ",Y=" + NumToText (YLoc) + DQ +
Message + DQ + "," + myColor + ", DNum=" + NumToText (DNum) ;

     Print (skt_Method_Header (App_Name, "TextLabel_Update", myStr)) ;
   end ;

   myTL  = TextLabel.Create(XYPoint.Create(XLoc, YLoc), Message, DNum)
;

   if  myTL  = NULL  then begin
   Print ("Error : TextLabel_Update, TheTL = NULL. Abort!") ;
     Return NULL ;
   end ; // error report
   myTL.Color   = Color.FromName (myColor) ;
   myTL.Persist  =  TRUE ;
   myTL.SubgraphResize += TextLabel_SubgraphResize ;
// as long as the DrawingObject is not NULL it is OK
// if it does not exist, no foul
   if  oldTL <> NULL  then begin
```

```
    oldTL.SubgraphResize -= TextLabel_SubgraphResize ;
    DrawingObjects.Delete (oldTL) ;
  end ;
  DrawingObjects.Add (myTL) ;

  Return myTL ;
end ; // "TextLabel_Update" method

// -----------------------------------------------------------

method String NumToText (Int Value)
// receives a method argument and return a string of it
Vars   :
 Int     Num,
 String Str ;
begin
  Num   = Value ;
  Str   = NumToStr (Num, 00) ;
  Return Str ;
end ; // "NumToText" method

// -----------------------------------------------------------

method String NumToText (Double Value, Int Decimals)
// receives a method argument and returns a string of it
// illustrates using two methods with the same name
// and different parameters via overloading

Vars   :
 Double Num,
 String Str ;
begin
  Num   = Value ;
  Str   = NumToStr (Num, Decimals) ;
  Return Str ;
end ; // "NumToText" method override

// -----------------------------------------------------------

method String Method_Header (String AppName, String MethodName, String
MethodArgs)
Vars   :
 String RetVal ;
begin
  if  Debug  then  Print (Method_Header (App_Name, "Method_Header",
AppName + "," + MethodName + "," + MethodArgs)) ;
  RetVal  = String.Format ("({00}.) {01} ({02})", AppName, MethodName,
MethodArgs) ;
  Return RetVal ;
end ; // "Method_Header" method

// ===========================================================
// Main Code Body
//============================================================

once begin
  App_Init () ;
end ; // Once, and only once

if  LastBarOnChart
and (BarStatus (01)  = 02   // closing tick
```

```
  or  BarStatus (01)  = 00)   // opening tick using "next bar"
then begin
  if  Show_Text  then begin
    TheTL  = TextLabel_Init (sgXLoc, sgYLoc, Message, myColor, DNum) ;
  end ;
end ; // end LastBarOnChart
```

All that code for one little snippet of text that says, "My Text." But it was worth it. In the code you see examples of using Debug, raising errors, specifying which DataStream to use, and adjusting as the subgraph resizes.

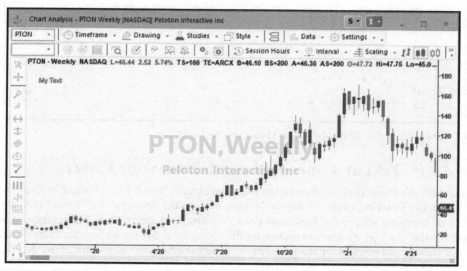

FIGURE 9.03—MyText TextLabel on a Chart

Let's change the `Data_Num` input and look at a chart with TSLA and AAPL on it and see where the **TextLabel** goes. Take a look at Figure 9.04 which shows that the **TextLabel** is now on Data2, just by changing an input.

Unlike text that you position by hand with the Text Drawing Tool, this text stays in place while you magnify or demagnify, scroll or squeeze the chart.

And, if you use the Remove Drawing Objects… under the Drawing menu, this text doesn't disappear, because it is an indicator, not text.

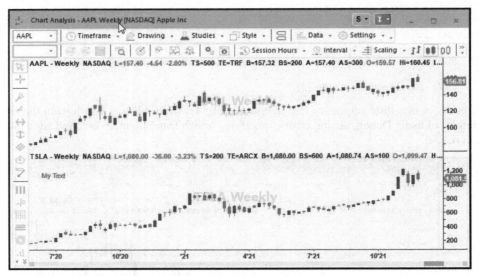

FIGURE 9.04—Now the TextLabel is on Data2 on the Left

Text at a Specific Location on Your Chart

I introduced the Floating Text routines in the previous chapter, but it bears further investigation now that we are in the Drawing Objects chapter. We are back to the function `OME_Floating_Text` that takes care of choosing where the **TextLabel** goes. We send it a string that is concatenated with the application name, the text we want to appear on the chart, the color the string should be on the chart, the font we choose and positioning information. This way the function takes care of the details and the main body code controls what we want to happen.

I'm going to repeat the code here, so you don't have to flip back and forth.

This code calls the function with each bar to allow for changing the value. The `TextToPlot` input is set to plot the Close as text on the chart. Since the close changes on each trade tick, we will call the function so that the text is updated. As noted above, since we are calling the function only once in the code as well as using the same parameters (i.e., the inputs), the function creates only one **TextLabel**.

To change the text color, font name, font size, percent from right, or percent from bottom, the function should be called with the same parameters (for example, using variables or inputs) so that a new instance of the function is not created that will, in turn, create a new **TextLabel**. Thus, variables (or input values as demonstrated by this code) should be used for the function parameters and if you want to change something like the color, change the variable that specifies the color and then call the function with the variable as the color parameter.

This example is repeated from an earlier chapter to help you in visualizing the concepts.

The function is listed below the next Example and is readily available on https://www.EasyLanguageOOEL.com and is called `OME_Floating_Text`.

EXAMPLE 9.09—Floating Text [OME_Floating_Text]

```
// =========================================================
// ===== OME_Floating_Text:=======
// =========================================================

Consts:
 String App_Type      ("Study"),
 String App_Name      ("OME_Hello_World!_Ex#07a")
 String App_Note      ("Hello from Sunny and Sam to the WHOLE World"),
 String App_Vers      ("01.01.00") ;
```

```
Vars  :
 String NL              (NewLine) ;

Once (LastBarOnChart) begin
   if OME_Floating_text (App_Name + NL + App_Note, "Black", "Arial",
10, 50, 50, FALSE) then ;
end ;
```

> ☑ I chose Black because I do NOT use charts with a black background – Your Results May Vary – change the default color in your code!

Okay. Here come the details, the OME_Floating_Text function again. See Figure 9.05 below. The net effect is to place the text on the middle of your chart and keep it there, even if you scroll backward or forward.

For positioning, the function detects a change in the size of the subgraph where the text is located and repositions the text, so we don't need to call the function from this code to ensure it stays in the correct position.

> ☑ "Floating Text" is a study available with TradeStation. I made it a User Function for greater versatility and sort of spiced it up. My original idea was to trap a return code from it but it does not quite function that way.

EXAMPLE 9.10—Function OME_Floating_Text [OME_Floating_Text]

```
// =========================================================
// ===== OME_Floating_Text function: ======================
// =========================================================
#Region - - - Declarations

using elSystem ;
using elSystem.Drawing ;
using elSystem.DrawingObjects ;

Inputs:
 string TextToFloat          (StringSimple),
 string TextColorString      (StringSimple),
 string TextFontName         (StringSimple),
 double TextFontSize         (NumericSimple),
 double XPercentFromRight     (NumericSimple),
 double YPercentFromBottom    (NumericSimple),
 bool   ShowTextInSubgraph    (TrueFalseSimple) ;

Vars  :
IntraBarPersist bool   InAChart            (FALSE),
IntraBarPersist bool   NotOpt              (FALSE),
IntraBarPersist double XDecimalFromRight   (0.00),
IntraBarPersist double YDecimalFromBottom  (0.00),
IntraBarPersist double SubgraphUpperLeftX  (0.00),
IntraBarPersist double SubgraphUpperLeftY  (0.00),
IntraBarPersist double SubgraphLowerRightX (0.00),
IntraBarPersist double SubgraphLowerRightY (0.00),
IntraBarPersist double TextLabelX          (0.00),
IntraBarPersist double TextLabelY          (0.00),
                TextLabel TextLabelToFloat  (NULL) ;

// =========================================================
#Region - - - Working Storage
// Working Storage
Consts:
```

```
  String App_Type   ("Function (Bool, Simple)"),
  String App_Name   ("OME_Floating_Text"),
  String App_Note   ("Creates Floating Text where we want and saying
what we want."),
  String App_Vers   ("01.00.00") ;

Vars  :
 Bool   Debug    (FALSE),
 Bool   RetVal   (FALSE);

#endRegion // Working Storage
#endRegion // Declarations

// ============================================================

#Region - - - myMethods

method void ErrorCheckInputValues ()
begin
  if  XPercentFromRight  <   000
   or XPercentFromRight   > 100
   or YPercentFromBottom <   000
   or YPercentFromBottom  > 100
  then begin
    throw  Exception.Create ("Text_FloatEx parameter out of range.
Text cannot be placed outside the boundaries of the chart, so the
XPercentFromRight and YPercentFromBottom parameters must have values
between 00 and 100.") ;
  end ;
end ; // "ErrorCheckInputValues" method

// ----------------------------------------------------------
// This totally does not work because InfoBox is Synchronius
// and does NOT wait for user input prior to returning.
// GREAT idea though...  Gold star for trying.
method void MakeSureItIsAChart (Bool isChart)
Vars  :
 Int    Choice ;
begin
  if  isChart  = FALSE
  then begin
    Choice  = OME_InfoBox ("TextLabels and other DrawingObjects are
only used on Charts. Click 'Yes' to continue or 'No' to abort.", "***
Not a Chart ***", 50, 50);
    if  Choice <  00  then
      throw  Exception.Create ("Program terminated by User Action.") ;
  end ;
end ; // "MakeSureItIsAChart" method

// ----------------------------------------------------------

method TextLabel TextLabel_Create ()
vars:
 TextLabel tempTextLabel ;
begin
  tempTextLabel  = TextLabel.Create (XYPoint.Create (00, 00),
TextToFloat) ;

  tempTextLabel.HStyle  = HorizontalStyle.Center ;
  tempTextLabel.VStyle  = VerticalStyle.Center ;
  tempTextLabel.Lock    =  TRUE ;
```

```
  // prevent inadverent moving
    tempTextLabel.ShowInPlotSubraph = ShowTextInSubgraph ;

  // Setting 'Persist' to true causes the text label to NOT be
  // deleted on an intrabar tick. The text label is created
  // once and positioned

    tempTextLabel.Persist  =  TRUE ;

    if  TextFontSize  > 00
      then  tempTextLabel.Font = Font.Create (TextFontName,
  TextFontSize) ;
    tempTextLabel.SubgraphResize += TextLabel_SubgraphResize ;
  // add the event handler

  // this is how the text label is "shown"; the text label is
  // added to the DrawingObjects collection; if you want to
  // remove the text label, you can use the Delete method of
  // the DrawingObjects class; DrawingObjects collection
  // is not available in RadarScreen (it is NULL)

    if  DrawingObjects <> NULL
      then  DrawingObjects.Add (tempTextLabel) ;

    return tempTextLabel ;
  end ; // "TextLabel_Create" method

  // ----------------------------------------------------------

method void TextLabel_SubgraphResize (Object sender,
SubgraphResizeEventArgs args)
begin
// this event fires upon initial running of the code and
// when the size of the subgraph is changed.
// The args give us the upper left and lower right locations
// of the subgraph.
// We will set these locations in variables that we will use
// to position the TextLabel based on the percentages passed
// in via the inputs.
  SubgraphUpperLeftX      = args.UpperLeft.X ;
  SubgraphUpperLeftY      = args.UpperLeft.Y ;
  SubgraphLowerRightX     = args.LowerRight.X ;
  SubgraphLowerRightY     = args.LowerRight.Y ;

  if  Debug  then  Print ("UL_X=", SubgraphUpperLeftX:2:0, ", Y= ",
SubgraphUpperLeftY:2:0, ", LR X=",
  SubgraphLowerRightX:2:0, ", Y=",SubgraphLowerRightY:2:0) ;

  TextLabel_SetLocation () ;
end ; // "TextLabel_SubgraphResize" method

  // ----------------------------------------------------------

method void TextLabel_SetColor ()
Vars :
 String myTextColor ;
begin
  myTextColor  = TextColorString ;
  if  GetBackgroundColor  =  Black
  and TextColorString      = "Black"
```

```
      then  myTextColor      = "White" ;
   if  GetBackgroundColor   =   White
  and TextColorString       = "White"
      then  myTextColor      = "Black" ;

   if Color.FromName (TextColorString).IsKnownColor
      then  TextLabelToFloat.Color  = Color.FromName (myTextColor) ;
 end ; // "TextLabel_SetColor" method

 // ----------------------------------------------------------

method void App_Init ()
begin
// shift the X decimal place only once:
   XDecimalFromRight    = XPercentFromRight  * 0.01 ;
// shift the Y decimal place only once:
   YDecimalFromBottom  = YPercentFromBottom * 0.01 ;
   InAChart  = GetAppInfo (aiApplicationType)  = cChart ;
   NotOpt    = skt_isOptimizing  = FALSE ;
   MakeSureItIsAChart (InAChart) ;
 end ; // "App_Init" method

 // ----------------------------------------------------------
#endRegion // myMethods

 // ==========================================================
#Region - - - Main Code Body
Once begin
   App_Init () ;
end ; // Once, and only once
if  InAChart
and LastBarOnChart
then begin
// On the close of each bar, apparently
// Print (App_Name, ", ", vrt_MMDDYYYY (Date), ", ", vrt_HHMM_pm
(Time), ", How often is this code being hit?") ;
   if  TextLabelToFloat  = NULL  then  TextLabelToFloat  =
TextLabel_Create () ;
//  ErrorCheckInputValues () ;
   TextLabelToFloat.TextString = TextToFloat ;

   if  TextFontSize > 00
      then  TextLabelToFloat.Font  = Font.Create (TextFontName,
TextFontSize) ;
   TextLabel_SetColor () ;
   TextLabel_SetLocation () ;
   RetVal  = TRUE ; //
end ; // We are on a chart else do not execute

 // ==========================================================
OME_Floating_Text  = RetVal ;
#endRegion // Main Code Body
 // ==========================================================
```

It bears repeating if you are wondering what the skt_ means and what those routines are. SKT are Sam's[44] initials, and these routines are proprietary to him. He has generously allowed me to print them here for your education. The first subroutine is skt_isOptimizing. It checks the chart to be sure you are not running an optimization before proceeding further. Routines with the initials vrt_ in front

---

[44] Samuel K. Tennis, sktennis@vista-research.com

of them stand for Sam's former company, Vista-Research and Trading.

EXAMPLE 9.11—skt_isOptimizing function

```
Once begin
  RetVal  = GetAppInfo (aiOptimizing)  = 01 ;
end ; // Once, and only once...
skt_isOptimizing  = RetVal ;
```

The next Example shows Sam's proprietary date conversion function, used in the code above. The function turns a TS date into a delimited string.

EXAMPLE 9.12—vrt_MMDDYYYY Date Conversion Function

This function reduces the input date in TS format to numbers, calculates the day, month, and year, and converts it to string output for our purposes.

```
//=== vrt_MMDDYYYY date conversion to string
Inputs: tDate (NumericSimple) ;

Vars  : chDD    (""),        chMM    (""),
         chYY    (""),        RetStr  ("") ;
Vars  : dd      (00),        mm      (00),        yy      (00) ;

// ---------------------------------------------------

dd = Round       (FracPortion (tDate *    0.01) * 100.0, 0) ;
mm = IntPortion  (FracPortion (tDate * 0.0001) * 100.0) ;
yy = IntPortion               (tDate * 0.0001) + 1900 ;

chDD = NumToStr (DD, 0) ;
chMM = NumToStr (MM, 0) ;
chYY = NumToStr (YY, 0) ;

if StrLen (chDD) < 2 then chDD = "0" + chDD ;
if StrLen (chMM) < 2 then chMM = "0" + chMM ;

RetStr = chMM + "/" + chDD + "/" + chYY ;

vrt_MMDDYYYY  = RetStr ;
```

After all of that, here is what the window looks like, see Figure 9.05 below.

FIGURE 9.05—Hello_World!_Ex#08a on a Chart

Unlike other text you might place on a chart with the Text tool, this text goes nowhere if you try to move it with the cursor. It stays in place right where the coordinates told it to be.

A note about the placement of our text. Coordinates of your screen start at the upper left at (0, 0) with the first coordinate being the horizontal identifier and the second coordinate the vertical coordinate. The screen is measured in pixels from the upper left.

HorizontalLine Class

This draws a **HorizontalLine** on a chart at a given price. The appearance may be altered and an alert set using appropriate properties. Horizontal lines are often used as an analytical drawing tool to identify support and resistance levels as well as to highlight trading ranges.

The following code snippet shows how to add a horizontal line to a chart at the Close of the current bar. To use this in an Analysis Technique, be sure that it is setup as described in **About Drawing Objects**.

```
myHLine = HorizontalLine.create (Close) ;
DrawingObjects.Add (myHLine) ;
```

Properties from both are available and allow custom formatting (width, style, color, etc.). In this next Example, the Color property is inherited from **DrawingObject**.

```
myHLine.Color = elSystem.Drawing.Color.Cyan ;
myHLine.Style = StyleType.dashed3 ;
```

NAMESPACE: elSystem.DrawingObjects

PROPERTIES

	Name	Type	Description
📇	Alert	object	References additional properties used to enable and configure alert criteria for the horizontal line. See PriceAlert and AlertConfiguration.
📇	Label	object	References the DrawingObjectLabel object for the line. (TS >= 10)
📇	Price	double	Gets or sets a double representing the Price value of the

	Name	Type	Description
			line.
📨	RightJustify	bool	True to right-justify the label associated with the line. (TS >= 10)
📨	ShowLabels	bool	True to show labels associated with the line. (TS >= 10)
📨	Style	enum	Gets or sets the style of the line. See the StyleType enumerated list. Usage example: StyleType.solid
📨	Weight	enum	Gets or sets the line weight from an enumerated list. See Weight for a list of values. Usage example: Weight.weight5

TABLE 9.13—HorizontalLine Properties

METHODS

	Name	Description
🔧	Create ()	Initializes a new instance of the class.
🔧	Create (Double)	Initializes a new instance of the HorizontalLine Class for a given Price .
🔧	Create (double, int)	Initializes a new instance of the HorizontalLine Class for a given Price and Data source.

TABLE 9.14—HorizontalLines Methods

INHERITANCE HIERARCHY

elSystem.Object
  elSystem.DotNetObject
   elSystem.elComponent
    elSystem.DrawingObjects.DrawingObject
     elSystem.DrawingObjects.HorizontalLine

Now let's look at some examples.

EXAMPLE 9.13—Declare Variables for Each Object Type

```
using elSystem.DrawingObjects ;
using elSystem ;
vars:
// declare myHorizLine1 as a HorizontalLine type:
   HorizontalLine myHorizLine1(null),
// declare myTrendLine1 as a TrendLine type):
   TrendLine myTrendLine1(null),
// declare bar number points 1 & 2:
   BNPoint BNPoint1 (null), BNPoint BNPoint2 (null) ;
```

Then you need to create an instance of each drawing object at the point locations specified.

EXAMPLE 9.14—Create an Instance of Two Drawing Objects

This is not a full listing, so the code is not in https://www.EasyLanguageOOEL.com.

```
// create a horizontal line at .02 below the last price:
myHorizLine1 = HorizontalLine.Create (last -0.02) ;
// create 1st TL point 10 bars to the left
// of the current bar:
myPoint1 = BNPoint.Create(BarNumber + MaxBarsBack - 10, close[10]) ;
// create second trendline point at current bar:
myPoint2 = BNPoint.Create (BarNumber + MaxBarsBack, close) ;
```

```
      // create a trend line and assign it to myTrendLine
      myTrendLine1 = TrendLine.Create (myPoint1,myPoint2) ;
```

The next example is simple in concept because it just requires an input to specify the HL_Price, where you want the line drawn. You input a price and the indicator draws a horizontal line at the designated price. Of course, you can get much more sophisticated by calculating pivot points, recent highs and lows etc. But you will be able to figure that out on your own by using this indicator as a template.

EXAMPLE 9.15—Code for Simple Horizontal Line [OME_HorizontalLine_Ex#01]

```
Using elSystem ;
Using elSystem.Drawing ;
Using elSystem.DrawingObjects ;

Inputs:
 Double HL_Price      (0.00) ;

Vars  :
 HorizontalLine myHL (NULL) ;

// Working Storage Section

Consts:
 String App_Type     ("Study"),
 String App_Name     ("OME_HorizontalLine_Ex#01"),
 String App_Note     ("OOEL Made Easy Example using a HorizontalLine
DrawingObject"),
 String App_Vers     ("01.00.00") ;

Vars  :
 String AlertStr     (""),
 Bool   doCmtry      (FALSE),
 Bool   doAlert      (FALSE),
 Bool   KeepGoing    ( TRUE),
 Bool   Debug        (FALSE),
 Double Dummy        (0.00) ;

method HorizontalLine HorizontalLine_Init (Double Price)
Vars  :
 HorizontalLine myHL ;
begin
  myHL  = HorizontalLine.Create (Price) ;
  myHL.Click          += HorizontalLine_Click ;
  myHL.SubgraphResize += HorizontalLine_SubgraphResize ;
  DrawingObjects.Add (myHL) ;
  Return myHL ;
end ; // "HorizontalLine_Init" method

// ------------------------------------------------------

method void HorizontalLine_Click (elSystem.Object sender,
elSystem.DrawingObjects.DrawingObjectEventArgs args)
begin
  Print ("HorizontalLine_Click") ; // print if line clicked
end ; // "HorizontalLine_Click" method

// ------------------------------------------------------

method void HorizontalLine_SubgraphResize (elSystem.Object sender,
elSystem.DrawingObjects.SubgraphResizeEventArgs args)
begin
```

```
   Print ("HorizontalLine_SubgraphResize") ;
// Print if chart resized
end ; // "HorizontalLine_SubgraphResize" method

// ==========================================================

Once begin
  myHL   = HorizontalLine_Init (HL_Price) ;
  KeepGoing  =  TRUE ;
end ; // Once, and only once

if  (CurrentBar <= 01)  then begin
end ; // first bar of data

if  KeepGoing  then begin
  if  (Date [00]  > Date [01])  then begin
  end ; // first bar of new day
end ; // keep going / walk forward
```

And, lo and behold a **HorizontalLine** appears on the chart at the input price.

FIGURE 9.06—Horizontal Line

HorizontalLines are very similar to **TrendLines** except that you must specify two points for a **TrendLine**, while a **HorizontalLine** needs only price.

Let's try drawing **VerticalLines** next and then we will get to **TrendLine**s.

VerticalLine Class

With this class you can place a vertical line object on a chart at a given time (**DTPoint**) or bar number (**BNPoint**). Appearance may be altered and an alert set using appropriate properties. A vertical line may be used as an analytical drawing tool used to identify a point in time on a chart.

The following code snippet shows how to create a vertical line based on a **DateTime** object. To use this in an AT be sure that it is setup as described in About Drawing Objects.

```
myDTPoint = DTPoint.Create(BarDateTime, 0);
myVLine = VerticalLine.create(myDTPoint);
DrawingObjects.Add(myVLine);
```

In this next Example, the Color and Line Style of the vertical line are changed. Note that the Color Property is inherited from **DrawingObject** while Style is a property of **VerticalLine**.

```
myVLine.Color = elSystem.Drawing.Color.Red ;
myVLine.Style = StyleType.solid ;
```

NAMESPACE: elSystem.DrawingObjects

PROPERTIES

	Name	Type	Description
📇	Alert	object	References additional properties used to enable and configure alert criteria for the vertical line. See TimeAlert and AlertConfiguration.
📇	Label	object	References the DrawingObjectLabel Object for the line.
📇	Position	double	Gets or sets the position of the vertical line as a drawing object point. See DOPoint for more information.
📇	ShowDate	bool	True to show the date associated with the line.
📇	ShowLabels	bool	True to show labels associated with the line.
📇	ShowTime	bool	True to show the time associated with the line.
📇	Style	enum	Gets or sets the style of the line. See the StyleType enumerated list. Usage example: StyleType.solid
📇	TopPlacement	bool	True places the label at the top of the vertical line; False at the bottom.
📇	Weight	enum	Gets or sets the line weight from an enumerated list. See Weight for a list of values. Usage example: Weight.weight5

TABLE 9.15—VerticalLine Class Properties

METHODS

	Name	Description
🔷	Create ()	Initializes a new instance of the class.
🔷	Create (object)	Initializes a new instance of the VerticalLine class at a DTPoint (date/time).
🔷	Create (object, int)	Initializes a new instance of the VerticalLine class at a DTPoint (date/time) and Data source.
🔷	Create (object)	Initializes a new instance of the VerticalLine class at a BNPoint (bar number).
🔷	Create (object, Int)	Initializes a new instance of the VerticalLine class at a BNPoint (bar number) and Data source.

TABLE 9.16—VerticalLine Class Methods

INHERITANCE HIERARCHY

elSystem.Object
  elSystem.DotNetObject
   elSystem.elComponent
    elSystem.DrawingObjects.DrawingObject
     elSystem.DrawingObjects.VerticalLine

EXAMPLE 9.16—Vertical Line on a Chart [OME_VerticalLine_Ex#01]

This example plots a vertical line on the bar of the Highest High of Bars_Ago bars.

```
Inputs:
 Int    Bars_Ago  (03) ;
```

```
Vars   :
 Int    BarsBack   (00) ;

Using elSystem ;
Using elSystem.Drawing ;
Using elSystem.DrawingObjects ;

Vars  :
 DTPoint      myDT   (NULL),
 VerticalLine myVL   (NULL) ;

// Working Storage Section
Consts:
 String App_Type    ("Study"),
 String App_Name    ("OME_Vertical_Line_Ex#01"),
 String App_Note    ("Vertical Line example using OOEL"),
 String App_Vers    ("01.01.00") ;

Vars  :
 String DQ          (DoubleQuote),
 String NL          (NewLine),
 Bool   Debug       (FALSE),
 Double Dummy       (0.00) ;

once begin
end ; // Once, and only once

if  LastBarOnChart  then begin
  BarsBack  = HighestBar (High, Bars_Ago) ;
  if  myVL  = NULL  then begin
    myDT = DTPoint.Create (BarDateTime [BarsBack], High [BarsBack]) ;
    myVL = VerticalLine.Create (myDT) ;
    DrawingObjects.Add    (myVL) ;
  end
  else begin
    DrawingObjects.Delete (myVL) ;
    myDT = DTPoint.Create (BarDateTime [BarsBack], High [BarsBack]) ;
    myVL = VerticalLine.Create (myDT) ;
    DrawingObjects.Add    (myVL) ;
  end ; // vertical line already created
end ;
```

FIGURE 9.07—Vertical Line Example #01

EXAMPLE 9.17—Vertical Line Example #02 [OME_VerticalLine_Ex#02]

This next example is identical in its resultant chart but uses a Method to initialize the **VerticalLine**.

```
Inputs:
 Int     Bars_Ago  (03) ;
Vars  :
 Int     BarsBack  (00) ;

Using elSystem ;
Using elSystem.Drawing ;
Using elSystem.DrawingObjects ;

Vars  :
 DTPoint      myDT  (NULL),
 VerticalLine myVL  (NULL) ;

// Working Storage Section
Consts:
 String App_Type   ("Study"),
 String App_Name   ("OME_Vertical_Line_Ex#02"),
 String App_Note   ("Vertical Line example using OOEL"),
 String App_Vers   ("01.01.00") ;

Vars  :
 String DQ         (DoubleQuote),
 String NL         (NewLine),
 Bool   Debug      (FALSE),
 Double Dummy      (0.00) ;

// =====================================================

method VerticalLine VerticalLine_Init (Int Offset)
Vars  :
 DTPoint      myDT,
 VerticalLine myVL ;
begin
  myDT  = DTPoint.Create (BarDateTime [Offset], High [Offset]) ;
```

```
  myVL  = VerticalLine.Create (myDT) ;
  DrawingObjects.Add (myVL) ;

  Return myVL ;
end ; // "VerticalLine_Init" method


// =======================================================

once begin
end ; // Once, and only once

if  LastBarOnChart  then begin
  BarsBack  = HighestBar (High, Bars_Ago) ;
  if  myVL <> NULL  then  DrawingObjects.Delete (myVL) ;
  myVL  = VerticalLine_Init (BarsBack) ;
end ; // simplified the logic
```

EXAMPLE 9.18—Vertical Line Ex #03 [OME_VerticalLine_Ex#03]

This study marks the Highest High in the first, second and third positions. It divides the **MaxBarsBack** buffer into three sections and plots a **VerticalLine** at each. In three different colors.

As a habit, Sam prefers to use **HighestBar** rather than **Highest(H,n)** because it yields more information. Not only do you get the High, but you also get the **BarsAgo** value.

```
Inputs:
 Int    Bars_Ago  (03) ;

Vars  :
 Int    BarsBack  (00) ;

Using elSystem ;
Using elSystem.Drawing ;
Using elSystem.DrawingObjects ;

Vars  :
 DTPoint      myDT  (NULL),
 VerticalLine myVL  (NULL) ;

// Working Storage Section
Consts:
 String App_Type    ("Study"),
 String App_Name    ("OME_Vertical_Line_Ex#01"),
 String App_Note    ("Vertical Line example using OOEL"),
 String App_Vers    ("01.01.00") ;

Vars  :
 String DQ          (DoubleQuote),
 String NL          (NewLine),
 Bool   Debug       (FALSE),
 Double Dummy       (0.00) ;

once begin
end ; // Once, and only once

if  LastBarOnChart  then begin
  BarsBack  = HighestBar (High, Bars_Ago) ;
  if  myVL  = NULL  then begin
    myDT  = DTPoint.Create (BarDateTime [BarsBack], High [BarsBack]) ;
    myVL  = VerticalLine.Create (myDT) ;
    DrawingObjects.Add    (myVL) ;
```

```
    end
    else begin
      DrawingObjects.Delete (myVL) ;
      myDT  = DTPoint.Create (BarDateTime [BarsBack], High [BarsBack]) ;
      myVL  = VerticalLine.Create (myDT) ;
      DrawingObjects.Add      (myVL) ;
    end ; // vertical line already created
  end ;
```

FIGURE 9.08—Three Colorful Vertical Lines [OME_VerticalLine_Ex#03]

TrendLine Class

With this class you can draw a trendline on a chart, through two points. The points may be time-based (**DTPoint**) or bar number-based (**BNPoint**). Appearance may be altered, and an alert enabled using appropriate properties. Trendlines are often used to track market direction and identify breakouts.

NAMESPACE: elSystem.DrawingObjects

PROPERTIES

	Name	Type	Description
	Alert	object	References additional properties used to enable and configure alert criteria for the trendline. See PriceAlert and Using Alerts for more information.
	EndPoint	object	Gets the ending point of the trendline as a DOPoint object.
	ExtLeft	bool	Gets or sets the extend left property. True to extend the trendline to the left.
	ExtRight	bool	Gets or sets the extend right property. True to extend the trendline to the right.
	Label	object	References the DrawingObjectLabel object for the line. (TS >= 10)
	RightJustify	bool	True to right-justify the label associated with the line. (TS >= 10)

	Name	Type	Description
🖾	ShowBarCount	bool	True to show the number of bars covered by the line (TS >= 10)
🖾	ShowLabels	bool	True to show labels associated with the line. (TS >= 10)
🖾	ShowPriceNetChange	bool	True to show the net price change from the start to the end of the line. (TS >= 10)
🖾	ShowPricePercentChange	bool	True to show the price percent change from the start to the end of the line. (TS >= 10)
🖾	ShowTimeSpan	bool	True to show the time span from the start to the end of the line. (TS >= 10)
🖾	StartPoint	object	Gets the starting point of the trendline as a DOPoint object.
🖾	Style	enum	Gets or sets the TrendLine style using a StyleType enumerator.
🖾	Weight	enum	Gets or sets the line weight from an enumerated list. See Weight for a list of values.

TABLE 9.17—TrendLine Class Properties

METHODS

	Name	Description
🔷	Create ()	Initializes a new instance of the class.
🔷	Create (DTPoint, DTPoint)	Initializes a new instance of the Trendline class. The first parameter is a DTPoint object representing the start point of the line; the second parameter is a DTPoint object representing the end point of the line.
🔷	Create (DTPoint, DTPoint, int)	Initializes a new instance of the Trendline class. The first parameter is a DTPoint object representing the start point of the line; the second parameter is a DTPoint object representing the end point of the line, and the third parameter is an integer representing the data number (data1 - 50).
🔷	Create (BNPoint, BNPoint)	Initializes a new instance of the Trendline class. The first parameter is a BNPoint object representing the start point of the line; the second parameter is a BNPoint object representing the end point of the line.
🔷	Create (BNPoint, BNPoint, int)	Initializes a new instance of the Trendline class. The first parameter is a BNPoint representing the start point of the line; the second parameter is a BNPoint object representing the end point of the line, and the third parameter is an integer representing the data number (data1 - 50).
🔷	GetValue (DateTime)	Returns the price for a specified DateTime object.
🔷	GetValue (BarNumber)	Returns the price value of the TrendLine at the specified absolute BarNumber.

	Name	Description
⌐◆	SetEndPoint (DTPoint)	Sets the TrendLine end point using a DTPoint object.
⌐◆	SetEndPoint (BNPoint)	Sets the TrendLine end point using a BNPoint object.
⌐◆	SetStartPoint (DTPoint)	Sets the TrendLine start point using a DTPoint object.
⌐◆	SetStartPoint (BNPoint)	Sets the TrendLine start point using a BNPoint object.

TABLE 9.18—TrendLine Class Methods

INHERITANCE HIERARCHY

```
elSystem.Object
  elSystem.DotNetObject
    elSystem.elComponent
      elSystem.DrawingObjects.DrawingObject
        elSystem.DrawingObjects.TrendLine
```

EXAMPLE 9.19—Specifying a TrendLine Directly with BNPoint

A **TrendLine** may be created and drawn from the Close of 20 bars ago to the Close of the last bar on the chart as follows.

```
myTrendLine1 = TrendLine.Create (BNPoint.Create(BarNumber +
MaxBarsBack - 20, close[20]), BNPoint.Create (BarNumber + MaxBarsBack,
close)) ;
```

This is just a snippet so you can see how it is coded.

EXAMPLE 9.20—Create a TrendLine and Add to a Chart [OME_TL_Ex#01]

☑ In examples where the name of the study is too long to fit on one line we have taken the liberty of shortening the name. For instance, OME_TL_Ex#01 is actually OME_TrendLine_Ex#01 on the website. This convention carries on throughout the book.

This next example draws two horizontal trendlines at the Opening Range (defined by the inputs `Beg_Time` and `End_Time`.) Here we have made the inputs in Eastern Time, but if you live in California like me the inputs should be 0630 and 0730. (I call it oh-dark-thirty).

```
Using elSystem ;
Using elSystem.Drawing ;
Using elSystem.DrawingObjects ;

Inputs:
  Int     Beg_Time   (0930),
  Int     End_Time   (1030) ;

Vars  :
  Bool    Time_OK    (FALSE),
  Int     ORB_Beg    (-01),
  Int     ORB_End    (-01),
  Double ORB_Hi      (0.00),
  Double ORB_Lo      (0.00) ;

// Working Storage Section
Consts:
  String App_Type      ("Study"),
  String App_Name      ("OME_TrendLine_Ex#01"),
```

```
    String App_Note      ("Opening Range Breakout example using
    TrendLine(s)"),
    String App_Vers      ("01.01.00") ;

  Vars  :
   String DQ            (DoubleQuote),
   String NL            (NewLine),
   Bool   Debug         (FALSE),
   Double Dummy         (0.00) ;

  // ========================================================
  Vars  :
   TrendLine  hiTL       (NULL),
   TrendLine  loTL       (NULL) ;

  method void Draw_Lines ()
  Vars  :
   DTPoint     BegDT,
   DTPoint     EndDT ;

  begin
    Print ("Draw_Lines") ;

  // Create the TrendLine for the high of the Opening Range
  // Create the PointValue for the beginning of the
  // TrendLine
    BegDT  = DTPoint.Create (BarDateTime [BarNumber - ORB_Beg], ORB_Hi)
  ;
    if  BegDT  = NULL  then begin
      Print ("Error: BegDT  = NULL - Abort!") ;
      Return ;
    end ;
  // Create the PointValue for the ending of the TrendLine
    EndDT  = DTPoint.Create (BarDateTime [BarNumber - ORB_End], ORB_Hi)
  ;
    if  EndDT  = NULL  then begin
      Print ("Error: EndDT  = NULL - Abort!") ;
      Return ;
    end ;
  // Create the TrendLine using the PointValues
  // created above
    hiTL   = TrendLine.Create (BegDT, EndDT) ;
    if  hiTL  = NULL  then begin
      Print ("Error: hiTL  = NULL - Abort!") ;
      Return ;
    end ;
    hiTL.Persist  =  TRUE ; // in case tick-by-tick enabled
  // Create the TrendLine for the Low of the Opening Range
    BegDT  = DTPoint.Create (BarDateTime [BarNumber - ORB_Beg], ORB_Lo)
  ;
    if  BegDT  = NULL  then begin
      Print ("Error: BegDT  = NULL - Abort!") ;
      Return ;
    end ;
    EndDT  = DTPoint.Create (BarDateTime [BarNumber - ORB_End], ORB_Lo)
  ;
    if  EndDT  = NULL  then begin
      Print ("Error: EndDT  = NULL - Abort!") ;
      Return ;
    end ;
```

```
  loTL   = TrendLine.Create (BegDT, EndDT) ;
  if  loTL  = NULL  then begin
    Print ("Error: loTL  = NULL - Abort!") ;
    Return ;
  end ;
  loTL.Persist  =  TRUE ; // in case tick-by-tick enabled
  DrawingObjects.Add (hiTL) ;
  DrawingObjects.Add (loTL) ;
end ; // "Draw_Lines" method

//==========================================================

once begin
end ; // Once, and only once

If  Time [00] >= Beg_Time
and Time [01] <  End_Time
  then  Time_OK  =  TRUE ;
// catch the first bar of the Opening Range

if  Time [00]  > End_Time
  then  Time_OK  = FALSE ;
// catch the first bar after the end of the Opening Range

if  Time_OK
and Time_OK [01]  = FALSE
then begin
  ORB_Beg  = BarNumber ;
// store the bar number of the first bar of Opening Range
  ORB_Hi  = High [00] ;
  ORB_Lo  =  Low [00] ;
end   //
else
if  Time_OK  then begin
  ORB_End  = BarNumber ;
// store the bar number of the last bar of Opening Range
  if  High [00]  > ORB_Hi  then  ORB_Hi  = High [00] ;
  if   Low [00] <  ORB_Lo  then  ORB_Lo  =  Low [00] ;
end ;

if  Time_OK [00]  = FALSE
and Time_OK [01]  =  TRUE
then begin
  Draw_Lines () ;
end ;
// we just determined the Opening Range and have all the
// data points stored
```

☑ The Persist property in the above example, as well as additional Properties, Methods, and Events not listed, are inherited from the DrawingObject Class.

FIGURE 9.09—Opening Range Breakout with TrendLines

The labels on the chart in Figure 9.09 above are due to my default settings of Show Label. Yours might not show like this. If not, and you want to see them, 🖰 Right-Click on the **TrendLine**, select No, and edit the defaults.

Starting with TradeStation version 10 you can control the Labels from within your code. Since most of the code was developed on TS 9.5 for backward compatibility, we have not included an example of that.

There are several more examples (bonus) of the series OME_TrendLine_Ex#0x which are on the website[45], but not included in this book. As the number of examples progresses the difficulty and sophistication rise. Enjoy!

Rectangle Class

The **Rectangle** Class draws a rectangle at a specified location on a chart. Appearance may be altered using appropriate properties. A rectangle is a non-analytical drawing tool used to highlight specific portions of a chart.

NAMESPACE: elSystem.DrawingObjects

PROPERTIES

	Name	Type	Description
🖼	EndPoint	object	Gets the end point as a DOPoint object. See DOPoint.
🖼	ExtLeft	bool	True to extend the rectangle to the left of the start point.
🖼	ExtRight	bool	True to extend the rectangle to the right of the end point.
🖼	FillColor	object	Gets or sets the fill color property. See **Color**.
🖼	FillPattern	enum	Gets or sets the fill pattern property using a FillPattern enumerator.
🖼	StartPoint	object	Gets the Rectangle object start point. See **DOPoint**.
🖼	Style	enum	Gets or sets the Rectangle border style using a StyleType enumerator.
🖼	Weight	enum	Gets or sets the Rectangle border weight using a Weight enumerator.

TABLE 9.19—Rectangle Class Properties

---

[45] www.EasyLanguageOOEL.com

METHODS

	Name	Description
▫◆	Create ()	Initializes a new instance of the **Rectangle** class.
▫◆	Create (DTPoint, DTPoint)	Initializes a new instance of the **Rectangle** class. The first parameter is a **DTPoint** object representing the starting point (upper left) of the rectangle. The second parameter is a **DTPoint** object representing the end point (lower right).
▫◆	Create (DTPoint, DTPoint, int)	Initializes a new instance of the **Rectangle** class. The first parameter is a **DTPoint** object representing the starting point (upper left) of the rectangle. The second parameter is a **DTPoint** object representing the end point (lower right), and the third parameter is an integer representing the data number (Data1 - 50).
▫◆	Create (BNPoint, BNPoint)	Initializes a new instance of the **Rectangle** class. The first parameter is a **BNPoint** object representing the starting point (upper left) of the rectangle. The second parameter is a **BNPoint** object representing the end point (lower right).
▫◆	Create (BNPoint, BNPoint, int)	Initializes a new instance of the **Rectangle** class. The first parameter is a **BNPoint** object representing the starting point (upper left) of the rectangle. The second parameter is a **BNPoint** object representing the end point (lower right), and the third parameter is an integer representing the data number (Data1 - 50).
▫◆	Create (XYPoint, XYPoint)	Initializes a new instance of the **Rectangle** class. The first parameter is a **XYPoint** object representing the starting point of a rectangle that contains the ellipse; the second parameter is a **XYPoint** object representing the end point (lower right).
▫◆	Create (XYPoint, XYPoint, int)	Initializes a new instance of the **Rectangle** class. The first parameter is a **XYPoint** object representing the starting point (upper left) of the rectangle. The second parameter is a **XYPoint** object representing the end point (lower right), and the third parameter is an integer representing the data number (data1 - 50).
▫◆	SetEndPoint (DTPoint)	Sets the **Rectangle** end point using a **DTPoint** object.
▫◆	SetEndPoint (BNPoint)	Sets the **Rectangle** end point using a **BNPoint** object.
▫◆	SetEndPoint (XYPoint)	Sets the **Rectangle** end point using a **XYPoint** object.
▫◆	SetStartPoint (DTPoint)	Sets the **Rectangle** start point using a **DTPoint** object.
▫◆	SetStartPoint (BNPoint)	Sets the **Rectangle** start point using a **BNPoint** object.
▫◆	SetStartPoint (XYPoint)	Sets the **Rectangle** start point using a **XYPoint** object.

TABLE 9.20—Rectangle Class Methods

INHERITANCE HIERARCHY

elSystem.Object
  elSystem.DotNetObject
    elSystem.elComponent
      elSystem.DrawingObjects.DrawingObject

elSystem.DrawingObjects.Rectangle

EXAMPLE 9.21—Drawing a Rectangle at a Fixed Location

The following code snippet shows how to draw a rectangle at a fixed location in a chart using **XYPoint** so that it is anchored to the window itself and will not scroll with the bars. In this case, the rectangle's upper left corner will be 150 pixels from the chart's left-side border and 50 pixels from the top border. The lower-right corner is 250 pixels from the left-side and 100 pixels from the top.

```
Vars  : Rectangle myXYRect (NULL) ;
myXYRect = Rectangle.create (XYPoint.Create(150, 50),
XYPoint.Create(250,100)) ;
DrawingObjects.Add (myXYRect) ;
```

Alternatively, you can use **BNPoint** to draw a rectangle between specified bar numbers or **DTPoint** to draw between date-time positions, so that the rectangle will scroll with the bars:

EXAMPLE 9.22—Using BNPoint to Draw a Rectangle [OME_Rectangle_BN]

This example provides a snippet of the code required. You may incorporate it into your own code.

```
Using elSystem ;
Using elSystem.DrawingObjects ;

Vars  :
 Rectangle MyBNRectangle (NULL),
 Rectangle MyDTRectangle (NULL) ;

If  (Currentbar  = 50)  then begin
  MyBNRectangle  = Rectangle.Create (BNPoint.Create (CurrentBar      +
MaxBarsBack, Highest (High, 50)), BNPoint.Create (CurrentBar – 50 +
MaxBarsBack,  Lowest ( Low, 50))) ;
  DrawingObjects.Add (MyBNRectangle) ;
end ;

If  (LastBarOnChart  = True) then begin
  MyDTRectangle  = Rectangle.Create (DTPoint.Create (BarDateTime[00],
Highest (High, 50)), DTPoint.Create (BarDateTime[49],  Lowest ( Low,
50))) ;
  DrawingObjects.Add (MyDTRectangle) ;
end ;
```

The following statements change the rectangle's border Color Property (inherited from DrawingObject) to cyan while FillPattern and FillColor set the background area to solid (pattern1) red.

```
myRectangle.Color = elSystem.Drawing.Color.Cyan ;
myRectangle.FillPattern = FillPattern.pattern1 ;
myRectangle.FillColor = elSystem.Drawing.Color.Red ;
```

To use this in an Analysis Technique, be sure that it is setup as described in About Drawing Objects.

EXAMPLE 9.23—Highlighting Opening Range with a Rectangle [OME_Rectangle_Ex#01]

```
Using elSystem ;
Using elSystem.Drawing ;
Using elSystem.DrawingObjects ;

Inputs:
 Int    Beg_Time    (0630),
 Int    End_Time    (0730),
 Int    hi_Color    (Green),
 Int    lo_Color    (Red),
 Int    Fill_Level  (128),
```

```
  String Fill_Note    ("Transparency of the fill (00-255 is solid)"),
  Int    Thickness    (01) ;

Vars :
  Bool   Time_OK      (FALSE),
  Int    ORB_Beg      (-01),
  Int    ORB_End      (-01),
  Double ORB_Hi       (0.00),
  Double ORB_Lo       (0.00) ;

// Working Storage Section
Consts:
  String App_Type     ("Study"),
  String App_Name     ("OME_Rectangle_Ex#01"),
  String App_Note     ("Opening Range Breakout example"),
  String App_Vers     ("01.02.00") ;

Vars :
  String DQ           (DoubleQuote),
  String NL           (NewLine),
  Bool   Debug        (FALSE),
  Double Dummy        (0.00) ;

// ======================================================
Vars :
  TrendLine hiTL      (NULL),
  TrendLine loTL      (NULL) ;

Vars :
  Rectangle Rect      (NULL),
  Int       LineColor (Blue),
  Int       FillColor (Yellow) ;

method void Draw_Rectangle ()
Vars :
  DTPoint   BegDT,
  DTPoint   EndDT ;
begin
  if Debug then Print ("Draw_Rectangle") ;
  BegDT = DTPoint.Create (BarDateTime [BarNumber - ORB_Beg], ORB_Hi)
;
  EndDT = DTPoint.Create (BarDateTime [BarNumber - ORB_End], ORB_Lo)
;
  Rect = Rectangle.Create (BegDT, EndDT) ;
  Rect.Color     = Color.FromArgb (LineColor) ;
  Rect.FillColor = Color.FromArgb (FillColor) ;
// set the FillColor to a numbered color
  Rect.FillColor = Color.FromArgb (Fill_Level, Rect.FillColor) ;
// set the transparency of the fill color to 75% (0-255)

  DrawingObjects.Add (Rect) ;
  Rect.Tag = "My Rectangle" ;
end ; // "Draw_Rectangle" method

method void Draw_Lines ()
Vars :
  DTPoint   BegDT,
  DTPoint   EndDT ;
// when these were declared local, they were instantiated
// on each call to the method hence, we were unable to
// delete the previous trendlines
```

```
begin
  if  Debug  then  Print ("Draw_Lines") ;

// remove the previous trendlines, if any
  if  hiTL <> NULL  then  DrawingObjects.Delete (hiTL) ;
  if  loTL <> NULL  then  DrawingObjects.Delete (loTL) ;

// Create the TrendLine for the high of
// the Opening Range
  BegDT  = DTPoint.Create (BarDateTime [BarNumber - ORB_Beg], ORB_Hi)
;
  if  BegDT  = NULL  then begin
    Print ("Error: BegDT  = NULL - Abort!") ;
    Return ;
  end ;
  EndDT  = DTPoint.Create (BarDateTime [BarNumber - ORB_End], ORB_Hi)
;
  if  EndDT  = NULL  then begin
    Print ("Error: EndDT  = NULL - Abort!") ;
    Return ;
  end ;
  hiTL    = TrendLine.Create (BegDT, EndDT) ;
  if  hiTL  = NULL  then begin
    Print ("Error: hiTL  = NULL - Abort!") ;
    Return ;
  end ;
  hiTL.ExtRight  = FALSE ;
// set the Entend Right Property to false
  hiTL.Lock       =  TRUE ;
  hiTL.Color      = Color.FromArgb (hi_Color) ;
  hiTL.Weight     = Thickness ;
// Create the TrendLine for the low of the Opening Range
  BegDT  = DTPoint.Create (BarDateTime [BarNumber - ORB_Beg], ORB_Lo)
;
  if  BegDT  = NULL  then begin
    Print ("Error: BegDT  = NULL - Abort!") ;
    Return ;
  end ;
  EndDT  = DTPoint.Create (BarDateTime [BarNumber - ORB_End], ORB_Lo)
;
  if  EndDT  = NULL  then begin
    Print ("Error: EndDT  = NULL - Abort!") ;
    Return ;
  end ;
  loTL    = TrendLine.Create (BegDT, EndDT) ;
  if  loTL  = NULL  then begin
    Print ("Error: loTL  = NULL - Abort!") ;
    Return ;
  end ;
  loTL.ExtRight  = FALSE ;
// set the Extend Right Property to false
  loTL.Lock       =  TRUE ;
  loTL.Color      = Color.FromArgb (lo_Color) ;
  loTL.Weight     = Thickness ;

  DrawingObjects.Add (hiTL) ;
  DrawingObjects.Add (loTL) ;
end ; // "Draw_Lines" method
```

6666

```
// ===========================================================

once begin
end ; // Once, and only once


If   Time [00] >= Beg_Time
and Time [01] <  End_Time
  then  Time_OK  =   TRUE ;
// catch the first bar of the Opening Range

if   Time [00]  > End_Time
  then  Time_OK  = FALSE ;
// catch the first bar after the end of the Opening Range

if   Time_OK
and Time_OK [01]  = FALSE
then begin
  ORB_Beg  = BarNumber ;
// store the bar number of the first bar of Opening Range
  ORB_Hi  = High [00] ;
  ORB_Lo  =  Low [00] ;
end    //
else
if   Time_OK  then begin
  ORB_End  = BarNumber ;
// store the bar number of the last bar of Opening Range
  if  High [00]  > ORB_Hi  then  ORB_Hi  = High [00] ;
  if   Low [00] <  ORB_Lo  then  ORB_Lo  =  Low [00] ;
end ;

if   Time_OK [00]  = FALSE
and Time_OK [01]  =  TRUE
then begin
//  Draw_Lines () ;
  Draw_Rectangle () ;
end ;
// we just determined the Opening Range and have all the
// data points stored

//Once skt_LastBarOnChart begin
// Error 1; Description: Assignment to a function not
// allowed.; Location: OME_ChartingHost; Line: 157
Once (skt_LastBarOnChart) begin // No Error, parenthesis required
  if  skt_PowerUser (CustomerID)
  and OME_Floating_text (App_Name + NL + App_Note, "Black", "Arial",
10, 50, 50, FALSE)  then ;
end ; // Once, and only once
```

And in Figure 9.10 below is the resultant chart:

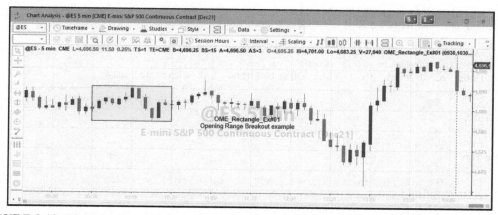

FIGURE 9.10—Opening Range Breakout Rectangles with Semi-Transparent Fill

☑ Rectangle Classes along with their Methods and Properties are in **Volume II—Reference Guide, Appendix III: Classes**.

EXAMPLE 9.24—Display a Rectangle Containing a Text Label [OME_TextRectangle]

This example displays a rectangle containing a text label at a fixed position in a chart.

```
// OME_TextRectangle
// Displays a rectangle containing a text label at a
//    fixed position in a chart

Using Charting ;
Using elSystem.Drawing ;
Using elSystem.DrawingObjects ;

Vars  :
ChartingHost myCH      (NULL),
Rectangle myRectangle (NULL),
// declares a rectangle drawing object
TextLabel myText       (NULL) ;
// declares a textlabel drawing object


method void ChartingHost_Init ()
begin
  myCH  = ChartingHost.Create () ;
  myCH.OnInitialUpdate += ChartingHost1_OnInitialUpdate ;
  myCH.OnSize += ChartingHost1_OnSize ;
end ; // "ChartingHost_Init" method

// plots the text rectangle when the chart window is
//    initialized
method void ChartingHost1_OnInitialUpdate (elSystem.Object sender,
charting.OnInitialUpdateEventArgs args)
begin
  PlotLabel (args.width, args.height) ;
  // plots the text rectangle
end ; // "ChartingHost1_OnInitialUpdate" method

// updates the text rectangle when the chart is resizsed
method void ChartingHost1_OnSize (elSystem.Object sender,
charting.OnSizeEventArgs args)
begin
  PlotLabel (args.width, args.height) ;
```

```
      // plots the text rectangle
   end ; // "ChartingHost1_OnSize" method

   // plots a rectangle containing a text label near the upper
   //   right corner of a chart
   Method void PlotLabel (int ChartWidth, int ChartHeight)
   Vars  :
    Int    x1,
    Int    y1,
    Int    w1,
    Int    h1 ;
   begin
     w1  = 125 ;
     // width of the rectangle (needs to be slightly wider
     //   than the text)
     h1  =  22 ;
     // height of the rectangle
     x1  = ChartWidth - 70 - w1 ;
     // x coordinate of the left edge of the rectangle
     y1  =  20 ;
     // y coordinate of the top edge of the rectangle

     // create the rectangle and text drawing objects if they
     //   don't exist
     If  myRectangle  = NULL  then begin
       // creates a rectangle using a pair of X,Y points
       myRectangle = Rectangle.Create (XYPoint.Create (x1, y1),
   XYPoint.Create (x1 + w1, y1 + h1)) ;
       myRectangle.Color  = Color.DarkCyan ;
       myRectangle.FillColor = Color.fromARGB (80, 00, 00, 255);
       // set to transparent blue
       myRectangle.Persist  =  TRUE ;
       // persist keeps the rectangle on the chart between tick
       //    updates
       DrawingObjects.Add (myRectangle) ;
       // draws the rectangle on the chart
       // creates a text string at an X,Y point inside
       //   the rectangle
       myText  = TextLabel.Create (XYPoint.Create (x1 + 05, y1 + 05),
   "Trades today: " + NumToStr (DailyTrades, 00)) ;
       myText.Color  = Color.White ;

       myText.Persist  =  TRUE ;
       // persist keeps the text label on the chart between
       //    tick updates
       DrawingObjects.Add (myText) ;
       // draws the text on the chart
       Print ("myRectangle  = NULL") ;
     end
     else begin
       // udpates the X,Y coordinates for an existing rectangle
       //    and text
       myRectangle.SetStartPoint (XYPoint.Create (x1, y1)) ;
       myRectangle.SetEndPoint   (XYPoint.Create (x1 + w1, y1 + h1)) ;
       myText.PointValue  = XYPoint.Create (x1 + 05, y1 + 05) ;

       DrawingObjects.Add (myText) ;
       // draws the text on the chart
       Print ("myRectangle <> NULL") ;
     end ; // myRectangle <> NULL
   end ; // "PlotLabel" method
```

```
once begin
  ChartingHost_Init () ;
end ; // Once, and only once

// updates the text string on every tick
If  myText <> NULL  then  myText.TextString  = "Trades today: " +
NumToStr (DailyTrades, 00) ;
```

FIGURE 9.11—Rectangle with a TextLabel

Ellipse Class

The **Ellipse** Class creates an instance of an **Ellipse** Object at a specified location and of a specified size on a chart. This Object is then added to the Chart by calling the **DrawingObjects.Add ()** Method.

Appearance may be altered using appropriate properties. An **Ellipse** is a non-analytical drawing tool used to highlight specific portions of a chart. If you specify a square shape instead of a rectangle, the ellipse will be a circle.

☑ Note that the points that define an ellipse are relative to left-side and right-side corners of an imaginary rectangle that bounds the ellipse.

NAMESPACE: elSystem.DrawingObjects

INHERITANCE HIERARCHY

elSystem.Object
 elSystem.DotNetObject
  elSystem.elComponent
   elSystem.DrawingObjects.DrawingObject
    elSystem.DrawingObjects.Ellipse

The following code snippet shows how to add an Ellipse to a chart at specific X-Y coordinates using **XYPoint**. Alternatively, the dimensions could be given using **BNPoint** or **DTPoint**. Again, this is just a snippet of code so you can see how it's used.

EXAMPLE 9.25—Create an Ellipse with XYPoint

```
Vars  : Ellipse myEllipse (NULL) ;
myEllipse = Ellipse.create (XYPoint.Create(150, 50),
XYPoint.Create(250,100)) ;
DrawingObjects.Add (myEllipse) ;
```

EXAMPLE 9.26—Create an Ellipse with BNPoint

You can use **BNPoint** to draw an **Ellipse** between specified bar numbers or **DTPoint** to draw between date-time positions, so that the **Ellipse** will scroll with the bars:

```
If  (CurrentBar  = 70)  then begin
//draw an ellipse from the current bar to the 40th bar back
  MyBNEllipse  = Ellipse.Create (BNPoint.Create (CurrentBar +
MaxBarsBack, Highest (High, 40)), BNPoint.Create (CurrentBar +
MaxBarsBack - 40, Lowest (Low, 40))) ;
  DrawingObjects.Add (MyBNEllipse) ;
End ;


If  (LastBarOnChart  = True)  then begin
// draw an ellipse from the last bar on the chart
// to the 50th bar ago
  MyDTEllipse  = Ellipse.Create (DTPoint.Create (BarDateTime[00],
Highest (High, 50)), DTPoint.Create (BarDateTime[50],  Lowest ( Low,
50))) ;
  DrawingObjects.Add (MyDTEllipse) ;
End ;
```

Properties allow custom formatting (width, style, color, etc.). In this example, the Color property (which describes line color of the Ellipse, not the fill color) is inherited from **DrawingObject** .

EXAMPLE 9.27—Changing the Color of an Ellipse

```
myEllipse.Color = elSystem.Drawing.Color.Cyan ;
myEllipse.FillPattern = FillPattern.pattern1 ;
```

To use this in an Analysis Technique, be sure that it is setup as described in About Drawing Objects.

EXAMPLE 9.28—Opening Range Breakout Using Ellipse [OME_Ellipse_Ex#01]

```
[LegacyColorValue = FALSE]

Using elSystem ;
Using elSystem.Drawing ;
Using elSystem.DrawingObjects ;

Inputs:
  Int    Beg_Time    (0630),
  Int    End_Time    (0730),
  Int    hi_Color    (Green),
  Int    lo_Color    (Red),
  Int    Thickness   (01) ;

// OOEL Variables
Vars  :
Ellipse myEllipse (NULL) ;

// Classic variables
Vars  :
  Bool    Time_OK    (FALSE),
  Int     ORB_Beg    (-01),
  Int     ORB_End    (-01),
  Double ORB_Hi      (0.00),
  Double ORB_Lo      (0.00) ;

// Working Storage Section
Consts:
  String App_Type    ("Study"),
  String App_Name    ("OME_Ellipse_Ex#01"),
```

```
   String App_Note      ("Opening Range Breakout example"),
   String App_Vers      ("01.00.00") ;

  Vars  :
  String DQ             (DoubleQuote),
  String NL             (NewLine),
  Bool   Debug          (FALSE),
  Double Dummy          (0.00) ;

  // =======================================================

  Vars  :
  Int          LineColor (Blue),
  Int          FillColor (Yellow) ;

method Ellipse Draw_Ellipse ()
Vars  :
 DTPoint      BegDT,
 DTPoint      EndDT,
 Ellipse      myEllipse ;
begin
  Print ("Draw_Ellipse") ;
  BegDT  = DTPoint.Create (BarDateTime [BarNumber - ORB_Beg], ORB_Hi)
;
  EndDT  = DTPoint.Create  (BarDateTime [BarNumber - ORB_End], ORB_Lo)
;
  myEllipse   = Ellipse.Create (BegDT, EndDT) ;
  myEllipse.Color      = Color.fromArgb (LineColor) ;
  myEllipse.FillColor  = Color.fromArgb (FillColor) ;          // set
the FillColor to a numbered color
//  myEllipse.FillColor  = Color.fromArgb (128, FillColor asType
Color) ; // set the transparancy of the fill color to 75% (0-255)

//Print (Color.fromArgb (128, 255, 215, 00).Name) ;
// Rect.FillColor  = Color.fromArgb (128, 255, 215, 00) ;
// Rect.FillColor  = Color.fromArgb (16776960) ;

  DrawingObjects.Add (myEllipse) ;
  myEllipse.Tag  = "My myEllipse" ;
  Return myEllipse ;
end ; // "Draw_Ellipse" method

  // =======================================================

once begin
end ; // Once, and only once

If  Time [00] >= Beg_Time
and Time [01] <  End_Time
  then  Time_OK  =  TRUE ;
// catch the first bar of the Opening Range

if  Time [00]  > End_Time
  then  Time_OK  = FALSE ;
// catch the first bar after the end of the Opening Range

if  Time_OK
and Time_OK [01]  = FALSE
then begin
  ORB_Beg  = BarNumber ;
```

```
// store the bar number of the first bar of Opening Range
  ORB_Hi  = High [00] ;
  ORB_Lo  =  Low [00] ;
end   //
else
if  Time_OK  then begin
  ORB_End  = BarNumber ;
// store the bar number of the last bar of Opening Range
  if  High [00]  > ORB_Hi  then  ORB_Hi  = High [00] ;
  if   Low [00] <  ORB_Lo  then  ORB_Lo  =  Low [00] ;
end ;

if  Time_OK [00]  = FALSE
and Time_OK [01]  =  TRUE
then begin
  myEllipse  = Draw_Ellipse () ;
end ;
// we just determined the Opening Range and have all the
// data points stored
```

FIGURE 9.12—Opening Range Breakout Using Ellipse

☑ The Properties and Methods of the Ellipse class are found in **Volume II—Reference Guide, Appendix III: Classes**.

Summary

In this chapter we have discovered the many types and styles available from the **DrawingObject** (DO) **Classes** from **TextLabel, TrendLine, VerticalLine, HorizontalLine,** to **Rectangle** and more. We have demonstrated moving them after they have been added to the chart, what happens when you extend your **TrendLine** to the right, and changing the **Color, Style** and **Weight**. We have filled a rectangle with color. There are so many useful ways you can use these modern objects; they are so much more versatile than the classic **TL_New** and **Text_New** functions. I feel sure each of you will have some idea of how these new abilities of yours may be applied to improve your technical skills.

SKT: As an example, I have **clients** who use tools they have commissioned me to write that drop **TrendLines** on the chart at the click of a **Button**. They then can move the **TrendLines** to the places they see support or resistance, and, upon the click of another **Button**, orders are placed at those values using a classic EasyLanguage Strategy.

CHAPTER 10

Host Classes

In This Chapter

- Introduction
- ChartingHost Class (Component)
- PlatformClientHost Class (Component)
- PortfolioHost Class (Component)
- RadarScreenHost Class (Component)
- StrategyHost Class (Component)
- Summary

Introduction

The base class for all these **Host** Classes (except **PortfolioHost**) is the **Host** Class—kind of obvious, I know, but it is a good place to start. Each of the **Host** Classes described in this chapter inherits the **HostName** Property and the **Create ()** Method of this **Host** Class.

These Classes all inherit the **elComponent** Class and its members, the Name Property, and the **Destroy ()** Method. Inheriting the **elComponent** Class means that the Classes of the object may be used with the ToolBox and Component Tray. TS Help states merely "The base class for a design component object". They can also be programmed using straight editing in the code editor (TDE).

I bring up the Inheritance subject to remind you that there are often 'hidden' members (Properties, Methods, Events and Operators) available under the Inheritance of a Class. This fact is true throughout OOEL so it must be fully understood. I have included the Inheritances with each class in this book and in **Volume II—Reference Guide**.

The **ChartingHost** and **RadarScreenHost** Classes also inherit from the **PlatformClientHost** Class including any Members (Properties, Methods and Events) it contains. This primarily gives the **ChartingHost** and **RadarScreenHost** access to the **ActiveAccountID**.

It is worth mentioning that the TradingApp (TA) does **not** have a TradingAppHost Class and is unable to directly access the CustomerID information. Using the GetAccountID Function will not return a usable value. A TradingApp must instead use an Object of the **AccountsProvider** Class to access this information.

All these higher-level Host classes have Events for which you can, and probably will need to, create the appropriate Event Handler Methods to make anything really productive using these tools.

An Event Handler allows you to process a click or a selection of an element, changes made to key values, a key down event, a window resizing or when a chart element is deleted or about to appear. The following tables illustrate the properties of the ChartingHost Class.

ChartingHost Class (Component)

The **ChartingHost** allows access to click events within a chart analysis window. Each event returns additional information using the matching event args class.

Note that the **ChartingHost** Class inherits both the **elComponent** Class and the **PlatformClientHost** Class.

NAMESPACE: Charting

PROPERTIES

	Name	Type	Description
🖅	BackColor	object	Get the Background Color of the chart. (TS >= 10)
🖅	ChartViewHasFocus	bool	True when the chart is active and has focus. (TS >= 10)
🖅	ClientWindow	object	Gets the current ChartWindow object.
🖅	CurrentSubgraph	int	Gets the number of the chart subgraph in which the study containing the StrategyHost is inserted. (TS >= 10)

TABLE 10.01—ChartingHost Class Properties

METHODS

	Name	Description
🔷	Create ()	Initializes a new instance of the class.
🔷	ScrollTo (object)	Scrolls the chart window to the specified time given by the DateTime object.
🔷	ScrollTo (int)	Scrolls the chart window to the specified bar number given as an integer. The bar number is the absolute bar number on the chart. **MaxBarsBack** is not considered.
🔷	SetChartViewFocus ()	Gives focus to the chart. (TS >= 10)

TABLE 10.02—ChartingHost Class Methods

EVENTS

	Name	Description
⚡	ChartElementClick	Occurs when a click occurs in a chart. See **ChartElementClickEventArgs** for the properties returned by the handler's args parameter.
⚡	ElementSelected	Occurs when an element is selected in a chart. See **ElementSelectedEventArgs** for the properties returned by the handler's args parameter.
⚡	OnInitialUpdate	Occurs on initial update. See **OnInitialUpdateEventArgs** for the properties returned by the handler's args parameter.
⚡	OnKeyDown	Occurs when a DownKey event occurs in a chart. See **HostKeyEventArgs** for the properties returned by the handler's args parameter. (TS >= 10)
⚡	OnKillFocus	Occurs when the chart loses focus. (TS >= 10)
⚡	OnSetFocus	Occurs when the chart receives focus. (TS >= 10)
⚡	OnSize	Occurs when the client window is resized. See **OnSizeEventArgs** for the properties returned by the handler's args parameter.
⚡	OrderElementMove	Occurs when an order element is moved. See OrderElementMoveEventArgs for the properties returned by the handler's args parameter.

	Name	Description
🔗	PreDeleteElement	Occurs when a chart element is about to be deleted. See PreDeleteElementEventArgs for the properties returned by the handler's args parameter.
🔗	PreShowElementMenu	Occurs when chart element menu is about to appear. See PreShowElementMenuEventArgs for the properties returned by the handler's args parameter.

TABLE 10.03—ChartingHost Class Events

INHERITANCE HIERARCHY

elSystem.Object
  elSystem.elComponent
  elSystem.Host
    platform.PlatformClientHost
     charting.ChartingHost

Finally, write the Method(s) to be called when a ChartElementClick event occurs.

EXAMPLE 10.01—Method for Reacting to a ChartElementClick Event

```
method void DOClick (Object sender, DrawingObjectEventArgs args)
begin
// Your code to handle a drawing object that has been
// clicked
End ;
```

EXAMPLE 10.02—Reacting to Events on a Chart [OME_ChartingHost_Ex#01]

You can open the Print Log window and it will report information on whatever object you click on the Background, a Bar, a Plot, a DrawingObject, etc. With a tad more programming you can report whether the **DrawingObject** was created manually, using **TL_New** or as a **DrawingObjects.TrendLine** Object.

```
// OOEL Declarations
Using elSystem ;
Using Charting ;

Vars :
 ChartingHost   myCH   (NULL) ;

Vars :
 Int    DecPlaces   (02) ;

// Working Storage Section
Consts:
 String App_Type    ("Study"),
 String App_Name    ("OME_ChartingHost_Ex#01"),
 String App_Note    ("Explore the ChartingHost Object"),
 String App_Vers    ("01.01.00") ;

Vars :
 String DQ      (DoubleQuote),
 String NL      (NewLine),
 Bool   Debug   (FALSE),
 Double Dummy   (0.00) ;

  ChartingHost myCH ;
begin
  Print ("ChartingHost_Init (" + DQ + App_Name + DQ + ")") ;
  myCH = ChartingHost.Create () ;
```

```
  if  myCH = NULL  then begin
    Print ("Error: " + DQ + App_Name + DQ + " ChartingHost_Init - myCH
= NULL!") ;
    Return NULL ;
  end ;
  myCH.ChartElementClick  += ChartingHost_ChartElementClick;
  myCH.ElementSelected    += ChartingHost_ElementSelected ;
  myCH.OnInitialUpdate    += ChartingHost_OnInitialUpdate ;
  myCH.OnSize             += ChartingHost_OnSize ;
  myCH.OrderElementMove   += ChartingHost_OrderElementMove ;
  myCH.PreDeleteElement   += ChartingHost_PreDeleteElement ;
  myCH.PreShowElementMenu += ChartingHost_PreShowElementMenu;

  Print (" Width = ", myCH.ClientWindow.Width:00:00, ", Height = ",
myCH.ClientWindow.Height:00:00) ;
  Return myCH ;
end ; // "ChartingHost_Init" method

// -------------------------------------------------------

method void ChartingHost_OnInitialUpdate (elSystem.Object sender,
charting.OnInitialUpdateEventArgs args)
// Event handler that is called on initial update.
// args Properties: Height, Width
begin
  Print (Method_Header (App_Name, "ChartingHost_OnInitialUpdate",
args.Width.toString () + "," + args.Height.toString ())) ;
  Print (" - myCH.ClientWindow: Width = ",
myCH.ClientWindow.Width:00:00, ", Height = ",
myCH.ClientWindow.Height:00:00) ;
  Print (" - args : Width = ", args.Width:00:00, ", Height = ",
args.Height:00:00) ;
end ; // "ChartingHost_OnInitialUpdate" method

// -------------------------------------------------------

method void ChartingHost_onSize (elSystem.Object sender,
charting.OnSizeEventArgs args)
// Event handler that is called when the client window
// is resized.
// args Properties: Height, Width
begin
  Print (Method_Header (App_Name, "ChartingHost_onSize",
args.Width.toString () + "," + args.Height.toString ())) ;
end ; // "ChartingHost_onSize" method

// -------------------------------------------------------

method void ChartingHost_OrderElementMove (elSystem.Object sender,
charting.OrderElementMoveEventArgs args)
// Event handler that is called when an order element
// moved. args Properties: Cancel, CurrentPrice, Element,
// IsReadOnly, TargetPrice
begin
  Print (Method_Header (App_Name, "ChartingHost_OrderElementMove",
         args.Cancel.toString () + "," + myFormat (args.Currentprice)
+ "," + DQ + args.Element.toString () + DQ + "," +
args.isReadOnly.toString () + "," + myFormat (args.TargetPrice))) ;
end ; // "ChartingHost_OrderElementMove" method

// -------------------------------------------------------
```

```
method void ChartingHost_PreDeleteElement (elSystem.Object sender,
charting.PreDeleteElementEventArgs args)
// Event handler that occurs when a chart element is
// about to be deleted.
// args Properties: Cancel, Element, IsReadOnly, Type
begin
  Print (Method_Header (App_Name, "ChartingHost_PreDeleteElement",
         args.Cancel.toString () + "," + args.Element.toString () +
"," + "," + args.isReadOnly.toString () + "," + DQ +
args.Type.toString () + DQ)) ;
  args.Cancel  =  TRUE ;
// this would prevent the object from being deleted.
end ; // "ChartingHost_PreDeleteElement" method

// ----------------------------------------------------------

method void ChartingHost_PreShowElementMenu (elSystem.Object sender,
charting.PreShowElementMenuEventArgs args)
// Event handler that occurs when chart element menu is
// about to appear.
// args Properties: Cancel, Element, IsKeyboard, IsReadOnly,
// Type, X, Y
begin
  Print (Method_Header (App_Name, "ChartingHost_PreShowElementMenu",
         args.Cancel.toString () + "," + "," + args.Element.toString
() + "," + args.IsKeyboard.toString () + "," +
args.isReadOnly.toString () + "," + args.Type.toString () + "," +
args.X.toString () + "," + args.Y.toString ())) ;
  args.Cancel  =  TRUE ;
// this will prevent the menu from being displayed.
end ; // "ChartingHost_PreShowElementMenu" method

// ----------------------------------------------------------

method String Method_Header (String AppName, String MethodName, String
MethodArgs)
Vars  :
 String RetVal ;
begin
  if  Debug  then  Print (Method_Header (App_Name, "Method_Header",
AppName + "," + MethodName + "," + MethodArgs)) ;
  RetVal  = String.Format ("({00}.) {01} ({02})", AppName, MethodName,
MethodArgs) ;
  Return RetVal ;
end ; // "Method_Header" method

// ----------------------------------------------------------

method String myFormat (Double Price)
Vars  :
 Double myNum ;
begin
  myNum  = Price ;
  Return vrt_Format (myNum) ;
end ; // "myFormat" method

// ----------------------------------------------------------

method String myDblToStr (Double NumIn)
```

```
Vars  :
 Double myNum ;
begin
  myNum  = NumIn ;
  Return NumToStr (myNum, DecPlaces) ;
end ; // "myDblToStr" method

// ---------------------------------------------------------

method String myIntToStr (Int NumIn)
Vars  :
 Int    myNum ;
begin
  myNum  = NumIn ;
  Return NumToStr (myNum, 00) ;
end ; // "myIntToStr" method

// =========================================================
// Main Code Section
// =========================================================

once begin
  App_Init () ;
end ; // Once, and only once

Once (skt_LastBarOnChart) begin // No Error
  if  OME_Floating_Text (App_Name + NL + App_Note, "Blue", "Arial",
10, 50, 50, FALSE)  then ;
end ; // Once, and only once
```

The chart below shows four drawing objects: a **VerticalLine**, a **TrendLine**, a Moving Average and a **TextLabel**. When you click on one of the objects, or even click on the data, a message will appear in the Print Log describing what action was taken, the date and time, and the x-y coordinates.

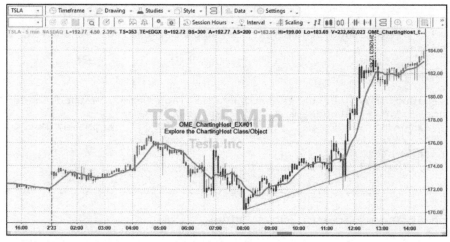

FIGURE 10.01—Chart with Objects Illustrating ChartingHost

Here is the output to the Print Log, showing that when you click on an object on the chart the code prints out location, date, and time as well as information on the type of object that was clicked upon.

```
(OME_ChartingHost_EX#01.) ChartingHost_ElementSelected ("charting.BackgroundVisualElement",true,true,"background")
(OME_ChartingHost_EX#01.) ChartingHost_ElementSelected ("charting.BackgroundVisualElement",true,false,"background")
(OME_ChartingHost_EX#01.) ChartingHost_ElementSelected ("charting.DrawingObjectVisualElement",true,true,"drawingobject")
(OME_ChartingHost_EX#01.) ChartingHost_ChartElementClick ( 389.69,"charting.DrawingObjectVisualElement", 389.69,3/30/2020 1:00:00 PM,"drawingobject")
```

FIGURE 10.02—Print Log After Clicking Vertical Line

PlatformClientHost Class (Component)

The **PlatformClientHost** allows access from a **ChartingHost** or **RadarScreenHost** to the currently active account number in TS and lets you set an event to monitor changes in the account number made by other components.

NAMESPACE: Platform

PROPERTIES

	Name	Type	Description
	ActiveAccountID	string	Gets the ID of the current account.
	ActiveAccountInfo	object	Gets the DynamicProperties object for the account.
	ClientWindow	object	Gets the Window of the current client.

TABLE 10.04—PlatformClientHost Properties

METHODS

	Name	Description
	Create ()	Initializes a new instance of the class.

TABLE 10.05—PlatformClientHost Methods

EVENTS

	Name	Description
	ActiveAccountChanged	Occurs whenever the account id is updated. See ActiveAccountChangeEventArgs for the properties returned by the handler's args parameters.

TABLE 10.06—PlatformClientHost Events

INHERITANCE HIERARCHY

elSystem.Object
  elSystem.DotNetObject
  elSystem.elComponent
   elSystem.Host
    platform.PlatformClientHost

```
ActiveAccountChanged event public ( elsystem.Obje
platform.ActiveAccountChangedEventArgs args )
```

FIGURE 10.03—ActiveAccountChanged

EXAMPLE 10.03—PlatformClientHost [OME_PlatformClientHost]

The **PlatformClientHost** Class is inherited by the **ChartingHost** Class and **RadarScreenHost** Class allowing it to receive information about the **ActiveAccountID**. However, the TradingApp does not have a **Host** class, let alone inherit the Host and **PlatformClientHost** classes, so it is not able to inherit this information. Instead, it must dumpster dive to get access to it. Nor does the **Portfolio** Class have access to this information. OK, Portfolio Maestro may not be used, but it seems that to issue real time trades, or **OrderTickets** (I cannot imagine why, as Portfolio Trading would be a very powerful feature). The TradingApp certainly deserves access to this information!

FIGURE 10.04—PlatformClientHost in the Dictionary

PortfolioHost Class (Component)

The **PortfolioHost** is the top-level portfolio object that is used to access portfolio state values when they are executed from a Portfolio Maestro (PM) Strategy Group. It gives programmatic access to many Properties of the Portfolio Maestro tool, if you are subscribed to it, within TS Platform.

There are no Events associated with the **PortfolioHost** Class.

> ☑ Portfolio objects are only for use with Portfolio Maestro and cannot be used with TS charts or other analysis tools.

NAMESPACE: PortfolioMaestro

PROPERTIES

	Name	Type	Description
📇	IsConnected	bool	True when Portfolio Maestro is connected.
📇	Portfolio	object	Accesses the PortfolioState properties for a strategy group in a portfolio.

TABLE 10.07—PortfolioHost Properties

METHODS

	Name	Description
◈	Create ()	Initializes a new instance of the class.

TABLE 10.08—PortfolioHost Methods

INHERITANCE HIERARCHY

elSystem.Object
  elSystem.DotNetObject
   elSystem.elComponent
    portfoliomaestro.PortfolioHost

EXAMPLE 10.04—Using the PortfolioHost [OME_PortfolioHost]

Sam says he has never had the opportunity or reason to use the **PortfolioHost** Class and has difficulty imagining a use. Since instantiating a member of this class will throw an error if it is not within Portfolio Maestro, and there is no reliable method to determine (using **GetAppInfo**) that this is an instance of Portfolio Maestro, he is at a loss for how to use this within any Strategy code—again, an example of not keeping up with the advances in TS—by several years.

In short, this class allows access to the Active Account Number in TS and monitors changes in the Account Number made by other components.

I believe you could try instantiating the class object and use a **Try…Catch** block to trap the resulting error. Who knows, I may have an "isPortfolioMaestro" User Function before this goes to press. If so, it will be in the download ELD file from www.EasyLanguageOOEL.com.

Nevertheless, ignoring Sam's grousing, here's an example of using the **PortfolioHost**. Note that this is a Strategy, not an Indicator.

```
Using elSystem ;
Using Platform ;
Using PortfolioMaestro ;
Using elSystem.IO ;

Inputs:
  String File_Spec ("C:\OME_Files\PMH.TXT") ;

Vars  :
 PortfolioHost  PMH (NULL),
 StreamWriter   SW  (NULL) ;

Vars  :
IntraBarPersist Bool  isPM  (FALSE) ;

// Working Storage Section

Consts:
 String App_Type    ("Strategy"),
 String App_Name    ("OME_PortfolioHost"),
 String App_Note    ("Sample code to demonstrate the creation and
execution of a PortfolioHost object"),
 String App_Vers    ("01.00.00") ;

Vars  :
 String DQ          (DoubleQuote),
 String NL          (NewLine),
 String CmtryStr    (""),
 String OrderStr    (""),
 Bool   doCmtry     (FALSE),
 Bool   Debug       (FALSE),
 Double Dummy       (0.00) ;

 // ======================================================

method void App_Init ()
```

```
begin
  Print ("App_Init") ;
  isPM  = skt_isPortfolioMaestro ;
// cannot reliably use GetSppinfo in this case
  if  isPM  then begin
    PMH  = Portfolio_Init () ;
  end ;
end ; // "App_Init" method

// -----------------------------------------------------------

method PortfolioHost Portfolio_Init ()
// PortfolioHost has no Events so I am not certain
// what to code...
Vars  :
 PortfolioHost myPMH ;
begin
  Print ("Portfolio_Init") ;
  myPMH  = PortfolioHost.Create () ;
  Return myPMH ;
end ; // "Portfolio_Init" method

// -----------------------------------------------------------

method void PM_Report ()
Vars  :
 StreamWriter SW ;
begin
  SW  = StreamWriter.Create (File_Spec,   TRUE) ;
  SW.WriteLine ("PM_Report") ;
  if  PMH.isConnected then begin
    SW.WriteLine ("PortfolioHost : isConnected = " + skt_Bool_Str
(PMH.isConnected) + ", Symbol = " + Symbol) ;
    SW.WriteLine ("Portfolio Property : ") ;
    SW.WriteLine ("PortfolioState : Includes Currency, Equity,
InitialCapital, Name, RealizedTrades, StrategyGroup, UnrealizedTrades,
Version.") ;
    SW.WriteLine ("PortfolioState : Currency = " +
PMH.Portfolio.Currency) ;
    SW.WriteLine ("PortfolioState : InitialCapital = $" + NumToStr
(PMH.Portfolio.InitialCapital, 02)) ;
    SW.WriteLine ("PortfolioState : Name  = " + PMH.Portfolio.Name) ;
    SW.WriteLine ("PortfolioState : RealizedTrades = " +
PMH.Portfolio.RealizedTrades.toString ()) ;
    SW.WriteLine ("PortfolioState : StrategyGroup = " +
PMH.Portfolio.StrategyGroup.toString ()) ;
    SW.WriteLine ("PortfolioState : UnrealizedTrades = " +
PMH.Portfolio.UnrealizedTrades.toString ()) ;
    SW.WriteLine ("PortfolioState : Version = " + NumToStr
(PMH.Portfolio.Version, 00) ;
  end
  else begin
    SW.WriteLine ("PortfolioHost not 'Connected' (to WHAT?).") ;
  end ;
  SW.Close () ;
end ; // "PM_Report" method

// ===========================================================

once begin
```

```
   App_Init () ;
   if  isPM  then begin
     PM_Report () ;
   end
   else begin
     Print (App_Name, " can only be used within Portfolio Maestro.") ;
   end ;
end ; // Once, and only once
```

The following figure shows some of the output from the **PortfolioHost** example, which went to the file specified: C:\OME_files\PMH.txt.

FIGURE 10.05—Portfolio Maestro Output from OME_PortfolioHost Example

RadarScreenHost Class (Component)

The **RadarScreenHost** allows access to mouse click events within a RadarScreen window, assuming you are subscribed to this feature. The event returns additional information from the event handler using the PlotClickEventArgs and CellClickEventArgs classes.

Note that the **RadarScreenHost** does not inherit the **elComponent** Class but it does inherit the **PlatformClientHost** Class.

NAMESPACE: Quote

EVENTS

	Name	Description
⚡	PlotClick	Occurs when a RadarScreen cell value is clicked. See PlotClickEventArgs for the properties returned by the handler's args parameter.

TABLE 10.09—RadarScreenHost Events

INHERITANCE HIERARCHY

elSystem.Object
  elSystem.DotNetObject
  elSystem.elComponent
   elSystem.Host
    platform.PlatformClientHost
     quote.RadarScreenHost

> ☑ One thing about the RadarScreenHost: you cannot click on the Symbol cell and trigger the event. It is described as a "static" cell and is not privy to normal operating procedures. In other words, it is impervious to mouse clicks as far as the RadarScreenHost is concerned.

OK, let us suppose our study plots an average, default on the close. We could write code so when you click on the **Open** column for any row (Symbol) each row recalculates using its respective **Open**. Of course, the concept extends to **High**, **Low**, **Close** etc.

For example, you could use the **GetAppInfo** function to determine the Row number of this specific symbol and test for that, rather than the symbol the way I did in my example.

EXAMPLE 10.05—RadarScreenHost [OME_RadarScreenHost]

This sample code demonstrates the creation and execution of a **RadarScreenHost** object. To illustrate its use, please apply it to a RS that has only a few symbols (10-20) and click on any of the cells to the right of the symbol column. The events triggered will be displayed in the Print Log. If you hold down the SHIFT, CTRL or ALT key it will report that in the Print Log as well.

```
{*
One note about the RadarScreenHost that I recently discovered is that
you can click in any cell except the Symbol (Column one). That is
described as a 'static' cell and is not privy to normal operating
procedures. In other words, it is impervious to mouse clicks as far as
the RSHost is concerned.
  Why the RadarScreen Generates an event for every row/symbol in the
window is (was) a mystery to me, I had really assumed it was specific
to one row. Silly me!
*}
Using elSystem ;
Using Platform ;
Using Quote ;

Vars  :
 RadarScreenHost  RSH (NULL) ;

Vars  :
IntraBarPersist Int EventCount (00),
IntraBarPersist Int AppType    (00),
IntraBarPersist Int ActiveRow  (00) ; /
/ row within RadarScreen, this symbol

// Working Storage Section
Inputs:
 Bool   ShowCmtry    (FALSE) ;

Consts:
 String App_Type     ("Study"),
 String App_Name     ("OME_RadarScreenHost"),
 String App_Note     ("Sample code to demonstrate the creation and
execution of a RadarScreenHost object"),
 String App_Vers     ("01.01.00") ;

Vars  :
 String DQ           (DoubleQuote),
 String NL           (NewLine),
 Bool   Debug        (FALSE),
 Double Dummy        (0.00) ;

// ========================================================

method void App_Init ()
```

```
begin
  Print ("App_Init") ;
  AppType    = GetAppInfo (aiApplicationType) ;
  if  AppType  = cRadarScreen  then begin
    ActiveRow  = GetAppInfo (aiRow) ;
    RSH = RadarScreen_Init () ;
  end
  else begin
    Print ("You may only create a RadarScreenHost within a RadarScreen
window.") ;
  end ;
end ; // "App_Init" method

// ----------------------------------------------------------

method RadarScreenHost RadarScreen_Init ()
Vars  :
 RadarScreenHost myRSH ;
begin
  Print ("RadarScreen_Init") ;
  myRSH  = RadarScreenHost.Create () ;
  myRSH.PlotClick += RSH_PlotClick ;
  Return myRSH ;
end ; // "RadarScreen_Init" method

// ----------------------------------------------------------

method void RSH_PlotClick (elSystem.Object sender,
quote.PlotClickEventArgs args)
// the PlotClick Event is triggered
// for EVERY member of the RadarScreen
// NOT JUST the row you click on, so one must filter
// the response.
begin
// either way works
//  if  args.Symbol  = Symbol  then begin
  if args.Row  = ActiveRow  then begin
    EventCount += 01 ;
    Print ("RSH_PlotClick Sym=", DQ + Symbol + DQ + ", Cnt=",
EventCount:2:0, ", CBar=", CurrentBar:2:0) ;

    Print ("CellClickEventArgs : Column = ", args.Column, ", Row = ",
args.Row, ", Symbol = ", args.Symbol, ", Value = ",
args.Value.toString ()) ;
    Print ("ClickEventArgs : Button = ", args.Button.toString (), ",
isKeyDown = ", args.isKeyDown [Key.Shift], ", isReadOnly = ",
args.isReadOnly, ", Value = ", args.Value.toString ()) ;
    Print ("KeyDown : Is the Alt key down? ", args.isKeyDown
[Key.Alt], ", Shift Key? ", args.isKeyDown [Key.Shift], ", Control
Key? ", args.isKeyDown [Key.Control]) ;
    Print ("PlotClickEventArgs : BooleanValue, DateVal, DoubleValue,
FormatStyle, IntegerVal, PlotName, PlotNumber, StringVal, StudyName,
Type") ;
    Print ("PlotClickEventArgs : FormatStyle = ",
args.FormatStyle.toString (), ", PlotName = ", args.PlotName.toString
(), ", PlotNumber = ", args.PlotNumber.toString (), ", StudyName = ",
args.StudyName.toString (), ", Type = ", args.Type.toString ()) ;
    // Print ("Data Types:  Type = ", args.Type.toString (),
args.BooleanValue.toString(), args.DateValue.toString(),
args.DoubleValue.toString(), args.IntegerValue.toString(),
```

```
args.StringValue.toString()) ;
    if args.Type = NativeDataType.BooleanVal then Print
("BooleanValue : ", args.BooleanValue.toString ()) ;
    if args.Type = NativeDataType.DateVal then Print
("DateValue    : ", args.DateValue  .toString (), ", ",
args.DateValue.ELDateTimeEx) ;
    if args.Type = NativeDataType.DoubleVal then Print
("DoubleValue  : ", args.DoubleValue .toString ()) ;
    if args.Type = NativeDataType.IntegerVal then Print
("IntegerValue : ", args.IntegerValue.toString ()) ;
    if args.Type = NativeDataType.StringVal then Print
("StringValue  : ", args.StringValue .toString ()) ;
  end
  else begin
    Print ("args.Symbol (" + DQ + args.Symbol + DQ + ") is NOT my
Symbol (", DQ + Symbol + DQ + ")!") ;
  end ;
end ; // "RSH_PlotClick" method

// =============================================================

once begin
  App_Init () ;
end ; // Once, and only once


Plot1 (InsideBar (High, Low),        "Boolean", Default) ;
Plot2 (Date,                         "Date",    Default) ;
Plot3 (Time,                         "Time",    Default) ;
Plot4 (Close,                        "Price",   Default) ;
Plot5 (RSI  (Close, 14),             "Double",  Default) ;
Plot6 (DayOfWeek (Date),             "Integer", Default) ;
Plot7 (skt_Month_Name (Month (Date)), "String", Default) ;

#beginCmtry
if CheckCommentary and ShowCmtry then begin
  CommentaryCL (skt_Commentary_Header (App_Type, App_Name, App_Note,
App_Vers)) ;

end ; // expert Commentary enabled for this bar
#end
```

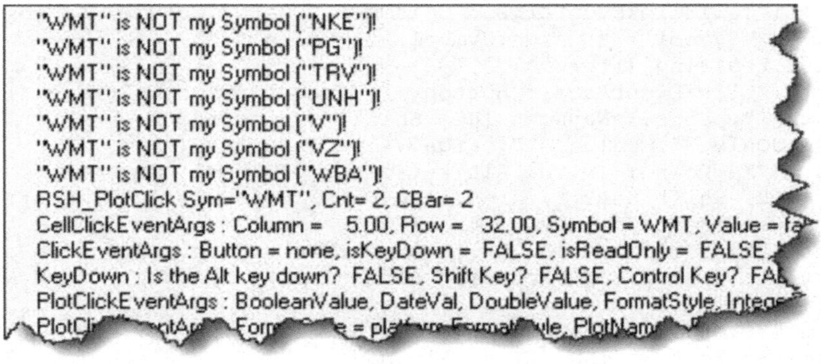

```
"WMT" is NOT my Symbol ["NKE"]!
"WMT" is NOT my Symbol ["PG"]!
"WMT" is NOT my Symbol ["TRV"]!
"WMT" is NOT my Symbol ["UNH"]!
"WMT" is NOT my Symbol ["V"]!
"WMT" is NOT my Symbol ["VZ"]!
"WMT" is NOT my Symbol ["WBA"]!
RSH_PlotClick Sym="WMT", Cnt= 2, CBar= 2
CellClickEventArgs : Column =  5.00, Row =  32.00, Symbol = WMT, Value = fa
ClickEventArgs : Button = none, isKeyDown = FALSE, isReadOnly = FALSE
KeyDown : Is the Alt key down? FALSE, Shift Key? FALSE, Control Key? FA
PlotClickEventArgs : BooleanValue, DateVal, DoubleValue, FormatStyle, Intege
PlotCli        ntAr   For        e = pla      Format  le, PlotNam
```

FIGURE 10.06—Print Log Output for RadarScreenHost

Symbol △	Interval	Last	Net Chg	Net %Chg	OME_RadarScreenHost						
					Boolean	Date	Time	Price	Double	Integer	String
Dow Jones Industrial Average											
RBLX	Daily	39.80	-0.04	-0.10%	FALSE	07/25/22	09:00:00 PM	39.16	47.580	1	July
$INDU	Daily	31,761.54	-228.46	-0.71%	FALSE	07/26/22	01:00:00 PM	31,761.54	60.657	2	July
WMT	Daily	122.38	-9.64	-7.30%	FALSE	07/25/22	09:00:00 PM	118.90	38.524	1	July
WBA	Daily	38.85	0.10	0.26%	FALSE	07/25/22	09:00:00 PM	38.22	47.852	1	July
DIS	Daily	100.95	-1.74	-1.69%	FALSE	07/25/22	09:00:00 PM	102.06	60.844	1	July
IBM	Daily	128.40	-0.14	-0.11%	FALSE	07/25/22	09:00:00 PM	128.10	30.713	1	July
HD	Daily	299.78	-6.37	-2.08%	FALSE	07/25/22	09:00:00 PM	300.49	75.864	1	July
ON	Daily	59.00	-0.34	-0.57%	FALSE	07/25/22	09:00:00 PM	58.99	78.360	1	July
MCD	Daily	256.80	6.42	2.56%	FALSE	07/25/22	09:00:00 PM	249.89	44.652	1	July
UNH	Daily	531.59	2.12	0.40%	FALSE	07/25/22	09:00:00 PM	528.71	60.583	1	July
HON	Daily	181.81	0.55	0.30%	TRUE	07/25/22	09:00:00 PM	181.00	68.837	1	July
MMM	Daily	141.00	6.88	5.13%	FALSE	07/25/22	09:00:00 PM	134.12	67.803	1	July
TSLA	Daily	787.00	-18.30	-2.27%	FALSE	07/25/22	09:00:00 PM	805.30	71.821	1	July
NKE	Daily	106.20	-3.08	-2.82%	FALSE	07/25/22	09:00:00 PM	107.40	55.983	1	July
TRV	Daily	160.86	0.88	0.55%	FALSE	07/25/22	09:00:00 PM	159.98	36.854	1	July
KO	Daily	63.13	0.94	1.51%	FALSE	07/25/22	09:00:00 PM	62.34	42.193	1	July
ESM22	Daily	3,667.50	3.74	0.10%	TRUE	06/17/22	02:00:00 PM	3,663.76	20.635	5	June
PG	Daily	144.27	0.28	0.19%	FALSE	07/25/22	09:00:00 PM	143.59	46.263	1	July
JNJ	Daily	173.68	1.22	0.71%	FALSE	07/25/22	09:00:00 PM	172.45	31.775	1	July
INTC	Daily	38.95	-0.21	-0.54%	FALSE	07/25/22	09:00:00 PM	39.27	67.720	1	July

FIGURE 10.07—RadarScreenHost with Plots

StrategyHost Class (Component)

The **StrategyHost** Class defines the structure for a **StrategyHost** object. The **StrategyHost** Class enables you to access much of the information from the dialog boxes used to customize your Strategy. It has some other neat features such as listing all Strategies available and listing all the Inputs for any Strategy you select, assuming you wrote the code to do so.

Sam has code for this, but it is too involved for this book. If you want access to it, it is extensive and is available for sale. You can purchase it on www.EasyLanguageOOEL.com at a very reasonable price.

NAMESPACE: Strategy

PROPERTIES

	Name	Type	Description
▤	Automation	object	References the values and settings related to the strategy automation settings. See **StrategyAutomation** in **Volume II** for properties.
▤	Backtesting	object	References the values and settings related to the strategy backtesting settings. See **StrategyBacktesting** in **Volume II** for properties.
▤	Connect	bool	True to open the connection to the strategy host events, otherwise False.
▤	Signals	object	References the signals associated with the strategies applied to the current chart. See **SignalList** in **Volume II** for properties.
▤	Strategies	object	References the strategies applied to the current chart. See **StrategyList** in **Volume II** for properties.

TABLE 10.10—StrategyHost Properties

METHODS

	Name	Description
⬥	Create ()	Initializes a new instance of the class

TABLE 10.11—StrategyHost Methods

EVENTS

	Name	Description
⚡	NewOrder	Occurs just after a strategy generates an order. This allows you to review your order and execute additional code, if desired, based on the order. See **StrategyNewOrderEventArgs** in **Volume II** for the properties returned by the handler's args parameter.
⚡	OrderFill	Occurs just after a strategy order is marked filled. This allows you to review your strategy position and execute additional code, if desired, based on the fill. See **StrategyFillOrderEventArgs** in **Volume II** for the properties returned by the handler's args parameter.
⚡	PreNewOrder	Occurs just before a strategy executes a specific order statement. This allows you to review your order values and execute additional code, if desired, before the strategy order is generated. See **StrategyNewOrderEventArgs in Volume II** for the properties returned by the handler's args parameter.
⚡	PrefillOrder	Occurs just before a strategy order is marked as filled. This allows you to review your fill assumptions and execute additional code, if desired, before the fill occurs. See **StrategyFillOrderEventArgs** in **Volume II** for the properties returned by the handler's args parameter.

TABLE 10.12—StrategyHost Events

INHERITANCE HIERARCHY

```
elSystem.Object
 elSystem.DotNetObject
  elSystem.elComponent
   strategy.StrategyHost
```

EXAMPLE 10.06—StrategyHost Example [OME_StrategyHost]

This code demonstrates the use of a **StrategyHost** to track new and filled orders. Further, it enters BarNumber shares for the order. I know, it's just a pretend strategy; who would want to place an order for "BarNumber" shares?

```
using elSystem ;
using Strategy ;

Vars  :
 StrategyHost SH          (NULL),
 SignalList    TheSigList (NULL),
 Signal        TheSignal  (NULL) ;

Vars  :
IntraBarPersist
 int    SignalNdx (00) ;

Consts:
 String Dt_Tm_FmtStr  ("%m/%d/%Y  %H:%M") ;
```

```
// Working Storage
Vars  :
 String App_Type   ("Strategy"),
 String App_Name   ("OME_StrategyHost"),
 String App_Note   ("Why do the NewOrder and FillOrder get hit
twice?"),
 String App_Vers   ("01.03.00") ;
Vars  :
 String CmtryStr   (""),
 String DQ         (DoubleQuote),
 String NL         (NewLine),
 Bool   DoCmtry    (FALSE),
 Bool   Debug      ( TRUE),
 Double Dummy      (0.00) ;

// =======================================================

method void App_Init ()
begin
  Print ("App_Init()") ;
  SH = New StrategyHost ;
  SH.Connect    =  TRUE ;
  TheSigList    = SH.Signals asType SignalList ;
  SH.NewOrder  += SH_NewOrder ;
  SH.OrderFill += SH_OrderFill ;
end ; // "App_Init" method

// -------------------------------------------------------

// Method fired when an order is filled
method void SH_OrderFill (elSystem.Object sender,
strategy.StrategyFillOrderEventArgs args)
begin
  Print (args.Date.Format (Dt_Tm_FmtStr),
" SH_OrderFill (", OrderDirection_toStr (args.OrderDirection),
", ", args.SignalIndex:1:0, ", ", args.Quantity:1:0,
",", args.AvgPrice, ",", args.TargetPrice, ")") ;
end ; // "SH_OrderFill" method

// -------------------------------------------------------

// Method fired when there is a new order
method void SH_NewOrder (elSystem. Object sender,
strategy.StrategyNewOrderEventArgs args)
begin
  Print (BarDateTime.Format (Dt_Tm_FmtStr),
" SH_NewOrder (", OrderDirection_toStr (args.OrderDirection),
", ", args.SignalIndex:1:0, ", ", args.RequestedQty:1:0,
",", args.TargetPrice, ") ", ) ;
end ; // "SH_NewOrder" method

// -------------------------------------------------------

method string OrderDirection_toStr (StrategyOrderDirection
myOrderDirection)
vars  :
 Bool   Debug,
 String myStr ;
begin
  Debug   = FALSE ; // suppress output
```

```
      if   Debug   then   Print ("OrderDirection_toStr (",
                         myOrderDirection.toString (), ")") ;
    switch   myOrderDirection   begin // StrategyOrderDirection
      case StrategyOrderDirection.unknown      {-01} :
        myStr  = "unknown" ;
      case StrategyOrderDirection.Buy          {+00} :
        myStr  = "Buy" ;
      case StrategyOrderDirection.Sell         {+01} :
        myStr  = "Sell" ;
      case StrategyOrderDirection.SellShort   {+02} :
        myStr  = "SellShort" ;
      case StrategyOrderDirection.BuyToCover {+03} :
        myStr  = "BuyToCover" ;
      Default                                    :
        myStr  = "Unknown" ;
    end ; // switch/case statement
    Return myStr ;
  end ; // "OrderDirection_toStr" method

  // ========================================================

  once begin
    App_Init () ;
    Print ;
    Print ("Initialization Complete (once begin)...Sym=", DQ, Symbol,
  DQ,
   ", ", DQ, skt_DataCompress_Str (DataCompression, BarInterval), DQ,
   ", BInt=", BarInterval:2:0, ", DComp=", DataCompression:2:0) ;
    Print ;
  end ; // first bar of data

  DoCmtry   = AtCommentaryBar ;
  if  DoCmtry  then  CmtryStr  = "" ;

  if  MarketPosition <  +01  then begin
    Buy         ("le.BNum") CurrentBar contracts next bar at High +
  TrueRange stop ;
  end ;
  if  MarketPosition  > -01  then begin
    Sell Short ("se.BNum") CurrentBar contracts next bar at  Low -
  TrueRange stop ;
  end ;

  if  (MarketPosition  = +01)  then begin
    if  (BarsSinceEntry <= 01)  then begin
    end ; // first bar of trade
  //Sell to Cover  ("lx.Cover") next bar at market ;
  //Sell to Cover  ("lx.Cover") next bar at market ;
  end ; // currently long

  if  (MarketPosition  = -01)  then begin
    if  (BarsSinceEntry <= 01)  then begin
    end ; // first bar of trade
  //Buy to Cover ("lx.Cover") next bar at market ;
  end ; // currently short

  #beginCmtry
  Inputs: ShowCmtry (FALSE) ;

  if  CheckCommentary and ShowCmtry  then begin
    CommentaryCL (skt_Commentary_Header (App_Type, App_Name, App_Note,
```

```
App_Vers),
                     skt_Commentary_Notes  (CmtryStr)) ;

end ; // expert Commentary enabled for this bar
#end
```

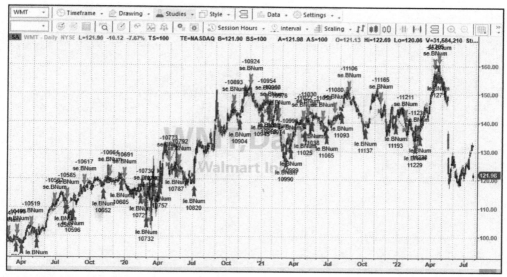

FIGURE 10.08—StrategyHost Example on a Chart

And next we have the printed output from the **StrategyHost** Example

```
07/22/2022   13:00  SH_NewOrder (Buy, 0, 13676,  76.00)
07/22/2022   13:00  SH_NewOrder (BuyToCover, 0, 13669,  76.00)
07/22/2022   13:00  SH_NewOrder (Buy, 0, 13676,  76.00)
07/25/2022   13:00  SH_OrderFill (BuyToCover, 0, 13669,  76.00,
76.00)
07/25/2022   13:00  SH_OrderFill (Buy, 0, 13676,  76.00,  76.00)
07/25/2022   13:00  SH_NewOrder (Sell, 1, 13676,  71.78)
07/25/2022   13:00  SH_NewOrder (SellShort, 1, 13677,  71.78)
07/25/2022   13:00  SH_NewOrder (Sell, 1, 13676,  71.78)
07/25/2022   13:00  SH_NewOrder (SellShort, 1, 13677,  71.78)
```

FIGURE 10.09—Output to the Print Log from the StrategyHost Strategy

Summary

In this chapter we have explored some of the **Host** classes including **ChartingHost**, **RadarScreenHost** and **PortfolioHost** and found various ways to manipulate objects of these classes in interesting, if not particularly useful, ways. The purpose of our sample code is to introduce you to what is there, what **Properties** and **Methods** are available and to start you thinking about ways you can make use of them for yourself. Once you know what the potential is your imagination can begin to devise great feats of derring-do which you will accomplish on your own. Use your imagination, have some fun and write some code. At first you might modify the examples we have provided and over time, you will be searching for even more ways you can manipulate these tools.

The **ChartingHost** Class in probably the most versatile of the **Host** Classes allowing you to catch mouse events and manipulate the objects on the chart. The other **Host** Class examples are so you can see how to set them up and learn from the code.

CHAPTER 11

Forms

In This Chapter

- Introduction
- Form Class
- Using WinForms Classes
- More About Control Classes
- Container Classes
- Adding a Form to Your EZL Code
- About the ToolBox
- About the Resource Editor
- Component Classes
- ContainerControl Class
- Control Class
- Adding a Form
- Editing a Form
- Summary

Introduction

The Resource Editor is useful for prototyping code, designing forms, positioning Controls where they look good and more. One caveat, either back up to ELD file, or save version control copies, frequently. I am a programmer and I want to make my code more readable. On way too many instances I have made some change, usually renaming something in the TDE, and found that my code now generates an error in the Read-Only DGC (Designer Generated Code).

You may find this is all you need. I know some programmers who never use the Resource Editor, writing all the code by hand (this is what Sam does for everything except **Forms**). I know some who use it start to finish. I use an alternate method.

I create my initial code (Study, Strategy or TradingApp) with 'Sandbox' appended to the name. Very frequently I copy the DGC and paste it within a comment block at the bottom of my code. When I get to the point, I no longer need to adjust control locations I create a NEW file, NOT 'Save As', of the same name omitting the 'Sandbox' portion. I copy and paste in the 'Sandbox' code. I now have a virgin body of code with no DGC in it. Now I copy (cut), block by block, the DGC from the comment at the bottom and paste it into the code body above. Eventually I am left with an empty comment block which I can delete. I have a dozen or so User Functions I have created, and I go through and replace, paragraph by paragraph, the voluminous generated code with my one line 'Button Create' or 'Checkbox Create' User Functions. This saves me hundreds or thousands of lines of code to scroll through. I also create a table of **Constants** for all the control settings such as Name, Text, Width, Height, XLoc, YLoc etc. that are required to create the controls. Now I can replicate one block of constants and add in X-more Labels, Y more TextBoxes, or whatever. Editing the XLoc and/or YLoc of these new objects, I find, is far easier and faster than struggling with the mouse to get them all aligned and labeled with meaningful names.

Form Class

The **Form** Class allows you to display a custom form window or dialog box as part of a TS AT, strategy, or TA.

NAMESPACE: elSystem.Windows.Forms

> ☑ If you create a Form in TS 10, or modify the form using the Resource Editor using TS 10, then the DGC will most likely not be usable on TS 9.5 unless you follow the process of removing the DGC and coding around the changes required.

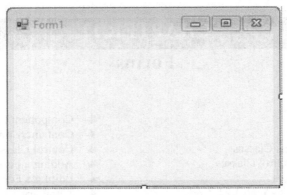

FIGURE 11.01—An Empty Form

PROPERTIES

	Name	Type	Description
	AcceptButton	object	Gets or sets the button object on the form that is clicked when the user presses the Enter key, regardless of which other control on the form has the focus. Note that the AcceptButton might not be activated if the currently selected control on the form intercepts the ENTER key and processes it. For example, a multiline text box control allows the Enter key to be pressed when it is selected to insert a new line character in the control.
	AutoScaleFactor	object	Gets the value indicating the automatic scaling being performed on a windows form. This reflects the factoring that needs to be performed on the controls based upon the Windows text sizing being "smaller", "medium", or "larger". If a form can resize TS automatically handles the refactoring of the form controls.
	CancelButton	object	Gets or sets the button control that is clicked when the user presses the ESC key.
	ClientSize	object	Gets or sets the size of the client area of the form.
	ControlBox	bool	True when a control box is displayed in the caption bar of the form.
	FormBorderStyle	enum	Gets or sets the border style of the form. See **FormBorderStyle** under **Form Class** for a list of possible values.
	Margin	object	Reserved for future use.
	MaximizeBox	bool	True indicates that the Maximize button is enabled in the caption bar of the form.
	MaximumSize	object	Gets or sets the maximum size to which the form can be resized.
	MinimizeBox	bool	True indicates that the Minimize button is enabled in the caption bar of the form.
	MinimumSize	object	Gets or sets the minimum size to which the form can be resized.

	Name	Type	Description
🖼️	Position	object	Gets or sets a Point object identifying the location of the upper left corner of the form in screen coordinates.
🖼️	RightToLeftLayout	bool	True when the form displays child controls from right-to-left.
🖼️	TabIndex	int	Not applicable to a form. (TS >= 10)
🖼️	TabStop	bool	Not applicable to a form. (TS >= 10)
🖼️	ToolTip	object	Represents a ToolTip object which is a small rectangular pop-up window that displays a brief description of a control's purpose when the user rests the pointer on the control. Note that the ToolTip object is automatically created. (TS >= 10)
🖼️	TopMost	bool	True when the form is to be displayed always-on-top of other windows.
🖼️	Visible	bool	True to make the form visible. False to hide it.
🖼️	WindowState	enum	Gets or sets the state of the window. See **FormWindowState** for a list of possible values.

TABLE 11.01—Form Class Properties

METHODS

	Name	Description
◆	Activate ()	Activates the form and gives it focus.
◆	Create ()	Creates a new instance of a form.
◆	Create (text, width, height)	Creates a new instance of a form. Parameters include the Text to appear on the title bar followed by the Width and Height of the control.
◆	Location (x, y)	Sets the coordinates of the upper-left corner of the control relative to the upper-left corner of its container.
◆	RemoveGradient ()	Removes the gradient.
◆	ResumeLayout ()	Resumes usual layout logic.
◆	SetLinearGradient (mode, startColor, endColor)	Creates a linear gradient listview background. See **LinearGradientMode** and **Color** for lists of possible values.
◆	SetRadialGradient (startColor, endColor)	Creates a radial gradient listview background. See **Color** for a list of possible values.
◆	Show ()	Displays the form.
◆	SuspendLayout ()	Temporarily suspends the layout logic for the control.

TABLE 11.02—Form Class Methods

EVENTS

> ☑ See EventArgs for the properties returned, if any, by the event handler's args parameter unless otherwise indicated.

	Name	Description
⚡	Activated	Occurs when the form is activated. (TS >= 10)
⚡	DockChanged	Occurs when the dock property of the form has changed.
⚡	FormClosed	Reserved for future use. See **FormClosedEventArgs** for event-specific properties.
⚡	FormClosing	Occurs when an undocked form is in the process of closing. See **FormClosingEventArgs** for event-specific properties
⚡	Resize	Occurs when a form is resized. See **EventArgs** for the properties returned by the handler's args parameter.
⚡	ResizeBegin	Occurs when a form resizing operation starts.
⚡	ResizeEnd	Occurs when a form resizing operation finishes.
⚡	Shown	Occurs when a form is shown. (TS >= 10)

TABLE 11.03—Form Class Events

INHERITANCE HIERARCHY

elSystem.Object
  elSystem.DotNetObject
   elSystem.elComponent
    elSystem.Windows.Forms.ELWFComponent
     elSystem.Windows.Forms.Control
      elSystem.Windows.Forms.ContainerControl
      elSystem.Windows.Forms.Form

Using WinForms Classes

The OOEL Classes contained in the WinForms Library allow you to create free-standing windows as part of an AT. Everything in the **winforms.ell** library is a control, at least as far as the topics we will cover in this chapter go. There are other things like **AnchorStyle**, **BorderRadius**, **AxisType** and more but we will not be covering them herein. The complete coverage of the more esoteric features of **Forms** will be covered in our next book, probably entitled something along the lines of "EasyLanguage OOEL Forms Made Easy!"

All the things from the ToolBox, which we can add to a **Form**, are Controls. Containers are used to group things like radio button and checkbox controls. Further, containers can be inside containers. The list of possibilities is endless and limited only by your imagination.

Containers (such as **Form**, **GroupBox**, **TabControl**, **TabPage** or **Panel**) are used to group and display controls (such as **Button**, **Label**, **NumericUpDown**, **ComboBox**, and more). The properties for each container and control object are accessed through OOEL either by making changes to your code or by using the Resource Editor and the Properties Editor. Consider the possibilities of grouping sections of your form to maneuver them more easily out of the way and then back in place again.

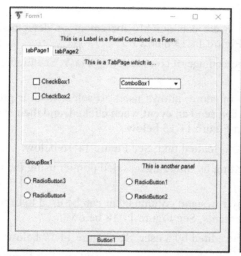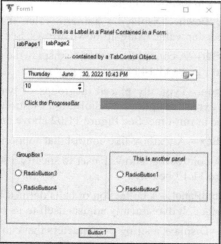

FIGURE 11.02—A Form with 2 Tabs and All the Pieces and Parts [OME_ContainerClass_DGC]

The code for the example in Figure 11.02 above is presented after all the controls are defined. Put a sticky note on this page because we will refer back to this Figure often.

Control Classes

To study these classes in their fullness please open **Volume II—Reference Guide** to the Classes section in **Appendix III** where they are all detailed. For the purposes of this chapter, we are only going to cover the simpler classes: **Button**, **CheckBox**, **RadioButton**, and **DataGridView**. Nevertheless, they are all listed below. We will leave those we don't cover in this chapter for the next book we write, which will cover all the elements of **Forms** and will be a more reasonable length. And might be titled something like *OOEL Forms Made Easy!*

The Classes for all the elements below may be found in **Volume II Reference Guide: Appendix III**.

Button—A push button that responds to a user's click by sending an event to the calling Analysis Technique. See Figure 11.02 above and Figure 11.03 below.

Chart—A chart that can be added to a Form or Panel for display of user-supplied data. See Figure 11.04 below.

CheckBox—A small box that can be checked or unchecked by the user. When clicked the **CheckBox** Object sends an event allowing the Analysis Technique to review the checked or unchecked state. See Figure 11.05 below.

ComboBox—Presents a list of items to a user from a drop-down list and sends an event when a selection is made. See Figure 11.02 above and Figure 11.06 below.

DataGridView—A grid that contains columns and rows. Which may contain numbers, strings and other objects. See Figure 11.07 below.

DateTimePicker—Displays a calendar control allowing users to conveniently select a date but if you want a time then you need to type it in via a custom format to a string value. See Figure 11.02 above.

FastSymbolLookupComboBox—A type of ComboBox that's useful for selecting stock, futures, or other asset symbols. As of this writing it appears to be nonfunctional and generates a fatal error. See Figure 11.09 below.

Label—Displays non-editable text on form. Labels can be used to provide descriptions or identify surrounding controls. See Figure 11.10 below.

LinkLabel—A control that acts like a hyperlink. See Figure 11.11 below.

ListView—Displays a collection of text items in a multi-column format. They send an event when a selection is made. See Figure 11.12 below.

NumericUpDown—Displays a numeric value that users can quickly increment or decrement at a predefined step value using up-down arrows. See Figure 11.13 below.

ProgressBar—A control that's used to display the percentage of completion of a task. See Figure 11.02 above and Figure 11.14 below.

RadioButton—Typically placed in groups of two or more, allows users to select from a group of mutually exclusive options. RadioButton Controls can send an event when clicked, and their state can be queried at run-time. See Figure 11.02 above and Figure 11.15 below.

RichTextBox—A textbox-like control that supports formatted text. See Figure 11.16 below.

Slider—A control that allows a user to specify a setting by dragging a scaled pointer using the mouse. See Figure 11.17 below.

TableLayoutPanel—A collection of cells defined by rows and columns that can be used to organize a user interface. It dynamically adjusts itself to its contents. See Figure 11.18 below.

TextBox—Displays a string of characters that can be edited by a user. See Figure 11.19 below.

WebBrowser—A control used to allow navigation to a web site from a user interface. See Figure 11.20 below.

WebView2—A Chromium-based alternative to the **WebBrowser** Control; useful for providing a browser interface to modern web sites. See Figure 11.21 below.

More About Control Classes

Here we have a bit more explanation and an example of each of the Control Classes so you can visualize them. Rather than list all of the individual Inheritance Hierarchies, Methods, Properties and Events with each example I refer you to **Volume II—Reference Guide** for details.

Button

Displays a push button control within a container in a form. A **Click** event is fired when the button is clicked.

The name of the button and size are specified when the object is instantiated using the Create Method.

NAMESPACE: elSystem.Windows.Forms

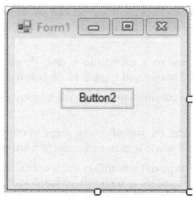

FIGURE 11.03—A Button in a Form

Chart

Serves as the root class of the **Chart** Control. To utilize the **Chart** Control, create it and add it to a form. Additionally, you will need to create one or more **ChartAreas** to define the areas where plotting will take place. You will also need to create one or more **ChartSeries**, which define the data to be displayed in the **ChartArea**. Optionally, axes and legends can be added.

NAMESPACE: elSystem.Windows.Forms

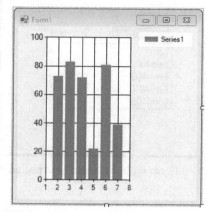

FIGURE 11.04—A Chart in a Form

CheckBox

Displays a **CheckBox** with associated text (optional) and allows you to toggle a check mark on/off. You may group check boxes, but unlike the **RadioButton** class, you may make multiple **CheckBox** selections within a group.

NAMESPACE: elSystem.Windows.Forms

While a grouped set of **RadioButton** Objects will toggle one off when you click the other, multiple check boxes can be checked.

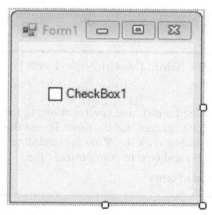

FIGURE 11.05—A Checkbox in a Form

ComboBox

A **ComboBox** contains a drop-down list of items (that you need to specify in your code). It is beneficial in your form for allowing the selection of pre-defined items.

NAMESPACE: elSystem.Windows.Forms

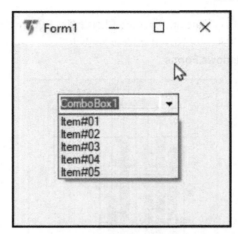

FIGURE 11.06—A ComboBox in a Form with the Selections pulled down.

DataGridView

The **DataGridView** Control allows you to display data in a tabular format. Similar to most controls, you start by creating a DataGridView and adding it to the form. Columns and rows can then be added using the **DataGridViewColumn** and **DataGridViewRow** classes. See Figure 11.07 below. [OME_DGV]

NAMESPACE: elSystem.Windows.Forms

	Default(TextBox)	Default(TextBox)
▶	0	1
	1	2
	2	3
	3	4
*		

FIGURE 11.07—A DataGridView [OME_DataGridView_Ex#01]

DateTimePicker

The **DateTimePicker** displays a calendar and time control allowing users to conveniently select a date and type in a time. Sorry, there is no "picker" for the time. To use this control simply use your arrow keys to scroll down the date and time or click the ▼ on the control to set dates and times. For the time field, you can also click on the field and type in your desired time.

NAMESPACE: elSystem.Windows.Forms

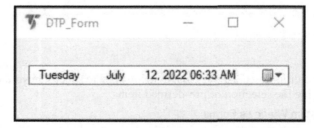

FIGURE 11.08—DateTimePicker in a Form [OME_Form_DateTimePicker]

FastSymbolLookupComboBox

Allows you to display a custom **ComboBox** that supports easy selection of symbols of the specified category. While the code for this example is available on www.EasyLanguageOOEL.com it comes with a caveat: at the time of this writing: it locks up TS. Buyer beware. We have turned in the error to TS, but it has not been fixed yet.

NAMESPACE: elSystem.Windows.Forms

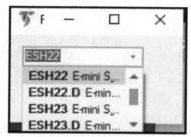

FIGURE 11.09—FastSymbolLookupComboBox in a Form [OME_FastSymbolLookupComboxBox]

☑ This example only works in TS version 10.0 or greater.

Label

Allows you to display a text string within a little box in a form (the little box is only visible in the Resource Editor). The default position for the box is Top Left. The text will wrap within the specified width and height of the control. Clipping will occur if the text wraps outside the specified width and height boundaries of the little box. The **TableLayoutPanel** below shows an example of a **Label**.

NAMESPACE: elSystem.Windows.Forms

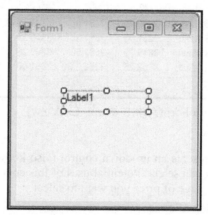

FIGURE 11.10—A Label in a Form

LinkLabel

The **LinkLabel** Class allows you to display text as a hyperlink. When clicked, the corresponding executable file or URL is run. Link color and color-after-visited may be set in your code.

NAMESPACE: elSystem.Windows.Forms

FIGURE 11.11—A LinkLabel in a Form

ListView

The **ListView** Class allows you to display a collection of items in a multi-column format. Header text can be included at the top of a column along with the ability to specify the width and horizontal alignment of each column.

NAMESPACE: elSystem.Windows.Forms

Unused	Date	Time	Open	High	Low	Close	Volume	
	07/06/2022	08:55pm	3850.75	3851.00	3849.75	3851.00	198	
	07/06/2022	09:00pm	3851.00	3851.25	3849.25	3849.50	142	
	07/06/2022	09:05pm	3849.75	3852.50	3849.25	3852.25	330	
	07/06/2022	09:10pm	3852.25	3853.25	3851.00	3851.00	141	

FIGURE 11.12—A ListView in a Form [OME_Form_ListView]

NumericUpDown

The **NumericUpDown** Class represents an up-down control (also known as a spin box) that displays numeric values from which you can select. Potential uses of this control include the number of bars, the number of ticks or the percentage of price you want to select.

NAMESPACE: elSystem.Windows.Forms

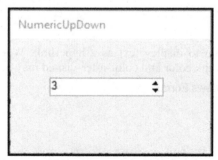

FIGURE 11.13—A NumericUpDown Control in a Form [OME_Form_NumericUpDown]

ProgressBar

The **ProgressBar** form control offers visual feedback on the progress of a long running process. Once created and added to a form or other control, the Minimum and Maximum properties can be set and then the Value property, some value between the Minimum and Maximum, is updated at various points throughout the calculation. Once the calculation is complete, it can be hidden, if used again, or destroyed if unwanted.

The Figure below shows a **ProgressBar** as it appears on a Form. To see a "fully formed" **ProgressBar** take a look at Figure 11.02—A Form with 2 Tabs and All the Pieces and Parts above. Clearly, since this isn't video, you can't see it moving and turning colors as it progresses, but when you add the indicator to your chart and the form appears, by clicking on it, it will show you the progress. See Figure 11.02.

NAMESPACE: elSystem.Windows.Forms

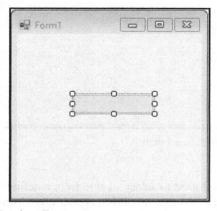

FIGURE 11.14—A ProgressBar in a Form

RadioButton

The **RadioButton** class is a form control that allows the user to select a single option from a group of choices when combined with other **RadioButton** controls. Unlike the **CheckBox** class, you may make only a single selection within a group of radiobuttons.

The Figure below shows a single **GroupBox** containing the **RadioButtons**. Figure 11.02—All the Pieces and Parts, shows two separate containers each with RadioButtons. The single action nature of these buttons in separate containers act alone. That is, the buttons in one container do not interact with the buttons in the other container.

NAMESPACE: elSystem.Windows.Forms

FIGURE 11.15—A Set of Radio Buttons in a GroupBox in a Form

RichTextBox

Supposedly the **RichTextBox** Class allows the user to display a rich-text string within a control in a form that can be edited by the user. Rich Text, as opposed to Plain Text, allows for formatting, images, colors and other markup. Rich Text is the default format of MS Word and even HTML. However, and this has also been reported to TS Engineering, it won't accept Rich Text at this time.

NAMESPACE: elSystem.Windows.Forms

FIGURE 11.16—A RichTextBox in a Form

Slider

The **Slider** class is a form control used to select a value from a defined range by dragging a "thumb" along a horizontal or vertical bar. To use the Slider, create it, set **Minimum** and **Maximum** values, frequency of tick marks, and an initial value. An event handler can also be supplied to allow an Analysis Technique to respond to changes in real-time.

It would be a novel idea to put labels beneath the **Slider** signifying the **Minimum** and **Maximum** values so your users could watch as the Slider progresses.

NAMESPACE: elSystem.Windows.Forms

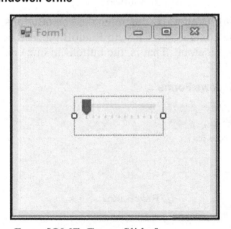

FIGURE 11.17—A Slider in a Form [OME_Form_Slider]

TableLayoutPanel

The **TableLayoutPanel** Class represents a panel that dynamically lays out its contents in a grid composed of rows and columns. The **TableLayoutPanel** control creates subsections within the panel that will maintain the sizes in either absolute or percentage values as a form is resized, without requiring additional code to move and size the individual sections. Notice how nicely you can get sections aligned with this configuration.

NAMESPACE: elSystem.Windows.Forms

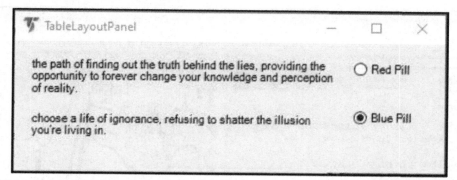

FIGURE 11.18—A TableLayoutPanel in a Form [OME_Form_TableLayoutPanel]

TextBox

The **TextBox** class is a form control that displays a text string within a container in a form that can be edited by the user. This box accepts Plain Text, as opposed to the **RichTextBox** above. The text will wrap within the specified width and height of the control. Scroll bars will appear if the text wraps outside the specified width and height boundaries.

NAMESPACE: elSystem.Windows.Forms

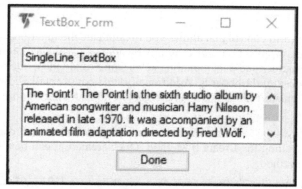

FIGURE 11.19—A TextBox in a Form [OME_Form_TextBox]

WebBrowser

The **WebBrowser** Class is a form control that allows you to duplicate Internet Explorer (IE) functionality inside of an EZL Application. For example, by adding a **WebBrowser** control to a form you can display external web resources and data including news stories and video, interactive tutorials, trading chat room access, and custom dashboards. Additionally, this control will allow you to programmatically create HTML Commentary, like the existing Analysis Commentary, but with much more flexibility and fewer restrictions.

Use of this control follows the same pattern as other EZL Form Controls. The control must be created prior to use by calling the **Create ()** Method or the **New** Reserved Word. Once created, it can be added to a Form using the **AddControl ()** Method.

The **WebBrowser** control includes features such as navigating to a URL, moving backwards and forwards through navigation history, searching, printing, and accessing browser properties.

Additionally, navigation and document loading events can be monitored.

Rather than print out the lengthy code for this example in this section, it is posted on www.EasyLanguageOOEL.com. You may download it there: [OME_WebBrowser].

NAMESPACE: elSystem.Windows.Forms

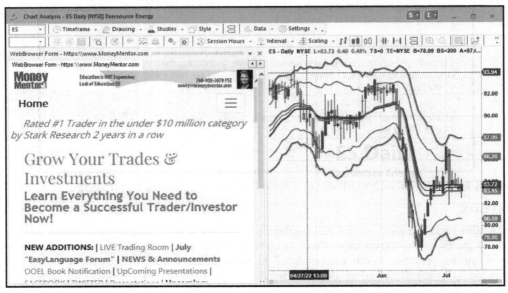

FIGURE 11.20—A WebBrowser in a Form with SunnyBands on a Chart

WebView2

The **WebView2** class is a form control that allows you to duplicate the functionality of Microsoft's Edge browser inside of an EZL Application. For example, by adding a **WebView2** control to a form you can display external web resources and data including news stories and video, interactive tutorials, trading chat room access, and custom dashboards. Additionally, this control will allow you to create HTML Commentary, like the existing Analysis Commentary, but with much more flexibility and fewer restrictions.

Use of this control follows the same pattern as other EZL WinForms controls. The control must be created prior to use by calling the **Create ()** Method. Once created, it can be added to a Form Object using its **AddControl ()** Method.

The **WebView2** control includes features such as navigating to a URL, reloading a web page, and moving backwards and forwards through navigation history. Additionally, navigation, document loading, and other events can be monitored (see the **Using Events** section, below).

NAMESPACE: elSystem.Windows.Forms

FIGURE 11.21—A WebView2 in a Form [OME_WebView2]

Container Classes

Form

A window in which to place the form's related Containers and Controls. When you add the indicator to a chart it displays a custom form window. The form itself is initially empty (see Figure 11.22 below) until you start placing controls in it.

NAMESPACE: elSystem.Windows.Forms

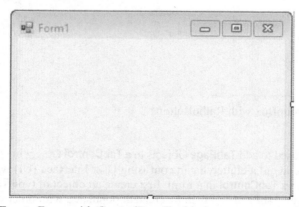

FIGURE 11.22—An Empty Form with ControlBox Enabled

Panel

A **Panel** Class is an area in which to visually place a form's related controls. It creates an area within a form for grouping controls. It is convenient for grouping elements that you might want to move together as a group as you design your form. That way you can "grab" the Panel and move all the elements at once. A panel allows you to make thing appear and disappear at will using the Visible and Active properties. By default, the Panel is bordered while a **GroupBox** is not.

NAMESPACE: elSystem.Windows.Forms

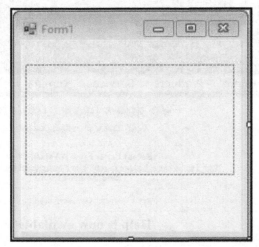

FIGURE 11.23—A Panel in a Form

GroupBox

The **GroupBox** Class allows you to create a **GroupBox** Object which defines an area used to visually group a form's related controls. In Figure 11.24 below you will see three **RadioButton** Objects grouped in a **GroupBox** so that clicking one will turn off the others.

NAMESPACE: elSystem.Windows.Forms

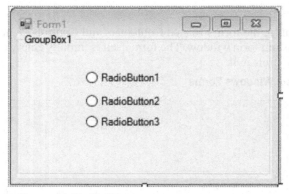

FIGURE 11.24—A GroupBox with RadioButtons

TabPage

The **TabControl** Cass is used to add **TabPage** Objects to a **TabControl** Object in your form. Tabs provide a way to save space and avoid a cluttered and confusing User Interface (UI) when many controls are needed in a form. To use a **TabControl** in a form, first create an object of type **TabControl** and add it to the Form. Objects of type **TabPage** can then be created, populated with other controls such as **Panel**, **Button**, **Label** and **CheckBox** Objects, and added to the **TabControl**. The currently selected tab is identified by the tab control's SelectedIndex property. To learn more about this, see **Volume II— Reference Guide** under **Classes** in **Appendix III**.

NAMESPACE: elSystem.Windows.Forms

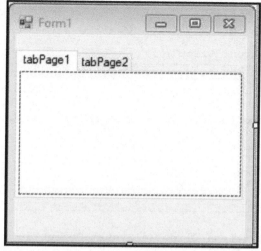

FIGURE 11.25—A Form with a TabControl and two TabPages

EXAMPLE 11.01—Code for Figure 11.02, All the Pieces and Parts of a Form [OME_Container]

```
method void Label1_Click (elSystem.Object sender, elSystem.EventArgs
args)
// EventArgs has no properties to explore
begin
  Print ("Label1_Click : This is another Label within another Panel.")
;
end ; // "Label1_Click" method

// ----------------------------------------------------------

method void Label2_Click (elSystem.Object sender, elSystem.EventArgs
args)
// EventArgs has no properties to explore
begin
  Print ("Label2_Click : This is a Label within a Panel.") ;
end ; // "Label2_Click" method

// ----------------------------------------------------------

method void Button1_Click (elSystem.Object sender, elSystem.EventArgs
args)
// EventArgs has no properties to explore
begin
  Print ("Button1_Click") ;
end ; // "Button1_Click" method

// ----------------------------------------------------------

method void RadioButton1_Click (elSystem.Object sender,
elSystem.EventArgs args)
// EventArgs has no properties to explore
begin
  Print ("RadioButton1_Click") ;
end ; // "RadioButton1_Click" method

// ----------------------------------------------------------
```

```
method void RadioButton2_Click (elSystem.Object sender,
elSystem.EventArgs args)
// EventArgs has no properties to explore
begin
  Print ("RadioButton2_Click") ;
end ; // "RadioButton2_Click" method

// ----------------------------------------------------------

method void RadioButton3_Click (elSystem.Object sender,
elSystem.EventArgs args)
// EventArgs has no properties to explore
begin
  Print ("RadioButton3_Click") ;
end ; // "RadioButton3_Click" method

// ----------------------------------------------------------

method void RadioButton4_Click (elSystem.Object sender,
elSystem.EventArgs args)
// EventArgs has no properties to explore
begin
  Print ("RadioButton4_Click") ;
end ; // "RadioButton4_Click" method

// ----------------------------------------------------------

method void ProgressBar1_Click (elSystem.Object sender,
elSystem.EventArgs args)
// EventArgs has no properties to explore
Vars   :
 Int    Loop,
 Int    Lopp ;
begin
  Print ("ProgressBar1_Click") ;
  for Loop  = ProgressBar1.Minimum
           to ProgressBar1.Maximum begin
    for Lopp  = 00 to 1000 begin
    end ; // for loop (inner) - just a visual delay
    ProgressBar1.Value  = Loop ;
  end ; // for loop (outer)
end ; // "ProgressBar1_Click" method

// ----------------------------------------------------------

method void DateTimePicker1_ValueChanged (elSystem.Object sender,
elSystem.EventArgs args)
// EventArgs has no properties to explore
begin
  Print ("DateTimePicker1_ValueChanged") ;
end ; // "DateTimePicker1_ValueChanged" method

// ----------------------------------------------------------

method void NumericUpDown1_ValueChanged (elSystem.Object sender,
elSystem.EventArgs args)
// EventArgs has no properties to explore
begin
  Print ("NumericUpDown1_ValueChanged") ;
end ; // "NumericUpDown1_ValueChanged" method
```

```
    // ------------------------------------------------------------

    method void ComboBox1_SelectedIndexChanged (elSystem.Object sender,
    elSystem.EventArgs args)
    // EventArgs has no properties to explore
    begin
      Print ("ComboBox1_SelectedIndexChanged") ;
    end ; // "ComboBox1_SelectedIndexChanged" method

    // ------------------------------------------------------------

    method void TabControl1_Selected (elSystem.Object sender,
    elSystem.Windows.Forms.TabControlEventArgs args)
    begin
      Print ("TabControl1_Selected Action=", args.Action.toString (), ",
    TabPage = ", args.TabPage.Name, ", TabPageIndex = ",
    args.TabPageIndex.toString ()) ;
    end ; // "TabControl1_Selected" method

    // ------------------------------------------------------------

    method void TabControl1_Deselected (elSystem.Object sender,
    elSystem.windows.forms.TabControlEventArgs args)
    // at least on TS 9.5 this event never seems to fire
    begin
      Print ("TabControl1_Deselected Action=", args.Action.toString (), ",
    TabPage = ", args.TabPage.Name, ", TabPageIndex = ",
    args.TabPageIndex.toString ()) ;
    end ; // "TabControl1_Deselected" method

    // ------------------------------------------------------------

    method void App_Init ()
    begin
      Print ("App_Init") ;
    // add dummy values to the ComboBox.
      ComboBox1.AddItem ("Item#01") ;
      ComboBox1.AddItem ("Item#02") ;
      ComboBox1.AddItem ("Item#03") ;
      ComboBox1.AddItem ("Item#04") ;
      ComboBox1.AddItem ("Item#05") ;
      Container_Form.TopMost  =  TRUE ;
    // setting this in the properties seemed to have no effect.
      Container_Form.AcceptButton  = Button1 ;

    // To get the date and Time you must set Format to Custom
    //   and CustomFormat to a format string shown below.
    //  DateTimePicker1.Format  = DateTimePickerFormat.Time ;
      DateTimePicker1.Format    = DateTimePickerFormat.Custom ;
      DateTimePicker1.CustomFormat  = "dddd MMMM dd, yyyy hh:mm tt" ;
    // AcceptButton does not appear to work
      Container_Form.AcceptButton  = Button1 ;
    // set the Reload button to be default for Enter
      Container_Form.Show () ;
    end ; // "App_Init" method

    // ============================================================

    Once begin
      App_Init () ;
```

```
end ; // Once, and only once
// =========================================================
```

Adding a Form to your EZL Code

To add a **Form** Class to your code, the easy way is to 🖱 Right-Click in your open TDE document and choose Add Form.

To use EZL form controls and containers, you must have the following elements:

Declare a variable for each container or control to be used. The class type of each variable must be appropriate for the object it will reference. Remember to include the identifier **"elSystem.Windows.Forms"** in front of the specific class type unless you have previously added a **Using** statement for the **Forms** namespace. In this example, form1 and button1 are the names of the variables being created.

```
Vars  : elSystem.windows.forms.Form form1(Null ),
//declare form1 as a Form type variable
       elSystem.windows.forms.Button button1(Null) ;
//declare button1 as a Button type variable
```

Create an instance of each container and control object by assigning it to the object variable created above.

```
form1 = Form.create("Form Heading", 100, 100) ;
//create a form container object and assign it to form1
button1 = Button.Create("MY BUTTON", 40, 30) ;
//create a button control object and assign it to button1
```

Add control objects (e.g., buttons) to a container object (e.g., form1).

```
form1.AddControl (button1) ;
```

Set the location property to specify the relative placement of a control within a container.

```
button1.Location (50, 50) ;
```

Add an event handler (a method to call when a control event occurs, such as when a button is clicked).

```
button1.Click += OnButton1Click ;
```

Finally, write the method(s) to be called when an event happens.

```
method void OnButton1Click (elSystem.Object sender, elSystem.EventArgs
args)
begin
//Your EasyLanguage code
end ;
```

INHERITANCE HIERARCHY

elSystem.Object
elSystem.Windows.Forms [ClassType]

About the ToolBox

The **ToolBox** includes a collection of components that may be placed into the AT currently open in the EZL editor simply by 🖱 Double-Clicking. Once in the editor, object-oriented code for the component is automatically generated. The Designer Generated Code (DGC) is protected (not intended to be edited directly) but the values contained in the component generated code can be modified using the Properties Editor.

ToolBox components are grouped into sections that may be expanded/collapsed using the **+/-** buttons next to each section tab title.

To add a new section tab to the ToolBox, click ▼ on the ToolBox title bar (or ⏷ Right-Click in a blank area of the ToolBox and select Add Tab). You can also ⏷ Right-Click on a tab to remove or rename a tab.

To add or remove components to a tabbed section of the ToolBox, ⏷ Right-Click on the tab and select **Choose Items**. From the **Choose ToolBox Items** dialog box, place a check mark next to items to be included and uncheck items to be removed. Click OK when done.

For components that are added to an AT, a separate read-only DGC file is created by the editor and can be viewed using the View → Designer Generated Code menu sequence from the TDE. The values in the designer generated code file are automatically updated when changes are made to components via the Properties Editor.

About the Resource Editor

The EZL Resource Editor is used to create or modify a form that is associated with an OOEL Study, TradingApp, or Strategy. Controls such as buttons, text boxes, etc. can be added to the form from the ToolBox and you can arrange the controls to fit anywhere within the form and change their appearance as desired. You can edit the properties of form controls using the Properties Editor, including assigning events to Event Handler Methods in your OOEL code.

The Resource Editor is a GUI environment that allows you to create forms without having to type all the code yourself. It's a very useful prototyping tool.

In the TDE, ⏷ Right-Click your code and select Add Form. In the ToolBox you ⏷ Double-Click on the control(s) that you want, and they appear on your Form. To relocate them, just drag them around. To change colors, styles, alignment etc., use the Properties Tab.

This subject will be covered more fully in our next book, specifically on Forms, titled something along the line of *OOEL Forms Made Easy!*

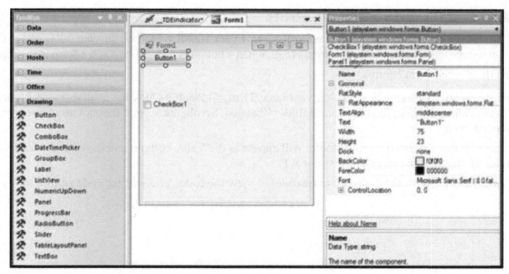

FIGURE 11.26—EZL Resource Editor

Additional Information

With the ToolBox you can easily insert drawing object components into a form by ⏷ double-clicking and dragging it where you want the control to be. Code for each object is automatically generated and appears in the DGC.

Use of the Resource Editor creates Designer Generated Code (DGC) which declares variables, instantiates objects, and sets up event handlers.

Properties and event handler linkage may be set in the Properties Editor. You can also do it in your code.

Adding a Form to an Analysis Technique

A form is added to an AT (Indicator, PaintBar, ShowMe, Strategy, TradingApp, etc.) using the following steps:

Open an existing AT (or create a new one) to which you want to add a form.

🖑 Right-Click anywhere in the AT and select **Add Form** from the shortcut menu.

A blank form will appear as a window in the editor and will be named `Form1` by default (for the first form).

To display the form as part of your study or strategy you'll also need insert a line of EZL code into your document that calls the **Show ()** Method for the specified form, such as:

```
Once Form1.Show () ;
```

Editing a Form

Once a Form has been attached to your AT you are ready to add controls to the form and edit their properties, as follows:

With a form selected, open the **ToolBox** and use the **WinForms** tab to view the available controls.

🖑 Double-Click on the name of a control (i.e., **Button**, **ComboBox**, etc.) in the ToolBox to add it to the form. The selected control will first appear in the upper-left corner of the form.

🖑 Drag the control to a new position in the form and re-size the control as desired.

With a control selected, go to the **Properties** panel to view, and change the text, appearance, and other properties for the control.

Using Events with Form Controls

Use the following steps to connect a control to an Event Handler Method in your EZL code. The method will be called when an event occurs (e.g., when a button is pressed or when a form is re-sized).

Select the desired form control.

In the **Properties Editor**, click the ⚡ Event icon. Then, 🖑 Double-Click the available event type in the Event column (Click, Resize, SelectedIndexChanged, Scroll, etc.). Note that not all controls have associated events.

The name of the generated Event Handler will appear in the Value column and the code for the Event Handler Method will be inserted into your AT.

🖑 Click the AT tab (or the appropriate cascade) to view the code. You will see code similar to:

```
method void CheckBox1_Click (elSystem.Object sender,
elSystem.EventArgs args)
begin
// Insert your EasyLanguage statements here
end ;
```

In this example, the method will run whenever a **CheckBox.Click** Event fires, indicating that the **CheckBox** was checked or unchecked.

Component Classes

To make it easier to add and use objects with EZL, some object classes are designed as components so that you can simply double-click on their icons in the **ToolBox** to add them into your AT. Once added, these objects are configured by using the **Properties Editor** (View → Toolbars → Properties).

Components automatically produce hidden Designer Generated Code (DGC) that is associated with your AT. You may view designer code, but you can't directly edit the code.

elComponent (EasyLanguage design component) is the base class for all Component objects except Windows.Forms Objects who instead inherit the class.

ELWFComponent (EasyLanguage WinForm design component) is the base class for Windows.Forms Components.

ContainerControl Class

A base class from which other forms container classes are derived. The **ContainerControl** Class includes the **Form**, **GroupBox**, **Panel**, **TabControl** and **TabPage** Classes. The members of the Form itself are detailed above in this chapter. All these containers are used to arrange your controls into logical groups.

NAMESPACE: elSystem.Windows.Forms

METHODS

	Name	Description
🔖	AddControl (control)	Adds the specified control to the ControlCollection of the container.

TABLE 11.04—ContainerControl Methods

INHERITANCE HIERARCHY

elSystem.Object
  elSystem.DotNetObject
    elSystem.elComponent
      elSystem.Windows.Forms.ELWFComponent
      elSystem.Windows.Forms.Control
        elSystem.Windows.Forms.ContainerControl

GroupBox Class

The **GroupBox** Class creates an area within a form for grouping controls, especially such as **RadioButton** Objects.

NAMESPACE: elSystem.Windows.Forms

PROPERTIES

	Name	Type	Description
🖼	FlatStyle	object	Gets or sets the flat style appearance of the GroupBox. See **FlatStyle** for a list of possible values.
🖼	UseCompatibleTextRendering	bool	True when the **System.Drawing.Graphics** class should be used to perform text rendering for compatibility with versions 1.0 and 1.1. of the .NET Framework; otherwise, False. The default is False.

TABLE 11.05—GroupBox Properties

METHODS

	Name	Description
🔖	Create ()	Initializes a new instance of a group box.

	Name	Description
⬧	Create (width,height)	Initializes a new instance of a group box. Parameters include the Width and Height of the control.

TABLE 11.06—GroupBox Methods

INHERITANCE HIERARCHY

elSystem.Object
　elSystem.DotNetObject
　　elSystem.elComponent
　　　elSystem.Windows.Forms.ELWFComponent
　　　　elSystem.Windows.Forms.Control
　　　　　elSystem.Windows.Forms.GroupBox

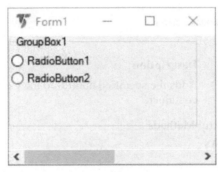

FIGURE 11.27—GroupBox with Radio Buttons in a Form

Panel Class

Creates an area within a form for grouping controls.

NAMESPACE: elSystem.Windows.Forms

PROPERTIES

	Name	Type	Description
🖳	AutoScroll	bool	True indicates that scroll bars automatically appear when the control contents are larger than the visible area.
🖳	BackgroundGradientStyle	object	Gets the style properties of the gradient background. See **BackGroundGradientStyle** and refer to the possible values for each property.
🖳	BorderRadius	object	Gets the BorderRadius object and related properties for the panel.
🖳	BorderStyle	enum	Sets or gets the style of the border. See **BorderStyle** for a list of possible values.

TABLE 11.07—Panel Properties

METHODS

	Name	Description
⬧	Create ()	Initializes a new instance of a panel.
⬧	Create (width, height)	Initializes a new instance of a panel. Parameters include the Width and Height of the control.

	Name	Description
▩◆	RemoveGradient ()	Removes the gradient.
▩◆	SetLinearGradient (mode, startColor, endColor)	Sets the control's background to a specified linear gradient mode, start color, and end color. See **LinearGradientMode** and Color for lists of possible values.
▩◆	SetRadialGradient (startColor, endColor)	Sets the control's background to a radial gradient using specified start color and end color. See **Color** for a list of possible values.

TABLE 11.08—Panel Methods

INHERITANCE HIERARCHY

elSystem.Object
  elSystem.DotNetObject
   elSystem.elComponent
    elSystem.Windows.Forms.ELWFComponent
     elSystem.Windows.Forms.Control
      elSystem.Windows.Forms.ContainerControl
       elSystem.Windows.Forms.Panel

EXAMPLE 11.02—Panel with TabControls, GroupBox with RadioButtons and Another Panel embedded [OME_Container_Class]

Refer back to Figure 11.02 to see both tabs and controls. The code for the **Container** Class is below.

```
Using elSystem ;
Using elSystem.Windows.Forms ;

// Working Storage

Consts:
  String App_Type   ("Study"),
  String App_Name   ("OME_Container_Class_DGC"),
  String App_Note   ("Demonstrate the various Container Classes"),
  String App_Vers   ("01.00.00") ;
Vars  :
  String DQ         (DoubleQuote),
  String NL         (NewLine),
  Double Dummy      (0.00) ;

// =======================================================

method void Label1_Click (elSystem.Object sender, elSystem.EventArgs
args)
// EventArgs has no properties to explore
begin
  Print ("Label1_Click : This is another Label within another Panel.")
;
end ; // "Label1_Click" method

// -------------------------------------------------------

method void Label2_Click( elSystem.Object sender, elSystem.EventArgs
args )
// EventArgs has no properties to explore
begin
  Print ("Label2_Click : This is a Label within a Panel.") ;
end ; // "Label2_Click" method
```

```
  // ----------------------------------------------------------

method void Button1_Click (elSystem.Object sender, elSystem.EventArgs
args)
// EventArgs has no properties to explore
begin
  Print ("Button1_Click") ;
end ; // "Button1_Click" method

  // ----------------------------------------------------------

method void RadioButton1_Click (elSystem.Object sender,
elSystem.EventArgs args)
// EventArgs has no properties to explore
begin
  Print ("RadioButton1_Click") ;
end ; // "RadioButton1_Click" method

  // ----------------------------------------------------------

method void RadioButton2_Click (elSystem.Object sender,
elSystem.EventArgs args)
// EventArgs has no properties to explore
begin
  Print ("RadioButton2_Click") ;
end ; // "RadioButton2_Click" method

  // ----------------------------------------------------------

method void RadioButton3_Click (elSystem.Object sender,
elSystem.EventArgs args)
// EventArgs has no properties to explore
begin
  Print ("RadioButton3_Click") ;
end ; // "RadioButton3_Click" method

  // ----------------------------------------------------------

method void RadioButton4_Click (elSystem.Object sender,
elSystem.EventArgs args)
// EventArgs has no properties to explore
begin
  Print ("RadioButton4_Click") ;
end ; // "RadioButton4_Click" method

  // ----------------------------------------------------------

method void ProgressBar1_Click (elSystem.Object sender,
elSystem.EventArgs args)
// EventArgs has no properties to explore
Vars  :
 Int    Loop,
 Int    Lopp ;
begin
  Print ("ProgressBar1_Click") ;
  for Loop  = ProgressBar1.Minimum to ProgressBar1.Maximum begin
    for Lopp  = 00 to 1000 begin
    end ; // for loop (inner)
    ProgressBar1.Value  = Loop ;
  end ; // for loop (outer)
```

```
  end ; // "ProgressBar1_Click" method

  // ------------------------------------------------------------

  method void DateTimePicker1_ValueChanged (elSystem.Object sender,
  elSystem.EventArgs args)
  // EventArgs has no properties to explore
  begin
    Print ("DateTimePicker1_ValueChanged") ;
  end ; // "DateTimePicker1_ValueChanged" method

  // ------------------------------------------------------------

  method void NumericUpDown1_ValueChanged (elSystem.Object sender,
  elSystem.EventArgs args)
  // EventArgs has no properties to explore
  begin
    Print ("NumericUpDown1_ValueChanged") ;
  end ; // "NumericUpDown1_ValueChanged" method

  // ------------------------------------------------------------

  method void ComboBox1_SelectedIndexChanged (elSystem.Object sender,
  elSystem.EventArgs args)
  // EventArgs has no properties to explore
  begin
    Print ("ComboBox1_SelectedIndexChanged") ;
  end ; // "ComboBox1_SelectedIndexChanged" method

  // ------------------------------------------------------------

  method void TabControl1_Selected (elSystem.Object sender,
  elSystem.windows.forms.TabControlEventArgs args)
  begin
    Print ("TabControl1_Selected Action=", args.Action.toString (), ",
  TabPage = ", args.TabPage.Name, ", TabPageIndex = ",
  args.TabPageIndex.toString ()) ;
  end ; // "TabControl1_Selected" method

  // ------------------------------------------------------------

  method void TabControl1_Deselected (elSystem.Object sender,
  elSystem.windows.forms.TabControlEventArgs args)
  // at least on TS 9.5 this event never seems to fire
  begin
    Print ("TabControl1_Deselected Action=", args.Action.toString (), ",
  TabPage = ", args.TabPage.Name, ", TabPageIndex = ",
  args.TabPageIndex.toString ()) ;
  end ; // "TabControl1_Deselected" method

  // ------------------------------------------------------------

  method void App_Init ()
  begin
    Print ("App_Init") ;
    ComboBox1.AddItem ("Item#01") ;
  // add dummy values to the ComboBox.
    ComboBox1.AddItem ("Item#02") ;
    ComboBox1.AddItem ("Item#03") ;
    ComboBox1.AddItem ("Item#04") ;
```

```
  ComboBox1.AddItem ("Item#05") ;
  Container_Form.TopMost   =   TRUE ;
// setting this in the properties seemed to have no effect.
  Container_Form.AcceptButton  = Button1 ;
  Container_Form.Show () ;
end ; // "App_Init" method

// ============================================================

Once begin
  App_Init () ;
end ; // Once, and only once
```

TabControl Class

The **TabControl** Class is used to add tabs to a form. Tabs provide a way to save space and avoid a cluttered and confusing User Interface when many controls are needed in a form. To use a tab control in a form, first create an object of type **TabControl** and add it to the form. Objects of type **TabPage** can then be created, populated with other controls such as buttons and checkboxes, and added to the Tab Control. The currently selected tab is identified by the Tab Control's SelectedIndex property.

NAMESPACE: elSystem.Windows.Forms

```
var: TabControl allTabs(null), TabPage myTab1(null) ;
// declare a TabControl and TabPage
{declare other form controls}

myTab1 = TabPage.Create("FirstTab",400,300) ;
// create a tab page with a button and label
myTab1.AddControl (aButton) ;
myTab1.AddControl (aLabel) ;

allTabs = TabControl.Create() ;
// create a tab control and add a tab page
allTabs.AddControl(myTab1) ;

{create other form controls and add them all to a form}
```

PROPERTIES

	Name	Type	Description
☞	Multiline	bool	Gets or sets a value that determines whether more than one line of tabs can be displayed. Set to True to allow more than one line of tabs. Set to False to not allow more than one line of tabs. (TS >= 10.0)
☞	SelectedIndex	int	Gets the zero-based index of the currently selected tab.
☞	SelectedTab	object	Gets or sets the selected **TabPage**.(TS >= 10.0)
☞	TabCount	int	Gets the number of tabs.
☞	TabPages	object	Gets a TabPageCollection that contains the TabControl's TabPages. (TS >= 10.0)

TABLE 11.09—TabControl Class Properties

METHODS

	Name	Description
☜	Create ()	Initializes a new instance of a **TabControl**.

	Name	Description
🔹	SelectTab (Index)	Makes the tab with the specified index number the current tab. (TS >= 10.0)
🔹	SelectTab (TabPage)	Makes the specified **TabPage** the current tab. (TS >= 10.0)
🔹	SelectTab (PageName)	Makes the tab with the specified name the current tab. (TS >= 10.0)

TABLE 11.10—TabControl Class Methods

EVENTS

	Name	Description
⚡	Deselected	Occurs when a tab is selected. See **TabControlEventArgs** for the properties returned by the handler's args parameter.
⚡	Selected	Occurs when a tab is selected. See **TabControlEventArgs** for the properties returned by the handler's args parameter.

TABLE 11.11—TabControl Class Events

INHERITANCE HIERARCHY

elSystem.Object
 elSystem.DotNetObject
  elSystem.elComponent
   elSystem.Windows.Forms.ELWFComponent
    elSystem.Windows.Forms.Control
     elSystem.Windows.Forms.ContainerControl
      elSystem.Windows.Forms.TabControl

TabPage Class

The **TabPage** Object represents a tab that is added to a **TabControl** which is on the Form. It can be populated with other controls, such as **Button** and **CheckBox** Objects.

NAMESPACE: elSystem.Windows.Forms

METHODS

	Name	Description
🔹	Create ()	Initializes a new instance of the class.
🔹	Create (text, width, height)	Initializes a new instance of a TabPage. Parameters include the Text string to appear on the tab followed by integer values for the page Width and Height.

TABLE 11.12—TabPage Class Methods

INHERITANCE HIERARCHY

elSystem.Object
 elSystem.DotNetObject
  elSystem.elComponent
   elSystem.Windows.Forms.ELWFComponent
    elSystem.Windows.Forms.Control
     elSystem.Windows.Forms.ContainerControl
      elSystem.Windows.Forms.TabPage

Control Class

The **Control** Class is a base class from which other form control classes are derived.

☑ When dealing with a form only Control Classes will be shown in the ToolBox as they are the only components usable in a form.

Figure 11.28 below shows the members of the **winforms.ell**, similar to but less extensive than Windows WinForms, and which resides in the Namespace **elSystem.Windows.Forms**. You might want to look up Windows WinForms on Google to expand your horizons.

NAMESPACE: elSystem.Windows.Forms

FIGURE 11.28—WinForms Controls Available in the ToolBox

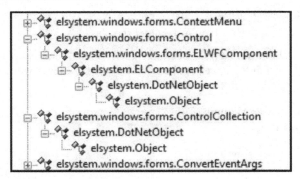

FIGURE 11.29—Control Shown in the Dictionary

PROPERTIES

	Name	Type	Description
🖼	Anchor	enum	Gets or sets the boundary of the parent container to which the control is anchored. See **AnchorStyles** for a list of possible values.

	Name	Type	Description
🖼	AutoSize	bool	True indicates that the control that is inherited from this class should resize itself based upon its contents.
🖼	BackColor	object	Gets or sets the background Color of a control.
🖼	BackgroundImage	object	Gets or sets the background Image displayed in the control.
🖼	BackgroundImageLayout	enum	Gets or sets how the BackgroundImage is oriented in the control. See **ImageLayout** for a list of values.
🖼	CanFocus	bool	True indicates that the control can receive focus.
🖼	ContainsFocus	bool	True if the control, or one of its child controls, currently has the input focus.
🖼	ControlLocation	object	Gets or sets the position of a control as a Point object.
🖼	Controls	object	Gets a collection of Control objects.
🖼	Dock	object	Gets or sets how a control is docked. See **DockStyle** for a list of values.
🖼	EffectiveBackColor	object	Gets the background Color actually being used. (TS >= 10.0)
🖼	EffectiveForeColor	object	Gets the foreground Color actually being used. (TS >= 10.0)
🖼	Enabled	bool	Gets or sets a value indicating if control can respond to user interaction.
🖼	Focused	bool	True if the control has input focus.
🖼	Font	object	Gets of sets the Font used to display text for a control.
🖼	ForeColor	object	Gets or sets the foreground Color of a control.
🖼	Height	int	Gets or sets the height of a control.
🖼	Margin	object	Gets or sets the space between controls. See **Padding**.
🖼	Padding	object	Gets or sets Padding within the control.
🖼	RightToLeft	enum	Gets or sets the text plotting direction. See **RightToLeft** for a list of values.
🖼	TabIndex	int	Gets or sets the tab order of the control within its container. (TS >= 10.0)
🖼	TabStop	bool	True indicates that the user can give the focus to this control using the TAB key. (TS >= 10.0)
🖼	Tag	object	Gets or sets an arbitrary object value that can be used to store custom information about a control.
🖼	Text	string	Gets or sets the text displayed in a control.
🖼	UseTheme	enum	Gets or sets the theme mode. See **UseThemeMode** for a list of values. (TS >= 10.0)

	Name	Type	Description
🖼️	UseWaitCursor	bool	True to use the wait cursor for the current control and all child controls.
🖼️	Visible	bool	Gets or sets a value indicating if control and its child controls are displayed.
🖼️	Width	int	Gets or sets the width of a control.

TABLE 11.13—Control Class Properties

METHODS

	Name	Description
🔷	BringToFront ()	Brings the control to the front of the z-order.
🔷	FindForm ()	Returns the form object in which the control is inserted or null if not inserted in any form. (TS >= 10.0)
🔷	Focus ()	True when the control has focus, otherwise False.
🔷	GetParent ()	Gets the parent object of a control.
🔷	Location (x, y)	Sets the x, y position of the control within its container.
🔷	PointToClient (p)	Computes the location of the specified screen Point into client coordinates.
🔷	PointToScreen (p)	Computes the location of the specified client Point into screen coordinates.

TABLE 11.14—Control Class Methods

EVENTS

	Name	Description
⚡	Click	Occurs when the control is clicked.
⚡	MouseEnter	Occurs when the mouse enters the control.

TABLE 11.15—Control Class Events

INHERITANCE HIERARCHY

elSystem.Object
  elSystem.DotNetObject
    elSystem.elComponent
      elSystem.Windows.Forms.ELWFComponent
      elSystem.Windows.Forms.Control

Button Class

Displays a push button control within a container in a form. A **Click** Event is fired when the button is pressed.

The name of the button and size are specified when the object is instantiated using the **Create ()** Method.

NAMESPACE: elSystem.Windows.Forms

PROPERTIES

	Name	Type	Description
🖼️	DisabledBackColor	object	Gets or sets the disabled button back color when OverrideDisabledColors = True. (TS >= 10.0)
🖼️	DisabledForeColor	object	Gets or sets the disabled button fore color when

	Name	Type	Description
			OverrideDisabledColors = True. (TS >= 10.0)
🖱	OverrideDisabledColors	bool	True potentially allows the disabled colors to take effect; False otherwise. (TS >= 10.0)

TABLE 11.16—Button Class Properties

METHODS

	Name	Description
◆	Create ()	Initializes a new instance of a Button.
◆	Create (text, width, height)	Initializes a new instance of a Button. Parameters include the Text to appear on the button followed by integer values for the button Width and Height.
◆	PerformClick ()	Generates a click event for a button. (TS >= 10.0)
◆	RemoveGradient ()	Removes the gradient.
◆	SetLinearGradient (mode, startColor, endColor)	Creates a linear gradient button background. See **LinearGradientMode** and Color for lists of possible values.
◆	SetRadialGradient (startColor, endColor)	Creates a radial gradient button background. See **Color** for a list of possible values.

TABLE 11.17—Button Class Methods

EVENTS

	Name	Description
⚡	KeyDown	Occurs when a key is pressed while the control has focus. See **KeyEventArgs** for the properties returned by the handler's args parameter. (TS >= 10.0)
⚡	KeyPress	Occurs when a key is pressed while the control has focus. See **KeyPressEventArgs** for the properties returned by the handler's args parameter. (TS >= 10.0)
⚡	KeyUp	Occurs when a key is pressed while the control has focus. See **KeyEventArgs** for the properties returned by the handler's args parameter. (TS >= 10.0)

TABLE 11.18—Button Class Events

INHERITANCE HIERARCHY

```
elSystem.Object
 elSystem.DotNetObject
  elSystem.elComponent
   elSystem.Windows.Forms.ELWFComponent
    elSystem.Windows.Forms.Control
     elSystem.Windows.Forms.ButtonBase
      elSystem.Windows.Forms.IButtonControl
       elSystem.Windows.Forms.Button
```

ButtonBase Class

The base class for button controls, including **Button**, **RadioButton**, and **CheckBox** Classes.

NAMESPACE: elSystem.Windows.Forms

PROPERTIES

	Name	Type	Description
🖳	FlatAppearance	object	Gets the appearance properties of a button. See **FlatButtonAppearance**.
🖳	FlatStyle	enum	Gets or sets the style of the button. See **FlatStyle** for a list of values.
🖳	Image	object	Gets or sets an image to be displayed on the button control.
🖳	ImageAlign	enum	Gets or sets the alignment of the button image. See **ContentAlignment** for a list of values.
🖳	TextAlign	enum	Gets or sets the alignment of the button control. See **ContentAlignment** for a list of values.
🖳	UseCompatibleTextRendering	bool	True indicates that text rendering should be compatible with previous release of Windows Forms, otherwise False.

TABLE 11.19—ButtonBase Class Properties

INHERITANCE HIERARCHY

elSystem.Object
  elSystem.DotNetObject
    elSystem.elComponent
      elSystem.Windows.Forms.ELWFComponent
        elSystem.Windows.Forms.Control
          elSystem.Windows.Forms.ButtonBase

CheckBox Class

Displays a **CheckBox** and allows you to toggle a check mark on/off. You may group check boxes, but unlike the **RadioButton** class, you may make multiple **CheckBox** selections within a group.

NAMESPACE: elSystem.Windows.Forms

PROPERTIES

	Name	Type	Description
🖳	Checked	bool	Gets or sets a value indicating whether the control is checked.

TABLE 11.20—CheckBox Class Properties

METHODS

	Name	Description
⬧	Create ()	Initializes a new instance of a CheckBox.
⬧	Create (text, width, height)	Initializes a new instance of a CheckBox. Parameters include the Text to appear next to the check box followed the Width and Height of the control.

TABLE 11.21—CheckBox Class Methods

EVENTS

	Name	Description
⚡	CheckedChanged	Occurs when the checked state of the Checked property changes. See **EventArgs** for the properties returned by the handler's args parameter. (TS >= 10.0)

TABLE 11.22—CheckBox Class Events

INHERITANCE HIERARCHY

elSystem.Object
 elSystem.DotNetObject
  elSystem.elComponent
   elSystem.Windows.Forms.ELWFComponent
    elSystem.Windows.Forms.Control
     elSystem.Windows.Forms.ButtonBase
      elSystem.Windows.Forms.CheckBox

ComboBox Class

Displays a **ComboBox** that contains a drop-down list of items.

NAMESPACE: elSystem.Windows.Forms

PROPERTIES

	Name	Type	Description
🖙	Count	int	Gets the number of items in the ComboBox list.
🖙	DropDownHeight	int	Gets or sets the height of the ComboBox.
🖙	DropDownStyle	enum	Gets or sets the style of the ComboBox. See **ComboBoxStyle** for a list of possible values.
🖙	DropDownWidth	int	Gets or sets the width of the ComboBox.
🖙	FlatStyle	enum	Gets or sets the flat style appearance of the ComboBox. See **FlatStyle** for a list of possible values.
🖙	SelectedIndex	int	Gets or sets the index of the selected ComboBox item.
🖙	SelectedItem	object	Gets the selected item from the ComboBox list.
🖙	SelectedText	string	Gets or sets the text that is selected in the editable portion of a ComboBox.
🖙	Sorted	bool	Sets or gets a value indicating if ComboBox items are sorted.

TABLE 11.23—ComboBox Class Properties

METHODS

	Name	Description
🔷	AddItem (string)	Adds a new ComboBox item using the provided text string.
🔷	Clear ()	Clears the contents from the ComboBox.
🔷	Create ()	Initializes a new instance of a ComboBox.
🔷	Create (text, width, height)	Initializes a new instance of a ComboBox. Parameters include the default Text to appear in the combo box followed the Width and Height of the control.
🔷	FindString (value)	Finds the first item in the combo box that starts with the specified string value. The search is not case sensitive.

	Name	Description
⬦	FindString (value, index)	Finds the first item in the combo box that starts with the specified string value starting after the specified index. The search is not case sensitive.
⬦	FindStringExact (value)	Finds the first item in the comb box that exactly matches the specified string value. The search is case sensitive.
⬦	RemoveItem (index)	Removes an item from the combo box at the index position.

TABLE 11.24—ComboBox Class Methods

EVENTS

	Name	Description
⚡	KeyDown	Occurs when a ComboBox is selected and a key on the keyboard is pressed down. See **KeyEventArgs** for the properties returned by the handler's args parameter.
⚡	KeyPress	Occurs when a ComboBox is selected and a key on the keyboard is pressed. See **KeyEventArgs** for the properties returned by the handler's args parameter.
⚡	KeyUp	Occurs when a ComboBox is selected and a key on the keyboard is released. See **KeyEventArgs** for the properties returned by the handler's args parameter.
⚡	SelectedIndexChanged	Occurs when a ComboBox item is selected or changed. See **EventArgs** for the properties returned by the handler's args parameter.

TABLE 11.25—ComboBox Class Events

INHERITANCE HIERARCHY

elSystem.Object
  elSystem.DotNetObject
   elSystem.elComponent
    elSystem.Windows.Forms.ELWFComponent
     elSystem.Windows.Forms.Control
      elSystem.Windows.Forms.ComboBox

DataGridView (DGV)

Represents a row in a **DataGridView** control. The Cells property contains a collection of cells in the row.

NAMESPACE: elSystem.Windows.Forms

After you add a **DataGridView** control to form, you can create rows and columns that contain data and add them directly to the DataGridView using the Rows and Columns properties. You can also use the Rows collection to access DataGridViewRow objects and the DataGridViewRow.Cells property to read or write cell values directly. After you add a DataGridView to a form (for example, `DataGridView1`), you add a row with two cells as follows:

EXAMPLE 11.03—Create a Simple DataGridView [OME_DataGridView_Ex#01]

```
#Region  - Declarations
Using tsData.Common ;
Using tsData.MarketData ;
Using elSystem ;
Using elSystem.Collections ;
Using elSystem.windows.forms ;
```

```
Consts:
 String App_Type ("TradingApp (Form)"),
 String App_Name ("OME_DataGridView_Ex#01"),
 String App_Note ("Demonstrate creating and populating a DataGridView
 and changing cells."),
 String App_Vers ("01.01.01") ;

Vars  :
 String DQ       (DoubleQuote),
 String NL       (NewLine),
 Bool   Debug    (FALSE),
 Double Dummy    (0.00) ;

#endRegion // Declarations
// ========================================================
#Region  - myMethods

// ====================== Methods ====================

method void AnalysisTechnique_Initialized     (elSystem.Object sender,
elSystem.InitializedEventArgs args)
begin
  Print (App_Name, ".AnalysisTechnique_Initialized     ") ;
end ; // "AnalysisTechnique_Initialized" method

// --------------------------------------------------------

method void AnalysisTechnique_UnInitialized   (elSystem.Object sender,
elSystem.UnInitializedEventArgs args)
begin
  Print (App_Name, ".AnalysisTechnique_UnInitialized   ") ;
end ; // "AnalysisTechnique_UnInitialized" method

// --------------------------------------------------------

method void AnalysisTechnique_WorkspaceSaving (elSystem.Object sender,
elSystem.WorkspaceSavingEventArgs args)
begin
  Print (App_Name, ".AnalysisTechnique_WorkspaceSaving ") ;
end ; // "AnalysisTechnique_WorkspaceSaving" method

// --------------------------------------------------------

method void myDGV_CellValueChanged (elSystem.Object sender,
elSystem.windows.forms.DataGridViewCellEventArgs args)
begin
  Print ("myDGV_CellValueChanged") ;
end ; // "myDGV_CellValueChanged" method

// --------------------------------------------------------

method void myDGV_Click (elSystem.Object sender,
elSystem.EventArgsargs)
begin
  Print ("myDGV_Click") ;
end ; // "myDGV_Click" method

// --------------------------------------------------------
```

```
method void myDGV_ColumnHeaderMouseClick (elSystem.Object sender,
elSystem.windows.forms.DataGridViewCellMouseEventArgs args)
begin
  Print ("myDGV_ColumnHeaderMouseClick") ;
end ; // "myDGV_ColumnHeaderMouseClick" method

// -------------------------------------------------------

method void myDGV_RowHeaderMouseClick (elSystem.Object sender,
elSystem.windows.forms.DataGridViewCellMouseEventArgs args)
begin
  Print ("myDGV_RowHeaderMouseClick") ;
end ; // "myDGV_RowHeaderMouseClick" method

// -------------------------------------------------------

method void myDGV_DataError (elSystem.Object sender,
elSystem.windows.forms.DataGridViewDataErrorEventArgs args)
begin
  Print ("myDGV_DataError") ;
end ; // "myDGV_DataError" method

// -------------------------------------------------------

method void myDGV_SelectionChanged (elSystem.Object sender,
elSystem.EventArgs args)
begin
  Print ("myDGV_SelectionChanged") ;
end ; // "myDGV_SelectionChanged" method

// -------------------------------------------------------

method void myDGV_CellClick (elSystem.Object sender,
elSystem.windows.forms.DataGridViewCellEventArgs args)
begin
  Print ("myDGV_CellClick (Col=", args.ColumnIndex:2:0,
                      ", Row=", args.RowIndex:2:0, ")") ;
// Increment_Cell (args.ColumnIndex, args.RowIndex) ;
  DGV_AssignCellValue (Sender asType DataGridView, args.ColumnIndex,
args.RowIndex, "new value") ;
end ; // "myDGV_CellClick" method

// -------------------------------------------------------

method DataGridViewColumn DGV_CreateCol ()
Vars  :
DataGridViewColumn Col ;
begin
  Print ("DGV_CreateCol") ;
  Col = DataGridViewColumn.Create ("Default(TextBox)");
  Col.SortMode = DataGridViewColumnSortMode.Automatic ;
// DataGridView1.Columns.Add(col);
  Return Col ;
end ; // "DGV_CreateCol" method

// -------------------------------------------------------

method DataGridViewRow DGV_CreateRow (Int myValue)
Vars  :
 Int    Loop,
DataGridViewRow Row ;
```

```
begin
  Print ("DGV_CreateRow") ;
  row = DataGridViewRow.Create ("") ;
  myDGV.Rows.Add (Row) ;
  row.Cells [00].Value  = NumToStr (myValue + 00, 00) ;
  row.Cells [01].Value  = NumToStr (myValue + 01, 00) ;

  Return Row ;
end ; // "DGV_CreateRow" method

// -------------------------------------------------------

method void DGV_AssignCellValue (DataGridView myDGV, Int ColNdx, Int
RowNdx, String myValue)
Vars  :
DataGridViewCell myCell ;
begin
  Print ("DGV_AssignCellValue (Col=", ColNdx:2:0,
                      ", Row=", RowNdx:2:0,
                      ", Value=", DQ, myValue, DQ, ")") ;

  myCell  = myDGV.Rows [RowNdx].Cells.Items [ColNdx] ;
  if  myCell.value isType String  then begin
// This line will directly update a cell in a DataGridView
    myDGV.Rows [RowNdx].Cells.Items [ColNdx].Value = myValue ;
  end ;
//  myDGV.Rows [RowNdx]  = myRow ;
end ; // "DGV_AssignCellValue" method

// -------------------------------------------------------

method void Increment_Cell (Int ColNdx, Int RowNdx)
Vars  :
 String myStr,
 Double myNum,
DataGridViewCell myCell,
DataGridViewRow myRow ;
begin
  Print ("Increment_Cell (Col=", ColNdx:2:0,
                     ", Row=", RowNdx:2:0, ")") ;

//  myRow   = myDGV.Rows [RowNdx] ;
  myCell  = myDGV.Rows [RowNdx].Cells.Items [ColNdx] ;
  if  myCell.value isType String  then begin
    myStr  = myCell.Value asType String ;
    myNum  = StrToNum (myStr) + 01 ;
    myStr  = NumToStr (myNum, 00) ;
// This line will directly update a cell in a DataGridView
    myDGV.Rows [RowNdx].Cells.Items [ColNdx].Value = myStr ;
  end ;
//  myDGV.Rows [RowNdx]  = myRow ;
end ; // "Increment_Cell" method

// -------------------------------------------------------

method DataGridView DGV_Init (DataGridView DGV)
Vars  :
 Int    Loop,
DataGridViewColumn            Col,
DataGridViewRow               DGVR ;
```

```
begin
  Print ("DGV_Init") ;
  if  DGV  = NULL  then  DGV = DataGridView.Create () ;
  if  DGV  = NULL  then begin
    Print ("Unable to create the DGV Object, Abort!") ;
    Return DGV ;
  end ;

  Col  = DGV_CreateCol () ;
  DGV.Columns.Add (Col) ; // Column00
  Col  = DGV_CreateCol () ;
  DGV.Columns.Add (Col) ; // Column01

  for Loop  = 00 to 03 begin
    DGVR    = DGV_CreateRow (Loop) ;
  end ; // for loop

  Return DGV ;
end ; // "DGV_Init" method

// ---------------------------------------------------------

method void Application_Init ()
begin
  Print ("Application_Init") ;
// they work without the "Self." as well
  Self.Initialized += AnalysisTechnique_Initialized ;
  Self.UnInitialized += AnalysisTechnique_UnInitialized ;
  Self.WorkspaceSaving += AnalysisTechnique_WorkspaceSaving ;
  myDGV  = DGV_Init (myDGV) ;

// Try putting this line in and taking it out again.
//   ie: replace 'Fill' with another option
// DockStyles: Bottom; Fill; Left; None; Right; Top;
  OME_DGV_Form.Dock  = DockStyle.Fill ;
  OME_DGV_Form.Anchor  = AnchorStyles.Top + AnchorStyles.Right ;

  OME_DGV_Form.Show () ;
end ; // "Application_Init" method
```

	Default(TextBox)	Default(TextBox)
▶	0	1
	1	2
	2	3
	3	4
*		

FIGURE 11.30—Simple DataGridView

PROPERTIES

	Name	Type	Description
🖎	Cells	object	Gets the collection of cells that populate the row. See **DataGridViewCellCollection**.
🖎	Frozen	bool	True when a row remains fixed when a user scrolls the DataGridView control vertically.

	Name	Type	Description
🖾	Height	int	Gets or sets the height of the row in pixels.
🖾	IsNewRow	bool	True if the row is a new row and False if the row is not a new row. The new row is the blank row at the bottom of the control when the DataGridView is set to allow users to add rows. This property should be checked prior to deleting/removing a row (i.e., ensure IsNewRow is False prior to removing) or an exception is thrown.
🖾	MinimumHeight	int	Gets or sets the minimum height of the row.
🖾	Resizable	enum	Gets or sets a TriState value indicating whether the row is resizable.
🖾	Selected	bool	True if the row is in a selected state.
🖾	Tag	object	Gets or sets a value or object that can be used to store data associated with the control.
🖾	Text	string	Gets the name of the row.

TABLE 11.26—DataGridView Properties

METHODS

	Name	Description
🐾	Create (string)	Initializes a new instance of the DataGridViewRow class.
🐾	SetCell (int, string)	Sets the value of the row's indicated cell.

TABLE 11.27—DataGridView Methods

INHERITANCE HIERARCHY

elSystem.Object
 elSystem.DotNetObject
  elSystem.elComponent
   elSystem.Windows.Forms.ELWFComponent
    elSystem.Windows.Forms.Control
     elSystem.Windows.Forms.DataGridView

EXAMPLE 11.04—Create a Calculator with DataGridView [OME_DGV_Ex#02]

```
#Region  - Declarations
using elSystem ;
using elSystem.windows.forms ;

Inputs:
 string iText1 ("DataGridView1") ;

// ----------------------------------------------------
// working Storage
Consts:
 String App_Type ("TradingApp"),
 String App_Name ("OME_DataGridView_Ex#02"),
 String App_Note ("Example DataGridView to enter and calculate
values"),
 String App_Vers ("01.01.00") ;

Vars  :
 String DQ        (DoubleQuote),
```

```
  String NL        (NewLine),
  Bool   Debug     (FALSE),
  Double Dummy     (0.00) ;

#endRegion // Declarations
#Region  - myMethods
// ================= Methods  ==========================

method void AnalysisTechnique_Initialized      (elSystem.Object sender,
elSystem.InitializedEventArgs args)
begin
  Print (App_Name, ".AnalysisTechnique_Initialized     ") ;
end ; // "AnalysisTechnique_Initialized" method


// -------------------------------------------------------

method void AnalysisTechnique_UnInitialized   (elSystem.Object sender,
elSystem.UnInitializedEventArgs args)
begin
  Print (App_Name, ".AnalysisTechnique_UnInitialized    ") ;
end ; // "AnalysisTechnique_UnInitialized" method

// -------------------------------------------------------method void
AnalysisTechnique_WorkspaceSaving (elSystem.Object sender,
elSystem.WorkspaceSavingEventArgs args)
begin
  Print (App_Name, ".AnalysisTechnique_WorkspaceSaving ") ;
end ; // "AnalysisTechnique_WorkspaceSaving" method

// -------------------------------------------------------

method void DataGridView_CellClick (elSystem.Object sender,
elSystem.windows.forms.DataGridViewCellEventArgs args)
begin
  Print ("DataGridView_CellClick (col=", args.ColumnIndex:2:0,
",row=", args.RowIndex:2:0, ")") ;
  if  args.ColumnIndex  = 02  then begin
    Calc_Numbers (args.RowIndex) ;
  end ; // should be the Calculate column
end ; // "DataGridView_CellClick" method

// -------------------------------------------------------

method void DataGridView_CellValueChanged (elSystem.Object sender,
elSystem.windows.forms.DataGridViewCellEventArgs args)
begin
  Print ("DataGridView_CellValueChanged") ;
end ; // "DataGridView_CellValueChanged" method

// -------------------------------------------------------

method void DataGridView_DataError (elSystem.Object sender,
elSystem.windows.forms.DataGridViewDataErrorEventArgs args)
begin
  Print ("DataGridView_DataError") ;
end ; // "DataGridView_DataError" method

// -------------------------------------------------------

method void Calc_Numbers (Int RowIndex)
Vars  :
```

```
        Double RetVal,
        String Cell_00,
        String Cell_01,
        Double Num_00,
        Double Num_01,
        Double Num_03,
        DataGridViewRow DGVR,
        DataGridViewRowCollection DGVRC ;
      begin
        DGVRC     = DataGridView1.Rows ;
        DGVR      = DGVRC [RowIndex] ;
        Cell_00   = DGVR.Cells[00].Text ;
        Cell_01   = DGVR.Cells[01].Text ;
        Num_00    = StrToNum (Cell_00) ;
        Num_01    = StrToNum (Cell_01) ;
        Num_03    = Num_00 + Num_01 ;
        DGVR.SetCell (03, NumToStr (Num_03, 04)) ;
      end ; // "Calc_Numbers" method


    // ================= Methods  =========================
    #endRegion // myMethods
    #Region  - Main_Code_Body
    // ================= Main Code Body  ==================

    Once begin
      Form1.Name  = "Calculator" ;
      Form1.Dock  = DockStyle.Fill ;
      Form1.Show () ;
    end ; // Once, and only once

    #endRegion // Main_Code_Body
```

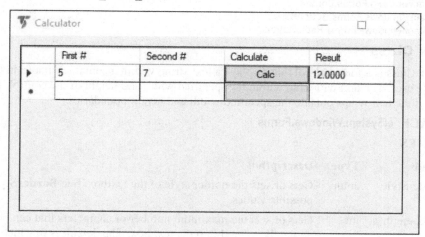

FIGURE 11.31—A Calculator Using DataGridView

RadioButton Class

The **RadioButton** class is a form control that allows the user to select a single option from a group of choices when combined with other **RadioButton** Controls. Unlike the **CheckBox** Class, you may make only a single selection within a group of **RadioButton** Objects.

NAMESPACE: elSystem.Windows.Forms

PROPERTIES

	Name	Type	Description
🖘	Checked	bool	Gets or sets a value indicating whether the control is checked.

TABLE 11.28—RadioButton Class Properties

METHODS

	Name	Description
❖	Create ()	Initializes a new instance of the control.
❖	Create (text, width, height)	Initializes a new instance of the control. Parameters include the text to be displayed followed by the width and height of the control.

TABLE 11.29—RadioButton Class Methods

EVENTS

	Name	Description
⚡	CheckedChanged	Occurs when the checked state of the radio button has changed. (TS >= 10.0)

TABLE 11.30—RadioButton Class Events

INHERITANCE HIERARCHY

elSystem.Object
  elSystem.DotNetObject
   elSystem.elComponent
    elSystem.Windows.Forms.ELWFComponent
     elSystem.Windows.Forms.Control
      elSystem.Windows.Forms.ButtonBase
       elSystem.Windows.Forms.RadioButton

TextBox Class

The **TextBox** Class is a form control that displays a text string within a container in a form that can be edited by the user. The text will wrap within the specified width and height of the control. Scroll bars will appear if the text wraps outside the specified width and height boundaries.

NAMESPACE: elSystem.Windows.Forms

PROPERTIES

	Name	Type	Description
🖘	BorderStyle	enum	Gets or sets the border style of the textbox. See **BorderStyle** for possible values.
🖘	MaxLength	int	Gets or sets the maximum number of characters that can be manually entered into the text box. The default is 0, which indicates no limit. (TS >= 10.0)
🖘	Multiline	bool	True to allow multiple lines of text in the control. False (default) ignores carriage returns and limits text to a single line.
🖘	ReadOnly	bool	True to make text read-only so that it cannot be edited by the user. False indicates that it can be edited.

TABLE 11.31—TextBox Class Properties

METHODS

	Name	Description
◆	Create ()	Initializes a new instance of a TextBox.
◆	Create (text, width, height)	Initializes a new instance of the control. Parameters include the text to be displayed followed by the width and height of the control.
◆	RemoveGradient ()	Removes the gradient.
◆	Select (start, length)	Gets a sub-string from the text box string based on the position of the start character and length of characters to select. (TS >= 10.0)
◆	SetLinearGradient (mode, startColor, endColor)	Creates a linear gradient textbox background using the specified mode and start/end colors. See **LinearGradientMode** and **Color** for lists of possible values.
◆	SetRadialGradient (startColor, endColor)	Creates a radial gradient textbox background using the specified start/end colors. See **Color** for a list of possible values.

TABLE 11.32—TextBox Class Methods

EVENTS

	Name	Description
⚡	KeyDown	Occurs when any key is pressed while the control has focus. See **KeyEventArgs** for the properties returned by the handler's args parameter.
⚡	KeyPress	Occurs when a character, space, or backspace key is pressed while the control has focus. See **KeyPressEventArgs** for the properties returned by the handler's args parameter.
⚡	KeyUp	Occurs when any key is released while the control has focus. See **KeyEventArgs** for the properties returned by the handler's args parameter.
⚡	TextChanged	Occurs when the text is changed. (TS >= 10.0)

TABLE 11.33—TextBox Class Events

INHERITANCE HIERARCHY

elSystem.Object
  elSystem.DotNetObject
   elSystem.elComponent
    elSystem.Windows.Forms.ELWFComponent
     elSystem.Windows.Forms.Control
      elSystem.Windows.Forms.TextBox

Adding a Form

A form is added to an Analysis Technique (Indicator, ShowMe, Strategy, TradingApp, etc.) using the following steps.

For the reader's convenience the following is repeated from **About the Resource Editor**, above.

Open an existing Analysis Technique (or create a new one) to which you want to add a form.

🖑 Right-Click anywhere in the Analysis Technique and select **Add Form** from the shortcut menu.

A blank form will appear on a tab in the editor and will be named Form1 by default (for the first form).

To display the form as part of your study or strategy you'll also need insert a line of EZL code into your document that calls the **Show()** Method for the specified form, such as:

```
Once form1.show () ;
```

This example uses OOEL Form Controls to display a custom window consisting of a form container and two controls, a button and textbox. A **Button** Click Event is set to call a method containing code that changes the text and button title.

The process of creating a custom form window consists of:

- declaring an object variable for each control
- creating a new instance of each control
- setting the location of controls within a form container
- setting parameters for the controls
- associating event methods with the controls
- adding controls to their container, and
- displaying the form.

Editing a Form

You may edit your Form in the EZL Editor directly or you can learn from the DGC and copy the parts you want into your code. You can edit your Form using the EasyLanguage Resource Editor DGC or you can use straight editing of the source code within the PowerEditor itself. Sam uses a combination of the two creating the initial Form using the Resource Editor in a 'sandbox' AT then when satisfied with the Form he creates a new document with the final name, copies the DGC code and pastes it in the document. He then copies and pastes the code into the appropriate sections of the editor window.

When I am working with these tools, I keep them all open on one window. Sam prefers to cascade windows and auto-hide the tabs. Each to his own. See Figure 11.32 below.

FIGURE 11.32—Multiple Views of Resource Editor, Properties and Outline

Summary

In this chapter we have introduced you to the **Form** Class and **Form Controls** as well as the ToolBox, and Resource Editor and their uses. We have talked about adding a Form and about the Resource Editor and **DataGridView**.

We could write a whole book on Forms alone. That's next. For the time being we leave this to you to explore and experiment with. If you run into difficulties, give us a call.[46]

---

[46] Sunny is at 1-760-908-3070 PT and you can reach Sam at sktennis@vista-research.com ET

CHAPTER 12
Provider Classes

In This Chapter
- Introduction
- Best Practices with DataProviders
- Summary

Introduction

This and the following chapter were written by the master at Data and Order Providers, Chris Davy.[47] We are enormously grateful. If you need help with these concepts, don't be shy about contacting him.

There are two main groups of data providers: market data and trading data. The data providers listed below must each be studied in-depth. They each have a specific set of information they make available to an application. Some are straight-forward and other quite complex with some unique and possibly un-anticipated behavior and limitations.

One should create small indicators to experiment with creating these providers and examining their properties and events.

Best Practices with Data Providers

The data providers handle the requesting of data from the TS servers.

Set all properties of a data provider before requesting it be loaded. Do not set properties of a data provider while it is loading or loaded.

Data Provider Events

All the data providers have two events:

- **StateChanged**—This event is raised whenever the state of the data provider changes. Having a **StateChanged** Event Handler Method will allow the code to detect a failed state.
- **Updated**—This event is raised when there is an update to the data which the data provider has been configured to receive.

Data Provider States

All data providers have four states in which they may exist.

- **Unloaded**—The data provider has been created but it has not been requested to load data.
- **Loading**—The data provider has been requested to load data by either setting its Load property to True or calling the **LoadProvider ()** Method.
- **Loaded**—The data provider has successfully retrieved the requested data from the TS servers.
- **Failed**—The data provider failed to load. This is typically the result of not properly setting its properties before requesting it be loaded.

> ☑ Do not attempt to retrieve data from a data provider before it has reached the loaded state. This will cause an exception.

A data provider has a **State** property that may be retrieved to determine its state. See the **DataState**

---

[47] Chris Davy c21tradingsystems@gmail.com

enumeration.

Data Provider Update Reasons

Various Data Providers may have different update reasons, so you'll need to refer to the Enumerations for specifics for that class. For instance:

DATASTATE ENUMERATION

Types of data states.

NAMESPACE: **tsData.Common**

ENUMERATED VALUES

	Name	Value
⊞	Failed	3
⊞	Loaded	2
⊞	Loading	1
⊞	Unloaded	0

TABLE 12.01—Enumerated Values for the DataState Enumeration

RealTime

Data providers can operate with the **RealTime** Property as True or False.

True indicates that as any of the requested data is updated, an updated event is to be raised.

False indicates no updated events are to be raised.

DataProviders and Functions

It is not advised to put data providers into functions. There are exceptions but generally it is not advised. Most trading code will need to know about the events from Data Providers. If one uses a function that creates a data provider and has the events defined within the function, the primary trading study will not receive those events and will therefore be unaware of critical events related to managing a trade.

Using Data Providers

Data providers operate asynchronously. This means when control is returned to the calling code immediately after a **LoadProvider ()** or **CloseProvider ()** call is made. There may be a time interval between calling the **LoadProvider ()** Method to load data and when that data is available. Data from the data provider cannot be accessed until the data provider is in the Loaded state. It is a good practice to use the **StateChanged** event to determine when the **DataProvider** is loaded.

Often it is necessary to ensure that a data provider is loaded before the bars begin to be referenced in a study. A study using a data provider can force the data provider to be loaded before continuing processing. This is important if the study needs the data available from the data provider for further calculations or actions.

To force a data provider to load, once the call to the **LoadProvider ()** Method is done, the next line would be:

```
if  DataProviderObject.State <> DataState.Unloaded
and DataProviderObject.State <> DataState.Failed
  then  Value99 = DataProviderObject.Count ;
// or some other numeric property of the data provider
```

This line will cause an exception since the count property of the data provider is null until the data provider reaches the loaded state. The platform catches this exception, waits until the data provider is loaded, and then restarts the study.

DO NOT enclose the calls to **LoadProvider** in a Try…Catch block as this will result in the study catching the exception and it not being passed on to the platform to restart the study once the data provider is loaded.

A **DataProvider** request results in the platform initiating the request and maintaining information about the request in the platform. The **DataProvider** initiated in the platform will continue receiving data for approximately 60 seconds after the **DataProvider** is closed. So, when the platform re-initializes your study after the Value99 line causes an exception and the platform **DataProvider** reaches the loaded state, when your EZL code again requests the loading of that provider, the platform **DataProvider** is already loaded and up to date, so the Value99 line of code does NOT cause an exception.

Depending upon what data providers a trading algorithm requires, this re-initialization may occur multiple times (such as for the **AccountsProvider** (AP), **PositionsProvider** (PP) and **OrdersProvider** (OP). Using this forced load is only appropriate at the startup of a study. Normally one would not want a study to re-initialize after running for some time. If a data provider is needed during processing after initialization, the code must request the loading of the data provider and wait for a **StateChanged** event indicating the data provider is loaded before attempting to use the data.

It is a best practice to not re-use a data provider. One should not close the provider, change some properties, and then load it. This can work with some data providers, like the **SymbolAttributesProvider** (SAP), but not with the **OrdersProvider**, **PriceSeriesProvider**(PSP), etc. It is best to create a new data provider in cases like this.

In some applications it may be appropriate to cascade through the providers due to data requirements. For example, you may need the **AccountsProvider** (AP) for the **AccountID** before the **PositionsProvider** (PP) or **OrdersProvider** (OP) can be loaded. An appropriate approach here is to request the loading of the PP from the **StateChanged** event of the AP once it is loaded.

The arguments for the events supply useful information.

Note that for the **Updated** event the args.Reason should be examined. The **InitialUpdate** reason will occur as the first Updated event and will typically not have any actual data associated with it. Hence it can usually be ignored.

Account Class

This Class accesses account information from a specified account when using an **AccountsProvider (AP)** component.

NAMESPACE: tsData.Trading

The **Updated** Event is called whenever a change occurs in the referenced data.

PROPERTIES

	Name	Type	Description
🖼	AccountID	string	Gets the ID (account number) of the account.
🖼	Alias	string	Gets the optional account name chosen by the user.
🖼	BDAccountEquity	double	Gets the value of beginning day account equity.
🖼	BDAcountNetWorth	double	Gets the value of beginning day account net worth.
🖼	BDCashBalance	double	Gets the value of beginning day cash balance.
🖼	BDDayTradingBuyingPower	double	Gets the value of beginning day DayTrading buying power.
🖼	BDOptionBuyingPower	double	Gets the value of beginning day option buying power.

	Name	Type	Description
	BDOptionLiquidationValue	double	Gets the value of beginning day option liquidation.
	BDOvernightBuyingPower	double	Gets the value of beginning day overnight buying power.
	BDUnrealizedPL	double	Gets the value of beginning day unrealized profit/loss.
	CanDayTrade	bool	True if day trading is allowed in the account, otherwise False.
	Currency	int	Gets an integer code indicating the currency of the account.
	ExtendedProperties	object	Gets the DynamicProperties object associated with the account.
	FourDaysTradeCount	int	Gets the number of trades from the past four days.
	HasValue	bool	True if the specified AccountField exists, otherwise False.
	IsDayTrader	string	True if the trader is a pattern day trader.
	Name	string	Gets the name of the account.
	OptionApprovalLevel	double	Gets the options approval level.
	RTAccountEquity	double	Gets the value of real-time account equity.
	RTAccountNetWorth	double	Gets the value of real-time account net worth.
	RTCashBalance	double	Gets the value of real-time cash balance.
	RTCostOfPositions	double	Gets the value of real-time cost of positions.
	RTDayTradingBuyingPower	double	Gets the value of real-time day trading buying power.
	RTInitialMargin	double	Gets the value of real-time initial margin.
	RTMaintenanceMargin	double	Gets the value of real-time maintenance margin.
	RTOptionBuyingPower	double	Gets the value of real-time option buying power.
	RTOptionLiquidationValue	double	Gets the value of real-time option liquidation value.
	RTOvernightBuyingPower	double	Gets the value of real-time overnight buying power.
	RTPurchasingPower	double	Gets the value of real-time purchasing power.
	RTRealizedPL	double	Gets the value of real-time realized profit/loss.
	RTUnrealizedPL	double	Gets the value of unrealized profit/loss.
	Status	string	Gets the status of the account.
	TodaysRTTradeEquity	double	Gets the value of today's real-time trade equity.
	Type	enum	Gets the account type. See AccountType for a

	Name	Type	Description
			list of possible values.
📷	UnclearedDeposits	double	Gets the value of uncleared deposits.
📷	UnsettledFund	double	Gets the value of unsettled funds.
📷	Value [fieldName]	double	Gets the value of the specified account field name.

TABLE 12.02—Account Class Properties

METHODS

	Name	Description
🔶	CanTradeSecurityOfType (type)	True if you can trade the specified type of security. See SecurityType for a list.

TABLE 12.03—Account Class Methods

EVENTS

	Name	Description
⚡	Updated	Occurs whenever the Account data is updated. See AccountUpdatedEventArgs for the properties returned by the handler's args parameter.

TABLE 12.04—Account Class Events

INHERITANCE HIERARCHY

elSystem.Object
  tsData.Trading.Account

AccountsProvider Class

The **AccountsProvider** (AP) exposes those accounts available with the current TS logon. Each account has properties that may be useful for monitoring buying power and account equity.

NAMESPACE: tsData.Trading

The **AccountsProvider** allows access to account information from one or more TS accounts that are associated with the provider. This information is like that found on the Balances tab of the TradeManager. The **Account** Class describes the properties available for a specific account. (See **Volume II—Reference Guide, Appendix III: Classes**.)

Typically, you will use the ToolBox to add a component to your Analysis Technique. 🖱 Double-Click the name **AccountsProvider** into your document from the ToolBox. The name of the provider appears in the Component Tray at the bottom of your document. By default, the name is followed by a number to identify multiple instances of the component.

Open the Properties Editor and locate the Accounts property under "Filters". A blank (default) Accounts filter property specifies that all your active TS accounts are to be included in the collection. Assigning a comma delimited list of account numbers to the Accounts filter property (i.e., "SIM12345, SIM67890") specifies that only those listed accounts are to be a part of the **Accounts** Collection queried by the **AccountsProvider**.

To reference property values for a specific Account Object in EZL code, use `Account[parameter]` followed by a dot operator (.) and the account property name. Parameter can be a numeric index (zero-based) that represents an Account Object within the provider account collection or a string containing a specific AccountID. Available Account properties including inherited properties will appear in the AutoComplete list as soon as you type the 'dot' after account[parameter]. Properties are also listed under **Account** class in the dictionary and in help.

For more specific information about the **AccountsProvider** Class see **Volume II—Reference Guide: Appendix III**.

EXAMPLE 12.01—Sample AccountsProvider Format

```
Value1=AccountsProvider1.Account[0].RTAccountNetWorth;
// gets the Real-Time Net Worth of first account [0]
// in the collection }
```

or

```
Value1=AccountsProvider1.Account["SIM12345"].BDCashBalance;
// gets the Beginning Day Cash Balance of a specific
// account number }
```

☑ The provider can only access accounts that are associated with the current TS logon and those that are indicated by the Accounts filter.

EXAMPLE 12.02—AccountsProvider Usage [OME_AccountsProvider]

This code is just a snippet but we are putting it in an ELD so you don't have to type it all. This method uses an **AccountsProvider** component to calculate the total real-time value of the accounts associated with your logon. For instance, on the chart below you will see that I have 3 accounts and a current account balance of $344,473. The results are plotted in the Subgraph as lines showing the number of accounts and the current balance. The drawback to this example is that it is scaled from -$300,000 to +$400,000 and the number of accounts is very much smaller than the accounts balance. To remedy this, just remove `Plot1` from the indicator and reset the scaling range.

```
method void AccountsProvider1_Updated( elSystem.Object sender,
tsData.Trading.AccountUpdatedEventArgs args )
{ the Updated event hander method is called when any Account property
changes }
variables:
tsData.Trading.Account myAccount,
// object variable used to access the values for each Account
double AcctValue,
// used to accumulate the total real-time net worth of all
// accounts
int Counter ;

begin
   if (AccountsProvider1.Count > 0) then
     begin
       AcctValue = 0;
       For Counter=0 to AccountsProvider1.Count-1
// reads each Account Object and adds the real-time value
// to the total
       begin
         myAccount = AccountsProvider1[Counter] ;
         AcctValue = AcctValue + myAccount.RTAccountNetWorth;
       end;
// displays the number of accounts and their total value
       Plot1(AccountsProvider1.Count,"Accts");
// remove Plot1 if the scaling concerns you
       Plot2(AcctValue,"TotalValue");
     end
   else
// display an error message if no accounts are found
     throw elSystem.Exception.Create ("No accounts available") ;
end ;
```

FIGURE 12.01—AccountsProvider Shows Three Accounts with Current Balance

For general information about providers, refer to Provider Classes in **Volume II—Reference Guide**: **Appendix III**.

PROPERTIES

	Name	Type	Description
	Account [index]	object	Gets the Account Object with the specified index.
	Account [accountID]	object	Gets the Account Object based on the specified AccountID string.
	Accounts	list	Gets or sets the TokenList filter that contains a comma-delimited list of specific accounts you want to query. All accounts are queried if the filter is blank.
	Count	int	Gets the total number of accounts in the provider's collection.
	Data	object	References the Accounts collection for the specified accounts.
	ExtendedFilter	object	Gets the DynamicProperties filter that may be applied to the data provider to select retrieved data based upon ExtendedProperties

TABLE 12.05—AccountsProvider Properties

METHODS

	Name	Description
	Contains (string)	True if the specified AccountID string is contained in the provider.
	Create ()	Initializes a new instance of AccountsProvider.
	GetAccountForSecurityOfType (type)	Returns an **Account** Object for an account that handles securities of the specified type. See **SecurityType** in **Volume II—Reference Guide, Appendix IV-- Enumerations**, for a list of possible values

TABLE 12.06—AccountsProvider Methods

EVENTS

	Name	Description
	Updated	Occurs whenever the Account data is updated. See **AccountUpdatedEventArgs**

Name	Description
	for the properties returned by the handler's args parameter.

TABLE 12.07—AccountsProvider Events

INHERITANCE HIERARCHY

elSystem.Object
  elSystem.DotNetObject
   elSystem.elComponent
    tsData.Common.DataProvider
     tsData.Trading.AccountsProvider

EXAMPLE 12.03—AccountsProvider [OME_AcctProvider]

In this example, for use in RadarScreen (RS), we display the number of accounts you have and the cumulative value of them. This information is independent of symbol. If you put it in a RS with lots of symbols the value will remain the same for each symbol. If you put it on a chart, you will get a real-time display of the total of your various accounts as a line on your chart.

```
Vars  :
 Bool   isRS   (FALSE) ;

// ============================================================

method void AccountsProvider1_Updated (elSystem.Object sender,
tsData.Trading.AccountUpdatedEventArgs args)
// the Updated event handler method is called when any
// Account property changes
Vars  :
tsData.Trading.Account myAccount,
// object variable used to access the values for each
// Account
double AcctValue,
// used to accumulate the total real-time net worth of
// all accounts }
int Loop ;
begin
   if  (AccountsProvider1.Count  > 00)  then begin
     AcctValue  = 00 ;
     For Loop  =  00 to AccountsProvider1.Count - 01
     // reads each Account Object and adds the real-time
     // value to the total
     begin
       myAccount   = AccountsProvider1 [Loop] ;
       AcctValue   = AcctValue + myAccount.RTAccountNetWorth ;
     end ; // for loop
     // displays the number of accounts and their total value
     if  isRS  then begin
       Plot1 (AccountsProvider1.Count, "Accts", Default, Default,
Default) ;
     end ;
     Plot2 (AcctValue, "TotalValue", Default, Default, Default) ;
   end
   else begin
     // display an error message if no accounts are found
     throw elSystem.Exception. Create ("No accounts available") ;
   end ; // count is zero
end ; // "AccountsProvider1_Updated" method

// ------------------------------------------------------------
```

```
method void AnalysisTechnique_Initialized (elSystem.Object sender,
elSystem.InitializedEventArgs args)
begin
   Print ("AnalysisTechnique_Initialized") ;
end ; // "AnalysisTechnique_Initialized" method

// -------------------------------------------------------

method void AnalysisTechnique_UnInitialized (elSystem.Object sender,
elSystem.UnInitializedEventArgs args)
begin
   Print ("AnalysisTechnique_UnInitialized") ;
end ; // "AnalysisTechnique_UnInitialized" method

// -------------------------------------------------------

method void AnalysisTechnique_WorkspaceSaving (elSystem.Object sender,
elSystem.WorkspaceSavingEventArgs args)
begin
   Print ("AnalysisTechnique_WorkspaceSaving") ;
end ; // "AnalysisTechnique_WorkspaceSaving" method

// ===========================================================

Once begin
   isRS  = GetAppInfo (aiAppID)  = cRadarScreen ;
end ; // Once, and only once
```

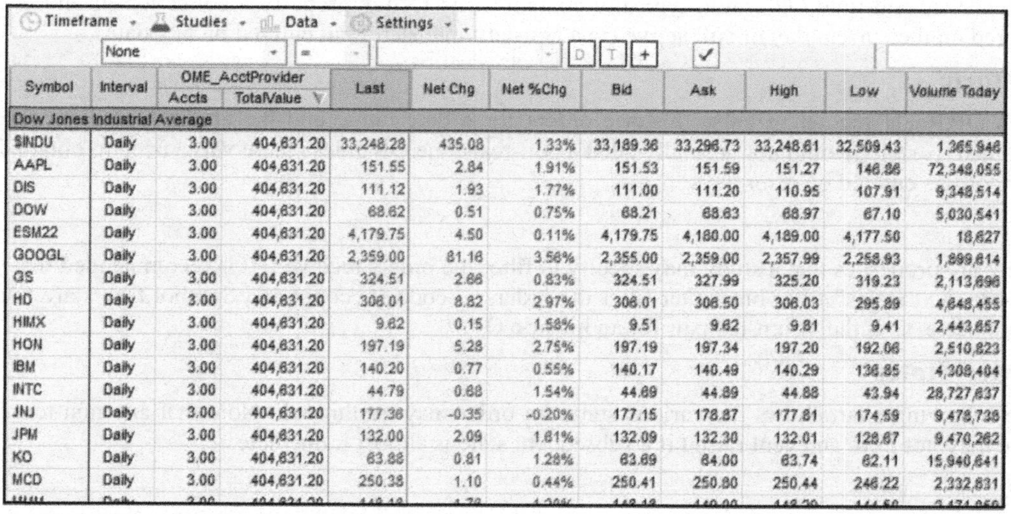

Symbol	Interval	OME_AcctProvider		Last	Net Chg	Net %Chg	Bid	Ask	High	Low	Volume Today
		Accts	TotalValue								
Dow Jones Industrial Average											
$INDU	Daily	3.00	404,631.20	33,248.28	435.08	1.33%	33,189.36	33,296.73	33,248.61	32,509.43	1,365,946
AAPL	Daily	3.00	404,631.20	151.55	2.84	1.91%	151.53	151.59	151.27	146.86	72,348,055
DIS	Daily	3.00	404,631.20	111.12	1.93	1.77%	111.00	111.20	110.95	107.91	9,348,514
DOW	Daily	3.00	404,631.20	68.62	0.51	0.75%	68.21	68.63	68.97	67.10	5,030,541
ESM22	Daily	3.00	404,631.20	4,179.75	4.50	0.11%	4,179.75	4,180.00	4,189.00	4,177.50	18,627
GOOGL	Daily	3.00	404,631.20	2,359.00	81.16	3.56%	2,355.00	2,359.00	2,357.99	2,258.93	1,899,614
GS	Daily	3.00	404,631.20	324.51	2.86	0.83%	324.51	327.99	325.20	319.23	2,113,696
HD	Daily	3.00	404,631.20	306.01	8.82	2.97%	306.01	306.50	306.03	295.89	4,648,455
HIMX	Daily	3.00	404,631.20	9.62	0.15	1.58%	9.51	9.62	9.81	9.41	2,443,657
HON	Daily	3.00	404,631.20	197.19	5.28	2.75%	197.19	197.34	197.20	192.06	2,510,823
IBM	Daily	3.00	404,631.20	140.21	0.77	0.55%	140.17	140.49	140.29	136.85	4,308,404
INTC	Daily	3.00	404,631.20	44.79	0.68	1.54%	44.69	44.89	44.88	43.94	28,727,637
JNJ	Daily	3.00	404,631.20	177.36	-0.35	-0.20%	177.15	178.87	177.81	174.59	9,478,738
JPM	Daily	3.00	404,631.20	132.00	2.09	1.61%	132.09	132.30	132.01	128.67	9,470,262
KO	Daily	3.00	404,631.20	63.88	0.81	1.28%	63.69	64.00	63.74	62.11	15,940,641
MCD	Daily	3.00	404,631.20	250.38	1.10	0.44%	250.41	250.80	250.44	246.22	2,332,831

FIGURE 12.02—AccountsProvider in RadarScreen

SymbolAttributesProvider Class

The **SymbolAttributesProvider** (SAP) has properties for a symbol. SAPs can be useful if the study needs to reference properties of multiple symbols.

Two properties for making a trading study independent of the user's time zone are **GMTExchangeOffset** and **GMTLocalOffset**.

The following statements display the type of security and exchange for the symbol in the Print Log.

```
Print (SymbolAttributesP1.SymbolType.tostring() ) ;
Print (SymbolAttributesP1.Exchange) ;
```

OrdersProvider Class

The **OrdersProvider** allows access to updated order information based on user specified filters from a list of specified TS accounts. This information is similar to that found on the Orders tab of the TradeManager. The **Order** class describes the properties available for a specific order.

The **OrdersProvider** (OP) can be one of the most useful data providers. It gives access to the orders that have been placed for the specified filters (accounts, symbols, states).

If you have multiple trading studies trading the same symbol, then tracking all the specific orders generated by the study and only utilizing these orders is a way to avoid having two studies interfere with each other's trading.

Note that the **OrdersProvider** retrieves orders with an **EnteredTime** within the "from-to" date range.

EXAMPLE 12.04—Using OrdersProvider

```
Value1 = OrdersProvider1.Order[0].Commission ;
// gets the commission of first order [0] in the collection.
```

or

```
Value1 = OrdersProvider1.Order["2-3105-2140"].LimitPrice;
// gets the Limit Price of a specific
// order id number.
```

See Volume II—Reference Guide, Appendix III: Classes for more information.

RealTime

With the OP.RealTime set to True, the OP can provide events whenever the state of an order is changed. This allows real-time monitoring of the status of orders. A study would typically have a real-time OP. A real-time OP would typically contain in its **Order** property a collection of any orders entered on the current day or still active (in a non-terminal state) but entered on any date.

Historic

With OP.RealTime set to False, historic orders for a date range and the applicable filters can be obtained. A study would not normally need a non-real-time OP unless there was a need to obtain data from orders entered on prior days.

Filters

There are properties that a study may specify to filter the orders received. It is recommended that you not use the "States" filter but rather filter the orders in code. Account and Symbol filters are totally appropriate, as is the "from-to" pair for an historic OP.

Order States

The following chart shows the various states an order may go through. Note that any non-terminal state may not have an event raised if a subsequent state is almost immediate.

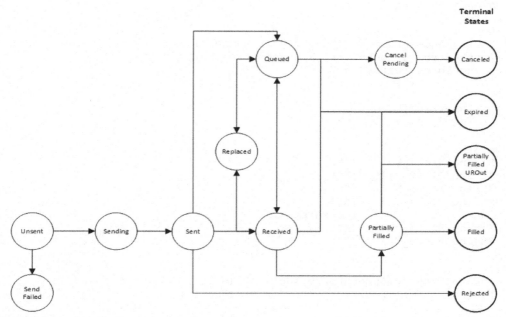

FIGURE 12.03—Flow Chart of Order States

Trade History

Often you will want to recreate the trade history for a symbol. The **OrdersProvider** in non-real-time mode (historical) is the key data provider for building a history of trades. With it, code can obtain all the historical orders in their final state (filled, canceled, etc.). You can then iterate (from oldest to latest) through all these orders to obtain the **AvgFilledPrice** and **FilledQuantity** and **Action** (buy, sell, etc.) from which P&L can be calculated.

If you only do day trades and the symbol is flat at the start and end of the day, then just select the from and to dates to be the day of interest and accumulate the P&L from the orders.

If you hold positions overnight or are currently in a position, then the issue is a bit more complicated. First use the **PositionsProvider** to find the current position, and then one must take a guess at how far back in history one wants to go. Then load the **OrdersProvider** with the "from" and "to" properties set to the appropriate dates and work backwards (current to oldest) through the orders to reconstruct positions, taking the current position into account. Note that the oldest trade being constructed may not be complete if the position actually started before the "from" date.

PositionsProvider Class

The **PositionsProvider** allows access to updated information about positions held for specified symbols and order types from a list of TS accounts. This information is similar to that found on the Positions tab of the TradeManager. The **Position** Class describes the properties available for a specific position.

Typically, you will use the ToolBox to add a component to your document. 🖱 Click and drag the name **PositionsProvider** into your document from the ToolBox. By default, the name of the provider appears in the component tray at the bottom of your document followed by a number (to help identify multiple instances of the component).

Note that the **PositionsProvider** (PP) and the **OrdersProvider** (OP) both can be used to monitor the position. However, since events are only processed one at a time and either the PP or OP may fire before the other, one generally should use one or the other to monitor the position.

EXAMPLE 12.05—Using PositionsProvider in RadarScreen [OME_R_PosnProvider]

This example uses a **PositionsProvider** component to reference position values for the current symbol.

```
Using tsData.Trading ;

Inputs:
 String AccountNumber ("Enter Acct Number") ;
// enter the account for which position information
// should be retrieved

Vars  :
IntraBarPersist
 String AcctName      ("") ;

Vars  :
 String Plot1_Val     (""),
 String Plot2_Val     (""),
 String Plot3_Val     (""),
 String Plot4_Val     (""),
 Int    Plot5_Clr     (DarkGreen),
 String Plot5_Val     (""),
 String Plot6_Val     ("") ;

Vars  :
 tsData.Trading.AccountsProvider  AP (NULL),
 tsData.Trading.PositionsProvider PP (NULL) ;

// Working Storage Section
Consts:
 String App_Type      ("Study"),
 String App_Name      ("OME_R_PosnProvider"),
 String App_Note      ("Example code demonstrating PositionsProvider in
RadarScreen"),
 String App_Vers      ("01.03.00") ;

Vars  :
 String DQ            (DoubleQuote),
 String NL            (NewLine),
 String CmtryStr      (""),
 Bool   doCmtry       (FALSE),
 Bool   Debug         (FALSE),
 Double Dummy         (0.00) ;

// ======================================================

method AccountsProvider AP_Init ()
Vars  :
 AccountsProvider AP ;
begin
  AP = AccountsProvider.Create () ;
//---------------------------
//AP
//---------------------------
  AP.Realtime = TRUE ;
  AP.TimeZone = tsdata.common.TimeZone.local ;
  AP.Name     = "AP" ;
  AP.Load     = TRUE ;
  Return AP ;
end ; // "AP_Init" method

// ------------------------------------------------------

method PositionsProvider PP_Init ()
Vars  :
```

```
     PositionsProvider PP ;
begin
//  PP = new tsdata.trading.PositionsProvider ;
   PP = tsdata.trading.PositionsProvider.Create () ;
   PP.Symbols   += Symbol ;
   if  Debug  then  Print ("#1 ", DQ, Symbol, DQ, ", AccountNumber=",
DQ, AccountNumber, DQ, ", AcctName=", DQ, AcctName, DQ, ", AcctName <>
'N/A'=", AcctName <> "N/A", ", PP.Accounts.isReadOnly=",
PP.Accounts.isReadOnly) ;
   PP.Accounts += AcctName ;
   PP.Types    += "Any" ;
   PP.Realtime  =  TRUE ;
   PP.TimeZone  = tsdata.common.TimeZone.local ;

//  PP.Accounts.IsReadOnly = true after the PositionsProvider
//  has loaded. You cannot change the accounts filter after
//  the provider has been loaded.
//  Before the PositionsProvider has been loaded,
//  PP.Accounts.IsReadOnly will be false.

   PP.Load  =  TRUE ;
   PP.Name  =  "PP" ;

   if  Debug  then  Print ("#2 ", DQ, Symbol, DQ, ", AccountNumber=",
DQ, AccountNumber, DQ, ", AcctName=", DQ, AcctName, DQ, ", AcctName <>
'N/A'=", AcctName <> "N/A", ", PP.Accounts.IsReadOnly=",
PP.Accounts.IsReadOnly) ;

   //---------------------------------------------
   //                    Events
   //---------------------------------------------
   PP.Updated      += PP_Updated ;
   PP.StateChanged += PP_StateChanged ;
   Return PP ;
end ; // "PP_Init" method

// ----------------------------------------------------

method void PP_Updated (elSystem.Object sender,
tsdata.trading.PositionUpdatedEventArgs args)
// the Updated event hander method is called whenever a
// Position property changes
Vars   :
 String PosAccountID,
 Double PcntOfAccount ;
begin
   if  Debug  then  Print ("PP_Updated) - Reason = ",
      args.Reason.toString (), ", Count - ", PP.Count:2:0) ;
// check to see if any position exists for the current symbol
// and plot position values
   if (args.Reason  = tsdata.trading.PositionUpdateReason.Added)
   and (PP.Count  > 00)
   then begin
     AcctName  = PP.Data [00].AccountID ;
     FillPlotValues () ;
   end   // Position Added or Real time update
   else
   if (args.Reason  =
tsdata.trading.PositionUpdateReason.RealTimeUpdate)
   and (PP.Count  > 00)
```

```
    then begin
      FillPlotValues () ;
    end   // Position Added or Real time update
    else
    if  (args.Reason  = tsdata.trading.PositionUpdateReason.Removed)
    and (PP.Count  = 00)
    then begin
      FillPlotValues () ;
    end ; // Position closed
end ; // "PP_Updated" method

// ------------------------------------------------------

method void PP_StateChanged (elSystem.Object sender,
tsdata.common.StateChangedEventArgs args)
Vars :
 String PosAccountID,
 Double PcntOfAccount ;
begin
  Print ("PP_StateChanged (OldState = ", args.OldState.toString (),
                          ", NewState- ", args.NewState.toString (),
")") ;
  if  args.NewState  =  tsdata.common.DataState.Loaded
  and (PP.Count  > 00)
  then begin
    AcctName  = PP.Data [00].AccountID ;
    FillPlotValues () ;
  end ;
end ; // "PP_StateChanged" method

// ------------------------------------------------------

method void FillPlotValues ()
Vars  :
 String PosAccountID,
 Double PcntOfAccount ;
begin
  if  Debug  then  Print ("FillPlotValues") ;
  if  (PP.Count  > 00)
  then begin
    PosAccountID  = PP.Position[00].AccountID ;
// calculate and plot pct. value of a stock account
    If  AP.Count  > 00
      then  PcntOfAccount  = PP.Position[00].MarketValue
            / AP.Account[PosAccountID].RTAccountNetWorth ;

    if  PP[00].OpenPL >= 0.00
      then  Plot5_Clr  = DarkGreen
      else  plot5_Clr  = Red ;

// plot properties associated with Position object '[00]'
    Plot1_Val  = PosAccountID ; // AcctName ;
    Plot2_Val  = NumToStr (PP.Position[00].Quantity,  00) ;
    Plot3_Val  = vrt_Format (PP.Position[00].AveragePrice) ;
    Plot4_Val  = NumToStr (PP.Position[00].MarketValue, 02) ;
    Plot5_Val  = NumToStr (PP.Position[00].OpenPL,      02) ;
    Plot6_Val  = NumToStr (PcntOfAccount * 100, 02) + " %" ;
  end
  else begin
//    Plot1_Val  = AcctName ;
    Plot2_Val  = "00" ;
```

```
       Plot3_Val   = "0.00" ;
       Plot4_Val   = "0.00" ;
       Plot5_Val   = "0.0" ;
       Plot6_Val   = "0.00" ;
     end  ;
     do_Plots () ;
  end ; // "FillPlotValues" method

  // -------------------------------------------------

  method void do_Plots ()
  begin
    Plot1 (Plot1_Val, "Account",   Default, Default, Default) ;
    Plot2 (Plot2_Val, "Qty",       Default, Default, Default) ;
    Plot3 (Plot3_Val, "EntPri",    Default, Default, Default) ;
    Plot4 (Plot4_Val, "Mkt Value", Default, Default, Default) ;
    Plot5 (Plot5_Val, "P/L",       Plot5_Clr, Default, Default) ;
    Plot6 (Plot6_Val, "% of Acct", Default, Default, Default) ;
  end ; // "do_Plots" method

  // ===================================================

  Once begin
    AP  = AP_Init () ;
    AcctName  = AccountNumber ;
    if  AcctName  = "Enter Acct Number"
      then  AcctName  = "" ;
    Plot1_Val  = AcctName ;
    Plot2_Val  = "00" ;
    Plot3_Val  = "0.00" ;
    Plot4_Val  = "0.00" ;
    Plot5_Val  = "0.00" ;
    Plot6_Val  = "0.00" ;
  //  do_Plots () ;
    PP  = PP_Init () ;
  end ; // Once, and only once

  do_Plots () ;
```

QuotesProviderClass

The **QuotesProvider** (QP) can supply real-time data for a symbol. The **QuotesProvider** allows access to updated information from the quotes data stream for a specified list of quote fields for a symbol. The **Updated** event is called whenever a change occurs in the quotes data.

Typically, you will use the ToolBox to add a component to your EZL document. ☝ Double-Click the name **QuotesProvider** into your document from the ToolBox. The name of the provider appears in the component tray at the bottom of your document. By default, the name is followed by a number to identify multiple instances of the component.

Open the Properties Editor and locate the **Symbol** and **Fields** Properties under **"Filters"**. Both are required fields. A comma delimited list of fields (e.g., "AskSize, DailyLimit"), specifies the values that will be available from the **QuotesProvider**.

To reference a property value for a **QuotesProvider** object in EZL code, use `QuotesProvider1` followed by a "dot operator", and the property name. Available **QuotesProvider** properties, including inherited properties, will appear in the AutoComplete list. To get data for one of the field names entered in the Properties Editor, use the "Quote" Property, followed by the field name within square brackets and double quotes["field name"]. Add a second "dot operator" and the type of the value to be returned.

```
Value1=QuotesProvider1.Quote["ask"].DoubleValue ;
// gets the Ask price for a specific symbol. Type MUST be
// known before using this.
```

For general information about providers, refer to **Provider Classes**.

PriceSeriesProvider Class (PSP)

The **PriceSeriesProvider** (PSP) can supply historical and real-time data for a symbol. The PSP is an alternative to having additional data streams in a chart. If the trading study will reside in a RadarScreen, the PSP is the only way to obtain historical data for symbols other than those in the RadarScreen.

> ☑ A PSP does not expose any historical data after the datetime of the current bar being processed in a chart. As new historic bars are processed, more data may be exposed. This is to prevent the study from "looking into the future" with a PSP. No events are raised for historic data.

Once the chart is processing the last bar on the chart in real-time, the **PSP** will expose its last interval and can raise events for updated PSP data.

EXAMPLE 12.06—Using AccountsProvider and PositionsProvider [OME_AP_PP]

The following is an example of using the **AccountsProvider** and the **PositionsProvider**.

It can be difficult getting started using order tickets, so here is a simple implementation of a strategy using only order tickets found on the TS Forum. There is no guarantee that it works as you might anticipate, so know that this is just an example to help get you started.

I've been running this on a 1-minute @ES chart in simulation mode.

The concept is to enter on the very short-term trend and then reverse the position if the trend reverses.

The indicator should be set to run end of bar (turn off tick-by-tick).

There is no exit, so anyone desiring one would have to add that themselves.

Be sure to enable order ticket objects in the setup, as shown in Figure 13.01 in the next chapter.

> ☑ The following code is from the TS Forum.

```
using elSystem.Collections ;
using elSystem ;
using tsData.Trading ;
using tsData.Common ;
using elSystem.IO ;
using elSystem.Windows.Forms ;
using elSystem.Drawing ;
using Charting ;

Input:
  double Price(Low),
  double Offset(0.00),
  bool   TradeOn(TRUE),
  string FileName("C:\OME_Files\OTFile01.txt") ;
Vars:
  double MA(Close) ;
Vars:
  Orders MyOrders (null),
  ReplaceTicket ReplTicket(null) ;

Vars:
  IntraBarPersist string    OrderTicketsFile
("\Users\Public\Documents\TradeLog\"),
  StreamWriter GoWrite (null) ;
Vars:
```

```
    IntraBarPersist double MktPos(0),
    IntraBarPersist string OrderID("") ;
  Vars:
    Vector OrderStorVctr (null),
    OrdersProvider OP1 ( NULL ),
    Orders StoredOrders (null),
    Order ActiveOrder (null),
    OrderIDFile (""),
    IntraBarPersist string MyOrderState (""),
    IntraBarPersist string ActiveOrderID(""),
    IntraBarPersist string MyOrderIDList(""),
    TokenList MyOPOrders(null),
    Order MyOrder(null),
    Order MySellOrder(null) ;
  Vars  :
    string MyOrderDirection(""),
    double MyOrderPrice(close),
    IntraBarPersist int OTMktPos(0) ;

//================================
//=== BUY ORDER EVENT HANDLER ===
//================================

method void OrderEH(Object sender, OrderUpdatedEventArgs args)
var: double FP ;
Begin
  Print (time:0:0," ",MyOrder.OrderID," ",
MyOrder.State.ToString()) ;
  If MyOrder.Action = OrderAction.Buy
  and MyOrder.State = OrderState.Filled then begin
    OTMktPos = OTMktPos + MyOrder.FilledQuantity;
    print(time:0:0,"    ","Buy"," ", MyOrder.AvgFilledPrice);
    FileWrite(DTS()+" |"+MyOrder.OrderID.ToString()+" |"+
MyOrder.State.ToString()+newline);
    MyOrder = null;
    Return ;
  end ;
  If MyOrder.Action = OrderAction.Sell
  and MyOrder.State = orderstate.Filled then begin
    OTMktPos = OTMktPos - MyOrder.FilledQuantity;
    Print (time:0:0,"   ","Sell",MyOrder.AvgFilledPrice) ;
    FileWrite(DTS()+" |"+ MyOrder.OrderID.ToString()+" |"+
MyOrder.State.ToString()+newline);
    MyOrder = null ;
    Return ;
  end ;
end ;

//================================
//=== ENTRY ORDER ===============
//================================
method void EntryOrder()
var: OrderTicket OrderTicket1, string SigText;
begin
  if  GetAppInfo(airealtimecalc) <> 01
   or OrderTicket.OrderPlacementEnabled = false
     then  Return ;
  OrderTicket1 = new OrderTicket() ;
..OrderTicket1.SymbolType = SecurityType.future ;
..OrderTicket1.Symbol = "ESU22" ;
```

```
..OrderTicket1.Account = getAccountID ;
..OrderTicket1.Quantity = 1 + absvalue(OTMktPos) astype int ;
..if MyOrderDirection = "Buy" then OrderTicket1.Action =
OrderAction.buy ;
  if MyOrderDirection = "Sell" then OrderTicket1.Action =
OrderAction.sell ;
  if MyOrderDirection = "Buy" then OrderTicket1.LimitPrice = close -
Offset ;
  if MyOrderDirection = "Sell" then OrderTicket1.LimitPrice = close +
Offset ;
    OrderTicket1.Type = OrderType.Limit ;
    OrderTicket1.Name = "OrderTicket1";
    MyOrder = OrderTicket1.send();
    MyOrder.Updated += OrderEH;
    FileWrite(DTS()+" |"+OrderTicket1.Action.ToString()+" |" +
OrderTicket1.Quantity.ToString () + " |"+
OrderTicket1.LimitPrice.ToString () + newline) ;
End ;


//===============================
//=== EXIT ORDER (N/A) ==========
//===============================
method void ExitOrder(string Sig)
Vars  : OrderTicket OrderTicket1, string SigText;
begin
   if  GetAppInfo (aiRealTimeCalc) <> 1 or
OrderTicket.OrderPlacementEnabled = false then return ;
  SigText = Sig+"SendExitTicket" ;
  OrderTicket1 = new OrderTicket () ;
  OrderTicket1.SymbolType = SecurityType.future ;
  OrderTicket1.Symbol = Symbol ;
  OrderTicket1.Account = GetAccountID ;
  OrderTicket1.Quantity = 1 + OTMktPos ;
  OrderTicket1.Action = OrderAction.Sell ;
  OrderTicket1.LimitPrice = close + Offset ;
  OrderTicket1.Type = OrderType.Limit ;
  OrderTicket1.Name = "OrderTicket1" ;
  MySellOrder = OrderTicket1.send();
  MySellOrder.Updated += OrderEH ;
end;


//============================================================
//=== METHOD TO RETURN DATE AND TIME STRING FOR THE COMPUTER

Method string DTS ()
Begin
  Return FormatDate ("MM/dd/yy", ComputerDateTime) + "|"
  + FormatTime ("hh:mm:ss", ComputerDateTime) ;
end ;


//============================================================
//=== METHOD TO WRITE TO FILE ================================
//============================================================

Method void FileWrite (string LineIn)
Begin
  GoWrite = new StreamWriter(OrderTicketsFile, True) ;
  GoWrite.AutoFlush = true ;
  GoWrite.Write(LineIn) ;
  GoWrite.close() ;
End ;
```

```
Once begin
  OrderTicketsFile += FileName;
end;

if BarStatus (01) = 02 then begin
  MA = Average (close, 20) ;
  plot1 (MA,"MA") ;

//==============================================================
//=== UPDATE ORDER IF IN RECEIVED STATE
//=== CANNOT DO REPLACE TICKET UNTIL THE FOLLOWING BAR
//=== Market Position <= 0
//==============================================================

  If  GetAppInfo (aiRealTimeCalc) = 01
  and BarStatus(1) = 2
  and MyOrder <> null
  and MyOrder.State = OrderState.Received
  and MktPos <= 0
  and MyOrderDirection = "Buy"
  and OrderTicket.OrderPlacementEnabled = true
  then begin
    ReplTicket = new replaceticket();
    ReplTicket.LimitPrice = Price - Offset;
    MyOrder.Replace(ReplTicket);
  end;

//==============================================================
//=== UPDATE ORDER IF IN RECEIVED STATE
//=== CANNOT DO REPLACE TICKET UNTIL THE FOLLOWING BAR
//=== Market Position >= 0
//==============================================================

  If GetAppInfo (aiRealTimeCalc) = 01
  and BarStatus (1) = 2
  and MySellOrder <> null
  and MySellOrder.State = orderstate.received
  and MktPos >= 0
  and MyOrderDirection = "Sell"
  and OrderTicket.OrderPlacementEnabled = true
  Then begin
    ReplTicket = new replaceticket();
    ReplTicket.LimitPrice = close + Offset;
    MySellOrder.Replace(ReplTicket);
  end;

  If BarStatus(1) = 2
  and GetAppInfo (airealtimecalc) = 01
  and TradeOn
  and Low > MA
  and OTMktPos <= 0
  and MyOrder = null
  then begin
    MyOrderDirection = "Buy";
    EntryOrder();
  end ;

  If BarStatus (01) = 02
  and GetAppInfo (airealtimecalc) = 01
```

```
and TradeOn
and High < MA
and OTMktPos >= 0
and MyOrder = null
then begin
   MyOrderDirection = "Sell";
   EntryOrder();
end ;
end ;
```

This code only makes sense when you have a Strategy on your chart or when you are placing orders that generate a fluctuation in the equity curve since it is plotting your account equity. To prepare the next figure I put my automated SunnyBands© Strategy on a chart of the EMini (ES) and let it run. The blue line in the center of the chart shows the accounts' equity as it progresses over time. Note that it shows all my accounts at once.

You will also see the arrows from the Strategy and, on the bottom, my DynamicMAV Histogram (DMA_H) plot. If you want to know more about the Indicator or the Strategy, go to https://www.moneymentor.com/products.html.

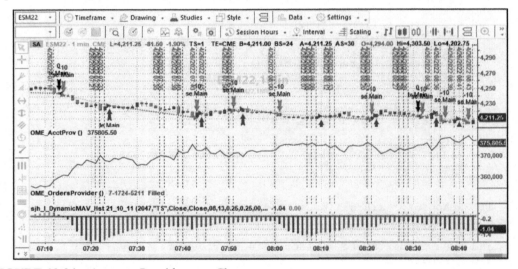

FIGURE 12.04—AccountsProvider on a Chart

Summary

This chapter and the next are largely written by Chris Davy[48] and we thank him for his generosity and expertise. The sample code was originated by Chris as well as the Best Practices section.

OrdersProvider and **DataProvider Classes** are sort of a specialty within OOEL and best handled by experts like Chris and Sam.

---

[48] Chris Davy may be reached at c21tradingsystems@gmail.com.

CHAPTER 13

Order Tickets & Data Providers

In This Chapter

- Introduction
- Benefits of Order Tickets
- Order Tickets & DataProviders
- Placing Orders with EasyLanguage
- Updating an Order
- Logging

- Factors of Design
- Enabling Order Placement Objects
- Order Class
- Examples of Order Tickets
- Summary

Introduction

It seems to be everyone's dream to have an automated system that does the chart monitoring and order placement by itself. Set it up once and leave. We all want an automated money-making machine.

That's a bit of a pipedream with complexities. While it is possible to code a program that places trades automatically, as far as I'm concerned it still must be monitored by someone. The electricity will flicker and connection with TS will be lost; the computer crashes from time to time, especially if you are running anything other than TS on it; TS loses data when your router flickers; TS itself sometimes encounters glitches. And there are times when even the most brilliant programmers don't anticipate the current market condition and take or close a trade you would or wouldn't have yourself. It might be alright while you run to the potty for a second, but don't expect it to respect your wishes while you sleep. For these, and more, reasons I don't leave my automated strategy alone. And I don't let it trade while I sleep.

While this chapter is largely devoted to Order Tickets, I must get into Data Providers (DP) a little bit herein, but the bulk of the Data Providers information was in the preceding chapter.

Credit where credit is due: most of the content of this chapter is gleaned from the works of Chris Davy[49]. He is the master of order tickets when it comes to OOEL, so why not learn from the best: Chris Davy?

In this chapter when Chris refers to "indicator" he means to say Analysis Technique when using Order Tickets.

Benefits of Order Tickets

Among the benefits of using **OrderTickets** (OT) are:

- Ability to submit true OSO and OCO OrderTickets.
- StopLimit orders are available.
- Easier coding for execution on tick-by-tick.
- All orders are resident on the TS servers, so a disconnect does not impact them.
- Time activation and deactivation rules.
- Price activation rules.
- Ability to send in orders at any time, not just on data ticks, including from event handlers. Of course, the market needs to be open for the order to be executed.
- Ability to send in a **Replace OrderTicket**, which either confirms the change or rejects the

---

[49] Christopher G. Davy c21tradingsystems@gmail.com

change request.
- Easy detection of rejected orders.
- Ability to confirm a cancel of an order before submitting a new one.
- True dynamic scaling in and scaling out are trivial with **OrderTickets**.
- Ability to trade multiple symbols from the same study.
- Ability to trade multiple trading algorithms on the same symbol in the same account, keeping everything separate.
- Avoid strategy-related dialog boxes that can halt trading until manually handled.

OrderTickets and DataProviders

Developing a study to perform trading and trade management chores requires the use of **OrderTickets** (OTs) to place orders and **DataProviders** (DPs) to monitor the actual trading.

These will require using an event-driven programming structure (EPS) as opposed to traditional top-down programming. Although the use of OTs and DPs give the developer significantly greater flexibility and control, this comes at the cost of significantly larger studies with greater complexity. Using traditional EZL strategies all the back-office work is done for you, things like knowing your current position, how many contracts you have on and your current open position profit.

There is additional functionality that will greatly benefit the study development. This includes such things as collections, WinForms and often file/directory I/O and XML.

There is no one specific template that will work with all trading algorithms. One must choose the types of OTs to be used, when they are used, and how specific DPs can be used to reach the desired objective.

Placing Orders with EasyLanguage

There are three basic approaches to placing orders within EZL.
- **Strategies** - Strategies have specific reserved words that are used exclusively in an EZL module of type Strategy. There are many reserved words for implementing a trading algorithm. There are some compromises when using a strategy to make their development easy. A strategy is essentially incompatible with both PlaceOrder functions and OrderTickets.
- **Data Providers and Functions** - It is not advised to put data providers into functions. Most trading code will need to know about the events from data providers. If one uses a function that creates a Data Provider and has the events defined within the function, the primary trading study will not receive those events and will therefore be unaware of critical events related to managing a trade.
- **OrderTickets and DataProviders** - **OrderTickets** and **DataProviders** offer the most functionality of all the methods. The cost is that the number of lines of code required is significantly greater and requires advanced programming techniques (object-oriented event-driven programming).

How They Compare

If you are proficient at developing strategies with EZL, there are some key differences you must think about in programming and trading with OrderTickets and DataProviders.

Code Execution

Most strategies are designed to execute on bar close, although if IntrabarOrderGeneration (IOG or IBOG) is enabled the strategy code executes on every tick. When a strategy executes it processes the lines of main body code from the top to the bottom and then stops executing on that data tick.

Indicators normally default to executing the code at the Close of the bar, but there is an option to have the calculations done on every tick.

However, much code execution happens as the Event Handlers fire asynchronously.

Unlike a strategy, the orders resulting from OTs are on the TS servers and the indicator does not need to be running for the trade to complete. The TS servers will handle them accordingly.

However, there are situations that would require the indicator to be executing, usually around situations in which the orders need to be modified based upon price activity or the passing of time.

A set of orders may be created that supports trailing stops, end-of-day exits, and stop adjustment based upon targets being hit, etc.

The compromise is often whether one wants all the orders to reside on the TS servers versus the need to update these orders based upon market activity.

Depending upon the reliability of one's Internet connection the need to have everything resident on the server may or may or may not be critical.

See the following websites for more information on event-driven programming.

https://en.wikipedia.org/wiki/Event-driven_architecture

https://medium.com/high-alpha/event-driven-architecture-a-primer-f636395d0295

https://www.confluent.io/blog/journey-to-event-driven-part-1-why-event-first-thinking-changes-everything/

Partial Fill Handling

If one is trading more than a quantity of 1, then there is the possibility of partial fills with limit orders. In case you are not familiar with different types of orders, before jumping in let me define two that we will cover in this section.

OSO means Order-Sends-Order. It is also known as Order-Triggers-Other. An OSO is a set of conditional orders stipulating that if one order executes (the primary order), then the other order(s) are automatically entered (the secondary order or orders).

An **OCO** order means One-Cancels-Other or Order-Cancels-Order. An OCO order is a pair of conditional orders stipulating that if one order executes, then the other order is automatically canceled. An OCO order often combines a stop order with a limit order on an automated trading platform. When either the stop or limit price is reached and the order is executed, the other order is automatically canceled.

If an **OSOOrderTicket** is utilized, then the orders resulting from the secondary order tickets are not made active until then entire entry quantity has been filled. If the entry order is only partially filled and the price moves away from the entry toward the exits, these exits are not active and therefore will not be filled, potentially resulting in missed profits or excessive losses.

If a simple **OrderTicket** is used for entry, then as it is partially filled, **OCOOrderTickets** or **BracketOrderTickets**[50] can be used to implement the target and/or stops for each partial fill. This avoids the issue of not having active exit brackets but does potentially result in more orders for handling exits. The exposure with this approach is the very small window of time in which there is a position without any exit bracket.

Order Submission

A Strategy may only submit an order on a data tick using IBOG or on the close of a bar without IBOG enabled. A Strategy may not submit an order from an event handler, such as a timer elapsed or a **GlobalDictionary ItemAdded** or **ItemChanged** Event. In a Strategy the code must submit the order every time the strategy executes, or the strategy engine will cancel the order.

An AT may submit an **OrderTicket** at any time, including from an event handler. Unlike a Strategy, the **OrderTicket** only needs to be sent once, not on every execution of the indicator. Zero or more Orders may result from the sending of an **OrderTicket**. Once the **OrderTicket** has been sent, all management of

---

[50] For definitions, see Glossary at https://www.moneymentor.com/glossary.html.

the trade must be accomplished by managing the Orders, most typically by handling the events that Orders raise indicating state changes of the Order. If the code needs to cancel an Order, there is an explicit **Cancel ()** Method that must be used to cancel the order.

A Strategy can be built for this purpose as well, assuming it does not use strategy keywords. A strategy which looks just like a study is a permissible use.

Order Lifetime

A Strategy must continue to send in an order on every execution of the strategy for that order to remain in place. Once an order is not re-sent, the strategy engine will initiate a cancel of that order.

When an indicator sends an **OrderTicket**, it only needs to do this once. Once the **OrderTicket** is received the generated Orders are resident on the TS servers and will remain there until some terminal state is reached, such as **Filled**, **Expired** or **Canceled**. See the **OrderState** Enumerated List.

A Strategy, sending a repeated order for every execution of the strategy, will initiate an order cancel once that order is no longer sent it. Conversely, when an order is sent in with an **OrderTicket** the code must explicitly cancel Orders.

Strategy orders are day orders. **OrderTicket** generated orders may have their duration specified, such as **Day** or **GTC**. See the **Duration** Property of the **Order** Class for more options.

Code Structure

A Strategy is typically designed to execute on bar close or every data tick. The code starts executing at the first line of body code and proceeds through the lines of code to the last line. In a Method or Once Block the code will execute as referenced, not from the top down.

An indicator's code will be mostly Methods and Event Handlers for various DataProviders and other OOEL classes, with few lines of body code.

Trading Information

A Strategy has access to many reserved words to allow the code to easily determine the state of the trade and prior trades. These are words like **MarketPosition**, **BarsSinceEntry**, **SetProfitTarget**, and other position related reserved words. They are essentially any of the reserved words in the Strategy Automation, Strategy Orders, Strategy Performance and Strategy Position groups under the **easylanguage.ell** section of the TDE Dictionary.

The code of the OrderTicket AT must obtain this information from various **DataProviders** and Classes and establish variables and collections to retain this information. A large portion of the code for a trading indicator will be associated with this endeavor.

Backtesting

There is no built-in functionality to perform backtesting with OrderTickets and DataProviders. One generally performs backtesting within TS using a Strategy. In using this more sophisticated OrderTicket/DataProviders structure you should have a Strategy to do the backtesting and an Indicator for the automation.

Sequence Management

With **OrderTickets** and **Orders** much of the sequencing of operations requires initiating a process and then waiting for some event to occur to initiate the next step. This asynchronous structure is very different from the typical synchronous nature of Strategies.

Technically a Strategy could be coded to do historical trades (beneficial for the Performance Report) and once the data becomes real-time could pass off execution to the **OrderTickets**.

An example of this is using the Load property of a Provider Class then the **StateChanged** and/or **Updated** Events to process the information once it has become available. Remember, Creating an Object does not necessarily mean it is immediately available for use. In some cases, the top-level object may not be Null but the properties you wish to access may not yet exist!

Updating an Order

In a Strategy an order is effectively updated by changing one or more properties of the reserved word that sends the order (order price, type of order or number of contracts/shares). The strategy assumes the old order was canceled (and not filled) and submits the new order.

With Order Tickets the code must build a **ReplaceTicket** and use the **Order.Replace** () Method to send in the replace request, and then wait for an **Order Updated Event** for that Order with an:

```
Order State/DetailState = Received/Received
```

or

```
Order State/StateDetail = Received/ChangeRequestRejected
```

and act accordingly. It is best to supply all the properties of a **ReplaceTicket**.

Only use the **Replace** Method after canceling any existing open orders or you could end up with more shares/contracts on than you intended.

Logging

When developing a large and often complex trading indicator, logging to a file should be one of the first major subsystems to include in the code. The logging should be verbose and as well structured as possible. This log will be a great benefit during the debugging and execution phases of the project. With a real-time system execution will happen quickly and there are no stopping things for a bit to examine the goings-on. The log file contents should contain a complete record of all actions taken by the software. This would include:

- Date/Time stamping every line
- Logging all input values
- Logging any chart or RadarScreen parameters, such as bartype, barinterval, symbol, etc.
- Logging all OrderTickets
- Logging all Order events
- Logging data prices at key action points
- Logging all critical and calculated values at key action points
- Logging any performance metrics

You may want each execution to have its own log file, timestamped to the second, or to have a new log file for each day or session.

> ☑ This is always a good practice to verify that you are indeed placing the orders you think you are.

Sam suggests the use of "=" signs to make your code more readable and easier to search. You can quickly isolate areas of concern with these breaks. Thus, you can easily scan for an area in time you wish to examine more closely.

Chris makes beautiful log files. To make this output fit on the page I must make the font smaller, but here's an example of his output:

EXAMPLE 13.01—Sample of a Chris Davy Log File

```
H|02/21/22 13:09:07|  0|INF|MAIN|INIT        |START      |
=========================================================
H|02/21/22 13:09:07|  1|INF|INIT|AMT         |LOGFILE    |
H|02/21/22 13:09:07|  2|INF|MAIN|INIT        |INFO       |Vsn #
H|02/21/22 13:09:07|  3|WRN|MAIN|INIT        |INFO       |Test
H|02/21/22 13:09:07|  4|INF|MAIN|INIT        |DONE       |Complete
H|02/21/22 13:09:07|  5|INF|MAIN|BARCLOSE    |CLOSEPRICE |22.65
```

```
H|02/21/22 13:09:07|   6|INF|MAIN|BARCLOSE    |HIGHPRICE  |23.28
H|02/21/22 13:09:07|   7|INF|MAIN|BARCLOSE    |LOWPRICE   |22.15
H|02/21/22 13:09:07|   8|FNC|FNCA|FUNCTION    |TEST       |Message
H|02/21/22 13:09:07|   9|INF|MAIN|BARCLOSE    |CLOSEPRICE |22.03
H|02/21/22 13:09:07|  10|INF|MAIN|BARCLOSE    |HIGHPRICE  |22.65
H|02/21/22 13:09:07|  11|INF|MAIN|BARCLOSE    |LOWPRICE   |21.65
H|02/21/22 13:09:07|  12|FNC|FNCA|FUNCTION    |TEST       |Message
```

Factors of Design

The overall design of indicator code to perform trading using **OrderTickets** and **DataProviders** depends upon several factors. Often the design must make compromises between the different factors. One must understand the different **OrderTicket** structures: simple, **OSO**, **OCO**, **Bracket** as well as **Replace** tickets and approaches for canceling orders or closing positions.

There is no single template for an OOEL-based trading study. The final design must reflect the various aspects of the trading algorithm.

The **Order** Class is listed below so you can see the multitude of choices and opportunities.

Enabling Order Placement Objects

For **OrderTickets** to be processed, when the study is inserted into a chart or RadarScreen, on the ⌖ Customize Indicator → General tab there is a checkbox with the label "Enable order placement objects". This box must be checked if **OrderTickets** are going to be used. See Figure 13.01 below.

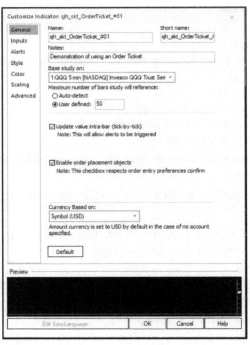

FIGURE 13.01—Check the box to "Enable order placement objects."

The state of the checkbox can be determined by checking the static property of the **OrderTicket** class. An **OrderTicket** object does not have to be created to perform this check. The following line of code does that checking:

```
if not OrderTicket.OrderPlacementEnabled  then RaiseRunTimeError
```

```
("Order Placement Objects not enabled") ;
```

Order Class

Listed in the tables below are the definitions for the structure for an object that represents an order.

NAMESPACE: tsData.Trading

PROPERTIES

	Name	Type	Description
	AccountID	string	Gets the ID of the account.
	Action	enum	Gets the type of order action. See **OrderAction** for a list of possible values.
	ActivationRules	object	Gets an activation rule for the order ticket. See **ActivationRules**.
	AdvanceOptions	string	Gets a string contained the advanced order settings.
	AllOrNone	bool	True to allow the order only if the entire quantity can be placed.
	AvgFilledPrice	double	Gets the average filled price for the current order.
	BuyMinusSellPlus	bool	True to allow buys to occur only on downticks and sells only on upticks.
	Child	int	Gets the child order with the specified index in an OCO/OSO order.
	ChildCount	int	Gets the number of children in an OCO/OSO order.
	Commission	double	Gets the commission paid in an order.
	Discretionary	bool	True to show an order's bid/ask at a lower/higher price than you are willing to pay.
	DiscretionaryAmount	double	Sets or gets the discretionary price increment used when **Discretionary** is True.
	Duration	string	Gets the duration of the order.
	Duration Date	datetime	Gets the duration date for GTD.
	ECNSweep	bool	True to route orders to ECNs only, bypassing all market makers.
	EnteredQuantity	int	Gets the quantity of shares or contracts requested for the order.
	EnteredTime	datetime	Gets the time when the order is placed.
	ExtendedProperties	object	Gets the DynamicProperties object associated with the Order.
	FilledQuantity	int	Gets the quantity of shares or contracts filled for the order.
	FilledTime	datetime	Gets the time when the order is filled.
	FirstSibling	object	Gets first Order object in the collection of sibling Orders. Note that all orders have at least one sibling, namely the order itself.
	GeneratingApplication	enum	Get the type of application that generated the Order. See **GeneratingApplication** for a list of possible

	Name	Type	Description
			values.
📧	HasValue	bool	True when specified field contains a value. False if no value.
📧	IfTouched	bool	True to specify a trigger event at which an order will be sent.
📧	IfTouchedPrice	double	The trigger price at which an IfTouched order is sent.
📧	IfTouchedPriceOffset	int	The IfTouched price offset value if using an 'auto' limit price style.
📧	IfTouchedPriceStyle	enum	The IfTouched price style. See PriceStyle for a list of possible values.
📧	LastSibling	object	Gets last Order object in the collection of sibling Orders. Note that all orders have at least one sibling, namely the order itself.
📧	LeftQuantity	int	Gets the number of unfilled shares or contracts for the current order.
📧	LimitPrice	double	Gets the limit price for a limit or stop limit order.
📧	LimitPriceOffset	int	Gets the limit price offset value if using an 'auto' limit price style for limit and stop limit orders.
📧	LimitPriceStyle	string	Gets the name of the limit price style for limit and stop limit orders.
📧	LotSize	int	Gets the size of the lot. Applicable only to forex orders.
📧	NextSibling	object	Gets the next Order object in the collection of sibling Orders, if one exists; otherwise null. Note that all orders have at least one sibling, namely the order itself.
📧	NonDisplay	bool	True if the current order is to be placed with the non-display option. See **Placing Non-Display Orders** in TS Platform Help.
📧	OCOGroupID	string	Gets the group name of the OCO group.
📧	OSOParentID	string	Gets the ID of the order that triggers the current order.
📧	OrderID	string	Gets the ID of the current order.
📧	Originator	string	Gets the account name that generates the order.
📧	Parent	order	Gets the parent order of the current order.
📧	Peg	enum	The enumeration for peg behavior. See **PegBehavior** for a list of possible values.
📧	PreviousSibling	object	Gets the previous Order object in the collection of sibling Orders, if one exists; otherwise, null. Note that all orders have at least one sibling, namely the order itself.
📧	Route	string	Gets the route for the order.

	Name	Type	Description
	ShowOnly	bool	True to place show only orders.
	ShowOnlyQuantity	int	Gets the size of a show only order. See **Show Only** in TS platform help.
	SiblingCount	int	Gets the number of siblings in an OCO/OSO order.
	SpreadName	string	Gets the spread name in an options order.
	State	enum	Gets the order state value. See **OrderState** for a list of possible values.
	StateDetail	enum	Gets the order state detail value. See **OrderStateDetail** for a list of possible values.
	StopPrice	double	Gets the stop price for a stop or stop limit order.
	StopPriceOffset	int	Gets the stop price offset value if using an 'auto' limit price style for stop and stop limit orders.
	StopPriceStyle	string	Gets the name of the stop price style for stop and stop limit orders.
	Symbol	string	Gets the symbol to trade.
	SymbolExtension	string	Gets the symbol extension for the Symbol to trade.
	TopLeftOrder	order	Gets the top-most and left-most node in an OCO/OSO order.
	TrailingStop	enum	Gets the trailing stop type. See **TrailingStopBehavior** for a list of possible values.
	TrailingStopAmount	double	Gets the trailing stop value.
	Type	enum	Get the order type. See **OrderType** for a list of possible values.
	Value	double	Gets the value of the specified OrderField.

TABLE 13.01—Order Class Properties

METHODS

	Name	Description
	ActionToString (action)	Gets a string representing a specified OrderAction.
	CanCancel ()	True if the Order can be canceled, otherwise False.
	Cancel ()	True to cancel the Order, otherwise False.
	Replace (replaceTicket)	Replaces the current Order with a new ReplaceTicket object. Returns True if the replacement Order was sent, otherwise False if replacement is not possible. Note that there may be cases when the original Order is filled before the replacement becomes active.
	StateToString (state)	Gets a string representing the state of the order based on a specified OrderState.
	TypeToString ()	Gets a string representing the order type based on a specified OrderType.

TABLE 13.02—Order Class Methods

EVENTS

	Name	Description
⚡	Updated	Occurs whenever the object is updated. See **OrderUpdatedEventArgs** for the properties returned by the handler's args parameter.

TABLE 13.03—Order Class Events

INHERITANCE HIERARCHY

elSystem.Object
  tsData.Order

Examples of Order Tickets

Typically, all **OrderTickets** are created in code rather than using templates from the ToolBox.

Also, methods are often used to create each type of **OrderTicket** with a number of parameters being passed in to tailor the **OrderTicket**. The following code samples show one approach to this. The methods return the **OrderTicket** constructed so that it can be included in more complex OrderTickets, such as an **OSOOrderTicket**.

The code presented here is for example only. The code does not represent a full working program and will not compile. It is for you to learn from and copy ideas from.

EXAMPLE 13.02—Entry Order Ticket [OME_EntryOrderTicket]i

```
//------------------------------------------------------------
//  Build Entry Order Ticket
//------------------------------------------------------------
method OrderTicket BuildEntryOrderTicket(string entryOrderType,
   string acct,
   string orderSymbol,
   OrderAction action,
   double orderEntryPrice,
   int extraEntryTicks,
   int entryDeactivationSeconds)

variables:
   OrderTicket OT,
   DateTime DT;
begin
   OT = OrderTicket.Create();
   OT.Account = acct;
   OT.Action = action;
   OT.Duration = "DAY";
   OT.Name = "OTE";
   OT.Quantity = 1;
   OT.Symbol = orderSymbol;
   OT.symboltype = Category;

   switch entryOrderType.Trim().ToUpper()
   begin
     case "MARKET", "MKT":
       OT.Type = OrderType.Market;
       OT.LimitPrice = 0;
       OT.LimitPriceStyle = PriceStyle.none;
       OT.LimitPriceOffset = 0;
       OT.StopPrice = 0;
       OT.StopPriceStyle = PriceStyle.none;
       OT.StopPriceOffset = 0;
```

```
    case "LIMIT", "LMT":
      OT.Type = OrderType.Limit;
      OT.LimitPrice = orderEntryPrice
      + extraEntryTicks * MinMove / PriceScale;
      OT.LimitPriceStyle = PriceStyle.none;
      OT.LimitPriceOffset = 0;
      OT.StopPrice = 0;
      OT.StopPriceStyle = PriceStyle.none;
      OT.StopPriceOffset = 0;

    case "STOPLIMIT", "SL":
      OT.Type = OrderType.StopLimit;
      OT.LimitPrice = orderEntryPrice
      + extraEntryTicks * MinMove / PriceScale;
      OT.LimitPriceStyle = PriceStyle.none;
      OT.LimitPriceOffset = 0;
      OT.StopPrice = orderEntryPrice
      + extraEntryTicks * MinMove / PriceScale;;
      OT.StopPriceStyle = PriceStyle.none;
      OT.StopPriceOffset = 0;
      if iInvalidEntryStopToMarket then OT.ConvertInvalidStopToMarket
= true;

    case "STOPMARKET", "SM":
      OT.Type = OrderType.StopMarket;
      OT.LimitPrice = 0;
      OT.LimitPriceStyle = PriceStyle.none;
      OT.LimitPriceOffset = 0;
      OT.StopPrice = orderEntryPrice
      + extraEntryTicks * MinMove / PriceScale;
      OT.StopPriceStyle = PriceStyle.none;
      OT.StopPriceOffset = 0;
      if iInvalidEntryStopToMarket then OT.ConvertInvalidStopToMarket
= true;

    default:
      Print(String.Format("BuildEntryOrderTicket: Unsupported order
type = {0}", entryOrderType.Trim().ToUpper()));

  End ; // switch/case statement

  //--------------------------------------------------------
  //  Add Deactivation rule
  //--------------------------------------------------------
  if entryOrderType.Trim().ToUpper() <> "MARKET"
    and entryDeactivationSeconds > 0 then
  begin
    DT = DateTime.Now;
    DT.AddSeconds(entryDeactivationSeconds);
    OT.ActivationRules.UseDeactivationTime = true;
    OT.ActivationRules.DeactivationTime = DT;
  End ;
  return OT ;
end ;
```

EXAMPLE 13.03—Target Order Ticket [OME_TargetOrderTicket]

Note that an entry **OrderTicket** is passed in as a parameter so that certain properties can be copied from the entry **OrderTicket** to assure consistency.

```
  //--------------------------------------------------------
```

```
// Build Target OrderTicket
//------------------------------------------------------------
method OrderTicket BuildTargetOrderTicket (OrderTicket ote,
  OrderAction exitAction,
  string exitOrderType,
  int priceOffset)
variables:
  OrderTicket OT ;
begin
  OT = OrderTicket.Create();
  OT.Account = OTE.Account;
  OT.Action = exitAction;
  OT.Duration = "GTC";
  OT.Name = "OTT";
  OT.Quantity = ote.Quantity;
  OT.Symbol = ote.Symbol;
  OT.SymbolType = ote.SymbolType;

  switch exitOrderType.Trim().ToUpper()
  begin
    case "LIMIT", "LMT":
      OT.Type = OrderType.Limit;
      OT.LimitPrice = 0;
      OT.LimitPriceStyle = PriceStyle.ParentPlus;
      OT.LimitPriceOffset = priceOffset;
      OT.StopPrice = 0;
      OT.StopPriceStyle = PriceStyle.none;
      OT.StopPriceOffset = 0;

    case "STOPLIMIT", "SL":
      OT.Type = OrderType.StopLimit;
      OT.LimitPrice = 0;
      OT.LimitPriceStyle = PriceStyle.ParentPlus;
      OT.LimitPriceOffset = priceOffset;
      OT.StopPrice = 0;
      OT.StopPriceStyle = PriceStyle.ParentPlus;
      OT.StopPriceOffset = priceOffset;

    case "STOPMARKET", "SM":
      OT.Type = OrderType.StopMarket;
      OT.LimitPrice = 0;
      OT.LimitPriceStyle = PriceStyle.None;
      OT.LimitPriceOffset = 0;
      OT.StopPrice = 0;
      OT.StopPriceStyle = PriceStyle.ParentPlus;
      OT.StopPriceOffset = priceOffset;

    default:
      Print (String.Format ("BuildTargetOrderTicket: Unsupported order
type = {0}", exitOrderType.Trim ().ToUpper())) ;

  end ; // switch/case statement

  return OT ;
end ;
```

EXAMPLE 13.04—Protect OrderTicket [OME_ProtectOrderTicket]

Note that an entry **OrderTicket** is passed in as a parameter so that certain properties can be copied from the entry **OrderTicket** to assure consistency.

```
//---------------------------------------------------------
//  Build Protect OrderTicket
//---------------------------------------------------------
method OrderTicket BuildProtectOrderTicket (string otName,
   OrderTicket ote,
   OrderAction exitAction,
   string exitOrderType,
   int priceOffset,
   TrailingStopBehavior trailingBehavior,
   double trailingAmount)
variables:
   OrderTicket OT;
begin
   OT = OrderTicket.Create();
   OT.Account = OTE.Account;
   OT.Action = exitAction;
   OT.Duration = "GTC";
   OT.Name = otName;
   OT.Quantity = ote.Quantity;
   OT.Symbol = ote.Symbol;
   OT.SymbolType = ote.SymbolType;

   switch exitOrderType.Trim().ToUpper()
   begin
     case "STOPMARKET", "SM":
       OT.Type = OrderType.StopMarket;
       OT.LimitPrice = 0;
       OT.LimitPriceStyle = PriceStyle.None;
       OT.LimitPriceOffset = 0;
       OT.StopPrice = 0;
       OT.StopPriceStyle = PriceStyle.ParentPlus;
       OT.StopPriceOffset = priceOffset;

     case "STOPLIMIT", "SL":
       OT.Type = OrderType.StopLimit;
       OT.LimitPrice = 0;
       OT.LimitPriceStyle = PriceStyle.ParentPlus;
       OT.LimitPriceOffset = priceOffset;
       OT.StopPrice = 0;
       OT.StopPriceStyle = PriceStyle.ParentPlus;
       OT.StopPriceOffset = priceOffset ;

     default:
       Print(String.Format("BuildProtectOrderTicket: Unsupported order
   type = {0}", exitOrderType.Trim().ToUpper ())) ;
   End ; // switch/case statement

   OT.TrailingStop = trailingBehavior;
   switch trailingBehavior
   begin
     case TrailingStopBehavior.Off:
       OT.TrailingStopAmount = 0;

     case TrailingStopBehavior.Points:
       OT.TrailingStopAmount = trailingAmount;

     case TrailingStopBehavior.Percentage:
       OT.TrailingStopAmount = trailingAmount;
   End ; // switch/case statement

   return OT ;
```

```
   end ;
```

EXAMPLE 13.05—Protect OrderTicket [OME_OSOOrderTicket]

The **Logs** Method is part of a logging system. References to strings are inputs.

```
method OSOOrderTicket BuildOSOOrderTicket (string entryOrderType,
   string acct,
   string orderSymbol,
   OrderAction entryAction,
   double orderEntryPrice,
   int entryDeactivationSeconds,
   int extraEntryTicks,
   string targetOrderType,
   int targetPriceOffset,
   string protectOrderType,
   int protectPriceOffset,
   int trailingStopTicks,
   int breakevenFloorTicks,
   string eodMinutes,
// TimeSpan <> null comparison is incorrect in EZL
   TimeSpan tsEODTime)
// May be null

variables:
   OrderAction ExitAction,
   OrderType EntryType,

   OSOOrderTIcket OTOSO,
   OCOOrderTicket OTOCO,
   OrderTicket OTE,
// Entry Order
   OrderTicket OTT,
// Target
   OrderTicket OTFP,
// Fixed Protect
   OrderTicket OTPTP,
// Point Trailing Protect
   OrderTicket OTBE,
// Breakeven
   OrderTicket OTEOD;
// End-of-day

begin
   //-----------------------------------------------------
   // Determine exit action
   //-----------------------------------------------------
   switch entryAction
   begin
     case OrderAction.Buy, OrderAction.BuyToCover:
       ExitAction = OrderAction.Sell ;
     case OrderAction.Sell, OrderAction.SellShort:
       ExitAction = OrderAction.BuyToCover ;
   end;

   //-----------------------------------------------------
   // Create OSO and OCO OrderTickets
   //-----------------------------------------------------
   OTOSO = OSOOrderTicket.Create();
   OTOCO = OCOOrderTicket.Create();
   OTOSO.SecondaryTickets += OTOCO;
```

```
//--------------------------------------------------------
//   Entry OrderTicket
//--------------------------------------------------------
OTE = BuildEntryOrderTicket(entryOrderType, acct, orderSymbol,
entryAction, orderEntryPrice, extraEntryTicks,
entryDeactivationSeconds) ;
  OTOSO.PrimaryTicket = OTE ;
  Logs(PrintDebug and PrintOT, AreaOT, OTE.Name,
    String.Format("C={0:FN} - {1}".Replace("FN", Fn), Close,
ELCFormatOrderTicket (OTE, DecimalPlaces))) ;

//--------------------------------------------------------
//   Target OrderTicket
//--------------------------------------------------------
if targetPriceOffset <> 0 then
begin
  OTT = BuildTargetOrderTicket (OTE, ExitAction, targetOrderType,
targetPriceOffset);
  OTOCO.Siblings += OTT ;
  Logs (PrintDebug and PrintOT, AreaOT, OTT.Name,
    String.Format ("C={0:FN} - {1}".Replace ("FN", Fn), Close,
ELCFormatOrderTicket (OTT, DecimalPlaces)));
  end ;

//--------------------------------------------------------
//   Fixed Protect OrderTicket
//--------------------------------------------------------
if protectPriceOffset <> 0 then
begin
  OTFP = BuildProtectOrderTicket("OTFP", OTE, ExitAction,
protectOrderType, protectPriceOffset,
    TrailingStopBehavior.Off, 0);
  OTOCO.Siblings += OTFP;
  Logs(PrintDebug and PrintOT, AreaOT, OTFP.Name, String.Format
("C={0:FN} - {1}".Replace ("FN", Fn), Close, ELCFormatOrderTicket
(OTFP, DecimalPlaces))) ;
  End ;

//--------------------------------------------------------
//   Trailing Protect OrderTicket
//--------------------------------------------------------
if  trailingStopTicks <> 00  then  begin
  OTPTP = BuildProtectOrderTicket("OTPTP", OTE, ExitAction,
protectOrderType, trailingStopTicks,
    TrailingStopBehavior.Points, AbsValue(trailingStopTicks *
MinMove / PriceScale));
  OTOCO.Siblings += OTPTP;
  Logs(PrintDebug and PrintOT, AreaOT, OTPTP.Name,
    String.Format("C={0:FN} - {1}".Replace("FN", Fn), Close,
ELCFormatOrderTicket(OTPTP, DecimalPlaces)));
  end ;

//--------------------------------------------------------
//   Breakeven OrderTicket
//--------------------------------------------------------
if breakevenFloorTicks <> 0 then
begin
  OTBE = BuildBreakevenOrderTicket(OTE, ExitAction,
breakevenFloorTicks, Close);
    If  OTBE <> null then  begin
```

```
      OTOCO.Siblings += OTBE;
      Logs (PrintDebug and PrintOT, AreaOT, OTBE.Name,
        String.Format ("C={0:FN} - {1}".Replace ("FN", Fn), Close,
ELCFormatOrderTicket (OTBE, DecimalPlaces))));
    end ;
  end ;

  //---------------------------------------------------------
  //  End Of Day Order
  //---------------------------------------------------------
  if iEODAtExch.Trim().Length > 0
    and iAllowEntryAfterExch <> iDisallowEntryAfterExch then
  begin
    OTEOD = BuildEODOrderTicket(OTE, ExitAction, tsEODTime);
    OTOCO.Siblings += OTEOD;
    Logs(PrintDebug and PrintOT, AreaOT, OTEOD.Name,
      String.Format ("C={0:FN} - {1}".Replace ("FN", Fn), Close,
ELCFormatOrderTicket (OTEOD, DecimalPlaces))) ;
  end ;

  return OTOSO ;
end ;
```

The above code calls a number of methods to build different **OrderTickets** that are added to the `OCOOrderTicket`. A few are included below:

EXAMPLE 13.06—Methods for Preceding OrderTickets [OME_OTMethods]

```
//---------------------------------------------------------
// The Breakeven order would need to be price-activated once
// the price has reached the floor amount
// of ticks in the profitable direction from the entry
// price.
// It would need to be a stop market order that then gets
// activated once the stop price (which is the entry price)
// has been reached.
//
// Price to be used for the entry price will be
// the limit price for a limit or
// stoplimit entry, or the close price for a market entry.
//---------------------------------------------------------

method OrderTicket BuildBreakevenOrderTicket(OrderTicket ote,
OrderAction exitAction, int breakevenTicks, double entryPriceToUse)

variables:
  OrderTicket OT,
  PriceActivationRule PAR;

begin
  try
    OT = OrderTicket.Create();
    OT.Account = OTE.Account;
    OT.Action = exitAction;
    OT.Duration = "GTC";
    OT.Name = "OTBE";
    OT.Quantity = ote.Quantity;
    OT.Symbol = ote.Symbol;
    OT.SymbolType = ote.SymbolType;
    OT.Type = OrderType.StopMarket;
```

```
PAR = PriceActivationRule.Create();
PAR.Symbol = ote.Symbol;
PAR.Trigger = OrderTriggerType.STT;
PAR.Name = "PARBE";
OT.ActivationRules.Rules.Add(PAR);

switch exitAction
begin
  case OrderAction.Buy, OrderAction.BuyToCover :
    OT.StopPrice = 0 ;
    OT.StopPriceStyle = PriceStyle.ParentPlus ;
    OT.StopPriceOffset = 0 ;
    PAR.Price = entryPriceToUse - breakevenTicks
        * MinMove / PriceScale ;
    PAR.ComparisonOperator = ComparisonOperator.LessEqual ;

  case OrderAction.Sell, OrderAction.SellShort:
    OT.StopPrice = 0;
    OT.StopPriceStyle = PriceStyle.ParentPlus;
    OT.StopPriceOffset = 0;
    PAR.Price = entryPriceToUse + breakevenTicks * MinMove /
PriceScale;
    PAR.ComparisonOperator = ComparisonOperator.GreaterEqual;
  End ; // switch/case statement

  return OT AccountsProvider;
catch (Exception ex)
  AddMessage(String.Format ("BuildBreakevenOrderTicket Error: {0}",
ex.Message)) ;
  return null ;
end ; // try/catch
end ; // method
```

In **Volume II—Reference Guide** you will find everything you need to complete this programming in **Appendix III: Classes** and **Appendix IV: Enumerations**.

Summary

Chris, in the above examples, has exposed us to an amazing amount of information. His rigorous methodology of reporting to a file displays his expertise and is worth dissecting and understanding. I do not personally apply precisely the same reporting standards, but I do have my methods, admittedly with the value of hindsight after learning from his example. He has introduced us to the **AccountsProvider**, **PositionsProvider** and **OrdersProvider** Classes as well as their sub-classes. Because Chris was part of the TS Team and has vastly more intimate acquaintance to the inner working of these Classes, we have bowed to his expertise and taken this opportunity to learn from a true master.

Note from Sam: I have, prior to reviewing his material for this chapter, written an extensive collection of Methods to delve into and report most every class and subclass covered herein but I have not tied them all together into a coherent and functioning whole. I wrote the Back Office code for System Writer, System Writer Plus and TS up through TS Version 4. It is a lot of work, and I am STILL tired. Chris claims it adds 10k lines of code to your basic Strategy rules and I believe him, though even that may be an underestimation. So far, I have not been able to envision a way to make it so standardized that I can have a copy-and-paste library to fit all needs and requirements. Maybe one day soon.

CHAPTER 14
Using Excel

In This Chapter

- Introduction
- Examples
- Summary

Introduction

Who would ever think that you could use Microsoft Excel from within OOEL? Built in. Well, you can, and thankfully so. This chapter shows you how. You can specify a workbook name and output real-time data to it from TS. You can then use Excel to conduct analyses on it that are not available in TS and optionally return the result back to your original (or another) AT

Naturally, Excel needs to be installed on your machine for this to work. It appears to work with all versions from Office 2007 through Office 365. Neither Excel nor the Workbook needs to be open, but the Workbook and the Worksheet must exist.

Examples

In the following example, we open Excel, a Workbook containing a Worksheet, read elements into a vector, read the length of a moving average from the Worksheet, and display the Close price demonstrating a two-way communication with Excel. Then we print the results to the Print Log.

EXAMPLE 14.01—Using Excel: [OME_Excel_Ex#01] and [DemoExcel.xlsx]

This example demonstrates reading from and writing to an Excel worksheet within a workbook from within EZL. This code and the Excel file were originally from a TradeStation demo and have been modified to meet our needs here.

At the beginning of the code, we put the MAV length into spreadsheet (cell I2). Next, we get the length from the spreadsheet and use it as the input to the moving average we plot on the chart.

The **Close** is written to cell E9 by EZL while cell I2 is read from the spreadsheet and used in EZL. Cells A1 : A10 are read from the spreadsheet and used in EZL.

There are five examples (in one example) of using Excel from within your EZL code. Example 00 puts the value of the `myLength` Input in cell I2; Example 01 loads data from Excel into an Array and a Vector, Example 02 gets a String value from E2; Example 03 stores the Close in E9; and Example 04 gets cell I2 for use as the moving average length.

```
// set the namespaces that will be used
using elSystem ;
using elSystem.Office.Excel ;
using elSystem.Collections ;

Inputs:
  String WorkbookPath     ("C:\OME_Files\"),
  String WorkbookName     ("DemoExcelClass"),
  String WorkbookExt      (".xlsx"),
// The path, filename, and extension must be correct
// for the file.
  String SheetName        ("Excel Demos"),
// sheet where the information is located
  Int    myLength         (20),
```

```
  Int    Dot_Color         (Green),
  Int    Line_Color        (Red),
  Bool   PrintToPrintLog ( TRUE),
  Bool   ClearTheLog       (FALSE) ;
// set to true to print array and vector values to print log

Vars  :
 String WorkbookFSpec     (WorkbookPath + WorkbookName + WorkbookExt),
 Int    Loop              (00),
 IntraBarPersist Bool RealTime (FALSE),
 IntraBarPersist MALen    (10),
 Workbook WB1             (NULL),  // Workbook object
 Vector MyDataVector      (NULL) ; // load vector from Excel

Arrays:
  MyDataArray[10] (00) ; // array to load from Excel

// Doing it this way, though completely proper, will prove
// slower because the "Once (GetAppInfo (aiRealTimeCalc)  = 01)"
// is executed on each bar of historical data until the condition
// is (finally) true on the last bar of data, potentially

//Once (GetAppInfo (aiRealTimeCalc)  = 01) begin
//  RealTime  =  TRUE ;
//end ; // Once, and only once

// Using this version it tests "if  LastBarOnChart" only on each bar
// of historical data until TRUE then sets the RealTime flag only
once.
// Well, sort of, it is not quite that simple...

if  LastBarOnChart
and RealTime  = FALSE
then begin
  RealTime  =  GetAppInfo (aiRealTimeCalc)  = 01 ;
end ;

once begin
  if  PrintToPrintLog and ClearTheLog  then  ClearPrintLog ;
// catenate the fully qualified file specification
  WorkbookFSpec  = WorkbookPath + WorkbookName + WorkbookExt ;
// instantiate a new Workbook object and set its properties
  WB1            = new Workbook ;
// create the new object
  WB1.FileName     = WorkbookFSpec ;
// assign it the File Specification
  WB1.Shared       = TRUE ; // Spreadsheet is shared
  WB1.Visible      = TRUE ; // Spreadsheet is visible
  WB1.Load         = TRUE ;
// load the spreadsheet from disk
  WB1.SaveOnClose  = FALSE ;
// do not save changes in this demo

//=========================================================
//   EXAMPLE 00 - Put the myLength Input (the Moving
//                Average Length) in CELL I2 VALUE
//=========================================================
  WB1.sheets[SheetName].CellsAsInt[09,02]  = MyLength ;

  MyDataArray [00]  = 00 ;
```

```
    // instantiate a new Vector
    MyDataVector  = new Vector ;
    MyDataVector.Push_Back (00) ;
    // this is done to put 00 in element 00. Elements 01 - 10
    // will be used so that the element number in the
    // vector matches the Excel row number.

    //====================================================
    //   EXAMPLE 01 - LOAD ARRAY AND VECTOR FROM EXCEL
    //====================================================
{*
   Load the array and the Vector from Cells A1:A10 in the workbook. The
0 element of the array is not used so the array index matches the
Excel row.
 *}
    for Loop = 01 to 10 begin
       // load the array - Excel cells are specified by
       // [Column,Row] so cell A1 is Column 1, Row 1 -> [1,1]
       MyDataArray[Loop]  = WB1.sheets[SheetName].CellsAsDouble[01,
Loop];
       // load the Vector
       MyDataVector.push_back (WB1.sheets[SheetName].CellsAsDouble[01,
Loop]) ;
    end ; // for loop

//============================================================
//    PRINT ARRAY AND VECTOR VALUES
//============================================================
   if  PrintToPrintLog  then begin
// print the name of the analysis technique
     print ("Analysis Technique -> ",
        AnalysisTechnique.Name.toString (), NewLine) ;

// Print the values from the array
     print (NewLine, "=========================",
           NewLine, "Array Values from Excel",
           NewLine, "=========================") ;
     for Loop = 01 to 10 begin
       print ("MyDataArray[", Loop:1:0, "] = ", MyDataArray[Loop]) ;
     end ; // for loop

   // print the values from the Vector
   print (NewLine, "=========================",
         NewLine, "Vector Values from Excel",
         NewLine, "=========================") ;
     for Loop = 01 to MyDataVector.Count - 01 begin
{*
A Vector holds objects, which can be one of many data types, such as
String, Int, Double, Order, OrderTicket, etc. so you must specify the
data type when you retrieve the value. This example is set up so that
Double values can be used, so the Vector element (specified with the
Item's property) is data-typed as a Double.
 *}
       Print ("MyDataVector.Items[", Loop:1:0, "] = ",
          MyDataVector.Items[Loop] asType Double) ;
     end ; // for loop
   end ; // if PrintToPrintLog
end ; // Once, and only once

//============================================================
//   EXAMPLE 02 - GET EXCEL CELL VALUE AS A STRING FROM E2
```

```
//============================================================
if  WB1.sheets[SheetName].CellsAsString[5,2] = "plot"
and LastBarOnChart
  then  Plot1 ( Low - MinMove/PriceScale, "ExcelPlot", Dot_Color,
Default, 04)
  else  NoPlot (01) ;

//============================================================
//  EXAMPLE 03 - POPULATE CELL E9 WITH THE CURRENT CLOSE
//============================================================
if  RealTime
  then  WB1.sheets[SheetName].CellsAsDouble[5,9] = Close ;

//============================================================
//  EXAMPLE 04 - GET CELL I2 VALUE for Moving Average Length
//============================================================
once  MALen  = WB1.sheets[SheetName].CellsAsInt [09, 02] ;
Plot2 (Average (Close, MALen), "MA", Line_Color, default, default) ;
```

This example prints **Vector** values to the Print Log, as seen here in Figure 14.01.

```
Analysis Technique -> OME_Excel_Ex#01
========================
Array Values from Excel
========================
MyDataArray[1]  =      0.00
MyDataArray[2]  =      0.00
MyDataArray[3]  =      0.00
MyDataArray[4]  =      0.00
MyDataArray[5]  =      0.00
MyDataArray[6]  =      0.00
MyDataArray[7]  =      0.00
MyDataArray[8]  =      0.00
MyDataArray[9]  =      0.00
MyDataArray[10] =       0.00


========================
Vector Values from Excel
========================
MyDataVector.Items[1]  =      0.00
MyDataVector.Items[2]  =      0.00
MyDataVector.Items[3]  =      0.00
MyDataVector.Items[4]  =      0.00
MyDataVector.Items[5]  =      0.00
MyDataVector.Items[6]  =      0.00
MyDataVector.Items[7]  =      0.00
MyDataVector.Items[8]  =      0.00
MyDataVector.Items[9]  =      0.00
MyDataVector.Items[10] =       0.00
```

FIGURE 14.01—Output from the Print Log

FIGURE 14.02—Moving Average Length Determined by Reading Spreadsheet

The next figure shows you the contents of the spreadsheet.

FIGURE 14.03—Using Excel from within EZL [OME_Excel_Ex#01] and [DemoExcelClass.xlsx]

EXAMPLE 14.02—Chart to Excel [OME_Chart_to_Excel]

Here's another example. This one is called OME_Chart_to_Excel.

The indicator opens an instance of Excel and sends information for each bar to Excel, one row per bar of data, including Date, Time, Close and NetChange.

```
Using elSystem.Office.Excel ;
// Namespace elSystem.Office.Excel
// Member of Library elSystem.ell

Inputs:
  String WorkBook_Path    ("C:\OME_Files\"),
  String WorkBook_Name    ("OME_OOEL_Examples"),
  String WorkBook_Ext     (".XLSX"),
  String WorkSheet_Name   ("OME_Chart_to_Excel"),
  Int    XLS_Row          (02),
  Int    XLS_Col          (01) ;
Consts:
  String Letters   ("ABCDEFGHIJKLMNOPQRSTUVWXYZ") ;

Arrays:
  String Col_Letters [026] ("") ;
```

```
Vars  : // Classic EasyLanguage variables
 Bool   WorkSheet_Valid (FALSE),
 String File_Spec        ("") ;

// Working Storage Section
Consts:
 String App_Type     ("Study"),
 String App_Name     ("OME_Chart_to_Excel"),
 String App_Note     ("Example sending price from Chart to Excel"),
 String App_Vers     ("01.02.00") ;

Vars :
 String DQ           (DoubleQuote),
 String NL           (NewLine),
 Bool   Debug        (FALSE),
 Double Dummy        (0.00) ;

// -----------------------------------------------------------
#Region - - - Analysis Technique
// -----------------------------------------------------------

method void App_Init ()
Vars  :
Int    Loop ;
begin
  Print (skt_Method_Header (App_Name, "App_Init" , "")) ;
  if  OME_Floating_Text (skt_Method_Header (App_Name, "App_Init" ,
""), "White", "Arial", 10, 50, 50, FALSE)  then ; // see Commentary
above

  File_Spec  = WorkBook_Path + WorkBook_Name + WorkBook_Ext ;
  Print (" - File_Spec = ", DQ, File_Spec, DQ) ;

  if  Debug  then  Print ("Number of Letters = ", Strlen
(Letters):2:0) ;
  for Loop  = 01 to StrLen (Letters) begin
    Col_Letters [Loop]  = MidStr (Letters, Loop, 01) ;
  end ; // for loop
  For Loop  = 01 to 26 begin
    if  Debug  then  Print ("Letter #", Loop:2:0, " = ", Col_Letters
[Loop]) ;
  end ; // for loop
end ; // "App_Init" method

// -----------------------------------------------------------
#endRegion // Analysis Technique

#Region - - - Excel_WorkBook
// -----------------------------------------------------------
// plot1(workbook1.sheets[1].CellsAsString[3,4]);

Vars  : // OOEL variables
 WorkBook myWB           (NULL),
 Sheet    mySheet        (NULL) ;

method WorkBook Excel_Init ()
Vars  :
 WorkBook WB ;
begin
```

```
    Print (skt_Method_Header (App_Name, "Excel_Init" , "")) ;
    WB  = WorkBook.Create () ;
    WB.FileName  = File_Spec ;
// The name of the Excel file on your computer.
    WB.Visible   =  TRUE ;
// True to display the spreadsheet when connected,
// otherwise False.
//  WorkSheet_Valid  = WB.Contains (WorkSheet_Name) ;
// True if the workbook contains a worksheet with the
// specified name, otherwise False.
    WB.Load  =  TRUE ;
// Indicates whether to open the connection to the
// Excel file.

    Return WB ;
end ; // "Excel_Init" method

// ----------------------------------------------------------
#endRegion // Excel_WorkBook
// ----------------------------------------------------------

Once begin
  App_Init () ;  ]// Initialize the AnalysisTechnique
  myWB  = Excel_Init () ; // Initialize the WorkBook
  Print ("The number of sheets in (" + DQ + "OME_Chart_to_Excel" + DQ
+ ") is ", myWB.SheetCount:2:0) ;

  WorkSheet_Valid  = myWB.Contains (WorkSheet_Name) ;
// True if the workbook contains a worksheet with the
// specified name, otherwise False.
  if  not WorkSheet_Valid  then begin
    Print ("WorkSheet name (" + DQ + WorkSheet_Name + DQ + ") is not
found, check Inputs and Spelling.") ;
  end
  else begin
    mySheet  = myWB.Sheets [WorkSheet_Name] ;
// The WorkSheet with the specified sheet name.
    Print ("Col 06, Row 04 = ", mySheet.CellsAsString [06, 04]) ;
  end ; // worksheet found

  mySheet.CellsAsString [XLS_Col + 00, XLS_Row - 01]  = "Date" ;
  mySheet.CellsAsString [XLS_Col + 01, XLS_Row - 01]  = "Time" ;
  mySheet.CellsAsString [XLS_Col + 02, XLS_Row - 01]  = "Close" ;
  mySheet.CellsAsString [XLS_Col + 03, XLS_Row - 01]  = "Net Change" ;
end ; // Once, and only once

mySheet.CellsAsString [XLS_Col + 00, XLS_Row + CurrentBar]  =
vrt_MMDDYYYY (Date) ;
mySheet.CellsAsString [XLS_Col + 01, XLS_Row + CurrentBar]  =
vrt_HHMM_pm (Time) ;
mySheet.CellsAsDouble [XLS_Col + 02, XLS_Row + CurrentBar]  = Close ;
if  CurrentBar  > 01 // and Currentbar <  10
then begin

// formula to compute the NetChange
  mySheet.CellsAsString [XLS_Col + 03, XLS_Row + CurrentBar]  = "=" +
Col_Letters [XLS_Col + 02] + NumToStr (XLS_Row + CurrentBar, 00)
+ " - " + Col_Letters [XLS_Col + 02] + NumToStr (XLS_Row + CurrentBar
- 01, 00) ;
end ;
```

```
// need to skip the first bar before activating the formula.
// The program opens an instance of Excel and populates a
// worksheet with date, time, close and the formula for the
// net change.
```

See Figure 14.04 below.

	A	B	C	D	E	F
1	Date	Time	Close	Net Change		
2						
3	18-May-21	02:00pm	4085.50			
4	19-May-21	02:00pm	4072.25	(13.25)		George
5	20-May-21	02:00pm	4114.25	42.00		
6	21-May-21	02:00pm	4114.75	0.50		
7	24-May-21	02:00pm	4156.75	42.00		
8	25-May-21	02:00pm	4148.50	(8.25)		
9	26-May-21	02:00pm	4156.00	7.50		
10	27-May-21	02:00pm	4162.00	6.00		
11	28-May-21	02:00pm	4165.50	3.50		
12	1-Jun-21	02:00pm	4161.00	(4.50)		
13	2-Jun-21	02:00pm	4167.25	6.25		
14	3-Jun-21	02:00pm	4153.25	(14.00)		
15	4-Jun-21	02:00pm	4189.75	36.50		
16	7-Jun-21	02:00pm	4187.50	(2.25)		
17	8-Jun-21	02:00pm	4187.50	0.00		

OME_Chart_to_Excel | OME_RadarScreen_to ...

FIGURE 14.04—Chart_to_Excel

EXAMPLE 14.03—RadarScreen to Excel [OME_RadarScreen_to_Excel]

This study exports the Date, Time, Close [0], Close[1] and the Net Change formula for each corresponding symbol/row of the RadarScreen to the Excel Worksheet. The Net Change requires the Close of one bar ago to compute the formula. The Net Change can only begin on the second bar of data since it requires the value of one bar ago to compute the formula.

```
Using elSystem.Office.Excel ;
// Namespace elSystem.Office.Excel Member of library
// elSystem.ell

Inputs:
 String WorkBook_Path    ("C:\OME_Files\"),
 String WorkBook_Name    ("OME_OOEL_Examples"),
 String WorkBook_Ext     (".XLSX"),
 String WorkSheet_Name   ("OME_RadarScreen_to_Excel"),
 Int    XLS_Row          (01),
 Int    XLS_Col          (00) ;

Arrays:
 String Row_Letters [026] ("") ;

Vars  : // Classic EasyLanguage variables
 Bool   WorkSheet_Valid (FALSE),
 String File_Spec       (""),
 String Formula         (""),
 Int    myRow           (00) ;

#Region - - - Working Storage
// Working Storage Section
Consts:
 String App_Type    ("Study"),
 String App_Name    ("OME_RadarScreen_to_Excel"),
```

```
  String App_Note      ("Example sending price from RadarScreen to
  Excel"),
  String App_Vers      ("01.02.00") ;

  Vars  :
  String DQ            (DoubleQuote),
  String NL            (NewLine),
  Bool   Debug         (FALSE),
  Double Dummy         (0.00) ;

  // ----------------------------------------------------------
  #endRegion // Working Storage
  #Region - - - Excel_WorkBook
  // ----------------------------------------------------------

  Vars  : // OOEL variables
   WorkBook myWB             (NULL),
   Sheet    mySheet          (NULL) ;

  // ----------------------------------------------------------

  method WorkBook Excel_Init ()
  Vars  :
   WorkBook WB ;
  begin
    Print (skt_Method_Header (App_Name, "Excel_Init" , Symbol)) ;
    WB  = WorkBook.Create () ;
    WB.FileName  = File_Spec ; // The name of the Excel file on your
  computer.
    WB.Visible   = TRUE ;
  // True to display the spreadsheet when connected,
  // otherwise False.
  //  WB.Visible   = FALSE ;
  // True to display the spreadsheet when connected,
  // otherwise False.
    WB.Shared  =  TRUE ;
    WB.Load  =  TRUE ; // Indicates whether to open the connection to
  the Excel file.

    Return WB ;
  end ; // "Excel_Init" method

  // ----------------------------------------------------------

  method void WB_FillData ()
  begin
    mySheet.CellsAsString [XLS_Col + 01, myRow]  = Symbol ;
    mySheet.CellsAsString [XLS_Col + 02, myRow]  = vrt_MMDDYYYY (Date) ;
    mySheet.CellsAsString [XLS_Col + 03, myRow]  = vrt_HHMM_pm (Time) ;
    mySheet.CellsAsDouble [XLS_Col + 04, myRow]  = Close [00] ;
    mySheet.CellsAsDouble [XLS_Col + 05, myRow]  = Close [01] ;

  // create the formula to compute the NetChange
    Formula  = "=" + Row_Letters [XLS_Col + 04] + NumToStr (myRow, 00)
            + "-" + Row_Letters [XLS_Col + 05] + NumToStr (myRow, 00) ;

  // place the formula in column F of this row
    mySheet.CellsAsString [XLS_Col + 06, myRow]  = Formula ;
  end ; // "WB_FillData" method

  // ----------------------------------------------------------
```

```
method void WB_doHeaders ()
begin
  if  XLS_Row  >  00   then begin
    mySheet.CellsAsString [XLS_Col + 01, XLS_Row]  = "Symbol" ;
    mySheet.CellsAsString [XLS_Col + 02, XLS_Row]  = "Date" ;
    mySheet.CellsAsString [XLS_Col + 03, XLS_Row]  = "Time" ;
    mySheet.CellsAsString [XLS_Col + 04, XLS_Row]  = "Close[0]" ;
    mySheet.CellsAsString [XLS_Col + 05, XLS_Row]  = "Close[1]" ;
    mySheet.CellsAsString [XLS_Col + 06, XLS_Row]  = "NetChng" ;
  end ; // print column headers if XLS_Row  > than zero
end ; // "WB_doHeaders" method

// -----------------------------------------------------------
#endRegion // Excel_WorkBook
// plot1 (workbook1.sheets[01].CellsAsString[03,04]) ;
// -----------------------------------------------------------

method void App_Init ()
Vars  :
 Int    Loop,
 String Letters ;
begin
  Print (skt_Method_Header (App_Name, "App_Init" , Symbol)) ;
  File_Spec  = WorkBook_Path + WorkBook_Name + WorkBook_Ext ;
  if  Debug  then  Print (" - File_Spec = ", DQ, File_Spec, DQ) ;
  Letters  = "ABCDEFGHIJKLMNOPQUSTUVWXYZ" ;
  if  Debug  then  Print ("Number of letters = ", Strlen
(Letters):0:0) ;
  for Loop  = 01 to 26 begin
    Row_Letters [Loop]  = MidStr (Letters, Loop, 01) ;
    if  Debug  then  Print ("#", Loop:2:0,
       ", ", DQ, MidStr (Letters, Loop, 01), DQ,
       ", ", DQ, Row_Letters [Loop], DQ) ;
  end ; // for loop

  myRow  = GetAppInfo (aiRow ) + XLS_Row ; // get the row for this
symbol
  myWB   = Excel_Init () ;

  WorkSheet_Valid  = myWB.Contains (WorkSheet_Name) ;
// True if the workbook contains a worksheet with the
// specified name, otherwise False.

  Print ("The number of sheets is ", myWB.SheetCount:2:0) ;
  if  WorkSheet_Valid  then begin
    Print ("Workbook contains ", DQ, Worksheet_Name, DQ) ;
  end
  else begin
    Print ("Workbook does not contain ", DQ, Worksheet_Name, DQ) ;
  end ;

  if  WorkSheet_Valid  then begin
// get the WorkSheet with the specified sheet name.
    mySheet  = myWB.Sheets [WorkSheet_Name] ;
    Print ("Col 06 (" + Row_Letters [06]
      + "), Row 06 = ", mySheet.CellsAsString [06, 06]) ;
  end ;
end ; // "App_Init" method
```

```
// --------------------------------------------------------
#Region - - - Main Code Body
// --------------------------------------------------------
once begin
  App_Init () ;
  WB_doHeaders () ;
end ; // Once, and only once

if  skt_LastBarOnChart  then begin
  WB_FillData () ;
end ; // once, on the last bar of data

// obligatory prlot statement
Plot1 (myRow, "Row#", Default, Default, Default) ;

// --------------------------------------------------------
#endRegion // Main Code Body
// --------------------------------------------------------
```

	A	B	C	D	E	F
1	Symbol	Date	Time	Close[0]	Close[1]	NetChng
2						
3	@ES	7/7/2022	05:00pm	3899.25	3848.25	51
4	@NQ	7/7/2022	05:00pm	12138.5	11880.25	258.25
5	@ES.D	7/7/2022	04:15pm	3898.75	3848.25	50.5
6	@NQ.D	7/7/2022	04:15pm	12138.5	11880.25	258.25
7	@NK	7/7/2022	05:00pm	26690	26300	390
8						
9	@VX	7/7/2022	05:00pm	26.85	27.2	-0.35
10	@US	7/7/2022	05:00pm	138.4063	139.7813	-1.375
11	@TY	7/7/2022	05:00pm	118.2656	119.0469	-0.78125
12	@ED	7/7/2022	05:00pm	96.735	96.76	-0.025
13	@GC	7/7/2022	05:00pm	1739.7	1736.5	3.2
14	@SI	7/7/2022	05:00pm	19.188	19.159	0.029
15	@PL	7/7/2022	05:00pm	865.8	840.9	24.9
16	@HG	7/7/2022	05:00pm	3.572	3.408	0.164
17	@CL	7/7/2022	05:00pm	102.73	98.53	4.2
18	@NG	7/7/2022	05:00pm	6.297	5.51	0.787
19	@HO	7/7/2022	05:00pm	3.6739	3.4106	0.2633
20	@RB	7/7/2022	05:00pm	3.4204	3.2366	0.1838
21	@DX	7/7/2022	05:00pm	106.959	106.898	0.061
22	@AD	7/7/2022	05:00pm	0.6844	0.67945	0.00495
23	@BP	7/7/2022	05:00pm	1.203	1.1941	0.0089
24	@CD	7/7/2022	05:00pm	0.7704	0.7668	0.0036
25	@EC	7/7/2022	05:00pm	1.02085	1.0235	-0.00265
26	@JY	7/7/2022	05:00pm	0.7383	0.73925	-0.00095

FIGURE 14.05—RadarScreen to Excel Output

Summary

In this chapter we have introduced you to the concepts for writing information to and reading information from Excel worksheets. It is left to the reader to find more useful reasons and methods to use this information. Creating simple output to, perhaps, be copied and pasted to a CSV file is simplistic…utilizing the computational powers of Excel is the end goal here and we leave it in your competent hands to discover usages far beyond what have been provided. Please post examples we may share with readers of this book! Currently I see no Events that may be triggered to tell TS when to retrieve data so it may all be up to Timer Events and chance until TS decides to strengthen this alliance.

I would also like to see TradeStation expand this functionality to include Google Sheets as well!

CHAPTER 15

Fundamental Data Fields

In This Chapter

- Introduction
- FundamentalFields Class
- Examples
- Summary

Introduction

Even though I am a technical trader I sometimes like to look at the technical elements of fundamental data. While most fundamental data is delayed, not by minutes but by days or weeks, the general trend is of interest to me.

The fields available are numerous, far beyond anything I can memorize. This chapter is one that should be browsed and then read so you can know what is available when you decide to explore fundamental fields. The primary reason for this chapter is to give you an easy place to find all these fundamental fields.

FundamentalFields Class and associated args are in **Volume II—Reference Guide** under **Classes**.

There are Classic EZL functions to access Fundamental Field data, but the OOEL FundamentalQuotesProvider (FQP) Methods are vastly more robust.

FundamentalFields Class

This class contains a list of fundamental quote field names that can be used to read a Quote["Name"] value from a **FundamentalQuotes** or **FundamentalQuotesProvider** collection of fields.

NAMESPACE: tsData.MarketData

Please see **Volume II—Reference Guide: Appendix III** for detailed information and a listing of fields available.

Numeric values are typically referenced as a DoubleValue, Date and Time as a .DateValue, and names/descriptions as a .StringValue. Refer to Value Type below to identify the type of property needed to read a specific Quote["Name"] value. These value types are also shown in the Example section of the EZL Dictionary Description pane for a specific field name.

Because some fundamental quotes contain history data from previous reporting periods, the Value Type properties must include an index that refers to the number of periods ago, where [0] is the last quote for current period, [1] is one period ago, etc. You can also use the **typeValueLast** property to read the last quote for the current period.

EXAMPLE 15.01—Plotting Fundamental Quotes Fields

```
Value1 = FundamentalQuotesProvider1.Quote["ATOT"].DoubleValue[1];
// gets the Total Assets from 1 report period ago
Value2 = FundamentalQuotesProvider1.Quote["AACR"].DoubleValue[0];
// gets the current period Accounts Receivable Net Trade
Plot1(FundamentalQuotesProvider1.Quote["YRAGODATE1"].DateValueLast)
// plots the date of the 1 Year Ago Price
Plot2(FundamentalQuotesProvider1.Quote["AskExchange"].StringValueLast)
// plots the exchange name of the last ask (offer)
```

Note that this is just a code snippet. It illustrates how to specify the fields.

EXAMPLE 15.02—Plotting EPS and P/E with Fundamental Quotes [OME_FQP_Ex#02]

This indicator is especially useful in RadarScreen, showing the Earnings Per Share (EPS) and Price/Earnings (P/E) Ratio.

```
Input: string iSymbol1 (symbol) ;
Input: string iFields1 ("F_TICKER, TTMBEPSXCL, PEINCLXOR, YRAGOPRC1,
YRAGODATE1") ;

method void FundamentalQuotesP1_Updated (elSystem.Object sender,
tsdata.marketdata.FundamentalQuoteUpdatedEventArgs
args)
 {the Updated event handler is called whenever a FundamentalQuote
property changes}
begin
  If FundamentalQuotesP1.Count>0 then begin
// plot the indexed FundamentalQuote based on the specified
// data type property for N periods ago
  Plot2(FundamentalQuotesP1.Quote[1].DoubleValue[0],"EPS") ;
  Plot3(FundamentalQuotesP1.Quote[2].DoubleValue[0],"P/E") ;
  Plot4(FundamentalQuotesP1.Quote[3].DoubleValue[0],"Yr Ago Price") ;
  Plot (FundamentalQuotesP1.Quote[4].DateValue[0].toString(), "Yr Ago
Date") ;
  end ;
end ;
```

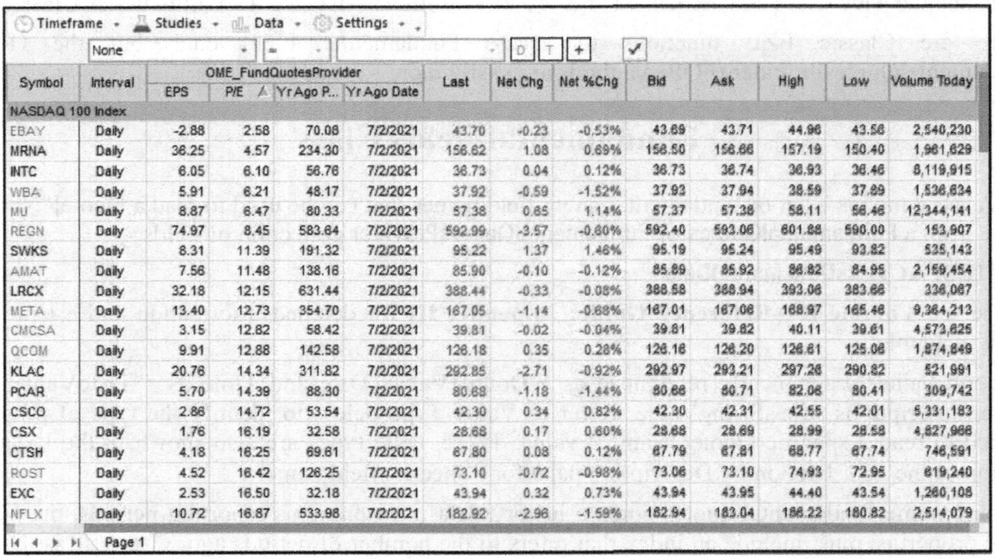

Symbol	Interval	OME_FundQuotesProvider				Last	Net Chg	Net %Chg	Bid	Ask	High	Low	Volume Today
		EPS	P/E	Yr Ago P...	Yr Ago Date								
NASDAQ 100 Index													
EBAY	Daily	-2.88	2.58	70.06	7/2/2021	43.70	-0.23	-0.53%	43.69	43.71	44.96	43.56	2,540,230
MRNA	Daily	36.25	4.57	234.30	7/2/2021	156.62	1.08	0.69%	156.50	156.66	157.19	150.40	1,961,629
INTC	Daily	6.05	6.10	56.76	7/2/2021	36.73	0.04	0.12%	36.73	36.74	36.93	36.46	8,119,915
WBA	Daily	5.91	6.21	48.17	7/2/2021	37.92	-0.59	-1.52%	37.93	37.94	38.59	37.89	1,536,634
MU	Daily	8.87	6.47	80.33	7/2/2021	57.38	0.65	1.14%	57.37	57.38	58.11	56.46	12,344,141
REGN	Daily	74.97	8.45	583.64	7/2/2021	592.99	-3.57	-0.60%	592.40	593.06	601.88	590.00	153,907
SWKS	Daily	8.31	11.39	191.32	7/2/2021	95.22	1.37	1.46%	95.19	95.24	95.49	93.82	535,143
AMAT	Daily	7.56	11.48	138.16	7/2/2021	85.90	-0.10	-0.12%	85.89	85.92	86.82	84.95	2,159,454
LRCX	Daily	32.18	12.15	631.44	7/2/2021	388.44	-0.33	-0.08%	388.58	388.94	393.06	383.66	336,067
META	Daily	13.40	12.73	354.70	7/2/2021	167.05	-1.14	-0.68%	167.01	167.06	168.97	165.46	9,364,213
CMCSA	Daily	3.15	12.82	58.42	7/2/2021	39.81	-0.02	-0.04%	39.81	39.82	40.11	39.61	4,573,625
QCOM	Daily	9.91	12.88	142.58	7/2/2021	126.18	0.35	0.28%	126.16	126.20	126.61	125.06	1,874,849
KLAC	Daily	20.76	14.34	311.82	7/2/2021	292.85	-2.71	-0.92%	292.97	293.21	297.28	290.82	521,991
PCAR	Daily	5.70	14.39	88.30	7/2/2021	80.68	-1.18	-1.44%	80.66	80.71	82.06	80.41	309,742
CSCO	Daily	2.86	14.72	53.54	7/2/2021	42.30	0.34	0.82%	42.30	42.31	42.55	42.01	5,331,183
CSX	Daily	1.76	16.19	32.58	7/2/2021	28.68	0.17	0.60%	28.68	28.69	28.99	28.58	4,827,966
CTSH	Daily	4.18	16.25	69.61	7/2/2021	67.80	0.08	0.12%	67.79	67.81	68.77	67.74	746,591
ROST	Daily	4.52	16.42	126.25	7/2/2021	73.10	-0.72	-0.98%	73.06	73.10	74.93	72.95	619,240
EXC	Daily	2.53	16.50	32.18	7/2/2021	43.94	0.32	0.73%	43.94	43.95	44.40	43.54	1,260,108
NFLX	Daily	10.72	16.87	533.98	7/2/2021	182.92	-2.98	-1.59%	182.94	183.04	186.22	180.82	2,514,079

Page 1

FIGURE 15.01—Fundamental Fields in RadarScreen

> ✒ Fundamental data for all fields may not be available for a specific symbol. It's recommended that you use the .HasQuoteData("ATOT") Method to determine if data is available for a specific quote using the current provider object before calculating or plotting a value.

PROPERTIES

Name	Description	Type	History
A1FCF	Free Cash Flow - 1st historical fiscal year	double	
A1FCFSHR	Free Cash Flow per share - most recent FY	double	

Name	Description	Type	History
A2FCFSHR	Free Cash Flow per share - most recent FY - 1	double	
A2NETMRGN	Net Profit Margin % - 2nd historical fiscal year	double	
AACR	Accounts Receivable - Trade, Net	double	yes
AAGA	Accumulated Goodwill Amortization	double	yes
AAII	Accrued Investment Income	double	yes
AAMT	Accumulated Intangible Amortization	double	yes
AARG	Accounts Receivable - Trade, Gross	double	yes
AASTTURN	Asset turnover - most recent fiscal year	double	
ABEPSXCLXO	EPS Basic excluding extraordinary items - most recent fiscal year	double	
ABVPS	Book value (Common Equity) per share - most recent fiscal year	double	
ACAC	Customer Acceptances	double	yes
ACAE	Cash & Equivalents	double	yes
ACAPSPPS	Capital Spending per Share, most recent fiscal year	double	
ACDB	Cash & Due from Banks	double	yes
ACFSHR	Cash Flow per share - most recent fiscal year	double	
ACFSHR2	Cash Flow per share - most recent fiscal year - 1	double	
ACOGS	Cost of goods sold - most recent fiscal year	double	
ACPC	Construction in Progress - Gross	double	yes
ACSH	Cash and Equivalents	double	
ACSHPS	Cash per share - most recent fiscal year	double	
ACURAST	Assets, current - most recent fiscal year	double	
ACURLIAB	Liabilities, current - most recent fiscal year	double	
ACURRATIO	Current ratio - most recent fiscal year	double	
ADCA	Discontinued Operations - Current Asset	double	yes
ADEBTEPS	Debt Service to EPS - most recent fiscal year	double	
ADEP	Accumulated Depreciation, Total	double	yes
ADEPEXP	Depreciation expense— (SCF) most recent fiscal year	double	
ADEPRESCFZ	Depreciation, accumulated—most recent fiscal year	double	

Name	Description	Type	History
ADFC	Deferred Charges	double	yes
ADGC	Deferred Gas Cost	double	yes
ADIV5YAVG	Dividend per Share—5-year average	double	
ADIVCHG	Dividend change %—year over year	double	
ADIVSHR	Dividend per share—most recent fiscal year	double	
ADOA	Discontinued Operations—LT Asset	double	yes
ADPA	Deferred Policy Acquisition Costs	double	yes
ADPL	Accumulated Depletion	double	yes
ADPT	Interest-Earning Deposits	double	yes
ADTA	Deferred Income Tax—Long Term Asset	double	yes
ADTC	Deferred Income Tax—Current Asset	double	yes
AEBIT	EBIT - most recent fiscal year	double	
AEBITD	EBITD - most recent fiscal year	double	
AEBITD2	EBITD - most recent fiscal year -1	double	
AEBITD5YR	EBITD Margin – 5-year average	double	
AEBITDMG	EBITD Margin—most recent fiscal year	double	
AEBT	Earnings Before Taxes—most recent fiscal year	double	
AEBTNORM	Earnings Before Taxes Normalized—most recent fiscal year	double	
AEPSCHG	EPS Change %—year over year	double	
AEPSINCLXO	EPS including extraordinary items - most recent fiscal year	double	
AEPSNORM	EPS Normalized - most recent fiscal year	double	
AEPSXCLXOR	EPS excluding extraordinary items - most recent fiscal year	double	
AEQI	LT Investment - Affiliate Companies	double	yes
AEXP	Exploration & Production	double	yes
AFFS	Fed Funds Sold/Sec. Purch under Resale Agreement.	double	yes
AFLB	FHLB Stock	double	yes
AFUL	Fuel - Inventory	double	yes
AGIS	Gas in Storage - Inventory	double	yes
AGROSMGN	Gross Margin - 1st historical fiscal year	double	

Name	Description	Type	History
AGROSMGN2	Gross Margin - 2nd historical fiscal year	double	
AGWG	Goodwill - Gross	double	yes
AGWI	Goodwill, Net	double	yes
AIFG	Inventories - Finished Goods	double	yes
AILR	LIFO Reserve	double	yes
AING	Intangibles - Gross	double	yes
AINT	Intangibles, Net	double	yes
AINTCOV	Interest coverage - most recent fiscal year	double	
AINTEXPZ	Interest expense - most recent fiscal year	double	
AINVENTORY	Inventory - most recent fiscal year	double	
AINVTURN	Inventory turnover - most recent fiscal year	double	
AIOT	Inventories - Other	double	yes
AIRC	Interest Receivable	double	yes
AIRM	Inventories - Raw Materials	double	yes
AITL	Total Inventory	double	yes
AIWP	Inventories - Work in Progress	double	yes
ALHS	Loans Held for Sale	double	yes
ALIC	Land/Improvements - Gross	double	yes
ALLA	Loan Loss Allowances	double	yes
ALTD2AST	LT debt/assets - most recent fiscal year	double	
ALTD2CAP	LT debt/total capital - most recent fiscal year	double	
ALTD2EQ	LT debt/equity - most recent fiscal year	double	
ALTDPS	LT debt/share - most recent fiscal year	double	
ALTI	LT Investments - Other	double	yes
ALTR	Note Receivable - Long Term	double	yes
AMEC	Machinery/Equipment - Gross	double	yes
ANI	Earnings after Taxes - most recent fiscal year	double	
ANIAC	Net Income available to common - most recent fiscal year	double	
ANIACINCLX	Total Income Net - most recent fiscal year	double	
ANIACNORM	Net Income Available to Common, Normalized - most recent fiscal year	double	

Name	Description	Type	History
ANICHG	Net Income Change % - year over year	double	
ANIEXCLXOR	Net Income excluding extraordinary items - most recent fiscal year	double	
ANIINCLXOR	Net Income including extraordinary items - most recent fiscal year	double	
ANINORM	Earnings After Taxes, Normalized—most recent fiscal year	double	
ANIPEREMP	Net Income/employee—most recent fiscal year	double	
ANLOAN	Loans, Net—most recent fiscal year	double	
ANLOANCHG	Loans, Net % Change - year over year	double	
ANNPERIODS	Number of historical periods - Annual	double	
ANPMGNPCT	Net Profit Margin % - 1st historical fiscal year	double	
ANRC	Natural Resources - Gross	double	yes
ANTL	Net Loans	double	yes
AOAS	Other Long-Term Assets	double	yes
AOAT	Other Assets	double	yes
AOCA	Other Current Assets	double	yes
AOEA	Other Earning Assets	double	yes
AOPC	Other Property/Plant/Equipment - Gross	double	yes
AOPMGNPCT	Operating margin - 1st historical fiscal year	double	
AOPMGNPCT2	Operating Margin - 2nd historical fiscal year	double	
AORC	Receivables - Other	double	yes
AORE	Other Real Estate Owned	double	yes
AOTI	Other Short-Term Investments	double	yes
APAYRATIO	Payout ratio - most recent fiscal year	double	
APAYRATIO2	Payout ratio - most recent fiscal year -1	double	
APBC	Buildings - Gross	double	yes
APBO	Pension Benefits - Overfunded	double	yes
APDA	Provision for Doubtful Accounts	double	yes
APEEXCLXOR	P/E excluding extraordinary items, most recent fiscal year	double	
APENORM	P/E Normalized, most recent fiscal year	double	
APLC	Leases - Gross	double	yes

Name	Description	Type	History
APPN	Property/Plant/Equipment, Total - Net	double	yes
APPY	Prepaid Expenses	double	yes
APR2REV	Price to Sales - most recent fiscal year	double	
APR2TANBK	Price to Tangible Book - most fiscal year	double	
APR2TANCE	Price to Tangible Book (common) - most recent fiscal year	double	
APRCFPS	Price to Cash Flow per share - most recent fiscal year	double	
APRE	Insurance Receivables	double	yes
APRFCFPS	Price to Free Cash Flow per Share - most recent fiscal year	double	
APRICE2BK	Price to Book - most recent fiscal year	double	
APRICE2TOTEQ	Price to Equity - most recent fiscal year	double	
APTC	Property/Plant/Equipment, Total - Gross	double	yes
APTMGNPCT	Pretax Margin - 1st historical fiscal year	double	
APTMGNPCT2	Pretax Margin - 2nd historical fiscal year	double	
AQUICKRATI	Quick Ratio - most recent fiscal year	double	
ARCA	Restricted Cash - Current	double	yes
ARCL	Restricted Cash - Long Term	double	yes
ARDEXP	Research and Development Expense - most recent fiscal year	double	
ARECTURN	Receivables Turnover - most recent fiscal year	double	
ARECVBL	Receivables - most recent fiscal year	double	
AREV	Revenue - most recent fiscal year	double	
AREVCHG	Revenue Change %, year over year	double	
AREVPEREMP	Revenue/Employee - most recent fiscal year	double	
AREVPS	Revenue/Share - most recent fiscal year	double	
AREVSTRT	Reinvestment Rate - most recent fiscal year	double	
ARII	Reinsurance - Asset	double	yes
AROA5YAVG	Return on Average Assets - 5 year average	double	
AROAPCT	Return on Average Assets - most recent fiscal year	double	
AROE5YAVG	Return on Average Equity - 5 year average	double	

Name	Description	Type	History
AROEPCT	Return on Average Equity - most recent fiscal year	double	
AROI5YRAVG	Return on Investment - 5 year average	double	
AROIPCT	Return on Investment - most recent fiscal year	double	
ARPI	Securities/Indebtedness of Related Parties	double	yes
ASAC	Separate Accounts - Assets	double	yes
ASEC	Total Investment Securities	double	yes
ASFS	Securities for Sale	double	yes
ASGA2REV	SG&A expenses / net sales - most recent fiscal year	double	
ASHM	Securities Held	double	yes
ASTI	Short Term Investments	double	yes
ASTR	Notes Receivable - Short Term	double	yes
ATA	Assets, Total - most recent fiscal year	double	
ATAA	Trading Account Assets	double	yes
ATACHG	Assets, Total % Change - year over year	double	
ATANBVDOLR	Book Value (tangible) in dollars - most recent fiscal year	double	
ATANBVPS	Book Value (tangible) per share - most recent fiscal year	double	
ATAXPD	Taxes Paid - most recent fiscal year	double	
ATAXRAT5YR	Tax Rate - 5 year average	double	
ATAXRATE	Tax Rate - most recent fiscal year	double	
ATAXRATE2	Tax Rate - most recent fiscal year -1	double	
ATCA	Total Current Assets	double	yes
ATCA_AYr10CAGR	Current Assets, 10 Year CAGR	double	
ATCA_AYr5CAGR	Current Assets, 5 Year CAGR	double	
ATGL	Total Gross Loans	double	yes
ATL	Liabilities, Total - most recent fiscal year	double	
ATOT	Total Assets	double	yes
ATOT_AMom	Total Assets, 10 Year Annual Trend Momentum %	double	
ATOT_AYr10Grth	Total Assets, 10 Year Annual Trend Growth %	double	

Name	Description	Type	History
ATOT_AYr10Vty	Total Assets, 10 Year Annual Trend Volatil %	double	
ATOT_IMom	Total Assets, 5 Year Interim Trend Momentum %	double	
ATOT_IYr5Grth	Total Assets, 5 Year Interim Trend Growth %	double	
ATOT_IYr5Vty	Total Assets, 5 Year Interim Trend Volatil %	double	
ATOTCE	Book Value (Common Equity) - most recent fiscal year	double	
ATOTD	Total Debt - most recent fiscal year	double	
ATOTD2AST	Total Debt/total assets - most recent fiscal year	double	
ATOTD2CAP	Total Debt/total capital - most recent fiscal year	double	
ATOTD2EQ	Total Debt/total equity - most recent fiscal year	double	
ATOTLTD	LT Debt (total) - most recent fiscal year	double	
ATOTSE	Shareholder Equity - most recent fiscal year	double	
ATRC	Total Receivables, Net	double	yes
AUNI	Unearned Income	double	yes
AUPD	Utility Plant Accumulated Depreciation	double	yes
AUPN	Utility Plant, Net	double	yes
AUTP	Utility Plant - Gross	double	yes
AUUR	Unbilled Utility Revenues	double	yes
AWCAPPSPR	Working Capital per share/Price - most recent fiscal year	double	
BasEpsExcX2P_A	EPS Excl. Extra Items, Basic/Price, FY	double	
BasEpsExcX2P_TTM	EPS Excl. Extra Items, Basic/Price, TTM	double	
BETA	Beta	double	
BETA_DOWN	Beta, Down	double	
BETA_UP	Beta, Up	double	
BETAW	3-Year Weekly Beta	double	
BETAW_DOWN	3-Year Weekly Beta, DOWN	double	
BETAW_UP	3-Year Weekly Beta, UP	double	
BVPS_AYr10CAGR	Book Value per Share, Total Equity, 10 Year CAGR	double	
BVPS_IAv2Yr3CAGR	Book Value per Share, Total Equity, 3 Year Interim CAGR	double	
BVPS_IAv2Yr5CAGR	Book Value per Share, Total Equity, 5 Year	double	

Name	Description	Type	History
	Interim CAGR		
BVTRENDGR	Book Value per Share growth rate, 5 year	double	
Capex2TotAst_A	Capital Expenditures/Total Assets, FY	double	
Capex2TotAst_TTM	Capital Expenditures/Total Assets, TTM	double	
CEIA	Equity In Affiliates	double	yes
CEq_AMom	Common Shareholders Equity, 10 Year Annual Trend Momentum %	double	
CEq_AYr10TrGrth	Common Shareholders Equity, 10 Year Annual Trend Growth %	double	
CEq_AYr10Vty	Common Shareholders Equity, 10 Year Annual Trend Volatil %	double	
CEq_IMom	Common Shareholders Equity, 5 Year Interim Trend Momentum %	double	
CEq_IYr5TrGrth	Common Shareholders Equity, 5 Year Interim Trend Growth %	double	
CEq_IYr5Vty	Common Shareholders Equity, 5 Year Interim Trend Volatil %	double	
CF_AYr10CAGR	Cash Flow, 10 Year CAGR	double	
CF_AYr3CAGR	Cash Flow, 3 Year CAGR	double	
CFMar_A	Cash Flow Margin, %, FY	double	
CFMar_AAvg5	Cash Flow Margin, %, 5 Year Average	double	
CFMar_IAvg3	Cash Flow Margin, %, 3 Year Average	double	
CFMar_TTM	Cash Flow Margin, %, TTM	double	
CFTRENDGR	Cash Flow Growth Rate, 5 year	double	
CGAP	U.S. GAAP Adjustment	double	yes
CGPD	General Partners' Distributions	double	yes
ChPctPAvg150Day	Price % Change Over 150 Day Average	double	
ChPctPAvg50Day	Price % Change Over 50 Day Average	double	
ChPctPriceMTD	Price % Change Month To Date	double	
ChPctPriceQTD	Price % Change Quarter To Date	double	
ChPctPriceWTD	Price % Change Week To Date	double	
CIAC	Income Available to Common Excl. Extra. Items	double	yes
CIAC_AYr10CAGR	Income Available to Common Excl. Extraordinary Items, 10 Year CAGR	double	

Name	Description	Type	History
CMEA	Miscellaneous Earnings Adjustment	double	yes
CMIN	Minority Interest	double	yes
COTC-10	COTC: Noncommercial Positions-Short (All)	double	yes
COTC-100	COTC: Traders-Total Reportable-Long (Other)	double	yes
COTC-101	COTC: Traders-Total Reportable-Short (Other)	double	yes
COTC-102	COTC: Concentration-Gross LT = 4 TDR-Long (All)	double	yes
COTC-103	COTC: Concentration-Gross LT =4 TDR-Short (All)	double	yes
COTC-104	COTC: Concentration-Gross LT =8 TDR-Long (All)	double	yes
COTC-105	COTC: Concentration-Gross LT =8 TDR-Short (All)	double	yes
COTC-106	COTC: Concentration-Net LT =4 TDR-Long (All)	double	yes
COTC-107	COTC: Concentration-Net LT =4 TDR-Short (All)	double	yes
COTC-108	COTC: Concentration-Net LT =8 TDR-Long (All)	double	yes
COTC-109	COTC: Concentration-Net LT =8 TDR-Short (All)	double	yes
COTC-11	COTC: Noncommercial Positions-Spreading (All)	double	yes
COTC-110	COTC: Concentration-Gross LT =4 TDR-Long (Old)	double	yes
COTC-111	COTC: Concentration-Gross LT =4 TDR-Short (Old)	double	yes
COTC-112	COTC: Concentration-Gross LT =8 TDR-Long (Old)	double	yes
COTC-113	COTC: Concentration-Gross LT =8 TDR-Short (Old)	double	yes
COTC-114	COTC: Concentration-Net LT =4 TDR-Long (Old)	double	yes
COTC-115	COTC: Concentration-Net LT =4 TDR-Short (Old)	double	yes
COTC-116	COTC: Concentration-Net LT =8 TDR-Long (Old)	double	yes
COTC-117	COTC: Concentration-Net LT =8 TDR-Short (Old)	double	yes
COTC-118	COTC: Concentration-Gross LT =4 TDR-Long (Other)	double	yes

Name	Description	Type	History
COTC-119	COTC: Concentration-Gross LT =4 TDR-Short(Other)	double	yes
COTC-12	COTC: Commercial Positions-Long (All)	double	yes
COTC-120	COTC: Concentration-Gross LT =8 TDR-Long (Other)	double	yes
COTC-121	COTC: Concentration-Gross LT =8 TDR-Short(Other)	double	yes
COTC-122	COTC: Concentration-Net LT =4 TDR-Long (Other)	double	yes
COTC-123	COTC: Concentration-Net LT =4 TDR-Short (Other)	double	yes
COTC-124	COTC: Concentration-Net LT =8 TDR-Long (Other)	double	yes
COTC-125	COTC: Concentration-Net LT =8 TDR-Short (Other)	double	yes
COTC-13	COTC: Commercial Positions-Short (All)	double	yes
COTC-14	COTC: Total Reportable Positions-Long (All)	double	yes
COTC-15	COTC: Total Reportable Positions-Short (All)	double	yes
COTC-16	COTC: Nonreportable Positions-Long (All)	double	yes
COTC-17	COTC: Nonreportable Positions-Short (All)	double	yes
COTC-18	COTC: Open Interest (Old)	double	yes
COTC-19	COTC: Noncommercial Positions-Long (Old)	double	yes
COTC-20	COTC: Noncommercial Positions-Short (Old)	double	yes
COTC-21	COTC: Noncommercial Positions-Spreading (Old)	double	yes
COTC-22	COTC: Commercial Positions-Long (Old)	double	yes
COTC-23	COTC: Commercial Positions-Short (Old)	double	yes
COTC-24	COTC: Total Reportable Positions-Long (Old)	double	yes
COTC-25	COTC: Total Reportable Positions-Short (Old)	double	yes
COTC-26	COTC: Nonreportable Positions-Long (Old)	double	yes
COTC-27	COTC: Nonreportable Positions-Short (Old)	double	yes
COTC-28	COTC: Open Interest (Other)	double	yes
COTC-29	COTC: Noncommercial Positions-Long (Other)	double	yes
COTC-30	COTC: Noncommercial Positions-Short (Other)	double	yes
COTC-31	COTC: Noncommercial Positions-Spreading	double	yes

Name	Description	Type	History
	(Other)		
COTC-32	COTC: Commercial Positions-Long (Other)	double	yes
COTC-33	COTC: Commercial Positions-Short (Other)	double	yes
COTC-34	COTC: Total Reportable Positions-Long (Other)	double	yes
COTC-35	COTC: Total Reportable Positions-Short (Other)	double	yes
COTC-36	COTC: Nonreportable Positions-Long (Other)	double	yes
COTC-37	COTC: Nonreportable Positions-Short (Other)	double	yes
COTC-38	COTC: Change in Open Interest (All)	double	yes
COTC-39	COTC: Change in Noncommercial-Long (All)	double	yes
COTC-40	COTC: Change in Noncommercial-Short (All)	double	yes
COTC-41	COTC: Change in Noncommercial-Spreading (All)	double	yes
COTC-42	COTC: Change in Commercial-Long (All)	double	yes
COTC-43	COTC: Change in Commercial-Short (All)	double	yes
COTC-44	COTC: Change in Total Reportable-Long (All)	double	yes
COTC-45	COTC: Change in Total Reportable-Short (All)	double	yes
COTC-46	COTC: Change in Nonreportable-Long (All)	double	yes
COTC-47	COTC: Change in Nonreportable-Short (All)	double	yes
COTC-48	COTC: % of Open Interest (OI) (All)	double	yes
COTC-49	COTC: % of OI-Noncommercial-Long (All)	double	yes
COTC-50	COTC: % of OI-Noncommercial-Short (All)	double	yes
COTC-51	COTC: % of OI-Noncommercial-Spreading (All)	double	yes
COTC-52	COTC: % of OI-Commercial-Long (All)	double	yes
COTC-53	COTC: % of OI-Commercial-Short (All)	double	yes
COTC-54	COTC: % of OI-Total Reportable-Long (All)	double	yes
COTC-55	COTC: % of OI-Total Reportable-Short (All)	double	yes
COTC-56	COTC: % of OI-Nonreportable-Long (All)	double	yes
COTC-57	COTC: % of OI-Nonreportable-Short (All)	double	yes
COTC-58	COTC: % of Open Interest (OI)(Old)	double	yes
COTC-59	COTC: % of OI-Noncommercial-Long (Old)	double	yes
COTC-60	COTC: % of OI-Noncommercial-Short (Old)	double	yes

Name	Description	Type	History
COTC-61	COTC: % of OI-Noncommercial-Spreading (Old)	double	yes
COTC-62	COTC: % of OI-Commercial-Long (Old)	double	yes
COTC-63	COTC: % of OI-Commercial-Short (Old)	double	yes
COTC-64	COTC: % of OI-Total Reportable-Long (Old)	double	yes
COTC-65	COTC: % of OI-Total Reportable-Short (Old)	double	yes
COTC-66	COTC: % of OI-Nonreportable-Long (Old)	double	yes
COTC-67	COTC: % of OI-Nonreportable-Short (Old)	double	yes
COTC-68	COTC: % of Open Interest (OI) (Other)	double	yes
COTC-69	COTC: % of OI-Noncommercial-Long (Other)	double	yes
COTC-70	COTC: % of OI-Noncommercial-Short (Other)	double	yes
COTC-71	COTC: % of OI-Noncommercial-Spreading (Other)	double	yes
COTC-72	COTC: % of OI-Commercial-Long (Other)	double	yes
COTC-73	COTC: % of OI-Commercial-Short (Other)	double	yes
COTC-74	COTC: % of OI-Total Reportable-Long (Other)	double	yes
COTC-75	COTC: % of OI-Total Reportable-Short (Other)	double	yes
COTC-76	COTC: % of OI-Nonreportable-Long (Other)	double	yes
COTC-77	COTC: % of OI-Nonreportable-Short (Other)	double	yes
COTC-78	COTC: Traders-Total (All)	double	yes
COTC-79	COTC: Traders-Noncommercial-Long (All)	double	yes
COTC-8	COTC: Open Interest (All)	double	yes
COTC-80	COTC: Traders-Noncommercial-Short (All)	double	yes
COTC-81	COTC: Traders-Noncommercial-Spreading (All)	double	yes
COTC-82	COTC: Traders-Commercial-Long (All)	double	yes
COTC-83	COTC: Traders-Commercial-Short (All)	double	yes
COTC-84	COTC: Traders-Total Reportable-Long (All)	double	yes
COTC-85	COTC: Traders-Total Reportable-Short (All)	double	yes
COTC-86	COTC: Traders-Total (Old)	double	yes
COTC-87	COTC: Traders-Noncommercial-Long (Old)	double	yes
COTC-88	COTC: Traders-Noncommercial-Short (Old)	double	yes
COTC-89	COTC: Traders-Noncommercial-Spreading (Old)	double	yes

Name	Description	Type	History
COTC-9	COTC: Noncommercial Positions-Long (All)	double	yes
COTC-90	COTC: Traders-Commercial-Long (Old)	double	yes
COTC-91	COTC: Traders-Commercial-Short (Old)	double	yes
COTC-92	COTC: Traders-Total Reportable-Long (Old)	double	yes
COTC-93	COTC: Traders-Total Reportable-Short (Old)	double	yes
COTC-94	COTC: Traders-Total (Other)	double	yes
COTC-95	COTC: Traders-Noncommercial-Long (Other)	double	yes
COTC-96	COTC: Traders-Noncommercial-Short (Other)	double	yes
COTC-97	COTC: Traders-Noncommercial-Spreading (Other)	double	yes
COTC-98	COTC: Traders-Commercial-Long (Other)	double	yes
COTC-99	COTC: Traders-Commercial-Short (Other)	double	yes
COTF-10	COTF: Noncommercial Positions-Short (All)	double	yes
COTF-100	COTF: Traders-Total Reportable-Long (Other)	double	yes
COTF-101	COTF: Traders-Total Reportable-Short (Other)	double	yes
COTF-102	COTF: Concentration-Gross LT = 4 TDR-Long (All)	double	yes
COTF-103	COTF: Concentration-Gross LT =4 TDR-Short (All)	double	yes
COTF-104	COTF: Concentration-Gross LT =8 TDR-Long (All)	double	yes
COTF-105	COTF: Concentration-Gross LT =8 TDR-Short (All)	double	yes
COTF-106	COTF: Concentration-Net LT =4 TDR-Long (All)	double	yes
COTF-107	COTF: Concentration-Net LT =4 TDR-Short (All)	double	yes
COTF-108	COTF: Concentration-Net LT =8 TDR-Long (All)	double	yes
COTF-109	COTF: Concentration-Net LT =8 TDR-Short (All)	double	yes
COTF-11	COTF: Noncommercial Positions-Spreading (All)	double	yes
COTF-110	COTF: Concentration-Gross LT =4 TDR-Long (Old)	double	yes
COTF-111	COTF: Concentration-Gross LT =4 TDR-Short (Old)	double	yes
COTF-112	COTF: Concentration-Gross LT =8 TDR-Long (Old)	double	yes

Name	Description	Type	History
COTF-113	COTF: Concentration-Gross LT =8 TDR-Short (Old)	double	yes
COTF-114	COTF: Concentration-Net LT =4 TDR-Long (Old)	double	yes
COTF-115	COTF: Concentration-Net LT =4 TDR-Short (Old)	double	yes
COTF-116	COTF: Concentration-Net LT =8 TDR-Long (Old)	double	yes
COTF-117	COTF: Concentration-Net LT =8 TDR-Short (Old)	double	yes
COTF-118	COTF: Concentration-Gross LT =4 TDR-Long (Other)	double	yes
COTF-119	COTF: Concentration-Gross LT =4 TDR-Short(Other)	double	yes
COTF-12	COTF: Commercial Positions-Long (All)	double	yes
COTF-120	COTF: Concentration-Gross LT =8 TDR-Long (Other)	double	yes
COTF-121	COTF: Concentration-Gross LT =8 TDR-Short(Other)	double	yes
COTF-122	COTF: Concentration-Net LT =4 TDR-Long (Other)	double	yes
COTF-123	COTF: Concentration-Net LT =4 TDR-Short (Other)	double	yes
COTF-124	COTF: Concentration-Net LT =8 TDR-Long (Other)	double	yes
COTF-125	COTF: Concentration-Net LT =8 TDR-Short (Other)	double	yes
COTF-13	COTF: Commercial Positions-Short (All)	double	yes
COTF-14	COTF: Total Reportable Positions-Long (All)	double	yes
COTF-15	COTF: Total Reportable Positions-Short (All)	double	yes
COTF-16	COTF: Nonreportable Positions-Long (All)	double	yes
COTF-17	COTF: Nonreportable Positions-Short (All)	double	yes
COTF-18	COTF: Open Interest (Old)	double	yes
COTF-19	COTF: Noncommercial Positions-Long (Old)	double	yes
COTF-20	COTF: Noncommercial Positions-Short (Old)	double	yes
COTF-21	COTF: Noncommercial Positions-Spreading (Old)	double	yes
COTF-22	COTF: Commercial Positions-Long (Old)	double	yes

Name	Description	Type	History
COTF-23	COTF: Commercial Positions-Short (Old)	double	yes
COTF-24	COTF: Total Reportable Positions-Long (Old)	double	yes
COTF-25	COTF: Total Reportable Positions-Short (Old)	double	yes
COTF-26	COTF: Nonreportable Positions-Long (Old)	double	yes
COTF-27	COTF: Nonreportable Positions-Short (Old)	double	yes
COTF-28	COTF: Open Interest (Other)	double	yes
COTF-29	COTF: Noncommercial Positions-Long (Other)	double	yes
COTF-30	COTF: Noncommercial Positions-Short (Other)	double	yes
COTF-31	COTF: Noncommercial Positions-Spreading (Other)	double	yes
COTF-32	COTF: Commercial Positions-Long (Other)	double	yes
COTF-33	COTF: Commercial Positions-Short (Other)	double	yes
COTF-34	COTF: Total Reportable Positions-Long (Other)	double	yes
COTF-35	COTF: Total Reportable Positions-Short (Other)	double	yes
COTF-36	COTF: Nonreportable Positions-Long (Other)	double	yes
COTF-37	COTF: Nonreportable Positions-Short (Other)	double	yes
COTF-38	COTF: Change in Open Interest (All)	double	yes
COTF-39	COTF: Change in Noncommercial-Long (All)	double	yes
COTF-40	COTF: Change in Noncommercial-Short (All)	double	yes
COTF-41	COTF: Change in Noncommercial Spreading (All)	double	yes
COTF-42	COTF: Change in Commercial-Long (All)	double	yes
COTF-43	COTF: Change in Commercial-Short (All)	double	yes
COTF-44	COTF: Change in Total Reportable-Long (All)	double	yes
COTF-45	COTF: Change in Total Reportable-Short (All)	double	yes
COTF-46	COTF: Change in Nonreportable-Long (All)	double	yes
COTF-47	COTF: Change in Nonreportable-Short (All)	double	yes
COTF-48	COTF: % of Open Interest (OI) (All)	double	yes
COTF-49	COTF: % of OI-Noncommercial-Long (All)	double	yes
COTF-50	COTF: % of OI-Noncommercial-Short (All)	double	yes
COTF-51	COTF: % of OI-Noncommercial-Spreading (All)	double	yes
COTF-52	COTF: % of OI-Commercial-Long (All)	double	yes

Name	Description	Type	History
COTF-53	COTF: % of OI-Commercial-Short (All)	double	yes
COTF-54	COTF: % of OI-Total Reportable-Long (All)	double	yes
COTF-55	COTF: % of OI-Total Reportable-Short (All)	double	yes
COTF-56	COTF: % of OI-Nonreportable-Long (All)	double	yes
COTF-57	COTF: % of OI-Nonreportable-Short (All)	double	yes
COTF-58	COTF: % of Open Interest (OI)(Old)	double	yes
COTF-59	COTF: % of OI-Noncommercial-Long (Old)	double	yes
COTF-60	COTF: % of OI-Noncommercial-Short (Old)	double	yes
COTF-61	COTF: % of OI-Noncommercial-Spreading (Old)	double	yes
COTF-62	COTF: % of OI-Commercial-Long (Old)	double	yes
COTF-63	COTF: % of OI-Commercial-Short (Old)	double	yes
COTF-64	COTF: % of OI-Total Reportable-Long (Old)	double	yes
COTF-65	COTF: % of OI-Total Reportable-Short (Old)	double	yes
COTF-66	COTF: % of OI-Nonreportable-Long (Old)	double	yes
COTF-67	COTF: % of OI-Nonreportable-Short (Old)	double	yes
COTF-68	COTF: % of Open Interest (OI) (Other)	double	yes
COTF-69	COTF: % of OI-Noncommercial-Long (Other)	double	yes
COTF-70	COTF: % of OI-Noncommercial-Short (Other)	double	yes
COTF-71	COTF: % of OI-Noncommercial-Spreading (Other)	double	yes
COTF-72	COTF: % of OI-Commercial-Long (Other)	double	yes
COTF-73	COTF: % of OI-Commercial-Short (Other)	double	yes
COTF-74	COTF: % of OI-Total Reportable-Long (Other)	double	yes
COTF-75	COTF: % of OI-Total Reportable-Short (Other)	double	yes
COTF-76	COTF: % of OI-Nonreportable-Long (Other)	double	yes
COTF-77	COTF: % of OI-Nonreportable-Short (Other)	double	yes
COTF-78	COTF: Traders-Total (All)	double	yes
COTF-79	COTF: Traders-Noncommercial-Long (All)	double	yes
COTF-8	COTF: Open Interest (All)	double	yes
COTF-80	COTF: Traders-Noncommercial-Short (All)	double	yes
COTF-81	COTF: Traders-Noncommercial-Spreading (All)	double	yes

Name	Description	Type	History
COTF-82	COTF: Traders-Commercial-Long (All)	double	yes
COTF-83	COTF: Traders-Commercial-Short (All)	double	yes
COTF-84	COTF: Traders-Total Reportable-Long (All)	double	yes
COTF-85	COTF: Traders-Total Reportable-Short (All)	double	yes
COTF-86	COTF: Traders-Total (Old)	double	yes
COTF-87	COTF: Traders-Noncommercial-Long (Old)	double	yes
COTF-88	COTF: Traders-Noncommercial-Short (Old)	double	yes
COTF-89	COTF: Traders-Noncommercial-Spreading (Old)	double	yes
COTF-9	COTF: Noncommercial Positions-Long (All)	double	yes
COTF-90	COTF: Traders-Commercial-Long (Old)	double	yes
COTF-91	COTF: Traders-Commercial-Short (Old)	double	yes
COTF-92	COTF: Traders-Total Reportable-Long (Old)	double	yes
COTF-93	COTF: Traders-Total Reportable-Short (Old)	double	yes
COTF-94	COTF: Traders-Total (Other)	double	yes
COTF-95	COTF: Traders-Noncommercial-Long (Other)	double	yes
COTF-96	COTF: Traders-Noncommercial-Short (Other)	double	yes
COTF-97	COTF: Traders-Noncommercial-Spreading (Other)	double	yes
COTF-98	COTF: Traders-Commercial-Long (Other)	double	yes
COTF-99	COTF: Traders-Commercial-Short (Other)	double	yes
CPFA	Pro Forma Adjustment	double	yes
CPIA	Interest Adjustment - Primary EPS	double	yes
CPRD	Preferred Dividends	double	yes
CSPTRENDGR	Capital Spending growth rate, 5 year	double	
DATEMRAP	Date for Financial statements - most recent fiscal year	date	
DATEMRQP	Date for financial statements - most recent quarter	date	
DATEPRELIM	Date for Preliminary update	date	
DCGD	Gross Dividends - Common Stock	double	yes
DCGD_TTMYr5Grth	Gross Dividends - Common Stock, 5 Year Interim Trend Growth %	double	
DCGD_TTMYr5Mom	Gross Dividends - Common Stock, 5 Year Interim Trend Momentum %	double	

Name	Description	Type	History
DCGD_TTMYr5Vty	Gross Dividends - Common Stock, 5 Year Interim Trend Volatil %	double	
DDPS1	Dividends per Share - Common Stock Primary Issue	double	yes
DDPS2	Dividends per Share - Common Stock Issue 2	double	yes
DDPS3	Dividends per Share - Common Stock Issue 3	double	yes
DDPS4	Dividends per Share - Common Stock Issue 4	double	yes
DebtCap_A	Total Debt Capital, LFY	double	
DebtCap_I	Total Debt Capital, LFI	double	
DIV	Dividends paid from SCF - most recent fiscal year	double	
Div2Ebitda_A	Dividends/EBITDA, FY	double	
Div2Ebitda_TTM	Dividends/EBITDA, TTM	double	
Div2Ocf_A	Dividends/Operating Cash Flow, FY	double	
Div2Ocf_TTM	Dividends/Operating Cash Flow, TTM	double	
DivCover_A	Dividend Coverage, FY	double	
DivCover_TTM	Dividend Coverage, TTM	double	
DIVGRPCT	Growth rate% - dividend, 3-year	double	
DIVNQ	Dividend - next quarterly declared	double	
DIVNQPDT	Dividend - next quarterly pay-date	date	
DIVNQXDT	Dividend - next quarterly ex-date	date	
DIVTREND10	Dividend growth rate, 10-year	double	
DIVTRENDGR	Dividend growth rate, 5-year	double	
DivYield_CurA	Current Dividend Yield - Common Stock Primary Issue, LFY	double	
DivYield_CurAnul	Current Dividend Yield - Common Stock Primary Issue, LFI, Annualized	double	
DivYield_CurTTM	Current Dividend Yield - Common Stock Primary Issue, LTM	double	
DivYield_IAvg3	Historic Dividend Yield - Common Stock Primary Issue, %, 3 Year Average	double	
DRECDATE	Dividend record date	date	
DVOLSHSOUT	Volume (daily) as a % of Shares Outstanding	double	
EADV	Advertising Expense	double	yes
EAMA	Amortization of Acquisition Costs	double	yes

Name	Description	Type	History
EAMI	Amortization of Intangibles	double	yes
EAML	Minimum Pension Liability Adjustment	double	yes
Ebitda_AYr10CAGR	Earnings Before Interest, Taxes, Depreciation, Amortization, 10-Year CAGR	double	
EBITDA_AYr10Grth	Earnings Before Interest, Taxes, Deprec, Amort, 10 Year Annual Trend Growth%	double	
EBITDA_AYr10Mom	Earnings Before Interest, Taxes, Deprec, Amort, 10 Year Annual Trend Momentum%	double	
EBITDA_AYr10Vty	Earnings Before Interest, Taxes, Deprec, Amort, 10 Yr Annual Trend Volatility%	double	
Ebitda_AYr3CAGR	Earnings Before Interest, Taxes, Depreciation,Amortization, 3-Year CAGR	double	
Ebitda_AYr5CAGR	Earnings Before Interest, Taxes, Depreciation,Amortization, 5-Year CAGR	double	
EBITDA_IYr5Vty	Earnings Before Interest, Taxes, Deprec, Amort, 5-Yr Interim Trend Volatility%	double	
Ebitda_TTM10CAGR	Earnings Before Interest, Taxes, Deprec, Amort, 10-Yr Interim CAGR	double	
EBITDA_TTM5Mom	Earnings Before Interest, Taxes, Deprec, Amort, 5-Yr Interim Trend Momentum %	double	
Ebitda_TTMY3CAGR	Earnings Before Interest, Taxes, Depreciation, Amortization, 3 Yr Interim CAGR	double	
Ebitda_TTMY5CAGR	Earnings Before Interest, Taxes, Depreciation, Amortization, 5 Yr Interim CAGR	double	
EBITDA_TTMY5Grth	Earnings Before Interest, Taxes, Deprec, Amort, 5 Yr Interim Trend Growth %	double	
Ebitda2BV_A	EBITDA/Total Equity, %, FY	double	
Ebitda2BV_AAvg5	EBITDA/Total Equity, %, 5 Year Average	double	
Ebitda2BV_IAvg3	EBITDA/Total Equity, %, 3 Year Average	double	
Ebitda2BV_TTM	EBITDA/Total Equity, %, TTM	double	
Ebitda2CEq_A	EBITDA/Common Shareholders Equity, %, FY	double	
Ebitda2CEq_AAvg5	EBITDA/Common Shareholders Equity, %, 5 Year Average	double	
Ebitda2CEq_IAvg3	EBITDA/Common Shareholders Equity, %, 3 Year Average	double	
Ebitda2CEq_TTM	EBITDA/Common Shareholders Equity, %, TTM	double	
EBITDA2EV	Current EBITDA/EV	double	
EBITDA2EV_A	Current EBITDA to EV, LFY	double	
EBITDA2EV_TTM	Current EBITDA to EV, LTM	double	

Name	Description	Type	History
Ebitda2TotAst_A	EBITDA/Total Assets, %, FY	double	
Ebitda2TtA_AAvg5	EBITDA/Total Assets, %, 5 Year Average	double	
Ebitda2TtA_IAvg3	EBITDA/Total Assets, %, 3 Year Average	double	
Ebitda2TtA_TTM	EBITDA/Total Assets, %, TTM	double	
EBITDAMar_IAvg3	EBITDA Margin, %, 3 Year Average	double	
ECAP	Interest Capitalized, Operating	double	yes
ECOR	Cost of Revenue	double	yes
EDEP	Depreciation	double	yes
EDOE	Operations & Maintenance	double	yes
EEXT	Excise Taxes Payments	double	yes
EFCA	Foreign Currency Adjustment	double	yes
EFEX	Fuel Expense	double	yes
EFFS	Fed Funds Sold/Secs. Sold under Repurch. Agrmnt.	double	yes
EFPR	Fuel Purchased for Resale	double	yes
EGLA	Loss (Gain) on Sale of Assets - Operating	double	yes
EIAS	Impairment-Assets Held for Sale	double	yes
EIAU	Impairment-Assets Held for Use	double	yes
EIBT	Income Before Tax	double	yes
EIBT_AYr10CAGR	Income Before Tax, 10 Year CAGR	double	
EIBT_AYr10Grth	Income Before Tax, 10 Year Annual Trend Growth %	double	
EIBT_AYr10Mom	Income Before Tax, 10 Year Annual Trend Momentum %	double	
EIBT_AYr10Vty	Income Before Tax, 10 Year Annual Trend Volatil %	double	
EIBT_AYr3CAGR	Income Before Tax, 3 Year CAGR	double	
EIBT_AYr5CAGR	Income Before Tax, 5 Year CAGR	double	
EIBT_TTMYr5Grth	Income Before Tax, 5 Year Interim Trend Growth %	double	
EIBT_TTMYr5Mom	Income Before Tax, 5 Year Interim Trend Momentum %	double	
EIBT_TTMYr5Vty	Income Before Tax, 5 Year Interim Trend Volatil %	double	

Name	Description	Type	History
EIEX	Interest Expense, Operating	double	yes
EIIN	Interest Income, Operating	double	yes
EINN	Interest Expense (Income), Net Operating	double	yes
EINV	Investment Income, Operating	double	yes
EIOB	Interest on Other Borrowings	double	yes
EIOD	Interest on Deposit	double	yes
ELAR	Labor & Related Expense	double	yes
ELBA	Losses, Benefits, and Adjustments	double	yes
ELIT	Litigation	double	yes
ELLP	Loan Loss Provision	double	yes
ENII	Net Interest Income	double	yes
EONT	Other, Net	double	yes
EOOE	Other Operating Expense	double	yes
EPAC	Amort. Of Policy Acquisition Costs	double	yes
EPOT	Property & Other Taxes	double	yes
EPPR	Purchased Power	double	yes
EPSCHNGIN	EPS Change % - prior quarter	double	
EPSCHNGYR	EPS Change % - most recent quarter 1 year ago	double	
EPSCHNGYRI	EPS Change % - year to date	double	
EpsExcEx2P_A	EPS Excl. Extra Items, Diluted/Price, FY	double	
EpsExcEx2P_AAvg5	EPS Excl. Extra Items, Diluted/Price, 5 Year Average	double	
EpsExcEx2P_IAvg3	EPS Excl. Extra Items, Diluted/Price, 3 Year Average	double	
EpsExcEx2P_TTM	EPS Excl. Extra Items, Diluted/Price, TTM	double	
EPSGRPCT	Growth rate% - EPS, 3 year	double	
EpsIncEx2P_A	EPS Incl. Extra Items, Diluted/Price, FY	double	
EpsIncEx2P_AAvg5	EPS Incl. Extra Items, Diluted/Price, 5 Year Average	double	
EpsIncEx2P_IAvg3	EPS Incl. Extra Items, Diluted/Price, 3 Year Average	double	
EpsIncEx2P_TTM	EPS Incl. Extra Items, Diluted/Price, TTM	double	
EpsNorm2P_A	EPS Normalized, Diluted/Price, FY	double	

Name	Description	Type	History
EpsNorm2P_TTM	EPS Normalized, Diluted/Price, TTM	double	
EPSTREND10	EPS growth rate, 10 year	double	
EPSTRENDGR	EPS growth rate, 5 year	double	
ERAD	Research & Development	double	yes
ERDW	Purchased R&D Written-Off	double	yes
ERES	Restructuring Charge	double	yes
ERII	Reinsurance - Expense	double	yes
ESGA	Selling/General/Administrative Expense	double	yes
ETOE	Total Operating Expense	double	yes
EUAC	Underwriting & Commissions	double	yes
EUGL	Unrealized Losses (Gains)	double	yes
EUIE	Other Unusual Expense (Income)	double	yes
Ev_AAvg5	Historic Enterprise Value, 5 Year Average	double	
Ev_AYr10CAGR	Historic Enterprise Value, 10 Year CAGR	double	
Ev_AYr10Grr	Historic Enterprise Value, 10 Year Annual Trend Growth %	double	
Ev_AYr10Mom	Historic Enterprise Value, 10 Year Annual Trend Momentum %	double	
Ev_AYr10Vty	Historic Enterprise Value, 10 Year Annual Trend Volatil %	double	
Ev_AYr3CAGR	Historic Enterprise Value, 3 Year CAGR	double	
Ev_AYr5CAGR	Historic Enterprise Value, 5 Year CAGR	double	
EV_Cur	Current Enterprise Value (EV)	double	
EV_CurA	Current Enterprise Value (EV), LFY	double	
EV_CurI	Current Enterprise Value (EV), LFI	double	
Ev_IAvg3	Historic Enterprise Value, 3 Year Average	double	
Ev_IYr10CAGR	Historic Enterprise Value, 10 Year Interim CAGR	double	
Ev_IYr3CAGR	Historic Enterprise Value, 3 Year Interim CAGR	double	
Ev_IYr5CAGR	Historic Enterprise Value, 5 Year Interim CAGR	double	
Ev_IYr5Grr	Historic Enterprise Value, 5 Year Interim Trend Growth %	double	
Ev_IYr5Mom	Historic Enterprise Value, 5 Year Interim Trend Momentum %	double	

Name	Description	Type	History
Ev_IYr5Vty	Historic Enterprise Value, 5 Year Interim Trend Volatil %	double	
EV2EBITDA_Cur	Current EV/EBITDA	double	
EV2EBITDA_CurA	Current EV/EBITDA, LFY	double	
EV2EBITDA_CurTTM	Current EV/EBITDA, LTM	double	
EV2FCF_Cur	Current EV/Free Cash Flow	double	
EV2FCF_CurA	Current EV/Free Cash Flow, LFY	double	
EV2FCF_CurTTM	Current EV/Free Cash Flow, LTM	double	
Ev2Focf_A	Historic Enterprise Value/Free Operating Cash Flow Excluding Dividends, FY	double	
Ev2Focf_AAvg5	Historic Enterprise Value/Free Operating Cash Flow Excl. Dividends, 5 Yr Avg	double	
Ev2Focf_Cur	Current EV/Free Operating Cash Flow Ex Dividends	double	
Ev2Focf_CurA	Current EV/Free Operating Cash Flow Ex Dividends, LFY	double	
Ev2Focf_CurTTM	Current EV/Free Operating Cash Flow Ex Dividends, LTM	double	
Ev2Focf_IAvg3	Historic Enterprise Value/Free Operating Cash Flow Excl. Dividends, 3 Yr Avg	double	
Ev2Focf_TTM	Historic Enterprise Value/Free Operating Cash Flow Excluding Dividends, TTM	double	
Ev2Mcap_A	EV/Market Cap, FY	double	
Ev2Mcap_I	EV/Market Cap, FI	double	
Ev2Rev_AAvg5	Historic Enterprise Value/Revenue, 5 Year Average	double	
EV2Rev_Cur	Current EV/Revenue	double	
EV2Rev_CurA	Current EV/Revenue, LFY	double	
EV2Rev_CurTTM	Current EV/Revenue, LTM	double	
Ev2Rev_IAvg3	Historic Enterprise Value/Revenue, 3 Year Average	double	
F_actinact	Active status	double	
F_company	Company name	string	
F_comptype	Company type	string	
F_country	Country code	string	
F_currency	Currency code	string	

Name	Description	Type	History
F_cusip	CUSIP	string	
F_exchange	Exchange code	string	
F_intexist	Interim financials exist	double	
F_isin	ISIN	string	
F_lstupdat	Last financial update	date	
F_mgind	Industry name	string	
F_mgindcod	Industry code	double	
F_mgindmne	Industry mnemonics	string	
F_mgsec	Sector name	string	
F_mgseccod	Sector code	double	
F_mgsecmne	Sector mnemonics	string	
F_mxsecid	MX Security Identifier	double	
F_region	Region code	string	
F_repno	Report number	string	
F_ric	RIC	string	
F_sedol	SEDOL	string	
F_ticker	Ticker symbol	string	
FCDP	Total Cash Dividends Paid	double	yes
FCDP_AYr10CAGR	Total Cash Dividends Paid, 10 Year CAGR	double	
FCDP_AYr5CAGR	Total Cash Dividends Paid, 5 Year CAGR	double	
FCSN	Common Stock, Net	double	yes
FDPC	Cash Dividends Paid - Common	double	yes
FDPC_AYr10CAGR	Cash Dividends Paid, Common, 10 Year CAGR	double	
FDPC_AYr5CAGR	Cash Dividends Paid, Common, 5 Year CAGR	double	
FDPP	Cash Dividends Paid - Preferred	double	yes
FDPT	Deposits	double	yes
FFCF	Other Financing Cash Flow	double	yes
FFFS	Federal Funds/REPOs	double	yes
FFLB	FHLB Borrowings	double	yes
FLASH	Flash Flag (indicates weather the "current" values come from a flash report)	double	

Name	Description	Type	History
FLDI	Long Term Debt Issued	double	yes
FLDN	Long Term Debt, Net	double	yes
FLDR	Long Term Debt Reduction	double	yes
FLOAT	Float	double	
FLOATPRC_Cur	Float as a Percent of Total Shares Outstanding	double	
FOCF_AYr10CAGR	Free Operating Cash Flow, 10 Year CAGR	double	
Focf_AYr10Grr	Free Operating Cash Flow Excluding Dividends, 10 Year Annual Trend Growth %	double	
FOCF_AYr10Grth	Free Operating Cash Flow, 10 Year Annual Trend Growth %	double	
FOCF_AYr10Mom	Free Operating Cash Flow, 10 Year Annual Trend Momentum %	double	
FOCF_AYr10Vty	Free Operating Cash Flow, 10 Year Annual Trend Volatil %	double	
FOCF_AYr3CAGR	Free Operating Cash Flow, 3 Year CAGR	double	
FOCF_AYr5CAGR	Free Operating Cash Flow, 5 Year CAGR	double	
Focf_TTMYr5Grr	Free Operating Cash Flow Excluding Dividends, 5 Year Interim Trend Growth %	double	
FOCF_TTMYr5Grth	Free Operating Cash Flow, 5 Year Interim Trend Growth %	double	
FOCF_TTMYr5Mom	Free Operating Cash Flow, 5 Year Interim Trend Momentum %	double	
FOCF_TTMYr5Vty	Free Operating Cash Flow, 5 Year Interim Trend Volatil %	double	
Focf2Rev_A	Free Operating Cash Flow/Revenue, FY	double	
Focf2Rev_AAvg5	Free Operating Cash Flow/Revenue, 5 Year Average	double	
Focf2Rev_IAvg3	Free Operating Cash Flow/Revenue, 3 Year Average	double	
Focf2Rev_TTM	Free Operating Cash Flow/Revenue, TTM	double	
FocfExD2Rev_A	Free Operating Cash Flow Ex Dividends/Revenue, FY	double	
FocfExD2RevAAvg5	Free Operating Cash Flow Ex Dividends/Revenue, 5 Year Average	double	
FocfExD2RevIAvg3	Free Operating Cash Flow Ex Dividends/Revenue, 3 Year Average	double	
FocfExD2RevTTM	Free Operating Cash Flow Ex Dividends/Revenue, TTM	double	
FocfExDAYr10CAGR	Free Operating Cash Flow Excluding Dividends,	double	

Name	Description	Type	History
	10 Year CAGR		
FocfExDAYr10Mom	Free Operating Cash Flow Excluding Dividends, 10 Yr Annual Trend Momentum %	double	
FocfExDAYr10Vty	Free Operating Cash Flow Excluding Dividends, 10 Yr Annual Trend Volatil %	double	
FocfExDAYr3CAGR	Free Operating Cash Flow Excluding Dividends, 3 Year CAGR	double	
FocfExDAYr5CAGR	Free Operating Cash Flow Excluding Dividends, 5 Year CAGR	double	
FocfExDTTMYr5Mom	Free Operating Cash Flow Excluding Dividends, 5 Yr Interim Trend Momentum %	double	
FocfExDTTMYr5Vty	Free Operating Cash Flow Excluding Dividends, 5 Yr Interim Trend Volatil %	double	
FOPX	Options Exercised	double	yes
FPRD	Issuance (Retirement) of Debt, Net	double	yes
FPSN	Preferred Stock, Net	double	yes
FPSS	Issuance (Retirement) of Stock, Net	double	yes
FRCP	Repurch./Retirement of Common/Preferred	double	yes
FRRC	Repurchase/Retirement of Common	double	yes
FRRP	Repurchase/Retirement of Preferred	double	yes
FSCP	Sale/Issuance of Common/Preferred	double	yes
FSDI	Short Term Debt Issued	double	yes
FSDN	Short Term Debt, Net	double	yes
FSDR	Short Term Debt Reduction	double	yes
FSIC	Sale/Issuance of Common	double	yes
FSIP	Sale/Issuance of Preferred	double	yes
FTDI	Total Debt Issued	double	yes
FTDR	Total Debt Reduction	double	yes
FTLF	Cash from Financing Activities	double	yes
FTST	Treasury Stock	double	yes
FWCV	Warrants Converted	double	yes
GAFI	Primary EPS Incl. Extra. Items	double	
GBAI	Basic EPS Incl. Extra. Items	double	
GBAS	Basic Weighted Average Shares	double	

Name	Description	Type	History
GBBF	Basic EPS Excl. Extra. Items	double	
GBFI	Primary Excl. Extra. Items	double	
GDAI	Diluted EPS Including ExtraOrd Items	double	
GDAJ	Dilution Adjustment	double	
GDBF	Diluted EPS Excluding ExtraOrd Items	double	
GDNI	Diluted Net Income	double	
GDWS	Diluted Weighted Average Shares	double	
GFAI	Fully Diluted EPS Including ExtraOrd Items	double	
GFBF	Fully Diluted EPS Excluding ExtraOrd Items	double	
GFDA	Dilution Adjustment	double	
GFDI	Fully Diluted Net Income	double	
GFDS	Fully Diluted Weighted Average Shares	double	
GMNTRENDGR	Gross Margin growth rate, 5 year	double	
GPAS	Primary Weighted Average Shares	double	
GPMar_IAvg3	Gross Profit Margin, Industrial,Utility, %, 3 Year Average	double	
GROSMGN5YR	Gross Margin - 5 year average	double	
HFFO	Funds From Operations - REIT	double	yes
HISTRELPE	Historical Relative P/E	double	
i_ADIV5YAVG	industry: Dividend per Share - 5 year average	double	
i_ADIVCHG	industry: Dividend change % - year over year	double	
i_AEBITD5YR	industry: EBITD Margin - 5 year average	double	
i_AEPSCHG	industry: EPS Change % - year over year	double	
i_AREVCHG	industry: Revenue Change %, year over year	double	
i_AROA5YAVG	industry: Return on average assets - 5 year average	double	
i_AROE5YAVG	industry: Return on average equity - 5 year average	double	
i_AROI5YRAVG	industry: Return on investment - 5 year average	double	
i_ATAXRAT5YR	industry: Tax Rate - 5 year average	double	
i_BETA	industry: Beta	double	
i_CSPTRENDGR	industry: Capital Spending growth rate, 5 year	double	

Name	Description	Type	History
i_DIVGRPCT	industry: Growth rate% - dividend, 3 year	double	
i_DIVTRENDGR	industry: Dividend growth rate, 5 year	double	
i_EPSCHNGYR	industry: EPS Change % - most recent quarter 1 year ago	double	
i_EPSGRPCT	industry: Growth rate% - EPS, 3 year	double	
i_EPSTRENDGR	industry: EPS growth rate, 5 year	double	
i_GROSMGN5YR	industry: Gross Margin - 5 year average	double	
i_IPCTHLDV	industry: Institutional percent held	double	
i_MARGIN5YR	industry: Net Profit Margin - 5 year average	double	
i_MKTCAP	industry: Market capitalization	double	
i_NITRENDGR	industry: Net Income growth rate, 5 year	double	
i_NPRICE	industry: Price - closing or last bid	double	
i_OPMGN5YR	industry: Operating Margin - 5 year average	double	
i_PAYOUT5YR	industry: Payout ratio - 5 year average	double	
i_PEEXCLXOR	industry: P/E excluding extraordinary items - TTM	double	
i_PEHIGH	industry: P/E excluding extraordinary items, High	double	
i_PELOW	industry: P/E excluding extraordinary items, Low	double	
i_PR04WKPCT	industry: Price - 04 week price percent change	double	
i_PR04WKPCTR	industry: Relative (S&P500) price percent change - 04 week	double	
i_PR13WKPCT	industry: Price - 13 week price percent change	double	
i_PR13WKPCTR	industry: Relative (S&P500) price percent change - 13 week	double	
i_PR1DAYPRC	industry: Price - 1 Day % Change	double	
i_PR26WKPCT	industry: Price - 26 week price percent change	double	
i_PR26WKPCTR	industry: Relative (S&P500) price percent change - 26 week	double	
i_PR2TANBK	industry: Price to Tangible Book - most recent quarter	double	
i_PR52WKPCT	industry: Price - 52 week price percent change	double	
i_PR52WKPCTR	industry: Relative (S&P500) price percent change - 52 week	double	
i_PR5DAYPRC	industry: Price - 5 Day % Change	double	

Name	Description	Type	History
i_PRICE2BK	industry: Price to Book - most recent quarter	double	
i_PRYTDPCT	industry: Price - YTD price percent change	double	
i_PTMGN5YR	industry: Pretax Margin - 5 year average	double	
i_QCSHPS	industry: Cash per share - most recent quarter	double	
i_QCURRATIO	industry: Current ratio - most recent quarter	double	
i_QLTD2EQ	industry: LT debt/equity - most recent quarter	double	
i_QQUICKRATI	industry: Quick ratio - most recent quarter	double	
i_QTOTD2EQ	industry: Total debt/total equity - most recent quarter	double	
i_REVCHNGYR	industry: Revenue Change % - most recent quarter 1 year ago	double	
i_REVGRPCT	industry: Growth rate% - Revenue, 3 year	double	
i_REVTRENDGR	industry: Revenue growth rate, 5 year	double	
i_TTMASTTURN	industry: Asset turnover - trailing 12 month	double	
i_TTMBEPSXCL	industry: EPS Basic excluding extraordinary items - trailing 12 month	double	
i_TTMEBITDMG	industry: EBITD Margin - trailing 12 month	double	
i_TTMEPSCHG	industry: EPS Change %, TTM over TTM	double	
i_TTMGROSMGN	industry: Gross Margin - trailing 12 month	double	
i_TTMINTCOV	industry: Interest coverage - trailing 12 month	double	
i_TTMINVTURN	industry: Inventory turnover - trailing 12 month	double	
i_TTMNIPEREM	industry: Net Income/employee - trailing 12 month	double	
i_TTMNPMGN	industry: Net Profit Margin % - trailing 12 month	double	
i_TTMOPMGN	industry: Operating margin - trailing 12 month	double	
i_TTMPAYRAT	industry: Payout ratio - trailing 12 month	double	
i_TTMPR2REV	industry: Price to sales - trailing 12 month	double	
i_TTMPRCFPS	industry: Price to Cash Flow per share - trailing 12 month	double	
i_TTMPRFCFPS	industry: Price to Free Cash Flow per Share - trailing 12 months	double	
i_TTMPTMGN	industry: Pretax margin - trailing 12 month	double	
i_TTMRECTURN	industry: Receivables turnover - trailing 12 month	double	
i_TTMREV	industry: Revenue - trailing 12 month	double	

Name	Description	Type	History
i_TTMREVCHG	industry: Revenue Change %, TTM over TTM	double	
i_TTMREVPERE	industry: Revenue/Employee - trailing 12 month	double	
i_TTMREVSTRT	industry: Reinvestment Rate - trailing 12 month	double	
i_TTMROAPCT	industry: Return on average assets - trailing 12 month	double	
i_TTMROEPCT	industry: Return on average equity - trailing 12 month	double	
i_TTMROIPCT	industry: Return on investment - trailing 12 month	double	
i_TTMTAXRATE	industry: Tax Rate - trailing 12 month	double	
i_VOL1DPRC	industry: Volume - 1 Day % Change	double	
i_YIELD	industry: Dividend Yield - indicated annual dividend divided by closing price	double	
IAD	Dividend rate, indicated annual	double	
IATMar_IAvg3	Income After Tax Margin, %, 3 Year Average	double	
IBAQ	Acquisition of Business	double	yes
IBTMar_IAvg3	Income Before Tax Margin, %, 3 Year Average	double	
ICEX	Purchase of Fixed Assets	double	yes
IFRE	Foreclosed Real Estate	double	yes
IIAN	Intangible, Net	double	yes
IIAQ	Purchase/Acquisition of Intangibles	double	yes
IICF	Other Investing Cash Flow	double	yes
IINP	Purchase of Investments	double	yes
IINS	Sale/Maturity of Investment	double	yes
IIVN	Investment, Net	double	yes
ILOA	Loans	double	yes
ILOR	Loans Origination - Investing	double	yes
INETNUMPUR	Institutional net shares purchased	double	
INETPURIN	Institutional net shares purchased - Prior Quarter	double	
INSNETPURC	Insider net shares bought	double	
INSNETTRAN	Insider net trades	double	
INSOWNERSH	Insider Ownership percent	double	
INUMPURC	Institutional shares bought	double	

Name	Description	Type	History
INUMPURCIN	Institutional shares bought - Prior Quarter	double	
INUMSHRS	Institutional number of shares owned	double	
INUMSHRSIN	Institutional number of shares owned - Prior Quarter	double	
INUMSOLD	Institutional shares sold	double	
INUMSOLDIN	Institutional shares sold - Prior Quarter	double	
IPCTHLD	Institutional percent held	double	
IPCTHLDIN	Institutional percent held - Prior Quarter	double	
IPOL	Policy Loans	double	yes
ISDC	Software Development Costs	double	yes
ISFA	Sale of Fixed Assets	double	yes
ISOB	Sale of Business	double	yes
ISOI	Sale of Intangible Assets	double	yes
ISPP	Principal Payments from Securities	double	yes
ITLI	Cash from Investing Activities	double	yes
ITOTNUM	Institutional number of shareholders	double	
LACC	Acceptances Outstanding	double	yes
LAEX	Accrued Expenses	double	yes
LAPB	Accounts Payable	double	yes
LBDT	Deferred Income Tax - LT Liability	double	yes
LCAV	Customer Advances	double	yes
LCLD	Current Port. of LT Debt/Capital Leases	double	yes
LCLO	Capital Lease Obligations	double	yes
LCPR	Commercial Paper	double	yes
LDBT	Total Deposits	double	yes
LDCL	Discontinued Operations - Curr Liability	double	yes
LDOL	Discontinued Operations - Liabilities	double	yes
LDPB	Dividends Payable	double	yes
LDTC	Deferred Income Tax - Current Liability	double	yes
LevFcf_AYr10Grr	Free Cash Flow, Levered, 10 Year Annual Trend Growth %	double	
LevFcf_AYr10Mom	Free Cash Flow, Levered, 10 Year Annual Trend	double	

Name	Description	Type	History
	Momentum %		
LevFcf_AYr10Vty	Free Cash Flow, Levered, 10 Year Annual Trend Volatil %	double	
LevFcf_TTMYr5Grr	Free Cash Flow, Levered, 5 Year Interim Trend Growth %	double	
LevFcf_TTMYr5Mom	Free Cash Flow, Levered, 5 Year Interim Trend Momentum %	double	
LevFcf_TTMYr5Vty	Free Cash Flow, Levered, 5 Year Interim Trend Volatil %	double	
LevFocf_AYr10Grr	Free Operating Cash Flow, Levered, 10 Year Annual Trend Growth %	double	
LevFocf_AYr10Mom	Free Operating Cash Flow, Levered, 10 Year Annual Trend Momentum %	double	
LevFocf_AYr10Vty	Free Operating Cash Flow, Levered, 10 Year Annual Trend Volatil %	double	
LevFocf_TTMY5Grr	Free Operating Cash Flow, Levered, 5 Year Interim Trend Growth %	double	
LevFocf_TTMY5Mom	Free Operating Cash Flow, Levered, 5 Year Interim Trend Momentum %	double	
LevFocf_TTMY5Vty	Free Operating Cash Flow, Levered, 5 Year Interim Trend Volatil %	double	
LFFP	Fed Funds Purch./Secs. Sold under Repurch. Agrmnt.	double	yes
LFLB	FHLB Advances	double	yes
LIBD	Interest Bearing Deposits	double	yes
LINR	Insurance Reserves	double	yes
Liq10DayAmt	Dollar Liquidity (10 day avg daily $ move price 1%)	double	
Liq10DayVol	Volume Liquidity (10 day avg daily shares move price 1%)	double	
LITC	Deferred Investment Tax Credit	double	yes
LLTD	Long Term Debt	double	yes
LLTL	Other Long Term Liabilities	double	yes
LMIN	Minority Interest	double	yes
LNID	Non-Interest Bearing Deposits	double	yes
LOBL	Other Bearing Liabilities	double	yes
LOCL	Other Current Liabilities	double	yes
LODP	Other Deposits	double	yes

Name	Description	Type	History
LOLB	Other Liabilities	double	yes
LOPB	Other Payables	double	yes
LOPF	Other Policyholders' Funds	double	yes
LOTB	Other Short Term Borrowings	double	yes
LotSize	Lot Size	string	
LPBA	Payable/Accrued	double	yes
LPBL	Pension Benefits - Underfunded	double	yes
LPLR	Policy Liabilities	double	yes
LRII	Reinsurance - Liability	double	yes
LRPA	Repurchase Agreements	double	yes
LRSV	Reserves	double	yes
LSAC	Separate Accounts - Liability	double	yes
LSDP	Security Deposits	double	yes
LSTB	Total Short Term Borrowings	double	yes
LSTD	Notes Payable/Short Term Debt	double	yes
LTCL	Total Current Liabilities	double	yes
LTCL_AYr10CAGR	Current Liabilities, 10 Year CAGR	double	
LTCL_IYr5CAGR	Current Liabilities, 5 Year CAGR	double	
LTLL	Total Liabilities	double	yes
LTLL_AMom	Total Liabilities, 10 Year Annual Trend Momentum %	double	
LTLL_AYr10CAGR	Total Liabilities, 10 Year CAGR	double	
LTLL_AYr10Grth	Total Liabilities, 10 Year Annual Trend Growth %	double	
LTLL_AYr10Vty	Total Liabilities, 10 Year Annual Trend Volatil %	double	
LTLL_AYr5CAGR	Total Liabilities, 5 Year CAGR	double	
LTLL_IMom	Total Liabilities, 5 Year Interim Trend Momentum %	double	
LTLL_IYr5Grth	Total Liabilities, 5 Year Interim Trend Growth %	double	
LTLL_IYr5Vty	Total Liabilities, 5 Year Interim Trend Volatil %	double	
LTTD	Total Long Term Debt	double	yes
LTTD_AMom	Long Term Debt, 10 Year Annual Trend Momentum %	double	

Name	Description	Type	History
LTTD_AYr10Grth	Long Term Debt, 10 Year Annual Trend Growth %	double	
LTTD_AYr10Vty	Long Term Debt, 10 Year Annual Trend Volatil %	double	
LTTD_IMom	Long Term Debt, 5 Year Interim Trend Momentum %	double	
LTTD_IYr5Grth	Long Term Debt, 5 Year Interim Trend Growth %	double	
LTTD_IYr5Vty	Long Term Debt, 5 Year Interim Trend Volatil %	double	
LTXP	Income Taxes Payable	double	yes
LUPR	Unearned Premium/Unearned Revenue	double	yes
MARGIN5YR	Net Profit Margin - 5 year average	double	
Mcap_AYr10CAGR	Historic Market Capitalization, Total Shares Outstanding, 10 Year CAGR	double	
Mcap_AYr10Grr	Hist Market Capitalization, Total Shares Out, 10 Yr Annual Trend Growth %	double	
Mcap_AYr10Mom	Hist Market Capitalization, Total Shares Out, 10 Yr Annual Trend Momentum %	double	
Mcap_AYr10Vty	Hist Market Capitalization, Total Shares Out, 10 Year Annual Trend Volatil %	double	
Mcap_AYr3CAGR	Historic Market Capitalization, Total Shares Outstanding, 3 Year CAGR	double	
Mcap_AYr5CAGR	Historic Market Capitalization, Total Shares Outstanding, 5 Year CAGR	double	
Mcap_IYr10CAGR	Historic Market Capitalization, Total Shares Outstanding, 10 Year Interim CAGR	double	
Mcap_IYr3CAGR	Historic Market Capitalization, Total Shares Outstanding, 3 Year Interim CAGR	double	
Mcap_IYr5CAGR	Historic Market Capitalization, Total Shares Outstanding, 5 Year Interim CAGR	double	
Mcap_IYr5Grr	Historic Market Capitalization, Total Shares Out, 5 Year Interim Trend Growth%	double	
Mcap_IYr5Mom	Historic Market Capitalization, Total Shares Out, 5 Yr Interim Trend Momentum%	double	
Mcap_IYr5Vty	Historic Market Capitalization, Total Shares Out, 5 Yr Interim Trend Volatil%	double	
METL	Employees	double	
METL_AYr10CAGR	Employees, Fiscal Year End, 10 Year CAGR	double	
METL_AYr5CAGR	Employees, Fiscal Year End, 5 Year CAGR	double	
MKTCAP	Market Capitalization	double	

Name	Description	Type	History
MNOS	Number of Common Shareholders	double	
MVOLSHSOUT	Volume (monthly) as a % of Shares Outstanding	double	
NAFC	Allowance for Funds Used during Const.	double	yes
NAMA	Amortization of Acquisition Costs	double	yes
NAMI	Amortization of Intangibles	double	yes
NAML	Minimum Pension Liability Adjustment	double	yes
NCCF	Credit Card Fees	double	yes
NCIN	Interest Capitalized, Non-Operating	double	yes
NDEP	Depreciation Expense	double	yes
NDPRELIM	Non Detailed Preliminary Flag	double	
NDTA	Dealer Trading Account Profit	double	yes
NDTL	Dealer Trading Account Loss	double	yes
NetDebt_A	Net Debt, LFY	double	
NetDebt_I	Net Debt, LFI	double	
NetDt_TTMAv2	Net Debt, Average TTM	double	
NetDt2Ebitda_A	Historic Net Debt/EBITDA, FY	double	
NetDt2Ebitda_TTM	Historic Net Debt/EBITDA, TTM	double	
NetDt2Ev_A	Net Debt/EV, FY	double	
NetDt2Ev_I	Net Debt/EV, FI	double	
NFAC	Fees & Commissions from Operations	double	yes
NFCA	Foreign Currency Adjustment	double	yes
NFCI	Foreign Currency Gains	double	yes
NFCL	Foreign Currency Losses	double	yes
NGLA	Gain (Loss) on Sale of Assets	double	yes
NHIG	Price - 12 month high	double	
NHIGDATE	12 Month High price date	date	
NIBX	Net Income Before Extra. Items	double	yes
NIBX_AYr10CAGR	Net Income Before Extraordinary Items, 10 Year CAGR	double	
NIBX_TTM	Net Income Before Extraordinary Items, TTM	double	
NIBX_TTMPop	Net Income Before Extraordinary Items, Period To Period % Change, TTM	double	

Name	Description	Type	History
NICF	Insurance Commissions, Fees & Premiums	double	yes
NICHNGIN	Net Income Change % - prior quarter	double	
NICHNGYR	Net Income Change % - most recent quarter 1 year ago	double	
NICHNGYRI	Net Income Change % - year to date	double	
NIEN	Interest Expense, Non-Operating	double	yes
NIGRPCT	Growth rate% - net income	double	
NIIN	Interest Income, Non-Operating	double	yes
NINC	Net Income	double	yes
NINC_AYr10Grth	Net Income Including Extraordinary Items, 10 Year Annual Trend Growth %	double	
NINC_AYr10Mom	Net Income Including Extraordinary Items, 10 Year Annual Trend Momentum %	double	
NINC_AYr10Vty	Net Income Including Extraordinary Items, 10 Year Annual Trend Volatil %	double	
NINC_TTMYr5Grth	Net Income Including Extraordinary Items, 5 Year Interim Trend Growth %	double	
NINC_TTMYr5Mom	Net Income Including Extraordinary Items, 5 Year Interim Trend Momentum %	double	
NINC_TTMYr5Vty	Net Income Including Extraordinary Items, 5 Year Interim Trend Volatil %	double	
NINN	Interest Income (Expense), Net Non-Operating	double	yes
NINV	Investment Income, Non-Operating	double	yes
NITRENDGR	Net Income growth rate, 5 year	double	
NLAR	Labor & Related Expenses	double	yes
NLIT	Litigation Expense	double	yes
NLOW	Price - 12 month low	double	
NLOWDATE	12 Month Low price date	date	
NOCS	Fees for Other Customer Services	double	yes
NOEX	Other Expense	double	yes
NONT	Other Non-Operating Income (Expense)	double	yes
NORE	Real Estate Operation Expense	double	yes
NORU	Other Revenue	double	yes
NPLG	Minimum Pension Liability Gain	double	yes

Name	Description	Type	History
NPLL	Minimum Pension Liability Loss	double	yes
NPMTRENDGR	Net Profit Margin growth rate, 5 year	double	
NPRICE	Price - closing or last bid	double	
NREG	Real Estate Operation Gain	double	yes
NRES	Restructuring Charge	double	yes
NSAC	Commissions & Fees from Securities Activities	double	yes
NSGL	Investment Securities Gains	double	yes
NSLL	Investment Securities Losses	double	yes
NUGG	Unrealized Gains	double	yes
NUGL	Unrealized Gains (Losses)	double	yes
NUIE	Other Unusual Expense	double	yes
NUII	Other Unusual Income	double	yes
NUNL	Unrealized Losses	double	yes
OACG	Accounting Change	double	yes
OACR	Accounts Receivable	double	yes
OAEX	Accrued Expenses	double	yes
OAMA	Amortization of Acquisition Costs	double	yes
OAMI	Amortization of Intangibles	double	yes
OAPB	Accounts Payable	double	yes
OBDT	Deferred Taxes	double	yes
OBEN	Policy Benefits/Liabilities	double	yes
Ocf2Capex_A	Operating Cash Flow/Capital Expenditures, FY	double	
Ocf2Capex_TTM	Operating Cash Flow/Capital Expenditures, TTM	double	
Ocf2Ce_A	Operating Cash Flow/Common Equity, FY	double	
Ocf2Ce_AAvg5	Operating Cash Flow/Common Equity, 5 Year Average	double	
Ocf2Ce_IAvg3	Operating Cash Flow/Common Equity, 3 Year Average	double	
Ocf2Ce_TTM	Operating Cash Flow/Common Equity, TTM	double	
Ocf2NetIntExp_A	Operating Cash Flow/Total Net Interest Expense, FY	double	
Ocf2Rev_A	Operating Cash Flow/Revenue, FY	double	

Name	Description	Type	History
Ocf2Rev_AAvg5	Operating Cash Flow/Revenue, 5 Year Average	double	
Ocf2Rev_IAvg3	Operating Cash Flow/Revenue, 3 Year Average	double	
Ocf2Rev_TTM	Operating Cash Flow/Revenue, TTM	double	
Ocf2TotLiab_A	Operating Cash Flow/Total Liabilities, FY	double	
Ocf2TotLiab_TTM	Operating Cash Flow/Total Liabilities, TTM	double	
OcfNetIntExp_TTM	Operating Cash Flow/Total Net Interest Expense, TTM	double	
OcfPD_TTMY10CAGR	Total Oper Cash Flow per Share, Avg. Diluted Shares Out, 10 Yr Interim CAGR	double	
OCFPS_A	Total Operating Cash Flow per Share, Avg. Diluted Shares Outstanding, FY	double	
OCFPS_AYr10CAGR	Total Operating Cash Flow per Share, Avg. Diluted Shares Out, 10 Year CAGR	double	
OCFPS_AYr3CAGR	Total Operating Cash Flow per Share, Avg. Diluted Shares Out, 3 Year CAGR	double	
OCFPS_AYr5CAGR	Total Operating Cash Flow per Share, Avg. Diluted Shares Out, 5 Year CAGR	double	
OcfPsD_TTMY3CAGR	Total Oper Cash Flow per Share, Avg. Diluted Shares Out, 3 Year Interim CAGR	double	
OcfPsD_TTMY5CAGR	Total Oper Cash Flow per Share, Avg. Diluted Shares Out, 5 Year Interim CAGR	double	
OcfPsrDil_TTM	Total Operating Cash Flow per Share, Avg. Diluted Shares Outstanding, TTM	double	
OCPD	Cash Payments	double	yes
OCRC	Cash Receipts	double	yes
ODPA	Amort. of Deferred Policy Acq. Costs	double	yes
ODPL	Depletion	double	yes
OEIA	Equity in Net Earnings (Loss)	double	yes
OIDO	Discontinued Operations	double	yes
OINR	Insurance Reserves	double	yes
OINV	Investment Securities, Gains/Losses	double	yes
OITL	Inventories	double	yes
OLLP	Loan Loss Provision	double	yes
OLOA	Loans, Gains/Losses	double	yes
OLOR	Loans Origination - Operating	double	yes

Name	Description	Type	History
OLOS	Loss Adjustment	double	yes
ONCI	Other Non-Cash Items	double	yes
ONET	Net Income/Starting Line	double	yes
ONET2OTLO_A	Net Income/Total Cash From Operating Activities, %, FY	double	
ONET2OTLO_TTM	Net Income/Total Cash From Operating Activities, %, TTM	double	
OOAL	Other Assets & Liabilities, Net	double	yes
OOAS	Other Assets	double	yes
OOCF	Other Operating Cash Flow	double	yes
OOLB	Other Liabilities	double	yes
OORE	Other Real Estate Owned	double	yes
OPAC	Deferred Policy Acquisition Costs	double	yes
OPBA	Payable/Accrued	double	yes
OpMar_IAvg3	Operating Profit Margin, %, 3 Year Average	double	
OPMGN5YR	Operating Margin - 5 year average	double	
OPPY	Prepaid Expenses	double	yes
OPRD	Purchased R&D	double	yes
OPTION	Optionable Stock Indicator	double	
OREF	Policy Refunds	double	yes
OREP	Reinsurance Payable	double	yes
ORER	Reinsurance Receivable	double	yes
OSOL	Sale of Loans	double	yes
OTLO	Cash from Operating Activities	double	yes
OTLO_AYr10CAGR	Total Cash From Operating Activities, 10 Year CAGR	double	
OTLO_AYr10Grth	Total Cash From Operating Activities, 10 Year Annual Trend Growth %	double	
OTLO_AYr10Mom	Total Cash From Operating Activities, 10 Year Annual Trend Momentum %	double	
OTLO_AYr10Vty	Total Cash From Operating Activities, 10 Year Annual Trend Volatil %	double	
OTLO_AYr3CAGR	Total Cash From Operating Activities, 3 Year CAGR	double	
OTLO_AYr5CAGR	Total Cash From Operating Activities, 5 Year	double	

Name	Description	Type	History
	CAGR		
OTLO_TTMYr5Grth	Total Cash From Operating Activities, 5 Year Interim Trend Growth %	double	
OTLO_TTMYr5Mom	Total Cash From Operating Activities, 5 Year Interim Trend Momentum %	double	
OTLO_TTMYr5Vty	Total Cash From Operating Activities, 5 Year Interim Trend Volatil %	double	
OTRA	Extraordinary Item	double	yes
OTXP	Taxes Payable	double	yes
OUIE	Unusual Items	double	yes
OUPR	Unearned Premiums	double	yes
P2BEpsIEx_AAvg5	Historic P/E Including Extraordinary Items, Avg. Basic Shares Out, 5 Yr Avg	double	
P2BEpsIEx_CurA	Current P/E Including Extraordinary Items, Basic, LFY	double	
P2BEpsIEx_CurTTM	Current P/E Including Extraordinary Items, Basic, LTM	double	
P2BEpsIEx_IAvg3	Historic P/E Including Extraordinary Items, Avg. Basic Shares Out, 3 Yr Avg	double	
P2BEpsXEx_AAvg5	Historic P/E Excluding Extraordinary Items, Avg. Basic Shares Out, 5 Yr Avg	double	
P2BEpsXEx_CurA	Current P/E Excluding Extraordinary Items, Basic, LFY	double	
P2BEpsXEx_CurTTM	Current P/E Excluding Extraordinary Items, Basic, LTM	double	
P2BEpsXEx_IAvg3	Historic P/E Excluding Extraordinary Items, Avg. Basic Shares Out, 3 Yr Avg	double	
P2CePsr_AAvg5	Historic Price to Common Equity, 5 Year Average	double	
P2CePsr_IAvg3	Historic Price to Common Equity, 3 Year Average	double	
P2EBITDA_CurA	Current Price to EBITDA/Share, Avg. Diluted Shares Outstanding, LFY	double	
P2EBITDA_CurTTM	Current Price to EBITDA/Share, Avg. Diluted Shares Outstanding, LFI	double	
P2EPSExX_AAvg5	Historic P/E Excluding Extraordinary Items, Avg. Diluted Shares Out, 5 Yr Avg	double	
P2EPSExX_CurTTM	Current P/E Excluding Extraordinary Items, LTM	double	
P2EPSExX_IAvg3	Historic P/E Excluding Extraordinary Items, Avg. Diluted Shares Out, 3 Yr Avg	double	

Name	Description	Type	History
P2EPSInX_AAvg5	Historic P/E Including Extraordinary Items, Avg. Diluted Shares Out, 5 Yr Avg	double	
P2EPSInX_CurA	Current P/E Including Extraordinary Items, LFY	double	
P2EPSInX_IAvg3	Historic P/E Including Extraordinary Items, Avg. Diluted Shares Out, 3 Yr Avg	double	
P2FCF_CurA	Current Price to Free Cash Flow/Share, LFY	double	
P2FCF_IAvg3	Historic Price to Free Cash Flow per Share, Avg. Diluted Shares Out, 3 Yr Avg	double	
P2FocfPsr_AAvg5	Hist Price to Free Oper Cash Flow per Share, Avg. Diluted Shares Out, 5 Yr Avg	double	
P2FocfPsr_IAvg3	Hist Price to Free Oper Cash Flow per Share, Avg. Diluted Shares Out, 3 Yr Avg	double	
P2FocfXDiv_AAvg5	Hist Price/Free Oper Cash Flow Ex Div per Share, Avg Diluted Shares Out, 5Yr Avg	double	
P2FocfXDiv_CurA	Current Price to Free Operating Cash Flow Ex Dividends/Share, LFY	double	
P2FocfXDiv_IAvg3	Hist Price/Free Oper Cash Flow Ex Div per Share, Avg Diluted Shares Out, 3Yr Avg	double	
P2FocfXDv_CurTTM	Current Price to Free Operating Cash Flow Ex Dividends/Share, LTM	double	
P2RevPsr_AAvg5	Historic Price to Revenue per Share, Avg. Diluted Shares Out, 5 Year Average	double	
P2RevPsr_IAvg3	Historic Price to Revenue per Share, Avg. Diluted Shares Out, 3 Year Average	double	
P2TanCePsr_AAvg5	Historic Price to Tangible Common Equity, 5 Year Average	double	
P2TanCePsr_IAvg3	Historic Price to Tangible Common Equity, 3 Year Average	double	
P2TanCEq_CurA	Current Price to Tangible Common Equity, LFY	double	
P2TanCEq_CurI	Current Price to Tangible Common Equity, LFI	double	
PAYOUT5YR	Payout ratio - 5 year average	double	
PayoutR_IAvg3	Dividend Payout Ratio, %, 3 Year Average	double	
PDATE	Pricing date	date	
PE5YRAVG	P/E excluding extordinary items, 5 Year Average	double	
PEBEXCLXOR	P/E Basic excluding extraordinary items - TTM	double	
PEEXCLXOR	P/E excluding extraordinary items - TTM	double	
PEHIGH	P/E excluding extraordinary items, High	double	
PEINCLXOR	P/E including extraordinary items - TTM	double	

Name	Description	Type	History
PELOW	P/E excluding extraordinary items, Low	double	
PPEBEXCLXO	P/E Basic excluding extraordinary items - prior trailing 12 month	double	
PPEEXCLXOR	P/E excluding extraordinary items - prior trailing 12 month	double	
PR04WKPCT	Price - 04 week price percent change	double	
PR04WKPCTR	Relative (S&P500) price percent change - 04 week	double	
PR13WKPCT	Price - 13 week price percent change	double	
PR13WKPCTR	Relative (S&P500) price percent change - 13 week	double	
PR1DAYPRC	Price - 1 Day % Change	double	
PR26WKPCT	Price - 26 week price percent change	double	
PR26WKPCTR	Relative (S&P500) price percent change - 26 week	double	
PR2TANBK	Price to Tangible Book - most recent quarter	double	
PR2TANCE	Price to Tangible Book (common) - most recent quarter	double	
PR52WKPCT	Price - 52 week price percent change	double	
PR52WKPCTR	Relative (S&P500) price percent change - 52 week	double	
PR5DAYPRC	Price - 5 Day % Change	double	
PRDASTD	Accounting standard used by company	string	
PRDAUDC	Auditor identifier	string	
PRDAUDO	Code for auditor opinion (annual financials)	string	
PRDCCCY	ISO code of converted currency	string	
PRDCRCY	ISO code for reporting currency	string	
PRDCUN	Period converted unit	string	
PRDLEN	Period length	double	
PRDLENC	Period length code - W:weeks, M:months	string	
PRDNUM	Period interim number	double	
PRDRATE	Current exchange rate between USD and reporting currency	double	
PRDSDT	Date when statement first added by Reuters Fundamentals	date	

Name	Description	Type	History
PRDSTYP	Statement type - income/balance sheet/cash flow	string	
PRDTYP	Period type - Annual:1, Interim:2	double	
PRDUN	Period reporting unit	string	
PRDUPDT	Update type - normal/reclassification/restatement	string	
PRDYEAR	Period fiscal year	double	
PRICE2BK	Price to Book - most recent quarter	double	
PRICE2BK2	Price to Book - most recent quarter, 1 year ago	double	
Price2BV_CurA	Current Price to Book, Total Equity, LFY	double	
Price2BV_CurI	Current Price to Book, Total Equity, LFI	double	
Price2Bvps_AAvg5	Historic Price to Book, Total Equity, 5 Year Average	double	
Price2Bvps_IAvg3	Historic Price to Book, Total Equity, 3 Year Average	double	
Price2EPS_CurA	Current P/E, LFY	double	
Price2EPS_IAvg3	Historic P/E, 3 Year Average	double	
PRICE2TOTEQ	Price to Equity - most recent interim period	double	
PriceAvg150Day	150 Day Average - Price	double	
PriceAvg200Day	200 Day Average - Price	double	
PriceAvg50Day	50 Day Average - Price	double	
PRYTDPCT	Price - YTD price percent change	double	
PRYTDPCTR	Relative (S&P500) price percent change - Year to Date	double	
PTMBEPSXCL	EPS Basic excluding extraordinary items - prior trailing 12 month	double	
PTMCFSHR	Cash Flow per share - prior trailing 12 month	double	
PTMEPSINCX	EPS including extraordinary items - prior trailing 12 month	double	
PTMEPSXCLX	EPS excluding extraordinary items - prior trailing 12 month	double	
PTMGN5YR	Pretax Margin - 5 year average	double	
PTMINTCOV	Interest coverage - prior trailing 12 month	double	
PTMNPMGN	Net Profit Margin % - prior trailing 12 month	double	
PTMPR2REV	Price to sales - prior trailing 12 month	double	
PTMPRCFPS	Price to Cash Flow per share - prior trailing 12 month	double	

Name	Description	Type	History
PTMRDEXP	Research and Development Expense - prior trailing 12 month	double	
PTMREV	Revenue - prior trailing 12 month	double	
PTMROAPCT	Return on average assets - prior trailing 12 month	double	
PTMROEPCT	Return on average equity - prior trailing 12 month	double	
QAML	Minimum Pension Liability Adjustment	double	yes
QASTTURN	Asset turnover - most recent quarter (annualized)	double	
QBEPSXCLXO	EPS Basic excluding extraordinary items - most recent quarter	double	
QBVPS	Book value (Common Equity) per share - most recent quarter	double	
QCAPSPPS	Capital Spending per Share. most recent quarter	double	
QCASH	Cash and Equiv., most recent quarter	double	
QCFSHR	Cash Flow per share - most recent quarter (annualized)	double	
QCFSHR2	Cash Flow per share - most recent quarter, 1 year ago	double	
QCFSHRNA	Cash Flow per share - most recent quarter (not annualized)	double	
QCFSHRNA2	Cash Flow per share - most recent quarter - 1 (not annualized)	double	
QCMS	Common Stock	double	yes
QCOGS	Cost of goods sold - most recent quarter	double	
QCOM	Other Comprehensive Income	double	yes
QCPS	Convertible Preferred Stock - Non Rdmble	double	yes
QCSHPS	Cash per share - most recent quarter	double	
QCSO1	Shares Outstanding - Common Stock Primary Issue	double	yes
QCSO2	Shares Outstanding - Common Issue 2	double	yes
QCSO3	Shares Outstanding - Common Issue 3	double	yes
QCSO4	Shares Outstanding - Common Issue 4	double	yes
QCTA	Translation Adjustment	double	yes
QCURAST	Assets, current - most recent quarter	double	
QCURLIAB	Liabilities, current - most recent quarter	double	
QCURRATIO	Current ratio - most recent quarter	double	

Name	Description	Type	History
QCURRATIO2	Current ratio - most recent quarter, 1 year ago	double	
QDEBTEPS	Debt Service to EPS - most recent quarter	double	
QDEPEXP	Depreciation expense - (SCF) most recent quarter	double	
QDEPRESCFZ	Depreciation, accumulated - most recent quarter	double	
QDPS	Dividend - most recent quarter	double	
QEBIT	EBIT - most recent quarter	double	
QEBITD	EBITD - most recent quarter	double	
QEBT	Earnings before taxes - most recent quarter	double	
QEDG	ESOP Debt Guarantee	double	yes
QEPSINCLXO	EPS including extraordinary items - most recent quarter	double	
QEPSXCLXOR	EPS excluding extraordinary items - most recent quarter	double	
QFCF	Free Cash Flow - most recent quarter	double	
QFCFSHR	Free Cash Flow per share - most recent quarter (annualized)	double	
QFCFSHR2	Free Cash Flow per share - most recent quarter, 1 year ago	double	
QFCFSHRNA	Free Cash Flow per share - most recent quarter (not annualized)	double	
QFCFSHRNA2	Free Cash Flow per share - most recent quarter - 1 (not annualized)	double	
QGPD	General Partner	double	yes
QGROSMGN	Gross Margin - most recent quarter	double	
QINTCOV	Interest Coverage - most recent quarter	double	
QINTEXPZ	Interest Expense - most recent quarter	double	
QINVENTORY	Inventory - most recent quarter	double	
QINVTURN	Inventory Turnover - most recent quarter (annualized)	double	
QLPD	Limited Partner	double	yes
QLTD2AST	LT Debt/Assets - most recent quarter	double	
QLTD2CAP	LT Debt/Total capital - most recent quarter	double	
QLTD2EQ	LT Debt/Equity - most recent quarter	double	
QLTD2EQ2	LT Debt/Equity - most recent quarter, 1 year ago	double	
QLTDPS	LT Debt/Share - most recent quarter	double	

Name	Description	Type	History
QNI	Earnings after Taxes - most recent quarter	double	
QNIAC	Net Income available to common - most recent quarter	double	
QNIPEREMP	Net Income/Employee - most recent quarter (annualized)	double	
QNLOAN	Loans, Net - most recent quarter	double	
QNLOANCHG	Loans, Net % Change - 1 year ago	double	
QNPMGNPCT	Net Profit Margin % - most recent quarter	double	
QOPMGNPCT	Operating Margin - most recent quarter	double	
QOTE	Other Equity	double	yes
QPAYRATIO	Payout Ratio - most recent quarter	double	
QPEHIGH	P/E excluding extraordinary items high, most recent quarter	double	
QPELOW	P/E excluding extraordinary items low, most recent quarter	double	
QPIC	Additional Paid-In Capital	double	yes
QPR2REV	Price to Sales - most recent quarter	double	
QPRCFPS	Price to Cash Flow per share - most recent quarter	double	
QPRS	Preferred Stock - Non Redeemable	double	yes
QPSO1	Shares Outstanding - Preferred Issue 1	double	yes
QPSO2	Shares Outstanding - Preferred Issue 2	double	yes
QPSO3	Shares Outstanding - Preferred Issue 3	double	yes
QPSO4	Shares Outstanding - Preferred Issue 4	double	yes
QPSO5	Shares Outstanding - Preferred Issue 5	double	yes
QPSO6	Shares Outstanding - Preferred Issue 6	double	yes
QPTMGNPCT	Pretax margin - most recent quarter	double	
QQUICKRAT2	Quick Ratio - most recent quarter, 1 year ago	double	
QQUICKRATI	Quick ratio - most recent quarter	double	
QRDEXP	Research and Development Expense - most recent quarter	double	
QRECTURN	Receivables turnover - most recent quarter (annualized)	double	
QRECVBL	Receivables - most recent quarter	double	
QRED	Retained Earnings (Accumulated Deficit)	double	yes

Name	Description	Type	History
QREV	Revenue - most recent quarter	double	
QREVPEREMP	Revenue/Employee - most recent quarter (annualized)	double	
QREVPS	Revenue/Share - most recent quarter (annualized)	double	
QREVPSNA	Revenue/Share - most recent quarter (not annualized)	double	
QREVSTRT	Reinvestment Rate - most recent quarter	double	
QROAPCT	Return on average assets - most recent quarter (annualized)	double	
QROEPCT	Return on average equity - most recent quarter (annualized)	double	
QROIPCT	Return on Investment - most recent quarter (annualized)	double	
QSGA2REV	SG&A expenses / net sales - most recent quarter	double	
QTA	Assets, total - most recent quarter	double	
QTACHG	Assets, total % Change - 1 year ago	double	
QTANBVDOLR	Book Value (tangible) in dollars - most recent quarter	double	
QTANBVPS	Book Value (tangible) per share - most recent quarter	double	
QTAXPD	Taxes Paid - most recent quarter	double	
QTAXRATE	Tax Rate - most recent quarter	double	
QTCO	Total Common Shares Outstanding	double	yes
QTEL	Total Liabilities & Shareholders' Equity	double	yes
QTL	Liabilities, Total - most recent quarter	double	
QTLE	Total Equity	double	yes
QTLE_AMom	Total Equity, 10 Year Annual Trend Momentum %	double	
QTLE_AYr10Grth	Total Equity, 10 Year Annual Trend Growth %	double	
QTLE_AYr10Vty	Total Equity, 10 Year Annual Trend Volatil %	double	
QTLE_IMom	Total Equity, 5 Year Interim Trend Momentum %	double	
QTLE_IYr5Grth	Total Equity, 5 Year Interim Trend Growth %	double	
QTLE_IYr5Vty	Total Equity, 5 Year Interim Trend Volatil %	double	
QTOTCE	Book Value (Common Equity) - most recent quarter	double	
QTOTCE2	Book Value (Common Equity) - most recent	double	

Name	Description	Type	History
	quarter 1 year ago		
QTOTD	Total Debt - most recent quarter	double	
QTOTD2AST	Total Debt/Total Assets - most recent quarter	double	
QTOTD2CAP	Total Debt/Total Capital - most recent quarter	double	
QTOTD2EQ	Total Debt/Total Equity - most recent quarter	double	
QTOTD2EQ2	Total Debt/Total Equity - most recent quarter, 1 year ago	double	
QTOTLTD	LT Debt (Total) - most recent quarter	double	
QTOTSE	Shareholder Equity - most recent quarter	double	
QTPN1	Treasury Shares - Preferred Primary Issue	double	yes
QTPN2	Treasury Shares - Preferred Issue 2	double	yes
QTPN3	Treasury Shares - Preferred Issue 3	double	yes
QTPN4	Treasury Shares - Preferred Issue 4	double	yes
QTPN5	Treasury Shares - Preferred Issue 5	double	yes
QTPN6	Treasury Shares - Preferred Issue 6	double	yes
QTPO	Total Preferred Shares Outstanding	double	yes
QTRPERIODS	Number of Historical Periods - Quarterly	double	
QTSC	Treasury Stock - Common	double	yes
QTSN1	Treas Shares - Common Stock Prmry Issue	double	yes
QTSN2	Treasury Shares - Common Issue 2	double	yes
QTSN3	Treasury Shares - Common Issue 3	double	yes
QTSN4	Treasury Shares - Common Issue 4	double	yes
QTSP	Treasury Stock - Preferred	double	yes
QUGL	Unrealized Gain (Loss)	double	
QWCAPPSPR	Working Capital per share/Price - most recent quarter	double	
RDPT	Interest on Deposits	double	yes
Reinvest_A	Reinvestment Rate, %, FY	double	
Reinvest_AAvg5	Reinvestment Rate, %, 5 Year Average	double	
Reinvest_IAvg3	Reinvestment Rate, %, 3 Year Average	double	
Reinvest_TTM	Reinvestment Rate, %, TTM	double	

Name	Description	Type	History
REOP	Electric Operations	double	yes
RetEarn_AY10Gw	Retained Earnings, 10 Year Annual Trend Growth %	double	
RetEarn_AY10Mom	Retained Earnings, 10 Year Annual Trend Momentum %	double	
RetEarn_AY10Vty	Retained Earnings, 10 Year Annual Trend Volatil %	double	
RetEarn_TTM5Gw	Retained Earnings, 5 Year Interim Trend Growth %	double	
RetEarn_TTMY5Mom	Retained Earnings, 5 Year Interim Trend Momentum %	double	
RetEarn_TTMY5Vty	Retained Earnings, 5 Year Interim Trend Volatil %	double	
RetOnCe_IAvg3	Return on Avg. Common Equity, %(Income Avail to Common Excl. Extra), 3Yr Avg	double	
RetOnTtAst_IAvg3	Return on Avg. Total Assets, % (Income After Tax), 3 Year Average	double	
RetOnTtCap_IAvg3	Return on Avg. Total Long Term Capital, % (Income After Tax), 3 Year Average	double	
RevBanks_A10Gw	Revenue, Banks, 10 Year Annual Trend Growth %	double	
RevBanks_AY10Mom	Revenue, Banks, 10 Year Annual Trend Momentum %	double	
RevBanks_AY10Vty	Revenue, Banks, 10 Year Annual Trend Volatil %	double	
RevBanks_TTM5Mom	Revenue, Banks, 5 Year Interim Trend Momentum %	double	
RevBanks_TTM5Vty	Revenue, Banks, 5 Year Interim Trend Volatil %	double	
RevBanks_TTMY5Gw	Revenue, Banks, 5 Year Interim Trend Growth %	double	
REVCHNGIN	Revenue Change % - prior quarter	double	
REVCHNGYR	Revenue Change % - most recent quarter 1 year ago	double	
REVCHNGYRI	Revenue Change % - year to date	double	
REVGRPCT	Growth rate% - Revenue, 3 year	double	
REVPS5YGR	Revenue/share (5 yr growth)	double	
REVTREND10	Revenue growth rate, 10 year	double	
REVTRENDGR	Revenue growth rate, 5 year	double	
REXT	Excise Tax Receipts	double	yes
RFFS	Fed Funds Sold/Secs. Sold under Resale Agrmnt.	double	yes

Name	Description	Type	History
RFLI	Interest & Fees on Loans	double	yes
RGOP	Gas Operations	double	yes
RINT	Interest Income, Non-Bank	double	yes
RISI	Interest & Dividends on Investment Securities	double	yes
RNBI	Other Non-Bank Income	double	yes
RNII	Net Investment Income	double	yes
RNIR	Other Non-Insurance Revenue	double	yes
RNTS	Net Sales	double	yes
RNUR	Other Non-Utility Revenue	double	yes
ROII	Other Interest Income	double	yes
ROIR	Other Insurance Revenue	double	yes
RORE	Other Revenue	double	yes
ROUR	Other Utility Revenue	double	yes
RPRE	Net Premiums Earned	double	yes
RPRW	Gross Premiums Written	double	yes
RREV	Gross Revenue	double	yes
RRGL	Realized Gains (Losses)	double	yes
RRII	Reinsurance - Income	double	yes
RSOP	Steam Operations	double	yes
RSRT	Sales Returns and Allowances	double	yes
RTAI	Trading Account Interest	double	yes
RTLR	Total Revenue	double	yes
RTLR_AYr10Grth	Total Revenue, 10 Year Annual Trend Growth %	double	
RTLR_AYr10Mom	Total Revenue, 10 Year Annual Trend Momentum %	double	
RTLR_AYr10Vty	Total Revenue, 10 Year Annual Trend Volatil %	double	
RTLR_TTMPop	Total Revenue, Period to Period % Change, TTM	double	
RTLR_TTMYr5Grth	Total Revenue, 5 Year Interim Trend Growth %	double	
RTLR_TTMYr5Mom	Total Revenue, 5 Year Interim Trend Momentum %	double	
RTLR_TTMYr5Vty	Total Revenue, 5 Year Interim Trend Volatil %	double	

Name	Description	Type	History
RTLRPS_AYr3CAGR	Revenue per Share, Avg. Diluted Shares Outstanding, 3 Year CAGR	double	
RWAT	Water Operations	double	yes
s_ADIV5YAVG	Sector: Dividend per Share - 5 year average	double	
s_ADIVCHG	Sector: Dividend change % - year over year	double	
s_AEBITD5YR	Sector: EBITD Margin - 5 year average	double	
s_AEPSCHG	Sector: EPS Change % - year over year	double	
s_AREVCHG	Sector: Revenue Change %, year over year	double	
s_AROA5YAVG	Sector: Return on average assets - 5 year average	double	
s_AROE5YAVG	Sector: Return on average equity - 5 year average	double	
s_AROI5YRAVG	Sector: Return on investment - 5 year average	double	
s_ATAXRAT5YR	Sector: Tax Rate - 5 year average	double	
s_BETA	Sector: Beta	double	
s_CSPTRENDGR	Sector: Capital Spending growth rate, 5 year	double	
s_DIVGRPCT	Sector: Growth rate% - dividend, 3 year	double	
s_DIVTRENDGR	Sector: Dividend growth rate, 5 year	double	
s_EPSCHNGYR	Sector: EPS Change % - most recent quarter 1 year ago	double	
s_EPSGRPCT	Sector: Growth rate% - EPS, 3 year	double	
s_EPSTRENDGR	Sector: EPS growth rate, 5 year	double	
s_GROSMGN5YR	Sector: Gross Margin - 5 year average	double	
s_IPCTHLDV	Sector: Institutional percent held	double	
s_MARGIN5YR	Sector: Net Profit Margin - 5 year average	double	
s_MKTCAP	Sector: Market capitalization	double	
s_NITRENDGR	Sector: Net Income growth rate, 5 year	double	
s_NPRICE	Sector: Price - closing or last bid	double	
s_OPMGN5YR	Sector: Operating Margin - 5 year average	double	
s_PAYOUT5YR	Sector: Payout ratio - 5 year average	double	
s_PEEXCLXOR	Sector: P/E excluding extraordinary items - TTM	double	
s_PEHIGH	Sector: P/E excluding extraordinary items, High	double	
s_PELOW	Sector: P/E excluding extraordinary items, Low	double	
s_PR04WKPCT	Sector: Price - 04 week price percent change	double	

Name	Description	Type	History
s_PR04WKPCTR	Sector: Relative (S&P500) price percent change - 04 week	double	
s_PR13WKPCT	Sector: Price - 13 week price percent change	double	
s_PR13WKPCTR	Sector: Relative (S&P500) price percent change - 13 week	double	
s_PR1DAYPRC	Sector: Price - 1 Day % Change	double	
s_PR26WKPCT	Sector: Price - 26 week price percent change	double	
s_PR26WKPCTR	Sector: Relative (S&P500) price percent change - 26 week	double	
s_PR2TANBK	Sector: Price to Tangible Book - most recent quarter	double	
s_PR52WKPCT	Sector: Price - 52 week price percent change	double	
s_PR52WKPCTR	Sector: Relative (S&P500) price percent change - 52 week	double	
s_PR5DAYPRC	Sector: Price - 5 Day % Change	double	
s_PRICE2BK	Sector: Price to Book - most recent quarter	double	
s_PRYTDPCT	Sector: Price - YTD price percent change	double	
s_PTMGN5YR	Sector: Pretax Margin - 5 year average	double	
s_QCSHPS	Sector: Cash per share - most recent quarter	double	
s_QCURRATIO	Sector: Current ratio - most recent quarter	double	
s_QLTD2EQ	Sector: LT debt/equity - most recent quarter	double	
s_QQUICKRATI	Sector: Quick ratio - most recent quarter	double	
s_QTOTD2EQ	Sector: Total debt/total equity - most recent quarter	double	
s_REVCHNGYR	Sector: Revenue Change % - most recent quarter 1 year ago	double	
s_REVGRPCT	Sector: Growth rate% - Revenue, 3 year	double	
s_REVTRENDGR	Sector: Revenue growth rate, 5 year	double	
s_TTMASTTURN	Sector: Asset turnover - trailing 12 month	double	
s_TTMBEPSXCL	Sector: EPS Basic excluding extraordinary items - trailing 12 month	double	
s_TTMEBITDMG	Sector: EBITD Margin - trailing 12 month	double	
s_TTMEPSCHG	Sector: EPS Change %, TTM over TTM	double	
s_TTMGROSMGN	Sector: Gross Margin - trailing 12 month	double	
s_TTMINTCOV	Sector: Interest coverage - trailing 12 month	double	

Name	Description	Type	History
s_TTMINVTURN	Sector: Inventory turnover - trailing 12 month	double	
s_TTMNIPEREM	Sector: Net Income/employee - trailing 12 month	double	
s_TTMNPMGN	Sector: Net Profit Margin % - trailing 12 month	double	
s_TTMOPMGN	Sector: Operating Margin - trailing 12 month	double	
s_TTMPAYRAT	Sector: Payout Ratio - trailing 12 month	double	
s_TTMPR2REV	Sector: Price to Sales - trailing 12 month	double	
s_TTMPRCFPS	Sector: Price to Cash Flow per share - trailing 12 month	double	
s_TTMPRFCFPS	Sector: Price to Free Cash Flow per Share - trailing 12 months	double	
s_TTMPTMGN	Sector: Pretax Margin - trailing 12 month	double	
s_TTMRECTURN	Sector: Receivables turnover - trailing 12 month	double	
s_TTMREV	Sector: Revenue - trailing 12 month	double	
s_TTMREVCHG	Sector: Revenue Change %, TTM over TTM	double	
s_TTMREVPERE	Sector: Revenue/Employee - trailing 12 month	double	
s_TTMREVSTRT	Sector: Reinvestment Rate - trailing 12 month	double	
s_TTMROAPCT	Sector: Return on average assets - trailing 12 month	double	
s_TTMROEPCT	Sector: Return on average equity - trailing 12 month	double	
s_TTMROIPCT	Sector: Return on investment - trailing 12 month	double	
s_TTMTAXRATE	Sector: Tax Rate - trailing 12 month	double	
s_VOL1DPRC	Sector: Volume - 1 Day % Change	double	
s_YIELD	Sector: Dividend Yield - indicated annual dividend divided by closing price	double	
SAMT	Amortization	double	yes
SANI	Total Adjustments to Net Income	double	yes
SBAI	Basic EPS Including Extraordinary Items*	double	yes
SBAS	Basic Weighted Average Shares*	double	yes
SBBF	Basic EPS Excluding Extraordinary Items*	double	yes
SBDA	Normalized EBITDA	double	
SBDT	Deferred Income Tax	double	yes
SBIT	Normalized EBIT	double	

Name	Description	Type	History
SBTR	Bank Total Revenue	double	
SBUYVOL	Insider Shares Purchased	double	
SCEX	Capital Expenditures	double	yes
SCEX_AYr10CAGR	Capital Expenditures, 10 Year CAGR	double	
SCIP	Cash Interest Paid	double	yes
SCL1	Std. Capital Lease Payments Due in Year 1	double	
SCL10	Std. Capital Lease Payments Due in Year 10	double	
SCL2	Std. Capital Lease Payments Due in Year 2	double	
SCL23	Std. Capital Lease Payments Due in Years 2 and 3	double	
SCL3	Std. Capital Lease Payments Due in Year 3	double	
SCL4	Std. Capital Lease Payments Due in Year 4	double	
SCL45	Std. Capital Lease Payments Due in Years 4 and 5	double	
SCL5	Std. Capital Lease Payments Due in Year 5	double	
SCL6	Std. Capital Lease Payments Due in Year 6	double	
SCL6B	Std. Capital Lease Payments Due in Year 6 and Beyond	double	
SCL7	Std. Capital Lease Payments Due in Year 7	double	
SCL8	Std. Capital Lease Payments Due in Year 8	double	
SCL9	Std. Capital Lease Payments Due in Year 9	double	
SCMS	Common Stock	double	yes
SCOR	Cost of Revenue, Total	double	yes
SCOR_AYr10CAGR	Cost of Revenue, Total, 10 Year CAGR	double	
SCOR_AYr3CAGR	Cost of Revenue, Total, 3 Year CAGR	double	
SCOR_AYr5CAGR	Cost of Revenue, Total, 5 Year CAGR	double	
SCOR_TTMYr10CAGR	Cost of Revenue, Total, 10 Year Interim CAGR	double	
SCOR_TTMYr3CAGR	Cost of Revenue, Total, 3 Year Interim CAGR	double	
SCOR_TTMYr5CAGR	Cost of Revenue, Total, 5 Year Interim CAGR	double	
SCSI	Cash and Short Term Investments	double	yes
SCTP	Cash Taxes Paid	double	yes
SCUI	Total Current Assets less Inventory	double	
SCUR	Current Ratio	double	

Name	Description	Type	History
SDAI	Diluted EPS Including Extraordinary Items*	double	yes
SDAJ	Dilution Adjustment*	double	yes
SDBF	Diluted EPS Excluding Extrordinary Items*	double	
SDBF_AYr10Grth	EPS Excl. Extraordinary, Avg Diluted Shares Out, 10 Yr Annual Trend Growth %	double	
SDBF_AYr10Mom	EPS Excl. Extraordinary, Avg Diluted Shares Out, 10 Yr Annual Trend Momentum %	double	
SDBF_AYr10Vty	EPS Excl. Extraordinary, Avg Diluted Shares Out, 10 Yr Annual Trend Volatil %	double	
SDBF_TTMYr5Grth	EPS Excl. Extraordinary, Avg Diluted Shares Out, 5 Yr Interim Trend Growth %	double	
SDBF_TTMYr5Mom	EPS Excl. Extraordinary, Avg Diluted Shares Out, 5 Yr Interim Trend Momentum %	double	
SDBF_TTMYr5Vty	EPS Excl. Extraordinary, Avg Diluted Shares Out, 5 Yr Interim Trend Volatil %	double	
SDED	Depreciation/Depletion	double	yes
SDEP	Depreciation	double	yes
SDNI	Diluted Net Income*	double	yes
SDPR	Depreciation/Amortization	double	yes
SDWS	Diluted Weighted Average Shares*	double	yes
SETR	Effective Tax Rate	double	
SFCF	Financing Cash Flow Items	double	yes
SFEE	Foreign Exchange Effects	double	yes
SGPP	Gross Margin	double	yes
SGRP	Gross Profit	double	yes
SGRPMar_A	Gross Profit Margin, %, FY	double	
SGRPMar_I	Gross Profit Margin, %, FI	double	
SGRPMar_IAvg3	Gross Profit Margin, %, 3 Year Average	double	
SGRPMar_TTM	Gross Profit Margin, %, TTM	double	
SharpeRatio3Yr	Sharpe Ratio 3 Year Weekly	double	
SharpeRatio5Yr	Sharpe Ratio 5 Year Monthly	double	
SHBOUTAVGQ	Shares outstanding Basic - average, most recent quarter	double	
SHSBOUTAVG	Shares outstanding Basic - average, most recent fiscal year	double	

Name	Description	Type	History
SHSBPTM	Shares outstanding Basic - average prior trailing 12 month	double	
SHSBTTM	Shares outstanding Basic - average trailing 12 month	double	
SHSOUT	Shares outstanding - current	double	
SHSOUTABS	Shares outstanding - BS, most recent fiscal year	double	
SHSOUTAVG	Shares outstanding - average, most recent fiscal year	double	
SHSOUTAVGQ	Shares outstanding - average, most recent quarter	double	
SHSOUTBS	Shares outstanding - BS, most recent quarter	double	
SHSOUTBS2	Shares outstanding - BS, most recent quarter 1 year ago	double	
SHSPTM	Shares oustanding - average prior trailing 12 month	double	
SHSTTM	Shares outstanding - average trailing 12 month	double	
SIAP	Net Interest Income after Loan Loss Provision	double	yes
SICF	Other Investing Cash Flow Items, Total	double	yes
SIEN	Interest Expense, Net Non-Operating	double	yes
SIEO	Interest Expense, Net Operating	double	yes
SIIB	Interest Income, Bank	double	yes
SIIN	Interest/Investment Income, Non-Operating	double	yes
SIIO	Interest/Investment Income, Operating	double	yes
SINV	Long Term Investments	double	yes
SLBA	Losses, Benefits, and Adjustments, Total	double	yes
SLD1	Std. Long Term Debt Maturing within 1 Year	double	
SLD10	Std. Long Term Debt Maturing in Year 10	double	
SLD2	Std. Long Term Debt Maturing in Year 2	double	
SLD23	Std. Long Term Debt Maturing in 2-3 Years	double	
SLD3	Std. Long Term Debt Maturing in Year 3	double	
SLD4	Std. Long Term Debt Maturing in Year 4	double	
SLD45	Std. Long Term Debt Maturing in 4-5 Years	double	
SLD5	Std. Long Term Debt Maturing in Year 5	double	
SLD6	Std. Long Term Debt Maturing in Year 6	double	

Name	Description	Type	History
SLD6B	Std. Long Term Debt Maturing in Year 6 and Beyond	double	
SLD7	Std. Long Term Debt Maturing in Year 7	double	
SLD8	Std. Long Term Debt Maturing in Year 8	double	
SLD9	Std. Long Term Debt Maturing in Year 9	double	
SLTL	Other Liabilities, Total	double	yes
SNCB	Net Cash - Beginning Balance	double	yes
SNCC	Net Change in Cash	double	yes
SNCE	Net Cash - Ending Balance	double	yes
SNCI	Non-Cash Items	double	yes
SNIE	Non-Interest Expense, Bank	double	yes
SNII	Non-Interest Income, Bank	double	yes
SNPM	Net Profit Margin	double	
SNTD	Net Debt	double	
SNUMPURC	Insider Buy Transactions	double	
SNUMSOLD	Insider Sell Transactions	double	
SOAT	Other Assets, Total	double	yes
SOBL	Other Bearing Liabilities, Total	double	yes
SOCA	Other Current Assets, Total	double	yes
SOCF	Changes in Working Capital	double	yes
SOCL	Other Current Liabilities, Total	double	yes
SOEA	Other Earning Assets, Total	double	yes
SOL1	Std. Operating Lease Payments Due in Year 1	double	
SOL10	Std. Operating Lease Payments Due in Year 10	double	
SOL2	Std. Operating Lease Payments Due in Year 2	double	
SOL23	Std. Operating Lease Payments Due in Years 2 and 3	double	
SOL3	Std. Operating Lease Payments Due in Year 3	double	
SOL4	Std. Operating Lease Payments Due in Year 4	double	
SOL45	Std. Operating Lease Payments Due in Years 4 and 5	double	
SOL5	Std. Operating Lease Payments Due in Year 5	double	

Name	Description	Type	History
SOL6	Std. Operating Lease Payments Due in Year 6	double	
SOL6B	Std.Operating Lease Payments Due in Year 6 and Beyond	double	
SOL7	Std. Operating Lease Payments Due in Year 7	double	
SOL8	Std. Operating Lease Payments Due in Year 8	double	
SOL9	Std. Operating Lease Payments Due in Year 9	double	
SOLA	Other Long Term Assets, Total	double	yes
SONT	Other, Net	double	yes
SOOE	Other Operating Expenses, Total	double	yes
SOPI	Operating Income	double	yes
SOPI_AYr10Grth	Operating Profit, 10 Year Annual Trend Growth %	double	
SOPI_AYr10Mom	Operating Profit, 10 Year Annual Trend Momentum %	double	
SOPI_AYr10Vty	Operating Profit, 10 Year Annual Trend Volatil %	double	
SOPI_TTMYr5Grth	Operating Profit, 5 Year Interim Trend Growth %	double	
SOPI_TTMYr5Mom	Operating Profit, 5 Year Interim Trend Momentum %	double	
SOPI_TTMYr5Vty	Operating Profit, 5 Year Interim Trend Volatil %	double	
SOPP	Operating Margin	double	
SORE	Other Revenue, Total	double	yes
SOTE	Other Equity, Total	double	yes
sp_ADIV5YAVG	SP500: Dividend per Share - 5 year average	double	
sp_ADIVCHG	SP500: Dividend change % - year over year	double	
sp_AEBITD5YR	SP500: EBITD Margin - 5 year average	double	
sp_AEPSCHG	SP500: EPS Change % - year over year	double	
sp_AREVCHG	SP500: Revenue Change %, year over year	double	
sp_AROA5YAVG	SP500: Return on average assets - 5 year average	double	
sp_AROE5YAVG	SP500: Return on average equity - 5 year average	double	
sp_AROI5YRAVG	SP500: Return on investment - 5 year average	double	
sp_ATAXRAT5YR	SP500: Tax Rate - 5 year average	double	
sp_BETA	SP500: Beta	double	
sp_CSPTRENDGR	SP500: Capital Spending growth rate, 5 year	double	

Name	Description	Type	History
sp_DIVGRPCT	SP500: Growth rate% - dividend, 3 year	double	
sp_DIVTRENDGR	SP500: Dividend growth rate, 5 year	double	
sp_EPSCHNGYR	SP500: EPS Change % - most recent quarter 1 year ago	double	
sp_EPSGRPCT	SP500: Growth rate% - EPS, 3 year	double	
sp_EPSTRENDGR	SP500: EPS growth rate, 5 year	double	
sp_GROSMGN5YR	SP500: Gross Margin - 5 year average	double	
sp_IPCTHLDV	SP500: Institutional percent held	double	
sp_MARGIN5YR	SP500: Net Profit Margin - 5 year average	double	
sp_MKTCAP	SP500: Market capitalization	double	
sp_NITRENDGR	SP500: Net Income growth rate, 5 year	double	
sp_NPRICE	SP500: Price - closing or last bid	double	
sp_OPMGN5YR	SP500: Operating Margin - 5 year average	double	
sp_PAYOUT5YR	SP500: Payout ratio - 5 year average	double	
sp_PEEXCLXOR	SP500: P/E excluding extraordinary items - TTM	double	
sp_PEHIGH	SP500: P/E excluding extraordinary items, High	double	
sp_PELOW	SP500: P/E excluding extraordinary items, Low	double	
sp_PR04WKPCT	SP500: Price - 04 week price percent change	double	
sp_PR04WKPCTR	SP500: Relative (S&P500) price percent change - 04 week	double	
sp_PR13WKPCT	SP500: Price - 13 week price percent change	double	
sp_PR13WKPCTR	SP500: Relative (S&P500) price percent change - 13 week	double	
sp_PR1DAYPRC	SP500: Price - 1 Day % Change	double	
sp_PR26WKPCT	SP500: Price - 26 week price percent change	double	
sp_PR26WKPCTR	SP500: Relative (S&P500) price percent change - 26 week	double	
sp_PR2TANBK	SP500: Price to Tangible Book - most recent quarter	double	
sp_PR52WKPCT	SP500: Price - 52 week price percent change	double	
sp_PR52WKPCTR	SP500: Relative (S&P500) price percent change - 52 week	double	
sp_PR5DAYPRC	SP500: Price - 5 Day % Change	double	
sp_PRICE2BK	SP500: Price to Book - most recent quarter	double	

Name	Description	Type	History
sp_PRYTDPCT	SP500: Price - YTD price percent change	double	
sp_PTMGN5YR	SP500: Pretax Margin - 5 year average	double	
sp_QCSHPS	SP500: Cash per share - most recent quarter	double	
sp_QCURRATIO	SP500: Current ratio - most recent quarter	double	
sp_QLTD2EQ	SP500: LT debt/equity - most recent quarter	double	
sp_QQUICKRATI	SP500: Quick ratio - most recent quarter	double	
sp_QTOTD2EQ	SP500: Total debt/total equity - most recent quarter	double	
sp_REVCHNGYR	SP500: Revenue Change % - most recent quarter 1 year ago	double	
sp_REVGRPCT	SP500: Growth rate% - Revenue, 3 year	double	
sp_REVTRENDGR	SP500: Revenue growth rate, 5 year	double	
sp_TTMASTTURN	SP500: Asset turnover - trailing 12 month	double	
sp_TTMBEPSXCL	SP500: EPS Basic excluding extraordinary items - trailing 12 month	double	
sp_TTMEBITDMG	SP500: EBITD Margin - trailing 12 month	double	
sp_TTMEPSCHG	SP500: EPS Change %, TTM over TTM	double	
sp_TTMGROSMGN	SP500: Gross Margin - trailing 12 month	double	
sp_TTMINTCOV	SP500: Interest coverage - trailing 12 month	double	
sp_TTMINVTURN	SP500: Inventory turnover - trailing 12 month	double	
sp_TTMNIPEREM	SP500: Net Income/employee - trailing 12 month	double	
sp_TTMNPMGN	SP500: Net Profit Margin % - trailing 12 month	double	
sp_TTMOPMGN	SP500: Operating Margin - trailing 12 month	double	
sp_TTMPAYRAT	SP500: Payout ratio - trailing 12 month	double	
sp_TTMPR2REV	SP500: Price to sales - trailing 12 month	double	
sp_TTMPRCFPS	SP500: Price to Cash Flow per share - trailing 12 month	double	
sp_TTMPRFCFPS	SP500: Price to Free Cash Flow per Share - trailing 12 months	double	
sp_TTMPTMGN	SP500: Pretax margin - trailing 12 month	double	
sp_TTMRECTURN	SP500: Receivables turnover - trailing 12 month	double	
sp_TTMREV	SP500: Revenue - trailing 12 month	double	
sp_TTMREVCHG	SP500: Revenue Change %, TTM over TTM	double	

Name	Description	Type	History
sp_TTMREVPERE	SP500: Revenue/Employee - trailing 12 month	double	
sp_TTMREVSTRT	SP500: Reinvestment Rate - trailing 12 month	double	
sp_TTMROAPCT	SP500: Return on average assets - trailing 12 month	double	
sp_TTMROEPCT	SP500: Return on average equity - trailing 12 month	double	
sp_TTMROIPCT	SP500: Return on investment - trailing 12 month	double	
sp_TTMTAXRATE	SP500: Tax Rate - trailing 12 month	double	
sp_VOL1DPRC	SP500: Volume - 1 Day % Change	double	
sp_YIELD	SP500: Dividend Yield - indicated annual dividend divided by closing price	double	
SPOL	Policy Liabilities	double	yes
SPRE	Total Premiums Earned	double	yes
SPRS	Preferred Stock - Non Redeemable, Net	double	yes
SPTM	Pretax Margin	double	
SQCK	Quick Ratio	double	
SREV	Revenue	double	yes
SREV_AYr10CAGR	Revenue, Primary, 10 Year CAGR	double	
SREV_AYr10Grth	Revenue, Primary, 10 Year Annual Trend Growth %	double	
SREV_AYr10Mom	Revenue, Primary, 10 Year Annual Trend Momentum %	double	
SREV_AYr10Vty	Revenue, Primary, 10 Year Annual Trend Volatil %	double	
SREV_AYr3CAGR	Revenue, Primary, 3 Year CAGR	double	
SREV_AYr5CAGR	Revenue, Primary, 5 Year CAGR	double	
SREV_TTMYr5Grth	Revenue, Primary, 5 Year Interim Trend Growth %	double	
SREV_TTMYr5Mom	Revenue, Primary, 5 Year Interim Trend Momentum %	double	
SREV_TTMYr5Vty	Revenue, Primary, 5 Year Interim Trend Volatil %	double	
SRPR	Redeemable Preferred Stock	double	yes
SSELLVOL	Insider shares sold	double	
SSGA	Selling/General/Administrative Expenses, Total	double	yes
STBP	Tangible Book Value per Share	double	

Name	Description	Type	History
STBV	Tangible Book Value	double	
STEC	Effect of Special Items on Income Taxes (STEC)	double	yes
STIE	Total Interest Expense	double	yes
STLD	Total Debt	double	yes
STLD_AMom	Total Debt, 10 Year Annual Trend Momentum %	double	
STLD_AYr10CAGR	Total Debt, 10 Year CAGR	double	
STLD_AYr10Grth	Total Debt, 10 Year Annual Trend Growth %	double	
STLD_AYr10Vty	Total Debt, 10 Year Annual Trend Volatil %	double	
STLD_AYr5CAGR	Total Debt, 5 Year CAGR	double	
STLD_IMom	Total Debt, 5 Year Interim Trend Momentum %	double	
STLD_IYr5Grth	Total Debt, 5 Year Interim Trend Growth %	double	
STLD_IYr5Vty	Total Debt, 5 Year Interim Trend Volatil %	double	
STSI	Total Special Items	double	yes
STXI	Total Extraordinary Items	double	yes
SUIE	Unusual Expense (Income)	double	yes
SUPN	Total Utility Plant, Net	double	yes
TanBV_AYr10CAGR	Tangible Book Value, Total Equity, 10 Year CAGR	double	
TanBV_AYr5CAGR	Tangible Book Value, Total Equity, 5 Year CAGR	double	
TanCe_AAvg5	Tangible Common Shareholders Equity, 5 Year Average	double	
TanCe_TTMAv2	Tangible Common Shareholders Equity, Average TTM	double	
TanCe_TTMAv2_Av3	Tangible Common Shareholders Equity, 3 Year Average	double	
TanCEq_A	Tangible Common Shareholders Equity, FY	double	
TanCEq_I	Tangible Common Shareholders Equity, FI	double	
TaxRate_IAvg3	Income Tax Rate, %, 3 Year Average	double	
TIAT	Income After Tax	double	yes
TIAT_AYr10CAGR	Income After Tax, 10 Year CAGR	double	
TIAT_AYr10Grth	Income After Tax, 10 Year Annual Trend Growth %	double	
TIAT_AYr10Mom	Income After Tax, 10 Year Annual Trend	double	

Name	Description	Type	History
	Momentum %		
TIAT_AYr10Vty	Income After Tax, 10 Year Annual Trend Volatil %	double	
TIAT_AYr3CAGR	Income After Tax, 3 Year CAGR	double	
TIAT_AYr5CAGR	Income After Tax, 5 Year CAGR	double	
TIAT_TTMYr5Grth	Income After Tax, 5 Year Interim Trend Growth %	double	
TIAT_TTMYr5Mom	Income After Tax, 5 Year Interim Trend Momentum %	double	
TIAT_TTMYr5Vty	Income After Tax, 5 Year Interim Trend Volatil %	double	
TI_SI	Short Interest	double	yes
TrdCycle_A	Average Net Trade Cycle (Days), FY	string	
TrdCycle_TTM	Average Net Trade Cycle (Days), TTM	string	
TTAX	Income Tax - Total	double	yes
TTMASTTURN	Asset turnover - trailing 12 month	double	
TTMBEPSXCL	EPS Basic excluding extraordinary items - trailing 12 month	double	
TTMCAPSPPS	Capital Spending per share, trailing 12 month	double	
TTMCFSHR	Cash Flow per share - trailing 12 month	double	
TTMCOGS	Cost of Good Sold - Trailing 12 month	double	
TTMDEBTEPS	Debt Service to EPS - trailing 12 month	double	
TTMDEPEXP	Depreciation expense - (SCF) trailing 12 month	double	
TTMDIVSHR	Dividends per Share - trailing 12 month	double	
TTMEBIT	EBIT - trailing 12 month	double	
TTMEBITD	EBITD - trailing 12 month	double	
TTMEBITDMG	EBITD Margin - trailing 12 month	double	
TTMEBITDPS	EBITD per share - trailing 12 month	double	
TTMEBT	Earnings before taxes - trailing 12 month	double	
TTMEPSCHG	EPS Change %, TTM over TTM	double	
TTMEPSINCX	EPS including extraordinary items - trailing 12 month	double	
TTMEPSXCLX	EPS excluding extraordinary items - trailing 12 month	double	
TTMFCF	Free Cash Flow - trailing 12 month	double	

Name	Description	Type	History
TTMFCFSHR	Free Cash Flow per share - trailing 12 month	double	
TTMGROSMGN	Gross Margin - trailing 12 month	double	
TTMINTCOV	Interest Coverage - trailing 12 month	double	
TTMINTEXP	Interest Expense - trailing 12 month	double	
TTMINVTURN	Inventory Turnover - trailing 12 month	double	
TTMNI	Earnings after Taxes - trailing 12 months	double	
TTMNIAC	Net Income available to common - trailing 12 months	double	
TTMNICHG	Net Income Change % - trailing 12 months	double	
TTMNIPEREM	Net Income/employee - trailing 12 month	double	
TTMNLOAN	Loans, Net - trailing 12 month	double	
TTMNPMGN	Net Profit Margin % - trailing 12 month	double	
TTMOCF3YGR	Cash from Operating Activities - 3 Year TTM Growth	double	
TTMOPMGN	Operating Margin - trailing 12 month	double	
TTMPAYRAT	Payout Ratio - trailing 12 month	double	
TTMPEHIGH	P/E excluding extraordinary items high, trailing 12 months	double	
TTMPELOW	P/E excluding extraordinary items low, trailing 12 months	double	
TTMPR2REV	Price to Sales - trailing 12 month	double	
TTMPRCFPS	Price to Cash Flow per share - trailing 12 month	double	
TTMPRFCFPS	Price to Free Cash Flow per Share - trailing 12 months	double	
TTMPTMGN	Pretax Margin - trailing 12 month	double	
TTMRDEXP	Research and Development Expense - trailing 12 month	double	
TTMRECTURN	Receivables Turnover - trailing 12 month	double	
TTMREV	Revenue - trailing 12 month	double	
TTMREVCHG	Revenue Change %, TTM over TTM	double	
TTMREVPERE	Revenue/Employee - trailing 12 month	double	
TTMREVPS	Revenue/Share - trailing 12 month	double	
TTMREVPS3YGR	Revenue/Share - 3 Year TTM Growth	double	
TTMREVSTRT	Reinvestment Rate - trailing 12 month	double	

Name	Description	Type	History
TTMROAPCT	Return on average assets - trailing 12 month	double	
TTMROEPCT	Return on average equity - trailing 12 month	double	
TTMROIPCT	Return on investment - trailing 12 month	double	
TTMSGA2REV	SG&A expenses / net sales - trailing 12 month	double	
TTMTA	Assets, total - trailing 12 month	double	
TTMTAXPD	Taxes paid - trailing 12 month	double	
TTMTAXRATE	Tax Rate - trailing 12 month	double	
UnlevFcf_AY10Gw	Free Cash Flow, Unlevered, 10 Year Annual Trend Growth %	double	
UnlevFcf_AY10Mm	Free Cash Flow, Unlevered, 10 Year Annual Trend Momentum %	double	
UnlevFcf_AY10Vty	Free Cash Flow, Unlevered, 10 Year Annual Trend Volatil %	double	
UnlevFcf_TTM5Vty	Free Cash Flow, Unlevered, 5 Year Interim Trend Volatil %	double	
UnlevFcf_TTMY5Gw	Free Cash Flow, Unlevered, 5 Year Interim Trend Growth %	double	
UnlevFcf_TTMY5Mm	Free Cash Flow, Unlevered, 5 Year Interim Trend Momentum %	double	
VADC	Deferred Revenue - Current	double	
VADL	Deferred Revenue - Long Term	double	
VADV	Advertising Expense, Supplemental	double	
VAGA	Accumulated Goodwill Amortization	double	
VAIA	Accumulated Intangible Amortization	double	
VAMA	Amortization of Acquisition Cost	double	yes
VAMI	Amortization of Intangibles	double	yes
VBES	Basic Normalized EPS	double	yes
VCAP	Interest Capitalized, Supplemental	double	yes
VCL1	Capital Lease Payments due in Year 1	double	
VCL2	Capital Lease Payments due in Year 2	double	
VCL3	Capital Lease Payments due in Year 3	double	
VCL4	Capital Lease Payments due in Year 4	double	
VCL5	Capital Lease Payments due in Year 5	double	
VCL6	Capital Lease Payments due in Year 6	double	

Name	Description	Type	History
VCL7	Capital Lease Payments due in Year 7	double	
VCL8	Capital Lease Payments due in Year 8	double	
VCL9	Capital Lease Payments due in Year 9	double	
VCLA	Capital Lease Payments due in Year 10	double	
VCLR	Capital Leases - Remaining Maturities	double	
VCTC	Current Tax - Total	double	
VCTD	Current Tax - Domestic	double	
VCTF	Current Tax - Foreign	double	
VCTL	Current Tax - Local	double	
VCTO	Current Tax - Other	double	
VCTR	Current Tax - Total	double	
VDEP	Depreciation, Supplemental	double	yes
VDES	Diluted Normalized EPS	double	yes
VDES_TTM	EPS, Normalized, Excl. Extraordinary Items, Avg. Diluted Shares Out, TTM	double	
VDTC	Deferred Tax - Total	double	
VDTD	Deferred Tax - Domestic	double	
VDTF	Deferred Tax - Foreign	double	
VDTL	Deferred Tax - Local	double	
VDTO	Deferred Tax - Other	double	
VDTR	Deferred Tax - Total	double	
VEEV	Stock Based Compensation Expense	double	yes
VEPS	Supplemental EPS	double	yes
VEXC	Capital Leases - Executory Costs	double	
VIAC	Normalized Income Available to Common	double	yes
VIAT	Normalized Income After Taxes	double	yes
VIAT_TTM	Income After Tax, Normalized, TTM	double	
VIEX	Interest Expense, Supplemental	double	yes
VINC	Capital Leases - Interest Costs	double	
VITN	Income Taxes Ex. Impact of Special Items	double	yes
VITT	Income Tax - Total	double	

Name	Description	Type	History
VLD1	Long Term Debt Maturing within 1 Year	double	
VLD2	Long Term Debt Maturing in Year 2	double	
VLD3	Long Term Debt Maturing in Year 3	double	
VLD4	Long Term Debt Maturing in Year 4	double	
VLD5	Long Term Debt Maturing in Year 5	double	
VLD6	Long Term Debt Maturing in Year 6	double	
VLD7	Long Term Debt Maturing in Year 7	double	
VLD8	Long Term Debt Maturing in Year 8	double	
VLD9	Long Term Debt Maturing in Year 9	double	
VLDA	Long Term Debt Maturing in Year 10	double	
VLDR	Long Term Debt - Remaining Maturities	double	
VOL1	Operating Lease Payments Due in Year 1	double	
VOL10DAVG	Volume - avg. trading volume for the last ten days	double	
VOL1DAVG	Volume - 1 Day Average	double	
VOL1DPRC	Volume - 1 Day % Change	double	
VOL2	Operating Lease Payments Due in Year 2	double	
VOL3	Operating Lease Payments Due in Year 3	double	
VOL3MAVG	Volume - avg. trading volume for the last 3 months	double	
VOL4	Operating Lease Payments Due in Year 4	double	
VOL5	Operating Lease Payments Due in Year 5	double	
VOL6	Operating Lease Payments Due in Year 6	double	
VOL7	Operating Lease Payments Due in Year 7	double	
VOL8	Operating Lease Payments Due in Year 8	double	
VOL9	Operating Lease Payments Due in Year 9	double	
VOLA	Operating Lease Payments Due in Year 10	double	
VOLR	Operating Leases - Remaining Payments	double	
VOTD	Domestic Tax - Other	double	
VOTF	Foreign Tax - Other	double	
VOTL	Local Tax - Other	double	
VOTO	Other Tax	double	

Name	Description	Type	History
VPFB	Basic EPS after Stock Based Comp. Expense	double	yes
VPFD	Diluted EPS after Stock Based Comp. Expense	double	yes
VPFI	Net Income after Stock Based Comp. Expense	double	yes
VPTI	Normalized Income Before Tax	double	yes
VRAD	Research & Development Exp, Supplemental	double	
VRTC	Total Capital %	double	
VRTO	Tier 1 Capital %	double	
VRWC	Total Risk-Weighted Capital	double	
VRXP	Rental Expenses	double	yes
VTCL	Total Capital Leases, Supplemental	double	
VTDT	Domestic Tax	double	
VTFT	Foreign Tax	double	
VTIT	Income Tax by Region - Total	double	
VTLD	Total Long Term Debt, Supplemental	double	
VTLT	Local Tax	double	
VTOL	Total Operating Leases, Supplemental	double	
VTOT	Other Tax	double	
WCapPS2Price_A	Working Capital per Share/Price, %, FY	double	
WCapPS2Price_I	Working Capital per Share/Price, %, FI	double	
X_LNG	Forex RollOver rate for Long positions	double	
X_SHT	Forex RollOver rate for Short positions	double	
XACG	Accounting Change	double	yes
XIDO	Discontinued Operations	double	yes
XNIC	Income Available to Common Incl. Extra. Items	double	yes
XSIT	Tax on Extraordinary Items	double	yes
XTRA	Extraordinary Item	double	yes
YIELD	Dividend Yield - indicated annual dividend divided by closing price	double	
YLD5YAVG	Dividend Yield - 5 Year Average	double	
YRAGODATE1	Price - year ago date	date	
YRAGOPRC1	Price - year ago	double	

Name	Description	Type	History
ZCPS	Redeemable Convertible Preferred Stock	double	yes
ZPSK	Redeemable Preferred Stock	double	yes
ZScoreM_A	ZScore, Manufacturing Weights, FY	double	
ZScoreM_AAvg5	ZScore, Manufacturing Weights, 5Year Average	double	
ZScoreM_I	ZScore, Manufacturing Weights, TTM	double	
ZScoreM_IAvg3	ZScore, Manufacturing Weights, 3Year Average	double	

TABLE 15.01—FundamentalFields Class Properties

INHERITANCE HIERARCHY

eISystem.Object
  tsData.MarketData.FundamentalFields

Now that you have memorized all the possible fundamental fields, I'll show you another example. This one was found in the TS help files.

EXAMPLE 15.03—Using FundamentalQuotesProvider to Report COTF-12 [OME_FQP_Ex#01]

In contrast to the above example this code retrieves and plots Commitment of Traders data either on a RadarScreen or a Chart.

```
Vars   :
FundamentalQuotesProvider FQP (NULL) ;

// Working Storage Section

Consts:
 String App_Type     ("Study"),
 String App_Name     ("OME_FQP_Ex#01"),
 String App_Note     ("OOEL example requesting CoT data using a
FundamentalQuotesProvider"),
 String App_Vers     ("01.02.01") ;

Vars   :
 String DQ           (DoubleQuote),
 String NL           (NewLine),
 Bool   Debug        (FALSE),
 Double Dummy        (0.00) ;

// =======================================================

method void App_Init ()
begin
  Print (skt_Method_Header (App_Name, "App_Init", Symbol + " " +
Field)) ;
// Call the Init method for the FundamentalQuotesProvider
  FQP  = FQP_Init (SymRoot, Field) ;
end ; // "App_Init" method

// -------------------------------------------------------

method FundamentalQuotesProvider  FQP_Init (String SymRoot, String
Field)
Vars   :
FundamentalQuotesProvider FQP ;
```

```
begin
  Print (skt_Method_Header (App_Name, "FQP_Init", "")) ;
// Instantiate the FundamentalQuotesProvider
  FQP  = FundamentalQuotesProvider.Create ()  ;
  FQP.Symbol        = SymRoot ;
// set the Symbol from the Input value
  FQP.RealTime      =  TRUE ;
  FQP.Fields       += Field ;
// set the Field(s) from the Input value
  FQP.StateChanged += FQP_StateChanged ;
  FQP.Updated      += FQP_Updated ;
  FQP.LoadProvider () ;

  Value99          = FQP.Count ;
// force it to load now.  May cause the code to restart
  Print ("Value99 = ", Value99:1:0) ;

  Return FQP ;
end ; // "FQP_Init" method

// ----------------------------------------------------

method void FQP_StateChanged (elSystem.Object sender,
tsdata.common.StateChangedEventArgs args)
Vars  :
 String Old_Str,
 String New_Str ;
begin
// Error 1; Description: method arguments cannot be used as
// inputs due to their life time;
// Location: OME_FQP_Ex#01; Line: 86
  Old_Str  = args.OldState.toString () ;
  New_Str  = args.NewState.toString () ;
  Print (skt_Method_Header (App_Name, "FQP_StateChanged", "Old=" +
Old_Str + " New=" + New_Str)) ;
  if  args.NewState  = tsdata.common.DataState.Loaded
  and args.OldState  = tsdata.common.DataState.Loading
  then begin
    Print ("FQP.Count = ", (sender asType
FundamentalQuotesProvider).Count:2:0 {, ", FQP.Quote.Count = ",
FQP.Quote[Field].Count:2:0} ) ;
    if  (sender asType FundamentalQuotesProvider).Count  > 00  then
begin
      if  (sender asType FundamentalQuotesProvider).Quote[Field]  =
NULL
        then  Print ("Quote  = NULL")
        else  Print ("FQP.Count = ", (sender asType
FundamentalQuotesProvider).Count:2:0,
             ", FQP.Quote.Count = ", (sender asType
FundamentalQuotesProvider).Quote[Field].Count:2:0) ;
    end ;
  end ; // loaded
end ; // "FQP_StateChanged" method

// ----------------------------------------------------

method void FQP_Updated (elSystem.Object sender,
tsdata.marketdata.FundamentalQuoteUpdatedEventArgs args)
Vars  :
 String Str ;
```

```
begin
// Error 1; Description: method arguments cannot be used as
// inputs due to their life time;
// Location: OME_FQP_Ex#01; Line: 86
  Str  = args.Reason.toString () ;
  Print (skt_Method_Header (App_Name, "FQP_Updated", "Reason=" + Str))
;
  switch args.reason begin
    case tsdata.marketdata.FundamentalUpdateReason.InitialUpdate : ;
    case tsdata.marketdata.FundamentalUpdateReason.RealtimeUpdate :
      Print ("RealTime Update for FundamentalQuotesProvider.") ;
  end ; // switch/case statement
end ; // "FQP_Updated" method

// =================================================

once begin
  App_Init () ;
end ; // Once, and only once

if  FQP.State  = tsdata.common.DataState.Loaded
and FQP.HasQuoteData (Field)
  then  Plot1 (FQP.Quote [Field].Value [BarDateTime] asType Double) ;
```

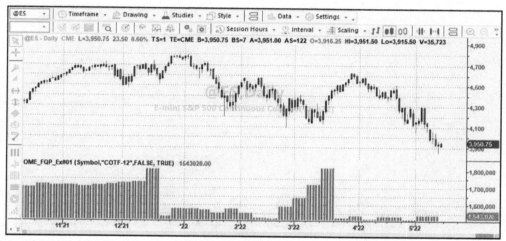

FIGURE 15.02—Commitment of Traders Using FundamentalQuotesProvider

Summary

In this chapter we have introduced you, ad nauseum, to the **FundamentalQuotesProvider** (FQP) Class and to about 100 pages of fundamental fields. Other than displaying Commitment of Traders (COT) data I have (personally or professionally) rarely found a need for fundamental data, though with RadarScreen I am certain a valuable comparative tool could be built, and with analytical attention paid to Fundamental Data a Technical Structure could be developed. See the OME_FQP_Ex#01 sample code for a practical example using the COT fundamental quote fields.

CHAPTER 16
Conclusion

W ell, we have certainly covered a lot of material. There is even more in **Volume II— Reference Guide**. All the reference material resides in the Appendices in Volume II. Practically anything you want to look up and learn is in that separate book. As you begin to refer to the alphabetical material in Volume II you will understand why I have broken 1,300 + pages into two volumes: you can keep both open at the same time on your desk, rather than flipping back and forth in a single book.

Having completed reading this book, it might be a good idea to go back to the beginning and read it again. Programming is not something you master with one read. You aren't going to shoot 100% of the baskets you try from the free-throw line without lots of practice.

This book is only the beginning. After practicing with the hundreds of examples herein you should pick up **Volume II—Reference Guide** and scan through the material to familiarize yourself with its contents. After that brief read whether you use the second volume or the Dictionary itself, you should go back and spend time with each term, each definition, and each concept so that when you have a task to accomplish you will remember that the help you need is in the Reference Guide.

It has been my distinct pleasure to work with and learn from Samuel K. Tennis in our long-into-the-night sessions with him in Florida and me in California meeting by Zoom. He is a master. Now I'm proficient at OOEL, though I wasn't when we began this effort on June 26, 2021. And it has been a great experience relaying it all to you, my readers.

We hope you profit from it!

Warmly,

Sy Sam

REFERENCE & CONTACTS

If you found this material interesting and of value, and want to explore further, herewith are some leads you might want to follow, and where you can find the people we have mentioned in the text.

Sunny J. Harris   www.moneymentor.com
sunny@moneymentor.com
1-760-908-3070 PT
Twitter: @SunnyJHarris
LinkedIn: linkedin.com/in/sunny-harris-018951a
Facebook: https://www.facebook.com/sunny.harris.773/

Samuel K. Tennis   www.vista-research.com
sktennis@vista-research.com
1-850-582-7342 (text)
Twitter: @SKTennis
LinkedIn: linkedin.com/in/sktennis
Facebook: https://www.facebook.com/sktennis/about

Christopher Davy   www.c21tradingsystemsinc.com
c21tradingsystems@gmail.com
1-214-460-5639

TradeStation   www.TradeStation.com   sales@TS.com
1-800-822-0512   1-954-652-7000

George Pruitt   www.georgepruitt.com
george.p.pruitt@gmail.com

Larry Williams   www.ireallytrade.com
larry@ireallytrade.com

Perry Kaufman   www.kaufmansignals.com
kaufmansignals@gmail.com

TABLE OF EXAMPLES

EXAMPLE 1.01—Classic EZL Print to File 5

EXAMPLE 1.02—OOEL Print to File 6

EXAMPLE 1.03—Diagnosing Proper Use of Data2 [OME_Data2] 7

EXAMPLE 1.04—Hello_World!_Ex#01 [Hello_World!_Ex#01] 15

EXAMPLE 1.05—Hello_World!_Ex#03 23

EXAMPLE 2.01—Variable Declarations 29

EXAMPLE 2.02—A Variety of String Formats [OME_Strings] 30

EXAMPLE 2.03—Input Declaration Statements 31

EXAMPLE 2.04—Declaring Variables 31

EXAMPLE 2.05—Variables 33

EXAMPLE 2.06—Declaring Pi as a Constant 33

EXAMPLE 2.07—Plotting a 10-bar Average of the Close [OME_3BarMAV] 34

EXAMPLE 2.08—Numeric Expressions 34

EXAMPLE 2.09—Using Parentheses for Clarification 35

EXAMPLE 2.10—Using AND and OR 36

EXAMPLE 2.11—Boolean Expressions Demonstrating Using NOT 36

EXAMPLE 2.12—Using NOT 36

EXAMPLE 2.13—If…Then Statement 37

EXAMPLE 2.14—Using NOT 38

EXAMPLE 2.15—If…Then 38

EXAMPLE 2.16—Else Begin 38

EXAMPLE 2.17—If…Then…Else 39

EXAMPLE 2.18—Using IFF to compare prices.. 39

EXAMPLE 2.19—Using IFF_Logic and IFF_String User Functions 40

EXAMPLE 2.20—Adding to a File with FileAppend 40

EXAMPLE 2.21—Deleting a File with FileDelete 40

EXAMPLE 2.22—Using Multiple Output Functions 43

EXAMPLE 2.23—Using a Wrapper Function [OME_f_ADX] 43

EXAMPLE 2.24—Turn Off Infinite Loop Detect 44

EXAMPLE 2.25—Simple Once Statement 44

EXAMPLE 2.26—Once Begin…End Block 44

EXAMPLE 2.27—Once Begin to Clear PrintLog 44

EXAMPLE 2.28—A Simple Begin…End Block 45

EXAMPLE 2.29—Complex Begin…End Block 45

EXAMPLE 2.30—Using the For Loop 46

EXAMPLE 2.31—A Simple Loop 46

EXAMPLE 2.32—Using For to Average Closing Values 46

EXAMPLE 2.33—A Function Using a For Loop [OME_f_ForLoop] 47

EXAMPLE 2.34—For Loops [OME_ForLoop]...47

EXAMPLE 2.35—DownTo 47

EXAMPLE 2.36—Illustration of To Structure 48

EXAMPLE 2.37—Structure of While 48

EXAMPLE 2.38—While Loop with No Ending Value..48

EXAMPLE 2.39—Using a While Loop to Put a Leading Zero on a String 49

EXAMPLE 2.40—Using the While Loop, to Find Inside Bars [OME_WhileLoop] 49

EXAMPLE 2.41—Using Strings 50

EXAMPLE 2.42—Using String Expressions 50

EXAMPLE 2.43—Manipulating Strings 50

EXAMPLE 2.44—Assigning DoubleQuote to DQ and NewLine to NL 51

EXAMPLE 2.45—Concatenating Strings to Place on Chart.....................................52

EXAMPLE 2.46—Converting EZL Dates to Strings 56

EXAMPLE 2.47—Another Date Format...56

EXAMPLE 2.48—Formatting Dates with Sam's Function 57

EXAMPLE 2.49—Converting Julian Time Date [OME_DateTime_Julian].................58

EXAMPLE 2.50—Using DateTime.Now with TimeSpan 62

EXAMPLE 2.51—Print Log TimeSpan Manipulations [OME_TimeSpan_Ex#01] 62

EXAMPLE 2.52—Custom Date and Time Formats [OME_DateTime_Ex#01] 69

EXAMPLE 2.53—String.Format in a Print statement..71

EXAMPLE 2.54—Composite Formatting [OME_StringManipulation] 72

EXAMPLE 2.55—Composite Formatting [OME_CompositeFormatting] 73

EXAMPLE 2.56—DateTime Examples [OME_DateTime]...77

EXAMPLE 2.57—Using Switch…Case to Designate Horizontal Styles....................83

EXAMPLE 2.58—Switch…Case with Begin…End 83

EXAMPLE 2.59—Using Switch and Case...84

EXAMPLE 2.60—Single-Dimension Array Declaration 88

EXAMPLE 2.61—Multi-Dimensional Array Declaration 88

EXAMPLE 2.62—Dynamic Array...88

EXAMPLE 2.63—Single-Dimension Array Declaration 89

EXAMPLE 2.64—Assigning Values to a Single-Dimension Array in a Loop 89

EXAMPLE 2.65—Retrieving Values from a Single-Dimension Array in a Loop 89

EXAMPLE 2.66—Multidimensional Array Declaration...89

EXAMPLE 2.67—Comparing Elements of an Array...90

EXAMPLE 2.68—Getting the Size of an Array...91

EXAMPLE 2.69—Changing the Size of a Dynamic Array...92

EXAMPLE 2.70—Adding the Values in a Dynamic Array 94

EXAMPLE 3.01—Adding Spaces to Your Strings 97

EXAMPLE 3.02—Alerts in SunnyBands© Indicator 99

EXAMPLE 3.03—Alerts from Sam's AME 100

EXAMPLE 3.04—Using RunCommand 102

EXAMPLE 3.05—Using RunCommandOnLastBar 102

EXAMPLE 3.06—Using At$ in a Strategy to Isolate the Signal Bar 103

EXAMPLE 3.07—Using At$ from AME 103

EXAMPLE 3.08—Using Analysis Commentary 103

EXAMPLE 3.09—A Real-World Example of Analysis Commentary 104

EXAMPLE 3.10—Testing HTML eMail Sending [OME_HTML_Email] 104

EXAMPLE 3.11—HTML Code to Link to a Website [OME_HTML2Website] 105

EXAMPLE 3.12—Two Examples of Custom Data Symbols 108

EXAMPLE 3.13—Using PlaySound 114

EXAMPLE 3.14—PlaySound on Key Reversal 114

EXAMPLE 3.15—Sunny's BingTicks© Indicator 115

EXAMPLE 3.16—Play a Video Clip at Commentary Bar 115

EXAMPLE 3.17—RaiseRunTimeError 116

EXAMPLE 3.18—Engaging the InfoBox 117

EXAMPLE 3.19—InfoBox with Two Moving Averages 117

EXAMPLE 3.20—Print Only on Last Bar 118

EXAMPLE 3.21—Printing Only on the First Bar of the Chart [OME_Hello_World! Ex#02] 118

EXAMPLE 3.22—Trading with Foreign Currencies (Forex) 124

EXAMPLE 4.01—Method to Plot Real-Time Equity 128

EXAMPLE 4.02—OOEL Coding Template [OME_CodingTemplate] 130

EXAMPLE 4.03—Employing Using Statements 139

EXAMPLE 5.01—Checking for Divide by Zero 151

EXAMPLE 5.02—Multiplying Instead of Dividing 151

EXAMPLE 5.03—Infinite Loop Detection 152

EXAMPLE 5.04—Using a Print Statement to Locate Errors 152

EXAMPLE 5.05—Printing DateTime, Open, High, Low and Close 152

EXAMPLE 5.06—Printing Data Between Selected Dates 152

EXAMPLE 5.07—The Minimum Code for Invoking Commentary 153

EXAMPLE 5.08—Minimum Code for Using Analysis Commentary 153

EXAMPLE 5.09—Using Debug [OME_Debug] 154

EXAMPLE 5.10—Using Try…Catch…Throw to Trap an Error [OME_TryCatchThrow] 157

EXAMPLE 5.11—Pseudo_Code Try…Catch…Finally 157

EXAMPLE 5.12—Throw a User-Defined Message 158

EXAMPLE 5.13—Trap Errors Using Try…Catch [OME_TryCatch] 158

EXAMPLE 6.01—Declaration with Override 159

EXAMPLE 6.02—Helper Methods [OME_HelperMethods] 160

EXAMPLE 6.03—Using Methods 162

EXAMPLE 7.01—Using CurrentBar <= 01 to Print a Single Line 166

EXAMPLE 7.02—Once and Only Once 166

EXAMPLE 7.03—Code for Printing on the Last Bar 167

EXAMPLE 7.04—Using the String.Format Method and a Vector [OME_Hello_World!_Ex#04] 168

EXAMPLE 7.05—Using StreamWriter to Create a File Within a Method [OME_Hello_World!_Ex#05a] 169

EXAMPLE 7.06—Using StreamReader and StreamWriter [OME_Hello_World!_Ex#05b] 170

EXAMPLE 7.07—Hello_World!_#06 Using StreamReader [OME_Hello_World!_Ex#06] 171

EXAMPLE 7.08—Hello_World!_#07 [OME_Hello_World!_Ex#07] 172

EXAMPLE 7.09—Hello_World! #07a [OME_Hello_World!_Ex#07a].................................175

EXAMPLE 7.10—Hello_World!_Ex#08a 177

EXAMPLE 7.11—Hello_World!_Ex #08b 178

EXAMPLE 8.01—Working with TokenList Objects 181

EXAMPLE 8.02—Using Two Dictionaries to Store Swing Highs & Swing Lows [OME_Swings_in_Dict_Ex#01] 183

EXAMPLE 8.03—Creating an Instance of GlobalDictionary 187

EXAMPLE 8.04—Creating an Instance of a Shared GlobalDictionary 187

EXAMPLE 8.05—Using GlobalDictionary with Pivots [OME_Swings_in_Dict_Ex#02] 188

EXAMPLE 8.06—Strategy Using Queue [OME_Queue_Ex#01] 194

EXAMPLE 8.07—Adding an Element to the Top of a Stack 198

EXAMPLE 8.08—Plotting a String from a Stack 198

EXAMPLE 8.09—Remove the Element at the Top of a Stack 198

EXAMPLE 8.10—Use a Stack to Store Trade Information [OME_Stack_Ex#01]....................198

EXAMPLE 8.11—Adding and Element to a Vector using Push_Back.................................204

EXAMPLE 8.12—Demonstrates Retrieving and Storing Values in a Vector 204

EXAMPLE 8.13—Demonstrates Two Ways of Removing an Item from a Vector 204

EXAMPLE 8.14—Analysis AppStorage Ex #01 [OME_AppStorage] 204

EXAMPLE 8.15—Using AppStorage to Output the Contents of Various Collections [OME_AppStorage_Report] 206

EXAMPLE 9.01—A Vanilla Moving Average [OME_MovAvg_Vanilla]..............................216

EXAMPLE 9.02—Code for Moving Average Strawberry [OME_MovAvg_StrwBry]................217

EXAMPLE 9.03—Preparation for Inserting Drawing Objects 222

EXAMPLE 9.04—Placing Drawing Objects on Your Chart...222

EXAMPLE 9.05—Defining a TrendLine with BNPoint 222

EXAMPLE 9.06—Method Shows How to Output Alert Configuration Settings.....................224

EXAMPLE 9.07—Method Illustrating Configuring a Notification 225

EXAMPLE 9.08—Using XYPoint to Anchor Text [OME_TextLabel_Ex#01].....................227

EXAMPLE 9.09—Floating Text [OME_Floating_Text] 232

EXAMPLE 9.10—Function OME_Floating_Text [OME_Floating_Text] 233

EXAMPLE 9.11—skt_isOptimizing function 237

EXAMPLE 9.12—vrt_MMDDYYYY Date Conversion Function 237

EXAMPLE 9.13—Declare Variables for Each Object Type...239

EXAMPLE 9.14—Create an Instance of Two Drawing Objects 239

EXAMPLE 9.15—Code for Simple Horizontal Line [OME_HorizontalLine_Ex#01] 240

EXAMPLE 9.16—Vertical Line on a Chart [OME_VerticalLine_Ex#01] 242

EXAMPLE 9.17—Vertical Line Example #02 [OME_VerticalLine_Ex#02] 244

EXAMPLE 9.18—Vertical Line Ex #03 [OME_VerticalLine_Ex#03] 245

EXAMPLE 9.19—Specifying a TrendLine Directly with BNPoint 248

EXAMPLE 9.20—Create a TrendLine and Add to a Chart [OME_TL_Ex#01] 248

EXAMPLE 9.21—Drawing a Rectangle at a Fixed Location 253

EXAMPLE 9.22—Using BNPoint to Draw a Rectangle [OME_Rectangle_BN] 253

EXAMPLE 9.23—Highlighting Opening Range with a Rectangle [OME_Rectangle_Ex#01]...... 253

EXAMPLE 9.24—Display a Rectangle Containing a Text Label [OME_TextRectangle]............ 257

EXAMPLE 9.25—Create an Ellipse with XYPoint 259

EXAMPLE 9.26—Create an Ellipse with BNPoint 260

EXAMPLE 9.27—Changing the Color of an Ellipse 260

EXAMPLE 9.28—Opening Range Breakout Using Ellipse [OME_Ellipse_Ex#01] 260

EXAMPLE 10.01—Method for Reacting to a ChartElementClick Event 265

EXAMPLE 10.02—Reacting to Events on a Chart [OME_ChartingHost_Ex#01] 265

EXAMPLE 10.03—PlatformClientHost [OME_PlatformClientHost] 269

EXAMPLE 10.04—Using the PortfolioHost [OME_PortfolioHost] 271

EXAMPLE 10.05—RadarScreenHost [OME_RadarScreenHost] 274

EXAMPLE 10.06—StrategyHost Example [OME_StrategyHost] 278

EXAMPLE 11.01—Code for Figure 11.02, All the Pieces and Parts of a Form [OME_Container] 299

EXAMPLE 11.02—Panel with TabControls, GroupBox with RadioButtons and Another Panel embedded [OME_Container_Class] 307

EXAMPLE 11.03—Create a Simple DataGridView [OME_DataGridView_Ex#01] 318

EXAMPLE 11.04—Create a Calculator with DataGridView [OME_DGV_Ex#02].............. 323

EXAMPLE 12.01—Sample AccountsProvider Format 336

EXAMPLE 12.02—AccountsProvider Usage [OME_AccountsProvider] 336

EXAMPLE 12.03—AccountsProvider [OME_AcctProvider] 338

EXAMPLE 12.04—Using OrdersProvider 340

EXAMPLE 12.05—Using PositionsProvider in RadarScreen [OME_R_PosnProvider] 341

EXAMPLE 12.06—Using AccountsProvider and PositionsProvider [OME_AP_PP] 346

EXAMPLE 13.01—Sample of a Chris Davy Log File 355

EXAMPLE 13.02—Entry Order Ticket [OME_EntryOrderTicket]i 360

EXAMPLE 13.03—Target Order Ticket [OME_TargetOrderTicket] 361

EXAMPLE 13.04—Protect OrderTicket [OME_ProtectOrderTicket] 362

EXAMPLE 13.05—Protect OrderTicket [OME_OSOOrderTicket].................................... 364

EXAMPLE 13.06—Methods for Preceding OrderTickets [OME_OTMethods] 366

EXAMPLE 14.01—Using Excel: [OME_Excel_Ex#01] and [DemoExcel.xlsx] 369

EXAMPLE 14.02—Chart to Excel [OME_Chart_to_Excel].. 373

EXAMPLE 14.03—RadarScreen to Excel [OME_RadarScreen_to_Excel] 376

EXAMPLE 15.01—Plotting Fundamental Quotes Fields 381

EXAMPLE 15.02—Plotting EPS and P/E with Fundamental Quotes [OME_FQP_Ex#02]...........382

EXAMPLE 15.03—Using FundamentalQuotesProvider to Report COTF-12 [OME_FQP_Ex#01] 451

TABLE OF FIGURES

FIGURE 1.01—Objects in Microsoft Word 9

FIGURE 1.02—TS When You First Open It 12

FIGURE 1.03—The TS Development Environment (TDE) 13

FIGURE 1.04—From the TDE: 🖱 File → New → Document Type 14

FIGURE 1.05—🖱 File → New → Indicator 15

FIGURE 1.06—Creating Hello_World!_Ex#01 Indicator 15

FIGURE 1.07—Print Log for HelloWorld#01 16

FIGURE 1.08—Finding the Print Command 18

FIGURE 1.09—Elucidating the Print Command 18

FIGURE 1.10—The Full Definition of Print 19

FIGURE 1.11—The Application Menu (Apps) 21

FIGURE 1.12—The Menu Bar 22

FIGURE 1.13—Output Bar 23

FIGURE 1.14—Using AutoComplete 24

FIGURE 1.15—AutoComplete PopUp 24

FIGURE 1.16—AutoComplete for Account 25

FIGURE 1.17—Introduction to the Dictionary 26

FIGURE 2.01—Strings on a Chart 52

FIGURE 2.02—Calculating with DateTime Values 61

FIGURE 2.03—Methods of the DateTime Class 62

FIGURE 2.04—Print Log Output for TimeSpan Manipulations 64

FIGURE 2.05—TimeSpan Class Members 65

FIGURE 2.06—Output in the Print Log 77

FIGURE 2.07—Output to the Print Log for DateTime Example 82

FIGURE 2.08—Output to the Print Log for DateTime Parse Example 82

FIGURE 2.09—DateTime Parse with Erroneous String 82

FIGURE 2.10—DateTime Display Examples 82

FIGURE 2.11—DateTime Comparison Examples 82

FIGURE 2.12—TimeSpan Examples 83

FIGURE 2.13—More DateTime Examples 83

FIGURE 2.14—Finding the Dictionary on the Toolbar 85

FIGURE 2.15—On First Clicking on the Dictionary Icon 85

FIGURE 2.16—The EasyLanguage.ell (Library) Menu 86

FIGURE 2.17—Visualizing a Vector 86

FIGURE 2.18—Visualizing a Two-Dimensional Array 87

FIGURE 3.01—The Alerts Box 98

FIGURE 3.02—The Configuration Box for Notification Preferences 98

FIGURE 3.03—SunnyBands 100

FIGURE 3.04—Alert on Bar Close 101

FIGURE 3.05—Analysis Commentary for the Code in Figure 3.08 105

FIGURE 3.06—HTML Link to Website [OME_HTML2Website] 106

FIGURE 3.07—SunnyBands Commentary Window 106

FIGURE 3.08—Third Party Data Menus 108

FIGURE 3.09—Add Symbol Dialog Box 110

FIGURE 3.10—Symbol Lookup 111

FIGURE 3.11—Add/Edit Data Source 112

FIGURE 3.12—Customize Your Symbol 112

FIGURE 3.13—Tell TS What Format Your Dates Are In 112

FIGURE 3.14—Error Message: Data Source Is Not Properly Formatted 113

FIGURE 3.15—Proper Formatting of Your Datafile 113

FIGURE 3.16—Gasoline Prices at the Pump vs Crude Light (through 2021) 114

FIGURE 3.17—InfoBox PopUp 117

FIGURE 3.18—Time and Sales Window for CSCO 119

FIGURE 4.01—Preview Level of the Dictionary 130

FIGURE 4.02—The Libraries in the First Level of the Dictionary 140

FIGURE 4.03—Namespaces and Their Descriptions 141

FIGURE 4.04—Second Level Shows Namespace tsOpt under eloptapi.ell 142

FIGURE 4.05—Cascading Menu Under tsopt 143

FIGURE 4.06—Button.Click Event from the Dictionary 146

FIGURE 5.01—Using HTML in Commentary 154

FIGURE 7.01—The results of the Hello_World!_Ex#01 Print statement 166

FIGURE 7.02—Printing Hello_World!_Ex#02 166

FIGURE 7.03—The Print Log for my first effort of Hello_World!_Ex#03 167

FIGURE 7.04—Update Value Intra-bar (tick-by-tick) Was Selected 167

FIGURE 7.05—Hello_World!_Ex#04 Output in the Print Log 169

FIGURE 7.06—Print Log Output from Hello_World!_Ex#05a 170

FIGURE 7.07—Contents of Scrap.txt File 171

FIGURE 7.08—Contents of C:\OME_Files\MyTextFile.txt 172

FIGURE 7.09—Print Log Output from Hello_World! #7 175

FIGURE 7.10—Chart for Hello_World!_#7a 176

FIGURE 7.11—Print Log for Example 7.09—Hello_World! #07a 177

FIGURE 7.12—Print Log Output from Hello_World!_Ex#08a 178

FIGURE 7.13—Output from Hello_World! #08b 179

FIGURE 8.01—Swing Highs and Swing Lows from the Dictionary 187

FIGURE 8.02—Results from the Print Log 187

FIGURE 8.03—Swings from the Dictionaries on a Chart 194

FIGURE 8.04—Output from the Print Log 194

FIGURE 8.05—Example 8.06 Output to Print Log 198

FIGURE 8.06—Stack Example #01 Output to Print Log 202

FIGURE 8.07—Analysis AppStorage 205

FIGURE 8.08—AppStorage Print Log 206

FIGURE 8.09—Output from Example 8.15: [OME_AppStorage_Ex#02] 211

FIGURE 9.01—A Vanilla Moving Average with Labels 217

FIGURE 9.02—Strawberry Moving Average Displays Lengths to the Right 218

FIGURE 9.03—MyText TextLabel on a Chart 231

FIGURE 9.04—Now the TextLabel is on Data2 on the Left 232

FIGURE 9.05—Hello_World!_Ex#08a on a Chart 238

FIGURE 9.06—Horizontal Line 241

FIGURE 9.07—Vertical Line Example #01 244

FIGURE 9.08—Three Colorful Vertical Lines [OME_VerticalLine_Ex#03] 246

FIGURE 9.09—Opening Range Breakout with TrendLines 251

FIGURE 9.10—Opening Range Breakout Rectangles with Semi-Transparent Fill 257

FIGURE 9.11—Rectangle with a TextLabel 259

FIGURE 9.12—Opening Range Breakout Using Ellipse 262

FIGURE 10.01—Chart with Objects Illustrating ChartingHost 268

FIGURE 10.02—Print Log After Clicking Vertical Line 269

FIGURE 10.03—ActiveAccountChanged 269

FIGURE 10.04—PlatformClientHost in the Dictionary 270

FIGURE 10.05—Portfolio Maestro Output from OME_PortfolioHost Example 273

FIGURE 10.06—Print Log Output for RadarScreenHost 276

FIGURE 10.07—RadarScreenHost with Plots 277

FIGURE 10.08—StrategyHost Example on a Chart 281

FIGURE 10.09—Output to the Print Log from the StrategyHost Strategy 281

FIGURE 11.01—An Empty Form 284

FIGURE 11.02—A Form with 2 Tabs and All the Pieces and Parts [OME_ContainerClass_DGC]
.... 287

FIGURE 11.03—A Button in a Form 288

FIGURE 11.04—A Chart in a Form 289

FIGURE 11.05—A Checkbox in a Form 289

FIGURE 11.06—A ComboBox in a Form with the Selections pulled down. 290

FIGURE 11.07—A DataGridView [OME_DataGridView_Ex#01] 290

FIGURE 11.08—DateTimePicker in a Form [OME_Form_DateTimePicker] 290

FIGURE 11.09—FastSymbolLookupComboBox in a Form
[OME_FastSymbolLookupComboxBox] 291

FIGURE 11.10—A Label in a Form 291

FIGURE 11.11—A LinkLabel in a Form 292

FIGURE 11.12—A ListView in a Form [OME_Form_ListView] 292

FIGURE 11.13—A NumericUpDown Control in a Form [OME_Form_NumericUpDown] 292

FIGURE 11.14—A ProgressBar in a Form 293

FIGURE 11.15—A Set of Radio Buttons in a GroupBox in a Form 293

FIGURE 11.16—A RichTextBox in a Form 294

FIGURE 11.17—A Slider in a Form [OME_Form_Slider]...294

FIGURE 11.18—A TableLayoutPanel in a Form [OME_Form_TableLayoutPanel] 295

FIGURE 11.19—A TextBox in a Form [OME_Form_TextBox]......................................295

FIGURE 11.20—A WebBrowser in a Form with SunnyBands on a Chart 296

FIGURE 11.21—A WebView2 in a Form [OME_WebView2] 297

FIGURE 11.22—An Empty Form with ControlBox Enabled 297

FIGURE 11.23—A Panel in a Form..298

FIGURE 11.24—A GroupBox with RadioButtons 298

FIGURE 11.25—A Form with a TabControl and two TabPages 299

FIGURE 11.26—EZL Resource Editor...303

FIGURE 11.27—GroupBox with Radio Buttons in a Form.....................................306

FIGURE 11.28—WinForms Controls Available in the ToolBox 312

FIGURE 11.29—Control Shown in the Dictionary 312

FIGURE 11.30—Simple DataGridView 322

FIGURE 11.31—A Calculator Using DataGridView..325

FIGURE 11.32—Multiple Views of Resource Editor, Properties and Outline 328

FIGURE 12.01—AccountsProvider Shows Three Accounts with Current Balance 337

FIGURE 12.02—AccountsProvider in RadarScreen...339

FIGURE 12.03—Flow Chart of Order States 341

FIGURE 12.04—AccountsProvider on a Chart...350

FIGURE 13.01—Check the box to "Enable order placement objects." 356

FIGURE 14.01—Output from the Print Log 372

FIGURE 14.02—Moving Average Length Determined by Reading Spreadsheet..............373

FIGURE 14.03—Using Excel from within EZL [OME_Excel_Ex#01] and [DemoExcelClass.xlsx]
....373

FIGURE 14.04—Chart_to_Excel..376

FIGURE 14.05—RadarScreen to Excel Output...379

FIGURE 15.01—Fundamental Fields in RadarScreen 382

FIGURE 15.02—Commitment of Traders Using FundamentalQuotesProvider 453

TABLE OF TABLES

TABLE 1.01—More Reserved Words 20

TABLE 2.01—Numeric Precision 31

TABLE 2.02—Frequently Used EZL Statements 34

TABLE 2.03—AND Truth Table 35

TABLE 2.04—OR Truth Table 36

TABLE 2.05—Logical Expression AND Truth Table 36

TABLE 2.06—Binary AND Truth Table 37

TABLE 2.07—String Functions 51

TABLE 2.08—Standard Numeric Format Strings 53

TABLE 2.09—Custom Numeric Format Strings 55

TABLE 2.10—Short Date Pattern 55

TABLE 2.11—Standard Date and Time Format Specifications 67

TABLE 2.12—Custom Date and Time Format Specifiers 69

TABLE 2.13—Dictionary Exploration Aid 84

TABLE 2.14—Array Compare Parameters 90

TABLE 2.15—Array_Copy Parameters 91

TABLE 2.16—Array_GetMaxIndex Parameters 91

TABLE 2.17—Array_GetType Parameters 92

TABLE 2.18—Array_SetMaxIndex Parameters 92

TABLE 2.19—Array_SetValName Parameters 93

TABLE 2.20—Array_Sort Parameters 94

TABLE 2.21—Array_Sum Parameters 94

TABLE 3.01—Useful Statements When Issuing Alerts 99

TABLE 3.02—RunCommand 101

TABLE 3.03—RunComandOnLastBar Parameters 102

TABLE 3.04—Chart Type Reserved Word Values 107

TABLE 3.05—Acceptable Field Names for 3rd Party Data 109

TABLE 3.06—Acceptable Date Formats 109

TABLE 3.07—Acceptable Time Formats 109

TABLE 3.08—InfoBox Parameters 116

TABLE 3.09—Time and Sales Condition/Subtype Reference 124

TABLE 4.01—AnalysisTechnique Properties 137

TABLE 4.02—AnalysisTechnique Methods 138

TABLE 4.03—AnalysisTechnique Events 138

TABLE 4.04—Dictionary Exploration Aid 145

TABLE 4.05—List of Provider Classes 147

TABLE 5.01—Exception Class Properties 155

TABLE 5.02—Exception Class Methods 155

TABLE 5.03—SystemException Class Properties 156

TABLE 5.04—SystemException Class Methods..156

TABLE 6.01—Overload Method..160

TABLE 8.01—Dictionary Class Properties 183

TABLE 8.02—Dictionary Class Methods 183

TABLE 8.03—Properties of the TokenList Class...203

TABLE 8.04—Methods of the TokenList Class 203

TABLE 8.05—Operators of the TokenList Class 203

TABLE 9.01—DrawingObject Properties 219

TABLE 9.02—DrawingObject Methods...220

TABLE 9.03—DrawingObject Events..220

TABLE 9.04—Object Class Methods 221

TABLE 9.05—Object Class Operators 221

TABLE 9.06—Alert Configuration Properties 224

TABLE 9.07—Alert Configuration Events..224

TABLE 9.08—AlertFrequency Enumeration 224

TABLE 9.09—Notification Class Properties 225

TABLE 9.10—Notification Class Methods 225

TABLE 9.11—TextLabel Properties 226

TABLE 9.12—TextLabel Methods..226

TABLE 9.13—HorizontalLine Properties..239

TABLE 9.14—HorizontalLines Methods 239

TABLE 9.15—VerticalLine Class Properties 242

TABLE 9.16—VerticalLine Class Methods 242

TABLE 9.17—TrendLine Class Properties 247

TABLE 9.18—TrendLine Class Methods..248

TABLE 9.19—Rectangle Class Properties 251

TABLE 9.20—Rectangle Class Methods...252

TABLE 10.01—ChartingHost Class Properties...264

TABLE 10.02—ChartingHost Class Methods...264

TABLE 10.03—ChartingHost Class Events 265

TABLE 10.04—PlatformClientHost Properties...269

TABLE 10.05—PlatformClientHost Methods...269

TABLE 10.06—PlatformClientHost Events...269

TABLE 10.07—PortfolioHost Properties 270

TABLE 10.08—PortfolioHost Methods 270

TABLE 10.09—RadarScreenHost Events 273

TABLE 10.10—StrategyHost Properties 277

TABLE 10.11—StrategyHost Methods 278

TABLE 10.12—StrategyHost Events 278

TABLE 11.01—Form Class Properties 285

TABLE 11.02—Form Class Methods 285

TABLE 11.03—Form Class Events 286

TABLE 11.04—ContainerControl Methods..305

TABLE 11.05—GroupBox Properties 305

TABLE 11.06—GroupBox Methods..306

TABLE 11.07—Panel Properties 306

TABLE 11.08—Panel Methods..307

TABLE 11.09—TabControl Class Properties 310

TABLE 11.10—TabControl Class Methods..311

TABLE 11.11—TabControl Class Events 311

TABLE 11.12—TabPage Class Methods 311

TABLE 11.13—Control Class Properties...314

TABLE 11.14—Control Class Methods 314

TABLE 11.15—Control Class Events 314

TABLE 11.16—Button Class Properties 315

TABLE 11.17—Button Class Methods 315

TABLE 11.18—Button Class Events 315

TABLE 11.19—ButtonBase Class Properties 316

TABLE 11.20—CheckBox Class Properties 316

TABLE 11.21—CheckBox Class Methods 316

TABLE 11.22—CheckBox Class Events 317

TABLE 11.23—ComboBox Class Properties 317

TABLE 11.24—ComboBox Class Methods..318

TABLE 11.25—ComboBox Class Events...318

TABLE 11.26—DataGridView Properties 323

TABLE 11.27—DataGridView Methods..323

TABLE 11.28—RadioButton Class Properties 326

TABLE 11.29—RadioButton Class Methods..326

TABLE 11.30—RadioButton Class Events 326

TABLE 11.31—TextBox Class Properties 326

TABLE 11.32—TextBox Class Methods 327

TABLE 11.33—TextBox Class Events 327

TABLE 12.01—Enumerated Values for the DataState Enumeration...............................332

TABLE 12.02—Account Class Properties 335

TABLE 12.03—Account Class Methods 335

TABLE 12.04—Account Class Events 335

TABLE 12.05—AccountsProvider Properties..337

TABLE 12.06—AccountsProvider Methods..337

TABLE 12.07—AccountsProvider Events...338

TABLE 13.01—Order Class Properties 359
TABLE 13.02—Order Class Methods 359
TABLE 13.03—Order Class Events 360
TABLE 15.01—FundamentalFields Class Properties 451

INDEX

- 20
.... 20
#BeginAlert.. 98, 99
#BeginCmtry...............................104, 105, 134
#BeginCmtryOrAlert 98
#End 99, 104, 105, 134
#EndRegion............77, 132, 162, 319, 374, 375
#Region 77, 132, 160, 178, 319, 374
(.... 20
) 20
* 20
*.wav File.. 114
*/ 28
. ... 33
. Dot Operator or Period................................ 32
.avi File 115
.csv File...................................2, 10, 86, 111
.dll File 10
.dop File 10, 107
.ela File 10
.eld File 10, 136
.eld Files 56
.ell Library 18
.elp File 10
.els File 10
.elx File 10
.html File 10
.ini File 10
.json File.. 11
.tmp File 11
.tsd File 11
.tsw File 11
.txt File 11
.wav File..............................11, 99, 114
.xlxs File 11
.xml File 11
/ 20
/* 28
// 16, 20, 28
: 87, 108
; 20, 31
[ ] 20, 168
[DemoExcel.xlsx] 369
[DemoExcelClass.xlsx] 373
[OME_3BarMAV] 34
[OME_AcctProvider].................................... 338
[OME_AP_PP] 346
[OME_AppStorage].................................... 204
[OME_AppStorage_Ex#02].................... 211
[OME_AppStorage_Report] 206
[OME_Chart_to_Excel].................................... 373
[OME_ChartingHost_Ex#01] 265

[OME_CodingTemplate] 130
[OME_CompositeFormatting] 73
[OME_Container] 299
[OME_Container_Class].................... 307
[OME_ContainerClass_DGC] 287
[OME_Data2].................................... 7
[OME_DataGridView_Ex#01] 290, 318
[OME_DateTime] 77
[OME_DateTime_Ex#01].................... 69
[OME_Debug] 154
[OME_DGV] 290
[OME_DGV_Ex#02] 323
[OME_Ellipse_Ex#01] 260
[OME_EntryOrderTicket].................... 360
[OME_Excel_Ex#01].................... 369, 373
[OME_f_ADX] 43
[OME_f_ForLoop] 47
[OME_FastSymbolLookupComboxBox] 291
[OME_Floating_Text].................... 232, 233
[OME_ForLoop].................................... 47
[OME_Form_DateTimePicker] 290
[OME_Form_ListView].................... 292
[OME_Form_NumericUpDown].................... 292
[OME_Form_Slider] 294
[OME_Form_TableLayoutPanel] 295
[OME_Form_TextBox].................... 295
[OME_FQP_Ex#01] 450
[OME_FQP_Ex#02] 382
[OME_Hello_World!_Ex#02] 118
[OME_Hello_World!_Ex#04] 168
[OME_Hello_World!_Ex#05a].................... 169
[OME_Hello_World!_Ex#05b] 170
[OME_Hello_World!_Ex#06] 171
[OME_Hello_World!_Ex#07] 172
[OME_Hello_World!_Ex#07a].................... 175
[OME_Hello_World!_Ex#08a].................... 177
[OME_Hello_World!_Ex#08b] 178
[OME_HelperMethods] 160
[OME_HorizontalLine_Ex#01] 240
[OME_HTML_Email] 104
[OME_HTML2Website].................... 105
[OME_MovAvg_Strawberry] 217
[OME_MovAvg_Vanilla].................... 216
[OME_OSOOrderTicket].................... 364
[OME_OTMethods] 366
[OME_PlatformClientHost] 269
[OME_PortfolioHost] 271
[OME_ProtectOrderTicket] 362
[OME_Queue_Ex#01] 194
[OME_R_PosnProvider].................... 341
[OME_RadarScreen_to_Excel].................... 376
[OME_RadarScreenHost] 274

[OME_Rectangle_BN].................................... 253
[OME_Rectangle_Ex#01]............................. 253
[OME_Stack_Ex#01].................................... 198
[OME_StrategyHost] 278
[OME_StringManipulation] 72
[OME_Strings].. 30
[OME_Swings_in_Dict_Ex#01] 183
[OME_Swings_in_Dict_Ex#02] 188
[OME_TargetOrderTicket] 361
[OME_TextLabel_Ex#01] 227
[OME_TextRectangle].................................. 257
[OME_TimeSpan_Ex#01] 62
[OME_TrendLine_Ex#01] 248
[OME_TrendLine_Ex#0x] 251
[OME_TryCatch] 158
[OME_TryCatchThrow]................................ 157
[OME_Vector_Ex#01] 204
[OME_VerticalLine_Ex#01]......................... 242
[OME_VerticalLine_Ex#02]......................... 244
[OME_VerticalLine_Ex#03]......................... 245
[OME_WebBrowser] 296
[OME_WebView2].. 297
[OME_WhileLoop] 49
‾ 33
‾ 38
{ 71
{ } 16, 20, 28
{ and } 71
} 71
~ 38
+ 20
+= 6, 203
+PREFIX:Symbol_Data............................. 108
< 20, 84
<= 20, 84
<> 20, 84, 221
= 20, 84, 221
-= 6
-= 203
> 20, 84
>= 20, 84
0 element.. 87
1 minute 110
1 tick... 110
10 minute 107
10 tick... 107
100 shares... 107
200 Day Average - Price 425
3rd Party Data 107, 108, 110
5-minute chart 100
A 20, 52
A Brief Interlude 84
A Brief Look at TokenLists 86
AAPL 231
Abbreviations... 10
Abort 117

Above Ask.. 120
AC 10, 152
AcceptButton 284
Account 124
Account [].. 337
Account Class 333
Account Object.. 25, 337
AccountID.................128, 333, 335, 337, 357
Accounts.. 335, 337
AccountsProvider.....128, 147, 263, 337, 346
AccountsProvider (AP) 333
AccountsProvider Class 335
ACKNOWLEDGMENTS........................ xxxi
Acquisition 120
Action 341, 357
ActionToString () 359
Activate () 285
Activated 286
ActivationRules.. 357
Active Account Number.............................. 271
ActiveAccountChanged 269
ActiveAccountChangeEventArgs................ 269
ActiveAccountID 263, 269
ActiveAccountInfo...................................... 269
ActivityBar........................... 13, 41, 136
Add ()...........................182, 183, 187, 203
Add Button 85
Add Form 303, 304, 327
Add Study 16
Add Symbol 110
Add Tab.. 148, 303
AddControl () 295, 296, 305, 310
AddEventArgs... 221
Adding a Form 327
Adding Drawing Objects to your EasyLanguage
   Code.. 214
AddItem ().............................. 309, 317
AddToMovieChain 116
ADIVSHR.. 384
Adobe Acrobat 8, 141
AdvanceOptions 357
ADX 43
aiApplicationType....................................... 236
aiOptimizing... 237
aiRealTimeCalc... 348
aiStrategyAuto.. 44
Alarm 97
AlarmEvent 146
Alert 99, 222, 223, 238, 242, 246
Alert Once per Bar 100
Alert.GlobalNotification 225
Alert.Notification 223
Alert.Notification.AudibleEnable 223
Alert.Notification.VisualEnable................. 223
AlertConfiguration 221, 222, 238, 242
AlertConfiguration Class.................... 223, 225

AlertEnabled 99

AlertEventArgs 221, 224

AlertFrequency 223

AlertFrequency Enumeration 224

Alerts.........................97, 99, 100, 215

Alerts for Drawing Objects 98, 222

Alerts Tab.................................... 97

Alias 333

Alice 8

Align 7

Align Text 83

Alignment 7

Alignment Component 72

Alignment of Cells in RadarScreen.............. 7

AllData.dop 107

AllOrNone................................... 357

ALT 274

AME 37

AME, *Ask Mr. EasyLanguage* 10, 39, 48

An 20

Analysis Commentary.27, 40, 97, 103, 104, 105, 126, 296

Analysis Commentary (AC)..................... 152

Analysis Commentary as a Debugging Tool. 152

Analysis Commentary Cursor 103

Analysis Commentary Tool 153

Analysis Technique.4, 5, 10, 22, 23, 41, 87, 304, 327

AnalysisTechnique Class 136, 204, 213, 214

AnalysisTechnique.Name.toString () 371

AnalysisTechnique_Initialized..................... 339

AnalysisTechnique_UnInitialized 339

AnalysisTechnique_WorkspaceSaving..319, 339

Anchor 312

AnchorStyle 286, 312

AND 35

Angled Brackets 88

AP, AccountsProvider......................... 10, 333

API 142

App_Init () 228

Appendices................................. 5, 24

Application Programming Interface............. 142

Apps...............................12, 21, 22, 119

AppStorage 4, 136, 137, 138, 139, 204, 205, 207, 208, 211

AppStorage.Contains ()......................207, 208

Arc 213

args....................................... 146

args.Action.toString 301

args.BooleanValue.toString ()...................... 275

args.Cancel.toString () 267

args.DateValue.toString () 275

args.DoubleValue.toString () 275

args.FormatStyle.toString () 275

args.Height.toString () 266

args.Reason 333

args.StudyName.toString ()...................... 275

args.TabPage.Name 301

args.Trigger.............................. 223

args.Triggered 224

args.Width.toString ()........................ 266

Array ..3, 27, 87, 88, 89, 139, 162, 181, 204, 371

Array or Collection Index 20

Array, Boolean 94

Array, Three-Dimensional 87

Array, Usage 89

Array_Compare 89, 90

Array_Copy............................. 89, 90

Array_GetMaxIndex 89, 91

Array_GetType 89, 91

Array_SetMaxIndex 89, 92

Array_SetValRange 89, 93

Array_Sort............................. 89, 93

Array_Sum 89, 94

ArrayName...................87, 88, 91, 92, 93, 94

Arrays...........................86, 87, 88, 89, 94, 182

Arrays, Dynamic 88

Arrays, Fixed Length 88

Arrays, Static 89

Arrow 213

ASCII 5, 50, 107, 108, 110

ASCII 3rd Party Data......................... 97

ASCII Character Codes........................ 3

ASCII Data................................. 107, 108

Ask 26

Ask Mr. EasyLanguage ....xxix, 2, 27, 39, 100

Ask, Best 118

AskSize 345

Assets 383, 388

asType 20

Asynchronous.............................. 354

At 20

AT 4, 10, 22, 23, 41, 87, 136, 304, 305, 369

At Ask 120

At Bid 120

At$ 97, 103

AT-Analysis Technique 5

atCommentaryBar 7, 103, 115, 133, 134, 153, 200, 201, 209

Attribute Statements......................... 20

Attributes................................. 124, 152

Attributes, Symbol 107

Attributes.ini 107

AudibleConfiguration 221, 225

AudibleEnable.............................. 225

Audio File 11

Audio Notifications.......................... 225

Auto Hide................................. 140

AutoComplete 24, 25

Auto-Detect................................ 166

Automation 277

AutoScaleFactor............................ 284

AutoScroll 306

AutoShow 219

AutoSize 313
Average 47, 216, 217
Average Directional Movement 43
Average Price 120
Average Price Trade 122
AvgFilledPrice 341, 357
AxisType 286
Axx 52
BackColor 264, 313
Background Color 264
BackgroundGradientStyle 306
BackgroundImage 313
BackgroundImageLayout 313
Backtesting 11, 125, 277, 354
Bad Tick 121
Balances 335
BarDateTime 57, 59, 64, 70, 72, 81, 215, 279
BarDateTime.toString () 152, 153
BarNumber 115, 166, 214, 222, 261, 278
BarsAgo 245
BarsAgo Reference 20
BarsBack 125, 139, 159
BarsSinceEntry 200, 280, 354
BarsSinceExit 124, 200
Base Currency 124
BaseCurrency 124
Based 20
Basket Index 120
Basket Order 21
BDAccountEquity 333
BDAcountNetWorth 333
BDCashBalance 333
BDDayTradingBuyingPower 333
BDOptionBuyingPower 333
BDOptionLiquidationValue 334
BDOvernightBuyingPower 334
BDUnrealizedPL 334
BegElementNum 93, 94
Begin 38, 44, 45, 86
Begin...End 37, 45, 46, 48, 83, 128, 166
Below Bid 120
Best Practices with Data Providers 331
Beta 389
Between Bid and Ask 120
Bid, Best 118
Bilat Block Trade 120
BingTicks 115, 126
Bitwise Binary Operator 37
Block Trade 120
BlueViolet 42
BNPoint 214, 215, 221, 222, 226, 241, 242, 246, 247, 252, 253, 259, 260
BNPoint.Create () 222, 239
Book Value 388, 429
Book Value per Share 389
Boolean 31, 32, 36, 39, 92, 93

Boolean Algebra 27, 35
Boolean Operators 35
Boolean, Array 94
BorderRadius 286, 306
BorderStyle 306, 326
Bracket Ordr 356
BracketOrderTickets 353
Break 86
Breakouts 246
BringToFront () 314
Brower, William (Bill) 27, 44
Browse Button 111
Browser 21
Bugs 151
Build 22
Built-In Function 41
Bunched Sold 120
Bunched Trade 120
Burst Basket 120
Button 287, 299, 304, 315, 328
Button Class 146, 314
Button.Create () 302
ButtonBase Class 315
Buy 13, 19, 20
Buy to Cover 280
BuyBuyBuy 115
BuyMinusSellPlus 357
BuyToCover 200
By 20
C# 28
C:\OME_Files\ 171, 373, 376
C:\OME_Files\myData.txt 40
C:\OME_Files\OTFile01.txt 346
C:\OME_Files\PMH.txt 271, 273
C:\OME_Files\Scrap.txt 170
C+ 28
C++ 28
c21tradingsystems@gmail.com 331, 351
CalcDate 57, 60
CalcTime 60
Calculations with Date and Time 60
Calendar 290
CanCancel () 359
Cancel 99
Cancel () 359
CancelButton 284
Canceled 120, 354
CanDayTrade 334
CanFocus 313
CanTradeSecurityOfType () 335
Capital Expenditures 435
Capital Expenditures/Total Assets 390
Capital Lease Obligations 413
Capital Leases 448
Caption 116
Carriage Return 10, 103, 153

Carriage Return + Line Feed 40
Case 83, 86
Cash 121
Cash and Equivalents 383
Cash Dividends Paid 406
Cash Flow 383, 390
Cash Flow per share 426
Catch 20, 80, 156, 157
Categorized 25
Category 84, 145, 154, 155
CCX/EFP Trade 121
CellClickEventArgs 4, 273
Cells 322
Cells, DataGridView 318
CellsAsString 375
Chart 287
Chart Analysis 14, 21, 107, 194
Chart Control 288
Chart Type Reserved Word Values 106
ChartArea 289
ChartElementClick 264, 266
ChartElementClick Event 265
ChartElementClickEventArgs 214, 264
Charting 144, 263, 265
Charting Tools Classic 153
Charting.ChartingHost 265
ChartingHost 4, 263, 265, 269, 281
ChartingHost Class 213, 263
ChartingHost Class (Component) 263
ChartingHost.Create () 257
ChartSeries 289
ChartViewHasFocus 264
ChartWindow 264
CheckAlert 99, 133
CheckBox 287, 289, 293, 304, 315, 316, 325
CheckBox Class 316
CheckBox.Click Event 304
CheckCommentary . 104, 152, 153, 201, 209, 280
Checked 224, 316, 326
CheckedChanged 317, 326
Child 357
ChildCount 357
Choose Items 148
CL 10, 153
Class 3, 4, 8, 84, 127, 129, 139, 141, 143, 145
Class Declaration 139, 144
Classes 3, 84, 127, 134, 142, 181, 211, 262
Classic Charting Tools 153
Clear () 183, 203, 317
Clear Triggered Alert on Bar Close 100
ClearDebug 154
ClearPrintLog 44, 45, 73, 78, 154
ClearTooltips () 219
Click 146, 220, 288, 314
Click Event 146, 273, 328
ClientSize 284
ClientWindow 264, 269

ClientWindow.Height 266
ClientWindow.Width 266
Clone () 203, 221
Close 19, 42, 109, 110, 373
Close Price 121
CloseProvider () 332
CmtryStr 104, 209
Coding Best Practices 2
Coding Template 2, 4, 29
Collection 3, 135, 182, 203
Collection Class 211
Collection Classes 182
Collections 4, 352
Collections: Dictionary, Vector etc. 181
Colon 108
Color . 7, 217, 219, 221, 232, 238, 241, 260, 291,
    307, 313, 327
Color Coded 23
Color Names 42
Color Tab 97
Color.fromARGB 218, 261
Color.fromName 236
ComboBox 286, 287, 289, 290, 301, 304, 309,
    317
ComboBox Class 317
ComboBox.AddItem () 301
Comma Delimited 345
Comma Separated Values, CSV 10, 172, 181
Command Line 102
Command Line Instruction 101
CommandOrMacro 101, 102
Comma-Separated List 202
Comment 16
Commentary 103, 104, 105, 106, 126, 152
Commentary Pointer 153
CommentaryBar 103
CommentaryCL .. 7, 103, 104, 153, 201, 209, 280
Comments 27, 28, 42
Commercial Paper 413
Commission 357
Commissions & Fees from Securities Activities
    418
Commitment of Traders 450
Common Stock 406, 436
Common Usage 42
Company Name 405
Compile 22
Compiler Directives 124
Component 135, 148
Component Classes 304
Component Tray 26, 135, 263, 335
Components 135, 206
Composite Format String 71
Composite Formatting 52, 55, 71
ComputerDate 57
ComputerDateTime 57, 59, 73
ComputerTime 57

CompuTrac xxvii
Concatenated 232
Concatenated Strings 153
Conclusion 5
Conditional 86
Conditions 37
Connect 277
Const 10, 33
Constant 33
Constants 27, 33, 283
ConstantValue 33
Constructor 135
Constructor Statement 144
Consts 33, 232, 254, 271, 319
Container 302, 309
Container Class 307
Container Classes 297
ContainerControl Class 305
Containers 286
Contains () 182, 183, 203, 337
ContainsFocus 313
Continuously 224
Control 302, 311
Control Class 311
Control Classes 287
ControlBox 284
ControlLocation 313
Controls 283, 298, 313
Conventions 9
Converting TS Formatted Dates 56
Copyright .... vii, ix
Cost of Goods Sold 383, 426
Cost of Revenue 436
COTC 391
COTF 395
Count 143, 181, 182, 183, 202, 219, 317, 337
Count Down 43
Count Up 43
Counter 46
Country Code 405
Courier 72
Courier New 9, 153
CPC™ Index 152
Create () 143, 144, 155, 156, 182, 183, 203,
    225, 226, 239, 242, 247, 252, 263, 264, 269,
    270, 278, 285, 295, 305, 306, 310, 311, 314,
    315, 316, 317, 323, 326, 327, 337
Credit Card Fees 416
CrLf 10
Cross Trade 121
Crossed 121
Crosses Above 36
Cruz, William R. (Bill) xxxi
Crypto Trading TApp 124
CSV 21, 172, 175, 181, 379
CTRL 274

CTRL-A 206
CTRL-ALT-DEL 151
CTRL-C 206
CTRL-R 167
CTRL-SHIFT-E 16, 40, 118, 165
Curly Braces 28
Curly Brackets 16, 28
Currency 52, 334
Currency Based On 124
Currency Code 405
Currency Conversion 97, 124, 126
CurrentBar 375
CurrentPrice 497
CurrentSubgraph 264
CustBuyMarket 102
Custom Basket Cross 121
Custom Date and Time Format Strings 55, 56
Custom Date Format Strings 67
Custom Format String 56
Custom Numeric Format Strings 52
Custom Time Format Strings 67
CustomerID 263
Customize Indicator 100
Daily 110
DailyLimit 345
Data 110, 155, 337
Data Order Parameter 107
Data Provider States 331
Data Providers 5, 332, 351
Data Providers, Using 332
Data Structures 7, 182
Data2 .... 7, 231
DataFile 110
DataGridView 10, 287, 290, 318, 319, 322, 323,
    329
DataGridView.Create () 322
DataGridViewCellCollection 322
DataGridViewRow 323
DataN 32, 88
DataNum 137
DataProvider 10, 332, 333
DataProviderObject.Count 332
DataProviders 147, 352, 354, 356
DataState 331
DataStream 231
DataStreams 137
DataType 32, 33, 88
Date 19, 57, 60, 66, 109, 110, 125, 373
Date and Time 56, 67
Date and Time as Integers 57
Date and Time Format Strings 55, 66
Date and Time Old School 57
Date and Time OOEL Style 59
Date References, OOEL 56
DateTime 67, 72, 241, 247, 264
DateTime Class 61

DateTime Related Tasks 77
DateTime, Double.........................56, 57, 58, 71
DateTime, Object.....4, 56, 57, 59, 62, 70, 73, 77
DateTime.Create 74
DateTime.Now...57, 75, 81
DateTime.Now.TimeOfDay.......................... 81
DateTime.Parse 80, 81
DateTimeOffset.. 67
DateTimePicker 287, 290, 300, 301, 309
DateTimeToString 58
DateToJulian 57
DateToString.. 59
DateToString () 73
Davy, Christopher G. (Chris)...xxxi, 1, 2, 12, 21, 29, 331, 350, 351
Day.. 354
Day of the Month 67
Day, Full Name 67
DayFromDate 58
DayOfMonth 57
DayOfWeek 57, 80
DayOfWeekFromDate 58
DaySessions.....................................497
Debug.................22, 31, 147, 154, 225, 231, 245
Debugging... 4, 151
Debugging with Analysis Commentary 152
Debugging, Exceptions and Error Handling 4
Decimal 52
Decimal Point.. 54
Decisions... 37
Declare Data Type 30
Default 83, 86, 133, 185, 216, 280, 338, 361, 362
Deferred Charges 384
Deferred Income Tax 384
Deferred Taxes.. 419
Definitive Guide to TradeStation's
  EasyLanguage & OOEL Programming..........
  .... xxix, 2
DeleteEventArgs 221
Delta-Neutral Trading Products 121
Depreciation... 402
Depreciation Expense 417
Dequeue ()... 194
Derivatively Priced 121
Description.. 25
Deselected 311
Designer Generated Code .10, 25, 135, 136, 148, 204, 206, 283, 302, 303, 305
DestArrayName 90, 91
DestElement.. 90, 91
Destroy () 263
Detail Pane 119
DGC ..10, 25, 135, 136, 148, 149, 204, 206, 283, 302, 303, 305, 307, 328
DGC-Designer Generated Code 5
DGV.....................................10, 318, 319
Dialog Box 352

Dict... 10
Dict.Add () 208
Dict.Contains () 207
Dictionary 207
Dictionary Class.......3, 4, 10, 137, 181, 182, 183, 187, 194, 204, 211
Dictionary Class (Collection)...................... 182
Dictionary Exploration Aid................. 25, 84, 86
Dictionary Tab 3, 4, 13, 16, 17, 18, 24, 25, 27, 60, 61, 70, 84, 85, 129, 140, 143, 145, 146, 148, 181, 354
Dictionary Unfolded..................................... 3
Dictionary vs GlobalDictionary 194
Dictionary.Create () 207
Digit Placeholder 54
DirMovement 43
DisabledBackColor 314
DisabledForeColor 314
Discretionary.. 1, 357
DiscretionaryAmount 357
Distribution 121
Divide by Zero 151
Dividend per Share..................................... 384
Dividends per Share 399
DLL 6
DMA 104, 497
DMA_H 350
DNTP 121
Dock 313
DockChanged.. 286
Docking... 140
DockStyle... 313
DOClick 222
doCmtry 103
Does 20
Donges, Diane.. xxxi
dop File 107
DOPoint 220, 226, 246, 247, 251
Dot Operator 127, 135, 335, 345
Double.. 31, 92
Double DateTime Format 58
Double Quotes.........................51, 55, 113, 345
DoubleQuote .10, 31, 50, 51, 168, 169, 207, 244, 245, 271, 279, 319, 323
DownKey 264
Download 10
DownTicks 19
DownTo 43, 45, 47, 48
DP 10, 351, 352
DQ-DoubleQuote Character............................ 10
Drawing.. 231
Drawing Classes.. 215
Drawing Menu 213
Drawing Object 4
Drawing Object Classes 213, 221
Drawing Object Classes, About 213
Drawing Objects 4, 7, 213, 232

480

Drawing Objects, Alerts 215
Drawing Tool 215, 227
Drawing Tools.................................... 4, 213
DrawingObject ..4, 214, 219, 220, 226, 238, 241, 250, 260, 265
DrawingObject Class 215, 220
DrawingObject Classes 222
DrawingObject Classes, About 214
DrawingObject Methods 221
DrawingObjectLabel Object 238, 242, 246
DrawingObjects 60, 137, 145, 213, 214, 222
DrawingObjects.Add () 214, 216, 230, 243, 246, 254, 259, 260, 261
DrawingObjects.Delete ()......218, 230, 243, 245, 246
DrawingObjects.TrendLine 265
DrawObjects.................................... 137, 221
Drobo 22
DropDownHeight 317
DropDownStyle 317
DropDownWidth 317
DTPoint....... 183, 215, 216, 221, 226, 241, 242, 244, 246, 247, 248, 252, 253, 259, 260
DTPoint.Create ()..243, 244, 245, 246, 254, 260, 261
Duration 357
Duration Date 357
Dynamic Link Library............................. 10
DynamicMAV Histogram 350
DynamicMovingAverage 104, 497
DynamicMovingAverage Histogram 497
DynamicProperties.................269, 337, 357
Earnings After Taxes.................385, 386, 427
Earnings Before Taxes 384
Easing Into EasyLanguage 27
Easing into Object-Oriented Programming 4
EasyLanguage ... ix, xxix, xxx, xxxi, 1, 2, 3, 5, 6, 16
EasyLanguage (EZL) 3
EasyLanguage (EZL) Brush-Up...................... 3
EasyLanguage Archive File 10
EasyLanguage Code Editor 23
EasyLanguage Coding Best Practices............ 29
EasyLanguage Components 148
EasyLanguage Dictionary 17
EasyLanguage Document File 10, 14
EasyLanguage Editor 21
EasyLanguage Intricacies........................... 3, 97
EasyLanguage Learning by Example 44
EasyLanguage Learning-by-Example Workbook
.... 27
EasyLanguage Optimization API 142
EasyLanguage Project File........................... 10
EasyLanguage Project XML 10
EasyLanguage Storage File 10
EasyLanguage Support................................ 12

EasyLanguage, EZL 3
EasyLanguage.ell 141, 354
EasyLanguage.ell Library 13, 17, 18, 60, 85, 140
ECNSweep 357
Edison, Thomas............................... 4, 151
Edit 22
Editor.. 21, 23
EffectiveBackColor................................. 313
EffectiveForeColor................................. 313
EFP 121
EFP Basis 121
EFP Block Trade 121
EFP/EFS Contra 121
EFR Trade 121
EFS Basis 121
EFS Block Trade 121
Elapsed 145
elCharting.ell Library 140
elComponent 263, 273, 305
ELD 10, 14, 336
ELDate 56
ELDateToString 51
ELDateToString () 50
Element 25
ElementSelected 146, 264, 266
ElementSelectedEventArgs 264
Ellipse 4, 213, 214, 215, 219, 221, 259, 260
Ellipse Class 259
Ellipse Object 215
Ellipse.Create () 259, 260, 261
elOptAPI.ell Library 141, 142
Else... 37, 45
elString.Format () 71
elSystem 61, 62, 73, 132, 136, 139, 144, 154, 155, 171, 206, 214, 220, 222, 227, 240, 244, 253, 260, 265, 271, 274, 278, 307
elSystem.AnalysisTechnique 138
elSystem.Collections 86, 132, 144, 168, 171, 173, 181, 182, 183, 198, 206
elSystem.Collections.Dictionary 183, 204
elSystem.Collections.Vector 204
elSystem.DateTime 70, 72
elSystem.DateTime Class 70
elSystem.DateTime.Now 71
elSystem.DotNetObject....... 220, 227, 239, 242, 248, 252, 259, 269, 271, 273, 278, 286, 305, 306, 307, 311, 314, 315, 316, 317, 318, 323, 326, 327, 338
elSystem.Drawing ...73, 132, 144, 217, 227, 238, 240, 242, 244, 260
elSystem.Drawing.Color 253
elSystem.DrawingObject........................... 222
elSystem.DrawingObjects 144, 214, 215, 216, 217, 222, 223, 224, 225, 227, 238, 240, 242, 244, 246, 251, 253, 259, 260
elSystem.DrawingObjects.[] 215

elSystem.DrawingObjects.AlertConfiguration 224

elSystem.DrawingObjects.DrawingObject... 215, 220, 227, 239, 242, 248, 252, 259

elSystem.DrawingObjects.Ellipse 259

elSystem.DrawingObjects.HorizontalLine.... 239

elSystem.DrawingObjects.Notification 225

elSystem.DrawingObjects.Rectangle 253

elSystem.DrawingObjects.TextLabel 227

elSystem.DrawingObjects.TrendLine 248

elSystem.DrawingObjects.VerticalLine 242

elSystem.elComponent 147, 220, 227, 239, 242, 248, 252, 259, 265, 269, 271, 273, 278, 286, 305, 306, 307, 311, 314, 315, 316, 317, 318, 323, 326, 327, 338

elSystem.ell Library 70

elSystem.Environment.Start 99

elSystem.EventArgs 224, 299, 307, 308, 309, 319

elSystem.Exception 155

elSystem.Exception.Create () 336, 338

elSystem.GlobalValueUpdatedEventArgs 177

elSystem.Host 265, 269, 273

elSystem.InitializedEventArgs 319, 339

elSystem.Int32 29

elSystem.IO ... 132, 144, 168, 169, 170, 171, 173, 175, 271

elSystem.Net 132

elSystem.Object 138, 146, 155, 156, 183, 203, 204, 215, 220, 224, 225, 226, 239, 242, 248, 252, 259, 265, 266, 269, 271, 273, 275, 278, 286, 299, 302, 305, 306, 307, 309, 311, 314, 315, 316, 317, 318, 319, 323, 326, 327, 335, 338, 360, 450, 452

elSystem.Office.Excel 144, 376

elSystem.SystemException 155, 156

elSystem.UnInitializedEventArgs 319, 339

elSystem.Windows.Forms 73, 132, 144, 283, 288, 289, 290, 291, 292, 293, 294, 295, 296, 297, 298, 302, 305, 306, 307, 310, 311, 312, 314, 315, 316, 317, 318, 323, 325, 326

elSystem.Windows.Forms [ClassType] 302

elSystem.Windows.Forms.Button 302, 315

elSystem.Windows.Forms.ButtonBase 315, 316, 317, 326

elSystem.Windows.Forms.CheckBox 317

elSystem.Windows.Forms.ComboBox 318

elSystem.Windows.Forms.ContainerControl 286, 305, 307, 311

elSystem.Windows.Forms.Control 286, 305, 306, 307, 311, 314, 315, 316, 317, 318, 323, 326, 327

elSystem.Windows.Forms.DataGridView 323

elSystem.Windows.Forms.DataGridViewCellEv entArgs 319

elSystem.Windows.Forms.ELWFComponent .. 286, 305, 306, 307, 311, 314, 315, 316, 317, 318, 323, 326, 327

elSystem.Windows.Forms.Form 286, 302

elSystem.Windows.Forms.GroupBox 306

elSystem.Windows.Forms.IButtonControl ... 315

elSystem.Windows.Forms.Panel 307

elSystem.Windows.Forms.RadioButton 326

elSystem.Windows.Forms.TabControl 311

elSystem.Windows.Forms.TabControlEventArg s 301, 309

elSystem.Windows.Forms.TabPage 311

elSystem.Windows.Forms.TextBox 327

elSystem.WorkspaceSavingEventArgs . 319, 339

elSystem.xml 132, 144

elSystem.xml.xmlDocument 157

ELWFComponent 305

EMailCheck 12

EmailEnable 225

Enable 224

Enable Alert 97, 100

Enable AutoComplete 24

Enabled 313

EncodeDate 59

EncodeTime 59

End 44, 45, 46

EndElementNum 93, 94

End-of-Day Exits 353

End-of-File, EOF 113

EndOfStream 172, 173

EndPoint 246, 251

enQueue () 194, 208

Enter 24

EnteredQuantity 357

EnteredTime 340, 357

EntryPrice 125

eNum 10, 25, 284

Enumerated List 144, 220

Enumerated Value 25

Enumeration 72, 84, 136, 145

Enumerators 136

EOF 113

EOO Trade 121

EPS 352, 383, 384

Equals () 221

Erase () 204

Error Codes 3

Error Handling 151

Escape Character 54

Esoteric Features 97

Eurex 120

Event 25, 84, 129, 135, 145, 146

Event Args 263

Event Handler 6, 25, 138, 143, 145, 146, 147, 205, 214, 222, 223, 263, 273, 303, 304, 347, 353, 354

Event Log 116, 157

482

Event Public 146
EventArgs 286, 317, 318
Event-Driven 146
Event-Driven Programming 352, 353
Event-Driven Programming Structure........ 352
Events 144, 145, 146, 263
Events Log 101, 102, 157
Excel 50, 107, 158, 369, 371, 373
Excel, Using within EZL............................... 5
Excellent! 21
Exception 136, 155, 156, 331
Exception Class.. 154
Exception.Create () 158
Exceptions 151, 154, 156
Exchange for Physical.................................. 121
Exchange for Physical Basis........................ 121
Exchange for Physical Block Trade 121
Exchange for Physical/Exchange for Swap
     Contra Block Trade 121
Exchange for Risk Trade............................. 121
Exchange for Swap Basis............................. 121
Exchange For Swap Block Trade. 121
Exchange of Options for Options Trade........ 121
ExitPrice.. 125
Expired... 354
Exponential 53
Exponential Notation 54
ExtendedFilter.. 337
ExtendedProperties 334, 357
Extensible Markup Language, XML 11
ExtLeft 246, 251
ExtRight 246, 251
EZL .... xxix, 1, 5, 6, 10, 14
EZL Icon 12
F3 ....10, 20, 21, 22
Facebook 142
Failed... 331
False 45
FalseVal 39
FastSymbolLookupComboBox............. 287, 291
FC... 10
Fibonacci 86
FIFO... 182
FIFO, First In First Out 194
File 22
File Extensions 10
File, Print to... 17
FileAppend... 40
FileDelete... 40
FileNotFoundException 157
FillColor... 251
Filled.. 354
FilledQuantity 341, 357
FilledTime.. 357
FillPattern.. 251
Filtered from Chart...................................... 121

Finally 20, 156, 157
Find in Files 23
FindForm () 314
FindString () 317, 318
FindStringExact () 318
Fired 223, 224
First In First Out, FIFO 182
FirstSibling.. 357
Fixed Width Font 72
Fixed-Length Array 88
Fixed-Point... 53
FlatAppearance 316
FlatStyle................................... 305, 316, 317
Float 31, 92, 406
Floating Text 232
Flush the Buffer... 169
Focus () 314
Focused 313
Font 217, 221, 226, 232, 313
Font Class.. 226
Font Size 232
Font.Create () 218, 235, 236
For 43, 44, 45, 46, 47, 48, 49
For...Begin 45
ForeColor 313
Foreword xxvii
Forex 120, 123
Form......3, 4, 141, 146, 283, 286, 287, 297, 302,
     305, 329
Form Class 283
Form Containers 302
Form Controls 295, 302, 328
Form T 121
Form with 2 Tabs and All the Pieces and Parts
     293
Form, Add 302
Form, Creating a Custom 328
Form, Editing 328
Form.AcceptButton...................................... 309
Form.Create () 302
Form1.Show () 301, 304, 310, 322, 325, 328
Format Item Syntax 71
Format Specifier 52
Format String Component 72
FormatDate... 59
FormatException 67
FormatString 72
Formatting DateTime 65
Formatting Types 72
FormBorderStyle.. 284
FormClosed 286
FormClosing... 286
Forum, TradeStation 2
Forum, TS 3
FourDaysTradeCount.................................... 334
FracPortion.. 237

French Braces.. 16, 28
Frequency.. 224
From Entry 103
Frozen 322
Fuel Expense 402
Full Date/Time Pattern............................... 66
Function 13, 41, 84, 102, 145
Functions, Multiple Output 42
Fundamental Data 381
Fundamental Data Fields.............................. 5
FundamentalFields Class 381
FundamentalQuotesProvider.................147, 452
FundamentalQuotesProvider.Create............. 451
GD.. 10
gDict... 10
gDict.Contains ()...................................... 191
General Date/Time Pattern........................... 66
General Partner 427
General Partners' Distributions 390
General Tab 97
GeneratingApplication 357
GetAccountForSecurityOfType ()................ 337
GetAccountID 263, 348
GetAppInfo 44, 58, 237, 271, 274, 275, 339,
      348, 378
GetBaseException () 155, 156
GetDataNum ()... 138
GetParent ()..138, 314
GetRGBValues 24
GetSessionName () 143
GetSymbolName 40
GetType () 221
GetValue ()... 247
Global Messaging Preferences 97
Global Notification Settings........................ 223
Global Variable Declarations 154
Global Variables 10
GlobalDictionary....... 4, 10, 159, 181, 182, 188,
      194, 207, 211, 353
GlobalDictionary Class 181, 182, 187
GlobalDictionary.Create ()........................... 207
GlobalNotification 224
GlobalValue 177, 178, 179
GMTExchangeOffset 339
GMTLocalOffset....................................... 339
Gradient 285, 327
Gradient Background 306
Gross Margin 427
Group Separator & Number Scaling 54
GroupBox......................286, 293, 298, 305
GroupBox Class 305
GTC 354
GTD 357
GV 10
Harris, Sunny J................................ vii, xxvii, 11
HasValue..334, 358
Height................................285, 311, 313, 323, 326

Hello World! 4, 5, 44, 165
Hello_World! #01 .... 4, 165
Hello_World! #02 166
Hello_World!_Ex#01 ....14, 118, 165
Hello_World!_Ex#02 117
Hello_World!_Ex#03 167
Hello_World!_Ex#05 169
Hello_World!_Ex#05a 171, 172
Hello_World!_Ex#06 171
Hello_World!_Ex#07 172
Hello_World!_Ex#07a 175
Hello_World!_Ex#08a 177
Hello_World!_Ex#08b 178
Help 22
HelpLink 155
Hexadecimal 53
High 19, 42, 109, 110
Highest 84, 245
Highest High 242
HighestBar 245
Historic Orders 340
Historical Values 30
HL 10
Hopper, Admiral Grace 4, 151
HorizontalLine 4, 10, 213, 214, 215, 221, 222,
      225, 239, 240, 241
HorizontalLine Class................................. 238
HorizontalLine Object................................ 215
HorizontalLine.Create () 214
HorizontalStyle 226
Host Class 263, 269, 281
Host Classes 4, 263
HostKeyEventArgs 264
HostName Property 263
Hot Lists 21
Hour 67
Hours and Minutes 68
HoursFromDateTime 58
HStyle 226
HTML 28, 104, 105, 153, 295, 296
HTML_HRef_Link 105
http://www.vista-research.com..................... 509
https://www.EasyLanguageOOEL.com 5, 14,
      184, 232
https://www.facebook.com/VistaResearch/ . 100,
      509
https://www.MoneyMentor.com 105, 350
https://www.TS-international.com/global/forex-
      trading/.. 124
HyperText Markup Language 10
Hypothetical Performance............................ 1, 8
IBOG... 10, 352
IBP 10
ID 219
IE 295
If 13, 38, 83, 86, 103
If...Then....................34, 37, 38, 39, 116

484

If...Then, Nested................................... 39
If...Then...Else....................... 37, 38, 39
If...Then...Else...Begin..................... 38
IFF.. 39
IFFLogic.. 39
IFFString... 39
IfTouched... 358
IfTouchedPrice................................... 358
IfTouchedPriceOffset........................ 358
IfTouchedPriceStyle.......................... 358
Image.. 316
ImageAlign.. 316
ImageLayout.. 313
Import/Export....................................... 14
In.. 20
Income After Tax 444
Income Before Tax 402
Income Tax - Total 448
Income Taxes Payable........................ 415
Index Component.................................. 71
Index Number 181
Index, Zero-Based............................... 203
IndexOf ().. 203
Indicator 13, 136
Indicators... 41
Industry Code...................................... 406
Infinite Loop 48, 151
InfiniteLoopDetect 44, 151
InfoBox 97, 116, 126
Inheritance.............................. 4, 145, 263
Initialized 138, 146
Initialized Event 136, 139, 206
InitialUpdate.. 333
InitialValue................................... 32, 88
InnerException 155
Input.. 25, 162
Input/Output 42, 43
Inputs Tab 97
Insert ()... 203, 204
Inside Bar 49, 87
Insider Buy Transactions................... 439
Insider Sell Transactions.................... 439
Insider Shares Purchased................... 435
Insider Shares Sold............................. 443
Instantiate.......................139, 144, 182, 370
InStr.. 51
Int... 29
Int64... 73
Integer 31, 92
Interest Bearing Deposits 414
Interest Expense 402
Interest Income.................................... 431
Intermarket Sweep 122
Internet Connection 353
Internet Explorer 295
IntPortion 50, 56, 237

IntrabarOrderGeneration 10, 11, 118, 352
IntraBarPersist.....10, 32, 88, 227, 271, 274, 278, 347
Intraday 12
Intraday Trade Detail 122
Invalid ScrArrayName or DestArrayName 91
Inventories.. 385
Inventory 385
Investment Income 418
Investment Securities Gains 418
Investment Securities Losses............ 418
IOG 11, 352
Is 20
ISBN vii
IsConnected... 270
IsDayTrader 334
IsNewRow.. 323
isReadOnly......................202, 266, 275, 343
isType... 20, 321
Item 202, 203
ItemAdded... 353
ItemChanged....................................... 353
Items... 183
j_Key.. 116
JavaScript.. 28
Julian 57
Julian Date.. 56
Julian Format.. 58
JulianToDate 50, 57, 58
Kagi.. 107
Kase.. 107
KeepGoing 132
Key Reversals.. 87
Key/Value Pairs 182
KeyDown 315, 318, 327
KeyEventArgs 315, 327
KeyPress............................. 315, 318, 327
KeyPressEventArgs........................315, 327
Keys 183
KeyUp 315, 318, 327
KeyWords 20
Label 238, 242, 246, 287, 291, 307
Labor & Related Expense 403, 418
Last Bar of Data 102
Last In First Out, LIFO 182
LastBarOnChart 52, 115, 117, 118, 134, 178, 179, 216, 218, 231, 233, 243, 245, 260, 372
LastSibling 358
LE 11
Left.. 7
LeftQuantity 358
LeftStr 51
LegacyColorValue 132
Level 1 Data 118, 119
Level 2 Data 118
Liabilities 383

LIBB 11
Library 3, 4, 18, 84, 85, 129, 140, 145
LIFO...182, 198, 385
Limit Order 359
Limit Price 340, 348, 358
LimitPrice 358
LimitPriceOffset... 358
LimitPriceStyle 358
Line Break 3 107
Line Feed 10, 103
Line Numbering 23
Line Numbers... 23
Line Style.. 241
Linear Gradient 327
LinearGradientMode 307, 315
LinkLabel 287, 291
ListView...287, 292
Literal String Delimiter 54
Litigation 403
Litigation Expense 418
Load 354
Loaded 331
Loading 331
LoadProvider ().....................331, 332, 333, 451
Location 111, 251, 259, 268, 328
Location ()..285, 314
Lock 219
Log File 355
Logging 364
Logging to a File 355
Logical Expression Operators 36
Long Date Pattern. 66
Long Entry 11
Long Exit 11
Long Term Debt...........................414, 415, 448
Long Time Pattern 67
Long-Term Assets 386
Long-Term Debt/Assets 385
Look Inside Bar Backtesting 11
Lookup 110
Loop 43, 49, 89, 204
LossCF 125
LotSize 358
Low 19, 42, 109, 110
LowerStr 51
Lowest 83
LX 11
Macro 101, 102
MakeNewMovieRef.. 115
Margin...284, 313
Market 39
Market Depth 21, 119
MarketDepthProvider...................................... 147
MarketPosition...............103, 125, 200, 280, 354
Martinez, Armando 61
Matrix.. 21
MaxBarsBack................152, 166, 214, 245, 264

MaxBarsBack, AutoDetect........................... 118
MaximizeBox 284
Maximum Execution Time 125
MaximumSize 284
MaxIndex 91, 92
MaxLength 326
MBB 11
Member 3, 24, 25, 26, 129, 134, 135, 159, 204
Member Association 24
Members 139, 145, 220, 223, 263
Members Pane 25
Menu 22
Menu Bar 22
Message.. 116, 155
MetaStock 107, 111
MetaStock Data 107
Method 3, 4, 20, 32, 84, 127, 128, 129, 135,
    139, 141, 145, 159, 215, 265, 354
Methods...4, 60, 71, 84, 127, 139, 144, 159, 162,
    227
Methods, Local... 139
Microsoft Edge... 296
Microsoft Excel........5, 11, 30, 50, 369, 371, 373
Microsoft Word 8
Middle 7
MidStr 51
Mille 54
MinimizeBox 284
MinimumHeight.. 323
MinimumSize 284
MinutesFromDateTime 58
MinutesToTime 60
Market Insights 12
Momentum 107
MoneyMentor.com.. 115
Month 57
Month, Day of 67
Month, Name of 68
Month/Day Pattern 66
MonthFromDateTime 58
Monthly.. 110
More on Vectors and Arrays 86
MouseEnter 314
Moved 220
Movie_ID 115
Moving 220
Moving Average, Strawberry 217
Mr. EasyLanguage xxx
Mr. OOEL 61
MSFT 110
MSFT.txt 110
MultiCore 187
Multiline..310, 326
Multiple Output Functions 42, 43
myDict.Contains ()....................................... 190
myEventHandler 6
myEventHandlerChain....................................... 6

MyFactor 34
MyFunc 41
MyValue 34
myWB.Contains () 375
Name 32, 334
Name of the Day 67
Name Property 263
Namespace 3, 4, 9, 25, 26, 61, 84, 127, 129,
   135, 136, 139, 140, 141, 143, 145, 214, 302
NaN 11
National Best Bid and Offer 119
NBBO 119
Nested If…Then 39
Net Income 418
Net Income/Employee 386
Net Profit 438
Net Profit Margin % 386
NetChange 373
New 20, 144, 295
NewLine.... 10, 31, 40, 51, 74, 81, 103, 153, 168,
   169, 176, 207, 244, 245, 271, 279, 319, 324,
   371
NewOrder 278
News 21
NewsProvider 147
Next Day 122, 123
NextSibling 358
NL 153
NL-NewLine Character 11
NonDisplay 358
NOT 36, 38, 375
Not Filled 355
Not Verified 21
Notepad 107
Notepad++ 107
Notification 221, 224
Notification Class 225
Notification Preferences 97
Null 3, 32, 181, 182, 218, 229, 244, 266, 322,
   346, 354, 358, 374
Number 53
Number of Common Shareholders 416
NumElements 90, 91
Numeric 31, 32
Numeric Expressions 34
Numeric Format Strings 52
NumericRef 42
NumericSimple 56
NumericUpDown 288, 292, 300
NumToStr 24, 40, 50, 51, 52, 56, 208, 218,
   230, 237, 268, 375
NumToText 228, 229, 230
Object.....3, 4, 127, 129, 134, 139, 141, 181, 215
Object Class 213, 215, 220
Object-Oriented 127

Object-Oriented EasyLanguage . xxix, xxxi, 1, 5,
   6, 9, 11, 17
Object-Oriented Programming 3, 7
Objects 8, 25, 72, 127, 144, 203, 213
Objects in a Vector 87
OCO 353, 357, 358
OCO Order 356
OCOGroupID 358
OCOOrderTicket 366
OCOOrderTickets 353
Odd Lot 122
Of 20
OME 11, 50
OME_DataGridView_Ex#02 323
OME_Floating_Text 175, 232, 233, 268
OME_Hello_World!_Ex#01 .... 14, 165
OME_Hello_World!_Ex#02 .... 97, 126
OME_Hello_World!_Ex#03 167
OME_Hello_World!_Ex#05a 169, 172
OME_Hello_World!_Ex#05b 170
OME_Hello_World!_Ex#06 171
OME_Hello_World!_Ex#07 172
OME_Hello_World!_Ex#07a 175
OME_Hello_World!_Ex#08a 177, 238
OME_Hello_World!_Ex#08b 178
OME_RoutineName 14
On 20
Once 40, 44, 86, 116, 154, 166, 224, 310
Once (skt_LastBarOnChart) 256
Once Begin 158, 241, 375
Once Begin…End 44, 166
Once Block 354
Once, and only once 256
OncePerBar 223, 224
OneAlert 99
One-Cancels-Other 353
OnInitialUpdate 264, 266
OnInitialUpdateEventArgs 264
OnKeyDown 264
OnKillFocus 264
OnSetFocus 264
OnSize 264, 266
OnSizeEventArgs 264
OOEL ....xxix, xxxi, 1, 2, 5, 6, 9, 11, 142
OP 11, 340
OP, OrdersProvider 333, 341
OP.RealTime 340
Open 19, 42, 109, 110, 125
Open Interest 110
Open Price 122
Open-Hi-Lo Lines 497
Opening Delay 122
Opening Range.............248, 250, 255, 256, 262
Opening Range Breakout 249, 260
Opening/Reopening Trade Detail................. 122
OpenInt.. 19, 109

Operating Margin 386
Operator 84, 129, 145
Optimization 7, 143
Optimizing with Data2 7
OptionApprovalLevel 334
Options 24
OptionStation Pro 21
OR 35
Order 356
Order Cancel 354
Order Class 357
Order Dependent 34
Order Object 357, 358
Order Submission 353
Order Tickets 5, 346, 351, 355
Order Tickets & Data Providers 5, 351
Order Updated Event 355
Order.Replace () 355
OrderAction 357, 359
OrderAction.Buy 347
OrderAction.Sell 347
Order-Cancels-Order 353
OrderElementMove 264, 266
OrderElementMoveEventArgs 264, 266
OrderField 359
OrderFill 278
OrderID 358
Orders 340, 354
Order-Sends-Order 353
OrdersProvider xxxi, 11, 147, 333, 340, 341, 347
OrdersProvider (OP) 333, 340
OrdersProvider Class 340
OrderState 359
OrderState.Filled 347
OrderState.Received 349
OrderTicket 11, 347, 353, 354, 356, 362
OrderTicket1.Action.ToString () 348
OrderTickets . 135, 147, 270, 351, 352, 354, 356, 360
Order-Triggers-Other 353
OrderType 359
OrderType.Limit 348
OrderUpdatedEventArgs 360
Originator 358
OSO 353, 357
OSO Order 356
OSOOrderTicket 353
OSOParentID 358
OT 11, 351, 352, 353
OTC 121
Out 20, 162
Out of Bounds 90
Out of Sequence 122
Outline 160
Output Bar 22
Outputs 43
Overload 230

Overloaded Methods 159
Override 20, 159, 206
OverrideDisabledColors 315
OverrideTooltips 219
Over-the-Counter 121
Padding 313
Pager_DefaultName 99
Pager_Send 99
PaintBar 13, 41, 136
Panel 286, 287, 297, 305
Panel Class 306
Parent 358
Partial Fill Handling 353
Partial Fills 353
Pascal 1, 3, 8
Pascal, Borland 1
Passed by Reference 42
Peek () 194, 198
Peg 358
PegBehavior 358
PennantFinder 497
Per Mille 54
Percent 53
Percentage Placeholder 54
Performance Report 354
PerformClick () 315
Persist 219, 250
PHW 497
Pi 33
Pivot 194
Pivot Points 87
Pixels 238, 253, 323
Place 20
PlaceOrder 352
Placing Non-Display Orders 358
Placing Text (Strings) on Your Chart 51
Plain Text 294
Platform 132, 144, 269, 271, 274
Platform.PlatformClientHost 265, 269, 273
PlatformClientHost 4, 263, 269, 273
PlatformClientHost (Component) 269
PlayMovieChain 97, 115, 116, 125
PlaySound 97, 99, 114, 126
Plot 13, 34
Plot1 336
PlotClick 273, 275
PlotClickEventArgs 4, 273
PM 270
PM-Portfolio Maestro 4
Point & Figure 107
Point Classes 215, 221
Points 219
PointToClient () 314
PointToScreen () 314
PointType 221, 226
PointValue 226
Pop () 198, 201

488

Pop_Back () 204
PopUpConfiguration 221
Portfolio 270
Portfolio Maestro 4, 22, 270, 271
PortfolioHost 4, 263, 271, 272, 273, 281
PortfolioHost Class 271
PortfolioHost Class (Component) 270
PortfolioMaestro 270, 271
PortfolioMaestro.PortfolioHost 271
PortfolioState 270
Pos_XPixels 116
Pos_YPixels 116
Position 242, 285
PositionsProvider ....xxxi, 147, 333, 341, 346
PositionsProvider (PP) 333
PositionsProvider Class 341
Potential Hourly Wage 497
PowerEditor 12, 21, 26
PP, PositionsProvider 333, 341
Precedence of Operators................................. 34
Precision Specifier 52
PreDeleteElement.................................... 265, 266
PreDeleteElementEventArgs 265, 267
Preface xxix
Preferred Stock 408
PrefillOrder 278
PREFIX 108
PreNewOrder 278
Prepaid Expenses 421
PreShowElementMenu.................265, 266, 267
PreShowElementMenuEventArgs................. 265
PreviousSibling 358
Price 238
Price - Year Ago 450
Price to Book 424
Price to Equity 425
Price to Sales 425
Price Variation Trade 123
Price/Earnings (P/E) Ratio 382
PriceAlert 221, 223, 238, 246
PriceCondition 223
PriceSeriesProvider 11, 147, 346
PriceSeriesProvider (PSP)............................. 333
PriceSeriesProvider Class 346
Prime 38
Print....... 9, 15, 17, 40, 55, 71, 73, 80, 118, 143,
    152, 166, 168, 170, 201, 205, 241, 299, 321
Print Log 4, 16, 17, 26, 40, 62, 72, 75, 77, 82,
    118, 147, 165, 166, 167, 169, 170, 171, 172,
    175, 176, 177, 178, 183, 187, 188, 194, 198,
    204, 265, 268, 274, 372
Print Log on First Bar 166
Print Log on Last Bar 167
Print to File.. 40
Print to Printer 40
Printer.. 17

Printing as a Debugging Tool........................ 152
Prior Reference Price 123
ProbabilityMap.. 13, 136
ProfitCF 125
ProgressBar 288, 293, 300, 308
Prompt for Editing.. 110
Properties 4, 127, 144, 205, 304
Properties Editor....... 25, 26, 147, 148, 302, 303,
    304, 335, 345
Properties Tab 303
Property 25, 84, 129, 135, 144, 145
Property & Other Taxes 403
Provider 147
Provider Class 4, 354
Provider Classes 147, 331, 346
Providers 135
Pruitt, George 27
PSP 11, 346
Push () 198, 208
Push_Back () 168, 170, 171, 173, 175, 176,
    196, 204, 208, 371
QP, QuotesProvider....................................... 345
Queue 137, 182, 196, 197, 207, 211
Queue Class.. 182, 194
Queue.Create () 207
Queue.Dequeue () 197
Queue.Enqueue ()... 196
Queue.Peek () 197
Queue.Peek ().GetType () 197
Queues 4
Quick Trade Bar 22
Quote 144, 273, 274
Quote Bar 119
Quote.RadarScreenHost 273
QuotesProvider.. 147, 345
QuotesProvider Class 345
RadarScreen 4, 7, 11, 14, 22, 107, 116, 194,
    211, 273, 338, 339, 346, 356
RadarScreen_Init () 275
RadarScreenHost........4, 263, 269, 273, 274, 281
RadarScreenHost Class (Component) 273
RadarScreenHost.Create () 275
RadioButton ..287, 288, 289, 293, 298, 299, 305,
    308, 315, 316, 325
RadioButton Class... 325
RaiseRunTimeError 97, 116, 126, 356
Raising Errors 231
Range 107
RE 11
Read/Write 182
ReadLine () 173
ReadOnly 326
Read-Only 182, 283, 303
Real Time Net Worth 128
RealTime 332
Real-Time.. 355

Real-Time Data 8, 119
Receivables 386, 387
Rectangle 4, 7, 213, 214, 215, 219, 221, 252
Rectangle Class 251
Rectangle Object 215
Rectangle.Color 253
Rectangle.Create () 253, 254
Rectangle.FillColor 253
Rectangle.FillPattern 253
Rectangle.SetEndPoint () 258
Rectangle.SetStartPoint () 258
Red 217
Ref. 162
ReferenceEquals () 221
Referred Quote 120, 123
Region 3, 127
Remove () 182, 183, 188, 203
Remove Button 85
Remove Drawing Objects 231
RemoveAt () 203
RemoveGradient () 285, 307, 315, 327
RemoveItem () 318
RemoveTooltipRow () 219
Renko 107
Repeat 50
Repeat…Until 43, 48, 49
Replace () 349, 355, 359
Replace OrderTicket 351, 356
ReplaceTicket 349, 355, 359
Research 22
Research and Development Expense 425, 428
Reserved Word 30, 31, 84, 145
Reserved Words 3, 9, 17, 19, 20, 27, 34
Reset Chart Scaling Range 6
Reset Scaling Range 6
Resizable 323
Resize 286
ResizeBegin 286
ResizeEnd 286
Resource Editor...4, 11, 136, 149, 283, 303, 328, 329
Restructuring Charge 418
ResumeLayout () 285
Return 128, 161
Return on Average Equity 388
Revenue/Employee 428
RFC1123 Pattern 66
RGB 42, 261
Rich Text 294
RichTextBox 288, 294, 295
Right 7
RightJustify 239, 246
RightStr 51
RightToLeft 313
RightToLeftLayout 285
Round 237
Round-Trip Date/Time Pattern 66

Route 358
RS. 11, 338
RSI 41
RSSProvider 147
RTAccountEquity 334
RTAccountNetWorth 334
RTCashBalance 334
RTCostOfPositions 334
RTDayTradingBuyingPower 334
RTInitialMargin 334
RTMaintenanceMargin 334
RTOptionBuyingPower 334
RTOptionLiquidationValue 334
RTOvernightBuyingPower 334
RTPurchasingPower 334
RTRealizedPL 334
RTUnrealizedPL 334
Ruggiero Jr, Murray 38
Rule 109, Amex 123
Rule 127 123
Rule 155 123
RunCommand 99, 101, 102
RunCommandOnLastBar 99, 102
Sales Returns and Allowances 432
Samuel K. Tennis vii
Sandbox....................149, 283, 328
SAP 11, 339
SAP, Symbol AtributesProvider 333
Scaling 6
Scaling Tab 97
Scanner 22
Scroll 304
Scroll Bars 306, 326
ScrollTo () 264
SE 11
Second 110
SecondsFromDateTime 58
Section. 54
Sector Code 406
Sector Name 406
Select () 327
Selected 311, 323
SelectedIndex 298, 310, 317
SelectedIndexChanged 304, 318
SelectedItem 317
SelectedTab 310
SelectedText 317
SelectNet 123
SelectTab () 311
Self 136
Self.Initialized 322
Self.UnInitialized 322
Self.WorkspaceSaving 322
Sell 13
Sell to Cover 280
Seller 123
SellSellSell 115

Semicolon 31, 45
Sender 146
Serializable 137, 182, 183
Series Function 42
Session 143
SetCell () 323
SetChartViewFocus () 264
SetEndPoint () 248, 252
SetLinearGradient () 285, 307, 315, 327
SetPointValue () 226
SetProfitTarget 354
SetRadialGradient () 285, 307, 315, 327
SetStartPoint () 248, 252
SetTooltipHeader () 220
SetTooltipRow () 220
Shareholder Equity 429
Shareholders Equity 390
Shares Outstanding 426, 428
Sharpe Ratio 437
SHIFT 274
Short Date Pattern 55, 66
Short Entry 11
Short Exit 11
Short Term Debt 408
Short Time Pattern 67
Shortcuts 97
Show () 285
Show Only Orders 358
ShowBarCount 247
ShowCmtry 104
ShowDate 242
ShowInformation 128
ShowInPlotSubgraph 219
ShowLabels 239, 242, 247
ShowMe 13, 41, 136
Shown 286
ShowOnly 358
ShowOnlyQuantity 359
ShowPriceNetChange 247
ShowPricePercentChange 247
ShowTime 242
ShowTimeSpan 247
Sibling 357
SiblingCount 359
Signals 277
Single 31
sjh 131
SJH 11
sjh_f_Colors 14
sjh_S_PositionsAsSpeech 115
Skip Words 19, 20, 27
skt 184, 236
SKT 11
skt Data Report Pro 505
skt Report Sender Unit 505
skt SPGC Report Pro 505

skt_AddTime 58
skt_AverageFC 41
skt_Commentary_Header 201, 276
skt_Commentary_Notes 201
skt_IFF_Str 201
skt_isOptimizing 236
skt_isPortfolioMaestro 272
skt_LastBarOnChart 268
skt_Method_Header 228, 374, 451
skt_Month_Name 276
skt_PowerUser 256
skt_RT_PL_Viewer 506
skt_ScrollTheChart 507
skt_ScrollTheChart_Docked 507
skt_Time_OK 200
sktennis@vista-research.com 104
Slater, Tim xxvii
Slider 288, 294
SMTP 98
Sold Last 123
Solid 242
Sortable Date/Time Pattern 66
Sorted 317
SortOrder 93, 94
SoundConfiguration 221
Source 155
Spaces 51, 97
Spin Box 292
Spinner 286
Split Trade 123
SpreadName 359
SrcArrayName 90, 91
SrcElement 90, 91
Support 12
Stack 137, 182, 198, 200, 207, 211
Stack Class 182, 198
Stack.Create () 207
Stack.Push () 200
Stacks 4
StackTrace 155, 156
Standard Date and Time Format Strings 66
Standard Numeric Format Strings 52
StartPoint 247, 251
State 359
State Change 145
StateChanged .146, 147, 331, 332, 333, 354, 451
StateChanged Event Handler 331
StateDetail 359
Statements 34
StateToString () 359
Status 334
Stock Option Trade 123
Stop 353
Stop Price Offset 359
StopLimit 351
Stopped 123

Stopped Stock 124
StopPrice 359
StopPriceOffset 359
StopPriceStyle 359
Strategies 13, 277, 352
Strategy 13, 41, 136, 144, 277
Strategy Group 270
Strategy Properties 124
Strategy.StrategyFillOrderEventArgs 279
Strategy.StrategyHost 278
Strategy.StrategyNewOrderEventArgs 279
StrategyHost 4, 264, 278, 281
StrategyHost Class (Component) 277
StreamReader 4, 169, 170, 171, 173, 204
StreamReader.Create () 158, 173, 174
StreamWriter 4, 160, 169, 170, 171, 175, 176,
    271, 348
StreamWriter.Create () 272
StreamWriter.Write () 160
StreamWriter.WriteLine () 71
String 30, 31, 32, 86, 92, 153, 183, 203
String Input 50
String Literal 50
String.Format () 30, 55, 59, 71, 72, 73, 74, 75,
    77, 160, 168, 179, 201
String.Split () 172, 179, 204
StringRef 42
Strings, Custom Date and Time Format 55
Strings, Custom Format 56
Strings, Custom Numeric Format 53
Strings, More About 50
Strings, Numeric Format 52
Strings, Standard Date and Time 55
StringSeries 30
StringSimple 30
StringToTime 59
StringValue 178, 179
StrLen 51, 237
StrToNum 51, 80
Studies 41
Study 13
Study Groups 13
Style 239, 241, 242, 247, 251
Style Tab 97
StyleType 220, 239, 242, 247
Subgraph 336
SubgraphResize 220
SubgraphResizeEventArgs 235
Subroutine 4, 159
Sunny J. Harris vii
sunny@moneymentor.com 498
SunnyBands© 51, 97, 99, 104, 106, 115, 126,
    153, 350, 497
SunnyBars 497
Support Classes 136
SuspendLayout () 285
Swing 194

Switch 83, 84, 86
Switch…Case 27, 83
SWP .... xxix, 11
SX 11
Symbol 110, 124, 359
Symbol Attribute 107
Symbol Customize 108
Symbol Data 108
Symbol Lookup 110
SymbolAttributesProvider 147, 339
SymbolAttributesProvider (SAP) 333
SymbolAttributesProvider Class 339
SymbolExtension 359
Symbolic Logic 35, 37
SymRoot.dop 107
Syntax Errors 21
System Class 136
System Writer .... xxx, 1, 8
System Writer Plus .... xxix, 1, 8, 11
System.Drawing.Graphics 305
SystemException Class 155
TA 11, 263
Tab, Add 303
TabControl 286, 298, 301, 305, 309, 310, 311
TabControl Class 310
TabControlEventArgs 309, 311
TabControl's TabPages 310
TabCount 310
TabIndex 285, 313
TableLayoutPanel 288, 291, 294
TabPage 286, 298, 305, 310, 311
TabPage Class 311
TabPageCollection 310
TabPages 310
Tabs 298
TabStop 285, 313
Tabula Rasa 13
Tag 219, 313, 323
TAG xxvii
TAG Seminars xxx
TApp 11
Targets 353
TargetSite 155, 156
TA-TradingApp 5
Tax Rate 388
Taxes Paid 429
Taxes Payable 421
TDE 2, 6, 11, 12, 16, 21, 23, 24, 26, 160, 263
Technical Analysis xxvii
Technical Analysis Group .... xxvii, xxx
Template 13, 14
Temporary File Extension 11
Tennis, Samuel K... vii, xxvii, xxix, xxx, xxxi, 1,
    11, 15, 39, 41, 100, 130, 198
Text 213, 313, 323
Text at a Specific Location 232
Text Centered on Chart 175

Text Drawing Tool 231
Text File 11
Text String 291
Text_New 57, 226, 262
Text_xxx 4
TextAlign 316
TextBox 288, 295
TextBox Class 326
TextChanged 327
TextLabel ..4, 213, 214, 215, 219, 221, 226, 227,
    228, 231, 232, 268
TextLabel Class 226
TextLabel Object 215
TextLabel.Create () 216, 218, 226
TextString 226
Than 20
The 20
Then 13, 86
Then Begin 38
Throw 20, 157
Tick-by-Tick 346, 351
Ticker Symbol 406
Ticks 19
Tilde 38
Time 19, 57, 58, 60, 66, 109, 261, 373
Time and Sales 22, 118, 119, 120
Time Zone 67
Time Zone Information 67
TimeAlert 221, 223, 242
TimeAndSalesProvider 147
Time-of-Day 59
Timer Events 379
Timer Object 145
TimerElapsed 146
TimeSpan 59, 61, 62, 64, 77
TimeSpan Class 62
TimeSpan.Create () 62, 63, 74
TimeSpan.FromELDateAndTime 64
TimeSpan_Init 63
TimeToMinutes 60
TimeToString (DateTime) 58
TL.VStyle 218
TL_GetAlert 99
TL_New 57, 262, 265
TL_SetAlert 99
TL_xxx 4
To 43, 45, 46, 47, 48
TodaysRTTradeEquity 334
TokenList ..4, 6, 86, 94, 172, 173, 181, 182, 202,
    204, 207, 337
TokenList Class 202
TokenList.Create () 207
Toolbar 22, 23, 119
ToolBox 3, 4, 5, 23, 26, 135, 148, 149, 263, 286,
    302, 303, 304, 312, 335, 345, 360
ToolBox, About 148, 302

Tools 22
Tools → Customize 22
ToolTip 219, 220, 285
TopLeftOrder 359
TopMost 285
TopPlacement 242
ToString () 29, 155, 156, 160, 203, 221
Total Debt Issued 408
Total Gross Loans 388
Total Income Net 385
Total Investment Securities 388
Trade History 341
TradeManager 22, 335, 340, 341
TradeManager Analysis 22
Trademarks ix
TradeStation .... xxx, xxxi, 11, 26, 27
TradeStation Desktop 11
TradeStation Development Environment .. 11, 12
TradeStation Forum 2
TradeStation Made Easy! ..... xxix, 2, 11, 27, 143
TradeStation Securities Group 1
TradeStation Tidbits 6
TradeStation Workspace File 11
Trading 101—How to Trade Like a Pro... xxix, 2
Trading 102—Getting Down to Business 2
Trading Account Assets 388
Trading Account Interest 432
TradingApp 5, 11, 13, 136, 263, 270
TradingApp Launcher 21
TradingApp Store 22
TradingApp Store Updates 22
TradingAppHost 263
TradingApps 12, 22
Trailing Stops 353
TrailingStop 359
TrailingStopAmount 359
Transparent 7
Treasury Shares 429
Treasury Stock 408
TrendLine 4, 141, 145, 183, 213, 214, 215,
    219, 221, 222, 241, 247, 248, 251, 268
TrendLine Class 246
TrendLine Object 215
TrendLine.Create () 214, 248, 255
True 45
TrueFalseRef 42
TrueVal 39
Truth Tables 35
Try 20, 79, 156, 157
Try...Catch Block 157, 271, 333
Try...Catch...Finally 156, 157, 158
Try...Catch...Throw 157, 158
TS .... xxx, 11
TS Data Network 107
TS Development Environment 2, 6, 16, 21
TS Securities Group 9

TS Servers.. 5
tsData 135, 143
tsData.Common73, 132, 144, 181, 202, 206, 332
tsData.Common.DataProvider 147, 338
tsData.Common.TokenList 203
tsData.MarketData 73, 144, 381, 452
tsData.MarketData.FundamentalFields 450
tsData.Order 360
tsData.Trading..........73, 139, 144, 333, 335, 357
tsData.Trading.Account 335
tsData.Trading.AccountsProvider 338
tsData.Trading.AccountUpdatedEventArgs .. 338
TSLA 231
TSME 11, 13
tsOpt Namespace................................. 142
tsopt.AvailableSessions.......................... 143
TradeStation Forum 12
Type 334, 359
Typecast 182
TypeToString () 359
Ultimate_F Compounding........................ 497
UnclearedDeposits 335
Unfolded 85
UnInitialize () 155
UnInitialized 138
UnInitialized Event 136, 138, 139, 206
Universal Full Date/Time Pattern 67
Universal Sortable Date/Time Pattern........... 67
Unknown Specifier 67
Unloaded 331
UnsettledFund 335
Until 50
Update Tick-by-Tick............................. 118
Update Value Intra-Bar.................101, 102, 114
Updated...... 146, 147, 178, 331, 333, 335, 337, 354, 360
Updated Event.................................. 345
UpdateEventArgs.............................. 221
Update-Intrabar 167
UpperStr.. 51
UpTicks 19
USDJPY 124
UseCompatibleTextRendering...............305, 316
Useful Methods 160
User Function......39, 41, 71, 136, 139, 159, 162, 283
User Interface (UI)............................. 298
UseTheme 313
UseThemeMode 313
UseWaitCursor............................... 314
Using 3, 20, 61, 77, 127, 139, 214, 222, 233, 302
Using Alerts 246
Using EasyLanguage 9.x................... 27
Using Excel.................................... 369
Using Methods 162
Using WinForms Classes 286
Utilization Monitor 97, 125, 126

Val.. 93
Value...................................87, 203, 359
Value [fieldName]............................. 335
Values 183
van Giessen, Pamela........................... xxxi
Var 31
VAR 11
Variable 31, 32
Variables 11, 27, 31
VarName 32, 33
Vars 31
Vector 3, 4, 86, 94, 137, 141, 156, 168, 171, 172, 175, 181, 182, 203, 207, 211, 371, 372
Vector Class 87, 182, 203
Vector Class (Collection).................... 181
Vector Collection, Add an Element 204
Vector of Vectors. 203
Vector.Create ()...................174, 175, 207
Vector.Insert () 204
Vector.Push_Back () 196, 200, 204
Vectors 86, 211
Verbose 9
Verified 21
Verify 4, 10, 20, 21, 22, 151, 152
Verify All 22
VerticalLine 4, 213, 214, 215, 221, 222, 223, 241, 242, 244, 268
VerticalLine Class........................... 241
VerticalLine Object......................... 215
VerticalLine.Create () 243, 245, 246
VerticalStyle 226
VerticalStyle.Center 218
Video... 115
View 22, 206
View Menu................................... 304
View g TradingApp Launcher................... 21
Visible 285, 314
Vista-Research and Trading................ 11, 237
Visual Notifications 225
VisualConfiguration 225
VisualEnable 225
VL 11
Void 127, 128, 157, 159, 162, 299, 304, 308
Volume...............................19, 109, 110, 125
Volume I 3
Volume II.. 3
Volume II—Reference Guide 3, 101, 129, 257
vrt 236
VRT 11
vrt_AddDate 57
vrt_Format................................... 201
vrt_HHMM_pm 56, 201
vrt_MMDDYYYY 56, 57, 104, 201, 375
VStyle 216, 226
Walk-Forward Optimizer 22
Was 20
WebBrowser 288, 295

494

Website Link for Supplemental Material 5
WebView2 .... 288, 296
Weekly 110
Weight....................................239, 242, 247, 251
What Is EasyLanguage.................................... 5
Where Is the Command?.............................. 3, 6
While......................43, 48, 49, 50, 171, 173, 201
While Loop 172
Who's On Top.. 497
Width...........................285, 311, 314, 326
Window 22
Window Position 140
Windows Forms 316
Windows WinForms 312
Windows.Forms Components 305
WindowState 285
WinForms 352
WinForms Tab, ToolBox 304
WinForms.ell Library....................286, 296, 312
Workbook 5, 369
Workbook.Create ().................................... 375
Workbook.Sheets 370
Worksheet 5, 374, 375
Workspaces 211
WorkspaceSaving............................... 137, 138

WorkspaceSaving Event 136, 139, 206
Wrapper Function.. 43
Write ().. 160, 174, 176
WriteLine ()................................... 176, 272
www.EasyLanguageOOEL.com .. 5, 10, 56, 271, 277, 296
www.facebook.com/VistaResearch/.............. 509
www.moneymentor.com 498
www.MoneyMentor.com 2, 42
www.moneymentor.com/products.html 497
www.Vista-Research.com 27
XLoc 283
xmlDocument... 157
XYPoint 215, 226, 252, 259
Year.. 57, 68
Year Month Pattern 67
YearFromDateTime 58
Yen.. 124
YLoc 283
Zero Placeholder 53
Zero-Based Index 203, 310
⌐⊕ 9
⌐⊕ File → New.. 23
⌐⊕ File → Open.. 23
⌐⊕ Tools → Options.................................... 24

PRODUCTS

S am and I have labored long and hard over many 3-hour nights of Tuesday and Thursday[51] meetings by Zoom for more than two years to bring you these books. And Sam has been doing the programming while Sunny has spent her days and nights writing. It has been a labor of love. We sincerely hope you will profit from our work. Please contact us to let us know what you think of our toils.

We are both EasyLanguage Programmers who love to help others. Whether you want us to code some of your ideas or teach you how to do it yourself, we are available.

Sunny is a Professional Trader and has been since 1981 through major bear and bull markets, as well as a Programmer & Mathematician. If you want to enhance your trading skills, give me a call (1-760-908-3070 PT).

Here we present a list of our most popular indicators for TradeStation, MultiCharts and NinjaTrader so you can consider getting them for your own.

Trade with My Software, for FREE:

Sunny J. Harris Products

There are additional products on www.moneymentor.com/products.html. These prices are current as of this writing. Be sure to check the website for current prices.

SunnyBands	$2,945
DynamicMovingAverage	$1,195
DynamicMovingAverage Histogram	$1,195
PHW (Potential Hourly Wage)	$895
Who's On Top	$995
DaySessions	$245
CurrentPrice	$95
Open-Hi-Lo Lines	$95
SunnyBars	$795
Ultimate_F Compounding	$6,995
PennantFinder	$195
WorldTime	$195

All Updates FREE, forever! One-time fee, no recurring charges. Anytime access to Sunny; just call.

Running both MultiCharts and TradeStation? Or TradeStation and NinjaTrader, or… Ask for our special pricing offer.

---

[51] Although for the last 6 months we were meeting Tuesday through Friday inclusive.

ACCOLADES

These are unsolicited emails from real clients.

"There are Instructors after Instructors out there willing to teach trading.

After numerous schools, seminars and Thousands of Dollars later, I was no closer to being a trader than the first day I walked into one of the Schools.

Most of the instructions and figures were on past performances. Drawing lines for supply and demand, when you already know the outcome, doesn't make you ready for trading. It is a recipe for disaster.

I was willing to take my losses (which were quite a sum of money) and find a job to pay for my losses.

Then I met Sunny.

From day one, after a brief conversation with Sunny, I knew I had the right person to teach me trading.

Sunny has a world of knowledge and is not afraid of sharing it with you. She can be stern at times but listen to what she says—it's for a reason. There are no short cuts to success! Everything she teaches you has a purpose.

Sunny will trade with you and may question your decision on why you took the trade. Even if you were right, she is making sure it wasn't a wild guess and you understand why you made the trade. You're not just another person to Sunny. Sunny is very passionate about what she does.

If Sunny can make a trader out of a kid from the Bronx, like me, she can work miracles."

- Billy Coyle

You can order any of these indicators at www.moneymentor.com or by emailing Sunny at sunny@moneymentor.com or even by calling me at 1-760-908-3070.

"Sunny, you're brilliant! You've got this thing solved. I made $10,000 just this week using SunnyBands." -Samuel S.

"I just finished watching the video [Trade Along with Sunny]. That was some very nice, calm trading. I was wondering where your stops were but noticed that you manage the trade precisely, without any second-guessing when you decide to close the trade. I've downloaded the manual and will put the rules next to my charts tomorrow to see how I might trade with them. Please keep me on your mailing list, I don't want to miss anything." -David P.

SunnyBands

ATR Bands Around My Proprietary DMA, Which Recalculates Its Length with Every Bar

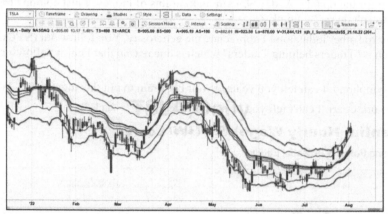

SunnyBands™ combine the beauty of Sunny's Dynamic Moving Average (DMA) with dynamic Average True Range bands on either side of the moving averages. The SunnyBands clearly show me where to get in and where to get out. In its simplest form, when an up candle (blue) penetrates the Upper Outer Band (UOB) to the upside and the next candle turns red and penetrates the UOB to the downside I go short or sell out of my long position. When red candles penetrate the Lower Outer Band (LOB) to the downside and subsequently turn blue and move back up inside the bands, I go long or exit my short trade.

"...using your bands now with great success! You're the best Sunny!" -Eric G.

"I'm getting a big kick out of the SunnyBands this morning. It's great when it all comes together. And as you said, your SunnyBands picks the tops perfectly." Frank Z.

DynamicMovingAvg (DMA) & DMA_Histogram

DMA_H Shows Exact Turning Point Signals

DMA_Histogram (DMA_H) displays the difference between the Purple and Gold MAVs as a colored histogram on the bottom of the chart. This indicator highlights the speed of the change of the moving averages by showing them in gold and red for up moves, and green and purple for down moves. This RadarScreen version of indicator fills the cells with the associated colors for the DMA_H and gives you a Direction (Dir) that highlights whether the symbol is currently moving up (//), down {\\}, up but has turned down (/\) or down but has turned up (\/). It is uncanny how quickly this indicator pegs market turns for all the symbols in your RadarScreen. The charting version (shown here) shows Gold when the Gold line is on top and Purple when the Purples line is on top.

The distinguishing feature of this indicator is that it shows turns quickly giving solid signals by turning from Purple to Green for long signals and Gold to Red for short signals. As always, I only take the signal when price confirms it.

> "Thank you for the update. And, yes, I am making lots of money. I just couldn't trade when the DMA wasn't there." – Frank Z.

> "Thanks for the other indicators! I appreciate the generosity. You follow our (SVOG Group) motto which is "Traders helping Traders" which is one reason that I enjoy following you."— Kurt S.

> "This is a symphony. I can tell you've used your big brain to put this together."—William P.

> "This is a work of art. I can't tell you how impressed I am." –Jack B.

PHW (Potential Hourly Wage) & PHW_Lower

Shows Ideal Turning Points & Potential Equity

PHW is Sunny's main research tool. I use it for marking yellow dots on all significant turning points. Then the indicator calculates: the date range of the symbol; Buy and Hold; the number of ideal trades; the ideal profit; and the PHW profit (which is 60% of the ideal). This is not a trading tool, but rather it is a research tool to help me trade better.

The PHW_Lower indicator goes on the lower subgraph of your chart and shows you how much profit was possible in previous trades. It's a great way to see how much you are leaving on the table. Are the ideal trades $500 and you are only keeping $125? Learn to quit getting out too early or too late with this fantastic tool.

Who's On Top

Gold and Purple Dots Illustrate Clearly Whether Gold or Purple is On Top

Do you have Sunny's DMA (Dynamic Moving Average) and ever wonder whether the Gold line is on top of the Purple, or vice versa? This indicator plots a series of Purple and Gold dots at the bottom of the chart showing exactly which is on top at the moment. Not only that, the purple and gold dots will lighten in color when the DMA is Flat, warning you to potential sideways action. This makes reading and deciding on positions much easier. I keep Who's On Top at the bottom of all my trading charts. Purple on Top means Bearishness while Gold on top signifies Bullishness.

DaySessions

Paint Day Session Bars a Different Color from After-Hours Session.

I like to know, at a glance, whether a test I ran produced trades in the day or night session. With this indicator, the DaySession bars are colored blue and red in this chart, while the Extended-Session bars are green and magenta. This makes life a lot easier for me, when I can tell which session I'm in at a glance.

"I love my Day Sessions candles. They really keep me focused on what the day and Globex sessions are." -Paul D.

CurrentPrice

Make it Really Easy to See Price Moves (Red Dot Signifies Last Price was Down)

Here's another tool that I programmed to make my trading life easier. I call it SM_CurrentPrice, for ShowMe the Current Price. This indicator puts a dot to the right of the current price. The dot is red if the last price movement was down, and a green dot shows that the last price movement was upward. If the dot is gray, then the price is unchanged. I prefer to watch the bouncing ball than to try and watch the edge of a candle.

"Until SunnyBands I hadn't found indicators that I could say "I can replace my job" and now

I have." –Robert W.

DayOpenHiLo

Easily See the Day's Open, High & Low (Often Important Support & Resistance).

Often the market will use the day's hi or low, or the opening values, as Support and Resistance. We often see price making a run for these values. I like to have the lines automatically drawn on my chart, so I can "predict" coming prices. It's another way I keep things easy. Note that the blue is the open, the red line is the low, while the high line is green. For the night sessions, the colors are light blue, magenta and light green. See how easy that is to read?

SunnyBars

See Volume Easily Displayed as the Width of the Candle

A more informative way of viewing CandleSticks. Each bar includes volume, as the width of the bar. Bars get wider as volume increases and narrower as volume decreases.

"I traded great on Thursday with SunnyBands! (on trial) But, on Friday I didn't have them and I got my butt handed to me!" -Dean J.

"I do like how you are straight forward and really seem to care about helping people succeed. I believe you stand apart in this industry." - Michael M.

"I want to say I loved those SunnyBands. I can tell that you've had 42 years of experience in day trading. I've gained 10% on my account value during this 7 day free trial period." –Devin T.

Ultimate-F Compounding

Watch your Trading Account Grow with Conservative Compounding

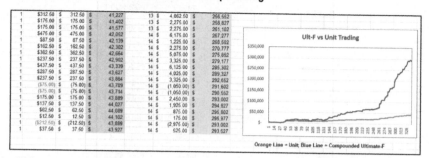

Orange Line = Unit; Blue Line = Compounded Ultimate-F

Based originally on the works of Ralph Vince, this function veers off from his in a subtle, yet extremely powerful way: it avoids the huge drawdowns and likelihood of ruin experienced by users of Ralph's optimal-f. My Ultimate-F function turns thousands into millions with its proper use with much lower drawdown. It is so phenomenal that it is only being offered for a short time, and at a hefty price. It's worth every penny and then some. Imagine your profitable system going from somewhat profitable to wildly profitable with the judicious use of compounding.

Pennant Finder

Easily find areas of Congestion. I like to Trade Pennant Breakouts.

Some people like to trade breakouts, rather than moving averages. This indicator was designed for a client who preferred to trade breakouts. The indicator marks areas of congestion with little triangles that show the top value and bottom value to use for breakouts. Notice how the market responds quickly when it penetrates one of the little red horizontal lines showing the edges of the Pennant.

"Sunny has a real talent for explaining complex ideas in simple terms." – James W.

"You stand behind your word and indicator. It has really helped me to stay in the trades longer and it works fantastic. Thanks for everything." –David N.

World Time

Easily see what time it is in any country. I have clients all over the world and now I can quickly see what time it is so I don't call them in the middle of the night!

Set up the countries and the time zone from GMT and you are all set. Any country, any time zone.

Samuel K. Tennis Products

These prices are current as of this writing. Be sure to check the website for current prices.

skt Data Report Pro $299

skt SPGC Report Pro $299

Data Report Pro and SPGC Report Pro Bundle $499

Real Time Profit Loss Viewer $495

Scroll the Chart $79.50

Scroll the Chart Docked...$149

Consulting & Custom Programming............................$180/hr

Data Report Pro

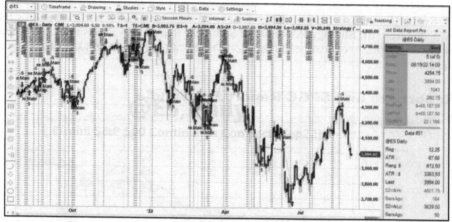

The Data Report will display, if the Report Sender Unit is active on the chart, information about the open position (Trade) or the most recently closed position. The Data Report will report market metrics on up to four data streams (Data1 - Data4). Adding these data series to the chart should not in any way impact the performance of any applied Strategies.

Use The Report Pro Bundle on every chart absolute must for keeping track of and testing Strategies in TradeStation.

Thanks Samuel, SB

The Report Pro Bundle should be part of TradeStation but is not. The Data Report Pro and SPGC Report Pro show you information that is usually only visible statically in the Strategy Performance Report, and other information as well. This is very useful in analyzing and understanding your strategies. -Neil Harrington

SPGC Report Pro

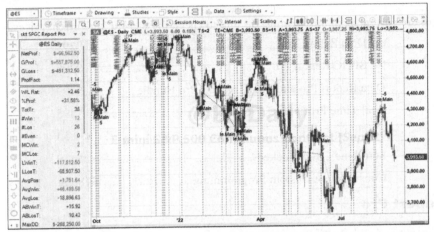

The SPGC Report (Strategy Performance at a Glance on the Chart) will report in real-time many the metrics available from the Strategy Performance Summary Report as well as the "Professional" metrics I have developed to overcome the decision TradeStation made to break up a position into separate trades.

Data Report Pro and SPGC Report Pro Bundle

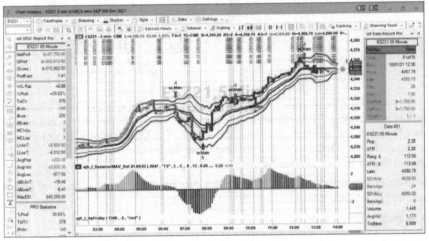

By default, the skt SPGC Report Pro shows up on the left of your chart while the skt Data Report Pro appears on the right of your chart. With this bundle you can display both on your chart, real-time.

The Data Report Pro will display information about the open position (Trade) or the most recently closed position if the Report Sender Unit is active on the chart. The Data Report will report market metrics on up to four data streams (Data1 - Data4). Adding these data series to the chart should not in any way impact the performance of any applied Strategies. The SPGC_Report will report in real-time many of the metrics available from the Strategy Performance Summary Report as well as the "Professional" metrics I have developed to overcome the decision TradeStation made to break up a position into separate trades.

Real Time Profit Loss Viewer

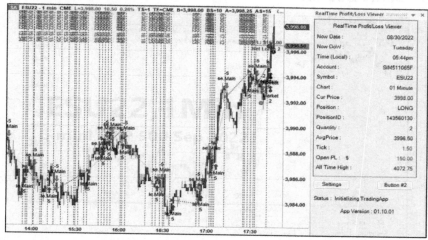

Sunny requested this product for her own real-time trading. She finds it exceptional while in a trade to closely monitor the statistics. It does not report the stats of your strategy, but rather it reports your real-time trades. It has two panels, "the answers and the questions." The "questions" are the Settings you desire. The "answers" are the real-time stats: symbol, timeframe, account, current price, position, quantity, average price, tick and open P/L. It keeps all the answers right up front on your chart, easy to access and easy to interpret.

"Scroll the Chart should be part of TradeStation but is not. Scroll the Chart is a simple but very useful tool that gives you many different ways to get to a part of your chart you want to get to. You know how frustrating it can be to get to a particular day and/or time or to a particular trade. Scroll the Chart gives you all those ways and others!" - Neil Harrington

Scroll the Chart

This Scroll the Chart application allows you to quickly move right to left and back by clicking the form and not wasting time with the chart scroll bar. You can even jump to specified locations, trades, or sessions.

Scroll the Chart Docked

Notice that the scroll tool is on the bottom of the chart, tucked away nice and tidy. This application allows you to quickly move right and left by clicking the form and not wasting time with the chart scroll bar. Additionally, this version is Docked at the location of your choice, left, right, bottom, or top of the chart.

Give us a call. Sunny and Sam are both available for a free consultation or questions. No project is too big or too small. Sunny is at 1-760-908-3070 PT or sunny@moneymentor.com and Sam is at sktennis@vista-research.com or 1-850-582-7342 (TEXT) ET.

Please contact us to let us know what you think of our toils. We wish you a profitable journey!

ABOUT THE AUTHORS

Dr. Sunny J. Harris is a professional trader (since 1981), mathematician, programmer, author, and host of several websites:

- https://www.moneymentor.com,
- https://www.sunnybands.com,
- http://www.tradestationmadeeasy.com and
- https://www.easylanguageOOEL.com, which is the website for these books.

Sunny has authored and published:

Trading 101—How to Trade Like a Pro,

Trading 102—Getting Down to Business,

Electronic Day Trading 101,

Getting Started in Trading,

TradeStation Made Easy!,

ghost written *Using EasyLanguage 9.x* for Murray Ruggiero,

and *Going Vegan!* for Linda Blair, and now

The Definitive Guide to TradeStation's EasyLanguage & OOEL Programming, Vol I & Vol II.

Listen to her Podcast: *The Sunny Harris Show* with Samuel K. Tennis where we visit famous gurus, traders and authors and get to know them personally.

Link to it here: https://www.moneymentor.com/podcast.html.

Sunny has been twice rated #1 trader (Commodity Trading Advisor) in the under $10 million category by Stark Research. Achieving 365.5% and 178% profits trading the S&P 500 futures.

Sunny lives in Southern California with her family and Pumpkin.

Get to know Sunny on these Podcasts:

- The Matt Kohrs Show
- Michael Filighera's Eye of the Storm
- Chat with Traders with Tessa Dao
- How to Trade It with Casey Stubbs
- The Daily Traders
- Desire to Trade with Etienne Crete
- Alternative Investments with Jackson Carr
- The Kook Jester Show
- Macro Jabber

Samuel K. Tennis is a professional programmer, author of *Ask Mr. EasyLanguage* and was the lead programmer and originator of TradeStation's predecessor System Writer. Sam is acknowledged as the world's leading authority on EasyLanguage programming. He continues to program for clients worldwide. His website is:

http://www.vista-research.com. and https://www.facebook.com/VistaResearch/

Samuel lives in Southern Florida with his family and Trixie. Unfortunately, during the period of writing of this book, I have to inform you that Trixie has met her match and flown off to that magical seed farm in the sky. Whether by anonymous hawk or friendly fire of the household dogs, we shall never know. And it matters not! She is missed by many!

Sam has a professional Vista-Research page on Facebook as well as a presence on Twitter and LinkedIn.

Made in the USA
Las Vegas, NV
13 November 2024

11648024R20295